Lecture Notes in Artificial Intelligence 10505

Subseries of Lecture Notes in Computer Science

Gabriele Kern-Isberner · Johannes Fürnkranz
Matthias Thimm (Eds.)

KI 2017: Advances in Artificial Intelligence

40th Annual German Conference on AI
Dortmund, Germany, September 25–29, 2017
Proceedings

 Springer

Editors
Gabriele Kern-Isberner
Fakultät für Informatik
Technische Universität Dortmund
Dortmund
Germany

Matthias Thimm
FB Informatik
Universität Koblenz
Koblenz, Rheinland-Pfalz
Germany

Johannes Fürnkranz 🆔
FB Informatik
TU Darmstadt
Darmstadt, Hessen
Germany

ISSN 0302-9743   ISSN 1611-3349   (electronic)
Lecture Notes in Artificial Intelligence
ISBN 978-3-319-67189-5   ISBN 978-3-319-67190-1   (eBook)
DOI 10.1007/978-3-319-67190-1

Library of Congress Control Number: 2017953421

LNCS Sublibrary: SL7 – Artificial Intelligence

Printed on acid-free paper

This Springer imprint is published by Springer Nature
The registered company is Springer International Publishing AG
The registered company address is: Gewerbestrasse 11, 6330 Cham, Switzerland

Preface

The German conference on Artificial Intelligence (abbreviated KI for "Künstliche Intelligenz") looks back on a long and fruitful history. The first official event took place in 1975, at that time a workshop of the KI working group of the German "Gesellschaft für Informatik" (association for computer science, GI). Before that, there were inofficial meetings, such as the "Fachtagung Kognitive Verfahren und Systeme", which was held in Hamburg in April 1973. The meeting has now developed into an annual conference for researchers in artificial intelligence, primarily from Germany and its neighboring countries but open to international participation.

This volume contains the papers presented at the 40th event in this series, which was held at the Technical University of Dortmund, September 25–29th, 2017. This year we received 73 valid submissions, an increase of 50% over last year. We were able to accept 20 papers as full research papers and 16 as short technical communications, yielding an acceptance rate of 27% for full papers and 49% overall. Due to the limited number of available slots in the conference schedule, we had to make difficult decisions and several worthy submissions had to be rejected or downgraded from full to short papers.

The Program Committee worked very hard to thoroughly review all the submitted papers and to provide action points to improve the papers. Despite the increased workload for the PC, almost all papers received three reviews, and only 10 papers had to be selected or rejected on the basis of only 2 reviews. The program chairs managed discussions amongst the reviewers, from which the final decisions emerged. As a result, the contributions cover a range of topics from, e.g., agents, robotics, cognitive sciences, machine learning, planning, knowledge representation, reasoning, and ontologies, with numerous applications in areas like social media, psychology, and transportation systems, reflecting the richness and diversity of our field.

In addition to the regular sessions, our program also featured three invited talks by Pierre Baldi (University of California, Irvine), Gerhard Brewka (University of Leipzig), and Luc De Raedt (Katholieke Universiteit Leuven), as well as an industrial session featuring a keynote by Wolfgang Wahlster (Saarland University), and a session composed of presentations of selected papers by German authors that have been presented at our international sister conferences AAAI and IJCAI in 2017.

In order to celebrate the 40th anniversary of the German Conference on Artificial Intelligence, the program also contained a historical session with a panel discussion. The session was hosted by Ulrich Furbach, and contained contributions from the panelists Katharina Morik, Hans-Helmut Nagel, Bernd Neumann, and Jörg Siekmann. After a short review of the history of computer science and artificial intelligence in Germany by the host, the panelists commented on their early AI-related activities and the relationship of these activities with the computer science community at that time. Finally, the development of the field in recent years and its future was reflected in an open forum.

For the first two days of the conference, our workshop and tutorial chair, Christoph Beierle (University of Hagen), organized a program of two workshops:

- ZooOperation Competition (Vanessa Volz, Christian Eichhorn)
- Formal and Cognitive Reasoning (Christoph Beierle, Gabriele Kern-Isberner, Marco Ragni, Frieder Stolzenburg)

During the workshops, many additional papers were presented, ideas discussed, and experiences exchanged. Moreover, the program also featured two tutorials:

- Defeasible Reasoning for Description Logics (Ivan Varzinczak)
- Knowledge Representation and Reasoning with Nilsson-Style Probabilistic Logics (Nico Potyka)

Organizing such a traditional conference is a very challenging but no less rewarding experience, which would not have been possible without the help of the many individuals who contributed to the success of this event. First and foremost, we would like to thank the authors and the reviewers for their excellent work, which forms the core of any such meeting. We also thank our workshop and tutorial chair, the invited speakers, the workshop chairs and tutorial presenters, and the participants of the historical session, all of which have already been listed above. Last but not least, special thanks go to the local organization team from the Technical University of Dortmund, Christian Eichhorn, Steffen Schieweck, and Marco Wilhelm without whom this conference would not have been possible.

July 2017

Gabriele Kern-Isberner
Johannes Fürnkranz
Matthias Thimm

Organization

General Chair

Gabriele Kern-Isberner   TU Dortmund, Germany

Program Chairs

Johannes Fürnkranz   TU Darmstadt, Germany
Matthias Thimm   University of Koblenz-Landau, Germany

Workshop and Tutorial Chair

Christoph Beierle   University of Hagen, Germany

Historial Session Chair

Ulrich Furbach   University of Koblenz-Landau, Germany

Local Chairs

Christian Eichhorn   TU Dortmund, Germany
Steffen Schieweck   TU Dortmund, Germany
Marco Wilhelm   TU Dortmund, Germany

Program Committee

Klaus-Dieter Althoff	DFKI/University of Hildesheim, Germany
Franz Baader	TU Dresden, Germany
Christian Bauckhage	Fraunhofer IAIS, Germany
Sven Behnke	University of Bonn, Germany
Christoph Beierle	University of Hagen, Germany
Ralph Bergmann	University of Trier, Germany
Leopoldo Bertossi	Carleton University, Germany
Chris Biemann	University of Hamburg, Germany
Gerhard Brewka	Leipzig University, Germany
Philipp Cimiano	Bielefeld University, Germany
Jürgen Dix	Clausthal University of Technology, Germany
Igor Douven	Paris-Sorbonne University, France
Didier Dubois	IRIT/RPDMP, France
Stefan Edelkamp	University of Bremen, Germany
Christian Guttmann	Nordic AI Institute/Karolinska Institute/ Univ. of New South Wales, Australia

Barbara Hammer	Bielefeld University, Germany
Malte Helmert	University of Basel, Switzerland
Andreas Hotho	University of Würzburg, Germany
Eyke Hüllermeier	University of Paderborn, Germany
Anthony Hunter	University College London, UK
Steffen Hölldobler	TU Dresden, Germany
Dietmar Jannach	TU Dortmund, Germany
Jean Christoph Jung	Universität Bremen, Germany
Kristian Kersting	TU Darmstadt, Germany
Oliver Kramer	Universität Oldenburg, Germany
Ralf Krestel	Hasso Plattner Institute/University of Potsdam, Germany
Thomas Lukasiewicz	University of Oxford, UK
Till Mossakowski	University of Magdeburg, Germany
Maurice Pagnucco	The University of New South Wales, Australia
Heiko Paulheim	University of Mannheim, Germany
Rafael Peñaloza	Free University of Bozen-Bolzano, Italy
Giuseppe Pirrò	Institute for High Performance Computing and Networking (ICAR-CNR), Italy
Henri Prade	IRIT/CNRS, France
Stefan Roth	TU Darmstadt, Germany
Günter Rudolph	TU Dortmund, Germany
Sebastian Rudolph	TU Dresden, Germany
Klaus-Dieter Schewe	Software Competence Center Hagenberg, Germany
Ute Schmid	University of Bamberg, Germany
Lars Schmidt-Thieme	University of Hildesheim, Germany
Lutz Schröder	Friedrich-Alexander-Universität Erlangen-Nürnberg, Germany
Christoph Schwering	University of New South Wales, Australia
Steffen Staab	University Koblenz-Landau/Univ. of Southampton, UK
Hannes Strass	Leipzig University, Germany
Heiner Stuckenschmidt	University of Mannheim, Germany
Thomas Stützle	Université Libre de Bruxelles, Germany
Paul Thorn	Heinrich-Heine-Universität Düsseldorf, Germany
Ingo J. Timm	University of Trier, Germany
Anni-Yasmin Turhan	TU Dresden, Germany
Jilles Vreeken	MPI for Informatics/Saarland University, Germany
Toby Walsh	NICTA/University of New South Wales, Australia
Stefan Woltran	TU Wien, Vienna

Additional Reviewers

Ahlbrecht, Tobias
Apeldoorn, Daan
Asaadi, Shima
Ayzenshtadt, Viktor
Barteld, Fabian
Bliem, Bernhard
Borgwardt, Stefan
Bremer, Jörg
Buga, Andreea
Dang, Hien
Dietz, Emmanuelle-Anna
Ecke, Andreas
Farazi, Hafez
Fiekas, Niklas
Flesca, Sergio
Grumbach, Lisa
Hassan, Teena Chakkalayil
Henzgen, Sascha
Houben, Sebastian
Huber, Steffen
Igarashi, Ayumi
Jugovac, Michael
Keller, Thomas
Knees, Peter

Koo, Seongyong
Kumar, Abhishek
Kutsch, Steven
Ludewig, Malte
Ma, Ning
Martin Garcia, German
Martinez-Gil, Jorge
Milde, Benjamin
Möller, Ralf
Müller, Gilbert
Nemes, Tania
Nesi, Monica
Neuhaus, Fabian
Nunes, Ingrid
Plaza, Enric
Pommerening, Florian
Sauerwald, Kai
Schweizer, Lukas
Seuß, Dominik
Siebers, Michael
Stram, Rotem
Wernhard, Christoph
Wirth, Christian
Zeyen, Christian

Keynotes

Deep Learning: Theory, Algorithms, and Applications in the Natural Sciences

Pierre Baldi

University of California, Irvine (UCI)
pfbaldi@ics.uci.edu

Abstract. The process of learning is essential for building natural or artificial intelligent systems. Thus, not surprisingly, machine learning is at the center of artificial intelligence today. And deep learning—essentially learning in complex systems comprised of multiple processing stages—is at the forefront of machine learning. In the last few years, deep learning has led to major performance advances in a variety of engineering disciplines from computer vision, to speech recognition, to natural language processing, and to robotics.

In this talk we will first address some fundamental theoretical issues about deep learning through the theory of local learning and deep learning channels. We will then describe inner and outer algorithms for designing deep recursive neural architectures to process structured, variable-size, data such as biological or natural language sequences, phylogenetic or parse trees, and small or large molecules in biochemistry. Finally we will present various applications of deep learning to problems in the natural sciences, such as the detection of exotic particles in high-energy physics, the prediction of molecular properties and reactions in chemistry, and the prediction of protein structures in biology.

Computational Models of Argument:
A Fresh View on Old AI Problems

Gerhard Brewka

Department of Computer Science, Leipzig University, Germany
brewka@informatik.uni-leipzig.de

Abstract. In the last two decades symbolic AI has seen a steady rise of interest in the notion of argument, an old topic of study in philosophy. This interest was fueled by a certain dissatisfaction with existing approaches in knowledge representation, especially default reasoning and inconsistency handling, and by the demands of applications in legal reasoning and related fields. The ultimate goal of computational argumentation is to enable the development of computer-based systems capable to support and to participate in argumentative activities. To this end one has to come up with formal models of the way we usually come to conclusions and make decisions, namely by

1. constructing arguments for and against various options,
2. establishing relationships among the arguments, most notably the attack relation, and
3. identifying interesting subsets of the arguments which represent coherent positions based on these relations.

In the talk we will highlight some of the main ideas and key techniques that have been developed in the field and show how they provide new ways of representing knowledge, handling inconsistencies, and reasoning by default. In particular, we will demonstrate how directed graphs with arbitrary edge labels, which are widely used to visualize argumentation and reasoning scenarios, can be turned into full-fledged knowledge representation formalisms with a whole range of precisely defined semantics.

Probabilistic Programming and its Applications

Luc De Raedt

Department of Computer Science, Katholieke Universiteit Leuven, Belgium
`luc.deraedt@cs.kuleuven.be`

Abstract. Probabilistic programs combine the power of programming languages with that of probabilistic graphical models. There has been a lot of progress in this paradigm over the past twenty years. This talk will introduce probabilistic logic programming languages [1], which are based on Sato's distribution semantics and which extend probabilistic databases. The key idea is that facts or tuples can be annotated with probabilities that indicate their degree of belief. Together with the rules that encode domain knowledge they induce a set of possible worlds. After an introduction to probabilistic programs, which will cover semantics, inference, and learning, the talk will sketch some emerging applications in knowledge based systems, in cognitive robotics and in answering probability questions. The first is concerned with learning rules in knowledge based systems such as CMU's Never Ending Language Learning [2], the second with learning probabilistic action definitions and using these for planning to grasp certain objects [3], the final one with the answering of challenging mathematical exercises about probability that are formulated in natural language [4].

References

1. De Raedt, L., Kimmig, A.: Probabilistic (logic) programming concepts. Mach. Learn. **100**(1), 5–47 (2015)
2. De Raedt, L., Dries, A., Thon, I., Van den Broeck, G., Verbeke, M.: Inducing probabilistic relational rules from probabilistic examples. In: Proceedings of the 25th International Joint Conference on Artificial Intelligence, IJCAI-15, pp. 1835–1843 (2015)
3. Nitti, D., Ravkic, I., Davis, J., De Raedt, L.: Learning the structure of dynamic hybrid relational models. In: Proceedings of the 22nd European Conference on Artificial Intelligence, ECAI-16, pp. 1283–1290 (2016)
4. Dries, A., Kimmig, A., Davis, J., Belle, V., De Raedt, L.: Solving probability problems in natural language. In: Proceedings of the 26th International Joint Conference on Artficial Intelligence, IJCAI-17, pp. 3981–3987 (2017)

Artificial Intelligence for Industrie 4.0

Wolfgang Wahlster

DFKI and Saarland University
www.dfki.de/~wahlster

Abstract. The transformative power of Artificial Intelligence (AI) for the fourth industrial revolution based on cyber-physical production systems is now recognized globally by highly industrialized nations. When we coined the term Industrie 4.0 in 2010, it was already clear to me that machine learning, semantic technologies, real-time action planning as well as plan recognition, collaborative robotics, and intelligent user interfaces are the scientific foundation for smart factories, smart products and smart services. AI is a key enabler for the next generation of smart manufacturing in Industrie 4.0, since it leads to a disruption in traditional workflows, supply chains, value creation, and business models in manufacturing and works towards empowering and expanding workforce expertise. The use of AI in manufacturing is paving the way to the synergistic collaboration between humans and robots in urban smart factories for mass customization [2]. In particular, we present recent results from our Industrie 4.0 projects at DFKI, including hybrid teams of human workers and collaborative robots, deep learning for predictive maintenance of networked production machines and for understanding human behaviors of shop floor workers, semantic technologies for worldwide interoperability of machine-to-machine communication in smart factories and logistics, human-aware and real-time production planning and scheduling for multiagent systems, intelligent industrial assistance systems for human workers, and proactive and situation-aware on-line help and training on the shop floor. The concept of active semantic product memories [3] that serve as digital twins invert the traditional production logic, since in Industrie 4.0 the emerging product is controlling its own production process in a service-oriented multiagent architecture. We discuss use cases from legacy factories which we have upgraded to Industrie 4.0 and show the comparative gains [1] in productivity, stock reduction, resource efficiency, retooling or changeover times, and job satisfaction.

References

1. Schuh, G., Anderl, R., Gausemeier J., ten Hompel, M., Wahlster, W. (eds.) Industrie 4.0 Maturity Index. Managing the Digital Transformation of Companies. Munich: Herbert Utz.
2. Wahlster, W.: Semantic technologies for mass customization. In: Wahlster, W., Grallert, HJ., Wess, S., Friedrich, H., Widenka, T. (eds.) Towards the Internet of Services, pp. 3–14. Springer, Heidelberg (2014)
3. Wahlster, W.: The semantic product memory: an interactive black box for smart objects. In: Wahlster (ed.) SemProM: Foundations of Semantic Product Memories for the Internet of Things, pp. 3–21. Springer, Heidelberg (2013)

Contents

Technical Communications

Full Technical Papers

Employing a Restricted Set of Qualitative Relations in Recognizing Plain Sketches

Ahmed M.H. Abdelfattah(✉) and Wael Zakaria

Faculty of Science, Ain Shams University, Cairo, Egypt
{ahabdelfattah,wael.zakarai}@sci.asu.edu.eg

Abstract. In this paper, we employ aspects of machine learning, computer vision, and qualitative representations to build a classifier of plain sketches. The paper proposes a hybrid technique for accurately recognizing hand-drawn sketches, by relying on a set of qualitative relations between the strokes that compose such sketches, and by taking advantage of two major perspectives for processing images. Our implementation shows promising results for recognizing sketches that have been hand-drawn by human participants.

Keywords: HOG feature learning · Qualitative representation · Sketch recognition

1 Introduction

An important challenge for artificial intelligence is the need to automatically recognize doodles that outline simple objects, which are sketched by normal people (i.e., humans with non-artistic capabilities). The importance stems form the spread and extensive availability of touch-enabled devices. Nowadays, these are everyone's most-preferred, multi-purpose, extensively-used tools. The automatic recognition, however, needs a glimpse of understanding that should be based on human experience (cf. [1]).

A hand-drawn sketch is broadly defined as a rapidly executed freehand drawing that is not usually intended as a finished work. There is still a challenging deficiency and broadness in formally defining sketches and their underlying terms. This is one major source of trouble for human-made machines (a.k.a. computers) to mechanically deal with human-made sketches (e.g., automatically generating or recognizing hand-drawn sketches of objects). For one, this kind of broadness neglects the inability of humans and machines to interact naturally, as they talk different languages and have very different representational forms of conceptual knowledge. This also omits a stream of aspects on sketching that need to be taken into consideration when intelligent computation is involved.

Techniques that traditionally recognize hand-drawn sketches follow one of two major perspectives for processing common sketches: raster and vector. The former considers a sketch as an image, from which a feature vector is built from

© Springer International Publishing AG 2017
G. Kern-Isberner et al. (Eds.): KI 2017, LNAI 10505, pp. 3–14, 2017.
DOI: 10.1007/978-3-319-67190-1_1

a histogram of oriented gradient (HOG) of pixels. Then, it uses a machine learning technique to build a classifier model. On the other hand, vector processing
deals with a sketch as a set of points, from which qualitative representations are
extracted to build a knowledge base of features, on which analogical processing
models can be applied for the recognition process.

This paper presents the results of an implementation of a hybrid technique for
such an initial recognition. The ideas are supported by the results of experiments,
conducted to test the roles of qualitative representations (QR) in recognizing
hand-drawn sketches [1,2]. The technique presented here goes somewhat down
into lower-level representations of sketches, where a sketch is treated as being
consisting of geometric shapes (i.e., sketch constituents) that have simple QR
features, such as relative sizes of geometric shapes, positional relations of any
successive pairs of geometric shapes, and similarity group of any number of
successive geometric shapes that have the same relative sizes.

1.1 The Constituents: An Abstraction

We define a **stroke** $s := \langle p_i \rangle_{i=1}^{n(s)}$ as a sequence of $n(s) \in \mathbb{N}$ tuples (points) that
are sequentially recorded between a pen-down and a pen-up events. Each tuple
p_i may simply be thought of as corresponding to the x_i- and y_i- coordinates
of the pixels composing s, including also a temporal parameter, t_i, to reflect
the time of drawing pixel p_i, for $1 \leq i \leq n(s)$. We also define a **sketch** as a
sequence of strokes, $\mathcal{S} = \langle s_1, s_2, \ldots, s_{m(\mathcal{S})} \rangle$, where i is the stroke number for
each $1 \leq i \leq m(\mathcal{S})$. Two strokes s_i and s_{i+1} are called *successive*. Figure 1a
gives an example of a sketch, $\mathcal{S}_{w_1} = \langle s_1, s_2, s_3, s_4, s_5, s_6, s_7 \rangle$ that contains seven
strokes (i.e., $m(\mathcal{S}_{w_1}) = 7$) corresponding to two successive "ellipses" (circles)
followed by five consecutive "line segments".

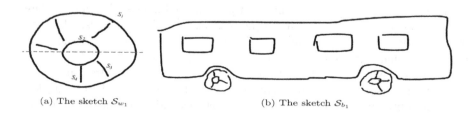

(a) The sketch $\mathcal{S}_{w_1}$ (b) The sketch $\mathcal{S}_{b_1}$

Fig. 1. Two hand-drawn sketches of two different objects: (a) a WHEEL object (which
is referred to in the text as $\mathcal{S}_{w_1}$, with some illustrative labels and a dashed line), and
(b) a BUS object (referred to as $\mathcal{S}_{b_1}$).

To assist the learner presented later in Sect. 2, we base the structuring on
a **feature space** that contains guiding information about all sketches of the
set of objects to be learnt (cf. Fig. 2). From all the sketched objects, we gather
and record a specific number of qualitative representational (QR) criteria (which
are limited in this paper to the following three kinds): *relative size*, *positional*

relation, and *similarity group*. Relative sizes measure the drawn strokes' metric lengths compared to that of the whole sketch they compose. The size of the (whole) sketch is measured by calculating the perimeter of the canvas that contains it. Based on this size, values ranging from zero to the perimeter's are discretized into intervals, each of which is assigned to one of seven **relative sizes** (cf. Sect. 2.2). A **positional relation** is a binary relation between (the centroids of) the two geometric shapes corresponding to successive strokes in a sketch. For a sketch $S = \langle s_1, s_2, \ldots, s_{m(S)} \rangle$, positional relations $s_i \, R \, s_{i+1}$ on $S \times S$ determine the location of a stroke s_{i+1}, relative to that of the stroke immediately sketched before it, s_i, for $1 \leq i < m(S)$. The positional relation R is one of the following nine:[1] equal ($\equiv$), up ($\uparrow$), right ($\rightarrow$), left ($\leftarrow$), up-left ($\nwarrow$), up-right ($\nearrow$), down ($\downarrow$), down-left ($\swarrow$), and down-right ($\searrow$). A **similarity group** is a collection of two or more successive geometric shapes of the same relative sizes. For instance, two successive ellipses can be combined in one group if they have the same relative size. We record, for each sketch $S = \langle s_1, s_2, \ldots, s_{m(S)} \rangle$, a constant number M of selected features that reflect the qualitative representation of a sketch $\mathbf{QR}(S)$. A QR feature vector, f_S, is used for recording numerical values $\langle f_i \rangle_{i=1}^M$ as representatives of the stored feature values. The features we use here have the fixed ordering $f_1, f_2, \ldots, f_M$ (cf. Sect. 2). If no stroke satisfies a given feature i, then $f_i := 0$. The feature vectors of all the N sketches (the learning sample) are collected in the feature space F. If $f_i \neq 0$, then the selected feature number i is satisfied by exactly f_i strokes (of each of the N sketches). The value $f_i \neq 0$ means that either (i) f_i represents the number of geometric shapes (for the corresponding relative size features), (ii) f_i represents the number of pairs of geometric shapes (for positional relation features), or (iii) f_i represents the number of n geometric shapes (for similarity group $n \geq 2$). Thus, the QR feature space F is a matrix of $N \times (M+1)$ integers, in which the N rows represent the N sketches (of the objects under consideration), while F's first M columns represent the M QR feature vectors of the sketches, and the $(M+1)^{\text{st}}$ column is a class value (e.g., the sketched object's label; cf. the "class value" column in the right part of Fig. 2).

1.2   The Constituents: An Example

The wheel in Fig. 1a has been sketched in the following order: outer circle/ellipse, inner ellipse, four lines started at down right and move clockwise. For this object, our technique extracts several features, such that the relative size of the outer ellipse is medium, the smaller ellipse is tiny, and the four lines are tiny. The positional relations between the outer circle and the inner circle is that the inner is equal to the outer (w.r.t. centroid positions), but the first line is down right of the inner ellipse, the second line is down left the first one, etc. The four lines are grouped together and create one group (cf. Sect. 1.1).

Let $S_{w_1} = \langle s_i \rangle_{i=1}^7$ represent the wheel sketch in Fig. 1a. Let s_1 and s_2 be the outer and inner "circles", respectively, and assume that their centroids have the

---

[1] Think of the 9 relations filling a 3×3 tic-tac-toe-like board: .

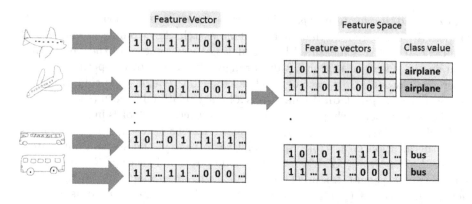

Fig. 2. Constructing the features space F from the N sketches.

same location. Let s_3 and s_4 be the right and left strokes, respectively, below the dashed line in the same figure (that is, s_4 is the line stroke immediately below the inner circle s_2, and s_3 is the stroke to its right in the figure[2]). Instead of the notation, $\equiv (s_2, s_1)$, of the positional relation "equal", we use the infix notation $s_2 \equiv s_1$ to indicate that s_2 is located at the same location of s_1. Since s_3 is a successor to s_2, and spatially located to the latter's "down-right", we write $s_2 \searrow s_3$. Similarly, $s_4 \nearrow s_3$ indicates that the semi-vertical line segment, s_4, comes "down-left" of (and successor to) the leaned line segment, s_3. The five consecutive line strokes $\langle s_i \rangle_{i=3}^{7}$ of the wheel $\mathcal{S}_{w_1}$ of Fig. 1a are successive and have the same relative size (which is "tiny" in this case). Therefore, these strokes are combined, forming a group labelled "*group of two or more lines*". The feature vector for $\mathcal{S}_{w_1}$ contains values that reflect the following features of the wheel in Fig. 1a: five tiny lines, one tiny circle, and one small circle. This means that the value of feature "tiny-line" is 4, of "tiny-circle" is 1, and of "small-circle" is 1. The similarity group labelled "*group of two circles*" has the value 1.

2   Methodology

We present a Qualitative Representation used for Sketch Recognition Technique, or *QuRSeR-Tech* for short, which builds its classification model by learning a restricted set of common qualitative representations between the primitive building blocks described in Sect. 1.1. QuRSeR-Tech is used for recognizing newly drawn sketches based on a previously given set of learning sketches (decomposed into the aforementioned primitives). It consists of two learning systems and, consequently, two kinds of datasets used for the learning purposes.

The first classifier utilizes HOG-based extracted features [3] for recognizing drawn strokes within geometric shapes. The **geometric shapes** are considered

---

[2] Note that the labeling of the strokes is intended to reflect the successiveness of the strokes; e.g., s_4 is sketched after s_3. This is vital, especially because the presented positional relations are not commutative (except $\equiv$, of course).

the low-level representation constituents of a sketch. The proposed geometric shapes in this paper are the following seven primitives: "line", "arc", "ellipse", "poly-line", "triangle", "rectangle", or "polygon". For each geometric shape, we collect a set of hand-drawn sketches describing it. These shapes are used as a training dataset in order to learn and build a classifier model that, in turn, is able to classify a given stroke as one of the geometric shapes. To that aim, we extract the features that discriminate each kind of image. The first dataset contains hand-drawn strokes (the learning samples), each of which is classified into one of the geometric shapes. The second classifier uses QR-based extracted features for recognizing a hand-drawn sketch to an object name. The second dataset contains hand-drawn sketches, each of which is classified into one of the **object names**, which are: "AIRPLANE", "BICYCLE", "BUS", or "HOUSE", in this paper.

2.1   StoG Classifier: The 1st Learner

The first learning system in QuRSeR-Tech is called *StrokeToGeometric-classifier* (StoG), which builds its classifier model to recognize a hand-drawn stroke. After that, all recognized geometric shapes and their qualitative representations are stored together, to build a new dataset that will be set as input for the second learning system (cf. Sect. 2.3).

The reader is reminded that Histogram of Gradient Orientation (HOG) is a method that is based on evaluating well-normalized local histograms of image gradient orientations in a dense grid. HOG's basic idea is that local object appearance and shape can often be characterized rather well by the distribution of local intensity gradients or edge directions, even without precise knowledge of the corresponding gradient or edge positions [3]. In order to extract HOG features of an image, one starts with describing the structure of the image from which the HOG features are extracted. Each gray image is represented by a matrix $\text{IMG}_{w \times h}$ of integer numbers, w and h, varying between 0 and 255, with $\text{IMG}(i,j)$ representing the intensity of the image at pixels $1 \leq i \leq w$ and $1 \leq j \leq h$. The image IMG is resized to $\text{IMG}'_{128 \times 128}$. A function, such as the *extractHOGFeatures*[3], can be applied to extract the HOG features of the resized image IMG', which gives the ability to set the values of its parameters depending on the needs. The output of this function is the extracted HOG features from a gray image $\text{IMG}'_{128 \times 128}$, which returns a 1-by-250 feature vector. These features encode local shape information from regions within an image. Therefore, for each image, we extract 250 features stored as an instance in the dataset. As a result, if we have k images, then we extract a feature space as a matrix called $\text{HogF}_{k \times 250}$, with one extra column attached that represents the class value (geometric shape) of each image. So the output is $\text{HogF}_{k \times 251}$.

A machine learning algorithm, particularly support vector machines (SVM), takes the extracted feature space HogF of all images as an input, and produces a classifier model called StrokeToGeometric-classifier (StoG) that is able to classify

---

[3] This is one of the predefined functions within the Matlab computer vision toolbox.

a drawn stroke to one of the geometric shapes mentioned earlier. In order to use StoG for testing an unknown classified image $UIM_{w \times M}$, the following steps are followed: (i) resize the image into $UIM'_{128 \times 128}$, (ii) extract its HOG features UIMHOG (which is a 1×250 vector), and (iii) apply StoG to UIMHOG, where the output will be the class value (geometric name) of the image. Figure 3 gives an example of a real case of a hand-drawn sketch (BUS), in which there are 15 strokes that have been drawn. StoG's application to each of the drawn strokes classifies them into: polygon, ellipse, ellipse, ellipse, line, line, line, ellipse, line, line, line, rectangle, rectangle, rectangle, and rectangle.

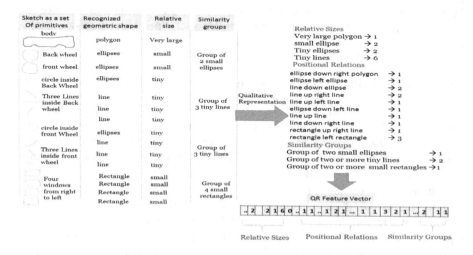

Fig. 3. QR feature vector of a sketched bus ($f_{S_{b_1}}$ of Fig. 1b).

2.2   QR Identification

One of the main goals is to study the role of qualitative representations in building a classifier model that recognizes hand-drawn sketches. We use three qualitative representations here.

Relative Sizes of Strokes (cf. Fig. 4a): The absolute size of a stroke $s := \langle p_i \rangle_{i=1}^{n(s)}$, called $size(s)$, is the accumulated distances between every two successive points p_i and p_{i+1} belonging to s (for $i < n(s)$). This can be formulated as $size(s) = \sum_{i=1}^{n(s)-1} \sqrt{(x_i - x_{i+1})^2 + (y_i - y_{i+1})^2}$. The relative size is also calculated for each stroke w.r.t. the sketch it belongs to. In our case, we use only relative sizes based on the discretization of the absolute size into one of the following seven discrete values: tiny, small, medium, semi medium, large, very large, huge. We conducted experiments with human subjects, in which the participants draw wheels of busses in different sizes, but almost always approximate a relative size (say "medium") w.r.t. the whole bus sketch. Furthermore, also based on our experiments, rectangles appear (as windows) in the sketches of a house object in large or very large relative sizes, whereas rectangles (as windows) in the sketches of bus objects appear in medium relative sizes (w.r.t. the whole BUS sketch). Figure 3 shows that the relative sizes of the drawn strokes: polygon, ellipse, ellipse, ellipse, line, line, line, ellipse, line, line, line, rectangle, rectangle, rectangle, and rectangle are very large, small, small, tiny, tiny, tiny, tiny, tiny, tiny, tiny, tiny, small, small, small, and small, respectively. We extracted 49 relative size features: for each one of the seven geometric shapes, we use seven relative size features. The relative size features, thus, are: tiny lines, ..., huge lines; tiny arcs, ..., huge arcs; ...; and tiny polygons, ..., huge polygons. In Fig. 3, the relative feature "very large polygon" is 1, which means that there is only one very large drawn polygon, and the relative size feature "tiny lines" is 6, which means that there are 6 drawn tiny lines.

Positional Relations (cf. Fig. 4b): A positional relation is calculated based on geometric properties of every two successive strokes, s_i and s_{i+1}, where the relation is calculated for s_{i+1} with respect to s_i (cf. Sect. 1.1). Thus, we make use of 441 features: $s_i \, R \, s_{i+1}$, where $R \in \{\equiv, \rightarrow, \leftarrow, \uparrow, \searrow, \nearrow, \downarrow, \swarrow, \searrow\}$ (i.e., $7 \times 9 \times 7 = 441$). An example is shown in Fig. 3, where the positional relation called "rectangle $\leftarrow$ rectangle" is set to 3, because there are three pairs of successive strokes having the same positional relation feature.

Similarity Groups (cf. Fig. 4c): A similarity group is inspired by the human vision system, and aims to create groups of similar successive strokes. A participant may, for instance, draw some lines —of similar relative sizes— inside a wheel, which are combined to form one group of (two or more) geometric shapes. Each of the 7 geometric shapes will have 2 kinds of similarity groups (namely, a group of two geometric shapes, or a group of two or more geometric shapes). Therefore, existing similarity groups are: group of two lines, group of two or more lines; group of two arcs, group of two or more arcs; ...; group of two polygons, group of two or more polygons (cf. Fig. 3). Hence, we extracted 14 features.

2.3 StOb Classifier: The 2nd Learner

The StOb classifier is a backbone of QuRSeR-Tech, and is used for classifying a hand-drawn sketch. This classifier is used to recognize a hand-drawn sketch, where it predicts the object name after each drawn stroke. The three kinds of extracted features for each sketch are stored together, forming a matrix called QR feature space F (cf. Sect. 1), with 504 features (i.e., 49 relative sizes, plus 441 positional relations, and 14 similarity groups). In order to build a classifier, we extract the same number of features for each sketch. This is achieved by building a feature space of all the possible 504 QR features, initialized to zero. Each time the system extracts a QR feature, it just adds +1 to the corresponding feature. Figure 5 summarizes the learning processes. While the subject is sketching an object, every stroke is classified into a geometric shape using the StoG-classifier. Then, using QR, a feature vector is built of three kinds of important features relative size, positional relation, and similarity.

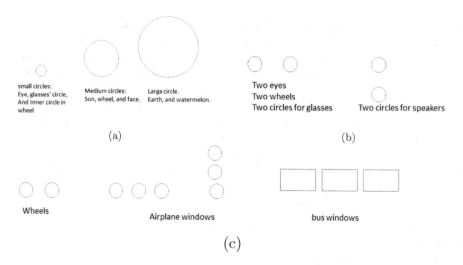

Fig. 4. The chosen kinds of QR: (a) Relative size examples. (b) Positional relation examples. (c) Similarity groups examples.

3 Experimental Results

We aim at building a classifier model that identifies hand-drawn sketches by recognizing their composing strokes and some qualitative interrelationships between those strokes. To that aim, we first try to define an abstract sketch in terms of the composing strokes, then employ the gathered interrelationships to learn specific sketches. The following two datasets have been collected through two experiments, conducted on human participants (see below), in order to provide the classification processes with as many realistic training datasets, from which the system can learn to build its model.

Hand-Drawn Geometric Shapes Dataset: In the first dataset, we collect hand-drawn strokes that represent the constituents of hand-drawn sketches, and then extract their HOG features to build the aforementioned HOG feature space. The strokes are classified into one of the seven geometric shapes suggested in this paper (cf. Sect. 2). A GUI interface has been implemented (in Matlab) for sketching and collecting hand-drawn geometric shapes. Using this interface, the experiment was conducted on human subjects, where each subject sketched all the geometric shapes with different scales, orientations, and positions. After collecting the hand-drawn geometric shapes, we converted them into HOG feature space.

   The core point is to apply one of the machine learning algorithms, particularly support vector machines SVM on the HOG feature space, to get a classifier (StoG) that is used for recognizing a newly sketched stroke and classifying it into one of the geometric shapes: line, arc, ellipse, poly-line, or polygon. The StoG classifier records an accuracy of 88.4% for recognizing a newly sketched

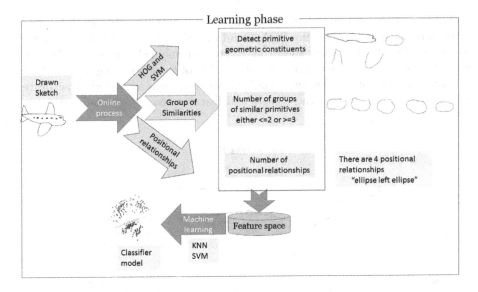

Fig. 5. The learning phase in QuRSeR-Tech.

hand-drawn geometric shape. Further analyses are made to classify the polygon into: triangle, rectangle, or polygon. This is done by extracting its HOG features, and comparing the latter with the features of the collected dataset using SVM. Figure 7a shows the StrokeToGeometric-Classifier's confusion matrix, in which the arc and ellipses can be recognized with accuracy greater than 90%, while the other shapes can be recognized with accuracy greater than 83%. Note that 10% of the poly-lines are recognized as polygons, so we use further processes to make sure that the shape is open or closed by calculating the (metric) distance between the start and last point of a drawn stroke.

Hand-Drawn Sketches Dataset: In this dataset, we collect hand-drawn sketches for four specific objects: AIRPLANE, BICYCLE, BUS, and HOUSE. Using the implemented GUI interface, another experiment has been conducted on 12 subjects, where each subject drew 20 sketches—five for each one of the four objects. The qualitative representation QR of all those sketches are extracted and stored in the QR feature space, F. By applying SVM to the feature space F, a sketchToObject-classifier is used for recognizing hand-drawn objects and classifying them into one of the 4 objects just mentioned. The sketchToObject-classifier have an accuracy of 80%. Figure 7b shows the StrokeToGeometric-Classifier's confusion matrix, in which all objects are classified correctly with percentage greater than 80%. In order to show the effect of each QR feature (namely: relative size, similarity group, and positional relation), we build and measure the accuracy of the following 7 models: relative size, similarity group, positional relation, relative size and similarity group, relative size and positional relation, similarity group and positional relation, and all QR. Figure 6 shows that for each of the 7 cases,

4 classifier models are tested (namely: linear SVM without using PCA for feature selection, linear SVM using PCA, Quadratic SVM without PCA, Quadratic SVM with PCA). The results show that the three combined QR feature plays an important role to achieve the best accuracy. One of the interesting observations is that, without using positional relations, we still have a somewhat accurate classifier. This implies that these particular features need more modifications.

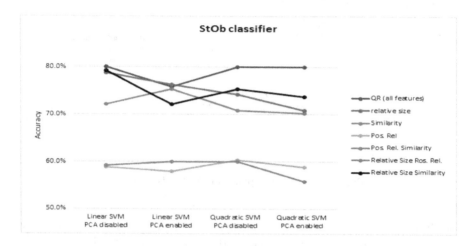

Fig. 6. SketchToObject classifiers accuracy

StoG classifier				
Arc	91%			4%	4%
ellipse		94%			6%
line	10%		86%	5%	
polyline	2%	2%	3%	84%	10%
polygon	3%	7%		3%	87%
	Arc	ellipse	line	polyline	polygon

(a)

StOb classifier			
Airplane	83%		10%	7%
Bicycle	8%	87%	5%	
Bus	13%	5%	68%	13%
House	8%	5%	5%	82%
	Airplane	Bicycle	Bus	House

(b)

Fig. 7. The confusion matrices of: (a) the StoG classifier, and (b) the StOb classifier, which result from implementing the proposed technique.

4   Conclusive Remarks

Understanding what plain sketches represent, in a way similar to what humans do, is a challenging problem for artificial intelligence. The representation of plain sketches using qualitative features seems to play a key role in mechanizing this understanding, because these features are usually stable across many transformations, and provide a natural approach compared to human perception and comparison. Qualitative models that can be used to represent sketches are traditionally based on two aspects. The first aspect is the way of segmenting an object's contour into meaningful edges. The second aspect is the level of detail for describing an object. The way of handling these aspects can distinguish one model from another.

Here, we proposed a hybrid distinguishing technique, called *QuRSeR-Tech*, which has been implemented to recognize hand-drawn sketches based on dealing with its constituents, the composing strokes, in an abstract way. The technique consists of two main stages that work on the abstracted, primitive constituents: the StoG classifier (that extracts HOG features of each stroke), and quadratic SVM (that is based on the HOG features for classifying the stroke into a geometric shape). To get a classifier with an acceptable accuracy, we set the parameters: cell size, block size, block overlap, number of bins, and the signed orientation to [4 4], [2 2], [50% 50%], 8, and false, respectively. The StoG classifier recorded 88.4% accuracy for recognizing the strokes to geometric shapes. The StOb classifier builds a new representation for the hand-drawn sketches by recording three kinds of qualitative representation: relative size, positional relation, and group of similarity. Based on this new representation and quadratic SVM, the StOb classifier is able to recognize plain sketches with accuracy 80%. Some comparative studies have been conducted to see the effect of each one of the three kinds of QR, in which we showed that the StOb classifier's accuracy will decrease if any of the mentioned representations is missing. In both of the two classifiers, we apply PCA to reduce the features to only the features that are highly correlated to the class value.

The results of the proposed technique seem promising to extend the technique's functionality to recognizing other sketches using the suggested set of qualitative relations (or an extended set thereof). The technique can, in the future, be used to gather more sketches and their composing strokes, learning also their QR interrelationships. The technique still needs to handle the cases when single strokes are disconnected, for some reason, resulting in more than one sub-stroke for one or more of the composing strokes. The conducted experiments, on which the results in this paper are built, are enhanced versions of those presented in [1,2], re-implemented to serve this paper's purpose, and tested on two workstations with Windows 10, Matlab 2016a with computer vision toolbox, and the classification learner application. All sketches have been collected via WACOM pens on WACOM touch screens. Some sketches from the dataset in [4] are used as guiding images to the participants.

It is worth mentioning that the ideas presented in this paper are in connection with others in the literature (such as [5–8], to mention a few). For example, [8] give a method based on fuzzy hybrid-based features to classify strokes into geometric primitives. A human computer interactive system is developed to determine the ambiguous results and revising the "missrecognitions". Their system is developed to classify eight specific primitive shapes. PaleoSketch is also a primitive shape recognizer that classifies single strokes into certain primitive geometric shapes (cf. [7]). Of the primitive geometric shapes that can be recognized are line, polyline, circle, ellipse, curve, arc, helix, and spiral (cf. [7]). A higher-level of qualitative representation based on *edge-cycles* is described in [6]. Edge-cycles are sequences of edges connected end-to-end, whose last edge connects back to the first. The results of the edge-cycle representation outperforms that of the edge-level representation —produced by CogSketch in [5]— in learning to classify hand-drawn sketches of everyday objects. Although the remarkable performance of edge-cycles representation, it has its own set of problems that can lead to misclassification of sketched concepts (cf. [6]).

Acknowledgements. The authors acknowledge the role of the Artificial Intelligence and Cognitive Science Lab that has recently been established at the Faculty of Science, Ain Shams University, Cairo, Egypt, supported by the Institute of Cognitive Science at the University of Osnabrück in Germany. The work in this paper is part of the activities of the JESICS project, which has been funded by the German Academic Exchange Service (DAAD) within the framework of the German-Arab Research partnerships Programme Line 4 under grant agreement 57247603.

References

1. Abdel-Fattah, A.M.H., Zakaria, W., Abdelghaffar, N., Abdelmoneim, N., Elsaadany, N., Schwering, A., Kühnberger, K.U.: Towards the modeling of sketch-based understanding: can computers interpret what non-artists draw? In: SHAPES 3.0 - The shape of Things, Larnaca, Cyprus, 2–6 November 2015 (2015)
2. Abdel-Fattah, A.M.H., Zakaria, W., Abdelghaffar, N., Abdelmoneim, N., Schneider, S., Kühnberger, K.U.: A preliminary assessment of conceptual salience for automatic sketching. In: The 4th International Workshop on Artificial Intelligence and Cognition. CEUR-WS (2016)
3. Dalal, N., Triggs, B., Schmid, C.: Human detection using oriented histograms of flow and appearance. In: Leonardis, A., Bischof, H., Pinz, A. (eds.) ECCV 2006. LNCS, vol. 3952, pp. 428–441. Springer, Heidelberg (2006). doi:10.1007/11744047_33
4. Eitz, M., Hays, J., Alexa, M.: How do humans sketch objects? ACM Trans. Graph. **31**(4), 1–10 (2012)
5. Lovett, A., Dehghani, M., Forbus, K.D.: Efficient learning of qualitative descriptions for sketch recognition. In: Proceedings of the 20th International Workshop on Qualitative Reasoning (2006)
6. McLure, M.D., Friedman, S.E., Lovett, A., Forbus, K.D.: Edge-cycles: a qualitative sketch representation to support recognition. In: Proceedings of the 25th International Workshop on Qualitative Reasoning (2011)
7. Paulson, B., Hammond, T.: Paleosketch: accurate primitive sketch recognition and beautification. In: Proceedings of the 13th International Conference on Intelligent User Interfaces, IUI 2008, pp. 1–10. ACM, New York (2008). http://doi.acm.org/10.1145/1378773.1378775
8. Wang, S., Wang, G., Gao, M., Yu, S.: Using fuzzy hybrid features to classify strokes in interactive sketches. Adv. Mech. Eng. **5** (2013). doi:10.1155/2013/259152

Interval Based Relaxation Heuristics for Numeric Planning with Action Costs

Johannes Aldinger$^{(\boxtimes)}$ and Bernhard Nebel

Department of Computer Science, University of Freiburg, Freiburg, Germany
{aldinger,nebel}@informatik.uni-freiburg.de

Abstract. Many real-world problems can be expressed in terms of states and actions that modify the world to reach a certain goal. Such problems can be solved by automated planning. Numeric planning supports numeric quantities such as resources or physical properties in addition to the propositional variables from classical planning. We approach numeric planning with heuristic search and introduce adaptations of the relaxation heuristics $h_{\max}$, h_{add} and h_{FF} to interval based relaxation frameworks. In contrast to previous approaches, the heuristics presented in this paper are not limited to fragments of numeric planning with instantaneous actions (such as linear or acyclic numeric planning tasks) and support action costs.

1 Introduction

Whereas domain-independent planning has proven successful, numeric quantities such as physical properties (e.g. velocity) and resources (e.g. fuel level) cannot be modeled in classical planning. As many real world problems feature numeric quantities, we aim to advance domain-independent planning by including numeric quantities, leading to *numeric planning*.

The performance of applying informed search algorithms such as hill-climbing or best-first search to planning depends on the quality of the underlying heuristic. One challenge is to design good heuristic estimators for numeric planning. We are interested in adapting the forward chaining *delete relaxation* heuristics $h_{\max}$, h_{add} and h_{FF} to numeric planning. The *delete relaxation* from classical planning ignores negative interactions between actions by neglecting delete effects: effects that falsify propositional variables. As such the set of achieved propositions grows monotonically, and heuristics can be computed in polynomial time. For numeric planning, intervals offer a way to compactly represent an over-approximation of arbitrarily many values that can be achieved by a variable.

Another challenge is that numeric actions are non-idempotent operations: applying the same numeric effect to a state more than once can yield a new distinct successor every time. This makes heuristics based on a basic *interval relaxation* only polynomial in the length of a shortest relaxed plan [13]. Recently, Aldinger et al. [2] proposed a more sophisticated interval-based relaxation framework for numeric planning that captures arbitrarily many repetitions of applying

© Springer International Publishing AG 2017
G. Kern-Isberner et al. (Eds.): KI 2017, LNAI 10505, pp. 15–28, 2017.
DOI: 10.1007/978-3-319-67190-1_2

a numeric action in one step. The plan existence problem in this *repetition relax-ation* is polynomial in the input for tasks with acyclic dependencies.

Previous work on numeric relaxation heuristics is either restricted to a frag-ment of numeric planning, e.g. Metric FF [13] is restricted to linear tasks whereas MIPS [9], Colin [8] and ENHSP [18] only deal with uniform action costs. The h_{max} and h_{add} variants of Scala et al. [17] correspond roughly to the *planning graph* approach with a *repetition relaxation* in this paper. We are interested in adaptations which offer heuristic guidance for *all* numeric planning tasks with instantaneous actions including actions with non-linear effects and non-uniform action cost. Notably, we are also interested in computing a h_{FF}-like heuristic, i.e., a heuristic basing its estimate on the extraction of valid relaxed plans.

In this paper, we explore the design space of numeric relaxation heuristics with regard to two relaxation methods (*interval* or *repetition* relaxation), two methods of aggregating heuristic costs (*max* and *sum*), and two search tech-niques for relaxed reachability (a *planning graph method* and *priority queues*). We identify tractable combinations and derive heuristics which also take action costs into account. We propose a new method to handle tasks with cyclic depen-dencies in the numeric effects which differs from Scala et al. [18]. Finally we present a generalization to the marking method of relevant operators used by h_{FF}, which explicates target values in the intervals to extract relaxed plans.

2   Interval Relaxation

A delete relaxation is a simplification of a planning instance where facts which are achieved once remain achieved. Thus, the set of achieved values grows monoton-ically. In relaxed classical planning, actions are idempotent and therefore, this growth is bounded by the number of actions in the planning task. In numeric planning, actions are non-idempotent operations and the number of values a variable can attain is unbounded even by executing a single action repeatedly. Aiming towards a tractable relaxation for numeric planning, intervals are an obvious choice to represent the achieved values of a variable, as they offer a compact representation. Furthermore, the number of action applications can be restricted as well. We discuss two relaxation frameworks that approach this challenge differently.

The depth of a relaxed planning graph is restricted to the length of a short-est relaxed plan, which allows us to compute an *interval relaxed* planning graph very much like in classical planning. However, desired heuristic properties (such as admissibility for h_{max}) can not be guaranteed in this framework. The *repeti-tion relaxation* uses a semi-symbolic representation of intervals to simulate the behavior of arbitrary many action repetitions at once. This makes relaxed actions idempotent, and the plan existence problem can be decided in polynomial time. In this section, we give a condensed overview of these relaxation frameworks, borrowing notation from Aldinger et al. [2].

Interval arithmetic [19] uses an upper and a lower bound to enclose the actual value of a number. Intervals $[\underline{x}, \overline{x}]$ contain all rational numbers from $\underline{x}$ to $\overline{x}$. We refer to the lower bound of an interval x by $\underline{x}$ and to the upper bound by $\overline{x}$. Intervals can be *closed* or *open* and we denote closed interval bounds by brackets $[\cdot,\cdot]$ and open interval bounds by parentheses $(\cdot,\cdot)$.

A numeric planning task $\Pi = \langle V_P, V_N, \mathcal{A}, \mathcal{I}, \mathcal{G}, \gamma \rangle$ is a 6-tuple, where V_P is a set of propositional variables with domain $\{true, false\}$, V_N is a set of numeric variables with domain $\mathbb{Q}^\infty := \mathbb{Q} \cup \{-\infty, \infty\}$, $\mathcal{A}$ is a set of actions, $\mathcal{I}$ the initial state, $\mathcal{G}$ a goal *condition* and $\gamma : \mathcal{A} \rightarrow \mathbb{Q}^+$ is a function assigning a strictly positive rational cost to each action. A *state* is a (full) mapping from variables $V := V_P \cup V_N$ to values from their respective domain. A *numeric expression* $(\xi_1 \circ \xi_2)$ is an arithmetic expression with operators $\circ \in \{+, -, \times, \div\}$ and expressions ξ_1 and ξ_2 recursively defined over variables V_N and constants from $\mathbb{Q}$. A *numeric constraint* $(\xi \trianglerighteq 0)$ compares numeric expressions ξ to 0 with $\trianglerighteq \in \{\geq, >, =\}$ and a (goal or action) *condition* is a conjunction of propositions and *numeric constraints*. *Numeric effects* are assignments $(v \circ= \xi)$ where v is a variable from V_N, $\circ= \in \{:=, +=, -=, \times=, \div=\}$ and ξ is a *numeric expression*. Actions in $\mathcal{A}$ have the form $\langle \text{pre}, \text{eff} \rangle$ and consist of a *condition* pre and a set of *effects* eff containing at most one truth assignment for each propositional variable and at most one *numeric effect* for each numeric variable.

The semantic of a numeric planning task is straightforward: conditions are satisfied in a state if all propositions evaluate to *true* and all numeric constraints are satisfied, where numeric expressions are evaluated recursively. The evaluation of expression ξ in state s is denoted by $s(\xi)$. Actions are *applicable* in a state, iff the precondition is satisfied and none of its effects causes a division by zero. The successor state s' obtained by applying an action in state s is s, expect for variables that appear in an *effect*. Propositional variables are assigned the new truth value and the values $s'(v_n)$ of each numeric variable v_n are evaluations of the expression on the right hand side of the effect in s applied to $s(v_n)$ according to the assignment operator. A *plan* π is a sequence of consecutively applicable actions that leads from $\mathcal{I}$ to a state satisfying $\mathcal{G}$.

We consider two relaxation frameworks: the *interval relaxation* and the *repetition relaxation*. Syntactically, they differ only slightly from the unrelaxed task. The domains of numeric variables V_N are now intervals. The interpretation of constants and the values of variables in the initial state are degenerate (one element) intervals. The semantics of both relaxations are based on interval arithmetic. Numeric expressions evaluate to intervals, and numeric constraints are satisfied, if numbers exist within these intervals that satisfy the constraint. Propositional effects that would set a variable to *false* are ignored.

Numeric effects ensure monotonicity by use of the convex union $r = x \sqcup y$ where $\underline{r} = \min(\underline{x}, \underline{y})$ and $\overline{r} = \max(\overline{x}, \overline{y})$. The successor state s' obtained by applying an action in s is again s, except for variables v that appear on the left hand side of numeric effects. These variables are mapped to $s'(v) = s(v) \sqcup \text{eval}(v)$, where eval$(v)$ is a relaxation dependent evaluation of the numeric effect. For the *interval relaxation*, eval(v) is the evaluation of the effect right-hand side, using interval arithmetic on the intervals from s. For the *repetition relaxation* eval(v) is the result of simulating arbitrary many repetitions of the effect in isolation.

The idea behind the *repetition relaxation* is that relaxed actions become idempotent if arbitrary many repetitions are handled at once. The evaluation of arbitrary many action applications does not have to be computed with an actual simulation. More efficiently, it is sufficient to consider the *behavior* of numeric effects. If an *additive* effect ($+=$ and $-=$) extends an interval bound of a variable in a state once, it can extend that bound to any value by applying the action multiple times. The repetition result of an additive effect only depends on whether the evaluated effect interval contains negative or positive numbers, but it does not depend on the amount. For multiplicative effects, the assignment can contract or expand depending on whether the effects intervals contains numbers with absolute value greater or less than 1 and switch signs if it contains negative elements. This observation allows us to decompose the evaluation of numeric effects into *behavior classes* $\mathcal{B} = \{(-\infty, -1), \{-1\}, (-1, 0), \{0\}, (0, 1), \{1\}, (1, \infty)\}$ and then unite these partial effects to obtain the interpretation of eval(v) in the *repetition relaxation*. Detailed semantics are found in the original paper [2]. We remark that the decomposition into *behavior classes* bases the evaluation eval(v) on the values of $s(v)$ before the application. As such, $s'(v)$ can hit new behavior classes. As the number of behavior classes is restricted, the repetition relaxed actions are "pseudo-idempotent": they can change up to three times (v has a different behavior if it is negative, zero or positive). Another source of non-idempotence comes from the interaction between actions which becomes especially problematic if these dependencies are cyclic. As such, the authors of the *repetition relaxation* deem it only feasible for tasks with acyclic dependencies.

2.1   Cyclic Dependencies

The interval which is reached by applying a numeric effect $v_n \circ= \xi$ *depends* on the values of all variables in ξ. This dependency relation induces a *dependency graph*. If the *dependency graph* is acyclic, sequences of actions are pseudo-idempotent as the values of the variables stabilize in topological order.

Cyclic dependencies can make sequences of actions non-idempotent. It is an open research question, whether the interval that is reached after repeatedly applying a sequence of actions causing a cycle can be determined in polynomial time. In order to enforce a topology nevertheless, we can break cycles by introducing auxiliary variables. The check for cycles can be done in polynomial time by algorithms checking for connected components in the dependency graph. In the heuristic, we include special cycle breaker actions which can reinsert the values of the auxiliary variables to the higher level original variable in a controlled manner. The implementation of these cycle breaker actions opens design space. Tractable heuristics have to bound the number of reinsertions.

The most coarse cycle breaker action sets changing variables to $(-\infty, \infty)$: an interval which can not be extended thus ensuring idempotence. A little more accurate is to only set an interval bound to infinity if the interval changed into the respective direction. This relates very much to the *additive effects transformation* [18], which compiles assignments $x := \xi$ into increase effects $x += \xi - x$. Both approaches relax cyclic effects even further by assuming that a shifted bound can be extended arbitrary often by the same margin. An advantage of our method is the restriction of cycle handling to the cycle breaker actions, which does not affect the preconditions of all other actions.

3   Numeric Planning Graph Heuristics

We want to solve a *delete relaxed* simplification of a planning problem in order to guide search in the original one. For classical planning, the relaxed plan existence problem is easy: starting from the initial state, we can iteratively apply all applicable actions to the relaxed state in parallel. The procedure terminates when a fix-point is reached. The *relaxed parallel planning graph* [14] is a graph representation of this planning procedure. It consists of alternating state layers of reachable propositions and action layers of actions which are applicable in that propositional state. The forward propagation heuristics h_{add} [5,6] and its admissible counterpart h_{max} [4] estimate the cost $\gamma(v_p)$ to achieve the propositions v_p for each achieving action a by $\gamma(v_p) := \min_a(\gamma(v_p), \gamma(a) + \gamma(\text{pre}(a)))$. Propositions that hold in the initial state are initialized to cost $\gamma(v_p) = 0$ and to $\gamma(v_p) = \infty$ otherwise. The action precondition cost $\gamma(\text{pre}(a))$ is an estimate of the cost of a set of propositions. The heuristics differ in how the cost of this set is estimated. For h_{max}, the most expensive proposition cost $\gamma(\text{pre}(a)) := \max_{v_p \in \text{pre}(a)} \gamma(v_p)$ is used, while h_{add} uses the *sum* of all preconditions $\gamma(\text{pre}(a)) := \sum_{v_p \in \text{pre}(a)} \gamma(v_p)$ instead. The h_{FF} heuristic [14] improves on h_{add} by *marking* actions that are required to compute the h_{add} estimate regressively, and as such it computes a relaxed plan, using its cost as h_{FF} estimate.

3.1   Heuristic Estimators for Numeric Planning

We discuss tractable extensions of the heuristics h_{max}, h_{add} and h_{FF} in the two interval based relaxation frameworks introduced in the previous section: the *interval relaxation* and the *repetition relaxation*. In a purely propositional setting, facts can be seen as variable-value pairs, where the value of propositional variables are subsets of $\{true, false\}$. Similarly, a "fact" for numeric planning is a variable-value pair where the values of numeric variables are intervals. In contrast to classical planning, there are infinitely many such variable-value pairs. Tractable heuristics have to restrict the number of considered numeric facts.

Numeric facts occur as *implicit preconditions* of the actions of the planning task. A numeric effect $v \circ = \xi$ can reach a certain interval $s'(v)$ by certain combinations of the intervals $s(v)$ and $s(\xi)$ before the application of the action. In general, there are infinitely many possible combinations of $s(v)$ and $s(\xi)$ to reach $s'(v)$ and thus, the pairs $\langle v, s(v) \rangle$ and all pairs of variables $\langle v_e, s(v_e) \rangle$ where v_e appears in the expression ξ are implicit preconditions. Similarly, numeric constraints $\xi \trianglerighteq 0$ can be satisfied by infinitely many target values $q_e \in s(\xi)$ satisfying $q_e \trianglerighteq 0$. These target values q_e can be reached by combinations of values of the variables in ξ, making them implicit preconditions, too.

A numeric relaxation heuristic has to ensure that first, values in the precondition enable the required values in the effect and second, that the number of considered numeric facts is bounded. We discuss a *planning graph* based and a *priority queue* based approach to restrict this number, both of which are motivated by the method of computing the cost formulas in classical planning.

The first approach is based on the parallel *planning graph* representation for relaxed planning. The considered facts are restricted to one variable-value pair for each variable in the state layers of the planning graph. For interval based planning, several parallel actions can alter the same variable, in which case the convex union of the individual results is used. The cost of a variable-value pair is again the cost of the cheapest achiever, and the cost of a set of such numeric facts is the sum or the maximum of each variable-value pair. Implicit preconditions from constraints and effects are included in the "fact set cost".

A different approach to restrict the considered numeric facts is to use a generalized Dijkstra algorithm for estimating the fact or fact set costs. Facts are processed according to a *priority queue* storing the cost to achieve them. As other actions can alter a variable while a new value is still in the priority queue, the considered numeric facts are convex unions of the effects values reachable at enqueue time and the variable's value at dequeue time.

Both approaches, the *planning graph* and the *priority queue* based approach restrict the number of considered variable-value pairs. Note that other approaches are conceivable, e.g. Scala et al. [17] discriminate facts by condition type. We will now discuss combinations of both approaches with *interval* or *repetition* relaxation which guarantee polynomial time bounds on the heuristic computation.

3.2   Heuristics Based on Planning Graphs

In the relaxed *planning graph*, the length of a shortest relaxed plan restricts the maximal number of layers required until the goal formula is satisfied for the first time. Therefore, heuristic cost estimations are polynomial in the output size $|\mathcal{A}| \times |\mathcal{V}| \times |\pi^\star|$ where $\pi^\star$ is a shortest (but not necessarily cheapest) plan. Variations of this approach are often used for numeric planning [7,9,13,18].

A weakness of this approach is that, for the *interval relaxation*, $h_{\max}$ does not compute admissible estimates in tasks with action costs, and the cost estimates for h_{add} can be higher than the estimates that would be computed by the formulas for classical planning. The reason is that a fact can be achieved at a better cost in a deeper layer in the planning graph. This is a problem for numeric planning, because no a priori bound can be given on how deep the better value could be found. Opposed to relaxed classical planning, where heuristic computation terminates when a fix-point is reached and no new facts are added or reached at a cheaper cost from one layer to the next, *interval relaxed* "facts" will usually not reach a fix-point. Instead, graph generation terminates as soon as the goal formula is satisfied for the first time. Admissibility of $h_{\max}$ can be enforced by setting the cost of all actions to the cheapest cost among action costs applicable in the current layer, which kind of obviates the use of action costs[1].

A combination of the *repetition relaxation* with the *planning graph* based variable-value pair selection strategy is not as promising as other combinations. The repetition relaxation is coarser than the interval relaxation as it aggregates arbitrary many repetitions. The planning graph approach is less accurate than the priority queue based approach when several actions of different cost alter the same variable: the result is the convex union of all individual results but the cost is the cost of the best achiever. The approach combines the downsides of the components without really making up for that.

3.3   Heuristics Based on Priority Queues

Priority queue based heuristics in the *interval relaxation* framework lack tractability as unboundedly many cheap actions can be processed before relevant ones.

The number of variable-value pairs which are inserted into the *priority queue* has to be bounded. Unfortunately, even *repetition relaxed* actions, or sequences thereof can be non-idempotent. Effects in the *repetition relaxation* are applied on the intervals fixed to the preceding state. Interactions of an action with itself are not considered when computing the behavior of the action. Similarly, a sequence of actions can be non-idempotent, even if every single action is idempotent. There are three sources of non-idempotence: variables hitting new behavior classes, interacting variables and, finally, cyclic dependencies between variables.

First, applying a numeric effect can cause a variable to hit a new behavior class. This type of non-idempotence does not impair tractability, as the behavior of a variable can change at most three times ($v > 0$, $v = 0$, $v < 0$).

Second, the result of a numeric effect depends on the variables in the assigned expression. As such, actions are reenqueued whenever an implicit precondition achieves a new value. For many planning tasks, the dependency relation between variables is acyclic. While the plan existence problem in the *repetition relaxation* is polynomial for acyclic tasks [2] this does not restrict the number of queue insertions polynomially. The problem occurs if cheap actions depend on many other more expensive actions which reside in topologically higher layers of the dependency graph. Theorem 1 of the Addendum to this paper [3] shows an example requiring exponentially many enqueue operations. The heuristic becomes tractable if actions which have an *implicit precondition* on a variable are only enqueued after all topologically higher variables have been processed. However, this means that variables in the lower layers have to wait for variables in a higher layer regardless of their cost. As the values achieved by the topologically higher variables might not be required, admissibility of h_{max} is impaired with this approach. For h_{add}, overestimating the heuristic value is acceptable, allowing us to

---

[1] Scala et al. [17] run into a similar problem using "asynchronous subgoaling" and have to set the cost of hard conditions to 0 to ensure admissibility of h_{max}.

block enqueuing of topologically lower variables until topologically higher variables are processed. A workaround for $h_{\max}$ is to compute $h_{\max}$ in two phases. In the first phase, maximally reachable intervals for all variables are determined, and tractability is ensured by delaying topologically lower variables. Then, in a second phase, the maximally reachable values from the first phase are used for the assign effects. Topological dependencies do not have to be respected with maximally reachable intervals, as now action sequences are idempotent.

The third source of idempotence are cycles in the *dependency graph*, which can be broken by introducing auxiliary variables as presented in Sect. 2.1.

Bounding non-idempotence ensures that *priority queue* based algorithms can compute *repetition relaxed* estimates for $h_{\max}$ and h_{add} in polynomial time.

3.4 h_{FF}-Based Heuristics

The h_{FF} heuristic computes a *relaxed plan*, and uses the cost of this plan as heuristic estimate. As in classical planning, this plan is computed *regressively* by greedily marking required facts and actions based on the h_{add} estimates. The marking procedure captures beneficial interactions such as an action enabling precondition facts of several others. Numeric planning offers even more room for improving h_{FF} over h_{add} by not having to fully enable *implicit preconditions*, as numeric facts do not necessarily have to enable the whole reachable interval. A major contribution of this paper is a generalization of the marking procedure to numeric planning, which selects explicit *target values* in the precondition fact intervals in order to determine the necessary part of numeric preconditions.

Example 1. Let $s_0(v_1) = [0,0]$ and $s_0(v_2) = [1,1]$ and actions $a_1 = \langle P, v_1 \mathrel{+}= v_2 \rangle$ and $a_2 = \langle \emptyset, v_2 := 5 \rangle$ with cost $\gamma(a_1) = 1$ and $\gamma(a_2) = 10$ having to satisfy a condition $\mathcal{C} : v_1 - 1 \geq 0$. Applying a_1 is sufficient to satisfy $\mathcal{C}$. However, as a_1 has a precondition P, a_2 could be applicable before a_1 making $s(v_2) = [1,5]$ with $\gamma = 10$. Explicating target values allows us to set $q_2 = 1$ for v_2, making h_{FF} chose $s_0(v_2) = [1,1]$ with $\gamma = 0$ instead, thus marking a_1 but not a_2.

For the *repetition relaxed* approach, explicating target values also allows to determine the actual number of repetitions required for each action, and thus, the *repetition relaxed* h_{FF} heuristic can compute an *interval relaxed* plan which is more accurate than accounting for relaxed actions only once.

The progression step generates a sequence of relaxed states with the property that the intervals for each variable are monotonically increasing and the last state satisfies the goal condition. Starting from the goal conditions, we explicate target values in these intervals regressively, while marking actions enabling them. The h_{FF} estimate is then the cost of marked actions.

3.5   Explication of Target Values

Given a sequence of relaxed states determined by a progressive reachability analysis and the actions achieving the respective reachable intervals, we want to explicate target values in these intervals so that the resulting plan has minimal cost. The explication procedure has to respect *local target value constraints* for each action, which ensure that all implicit and explicit preconditions of the action are satisfied and that the action achieves the desired values. These *local target value constraints* generate a set of feasible sub-intervals, where each choice of an explicit target value can lead to some relaxed plan.

The *global target value optimization problem* is then an optimization problem that selects target values in the feasible sub-intervals which minimize the cost of the resulting relaxed plan. Each target value choice influences the *local target value constraints* of all preceding states. The global target value optimization problem is NP-complete (see Theorem 2 of the Addendum [3]) and we will therefore propose approximate target value selection strategies for the local constraints and drop the requirement that the extracted plan has to be optimal.

The sequence of relaxed states starts in a state s_0 consisting of degenerate point intervals, the state for which the h_{FF} estimate has to be computed. The generated relaxed state sequence depends on the progression method: with the planning graph approach, relaxed states are the "fact layers" of the planning graph, whereas with a priority queue based approach the states are given by all intervals reachable with cost equal to the priority at enqueue time. The last state of the reachability sequence satisfies the goal condition.

The *local target value constraints* ensure that for each numeric effect of a given action a, all implicit and explicit preconditions are satisfied in the relaxed state before the application of the action, and that the execution of its numeric effects enables the target values desired from the global optimization component.

Three basic target value conditions ensure satisfaction of a *local target value constraint* of an action: Its explicit preconditions have to be satisfied (1). This requires numeric expressions evaluate to a desired target value (2). Finally, the numeric effects have to reach the desired target value (3). These basic target value conditions then restrict the intervals of the preceding state by sub-intervals containing feasible selection choices for the global target value optimization.

The first basic target value condition has to ensure that a constraint $\xi \unrhd 0$ is satisfied in the state $s(\xi)$ preceding the action. We know that the action is applicable in the progression $s \vDash s(\xi) \unrhd 0$. Therefore, the feasible sub-intervals $s(\xi) \cap [0, \infty)$ for "$\geq$", $s(\xi) \cap (0, \infty)$ for "$>$" or $s(\xi) \cap [0, 0]$ for "$=$" are non-empty.

Example 2. Let ξ evaluate to $s(\xi) = [-2, 3]$. The constraint $\xi \geq 0$ can be satisfied by any value in the feasible sub-interval $[0, 3]$, the result of $[-2, 3] \cap [0, \infty)$.

The second basic target value condition has to ensure that a *numeric expression* $\xi_1 \circ \xi_2$ evaluates to the target value q. Feasible sub-intervals can be obtained by first determining potential partners which make the expression evaluate to q by solving the equations $I_1 \circ s(\xi_2) = s(q)$ and $s(\xi_1) \circ I_2 = s(q)$ for I_1 or I_2 respectively, where I_1 and I_2 are intervals containing all numbers that have a partner in $s(\xi_2)$ or $s(\xi_1)$ respectively so that the expression evaluates to q. The feasible sub-intervals for the optimization component are then $s(\xi_1) \cap I_1$ and $s(\xi_2) \cap I_2$. Special care has to been taken if the inversely reachable partner "intervals" come from a division by an interval containing 0, an interval operation which can cause gaps in the resulting interval. We cannot relax the partner property, and therefore, the respective partner interval I_1 or I_2 is split.

Example 3. Let $s(\xi_1) = [-1, \frac{1}{2}]$ and $s(\xi_2) = [-3, 2]$ for $\xi_1 \times \xi_2$ enabling $q = 2$. The partner interval $I_1 = [2, 2] \div [-3, 2]$ is split into $I_1^1 = [2, 2] \div [-3, 0) = (-\infty, -\frac{2}{3}]$ and $I_1^2 = [2, 2] \div (0, 2] = [1, \infty)$. The partner interval $I_2 = [2, 2] \div [-1, \frac{1}{2}]$ is split into $I_2^1 = [2, 2] \div [-1, 0) = (-\infty, -2]$ and $I_2^2 = [2, 2] \div (0, \frac{1}{2}] = [4, \infty)$. The feasible sub-intervals are then $s(\xi_1) \cap I_1^1 = [-1, -\frac{2}{3}]$ and $s(\xi_2) \cap I_2^1 = [-3, -2]$ as the disjunctions $s(\xi_1) \cap I_1^2$ and $s(\xi_2) \cap I_2^2$ are empty.

Finally, the third basic target value condition ensures that a *numeric effect* $v \circ= \xi$ reaches the desired target value q, where reaching a target value has to be considered in a relaxed sense respecting the underlying relaxation semantics (repetition or interval relaxation). For the *interval relaxation*, this third basic type can be reduced to the second basic target value condition by interpreting the assignment $v \circ= \xi$ as an assignment of the expression $v := v \circ \xi$ with the appropriate assignment operator. This expression $v \circ \xi$ (or only ξ in the case of $:=$) has then to reach the required target value q. Care has to be taken here if the target value q was only reached because of the convex union of the relaxation semantics. When searching for partner intervals I_1 and I_2 we can use intervals $(-\infty, q]$ or $[q, \infty)$ instead of the degenerate interval $[q, q]$, where the diverging bound depends on whether the addition of q extends the upper or the lower bound of the value of v in the previous state $q > \overline{s(v)}$ or $q < \underline{s(v)}$. These values are larger (smaller) than needed and contain q because of the convex union.

Example 4. Let $s(v) = [0, 0]$ be assigned an expression $s(\xi) = [1, 2]$ by a numeric effect $v += \xi$ and let the required target value $q = \frac{1}{2}$. The corresponding expression $[0, 0] + [1, 2]$ evaluates to $[1, 2]$ which does not contain $q = \frac{1}{2}$. The partner intervals I_1 and I_2 use $[\frac{1}{2}, \infty)$ for q and we obtain $I_1 = [\frac{1}{2}, \infty) - [1, 2] = [-\frac{3}{2}, \infty)$ and $I_2 = [\frac{1}{2}, \infty) - [0, 0] = [\frac{1}{2}, \infty)$ So the target values can be chosen in $[0, 0] \cap [-\frac{3}{2}, \infty) = [0, 0]$ for $s(v)$ and $[1, 2] \cap [\frac{1}{2}, \infty) = [1, 2]$ for $s(\xi)$.

For the *repetition relaxation*, the feasible sub-intervals are intersections of the behavior classes involved to establish the desired target value with the value in the preceding state. The number of required repetitions is determined analogously to the repetitions from Theorem 6 of Aldinger et al. [2].

With these three basic target value conditions we can ensure that the propagation of values satisfying the *local target value constraints* leads to the desired target value. The explication process can propagate a list of feasible sub-intervals for the implicit and explicit preconditions to the previous layer.

The *global target value optimization problem* is now the problem to find a cost minimal set of target values for each feasible sub-interval of the *local target value constraints*. The cost of a target value is the cost of the achieving action (multiplied by the number of required repetitions for the repetition relaxation) plus the constraint cost of all of its (implicit and explicit) preconditions.

Determining target values in the feasible sub-intervals optimally is intractable. Therefore, our explication process selects locally promising target values. The values of all variables have to reach the point intervals from s_0 at the end of the regression procedure, making proximity to the starting values $s_0(v)$ an indicator for good target values. An exception to this rule are open intervals in the *repetition relaxation*. As open intervals are only generated by contracting effects, values close to open interval bounds can only be reached by applying the contraction repeatedly and it is advisable to keep a safety margin to open interval bounds.

4 Implementation and Experiments

The Fast Downward planning system [12] is a modular planning system that is widely used in classical planning. We extend Fast Downward to support numeric planning from PDDL 2.1, layer 2 [10] as well as selected features from PDDL 3 such as global constraints. The original Fast Downward does not support floating point numbers and thus, major modifications had to be performed.

While classical planning tasks are restricted to actions with integer valued action costs, numeric planning tasks come with more sophisticated metric expressions instrumenting over several variables. Numeric Fast Downward (NFD) supports linear state-independent instrumentation effects [7], which are evaluated in the initial state and compiled into a rational valued action cost. Instrumentation variables are detected automatically and stored separately which allows search algorithms to prune states that only differ in these variables.

We implemented the heuristics $h_{\max}$, h_{add} and h_{FF} in the two most promising combinations of relaxation and "fact" selection scheme identified in the previous section: the *planning graph* approach in an *interval relaxation* (identified by the superscript h^{gi}) and the *priority queue* based approach in the *repetition relaxation* (identified by the superscript h^{qr}).

4.1 Experiments

We performed experiments on various numeric domains [1,11,16] comparing NFD to Metric FF [13] and two configurations of ENHSP: subgoaling with redundant constraints $\hat{h}^{radd}_{hbd+}$ [17] and h_{AIBR} [18]. We used greedy best first search for all NFD heuristics. Experiments were run on a cluster with a timeout of 30 min for each instance. Table 1 shows the number of solved instances on various domains. A star indicates errors in ENHSPs preprocessing component.

Our heuristics perform slightly worse than Metric FF for the planning domains that both planners can solve. In principle, the heuristic estimates from h^{gi}_{FF} should resemble Metric FF most. Differences can probably be attributed to different search algorihms. Metric FF is restricted to linear tasks and cannot find solutions for nonlinear problems such as geo-rovers or jumpbot. ENHSP excels at block-grouping and performs roughly as good as most NFD configurations on the domains both planners can solve. ENHSP ignores action costs and uses unit cost actions instead. There was no domain in the benchmarks which exploits this weakness. The *priority queue* based *repetition relaxed* h^{qr}_{FF} heuristic does

Table 1. Solved instances on various numeric domains

Domain	Metric FF	ENHSP		NFD			
		$\hat{h}^{radd}_{hbd+}$	h_{AIBR}	h^{gi}_{add}	h^{qr}_{add}	h^{gi}_{FF}	h^{qr}_{FF}
Block-grouping (192)	22	**122**	62	15	18	14	28
Counters (78)	**36**	14	34	21	11	21	31
Depots (22)	**20**	⋆	⋆	7	10	10	11
Driverlog (40)	**34**	⋆	⋆	29	31	30	30
Farmland (50)	9	0	**50**	17	10	19	23
Geo-rovers (21)	0	⋆	⋆	1	0	1	**2**
Jumpbot (20)	0	3	15	**17**	0	15	13
Plant-watering (51)	**22**	12	**22**	0	15	0	15
Rovers (20)	**12**	⋆	⋆	0	3	1	4
Satellite (40)	26	21	22	12	23	19	**29**
Settlers (20)	**9**	⋆	⋆	0	0	0	2
Sokoban (325)	0	37	0	**70**	**70**	69	**70**
Zenotravel (20)	**20**	⋆	⋆	7	7	8	9
Sum (899)	210	209	205	196	198	207	**267**

not only solve most instances, but it also solves several instances in each of the domains, indicating that our heuristics offer guidance for all domains.

The jumpbot domain [1] is particularly interesting as it models physical properties in a dynamic world. It features cyclic, non-linear effects for turning, accelerating or deccelerating the robot, as well as classical preconditions. Therefore, it can neither be solved by control engineering [15] nor by planners requiring linear tasks such as Metric FF.

5   Conclusion

We discussed different approaches to tractable heuristics for interval relaxed numeric planning and considered different relaxation frameworks: the *interval relaxation* and the *repetition relaxation* with different restriction schemes for the variable-value pairs considered during heuristic exploration: one motivated from the *planning graph*, another from a *priority queue*. We highlighted critical combinations that impair tractability of the heuristic or restrict algorithms to a subset of numeric planning tasks. Furthermore, we generalized the marking procedure of h_{FF}.

We implemented the well known planning graph heuristics h_{max}, h_{add} and h_{FF} from classical planning in these frameworks and established heuristics which are suitable for all numeric planning tasks expressible in PDDL 2.1, layer 2. We showed experimentally that the general heuristics can find plans even for planning tasks with cycles, non-linear effects and action costs, providing a baseline for future approaches.

Acknowledgments. This work was supported by the DFG through grants EXC1086 (BrainLinks-BrainTools) and NE 623/13-2 (HYBRIS-2).

References

1. Aldinger, J.: The Jumpbot domain for numeric planning. Technical report 279, University of Freiburg (2016)
2. Aldinger, J., Mattmüller, R., Göbelbecker, M.: Complexity of interval relaxed numeric planning. In: Hölldobler, S., Krötzsch, M., Peñaloza, R., Rudolph, S. (eds.) KI 2015. LNCS (LNAI), vol. 9324, pp. 19–31. Springer, Cham (2015). doi:10.1007/978-3-319-24489-1_2
3. Aldinger, J., Nebel, B.: Addentum to 'Interval Based Relaxation Heuristics for Numeric Planning with Action Costs'. Technical report 280, University of Freiburg (2017)
4. Bonet, B., Geffner, H.: Planning as heuristic search: new results. In: Biundo, S., Fox, M. (eds.) ECP 1999. LNCS (LNAI), vol. 1809, pp. 360–372. Springer, Heidelberg (2000). doi:10.1007/10720246_28
5. Bonet, B., Geffner, H.: Planning as heuristic search. Artif. Intell. **129**(1–2), 5–33 (2001)
6. Bonet, B., Loerincs, G., Geffner, H.: A robust and fast action selection mechanism for planning. In: Proceedings of the 14th National Conference on Artificial Intelligence and 9th Innovative Applications of Artificial Intelligence Conference (AAAI 1997/IAAI 1997), 27–31 July 1997, pp. 714–719 (1997)
7. Coles, A., Coles, A., Fox, M., Long, D.: A hybrid LP-RPG heuristic for modelling numeric ressource flows in planning. J. Artif. Intell. Res. **46**, 343–412 (2013)
8. Coles, A., Fox, M., Long, D., Smith, A.: A hybrid relaxed planning graph-LP heuristic for numeric planning domains. In: Proceedings of the 20th International Conference on Automated Planning and Search (ICAPS 2008) (2008)
9. Edelkamp, S.: Generalizing the relaxed planning heuristic to non-linear tasks. In: Biundo, S., Frühwirth, T., Palm, G. (eds.) KI 2004. LNCS (LNAI), vol. 3238, pp. 198–212. Springer, Heidelberg (2004). doi:10.1007/978-3-540-30221-6_16
10. Fox, M., Long, D.: PDDL2.1: an extension to PDDL for expressing temporal planning domains. J. Artif. Intell. Res. **20**, 61–124 (2003)
11. Francès, G., Geffner, H.: Modeling and computation in planning: better heuristics from more expressive languages. In: Proceedings of the 25th International Conference on Automated Planning and Scheduling (ICAPS 2015) (2015)
12. Helmert, M.: The fast downward planning system. J. Artif. Intell. Res. **26**, 191–246 (2006)
13. Hoffmann, J.: The metric-FF planning system: translating 'Ignoring Delete Lists' to numeric state variables. J. Artif. Intell. Res. **20**, 291–341 (2003)
14. Hoffmann, J., Nebel, B.: The FF planning system: fast plan generation through heuristic search. J. Artif. Intell. Res. **14**, 253–302 (2001)
15. Löhr, J., Eyerich, P., Keller, T., Nebel, B.: A planning based framework for controlling hybrid systems. In: Proceedings of the 22nd International Conference on Automated Planning and Scheduling (ICAPS 2012) (2012)
16. Long, D., Fox, M.: An overview and analysis of the results of the 3rd international planning competition. J. Artif. Intell. Res. **20**, 1–59 (2003)

17. Scala, E., Haslum, P., Thiébaux, S.: Heuristics for numeric planning via subgoaling. In: Proceedings of the 25th International Joint Conference on Artificial Intelligence (IJCAI 2016), pp. 655–663 (2016)
18. Scala, E., Haslum, P., Thiébaux, S., Ramírez, M.: Interval-based relaxation for general numeric planning. In: Proceedings of the 22nd European Conference on Artificial Intelligence (ECAI 2016), pp. 655–663 (2016)
19. Young, R.C.: The algebra of many-valued quantities. Math. Ann. **104**, 260–290 (1931)

Expected Outcomes and Manipulations in Online Fair Division

Martin Aleksandrov[1,2,3]($\boxtimes$) and Toby Walsh[1,2,3]

[1] UNSW Sydney, Kensington, Australia
[2] Data61, CSIRO, Melbourne, Australia
{martin.aleksandrov,toby.walsh}@data61.csiro.au
[3] TU Berlin, Berlin, Germany

Abstract. Two simple and attractive mechanisms for the fair division of indivisible goods in an online setting are LIKE and BALANCED LIKE. We study some fundamental computational problems concerning the outcomes of these mechanisms. In particular, we consider what expected outcomes are *possible*, what outcomes are *necessary* and how to compute their *exact* outcomes. In general, we show that such questions are more tractable to compute for LIKE than for BALANCED LIKE. As LIKE is strategy proof but BALANCED LIKE is not, we also consider the computational problem of how, with BALANCED LIKE, an agent can compute a strategic bid to improve their outcome. We prove that this problem is intractable in general.

1 Introduction

Fair division is a fundamental problem in allocating resources among competing agents. Many practical fair division problems are online. We present two such settings. For example, in a food bank, we must start allocating food as it is donated. It is too late to wait until the end of the day before we start distributing the food to charities. As a second example, in allocating deceased organs to patients we must match newly donated organs swiftly. We cannot wait till more organs arrive before deciding on the precise match.

Motivated by such problems, Walsh has proposed a simple online model for the fair division of indivisible items in which the items arrive over time [19]. Aleksandrov et al. analysed two simple and attractive randomized mechanisms for such fair division problems: LIKE and BALANCED LIKE [1]. The LIKE mechanism allocates an arriving item uniformly at random between the agents that "like" it. It satisfies equal treatment of equals, and it is both strategy proof and envy free ex ante [1]. Indeed, any mechanism that is envy free ex ante assigns items to agents with the same probabilities as LIKE does. However, the LIKE mechanism is not very fair ex post as it can possibly allocate all items to one agent. The BALANCED LIKE mechanism is fairer. It allocates an arriving item uniformly at random between the agents that "like" it who have the fewest items currently. BALANCED LIKE bounds the envy one agent has for another's allocation ex post. However, this comes at the price of no longer being strategy proof

© Springer International Publishing AG 2017
G. Kern-Isberner et al. (Eds.): KI 2017, LNAI 10505, pp. 29–43, 2017.
DOI: 10.1007/978-3-319-67190-1_3

in general [1]. When restricted to 2 agents and 0/1 utilities, BALANCED LIKE is strategy proof. These mechanisms are simple and satisfy many desirable axioms. For these reasons, we now turn attention to their computational properties.

In practice, it may be difficult to query the agents each time an item arrives. The chair will often collect the preferences of the agents in advance, and allocate items to agents as they arrive. There are several settings where it is reasonable to suppose that the chair does that. For instance, in the food bank problem, a good proxy for the utility of an item to a charity that likes it might simply be its retail price. This is public information. As a second example, in deceased organ matching, the utility of allocating an organ to a patient might be computed from a simple formula that takes account of the age of the organ, the age of the patient and a number of other medical factors. This is again public information. The chair might then be interested in what outcomes are possible, necessary or exact based on these declared preferences. For example, the chair might be concerned that agents receive enough utility or particular essential items. Alternatively, the chair might want to be sure that a favored agent gets a particular item. Also, they might even want to give similar utility to each agent or bias the future allocation in case some agents receive only a few items and are promised to receive more in expectation.

There are two sources of uncertainty in deciding these outcomes. First, both mechanisms are randomized. Therefore each mechanism returns a probability distribution over actual outcomes. Second, as the problem is online, the arrival order of items is typically unknown. We consider here the problem of the chair computing what outcomes are possible, necessary or exact depending on both sources of uncertainty. In particular, we focus on computing whether an agent can possibly or necessarily receive a given expected utility. These results easily translate into whether an agent can possibly or necessarily receive a given item. We simply give most of the agent's utility to that item. Also, as all our results hold in the case of binary utilities, they can also be viewed as computing whether an agent can possibly or necessarily receive a given expected number of items. Whilst some of our results consider general utilities, such utilities are mainly used to compare outcomes and do not need to be elicited explicitly. General utilities are not used when bidding or allocating items. Such "like" and "not like" reporting has advantages. It is simple, does not require costly eliciting of utilities of agents for items and it also leads to mechanisms with nice axioms.

Our contributions: We consider three settings: the chair knows the arrival ordering of items, the arrival ordering is drawn from some probability distribution, and the allocation of past items is known. In all settings, we study the problem of the chair computing possible, necessary and exact outcomes of LIKE and BALANCED LIKE. For both mechanisms, these problems are intractable even with 2 agents and when the ordering of items is not fixed. In contrast, with any number of agents, computing each of these outcomes is tractable for LIKE and intractable for BALANCED LIKE when the ordering of items is fixed. Interestingly, computing outcomes with BALANCED LIKE becomes tractable in this setting only when restricted to 2 agents. Further, computing outcomes is tractable for both mechanisms at a certain moment of time when a new item arrives supposing the allocation of past items is known. In addition, we study a closely related problem of whether an agent can manipulate these mechanisms by strategically misreporting their preferences. Our computational results have a number of interesting consequences. For example, recall that the BALANCED LIKE mechanism is fairer but not strategy proof. However, we show that computing a manipulation of this mechanism is intractable in general.

2   Preliminaries

We next provide basic definitions of online instances, the LIKE and BALANCED LIKE mechanisms and their outcomes.

Allocation instance: An *instance* $\mathcal{I} = (A, O, U, \Delta)$ of an online fair division problem has (1) a set A of *agents* $a_1, \ldots, a_n$, (2) a set O of indivisible *items* $o_1, \ldots, o_m$, (3) a matrix $U = (u_{ik})_{m \times n}$ where u_{ik} is the *cardinal utility* of agent a_i for item o_k and (4) a matrix $\Delta = (\delta_{kj})_{m \times m}$ where δ_{kj} is a *probability* that item o_k arrives in moment j.

We consider *binary* utilities and *general* rational non-negative utilities. We say that agent a_i *likes* item o_k if $u_{ik} > 0$. Further, we assume that one item arrives in each moment j, i.e. $\sum_{k=1:m} \delta_{kj} = 1$.

Online setting: Suppose items o_1 to o_j have arrived at moments 1 to j, respectively. Given $o = (o_1, \ldots, o_j)$, let $\Delta(o)$ be its probability, $\pi(j, o)$ the current allocation of these items to agents, $p(\pi(j, o))$ its probability and $u_i(\pi(j, o))$ the additive utility of agent a_i for the items they receive in $\pi(j, o)$. Now, suppose that item o_k arrives at moment $(j+1)$ with probability $\delta_{k(j+1)}$ when each agent a_i places a rational non-negative *bid* v_{ik} for this item and a *mechanism* then decides its allocation to a *feasible* agent in an *online* manner, i.g. given $\pi(j, o)$ and *no* information about future items.

Mechanisms: We consider the randomized LIKE and BALANCED LIKE mechanisms from [1]. With the LIKE mechanism, agent a_i is feasible for item o_k if $v_{ik} > 0$. With the BALANCED LIKE mechanism, agent a_i is feasible for item o_k if $v_{ik} > 0$ and have so far received fewest items given $\pi(j, o)$ among those agents that bid positively for item o_k. Let the number of feasible agents be f_k. The probability that a feasible agent a_i is allocated item o_k is equal to $1/f_k$.

Possible, necessary and exact outcomes: We consider *expected* probabilities depending on what information is available to the chair. If the allocation $\pi(j, o)$ is the only available information, we use $p_i(j + 1, \pi(j, o))$ for the *probability* of agent a_i for the item that arrives at moment $(j + 1)$. If the order o is the only available information, we use $p_i(j + 1, o)$ for the *probability* of agent a_i for the item that arrives at moment $(j + 1)$. It is equal to $\sum_{\pi(j,o)} p(\pi(j, o)) \cdot p_i(j + 1, \pi(j, o))$. If there is no information about o or $\pi(j, o)$, we use $p_i(j + 1)$ for the *probability* of agent a_i for the item that arrives at moment $(j + 1)$. It is equal to $\sum_o \Delta(o) \cdot p_i(j + 1, o)$. We next define expected utilities of agents for items in each of these settings. Given $\pi(j, o)$, we use $u_{ij}(\pi(j, o))$ for the *utility* of agent a_i. It is equal to $u_i(\pi(j, o)) + p_i(j + 1, \pi(j, o))$. Given o, we use $u_{ij}(o)$ for the *utility* of agent a_i. It is equal to $\sum_{\pi(j,o)} p(\pi(j, o)) \cdot u_i(\pi(j, o))$. Given Δ, we use $u_{ij}(\Delta)$ for the *utility* of agent a_i. It is equal to $\sum_o \Delta(o) \cdot u_{ij}(o)$.

The *probability (or utility)* of agent a_i at moment j is *possible* if their probability (or utility) is positive. The outcome of agent a_i at moment j is *necessary* at least some rational number k if their probability (or utility) is at least k. We also say that the outcome of agent a_i at moment j is *exact* if we want to compute the exact value of their probability (or utility).

We study the complexity of computing possible, necessary and exact outcomes. For a mechanism that allocates all items to agents that like them, note that possible and necessary outcomes are directly related. For this reason, we only study necessary and exact outcomes. Our results for possible outcomes are inherited. We next show this relation.

Suppose we ask if $p_i(j + 1) > 0$ holds. This is true iff there is an ordering o and allocation $\pi(j, o)$ of the first j items such that $p_i(j + 1, \pi(j, o)) > 0$. We therefore conclude that $p_i(j + 1) > 0$ iff $p_i(j + 1) \geq \epsilon$ where $0 < \epsilon \leq \min_{o, \pi(j, o)} \Delta(o) \cdot p(\pi(j, o)) \cdot p_i(j + 1, \pi(j, o))$. Note that this minimum value is positive and, consequently, such ϵ always exists. Such a relation is not true for utilities. For the utility of agent a_i, we have that $u_{ij}(\Delta) > 0$ holds iff agent a_i bids positively for at least one item and at least one item arrives. This problem is easy to decide. However, deciding if $u_{ij}(\Delta) \geq k$ holds might not be so easy.

Recall that we consider three settings: when the past allocation of items to agents is known, when the ordering of items is unknown and when the ordering of items is known. We next observe that all outcomes are tractable in the setting when the past allocation is known, *fixed* and *no* information about future items is available.

Items arriving online: Let us suppose that the first j items have arrived and their allocation be $\pi(j, o)$. Suppose now that item o_k arrives at moment $(j + 1)$. For both LIKE and BALANCED LIKE, the *exact* value of $p_i(j + 1, \pi(j, o))$ is equal to $\sum_{k=1:m} \delta_{k(j+1)} \cdot (1/f_k)$ and the *exact* value of $u_i(\pi(j, o))$ is equal to the sum of the cardinal utilities of agent a_i for the items they are allocated in $\pi(j, o)$. Both of these exact outcomes, the value of $u_{ij}(\pi(j, o))$ and therefore any *possible* and *necessary* outcomes in this setting can be computed in $\mathcal{O}(m \cdot n)$ time and space.

We use popular reductions and computational problems from computational complexity, graph theory and set theory in order to show our hardness results.

Computational complexity: We use complexity classes of decision and counting problems such as P, NP, coNP and #P, and mappings such as *Karp*, *Turing*, *parsimonious* and *arithmetic* reductions [7,16,17].

Graph theory: Let G be an undirected bipartite graph. A *matching* μ in G is a set of vertex-disjoint edges. We say that μ *matches* a vertex if there is an edge in it that is incident with the vertex. Matching μ is *maximal* if it is no longer a matching once some other edge is added to it. Matching μ is *perfect* if it matches all vertices in G. Given a graph G and a number k, the *minimum size maximal matching problem* is to decide if there is a matching μ in G with $|\mu| \leq k$. It is NP-hard on various bipartite graphs [9,15]. Given a graph G, the *counting perfect matchings problem* is to output the number of perfect matchings in G. It is #P-hard on various bipartite graphs [14,18].

Set theory: Let S be a set of integers and b, c be integers. A (b,c)-subset of S is a subset of S whose elements sum up to b and its cardinality is c. The (b,c)-*subset sum problem* is to decide if there is a (b,c)-subset of S. Note that there is a (b,c)-subset of S for at least one $c \in [1, |S|]$ iff there is a subset of S whose elements sum up to b. The latter problem is the NP-hard b-*subset sum problem* [11].

This paper is structured as follows. In Sect. 3, the items are drawn from some known probabilistic distribution Δ. For example, such distribution in the food bank problem could be estimated based on historical data. In Sect. 4, we suppose the ordering o in which the items will arrive is fixed, i.e. for each moment j, we have that $\delta_{kj} = 1$ holds for exactly one item o_k. Again, in the food bank problem, some charities donate certain items on a regular basis and only at specific moments. In Sect. 5, we consider problems of computing manipulations of these mechanisms.

3   Items Arriving from a Distribution

We suppose the agents act sincerely and begin with the case when the chair knows the utilities *but* the items come from a distribution Δ whose size is polynomial in n and m.

STOCHASTICEXACTUTILITY	STOCHASTICNECESSARYUTILITY
Input: $\mathcal{I} = (A, O, U, \Delta)$, a_i.	Input: $\mathcal{I} = (A, O, U, \Delta)$, a_i, $k \in \mathbb{Q}$.
Output: $u_{im}(\Delta)$.	Question: $u_{im}(\Delta) \geq k$?

The stochastic exact outcomes of LIKE and BALANCED LIKE are #P-hard with just two agents. Our reduction is motivated by the food bank problem. Let m items be donated by m suppliers and not each of the suppliers can donate each of the items. This relation could be viewed as an undirected bipartite graph. The items are in one partition. The suppliers are in another partition. Let us enumerate them from 1 to m. There is an edge between an item and a supplier if the supplier donates the item. Each perfect matching in the graph then can be viewed as an ordering w.r.t. the enumeration of the suppliers in which each of the m different suppliers donates exactly one of the m different items. At the beginning of the day, the chair does not know the actual order in which the suppliers will donate items but they can estimate it by computing an estimate δ_{kj} for each item o_k and moment j. Based on past data whose size is polynomial in m, one such estimate could be the number of days of past data in which each of the m items is donated from a different supplier amongst the m suppliers divided by the total number of days of past data. We give a reduction from the *counting perfect matchings problem* to STOCHASTICEXACTUTILITY.

Reduction 1. Let G be a (3-regular) bipartite graph with M vertices in each partition. The allocation instance $\mathcal{I}_G$ has:

- **Agents:** agents a_1 and a_2 (i.e. 2 agents),
- **Items:** items o_1 to o_M (i.e. M items),
- **Utilities:** $u_{ij} = 1$ for each a_i and o_j, and
- **Distribution:** $\delta_{kj} = 1/M$ for each o_k and j.

Theorem 1. *With $n = 2$ agents, 0/1 utilities and the* LIKE *or* BALANCED LIKE *mechanism, problem* STOCHASTICEXACTUTILITY *is #P-hard under arithmetic reductions.*

Proof. WLOG, the set of orderings of items is equal to the set of perfect matchings in G united with the set of o_ϵ that reveals no items. Each ordering o_M that reveals M items corresponds to a perfect matching in G w.r.t. the enumeration of the suppliers in G. We suppose the items arrive independently of each other and across the different time moments. Consequently, ordering o_M occurs with probability $1/M^M$ and the expected utility $u_{iM}(o_M)$ is $M/2$ with both mechanisms as both agents have the same utilities for items. The ordering o_ϵ reveals 0 items. It occurs with probability 1 minus $(1/M^M)$ multiplied by the number of perfect matchings in G and $u_{i0}(o_\epsilon)$ is 0 with both mechanisms as no items are revealed. We quickly obtain that $u_{iM}(\Delta)$ is equal to $(1/M^M) \cdot (M/2)$ multiplied by the number of perfect matchings in G. The result follows. □

We further showed that stochastic necessary outcomes of these mechanisms are NP-hard with just two agents. We omit the complete proof for reasons of space but we give the main reduction which is from the (b, c)-*subset sum problem*. Given set of integers $S = \{n_1, \ldots, n_M\}$ and integers b and c, we construct instance $\mathcal{I}_{S,b,c}$: (1) agents a_1 and a_2, (2) item o_k for each $n_k \in S$, (3) agent a_i values item o_k with n_k, and (4) $\delta_{kj} = 1/M$ for each item o_k and moment j. The instance of STOCHASTICNECESSARYUTILITY has $\mathcal{I}_{S,b,c}$, agent a_i and constant $k = (1/M^c) \cdot (b/2)$. Let us order each subset of S w.r.t. the enumeration $(1, \ldots, M)$. The set of orderings is now equal to the set of ordered (b, c)-subsets of S united with the set of o_ϵ that reveals no items. Similarly to the proof of Theorem 1, it should be easy now for the reader to show that there is a (b, c)-subset of S iff $u_{iM}(\Delta) \geq k$.

4   Items Arriving from a Fixed Ordering

We again suppose the agents act sincerely and next consider the case that the chair knows the utilities *and* the arrival ordering of future items. This corresponds to the case when exactly one item arrives with probability of one at each moment in time.

EXACTUTILITY	NECESSARYUTILITY
Input: $\mathcal{I} = (A, O, U, o)$, a_i.	Input: $\mathcal{I} = (A, O, U, o)$, a_i, $k \in \mathbb{Q}$.
Output: $u_{im}(o)$.	Question: $u_{im}(o) \geq k$?

4.1 The Case of $n > 2$ Agents

Let there be $n > 2$ agents. Interestingly, the outcomes of the LIKE mechanism become tractable whereas the ones of the BALANCED LIKE mechanism remain intractable even when the ordering is fixed.

Exact Outcomes. Let us start with the LIKE mechanism. This mechanism does not keep track of the allocation of past items. As a result, any agent is feasible for each next item supposing they like this item. Indeed, all exact outcomes are tractable with this mechanism for this reason.

Observation 1. *With general utilities and the* LIKE *mechanism, problem* EXACTUTILITY *is in* P.

Proof. The probability $p_i(j, o)$ of agent a_i for item o_j is $1/n_j$ where n_j is the number of agents that like the item. Their utility $u_{im}(o)$ can be given as $\sum_{j=1}^{m}(1/n_j) \cdot u_{ij}$. □

We continue with exact allocations for the BALANCED LIKE mechanism and give a parsimonious reduction from *counting perfect matchings problem* to EXACTUTILITY. The counting problem remains in #P-hard even on 3-regular undirected bipartite graphs in [8]. Our reduction is very insightful because it provides a very tight bound on the complexity of EXACTUTILITY (i.e. 0/1 utilities, each agent likes at most 4 items, each item except one is liked by at most 3 agents, each pair of agents like at most 3 items in common, the ordering is fixed, etc.).

Reduction 2. Let G be a 3-regular bipartite graph, $u_1, \ldots, u_N$ be the vertices from one of its partitions and $v_1, \ldots, v_N$ the vertices from the other one of its partitions. For each vertex u_i, let v_{i1}, v_{i2}, v_{i3} denote the vertices connected to it and $e_{3 \cdot (i-1)+1} = (u_i, v_{i1})$, $e_{3 \cdot (i-1)+2} = (u_i, v_{i2})$, $e_{3 \cdot (i-1)+3} = (u_i, v_{i3})$ the edges incident with it. Each edge e_k can be represented as (u_i, v_j) for some $u_i \in \{u_1, \ldots, u_N\}$ and $v_j \in \{v_{i1}, v_{i2}, v_{i3}\}$. We use the graph and next construct the online allocation instance $\mathcal{E}_G$ as follows:

- **Agents:** 1 agent a_k per edge e_k and 3 special agents $a_{3 \cdot N+1}$, $a_{3 \cdot N+2}$ and $a_{3 \cdot N+3}$ (i.e. $3 \cdot N + 1$ agents),
- **Items:** 1 item per vertex v_j, 2 items u_{i1}, u_{i2} per vertex u_i and 3 special items w and x (i.e. $3 \cdot N + 2$ items),
- **Non-zero utilities:** for $i \in [1, N], j \in \{1, 2, 3\}$, **agent** $a_{3 \cdot (i-1)+j}$ has utility 1 for items $v_{ij}, u_{i1}, u_{i2}, x$; **agent** $a_{3 \cdot N+1}$ has utility 1 for items w, x, and
- **Ordering:** $o = (v_1 \ldots v_N u_{11} u_{12} \ldots u_{N1} u_{N2} w x)$.

We highlight the main idea behind the proof of the next Lemma 1. Basically, we showed that computing the number of allocations of the first $3 \cdot N + 1$ items in o in which each agent receives exactly one item is in #P-complete.

Lemma 1. *With the* BALANCED LIKE *mechanism, the number of allocations in $\mathcal{E}_G$ in which agent $a_{3 \cdot N + 1}$ is feasible for item x is equal to 2^N times the number of perfect matchings in G. Computing it is in #P-hard under arithmetic reductions.*

Proof. By construction, each item v_j is liked by three different agents and, hence, each allocation of $v_1, \ldots, v_N$ gives these items to N different agents among $a_1, \ldots, a_{3 \cdot N}$. Consider then an allocation of $v_1, \ldots, v_N$ such that, for each vertex u_i, either agent $a_{3 \cdot (i-1)+1}$ gets item v_{i1} or agent $a_{3 \cdot (i-1)+2}$ gets item v_{i2} or agent $a_{3 \cdot (i-1)+3}$ gets item v_{i3}. We say that such an allocation of $v_1, \ldots, v_N$ has *perfect* matches for vertices $u_1, \ldots, u_N$ because exactly one agent per triplet $a_{3 \cdot (i-1)+1}, a_{3 \cdot (i-1)+2}, a_{3 \cdot (i-1)+3}$ gets an item among $v_1, \ldots, v_N$. In fact, there is a perfect matching in G over $v_1, \ldots, v_N$ and $u_1, \ldots, u_N$ iff there is an allocation in $\mathcal{E}_G$ of $v_1, \ldots, v_N$ that has perfect matches for $u_1, \ldots, u_N$. Furthermore, this is a 1-to-1 parsimonious correspondence. Each allocation π in $\mathcal{E}_G$ of the first $3 \cdot N + 1$ items in o in which each agent among $a_1, \ldots, a_{3 \cdot N}, a_{3 \cdot N + 1}$ receives exactly one item occurs with positive probability. We call π *perfect allocation* over the first $3 \cdot N + 1$ items in o. We show that there is an allocation in $\mathcal{E}_G$ of $v_1, \ldots, v_N$ that has perfect matches for $u_1, \ldots, u_N$ iff there are 2^N perfect allocations such as π in $\mathcal{E}_G$. Moreover, this is a 1-to-2^N arithmetic correspondence. In other words, we show that the number of perfect allocations such as π in $\mathcal{E}_G$ is equal to 2^N times the number of perfect matchings in G.

First, let us consider one discrete allocation π_1 in $\mathcal{E}_G$ of $v_1, \ldots, v_N$ that has perfect matches for $u_1, \ldots, u_N$. The allocation π_1 occurs with positive probability because $v_1, \ldots, v_N$ are liked by disjoint sets of three agents. WLOG, suppose that π_1 is such that, for each u_i, agent $a_{3 \cdot (i-1)+1}$ receives their corresponding item v_{i1}. The allocation π_1 can be extended by the mechanism to two discrete allocations w.r.t. each u_i: (1) agent $a_{3 \cdot (i-1)+2}$ gets item u_{i1} and agent $a_{3 \cdot (i-1)+3}$ gets item u_{i2} or (2) agent $a_{3 \cdot (i-1)+2}$ gets item u_{i2} and agent $a_{3 \cdot (i-1)+3}$ gets item u_{i1}. By the preference structure, π_1 can then be extended by the mechanism to 2^N perfect allocations in $\mathcal{E}_G$. Note that each of these perfect allocations necessarily gives item w to agent $a_{3 \cdot N + 1}$ because only they like it. Second, consider one perfect allocation in $\mathcal{E}_G$. It must be the case that it extends some discrete allocation of $v_1, \ldots, v_N$ that has perfect matches for $u_1, \ldots, u_N$. To show this, consider a discrete allocation π_2 of $v_1, \ldots, v_N$ that has not perfect matches for $u_1, \ldots, u_N$. Hence, π_2 is such that at least two of the agents $a_{3 \cdot (i-1)+1}, a_{3 \cdot (i-1)+2}, a_{3 \cdot (i-1)+3}$ for some vertex u_i receive their corresponding items v_{i1}, v_{i2}, v_{i3} of $v_1, \ldots, v_N$. Therefore, each allocation of all items that extends π_2 by using the mechanism gives item u_{i1} or item u_{i2} to one of the agents $a_{3 \cdot (i-1)+1}, a_{3 \cdot (i-1)+2}, a_{3 \cdot (i-1)+3}$ as their second item. As a consequence, in each such allocation, there is another agent with zero items after round $3 \cdot N + 1$. We conclude that each such extension of π_2 is not a perfect allocation in $\mathcal{E}_G$.   □

Theorem 2. *With $n > 2$ agents, 0/1 utilities and the* BALANCED LIKE *mechanism, problem* EXACTUTILITY *is in #P-hard under arithmetic reductions.*

Proof. Let us consider allocation $\pi = \pi(3 \cdot N + 1, o)$ of the first $3 \cdot N + 1$ items in o in which each agent among $a_1, \ldots, a_{3 \cdot N}, a_{3 \cdot N+1}$ receives exactly one item. Note that agent $a_{3 \cdot N+1}$ gets item x with positive conditional probability only given such allocations because all agents like item x. By the preference structure, we conclude that π occurs with probability $p(\pi) = (1/3^N) \cdot (1/2^N)$. The conditional probability $p_i(x|\pi)$ of agent $a_{3 \cdot N+1}$ for item x given π is equal to $1/(3 \cdot N + 1)$ because all agents $a_1, \ldots, a_{3 \cdot N}, a_{3 \cdot N+1}$ like item x. The conditional probability of agent $a_{3 \cdot N+1}$ for item x is 0 given any other allocation. Therefore, $p_{3 \cdot N+1}(x, o)$ is equal to $(1/3^N) \cdot (1/2^N) \cdot (1/(3 \cdot N + 1))$ multiplied by the number of allocations such as π in which agent $a_{3 \cdot N+1}$ is feasible for item x. Finally, the expected utility $u_{(3 \cdot N+1)(3 \cdot N+3)}(o) = p_{3 \cdot N+1}(w, o) + p_{3 \cdot N+1}(x, o)$. We have that $p_{3 \cdot N+1}(w, o) = 1$ because only agent $a_{3 \cdot N+1}$ likes item w and the mechanism allocates each item to an agent. The result follows by Lemma 1. $\square$

Necessary Outcomes. The tractability of the exact allocations of the LIKE mechanism entails the tractability of its necessary allocations. By Observation 1, we conclude the next immediate result.

Observation 2. *With general utilities and the* LIKE *mechanism, problem* NECESSARYUTILITY *is in* P.

We next focus on the necessary outcomes of the BALANCED LIKE mechanism. We give a Karp reduction from *minimum size maximal matching problem* to the negation of NECESSARYUTILITY. The minimum size maximal matching problem is shown to be NP-hard on subdivision graphs of degree at most 3 in [12].

Reduction 3. Let us have a subdivision graph G of degree at most 3 and integer r. The graph G is bipartite with vertices $u_1, \ldots, u_N$ of degree exactly 2 and vertices $v_1, \ldots, v_M$ of degree at most 3. WLOG, we can assume that $N \geq M$ and there are no two vertices from U that are connected to the same two vertices from V. We construct an allocation instance $\mathcal{P}_{G,r}$ as follows:

- **Agents:** 2 agents u_{i1}, u_{i2} per u_i and agents $a_1, \ldots, a_{N-r}, b_1, \ldots, b_M$ and c (i.e. $3 \cdot N + M - r + 1$ agents),
- **Items:** 1 item per v_j and items $x_1, \ldots, x_N, y_1, \ldots, y_N, z_1, \ldots, z_{N-r}$ and w (i.e. $3 \cdot N + M - r + 1$ items),
- **Non-zero utilities:** for each $i \in [1, N], j \in \{1, 2\}$, agent u_{ij} has utility 1 for items $x_i, v_{ij}, y_i, z_1, \ldots, z_{N-r}$; for each $i \in [1, N-r]$, agent a_i has utility 1 for items $x_1, \ldots, x_N$; agents $b_1, \ldots, b_M$ have each utility 1 for item w; agent c has utility 1 for items z_{N-r}, w, and
- **Ordering:** $o = (x_1 \ldots x_N v_1 \ldots v_M y_1 \ldots y_N z_1 \ldots z_{N-r} w)$.

The expected utility of each of the agents $b_1, \ldots, b_M$ is at least $1/M$ iff $p_c(w, o) = 0$. This observation holds because each of the agents b_1 to b_M have

equal utilities for items in which case they receive item w with the same probability which apparently is also equal to their expected utility as this is the only
item they like. Theorem 3 follows from this observation.

Theorem 3. *With $n > 2$ agents, 0/1 utilities and the* BALANCED LIKE *mechanism, problem* NECESSARYUTILITY *is in* coNP-*hard under Turing reductions.*

Proof. There is a maximal matching in G of cardinality at most r iff there is an
allocation in $\mathcal{P}_{G,r}$ in which agent c receives item w iff $p_c(w, o) > 0$. The second
"iff" is trivial. We, therefore, focus on the first "iff". The "only if" direction is
easier to show and, for reasons of space, we only show the more difficult "if"
direction. Suppose next that π is an allocation of all items in $\mathcal{P}_{G,r}$ in which
agent c receives item w.

1. Item w is allocated in π to agent c as their first item. To see this, suppose
   they also get some items among z_{N-r}. Now, they would not be feasible when
   item w arrives as agents $b_1, \ldots, b_M$ have zero items in π and the mechanism
   would have given item w to an agent among $b_1, \ldots, b_M$ and not to agent c.
2. Prior to item w in π, agent c have received zero items. Hence, items
   $z_1, \ldots, z_{N-r}$ are allocated in π to $N - r$ agents as their first items. By the
   preferences, these agents are from different pairs among $u_{11}, u_{12}, \ldots, u_{N1}, u_{N2}$
   because, for each pair of agents u_{i1}, u_{i2}, either u_{i1} or u_{i2} is forced to get item
   y_i. WLOG, let us assume that agents $u_{11}, \ldots, u_{(N-r)1}$ get items $z_1, \ldots, z_{N-r}$
   in π.
3. Prior to item z_1 in π, agents $u_{11}, \ldots, u_{(N-r)1}$ have zero items. Hence, $N - r$
   items among $y_1, \ldots, y_N$ are allocated in π to $u_{12}, \ldots, u_{(N-r)2}$ as their first
   items. These items are $y_1, \ldots, y_{N-r}$. For i in $[N-r+1, N]$, we note that item
   y_i is allocated in π to either u_{i1} or u_{i2} as their first or second item.
4. Prior to item y_1 in π, agents $u_{11}, u_{12}, \ldots, u_{(N-r)1}, u_{(N-r)2}$ have zero items.
   By the preferences, agents $a_1, \ldots, a_{N-r}$ must then receive items $x_1, \ldots, x_{N-r}$
   in π. For i in $[N-r+1, N]$, item x_i is allocated in π to either u_{i1} or u_{i2}, say u_{i2}.
   We conclude that agents $u_{(N-r+1)1}, \ldots, u_{N1}$ have zero items prior to item
   v_1 in π. Moreover, only agents $u_{(N-r+1)1}, u_{(N-r+1)2}, \ldots, u_{N1}, u_{N2}$ receive
   items $v_1, \ldots, v_M$ in π. Finally, only $l \leq r$ agents among $u_{(N-r+1)1}, \ldots, u_{N1}$
   get items in π among $v_1, \ldots, v_M$ as first items as some of these agents
   might like the same items among $v_1, \ldots, v_M$. WLOG, let these agents be
   $u_{(N-l+1)1}, \ldots, u_{N1}$ and they are allocated in π items $v_1, \ldots, v_l$ as first items.

The constructed set $\mu_\pi = \{(u_{N-l+1}, v_1), \ldots, (u_N, v_l)\}$ contains only edges
from the graph G which are vertex-disjoint. Therefore, this set is a matching in G. Moreover, the cardinality of this set is l at most r. We next show
that μ_π is a maximal matching. For the sake of contradiction, suppose that μ_π
remains a matching if we add a new edge to it, say (u, v). The edge (u, v) is
vertex-disjoint with the edges in μ_π. This means that vertex u is not among
$u_{N-l+1}, \ldots, u_N$ and vertex v is not among $v_1, \ldots, v_l$. Hence, vertex u is among
$u_1, \ldots, u_{N-l}$. In the allocation π, agents $u_{11}, u_{12}, \ldots, u_{(N-r)1}, u_{(N-r)2}$ do not

receive any items among $v_1, \ldots, v_M$. This implies that all these agents are feasible for the items they like among $v_1, \ldots, v_M$ but they do not get them in π. As agents $u_{(N-l+1)1}, \ldots, u_{N1}$ get items $v_1, \ldots, v_l$ as their first items, we conclude that some agents among $u_{(N-l+1)1}, u_{(N-l+1)2} \cdots, u_{N1}, u_{N2}$ receive items v_{l+1}, $\ldots, v_M$ as their second items. Therefore, it must be the case that all agents $u_{11}, u_{12}, \ldots, u_{(N-r)1}, u_{(N-r)2}$ do not like any item among $v_{l+1}, \ldots, v_M$. Otherwise, the mechanism would allocate some of these items to agents among u_{11}, u_{12}, $\ldots, u_{(N-r)1}, u_{(N-r)2}$. This is just the way in which the mechanism works. And, we reached a contradiction with the existence of the allocation π. Finally, in the graph G, vertices $u_1, \ldots, u_{N-r}$ are connected only to vertices among $v_1, \ldots, v_l$. Hence, v is among $v_1, \ldots, v_l$. This fact contradicts that $\mu_\pi \cup \{(u, v)\}$ is a matching. □

4.2 The Case of 2 Agents

By Observations 1 and 2, the outcomes of LIKE are tractable. Surprisingly, in contrast to Theorems 1, 2 and 3, the outcomes of BALANCED LIKE become tractable with only two agents and when the ordering of items is fixed.

Theorem 4. *With $n = 2$ agents, general utilities and the* BALANCED LIKE *mechanism, problems* EXACTUTILITY *and* NECESSARYUTILITY *are in* P.

Proof. We use a dynamic program. Each state $s = (p, q)$ in it encodes that agent a_1 has p items, agent a_2 has q items, and its probability $p(s)$. By induction, we show that there are at most 2 different states after each allocation round. In the base case, consider round 1. There are at most 2 states after this round depending on whether both a_1 and a_2 or only one of them like the first item. In the hypothesis, consider round j and suppose there are at most two states after round j. In the step case, consider round $j + 1$. Now, there are two cases. In the first one, there is only one state after round j. The result follows by the base case. In the second case, there are two states after round j. Let these be (p, q) and $(p - 1, q + 1)$ where $p + q = j$. If only one agent likes item o_{j+1}, each state transits into a new state and the result follows. If both a_1 and a_2 like item o_{j+1}, we consider four sub-cases depending on the difference $p - q$: (1) (p, q) and $(p-1, q+1)$ for $p-q > 2$, (2) $(q+2, q)$ and $(q+1, q+1)$ for $p-q = 2$, (3) $(q+1, q)$ and $(q, q + 1)$ for $p - q = 1$ and (4) (q, q) and $(q - 1, q + 1)$ for $p - q = 0$. For sub-case (1), each state transits into one new state with the same probability. For sub-case (2), $(q + 2, q)$ transits into $(q + 2, q + 1)$, and $(q + 1, q + 1)$ into $(q + 2, q + 1)$ and $(q + 1, q + 2)$. For sub-case (3), both states transit into the same new state with probability 1. For sub-case (4), (q, q) transits into $(q, q + 1)$ and $(q + 1, q)$, and $(q - 1, q + 1)$ into $(q, q + 1)$. We conclude that there are at most two different states after round $j + 1$ in each sub-case.

The probability $p_1(j + 2, o)$ is equal to $\sum_{s_{j+1}} p(s_{j+1}) \cdot p(a_1 \text{ gets } o_{j+2}|s_{j+1})$ where s_{j+1} is such a state after round $j + 1$ in which agent a_1 is feasible for item o_{j+2}. The conditional probability $p(a_1 \text{ gets } o_{j+2}|s_{j+1})$ of agent a_1 for item o_{j+2} is (i) 0 or 1 in sub-case (1), (ii) 0, 1/2 or 1 in sub-case (3) and (iii) the probability of the state in which they are feasible in sub-cases (2) and (4). We can compute the states, their probabilities and hence the probabilities of agents and their utilities in $\mathcal{O}(m)$ space and time. □

5   Manipulations

We next consider how agents can act strategically. The LIKE mechanism is strategy-proof and hence agents have an incentive to bid sincerely for items. In contrast, the BALANCED LIKE mechanism is not strategy-proof and agents can have an incentive to bid strategically for items [1]. We thus focus on strategic misreporting of bids with BALANCED LIKE. In particular, we study the worst case when the utilities and the ordering of the items are known to the misreporting agent. Any complexity results, in this case, provide lower bounds on the complexity in the case of partial or probabilistic information. We formulate the next problems where $u_{im}(v^i, o)$ denotes the utility of agent a_i supposing their bid vector is $v^i = (v_{i1}, \ldots, v_{im})$ and the other agents bid sincerely. Let $u^i = (u_{i1}, \ldots, u_{im})$ denotes their sincere bid vector.

EXACTMANIPULATION
Input: $\mathcal{I} = (A, O, U, o)$, a_i, u^i, v^i.
Output: $u_{im}(v^i, o) - u_{im}(u^i, o)$.

NECESSARYMANIPULATION
Input: $\mathcal{I} = (A, O, U, o)$, a_i, v^i, u^i, $k \in \mathbb{Q}$.
Question: $u_{im}(v^i, o) - u_{im}(u^i, o) \geq k$?

Theorem 5. *With $n > 2$ agents, 0/1 utilities and the BALANCED LIKE mechanism, problem EXACTMANIPULATION is in #P-hard under arithmetic reductions.*

Proof. Consider instance $\mathcal{E}_G$. Let us modify this instance a bit. We add one new item z between items w and x in the ordering o such that only agent $a_{3 \cdot N + 1}$ likes z with 1. Let $\mathcal{F}_G$ denote this new instance. Suppose that all agents in $\mathcal{F}_G$ bid sincerely. Thus, agent $a_{3 \cdot N+1}$ receives each of the items w and z each with probability 1 because they are the only agent who likes them. However, they receive item x with probability 0. Therefore, $u_{(3 \cdot N+1)(3 \cdot N+3)}(u^{(3 \cdot N+1)}, o) = 2$. Suppose that all agents in $\mathcal{F}_G$ bid sincerely except agent $a_{3 \cdot N+1}$ who bids strategically 0 for item z. Let $v^{(3 \cdot N+1)}$ be their bidding vector in this case. We can now remove item z because no agent bids positively for it. But, then we obtain instance $\mathcal{E}_G$. By Theorem 2, we have $u_{(3 \cdot N+1)(3 \cdot N+3)}(v^{(3 \cdot N+1)}, o) = 1 + p_{3 \cdot N+1}(x, o)$. The instance of EXACTMANIPULATION uses instance $\mathcal{F}_G$, agent $a_{3 \cdot N+1}$ and vectors $u^{(3 \cdot N+1)}$ and $v^{(3 \cdot N+1)}$. Its hardness follows by Theorem 2. □

Observe that the truthful report of agent $a_{3 \cdot N+1}$ in the proof of Theorem 5 leads to their utility being 2 whereas their insincere report leads to their utility being at most 2. Hence, their strategic move cannot lead to an increase in their utility but the computation of the exact difference in utility is intractable. However, as we discuss next, computing an exact profitable insincere report that leads to such an increase is also intractable.

Necessary manipulations might be easy even when exact manipulations are hard. For example, in the proof of Theorem 5, suppose that agent $a_{3 \cdot N+1}$ has cardinal utility for item x that is strictly greater than $(3^N).(3N + 1)$. If they bid sincerely, their expected utility is 2. If they bid strategically zero for item z, their expected utility is strictly greater than 2. This *necessary* increase can be decided in polynomial time but computing the *exact* increase is intractable. However, necessary manipulations are also in general not always easy even if we ask merely for any increase in the expected utility of a given agent.

Theorem 6. *With $n > 2$ agents, 0/1 utilities and the* BALANCED LIKE *mechanism, problem* NECESSARYMANIPULATION *is in* coNP-*hard under Turing reductions.*

Proof. Consider instance $\mathcal{P}_{G,r}$. Suppose all agents bid sincerely. Hence, $u_{c(3N+M-r+1)}(u^c, o) = p_c(z_{N-r}, o) + p_c(w, o)$. Suppose all agents bid sincerely except agent c who bids strategically 0 for item w. Let their bidding vector be v^c. We have that $u_{c(3N+M-r+1)}(v^c, o) = p_c(z_{N-r}, o)$. The instance of NECESSARYMANIPULATION uses as input instance $\mathcal{P}_{G,r}$, agent c, vectors v^c and u^c, and rational number $k = 0$. We conclude that $u_{c(3N+M-r+1)}(v^c, o) - u_{c(3N+M-r+1)}(u^c, o) \geq 0$ iff $p_c(w, o) = 0$. The result follows by Theorem 3. □

Another definition of the manipulation problem is whether a player can possibly increase their utility by insincere reporting, rather than computing the necessary or exact gain. Observe that in the proof of Theorem 6, we have that $u_{c(3N+M-r+1)}(u^c, o) - u_{c(3N+M-r+1)}(v^c, o) > 0$ iff $p_c(w, o) > 0$. We conclude that possible manipulations are also intractable in general by the proof of Theorem 3. Finally, by Theorem 4, we conclude that possible, necessary and exact manipulations are easy with just two agents and items arriving from a fixed ordering. By Theorem 1 and the discussion after it, we conclude that necessary and exact manipulations are hard with two agents and items arriving from a distribution.

6 Related Work and Conclusion

We studied the worst-case computational complexity of possible, necessary and exact outcomes returned by the LIKE and BALANCED LIKE mechanisms supposing agents act sincerely. With LIKE, there is no benefit for agents to act strategically. With BALANCED LIKE, the agents might be strategic but we proved that computing a manipulation is computationally intractable in general. Some results are however tractable for the case of 2 agents. Our study of the online allocations returned by the LIKE and BALANCED LIKE mechanisms is in-line with many results in offline fair division, voting theory and partial tournaments where possible, necessary and exact outcomes play crucial role; see e.g. [2,4,5,20]. Our results provide a stepping stone towards better understanding strategic behavior. A number of works already considered such behavior for offline mechanisms; see e.g. [3,6]. Another interesting future directions would be to estimate the outcomes of our mechanisms or to look at fixed-parameter tractable algorithms for these problems [10,13,15].

References

1. Aleksandrov, M., Aziz, H., Gaspers, S., Walsh, T.: Online fair division: analysing a food bank problem. In: Proceedings of IJCAI 2015, Buenos Aires, Argentina, pp. 2540–2546, 25–31 July 2015. http://ijcai.org/papers15/Abstracts/IJCAI15-360. html

2. Aziz, H., Brill, M., Fischer, F.A., Harrenstein, P., Lang, J., Seedig, H.G.: Possible and necessary winners of partial tournaments. J. Artif. Intell. Res. (JAIR) **54**, 493–534 (2015). http://dx.doi.org/10.1613/jair.4856

3. Aziz, H., Gaspers, S., Mackenzie, S., Mattei, N., Narodytska, N., Walsh, T.: Equilibria under the probabilistic serial rule. In: Proceedings of IJCAI 2015, Buenos Aires, Argentina, pp. 1105–1112, 25–31 July 2015. http://ijcai.org/papers15/Abstracts/IJCAI15-160.html

4. Aziz, H., Walsh, T., Xia, L.: Possible and necessary allocations via sequential mechanisms. In: Proceedings of IJCAI 2015, Buenos Aires, Argentina, pp. 468–474, 25–31 July 2015. http://ijcai.org/papers15/Abstracts/IJCAI15-072.html

5. Bachrach, Y., Betzler, N., Faliszewski, P.: Probabilistic possible winner determination. In: Proceedings of AAAI 2010, Atlanta, Georgia, USA, 11–15 July 2010

6. Bouveret, S., Lang, J.: Manipulating picking sequences. In: ECAI 2014–21st European Conference on Artificial Intelligence, Prague, Czech Republic - Including PAIS, pp. 141–146, 18–22 August 2014. http://dx.doi.org/10.3233/978-1-61499-419-0-141

7. Bürgisser, P.: Completeness and Reduction in Algebraic Complexity Theory. Algorithms and Computation in Mathematics. Springer, New York (2000). http://opac.inria.fr/record=b1099577

8. Dagum, P., Luby, M.: Approximating the permanent of graphs with large factors. Theor. Comput. Sci. **102**(2), 283–305 (1992)

9. Demange, M., Ekim, T.: Minimum maximal matching is NP-hard in regular bipartite graphs. In: Agrawal, M., Du, D., Duan, Z., Li, A. (eds.) TAMC 2008. LNCS, vol. 4978, pp. 364–374. Springer, Heidelberg (2008). doi:10.1007/978-3-540-79228-4_32

10. Downey, R.G., Fellows, M.R.: Fundamentals of Parameterized Complexity. Texts in Computer Science. Springer, London (2013). https://doi.org/10.1007/978-1-4471-5559-1

11. Garey, M.R., Johnson, D.S.: Computers and Intractability: A Guide to the Theory of NP-Completeness. W. H. Freeman, New York (1979)

12. Horton, J.D., Kilakos, K.: Minimum edge dominating sets. SIAM J. Discrete Math. **6**(3), 375–387 (1993). http://dx.doi.org/10.1137/0406030

13. Jerrum, M., Sinclair, A.: Approximating the permanent. SIAM J. of Comp. **18**(6), 1149–1178 (1989). http://dx.doi.org/10.1137/0218077

14. Okamoto, Y., Uehara, R., Uno, T.: Counting the number of matchings in chordal and chordal bipartite graph classes. In: Paul, C., Habib, M. (eds.) WG 2009. LNCS, vol. 5911, pp. 296–307. Springer, Heidelberg (2010). doi:10.1007/978-3-642-11409-0_26

15. Sabán, D., Sethuraman, J.: The complexity of computing the random priority allocation matrix. Math. Oper. Res. **40**(4), 1005–1014 (2015)

16. Turing, A.M.: On computable numbers, with an application to the Entscheidungsproblem. J. Proc. Lond. Math. Soc. **2**(42), 230–265 (1936). http://www.cs.helsinki.fi/u/gionis/cc05/OnComputableNumbers.pdf

17. Valiant, L.G.: The complexity of computing the permanent. Theor. Comput. Sci. **8**, 189–201 (1979). http://dx.doi.org/10.1016/0304-3975(79)90044-6

18. Valiant, L.G.: The complexity of enumeration and reliability problems. SIAM J. Comput. **8**(3), 410–421 (1979). http://dx.doi.org/10.1137/0208032

19. Walsh, T.: Challenges in resource and cost allocation. In: Proceedings of 29th AAAI 2015, Austin, Texas, USA, pp. 4073–4077, 25–30 January 2015. http://www.aaai. org/ocs/index.php/AAAI/AAAI15/paper/view/9927

20. Xia, L., Conitzer, V.: Determining possible and necessary winners given partial orders. J. Artif. Intell. Res. (JAIR) **41**, 25–67 (2011)

Most Competitive Mechanisms
in Online Fair Division

Martin Aleksandrov[(⊠)] and Toby Walsh

UNSW Sydney and Data61, CSIRO and TU Berlin, Berlin, Germany
{martin.aleksandrov,toby.walsh}@data61.csiro.au

Abstract. This paper combines two key ingredients for online algorithms - *competitive analysis* (e.g. the competitive ratio) and *advice complexity* (e.g. the number of advice bits needed to improve online decisions) - in the context of a simple online fair division model where items arrive one by one and are allocated to agents via some mechanism. We consider four such online mechanisms: the popular RANKING matching mechanism adapted from online bipartite matching and the LIKE, BALANCED LIKE and MAXIMUM LIKE allocation mechanisms firstly introduced for online fair division problems. Our first contribution is that we perform a competitive analysis of these mechanisms with respect to the expected size of the matching, the utilitarian welfare, and the egalitarian welfare. We also suppose that an oracle can give a number of advice bits to the mechanisms. Our second contribution is to give several impossibility results; e.g. *no* mechanism can achieve the egalitarian outcome of the optimal offline mechanism supposing they receive partial advice from the oracle. Our third contribution is that we quantify the competitive performance of these four mechanisms w.r.t. the number of oracle requests they can make. We thus present a *most competitive* mechanism for each objective.

1 Introduction

Competitive analysis is a well-known technique to measure the quality of online versus offline decisions [4,20]. *Online* decisions are irrevocable (i.e. we cannot change past decisions) and instantaneous (i.e. we cannot use future knowledge). *Offline* decisions are made supposing the entire problem information is available. Competitive analysis has been applied in various areas during the years, e.g. online bipartite matching, online stochastic matching, online sequential allocation, online sequential bin packing, online scheduling [1,10,11,13,14].

For some online problems, quite successful algorithms are already known under particular assumptions about the arriving input (e.g. [7]). For other problems, this is unfortunately not the case. For example, in the uniform knapsack problem, any deterministic online algorithm without advice has an unbounded competitive ratio. Interestingly, with just one bit of advice, it is possible to implement a 2-competitive algorithm for this problem [15]. In general, we can increase the competitive ratio of any online algorithm by giving it enough advice. This motivates the development of novel frameworks such as *advice complexity*.

© Springer International Publishing AG 2017
G. Kern-Isberner et al. (Eds.): KI 2017, LNAI 10505, pp. 44–57, 2017.
DOI: 10.1007/978-3-319-67190-1_4

An online algorithm has now an access to an *oracle tape* for the problem of interest and can request an *advice string* when making a decision. The oracle is normally assumed to have an unlimited computational power but the number of bits in the advice string must be polynomially bounded in the size of the input offline problem. For a detailed survey on advice complexity, we refer to [5]. Advice complexity is also related to *semi-online* and *look-ahead* algorithms that suppose some of the input is available [19].

This raises a number of questions. How many advice bits are sufficient to increase the competitive ratio of an online algorithm to a certain threshold? How many bits are needed to match an *optimal* offline algorithm? For example, in the popular paging problem, to achieve offline optimality with an online algorithm we need $\lceil \log_2 k \rceil$ bits of advice to specify which page to delete from the buffer of size k. This results in advice complexity of $n \cdot \lceil \log_2 k \rceil$ for instances with n requests, whereas it is shown that $n + k$ bits of advice suffice [3,8]. As another example, in online bipartite matching with a graph of size n (i.e. the number of vertices in a partition), a corresponding deterministic online algorithm is optimal (w.r.t. the expected matching size) whenever it has an access to $\lceil \log_2 n! \rceil$ but not less advice bits [17].

Here, for the first time, we introduce techniques from competitive analysis *and* advice complexity into online fair division. Online fair division is an important and challenging problem facing society today due to the uncertainty we may have about future resources, e.g. deceased organs to patients, donated food to charities, electric vehicles to charging stations, tenants to houses, even students to courses, etc. We often cannot wait until the end of the year, week or even day before starting to allocate incoming resources. For example, organs cannot be kept too long on ice or products cannot be stored in the warehouse before distributing to a food bank [21,22]. We extend past work by asking how many advice bits are needed to increase the welfare.

Advice helps us understand how the competitive ratio depends on uncertainty about the future. It can be based on information about past or future items. For example, consider the allocation of food donations to charities by a central decision maker. A number of contractors usually donate food on a regular basis and at specific times so the decision maker knows when some of the items will arrive. Also, each item could have a *type* that is the set of charities that like the item. The oracle might then keep track on the item types that have arrived in the past and thus bias the allocation of the new item type whenever possible. As another example, consider the allocation of deceased organs to patients. The administrator of a hospital might know what organs will arrive that can be exchanged with a neighboring hospital. They might use this offline information to improve significantly the best local online match for the current organ. Further, the oracle could keep track of how long patients are in the waiting list and thus bias the future organ matching decisions based on this information under various constraints, e.g. a patient should not wait for an organ more than 30 days, a patient who arrived at time moment 10 to the waiting list should receive organs earlier than a patient who arrived after time moment 10, etc.

Our contributions: Our work is novel for several reasons. For example, we combine advice complexity and competitive analysis in the context of online fair division. As another example, we study multiple objectives and online competitiveness of mechanisms. We first observe a 1-to-1 correspondence between online bipartite matching and online fair division. By using this correspondence, we can transfer and significantly extend objectives and algorithms from online bipartite matching to online fair division and vice versa. This is useful for a number of reasons. For example, agents in fair division have preferences and can be strategic which is an aspect not typically considered in bipartite matching. As a second example, allocations may be more difficult to find than matchings if we want them to satisfy multiple fairness and efficiency criteria. We thus view algorithms for online bipartite matching as *mechanisms* for online fair division. Following this, we study the competitive performance of the popular matching RANKING mechanism and the attractive LIKE, BALANCED LIKE and MAXIMUM LIKE allocation mechanisms w.r.t. three different objectives: the *expected matching size*, the *utilitarian welfare* and the *egalitarian welfare*. We consider three settings, namely online fair division setting *without advice*, *with full advice* and *with partial advice*. In each of these settings, we analyse these four mechanisms and present a most competitive mechanism for each objective supposing adversarial input. We further plot their competitive ratios. We finally proved that there is no mechanism that maximizes the expected matching size or the egalitarian welfare and uses less than full advice.

The next Sect. 2 provides the notions, the mechanisms and the objectives that we use throughout the paper. In Sects. 3, 4 and 5, we report our results for the online setting without advice, the online setting with full advice and the online setting with partial advice, respectively. Finally, we discuss related work, future work and conclude in Sect. 6.

2 Preliminaries

Online bipartite matching instance: An *instance* $\mathcal{G}$ has (1) a set of n "boy" vertices, (2) a set of m "girl" vertices, (3) a *weight* matrix where the (i,j)-th cell contains the *weight* of the edge between vertices the i-th "boy" vertex and the j-th "girl" vertex, and (4) a *sequence* of the "girl" vertices. We consider *binary* (i.e. unweighted graph) and *non-negative* (i.e. weighted graph) weights.

Online fair division instance: An *instance* $\mathcal{I}$ has (1) a set A of *agents* $a_1, \ldots, a_n$, (2) a set O of indivisible *items* $o_1, \ldots, o_m$, (3) *utility* matrix $U = (u_{ij})_{n \times m}$ where u_{ij} is the private *utility* of agent a_i for item o_j, and (4) *ordering* o of the items. We consider *binary* and *general* non-negative rational utilities.

Online setting: Let $\mathcal{G}_{\mathcal{I}} = (A, O, U, o)$ be the online bipartite graph associated with $\mathcal{I}$. We suppose that ordering o reveals item o_j in round j when each agent a_i bids a rational non-negative value v_{ij} for item o_j and a *mechanism* allocates item o_j to an agent. Further, we assume that the ordering o is adversarial which captures the worst-case arrival sequences.

Fair division axioms: A mechanism is *strategy-proof* if, with complete information, no agent can misreport their utilities and thus increase their expected outcome. Agent a_1 *envies (ex ante) ex post* agent a_2 if a_1 assigns greater (expected) utility to the (expected) allocation of a_2 than to their own (expected) allocation. A mechanism is *bounded envy-free (ex ante) ex post with r* if no agent envies (ex ante) ex post another one with more than r given the (expected) allocation returned by the mechanism. A mechanism is *(ex ante) ex post Pareto efficient* if its returned (expected) allocation is Pareto optimal.

Mechanisms: We use an oracle tape to specify some of the behavior of the optimal offline mechanism. An *online* mechanism M does not consult the oracle tape and makes the current decision supposing the past decisions are irrevocable and no information about future items is available. By comparison, its modification ADVICED M can at each round decide whether to consult the oracle or not. If "yes", the oracle encodes the identifier of the agent that should receive the item on the advice tape when the mechanism reads the tape and allocates the item to the adviced agent. If "no", ADVICED M runs M to allocate the current item. There are two extreme cases. If ADVICED M does not read the oracle tape at any round, then its performance coincides with the one of M. If ADVICED M reads the oracle tape at each round, then its performance coincides with the one of an optimal offline mechanism.

We consider four online mechanisms. The MAXIMUM LIKE mechanism allocates each item o_j uniformly at random to an agent with the greatest bid for o_j. The RANKING mechanism from [13] picks a strict priority ordering over the agents uniformly at random and allocates each item o_j to an agent that has positive bid for it, has not been allocated items previously and has the greatest priority. We further use the LIKE and BALANCED LIKE mechanisms from [2]. The LIKE mechanism allocates each item o_j uniformly at random to an agent that bids positively for the item. The BALANCED LIKE mechanism allocates each item o_j uniformly at random to an agent among those agents who bid positively for the item and have been allocated fewest items previously. We modify these four mechanisms to read advice bits from the oracle tape: ADVICED MAXIMUM LIKE, ADVICED RANKING, ADVICED LIKE and ADVICED BALANCED LIKE.

These mechanisms satisfy many nice axioms. For example, MAXIMUM LIKE is Pareto efficient. In fact, it is one of a few Pareto efficient mechanisms but unfortunately it is not strategy-proof or envy-free. LIKE is strategy-proof and envy-free ex ante. In fact, each envy-free ex ante mechanism assigns probabilities for items to agents as LIKE does. However, LIKE is not envy-free ex post. In contrast, BALANCED LIKE mechanism bounds the envy ex post. Interestingly, with 0/1 utilities, it is also Pareto efficient and envy-free ex ante. We further analysed the matching RANKING mechanism from a fair division point of view. For example, it is strategy-proof, envy-free ex ante and bounds the envy ex post but only with simple 0/1 utilities. However, it is not Pareto efficient in this setting as it may discard items. These axiomatic properties are well-understood. We, therefore, turn attention to the competitive properties of these mechanisms.

Objectives: Given instance $\mathcal{I}$, each mechanism induces a probability distribution over a set $\Pi_{\mathcal{I}}$ of allocations. The *expected matching size* $\overline{k}(\mathcal{I})$ is equal to $\sum_{\pi \in \Pi_{\mathcal{I}}} p(\pi) \cdot k(\pi)$ where $p(\pi)$ is the probability of allocation π and $k(\pi)$ is the number of agents that are allocated items in π. The *expected utility* $\overline{u}_i(\mathcal{I})$ of agent a_i is $\sum_{j=1}^{m} p_i(j, \mathcal{I}) \cdot u_{ij}$ where $p_i(j, \mathcal{I})$ is the expected probability of agent a_i for item o_j. The *utilitarian welfare* $\overline{u}(\mathcal{I})$ is equal to $\sum_{i=1}^{n} \overline{u}_i(\mathcal{I})$. The *egalitarian welfare* $\overline{e}(\mathcal{I})$ is equal to $\min_{i=1}^{n} \overline{u}_i(\mathcal{I})$.

Example 1 (Upper-triangular instance). *Consider $\mathcal{I}$ with n agents, n items and let each agent a_i has utilities equal to 1 for items o_1 to o_{n-i+1}. For a deterministic mechanism that allocates all items to agents that like them, we have that $\overline{k}(\mathcal{I}) \in \{1, 2, \ldots, n\}$, $\overline{u}(\mathcal{I}) = n$ and $\overline{e}(\mathcal{I}) \in \{0, 1\}$.* □

Performance measures: We use the objectives in order to define three statistics to measure the performance of online mechanisms over all instances.

$$(ES) \min_{\mathcal{I}} \overline{k}(\mathcal{I}) \tag{1}$$

$$(UW) \min_{\mathcal{I}} \overline{u}(\mathcal{I}) \tag{2}$$

$$(EW) \min_{\mathcal{I}} \overline{e}(\mathcal{I}) \tag{3}$$

Online ratios with advice: We say that an online mechanism M has an *offline (online) competitive ratio* $c(m)$ with m advice bits w.r.t. welfare W if, for an instance $\mathcal{I}$ and an ordering o of m items, we have that $W(OPT_{off(on)}) \leq c(m) \cdot W(M(\mathcal{I})) + b(m)$ holds where $b(m)$ is an additive constant and $OPT_{off(on)}$ is the optimal offline (online) mechanism. Note that the OPT_{off} mechanism does not depend on the ordering of the items whilst OPT_{on} does. A mechanism M is *most $c(m)$-competitive* w.r.t. welfare W if M has a competitive ratio $c(m)$ w.r.t. W and each other mechanism has a competitive ratio that is at least $c(m)$. We say that M_1 is *strictly better* than M_2 on a set of instances if the welfare value of M_1 is not lower than the one of M_2 on all instances from the set, and greater than the one of M_2 on some instances from the set. We say that M_1 and M_2 are *incomparable* if M_1 is strictly better than M_2 on some instances and M_2 is strictly better than M_1 on some other instances.

We suppose throughout the paper that agents *sincerely* report their utilities for items. Also, we assume that each agent has positive utility for at least one item and each item is liked by at least one agent. We show our results for the case when $m = n$ and there is a *perfect allocation* in $\mathcal{I}$ (or *perfect matching* in $\mathcal{G}_{\mathcal{I}}$), i.e. an allocation in which each agent receives exactly one item that they like. However, we also draw conclusions for the case when $m > n$ and there is an allocation in which each agent receives at least one item that they like. Finally, we extended all our results to the case when the maximum number of agents that receive items that they like in each possible allocation is $k < n$ (or *maximum matching* in $\mathcal{G}_{\mathcal{I}}$ of cardinality $k < n$). However, we omit these results for reasons of space.

3   Online Fair Division Without Advice

We study the competitiveness of our four online mechanisms w.r.t. to the optimal offline mechanism for the expected matching size (ES), the utilitarian welfare (UW) and the egalitarian welfare (EW). The optimal *offline* mechanism returns an allocation in which each agent receives exactly one item for (ES), an allocation in which each item is received by an agent that values it most for (UW) and a perfect allocation that maximizes the egalitarian welfare for (EW).

3.1   Expected Matching Size

A mechanism that maximizes the objective $\overline{k}(\mathcal{I})$ also maximizes both $\overline{u}(\mathcal{I})$ and $\overline{e}(\mathcal{I})$ simultaneously when agents have simple binary utilities. By Theorem 2 from [17], no deterministic online mechanism can maximize (ES). We, therefore, turn our attention to randomized mechanisms for (ES). By [13], the RANK-ING mechanism is most competitive for (ES) with expected matching size of $n \cdot (1 - \frac{1}{e}) + o(n)$ when the arriving sequence is adversarial. Its competitive ratio is $1 + \frac{1}{e-1}$. For this reason, we next report the competitive ratios of BALANCED LIKE, LIKE and MAXIMUM LIKE with respect to the optimal offline mechanism and RANKING. The optimal offline mechanism returns a matching of expected size n.

Theorem 1. *The* LIKE *and* BALANCED LIKE *mechanisms are 2-competitive and* $2 \cdot (1 - \frac{1}{e})$*-online competitive whereas the* MAXIMUM LIKE *mechanism is* n*-competitive and* $n \cdot (1 - \frac{1}{e})$*-online competitive for (ES).*

Proof. For BALANCED LIKE, consider the RANDOM mechanism that allocates each next item uniformly at random to an agent among those with 0 items. If no such agent exists for the current item, then RANDOM discards the item. The BALANCED LIKE mechanism can be seen as a *completion* of RANDOM, i.e. BALANCED LIKE allocates even the items that RANDOM discards. It is easy to prove that the expected matching sizes of BALANCED LIKE and RANDOM are the same for each instance. Therefore, the BALANCED LIKE and RANDOM mechanisms achieve the same expected matching size for each instance. By [13], the minimum such size is equal to $\frac{n}{2} + o(\log_2 n)$.

For LIKE, consider n agents, n items. Suppose that each agent likes the first $n/2$ items. The remaining $n/2$ items are chosen by the adversary. We have that $k \in [1, n/2]$ different agents are allocated the first $n/2$ items. The adversary then chooses the next $n/2$ items in such a way so that $n/2$ different agents like them and k of them are the ones matched the first $n/2$ items. The expected matching size is $\frac{n}{2} + o(\log_2 n)$. There could be instances, however, when this size is lower.

For MAXIMUM LIKE, consider an instance with n agents and n items. Let us suppose that all agents have positive utilities for all items but only agent a_1 has the greatest utility for each item. The mechanism gives all items to agent a_1 and thus achieves a matching size of 1. Note that this is the worst possible outcome. For each instance, the expected matching size of this mechanism is at least 1 because it allocates all items to at least one agent. □

Observation 1. *The* RANKING *mechanism is strictly better than the* BALANCED LIKE *mechanism which is strictly better than the* LIKE *mechanism for (ES).*

For RANKING and BALANCED LIKE, the result in Observation 1 follows immediately from Theorem 1. By Lemma 1, BALANCED LIKE is at least as competitive than LIKE for each instance. For some instances, BALANCED LIKE is more competitive than LIKE. Hence, BALANCED LIKE is strictly better than LIKE.

Lemma 1. *Let* π_j *be an allocation of items* o_1 *to* o_j, *and* ρ_j *and* σ_j *extend* π_j *to all items by using* BALANCED LIKE *and* LIKE, *respectively. Further, let* $b(\rho_j)$ *and* $l(\sigma_j)$ *be their probabilities. For each instance,* $j \in [1, n]$ *and* π_j, *we have that* $\sum_{\rho_j} b(\rho_j) \cdot k(\rho_j) \geq \sum_{\sigma_j} l(\sigma_j) \cdot k(\sigma_j)$ *holds.*

RANKING outperforms MAXIMUM LIKE in general over all instances. In contrast, there are instances on which MAXIMUM LIKE outperforms RANKING. We illustrate this in Example 2.

Example 2 (Expected matching incomparabilities). *Consider the fair division of 2 items between 2 agents. Let* $u_{11} = 2, u_{12} = 0, u_{21} = 1, u_{22} = 2$. *The expected matching sizes of* MAXIMUM LIKE *and* RANKING *are* 2 *and* 3/2.   □

If $m > n$, our results hold as well. We conclude that RANKING is more competitive than BALANCED LIKE, LIKE and MAXIMUM LIKE for (ES) in the worst case.

3.2   Utilitarian Welfare

In general, the utilitarian welfare can be maximized even online with no information about future items. One most competitive online mechanism that achieves the optimal offline welfare is MAXIMUM LIKE. Hence, the offline and online competitive ratios of online mechanisms conflate to just one competitive ratio.

Proposition 1. *With general utilities, the* MAXIMUM LIKE *mechanism maximizes (UW).*

Proof. MAXIMUM LIKE allocates each next item in the ordering to an agent with the greatest utility for the item. The returned online welfare value coincides with the maximum possible offline value of this welfare, i.e. the maximum utility sum over the items.   □

The result in Proposition 1 is straightforward in our setting but there are fair division settings in which optimizing the utilitarian welfare is intractable even *offline* when the entire problem input information is available [18]. We, therefore, find our result fundamental. On the other hand, with binary utilities, note that each mechanism that gives all items to agents that like them maximizes the utilitarian welfare. Indeed, BALANCED LIKE and LIKE do maximize it whereas RANKING does not because it might discard items.

Observation 2. *With 0/1 utilities, the* BALANCED LIKE *and* LIKE *mechanisms are strictly better than the* RANKING *mechanism for (UW).*

With general utilities, LIKE is n-competitive; see the example in the proof of Theorem 9 from [2]. By comparison, RANKING and BALANCED LIKE are not competitive from a utilitarian perspective even with just two agents and two items. We illustrate these results in Example 3.

Example 3 (Utilitarian non-competitiveness). *Consider the fair division of 2 items to 2 agents. Let $u_{11} = 0, u_{12} = 1, u_{21} = 1, u_{22} = u$. The optimal offline utilitarian welfare is $u + 1$ whereas the one of* BALANCED LIKE *and* RANKING *is 2. Their ratios go to ∞ as u goes to ∞.* $\quad\square$

Our Example 3 is in-line with an impossibility example and an impossibility remark presented by [14] for online weighted bipartite matching. These show that there is no deterministic or randomized online algorithm that maximizes (or minimizes) the *perfect utilitarian welfare* (the sum of the utilities in a perfect allocation) where the competitive ratio of the algorithm depends only on the number of agents n. In contrast, our utilitarian welfare objective (UW) is different because its maximum value could be obtained by allocating all items to a single agent. As a result, MAXIMUM LIKE is a mechanism whose competitive ratio does not depend even on n and LIKE is a mechanism whose competitive ratio depends solely on n.

If $m > n$, the MAXIMUM LIKE mechanism remains optimal for (UW). We used the argument in the proof of Theorem 9 from [2] to construct an example and show that LIKE remains n-competitive. Both RANKING and BALANCED LIKE remain not competitive; see the example in the proof of Theorem 10 from [2]. We conclude that MAXIMUM LIKE is more competitive than RANKING, BALANCED LIKE and LIKE for (UW) in any case.

3.3   Egalitarian Welfare

In this section, we optimize the egalitarian welfare. It is easy to see that there is no deterministic online mechanism that maximizes the egalitarian welfare. We focus therefore on randomized mechanisms.

With binary utilities, both LIKE and BALANCED LIKE are n-competitive from an egalitarian perspective; see Example 1. Moreover, MAXIMUM LIKE is equivalent to LIKE and hence it is also n-competitive. With general utilities, MAXIMUM LIKE is unfortunately not competitive at all even with just two agents and two items. See Example 4 for this simple result.

Example 4 (Egalitarian non-competitiveness). *Consider the fair division of 2 items to 2 agents. Let $u_{11} = 2, u_{12} = 2, u_{21} = 1, u_{22} = 1$. An optimal offline egalitarian mechanism gives say item o_1 to agent a_1 with probability 1 and item o_2 to agent a_2 with probability 1. Its egalitarian welfare is equal to 1.* MAXIMUM LIKE *gives items o_1 and o_2 to agent a_1 with probability 1. Its welfare is equal to 0. Hence, its ratio is ∞.* $\quad\square$

Interestingly, with general utilities, LIKE, BALANCED LIKE and RANKING are all most n-competitive from an egalitarian perspective.

Theorem 2. *With general utilities, the* BALANCED LIKE, LIKE *and* RANKING *mechanisms are most n-competitive for (EW).*

Proof. The mechanisms have competitive ratios of n. Consider instance $\mathcal{I}$, agent a_i and the first item o_j in the ordering such that agent a_i has positive utility for it. We show that $\bar{e}(\mathcal{I})$ is at least $\frac{1}{n}$. With LIKE, we have that the probability $p_i(j, \mathcal{I})$ of agent a_i for item o_j is equal to $1/n_j$ where n_j is the number of agents that like item o_j. Since $n_j \leq n$, we have $p_i(j, \mathcal{I}) \geq 1/n$. With BALANCED LIKE and RANKING, the worst case for agent a_i is when they have been allocated 0 items prior round j and all agents together have positive utilities for item o_j. Therefore, we have $p_i(j, \mathcal{I}) \geq 1/n_j \geq 1/n$. Hence, agent a_i receives expected utility of at least $\frac{1}{n}$. This lower bound is achieved in Example 1.

Next, we confirm that every other mechanism has competitive ratio at least n. Consider the upper-triangular instance from Example 1 and a mechanism M. If M shares the probability for the first item uniformly at random, then its competitive ratio is equal to $\frac{1}{n}$. If M shares the probability for the first item not uniformly at random, then its competitive ratio is lower than $\frac{1}{n}$. Suppose that M gives the first item to agent a_n with probability $p > \frac{1}{n}$. The probability of some other agent must be smaller than $\frac{1}{n}$ as these probability values sum up to at most 1. WLOG, suppose that the probability q of agent a_1 for this first item is one such value smaller than $\frac{1}{n}$. The egalitarian welfare on the upper-triangular instance is then p. However, consider next the *lower-triangular* instance, i.e. agent a_i likes items o_1 to o_i. The mechanism gives expected utility of $q < \frac{1}{n}$ to agent a_1. This value is also the welfare on the lower-triangular instance. M has competitive ratio of $1/q$ because the optimal offline welfare is 1.   □

Observation 3. *With 0/1 utilities, the* RANKING *mechanism is strictly better than the* BALANCED LIKE *mechanism which is strictly better than the* LIKE *mechanism for (EW).*

Observation 3 can be shown similarly as Observation 1. Surprisingly, there are instances on which MAXIMUM LIKE outperforms all the other three mechanisms even though it is not competitive in general. See Example 5 for this result.

Example 5 (Egalitarian incomparabilities). *Let $\mathcal{I}$ has 2 items, 2 agents and $u_{11} = 2, u_{12} = 1, u_{21} = 1, u_{22} = 2$. The value of $\bar{e}(\mathcal{I})$ of* MAXIMUM LIKE *is 2 whereas the value of $\bar{e}(\mathcal{I})$ of* BALANCED LIKE, LIKE *or* RANKING *is equal to 3/2.*   □

If $m > n$, RANKING and BALANCED LIKE become not competitive; see the example in the proof of Theorem 10 from [2]. LIKE however remains most n-competitive; see the example in the proof of Theorem 9 from [2]. We conclude that LIKE is more competitive than RANKING, BALANCED LIKE, MAXIMUM LIKE for (EW) in the worst case.

4 Online Fair Division with Full Advice

We next study most competitive adviced mechanisms for the expected matching size (ES), the utilitarian welfare (UW) and the egalitarian welfare (EW). By Proposition 1, there is a deterministic online mechanism that maximizes (UW) even without any advice. We, therefore, focus on (ES) and (EW).

We assume that the oracle specifies on the tape a different agent for each of the n items. Such an encoding requires $\lceil \log_2 n! \rceil$ advice bits. By Theorem 1 from [17], there is a deterministic online mechanism that uses $\lceil \log_2 n! \rceil$ advice bits and maximizes (ES). By Theorem 2 from [17], no deterministic online mechanism can use less than $\lceil \log_2 n! \rceil$ advice bits and maximize (ES). These two results are inherited for (EW) as well. Interestingly, we next prove that no randomized online mechanism can use less than $\lceil \log_2 n! \rceil$ advice bits and maximize either objective (ES) or (EW).

Theorem 3. *There is* **no** *randomized online algorithm that uses less than* $\lceil \log_2 n! \rceil$ *advice bits and maximizes (ES). Even with 0/1 utilities, there is* **no** *randomized online algorithm that uses less than* $\lceil \log_2 n! \rceil$ *advice bits and maximizes (EW).*

Proof. For (ES), suppose that there is such a mechanism. The maximum value of (ES) is n. Let π be an allocation returned by the mechanism and $p(\pi)$ its probability. Recall that $k(\pi) \leq n$ denotes the number of different agents that receive items in π. If $\sum_\pi p(\pi) < 1$ holds, then we conclude that $\sum_\pi p(\pi) \cdot k(\pi) < n$ holds. Therefore, the mechanism does not maximize (ES) which is a contradiction. Consequently, $\sum_\pi p(\pi) = 1$ holds. But, now we have that $\sum_\pi p(\pi) \cdot k(\pi) < n$ iff $k(\pi) < n$ for some π returned by the mechanism. Therefore, as the mechanism maximizes (ES), we conclude that $k(\pi) = n$ for each π. To sum up, the mechanism returns only perfect allocations and their probabilities sum up to 1. We can define now a deterministic online mechanism given one π returned by the randomized online mechanism. This deterministic online mechanism also uses less than $\lceil \log_2 n! \rceil$ advice bits and maximizes (ES). This is in contradiction with Theorem 2 from [17]. This result holds even with more items than agents.

For (EW) and binary utilities, suppose that there is such a mechanism. Hence, each agent receives an expected utility of 1 and the probability of 1 for each item is shared completely between agents that like the item. Given instance $\mathcal{I}$, consider the *random assignment* matrix $P(\mathcal{I}) = (p_i(j, \mathcal{I}))_{n \times n}$ of this mechanism. The matrix $P(\mathcal{I})$ is *bistochastic* because $\sum_{i=1}^{n} p_i(j, \mathcal{I}) = 1$ for each j and $\sum_{j=1}^{n} p_i(j, \mathcal{I}) = 1$ for each i hold. By the famous result of Birkhoff, every bistochastic matrix is a convex combination of permutation matrices [6]. Each permutation matrix corresponds to a perfect allocation in $\mathcal{I}$. There could be multiple combinations for the same bistochastic matrix. For each such combination, we can define a randomized online algorithm that uses less than $\lceil \log_2 n! \rceil$ advice bits and maximizes (ES). This is in contradiction with the previous result. This result holds even with more items than agents. $\square$

5   Online Fair Division with Partial Advice

In this section, we report the reciprocal ratios of the mechanisms. We assume that the oracle specifies agents for $k < m$ items. We start with the case when $m = n$. For (ES), the oracle specifies a different agent for each of the first k items. An efficient encoding requires $\lceil \log_2 k! \rceil$ advice bits. If $k = n - 1$, ADVICED RANKING and ADVICED BALANCED LIKE are optimal because they keep track on the past allocation whereas ADVICED MAXIMUM LIKE and ADVICED LIKE have ratios $1 - \frac{1}{n}$ and $1 - \frac{1}{n} + \frac{1}{n^2}$. If $k < n - 1$, we next report their ratios.

Theorem 4. *With $\lceil \log_2 k! \rceil$ advice bits, ADVICED RANKING is most $\frac{(e-1)n+k}{en}$-competitive for (ES).*

Proof. The mechanism has two components: (1) one that allocates items deterministically and (2) another one that allocates items according to RANKING. Let the entire input graph be $\mathcal{G}_\mathcal{I}$ with n vertices in each partition. Let us remove the k deterministically decided vertices from both partitions together with their edges from $\mathcal{G}_\mathcal{I}$. Now, consider the remaining bipartite sub-graph with $(n - k)$ vertices in each partition. This graph has perfect matching of size $(n - k)$ and RANKING matches vertices in this graph. Therefore, the expected matching size of RANKING on this smaller graph is $(n - k) \cdot (1 - \frac{1}{e}) + o(n - k)$. We conclude that this size for ADVICED RANKING is $k + (n - k) \cdot (1 - \frac{1}{e}) + o(n - k)$.

By Theorem 1 from [17], the deterministic component of ADVICED RANKING maximizes (ES) on the bipartite sub-graph of $\mathcal{G}_\mathcal{I}$ that contains the adviced $2 \cdot k$ vertices. By [13], we conclude that the randomized component of ADVICED RANKING maximizes (ES) on the bipartite sub-graph of $\mathcal{G}_\mathcal{I}$ that contains the remaining unadviced $2 \cdot (n - k)$ vertices.   □

By Theorem 2 from [17] and our Theorem 3, there is no mechanism that uses less than $\lceil \log_2 k! \rceil$ advice bits and has a greater competitive ratio than ADVICED RANKING with $\lceil \log_2 k! \rceil$ advice bits. We also obtained that the offline ratios of ADVICED MAXIMUM LIKE, ADVICED BALANCED LIKE and ADVICED LIKE for (ES) and $k \in [1, n - 1)$ are $\frac{k}{n}$, $\frac{k+n}{2n}$ and at most $\frac{k+n}{2n}$. Their online ratios are $\frac{ek}{(e-1)n+k}$, $\frac{e(k+n)}{2(e-1)n+2k}$ and at most $\frac{e(k+n)}{2(e-1)n+2k}$. In Fig. 1, we plot these ratios for $n = 10$ agents and $k \in [0, n]$ oracle calls.

For (UW), (EW) and 0/1 utilities, the oracle specifies a different agent for each of the first k items. For (UW) and general utilities, the oracle specifies an agent for each of k most valued items. The worst case for ADVICED RANKING and ADVICED BALANCED LIKE is when the adviced allocation biases the allocation of future items towards agents who receive negligibly small utilities for these items. Instead, ADVICED LIKE allocates each such unadviced item to an agent with probability at least $\frac{1}{n}$. ADVICED MAXIMUM LIKE optimizes (UW) by Proposition 1. For (EW) and general utilities, the oracle computes an allocation of k items to agents that maximizes the egalitarian welfare and then specifies the k agents for the k items in this computed allocation. ADVICED RANKING and ADVICED BALANCED LIKE focus on agents with zero and fewest items whereas

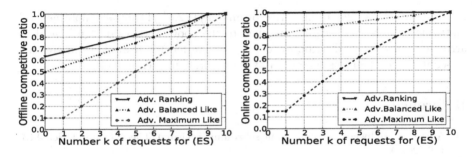

Fig. 1. (left) w.r.t optimal offline mechanism, (right) w.r.t. ADVICED RANKING

ADVICED LIKE and ADVICED MAXIMUM LIKE perform as LIKE and MAXIMUM LIKE.

We next consider the case when $m > n$. For (ES), we conclude the same results as above. For (UW), (EW) and 0/1 utilities, we assume that the oracle specifies k agents for the first k items in the ordering for which the k agents are different. For (UW), (EW) and general utilities, the oracle specifications are as in the case when $m = n$. We summarize all ratios in Table 1.

Table 1. Ratios for $k \in [0, m)$ adviced items and $l \in [1, n)$ adviced agents: (b) - binary utilities, (g)-general utilities.

Mechanism	(UW)-b $m \geq n$	(UW)-g $m \geq n$	(EW)-b $m \geq n$	(EW)-g $m = n$	(EW)-g $m > n$
ADV.MAX.LIKE	1	1	$\frac{1}{n}$	0	0
ADV.BAL.LIKE	1	$\frac{k}{m}$	$\frac{1}{n-l}$	$\frac{1}{n-l}$	0
ADV.LIKE	1	$\frac{k}{m} + \frac{1}{n} - \frac{k}{nm}$	$\frac{1}{n}$	$\frac{1}{n}$	$\frac{1}{n}$
ADV.RANKING	$\leq \frac{n}{m}$	$\frac{k}{m}$	$\frac{1}{n-l}$	$\frac{1}{n-l}$	0

6   Related Work and Conclusions

We combined competitive analysis, advice complexity and online fair division. Our results are simple but fundamental to understand better the interface between matching and fair division problems. In conclusion, the chair might use ADVICED RANKING for (ES), ADVICED MAXIMUM LIKE for (UW) and ADVICED LIKE or ADVICED BALANCED LIKE for (EW). We quantify the offline and online performance of these mechanisms with respect to the number of advice bits they can read from an oracle tape. We also presented two impossibility results and closed an open question from [17].

In future, we will analyse other b-matching mechanisms from a fair division viewpoint [11,12]. Also, we can explore more objectives (e.g. the Nash welfare)

or competitive measures (e.g. price of anarchy) [2,9]. There are more general matching models with weights attached to the "boy" vertices or "girl" vertices arriving from a known distribution or a random order [16]. It would be interesting to see if our mechanisms remain most competitive in such models.

References

1. Albers, S., Hellwig, M.: Semi-online scheduling revisited. Theor. Comput. Sci. **443**, 1–9 (2012)
2. Aleksandrov, M., Aziz, H., Gaspers, S., Walsh, T.: Online fair division: analysing a food bank problem. In: Proceedings of the Twenty-Fourth IJCAI 2015, Buenos Aires, Argentina, pp. 2540–2546, 25–31 July 2015
3. Böckenhauer, H.-J., Komm, D., Královič, R., Královič, R., Mömke, T.: On the advice complexity of online problems. In: Dong, Y., Du, D.-Z., Ibarra, O. (eds.) ISAAC 2009. LNCS, vol. 5878, pp. 331–340. Springer, Heidelberg (2009). doi:10. 1007/978-3-642-10631-6_35
4. Borodin, A., El-Yaniv, R.: Online Computation and Competitive Analysis. Cambridge University Press, Cambridge (1998)
5. Boyar, J., Favrholdt, L.M., Kudahl, C., Larsen, K.S., Mikkelsen, J.W.: Online algorithms with advice: a survey. SIGACT News **47**(3), 93–129 (2016)
6. Brualdi, R.: Combinatorial Matrix Classes. No. 13 in Combinatorial Matrix Classes, Cambridge University Press (2006). https://books.google.de/books? id=xdP9d8S1BxQC
7. Brubach, B., Sankararaman, K.A., Srinivasan, A., Xu, P.: New algorithms, better bounds, and a novel model for online stochastic matching. In: 24th Annual European Symposium on Algorithms, ESA, Aarhus, Denmark, pp. 1–16, 22–24 August 2016
8. Dobrev, S., Královic, R., Pardubská, D.: Measuring the problem-relevant information in input. Int. Tromb. Assoc. **43**(3), 585–613 (2009)
9. Freeman, R., Zahedi, S.M., Conitzer, V.: Fair social choice in dynamic settings. Paper presented at the 3rd (EXPLORE) Workshop, 15th AAMAS Conference 2016, Singapore, 9–10 May 2016
10. György, A., Lugosi, G., Ottucsák, G.: On-line sequential bin packing. J. Mach. Learn. Res. **11**, 89–109 (2010)
11. Jaillet, P., Lu, X.: Online stochastic matching: new algorithms with better bounds. Math. Oper. Res. **39**(3), 624–646 (2014)
12. Kalyanasundaram, B., Pruhs, K.: An optimal deterministic algorithm for online b-matching. Theor. Comput. Sci. **233**(1–2), 319–325 (2000)
13. Karp, R.M., Vazirani, U.V., Vazirani, V.V.: An optimal algorithm for on-line bipartite matching. In: Proceedings of 22nd Annual ACM Symposium on Theory of Computing, Baltimore, Maryland, USA, pp. 352–358, 13–17 May 1990
14. Khuller, S., Mitchell, S.G., Vazirani, V.V.: On-line algorithms for weighted bipartite matching and stable marriages. Theor. Comput. Sci. **127**(2), 255–267 (1994)
15. Marchetti-Spaccamela, A., Vercellis, C.: Stochastic on-line knapsack problems. Math. Program. **68**, 73–104 (1995)
16. Mehta, A.: Online matching and ad allocation. Found. Trends Theor. Comput. Sci. **8**(4), 265–368 (2013)
17. Miyazaki, S.: On the advice complexity of online bipartite matching and online stable marriage. Inf. Process. Lett. **114**(12), 714–717 (2014)

18. Nguyen, N., Nguyen, T.T., Roos, M., Rothe, J.: Computational complexity and approximability of social welfare optimization in multiagent resource allocation. Auton. Agents Multi-Agent Syst. **28**(2), 256–289 (2014)
19. Seiden, S.S., Sgall, J., Woeginger, G.J.: Semi-online scheduling with decreasing job sizes. Oper. Res. Lett. **27**(5), 215–221 (2000)
20. Sleator, D.D., Tarjan, R.E.: Amortized efficiency of list update and paging rules. Commun. ACM **28**(2), 202–208 (1985)
21. Walsh, T.: Allocation in practice. In: Lutz, C., Thielscher, M. (eds.) KI 2014. LNCS (LNAI), vol. 8736, pp. 13–24. Springer, Cham (2014). doi:10.1007/978-3-319-11206-0_2
22. Walsh, T.: Challenges in resource and cost allocation. In: Proceedings of 29th AAAI 2015, Austin, Texas, USA, pp. 4073–4077, 25–30 January 2015. http://www.aaai.org/ocs/index.php/AAAI/AAAI15/paper/view/9927

A Thorough Formalization of Conceptual Spaces

Lucas Bechberger[✉] and Kai-Uwe Kühnberger

Institute of Cognitive Science, Osnabrück University, Osnabrück, Germany
{lucas.bechberger,kai-uwe.kuehnberger}@uni-osnabrueck.de

Abstract. The highly influential framework of conceptual spaces provides a geometric way of representing knowledge. Instances are represented by points in a high-dimensional space and concepts are represented by convex regions in this space. After pointing out a problem with the convexity requirement, we propose a formalization of conceptual spaces based on fuzzy star-shaped sets. Our formalization uses a parametric definition of concepts and extends the original framework by adding means to represent correlations between different domains in a geometric way. Moreover, we define computationally efficient operations on concepts (intersection, union, and projection onto a subspace) and show that these operations can support both learning and reasoning processes.

Keywords: Conceptual spaces · Star-shaped sets · Fuzzy sets

1 Introduction

One common criticism of symbolic AI approaches is that the symbols they operate on do not contain any meaning: For the system, they are just arbitrary tokens that can be manipulated in some way. This lack of inherent meaning in abstract symbols is called the "symbol grounding problem" [17]. One approach towards solving this problem is to devise a grounding mechanism that connects abstract symbols to the real world, i.e., to perception and action.

The framework of conceptual spaces [15,16] attempts to bridge this gap between symbolic and subsymbolic AI by proposing an intermediate conceptual layer based on geometric representations. A conceptual space is a high-dimensional space spanned by a number of quality dimensions that are based on perception and/or subsymbolic processing. Convex regions in this space correspond to concepts. Abstract symbols can thus be grounded in reality by linking them to regions in a conceptual space whose dimensions are based on perception.

The framework of conceptual spaces has been highly influential in the last 15 years within cognitive science and cognitive linguistics [13,14,31]. It has also sparked considerable research in various subfields of artificial intelligence, ranging from robotics and computer vision [8–10] over the semantic web and ontology integration [2,12] to plausible reasoning [11,27].

One important question is however left unaddressed by these research efforts: How can an (artificial) agent learn about meaningful regions in a conceptual space purely from unlabeled perceptual data?

© Springer International Publishing AG 2017
G. Kern-Isberner et al. (Eds.): KI 2017, LNAI 10505, pp. 58–71, 2017.
DOI: 10.1007/978-3-319-67190-1_5

Our approach for solving this concept formation problem is to devise an incremental clustering algorithm that groups a stream of unlabeled observations (represented as points in a conceptual space) into meaningful regions.

In this paper, we point out that Gärdenfors' convexity requirement prevents a geometric representation of correlations. We resolve this problem by using star-shaped instead of convex sets. Our mathematical formalization defines concepts in a parametric way that is easily implementable. We furthermore define computationally efficient operations on these concepts, which can support both machine learning and reasoning processes. This paper therefore lays the foundation for our work on concept formation.

The remainder of this paper is structured as follows: Sect. 2 introduces the general framework of conceptual spaces and points out a problem with the notion of convexity. Section 3 describes our formalization of concepts as fuzzy star-shaped sets. In Sect. 4, we define operations on these sets and in Sect. 5 we show that they can support both machine learning and reasoning processes. Section 6 summarizes related work and Sect. 7 concludes the paper. Proofs of our propositions are provided in an appendix available online at http://lucas-bechberger. de/appendix-ki-2017/.

2   Conceptual Spaces

2.1   Definition of Conceptual Spaces

This section presents the cognitive framework of conceptual spaces as described in [15] and introduces our formalization of dimensions, domains, and distances.

A conceptual space is a high-dimensional space spanned by a set D of so-called "quality dimensions". Each of these dimensions $d \in D$ represents a way in which two stimuli can be judged to be similar or different. Examples for quality dimensions include temperature, weight, time, pitch, and hue. We denote the distance between two points x and y with respect to a dimension d as $|x_d - y_d|$.

A domain $\delta \subseteq D$ is a set of dimensions that inherently belong together. Different perceptual modalities (like color, shape, or taste) are represented by different domains. The color domain for instance consists of the three dimensions hue, saturation, and brightness.

Gärdenfors argues based on psychological evidence [5, 28] that distance within a domain δ should be measured by the weighted Euclidean metric:

$$d_E^{\delta}(x, y, W_{\delta}) = \sqrt{\sum_{d \in \delta} w_d \cdot |x_d - y_d|^2}$$

The parameter W_{δ} contains positive weights w_d for all dimensions $d \in \delta$ representing their relative importance. We assume that $\sum_{d \in \delta} w_d = 1$.

The overall conceptual space CS is defined as the product space of all dimensions. Again, based on psychological evidence [5, 28], Gärdenfors argues that distance within the overall conceptual space should be measured by the weighted

Manhattan metric d_M of the intra-domain distances. Let Δ be the set of all domains in CS. We define the distance within a conceptual space as follows:

$$d_C^\Delta(x, y, W) = \sum_{\delta \in \Delta} w_\delta \cdot d_E^\delta(x, y, W_\delta) = \sum_{\delta \in \Delta} w_\delta \cdot \sqrt{\sum_{d \in \delta} w_d \cdot |x_d - y_d|^2}$$

The parameter $W = \langle W_\Delta, \{W_\delta\}_{\delta \in \Delta}\rangle$ contains W_Δ, the set of positive domain weights w_δ. We require that $\sum_{\delta \in \Delta} w_\delta = |\Delta|$. Moreover, W contains for each domain $\delta \in \Delta$ a set W_δ of dimension weights as defined above. The weights in W are not globally constant, but depend on the current context. One can easily show that $d_C^\Delta(x, y, W)$ with a given W is a metric.

The similarity of two points in a conceptual space is inversely related to their distance. Gärdenfors expresses this as follows :

$$Sim(x, y) = e^{-c \cdot d(x,y)} \quad \text{with a constant } c > 0 \text{ and a given metric } d$$

Betweenness is a logical predicate $B(x, y, z)$ that is true if and only if y is considered to be between x and z. It can be defined based on a given metric d:

$$B_d(x, y, z) : \iff d(x, y) + d(y, z) = d(x, z)$$

The betweenness relation based on d_E results in the line segment connecting the points x and z, whereas the betweenness relation based on d_M results in an axis-parallel cuboid between the points x and z. We can define convexity and star-shapedness based on the notion of betweenness:

Definition 1 *(Convexity). A set $C \subseteq CS$ is* convex *under a metric*

$$d : \iff \forall x \in C, z \in C, y \in CS : (B_d(x, y, z) \to y \in C)$$

Definition 2 *(Star-shapedness). A set $S \subseteq CS$ is* star-shaped *under a metric d with respect to a set*

$$P \subseteq S : \iff \forall p \in P, z \in S, y \in CS : (B_d(p, y, z) \to y \in S)$$

Gärdenfors distinguishes properties like "red", "round", and "sweet" from full-fleshed concepts like "apple" or "dog" by observing that properties can be defined on individual domains (e.g., color, shape, taste), whereas full-fleshed concepts involve multiple domains.

Definition 3 *(Property). A natural property is a convex region of a domain in a conceptual space.*

Full-fleshed concepts can be expressed as a combination of properties from different domains. These domains might have a different importance for the concept which is reflected by so-called "salience weights". Another important aspect of concepts are the correlations between the different domains [20], which are important for both learning [7] and reasoning [21, Chap. 8].

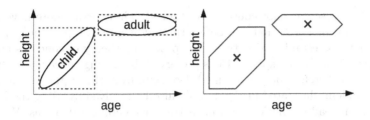

Fig. 1. Left: Intuitive way to define regions for the concepts of "adult" and "child" (solid) as well as representation by using convex sets (dashed). Right: Representation by using star-shaped sets with central points marked by crosses.

Definition 4 *(Concept). A natural concept is represented as a set of convex regions in a number of domains together with an assignment of salience weights to the domains and information about how the regions in different domains are correlated.*

2.2 An Argument Against Convexity

Gärdenfors [15] does not propose any concrete way for representing correlations between domains. As the main idea of the conceptual spaces framework is to find a geometric representation of conceptual structures, we think that a geometric representation of these correlations is desirable.

Consider the left part of Fig. 1. In this example, we consider two domains, age and height, in order to define the concepts of child and adult. We would expect a strong correlation between age and height for children, but no such correlation for adults. This is represented by the two solid ellipses.

Domains are combined by using the Manhattan metric and convex sets under the Manhattan metric are axis-parallel cuboids. Thus, a convex representation of the two concepts results in the dashed rectangles. This means that we cannot geometrically represent correlations between domains if we assume that concepts are convex and that the Manhattan metric is used. We think that our example is not a pathological one and that similar problems will occur quite frequently when encoding concepts. From a different perspective, also Hernández-Conde has recently argued against the convexity constraint in conceptual spaces [18].

If we only require star-shapedness instead of convexity, we can represent the correlation of age and height for children in a geometric way. This is shown in the right part of Fig. 1: Both sketched sets are star-shaped under the Manhattan metric with respect to a central point. Although the star-shaped sets do not exactly correspond to our intuitive sketch in the left part of Fig. 1, they definitely are an improvement over the convex representation.[1]

---

[1] The weaker requirement of star-shapedness allows us to "cut out" some corners from the rectangle. This enables us to geometrically represent correlations.

Star-shaped sets cannot contain any "holes". They furthermore have a well defined central region P that can be interpreted as a prototype. Thus, the connection that was established between the prototype theory of concepts and the framework of conceptual spaces [15] is preserved. Replacing convexity with star-shapedness is therefore only a minimal departure from the original framework.

The problem illustrated in Fig. 1 could also be resolved by using the Euclidean metric instead of the Manhattan metric for combining domains. We think however that this would be a major modification of the original framework. For instance, if the use of the Manhattan metric is abolished, the usage of domains to structure the conceptual space loses its main effect of influencing the overall distance metric. Moreover, psychological evidence [5,28,29] indicates that human similarity ratings are reflected better by the Manhattan metric than by the Euclidean metric if different domains are involved (e.g., stimuli differing in size and brightness). As a psychologically plausible representation of similarity is one of the core principles of the conceptual spaces framework, these findings should be taken into account. Furthermore, in high-dimensional feature spaces the Manhattan metric provides a better relative contrast between close and distant points than the Euclidean metric [3]. If we expect the number of domains to be large, this also supports the usage of the Manhattan metric from an implementational point of view.

Based on these arguments, we think that weakening the convexity assumption is a better option than abolishing the use of the Manhattan metric.

3   A Parametric Definition of Concepts

3.1   Preliminaries

Our formalization is based on the following insight:

Lemma 1. *Let $C_1, ..., C_m$ be convex sets in CS under some metric d and let $P := \bigcap_{i=1}^{m} C_i$. If $P \neq \emptyset$, then $S := \bigcup_{i=1}^{m} C_i$ is star-shaped under d w.r.t. P.*

Proof. Obvious (see also [30]). ∎

We will use axis-parallel cuboids as building blocks for our star-shaped sets. They are defined in the following way:

Definition 5 *(Axis-parallel cuboid). We describe an axis-parallel cuboid[2] C as a triple $\langle \Delta_C, p^-, p^+ \rangle$. C is defined on the domains $\Delta_C \subseteq \Delta$, i.e. on the dimensions $D_C = \bigcup_{\delta \in \Delta_C} \delta$. We call p^-, p^+ the support points of C and require:*

$$\forall d \in D_C : p_d^+, p_d^- \notin \{+\infty, -\infty\} \quad \wedge \quad \forall d \in D \setminus D_C : p_d^- := -\infty \wedge p_d^+ := +\infty$$

Then, we define the cuboid C in the following way:

$$C = \{x \in CS \mid \forall d \in D : p_d^- \leq x_d \leq p_d^+\}$$

---

[2] We will drop the modifier "axis-parallel" from now on.

Lemma 2. *A cuboid C is convex under d_C^A, given a fixed set of weights W.*

Proof. It is easy to see that cuboids are convex with respect to d_M and d_E. Based on this, one can show that they are also convex with respect to d_C^A, which is a combination of d_M and d_E.

Our formalization will make use of fuzzy sets [32], which can be defined in our current context as follows:

Definition 6 *(Fuzzy set). A fuzzy set $\widetilde{A}$ on CS is defined by its membership function $\mu_{\widetilde{A}} : CS \to [0,1]$.*

Note that fuzzy sets contain crisp sets as a special case where $\mu_{\widetilde{A}} : CS \to \{0,1\}$. For each $x \in CS$, we interpret $\mu_{\widetilde{A}}(x)$ as degree of membership of x in $\widetilde{A}$.

Definition 7 *(Alpha-cut). Given a fuzzy set $\widetilde{A}$ on CS, its α-cut $\widetilde{A}^\alpha$ for $\alpha \in [0,1]$ is defined as follows:*

$$\widetilde{A}^\alpha = \{x \in CS \mid \mu_{\widetilde{A}}(x) \geq \alpha\}$$

Definition 8 *(Fuzzy star-shapedness). A fuzzy set $\widetilde{A}$ is called star-shaped under a metric d with respect to a (crisp) set P if all of its α-cuts $\widetilde{A}^\alpha$ are either empty or star-shaped under d w.r.t. P.*

One can also generalize the ideas of subsethood, intersection, and union from crisp to fuzzy sets. We adopt the most widely used definitions:

Definition 9 *(Operations on fuzzy sets). Let $\widetilde{A}, \widetilde{B}$ be two fuzzy sets defined on CS.*

- *Subsethood:* $\widetilde{A} \subseteq \widetilde{B} : \iff (\forall x \in CS : \mu_{\widetilde{A}}(x) \leq \mu_{\widetilde{B}}(x))$
- *Intersection:* $\forall x \in CS : \mu_{\widetilde{A} \cap \widetilde{B}}(x) := \min(\mu_{\widetilde{A}}(x), \mu_{\widetilde{B}}(x))$
- *Union:* $\forall x \in CS : \mu_{\widetilde{A} \cup \widetilde{B}}(x) := \max(\mu_{\widetilde{A}}(x), \mu_{\widetilde{B}}(x))$

3.2 Fuzzy Simple Star-Shaped Sets

By combining Lemmas 1 and 2, we see that any union of intersecting cuboids is star-shaped under d_C^A. We use this insight to define simple star-shaped sets (illustrated in Fig. 2):

Definition 10 *(Simple star-shaped set). We describe a simple star-shaped set S as a tuple $\langle \Delta_S, \{C_1, \ldots, C_m\} \rangle$. $\Delta_S \subseteq \Delta$ is a set of domains on which the cuboids $\{C_1, \ldots, C_m\}$ (and thus also S) are defined. We further require that the central region $P := \bigcap_{i=1}^m C_i \neq \emptyset$. Then the simple star-shaped set S is defined as*

$$S := \bigcup_{i=1}^m C_i$$

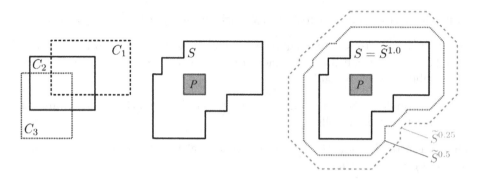

Fig. 2. Left: Three cuboids C_1, C_2, C_3 with nonempty intersection. Middle: Resulting simple star-shaped set S based on these cuboids. Right: Fuzzy simple star-shaped set $\widetilde{S}$ based on S with three α-cuts for $\alpha \in \{1.0, 0.5, 0.25\}$. (Color figure online)

In practice, it is often not possible to define clear-cut boundaries for concepts and properties. It is, for example, very hard to define a generally accepted crisp boundary for the property "red". We therefore use a fuzzified version of simple star-shaped sets for representing concepts, which allows us to define imprecise concept boundaries. This usage of fuzzy sets for representing concepts has already a long history (cf. [6,13,22,26,33]). We use a simple star-shaped set S as a concept's "core" and define the membership of any point $x \in CS$ to this concept as $\max_{y \in S} Sim(x, y)$:

Definition 11 *(Fuzzy simple star-shaped set). A fuzzy simple star-shaped set $\widetilde{S}$ is described by a quadruple $\langle S, \mu_0, c, W \rangle$ where $S = \langle \Delta_S, \{C_1, \ldots, C_m\} \rangle$ is a non-empty simple star-shaped set. The parameter $\mu_0 \in (0, 1]$ controls the highest possible membership to $\widetilde{S}$ and is usually set to 1. The sensitivity parameter $c > 0$ controls the rate of the exponential decay in the similarity function. Finally, $W = \langle W_{\Delta_S}, \{W_\delta\}_{\delta \in \Delta_S} \rangle$ contains positive weights for all domains in Δ_S and all dimensions within these domains, reflecting their respective importance. We require that $\sum_{\delta \in \Delta_S} w_\delta = |\Delta_S|$ and that $\forall \delta \in \Delta_S : \sum_{d \in \delta} w_d = 1$.*

The membership function of $\widetilde{S}$ is then defined as follows:

$$\mu_{\widetilde{S}}(x) = \mu_0 \cdot \max_{y \in S}(e^{-c \cdot d_C^{\Delta_S}(x, y, W)})$$

The sensitivity parameter c controls the overall degree of fuzziness of $\widetilde{S}$ by determining how fast the membership drops to zero. The weights W represent not only the relative importance of the respective domain or dimension for the represented concept, but they also influence the relative fuzziness with respect to this domain or dimension. Note that if $|\Delta_S| = 1$, then $\widetilde{S}$ represents a property, and if $|\Delta_S| > 1$, then $\widetilde{S}$ represents a concept.

The right part of Fig. 2 shows a fuzzy simple star-shaped set $\widetilde{S}$. In this illustration, the x and y axes are assumed to belong to different domains, and are combined with the Manhattan metric using equal weights.

Proposition 1. *Any fuzzy simple star-shaped set* $\widetilde{S} = \langle S, \mu_0, c, W \rangle$ *is star-shaped with respect to* $P = \bigcap_{i=1}^{m} C_i$ *under* $d_C^{\Delta s}$.

Proof. See appendix (http://lucas-bechberger.de/appendix-ki-2017/).

4 Operations on Concepts

In this section, we define some operations on concepts (i.e., fuzzy simple star-shaped sets). The set of all concepts is closed under each of these operations.

4.1 Intersection

If we intersect two simple star-shaped sets S_1, S_2, we simply need to intersect their cuboids. As an intersection of two cuboids is again a cuboid, the result of intersecting two simple star-shaped sets can be described as a union of cuboids. It is simple star-shaped if these resulting cuboids have a nonempty intersection. This is only the case if the central regions P_1 and P_2 of S_1 and S_2 intersect.[3]

However, we would like our intersection to result in a simple star-shaped set even if $P_1 \cap P_2 = \emptyset$. Thus, when intersecting two star-shaped sets, we might need to apply some repair mechanism in order to restore star-shapedness.

We propose to extend the cuboids C_i of the intersection in such a way that they meet in some "midpoint" $p^* \in CS$ (e.g., the arithmetic mean of their centers). We create extended versions C_i^* of all C_i by defining their support points like this:

$$\forall d \in D : p_{id}^{-*} := \min(p_{id}^{-}, p_d^*), \quad p_{id}^{+*} := \max(p_{id}^{+}, p_d^*)$$

The intersection of the resulting C_i^* contains at least p^*, so it is not empty. This means that $S' = \langle \Delta_{S_1} \cup \Delta_{S_2}, \{C_1^*, \ldots, C_{m^*}^*\} \rangle$ is again a simple star-shaped set. We denote this modified intersection (consisting of the actual intersection and the application of the repair mechanism) as $S' = I(S_1, S_2)$.

We define the intersection of two fuzzy simple star-shaped sets as $\widetilde{S}' = I(\widetilde{S}_1, \widetilde{S}_2) := \langle S', \mu_0', c', W' \rangle$ with:

- $S' := I(\widetilde{S}_1^{\alpha'}, \widetilde{S}_2^{\alpha'})$ (where $\alpha' = \max\{\alpha \in [0,1] : \widetilde{S}_1^{\alpha} \cap \widetilde{S}_2^{\alpha} \neq \emptyset\}$)
- $\mu_0' := \alpha'$
- $c' := \min(c^{(1)}, c^{(2)})$
- W' with weights defined as follows (where $s, t \in [0,1]$)[4]:

$$\forall \delta \in \Delta_{S_1} \cap \Delta_{S_2} : \left((w_\delta' := s \cdot w_\delta^{(1)} + (1-s) \cdot w_\delta^{(2)}) \right.$$

$$\left. \wedge \forall d \in \delta : (w_d' := t \cdot w_d^{(1)} + (1-t) \cdot w_d^{(2)}) \right)$$

$$\forall \delta \in \Delta_{S_1} \setminus \Delta_{S_2} : \left((w_\delta' := w_\delta^{(1)}) \wedge \forall d \in \delta : (w_d' := w_d^{(1)}) \right)$$

$$\forall \delta \in \Delta_{S_2} \setminus \Delta_{S_1} : \left((w_\delta' := w_\delta^{(2)}) \wedge \forall d \in \delta : (w_d' := w_d^{(2)}) \right)$$

---

[3] Note that if $D_{S_1} \cap D_{S_2} = \emptyset$, then $P_1 \cap P_2 \neq \emptyset$.

[4] In some cases, the normalization constraint of the resulting domain weights might be violated. We can enforce this constraint by manually normalizing them.

When taking the combination of two somewhat imprecise concepts, the result should not be more precise than any of the original concepts. As the sensitivity parameter is inversely related to fuzziness, we take the minimum. If a weight is defined for both original sets, we take a convex combination, and if it is only defined for one of them, we simply copy it.

Note that for $\alpha' < \max(\mu_0^{(1)}, \mu_0^{(2)})$, the α-cuts $\widetilde{S}_1^{\alpha'}$ and $\widetilde{S}_2^{\alpha'}$ are still guaranteed to be star-shaped, but not necessarily simple star-shaped. In order to be still well-defined, the modified crisp intersection I will in this case first compute their "ordinary" intersection, then approximate this intersection with cuboids (e.g., by using bounding boxes) and finally apply the repair mechanism.

4.2   Union

As each simple star-shaped set is defined as a union of cuboids, the union of two such sets can also be expressed as a union of cuboids. However, the resulting set is not necessarily star-shaped – only if the central regions of the original simple star-shaped sets intersect. So after each union, we might again need to perform a repair mechanism in order to restore star-shapedness. We propose to use the same repair mechanism that is also used for intersections. We denote the modified union as $S' = U(S_1, S_2)$.

We define the union of two fuzzy simple star-shaped sets as $\widetilde{S}' = U(\widetilde{S}_1, \widetilde{S}_2) := \langle S', \mu_0', c', W' \rangle$ with:

- $S' := U(S_1, S_2)$
- $\mu_0' := \max(\mu_0^{(1)}, \mu_0^{(2)})$
- c' and W' as described in Sect. 4.1

Proposition 2. *Let $\widetilde{S}_1 = \langle S_1, \mu_0^{(1)}, c^{(1)}, W^{(1)} \rangle$ and $\widetilde{S}_2 = \langle S_2, \mu_0^{(2)}, c^{(2)}, W^{(2)} \rangle$ be two fuzzy simple star-shaped sets. If we assume that $\Delta_{S_1} = \Delta_{S_2}$ and $W^{(1)} = W^{(2)}$, then $\widetilde{S}_1 \cup \widetilde{S}_2 \subseteq U(\widetilde{S}_1, \widetilde{S}_2) = \widetilde{S}'$.*

Proof. See appendix (http://lucas-bechberger.de/appendix-ki-2017/).

4.3   Subspace Projection

Projecting a cuboid onto a subspace results in a cuboid. As one can easily see, projecting a simple star-shaped set S onto a subspace results in another simple star-shaped set. We denote the projection of S onto domains $\Delta_{S'} \subseteq \Delta_S$ as $S' = P(S, \Delta_{S'})$.

We define the projection of a fuzzy simple star-shaped set $\widetilde{S}$ onto domains $\Delta_{S'} \subseteq \Delta_S$ as $\widetilde{S}' = P(\widetilde{S}, \Delta_{S'}) := \langle S', \mu_0', c', W' \rangle$ with:

- $S' := P(S, \Delta_{S'})$
- $\mu_0' := \mu_0$
- $c' := c$
- $W' := \langle \{|\Delta_S'| \cdot \frac{w_\delta}{\sum_{\delta' \in \Delta_{S'}} w_{\delta'}}\}_{\delta \in \Delta_{S'}}, \{W_\delta\}_{\delta \in \Delta_{S'}} \rangle$

Note that we only apply minimal changes to the parameters: μ_0 and c stay the same, only the domain weights are updated in order to not violate their normalization constraint.

Projecting a set onto two complementary subspaces and then intersecting these projections again in the original space yields a superset of the original set. This is intuitively clear for simple star-shaped sets and can also be shown for fuzzy simple star-shaped sets under one additional constraint:

Proposition 3. *Let* $\widetilde{S} = \langle S, \mu_0, c, W \rangle$ *be a fuzzy simple star-shaped set. Let* $\widetilde{S}_1 = P(\widetilde{S}, \Delta_1)$ *and* $\widetilde{S}_2 = P(\widetilde{S}, \Delta_2)$ *with* $\Delta_1 \cup \Delta_2 = \Delta_S$ *and* $\Delta_1 \cap \Delta_2 = \emptyset$. *Let* $\widetilde{S}' = I(\widetilde{S}_1, \widetilde{S}_2)$ *as described in Sect. 4.1. If* $\sum_{\delta \in \Delta_1} w_\delta = |\Delta_1|$ *and* $\sum_{\delta \in \Delta_2} w_\delta = |\Delta_2|$, *then* $\widetilde{S} \subseteq \widetilde{S}'$.

Proof. See appendix (http://lucas-bechberger.de/appendix-ki-2017/).

5 Supported Applications

5.1 Machine Learning Process: Clustering

The operations described in Sect. 4 can be used by a clustering algorithm in the following way:

The clustering algorithm can create and delete fuzzy simple star-shaped sets. It can move and resize an existing cluster as well as adjust its form by modifying the support points of the cuboids that define its core. One must however ensure that such modifications preserve the non-emptiness of the cuboids' intersection. Moreover, a cluster's form can be changed by modifying the parameters c and W: By changing c, one can control the overall degree of fuzziness, and by changing W, one can control how this fuzziness is distributed among the different domains and dimensions. Two neighboring clusters $\widetilde{S}_1, \widetilde{S}_2$ can be merged into a single cluster by unifying them. A single cluster can be split up into two parts by replacing it with two smaller clusters.

So clusters can be created, deleted, modified, merged, and split – which is sufficient for defining a clustering algorithm.

5.2 Reasoning Process: Concept Combination

The operations defined in Sect. 4 can also be used for combining concepts.

The modified intersection $I(\widetilde{S}_1, \widetilde{S}_2)$ roughly corresponds to a logical "AND": Intersecting "green" with "blue" results in the set of all colors that are both green and blue to at least some degree. The modified union $U(\widetilde{S}_1, \widetilde{S}_2)$ can be used to construct higher-level categories: For instance, the concept of "fruit" can be obtained by the unification of "apple", "banana", "pear", "pineapple", etc.

Gärdenfors [15] argues that adjective-noun combinations like "green apple" or "purple banana" can be expressed by combining properties with concepts. This is supported by our operations of intersection and subspace projection:

In combinations like "green apple", property and concept are compatible. We expect that their cores intersect and that the μ_0 parameter of their intersection is therefore relatively large. In this case, "green" should narrow down the color information associated with the "apple" concept. This can be achieved by simply computing their intersection.

In combinations like "purple banana", property and concept are incompatible. We expect that their cores do not intersect and that the μ_0 parameter of their intersection is relatively small. In this case, "purple" should replace the color information associated with the "banana" concept. This can be achieved by first removing the color domain from the "banana" concept (through a subspace projection) and by then intersecting this intermediate result with "purple".

As one can see from this short discussion, our formalized framework is also capable of supporting reasoning processes.

6   Related Work

This work is of course not the first attempt to devise an implementable formalization of the conceptual spaces framework.

An early and very thorough formalization was done by Aisbett and Gibbon [4]. Like we, they consider concepts to be regions in the overall conceptual space. However, they stick with Gärdenfors' assumption of convexity and do not define concepts in a parametric way. Their formalization targets the interplay of symbols and geometric representations, but it is too abstract to be implementable.

Rickard et al. [24, 25] provide a formalization based on fuzziness. They represent concepts as co-occurrence matrices of properties. By using some mathematical transformations, they interpret these matrices as fuzzy sets on the universe of ordered property pairs. Their representation of correlations is not geometrical: They first discretize the domains (by defining properties) and then compute the co-occurrences between these properties. Depending on the discretization, this might lead to a relatively coarse-grained notion of correlation. Moreover, as properties and concepts are represented in different ways, one has to use different learning and reasoning mechanisms. Their formalization is also not easy to work with due to the complex mathematical transformations involved.

Adams and Raubal [1] represent concepts by one convex polytope per domain. This allows for efficient computations while being potentially more expressive than our cuboid-based representation. The Manhattan metric is used to combine different domains. However, correlations between different domains are not taken into account as each convex polytope is only defined on a single domain. Adams and Raubal also define operations on concepts, namely intersection, similarity computation, and concept combination. This makes their formalization quite similar in spirit to ours. One could generalize their approach by using polytopes that are defined on the overall space and that are convex under the Euclidean and star-shaped under the Manhattan metric. However, we have found that this requires additional constraints in order to ensure starshapedness. The number of these constraints grows exponentially with the number of dimensions.

Each modification of a concept's description would then involve a large constraint satisfaction problem, rendering this representation unsuitable for learning processes. Our cuboid-based approach is more coarse-grained, but it only involves a single constraint, namely that the intersection of the cuboids is not empty.

Lewis and Lawry [19] have recently formalized conceptual spaces using random set theory. They define properties as random sets within single domains and concepts as random sets in a boolean space whose dimensions indicate the presence or absence of properties. Their approach is similar to ours in using a distance-based membership function to a set of prototypical points. However, their work focuses on modeling concept combinations and does not explicitly consider correlations between domains.

Many practical applications of conceptual spaces (e.g., [10–12,23]) use only partial ad-hoc implementations of the conceptual spaces framework which usually ignore some important aspects of the framework (e.g., the domain structure).

Finally, we can relate our work to statistical relational learning (SRL): Our geometric representation of concepts is a complex data structure (in SRL one typically uses logics for this) that is augmented with soft computing in the form of fuzziness (similar to the usage of probability theory in SRL).

7   Conclusion and Future Work

In this paper, we proposed a new formalization of the conceptual spaces framework. We aimed to geometrically represent correlations between domains, which led us to consider the more general notion of star-shapedness instead of Gärdenfors' favored constraint of convexity. We defined concepts as fuzzy sets based on intersecting cuboids and a similarity-based membership function. Moreover, we provided different computationally efficient operations and illustrated that these operations can support both learning and reasoning processes.

This work is mainly seen as a theoretical foundation for an actual implementation of the conceptual spaces theory. In future work, we will enrich this formalization with additional operations. Moreover, we will devise a clustering algorithm that will work with the proposed concept representation. Both the mathematical framework presented in this paper and the clustering algorithm will be implemented and tested in practice which will provide valuable feedback.

References

1. Adams, B., Raubal, M.: A metric conceptual space algebra. In: Hornsby, K.S., Claramunt, C., Denis, M., Ligozat, G. (eds.) COSIT 2009. LNCS, vol. 5756, pp. 51–68. Springer, Heidelberg (2009). doi:10.1007/978-3-642-03832-7_4
2. Adams, B., Raubal, M.: Conceptual Space Markup Language (CSML): towards the cognitive semantic web. In: IEEE International Conference on Semantic Computing, September 2009

3. Aggarwal, C.C., Hinneburg, A., Keim, D.A.: On the surprising behavior of distance metrics in high dimensional space. In: Van den Bussche, J., Vianu, V. (eds.) ICDT 2001. LNCS, vol. 1973, pp. 420–434. Springer, Heidelberg (2001). doi:10.1007/ 3-540-44503-X_27

4. Aisbett, J., Gibbon, G.: A general formulation of conceptual spaces as a meso level representation. Artif. Intell. **133**(1–2), 189–232 (2001)

5. Attneave, F.: Dimensions of similarity. Am. J. Psychol. **63**(4), 516 (1950)

6. Bělohlávek, R., Klir, G.J.: Concepts and Fuzzy Logic. MIT Press, Cambridge (2011)

7. Billman, D., Knutson, J.: Unsupervised concept learning and value systematicitiy: a complex whole aids learning the parts. J. Exp. Psychol. Learn. Mem. Cogn. **22**(2), 458–475 (1996)

8. Chella, A., Dindo, H., Infantino, I.: Anchoring by imitation learning in conceptual spaces. In: Bandini, S., Manzoni, S. (eds.) AI*IA 2005. LNCS, vol. 3673, pp. 495–506. Springer, Heidelberg (2005). doi:10.1007/11558590_50

9. Chella, A., Frixione, M., Gaglio, S.: Conceptual spaces for computer vision representations. Artif. Intell. Rev. **16**(2), 137–152 (2001)

10. Chella, A., Frixione, M., Gaglio, S.: Anchoring symbols to conceptual spaces: the case of dynamic scenarios. Robot. Auton. Syst. **43**(2–3), 175–188 (2003)

11. Derrac, J., Schockaert, S.: Inducing semantic relations from conceptual spaces: a data-driven approach to plausible reasoning. Artif. Intell. **228**, 66–94 (2015)

12. Dietze, S., Domingue, J.: Exploiting conceptual spaces for ontology integration. In: Data Integration Through Semantic Technology (DIST 2008) Workshop at 3rd Asian Semantic Web Conference (ASWC 2008) (2008)

13. Douven, I., Decock, L., Dietz, R., Égré, P.: Vagueness: a conceptual spaces approach. J. Philos. Logic **42**(1), 137–160 (2011)

14. Fiorini, S.R., Gärdenfors, P., Abel, M.: Representing part-whole relations in conceptual spaces. Cogn. Process. **15**(2), 127–142 (2013)

15. Gärdenfors, P.: Conceptual Spaces: The Geometry of Thought. MIT Press, Cambridge (2000)

16. Gärdenfors, P.: The Geometry of Meaning: Semantics Based on Conceptual Spaces. MIT Press (2014)

17. Harnad, S.: The symbol grounding problem. Phys. D Nonlinear Phenom. **42**(1–3), 335–346 (1990)

18. Hernández-Conde, J.V.: A case against convexity in conceptual spaces. Synthese **193**, 1–27 (2016)

19. Lewis, M., Lawry, J.: Hierarchical conceptual spaces for concept combination. Artif. Intell. **237**, 204–227 (2016)

20. Medin, D.L., Shoben, E.J.: Context and structure in conceptual combination. Cogn. Psychol. **20**(2), 158–190 (1988)

21. Murphy, G.: The Big Book of Concepts. MIT Press, Cambridge (2002)

22. Osherson, D.N., Smith, E.E.: Gradedness and conceptual combination. Cognition **12**(3), 299–318 (1982)

23. Raubal, M.: Formalizing conceptual spaces. In: Third International Conference on Formal Ontology in Information Systems, vol. 114, pp. 153–164 (2004)

24. Rickard, J.T.: A concept geometry for conceptual spaces. Fuzzy Optim. Decis. Making **5**(4), 311–329 (2006)

25. Rickard, J.T., Aisbett, J., Gibbon G.: Knowledge representation and reasoning in conceptual spaces. In: 2007 IEEE Symposium on Foundations of Computational Intelligence, April 2007

26. Ruspini, E.H.: On the semantics of fuzzy logic. Int. J. Approx. Reason. **5**(1), 45–88 (1991)
27. Schockaert, S., Prade, H.: Interpolation and extrapolation in conceptual spaces: a case study in the music domain. In: Rudolph, S., Gutierrez, C. (eds.) RR 2011. LNCS, vol. 6902, pp. 217–231. Springer, Heidelberg (2011). doi:10.1007/978-3-642-23580-1_16
28. Shepard, R.N.: Attention and the metric structure of the stimulus space. J. Math. Psychol. **1**(1), 54–87 (1964)
29. Shepard, R.N.: Toward a universal law of generalization for psychological science. Science **237**(4820), 1317–1323 (1987)
30. Smith, C.R.: A characterization of star-shaped sets. Am. Math. Mon. **75**(4), 386 (1968)
31. Warglien, M., Gärdenfors, P., Westera, M.: Event structure, conceptual spaces and the semantics of verbs. Theor. Linguist. **38**(3–4), 159–193 (2012)
32. Zadeh, L.A.: Fuzzy sets. Inf. Control **8**(3), 338–353 (1965)
33. Zadeh, L.A.: A note on prototype theory and fuzzy sets. Cognition **12**(3), 291–297 (1982)

Propagating Maximum Capacities
for Recommendation

Ahcène Boubekki[1,2]([⊠]), Ulf Brefeld[1], Cláudio Leonardo Lucchesi[3],
and Wolfgang Stille[4]

[1] Leuphana University of Lüneburg, Lüneburg, Germany
{boubekki,brefeld}@leuphana.de, boubekki@dipf.de
[2] German Institute for Educational Research, Frankfurt, Germany
[3] Universidade Federal de Mato Grosso do Sul, Campo Grande, Brazil
lucchesi@gmail.com
[4] Technische Universität Darmstadt, Darmstadt, Germany
stille@ulb.tu-darmstadt.de

Abstract. Neighborhood-based approaches often fail in sparse scenarios; a direct implication for recommender systems exploiting co-occurring items is often an inappropriately poor performance. As a remedy, we propose to propagate information (e.g., similarities) across the item graph to leverage sparse data. Instead of processing only directly connected items (e.g. co-occurrences), the similarity of two items is defined as the maximum capacity path interconnecting them. Our approach resembles a generalization of neighborhood-based methods that are obtained as special cases when restricting path lengths to one. We present two efficient online computation schemes and report on empirical results.

Keywords: Recommender systems · Information propagation · Maximum capacity paths · Co-occurrence · Sparsity · Cold-start problem

1 Introduction

Recommender systems often utilize co-occurrences of items to pass information between users and items. The underlying idea is that users sharing many items are considered similar and that an item is likely being recommended when it frequently co-occurs with an actually viewed one. Many systems use explicit co-occurrences of items to compute recommendations [13,16,19,28], but also collaborative methods such as neighborhood-based approaches [15,23] and matrix factorisation techniques [5,12,21] inherently ground on leveraging co-occurrence data.

However, the glory of collaborative filtering is quickly turned into a major limitation in the presence of sparsity; the cold-start problem being only one extreme case of this observation. If two items never explicitly co-occur in the data, they cannot be utilized by the recommendation engine at all. In large systems, co-occurrence matrices are naturally large-scale, but sparse. The sparsity

© Springer International Publishing AG 2017
G. Kern-Isberner et al. (Eds.): KI 2017, LNAI 10505, pp. 72–84, 2017.
DOI: 10.1007/978-3-319-67190-1_6

however does not change much over time due to the fact that the size of the matrix grows quadratically in the steadily increasing number of items, but the number of matrix entries increases only linearly in the number of co-occurring items. In practice, block structures are frequently observed. This implies several strongly connected components (e.g., genres, subjects, categories) that are again loosely connected to each other.

The cold-start problem appears in many situations, e.g., at the very beginning of collecting data, or when adding new items or new users. In the first case, not enough information has yet been collected to distinguish items. In the latter cases, the new items and users are isolated and connect to the others with only a few edges. In these scenarios, user tendencies cannot be inferred with high confidence; hence, co-occurrence-based methods are prone to fail and new techniques are required to extend neighborhoods of items appropriately.

In this paper, we study recommender systems for sparse settings to tackle cold-start problems and data sparsity. To increase the item neighborhood, we propose to leverage the transitive hull of all maximum capacity paths in the item graph, such that local item neighborhoods are extended to other connected components of the item graph. By doing so, co-occurrences are propagated through the item graph and similarities between all items, that are connected by at least one path, can be computed. We present two efficient online algorithms for integral as well as arbitrary capacities, respectively. We empirically evaluate our approaches on synthetic and standard datasets. In controlled cold-start scenarios, we identify limitations of collaborative filtering-based methods and show that the proposed approaches lead to better and more precise results.

The remainder is structured as follows. Section 2 reviews related work and Sect. 3 introduces the problem setting. We present our main contribution in Sect. 4. Section 5 reports on our empirical results and Sect. 6 concludes.

2 Related Work

Neighborhood-based collaborative filtering (CF) methods are perhaps the most widely used type of recommender systems. Although user-based approaches are not practical in real settings because of scalability issues [23], item-based collaborative filtering is very common. Besides being conceptually simple, a major advantage of CF-based approaches is the similarity measure that can be adapted to a problem at-hand. Common choices are for instance co-occurrence, cosine, correlation, Pearson, as well as hybrid similarity measures [1].

Co-occurrence data is frequently the basis for recommender systems [16,28] and approaches range from co-occurrence data sampled from random walks in item-item graphs [13] to generalizations of the aspect model [10] by considering three-way co-occurrences between users, items and item content [19]. The resulting generative models may also address cold-start problems [24].

Intrinsically, matrix factorization approaches [14,22] are neighborhood-based algorithms as well; high dimensional vectors are embedded in compact spaces by low dimensional (linear) transformations while preserving the notion of similarity. This class of algorithms performs well when the amount of training data is sufficiently large, but causes problems when data is sparse. Examples for such sparse scenarios are again cold-start and cross-selling problems [27]. With respect to collaborative filtering, this problem is handled by using additional information on the user like age, gender, etc. [4]. Another approach is to consider transitivity closures of item-graphs [2]. An application to recommender system is for example proposed in [25] using a Jaccard similarity measure.

To address recommendation in sparse scenarios, we rephrase the task as a propagation problem in an item-graph [6]. Drawing from network flow theory, we focus on the maximum capacity path [11,18] between two items. In general, using the maximum flow model would be appropriate as well, but as graphs in our application are usually very large, but sparse, the additional complexity spent on flow algorithms does not seem to be adequate with respect to the fact that in sparse scenarios, there is only one path at all, if a connection between items exists at all.

Maximum capacities have been used together with recommender systems by Malucelli et al. [17] before. The authors define similarity as the solution of a bi-criterion path problem [9] that is computed using a Dijkstra-based algorithm. Unfortunately, the authors choose some cumbersome definitions instead of linking their contribution to graph theory, and do not investigate the effect of sparsity. Unfortunately, the proposed algorithm has a complexity of $\mathcal{O}(n^4)$, thus rendering its application infeasible in large-scale scenarios. Nevertheless, it is a useful approach for small-scale problems. We review their contribution in Sect. 3.3 and use the algorithm as a baseline in Sect. 5.

3 Preliminaries

3.1 Rationale

The rationale behind our approach is as follows. Considering weighted graphs, we require a function that translates the transitive closure in the binary case to weighted problems. Shortest path trees are such a translation in case of an additive weight function. However, we do not have additive weights in our case, otherwise the applied measure (e.g. co-occurrence) would increase with the number of edges on a path, which is counterintuitive.

There are approaches normalizing shortest paths by the number of hops they consist of, i.e. computing the average weight of a path. This is not reasonable either as paths consisting of many strongly weighted edges and just one lowly weighted (bridging) edge, have a strong average weight despite of the fact that they virtually decompose into two connected components. Multiplicative approaches are not appropriate either as the weight of the path might be lower than the lowest weight of one of its edges, in particular when it is normalized by the number of hops.

Therefore, we focus on the minimum weight of the path's edges for correlating two items interconnected by that path. This choice seems appropriate as the weights of transitive connections between two nodes are independent of the length of the path in the first place. Bottlenecks are addressed in a reasonable way: the weight of the transitive connection is determined by the lowest weighted edge it contains. Eventually, for two nodes u and v, we consider the connecting path that has the highest minimum edge weight among all other connection path, i.e. the *maximum capacity path*.

3.2   Maximum Capacities

Let $G = (V, E)$ be a weighted graph, where V is a set of n nodes and E a set of m edges. Furthermore, let $A = (a_{ij})$ be its related adjacency matrix. In order to ease the following definitions, we assume without loss of generality that G is acyclic, and all self similarities are set to infinity (i.e. $a_{ii} = \infty$)[1]. The capacity of a path is defined as follows.

Definition 1 (Capacity). *Let $p = ((u, u_1), \ldots, (u_{l-1}, v))$ be a path between two vertices $u = u_0$ and $v = u_l$. The capacity, $c(p)$, of p is defined as the minimum weight of its edges:*

$$c(p) := \min_{(u_k, u_{k+1}) \in p} \left(a_{u_k u_{k+1}} \right).$$

Since there may be more than just one connecting path for a pair of nodes, we regard the path that implies the maximum capacity among all paths.

Definition 2 (Maximum Capacity). *Let $\mathcal{P}_{uv} = \{p_0, \ldots, p_k\}$ be the set of all the paths between u and v. The maximum capacity, $mc(u, v)$, between u and v is defined as maximum of all the paths capacities in $\mathcal{P}_{uv}$:*

$$mc(u, v) := \max_{p \in \mathcal{P}_{uv}} \left(c(p) \right).$$

Computing maximum capacity paths with a minimum number of hops using max-min matrix products is prohibitively expensive with a complexity of $\mathcal{O}(n^4)$. The Dijkstra algorithm is able to efficiently compute maximum capacity paths from a dedicated start node in $\mathcal{O}(n \log(n) + m)$. This amounts to $\mathcal{O}(n^2 \log(n) + mn)$ when considering shortest paths between all pairs of nodes. Before we introduce two efficient algorithms in Sect. 4, we briefly review the bi-criterion shortest path approach by [17].

3.3   Bi-criterion Shortest Path

Malucelli et al. [17] propose a capacity-based algorithm for recommendation. Their algorithm also considers the transitive closure of the graph, however the edge weights are given by solutions of a bi-criterion shortest path optimization problems, as shown in the following definition.

---

[1] Note that paths are usually cycle free by definition and capacities do not change by repeating cycles.

Definition 3 (Bi-criterion Capacity). *Let* $\mathcal{P}_{uv} = \{p_0, ..., p_k\}$ *be the set of all the paths between* u *and* v. *The length of a path* p *is denoted as* $\lambda(p)$ *and its capacity as* $c(p)$. *The* bi-criterion capacity, $bc(u,v)$, *between* u *and* u *is defined as follows:*

$$bc(u, v) := \max_{c(p)} \left(\frac{c(p)}{\lambda(p)} \right).$$

One problem with this approach is the fact that the same result (maximum capacity paths with a minimum number of hops) might be computed by a much simpler algorithm: (i) compute (all) maximum capacity paths (e.g. by using Dijsktra), and (ii) finally choose the one with the minimum number of hops. This can be achieved in $\mathcal{O}(n^3)$ in total, whereas the approach proposed in [17] takes $\mathcal{O}(n^4)$ and is much more complex to implement.

Note that similar problems have been studied in [7]. In this paper, we use the bi-objective label correcting algorithm with node-selection introduced by [26]. See [20] for an extensive review.

4   Maximum Capacity Algorithms

The following two sections are dedicated to two online algorithms that efficiently compute maximum capacity paths. Section 4.1 approaches the problem by a bucket style approach in case all weights are integral. Section 4.2 uses a tree-based approach and works with arbitrary edge weights.

4.1   Max Capacity Buckets

The basic idea is to consider the sub-graphs G_α of G, referred to as *buckets*, containing all the edges with weights higher than a given $\alpha \in \mathbb{N}_0$. In theory, α might be a real number, however in practice it can only be an integer as each of them needs to be stored separately. Note that $G_0 = G$. As the graphs G_α are acyclic and not necessarily connected, they can also be seen as forests.

$$G_\alpha = (V_\alpha, E_\alpha) \text{ such that } \begin{cases} E_\alpha := \{(i,j) \in E : a_{ij} > \alpha\} \\ V_\alpha := \{i \in V, j \in V : (i,j) \in E_\alpha\}. \end{cases}$$

The update of the buckets is straightforward. When the user views a new item v, edge to previously seen item (u, v) are updated as follows:

- the adjacency of the undirected edge is increased by one: $a_{uv} = a_{uv} + 1$,
- if not in $V_{a_{uv}}$, the nodes u and v are added to $G_{a_{uv}}$ as trivial trees,
- finally, the connected components containing u and v are merged: the root of the smallest tree becomes a child of the other root.

The maximum capacity between two nodes u and v is given by the biggest index of the buckets containing u and v.

$$mc(u, v) := \max (\alpha \; : \; (u, v) \in V_\alpha)$$

Graphs are implemented as dictionaries to leverage speed of their key search. The first step is just a modification or a creation of keys in a dictionary that is $\mathcal{O}(1)$ in average. The next step check if nodes are in a subgraph. In case of a positive answer this is done in constant time. However as weights grow, it will occur that at least one of the nodes will return a negative answer. The test will then have gone through all the keys at a linear cost of $\mathcal{O}(n)$. The final step needs to find the roots of two trees which can be done in $\mathcal{O}(\log n)$. Merging is performed by altering the property of the nodes which is constant $\mathcal{O}(1)$. In total, an update has a complexity of $\mathcal{O}(n + \log(n))$.

The evaluation of the maximum capacity between two nodes is done by browsing the buckets in increasing weight order until one of the nodes is not included anymore. Again, the respective test in each sub-graph requires in average $\mathcal{O}(1)$. The search stops when a test is negative, in which case we have costs $\mathcal{O}(n)$. Hence the overall complexity of the maximum capacity is $\mathcal{O}(a^\star + n)$, where $a^\star$ is the largest weight given by $a^\star := \max_{(u,v) \in E}(a_{uv})$. Note that the computation could be sped up by starting the search from $G_{a_{uv}}$ as the maximum capacity cannot be smaller than the weight of the direct edge, if it exists.

4.2   Max Capacity Trees

The well-known and efficient label correcting algorithm, known as *Dijkstra's Algorithm* [3], for the computation of shortest paths in directed graphs from a source node s might be easily adapted for the computation of maximum capacity paths. The distances/maximum capacities need to be initialized with $-\infty$ instead of ∞. Paths are then built using the following alternative update scheme preserving time and space complexity, where π is the predecessor function:

> **for each** neighbor v of u:
>   **if** $mc(s, v) > \min\{mc(s, u); a_{uv}\}$:
> $mc(s, v) := \min\{mc(s, u); a_{uv}\}$
> $\pi(v) := u$
>   **end if**

The algorithm yields a tree rooted at some specified start node s containing all nodes of the item graph, each with a label determining the capacity of the unique (maximum capacity) path to the root node s. The algorithm is computed several times such that each node of the graph becomes the start node exactly once. We obtain n rooted maximum capacity trees. The runtime of Dijkstra amounts to $\mathcal{O}(m + n \log n)$, where $n = |V|$, and $m = |E|$, so this yields to $\mathcal{O}(nm + n^2 \log n)$ for the all-pairs variant.

Runtime complexity might be reduced to $\mathcal{O}(n^3)$ in total by using an *all-pairs shortest path algorithm*, for example the *Floyd-Warshall* algorithm, which makes use of two $n \times n$ matrices: a capacity matrix MC stating the maximum capacities $mc(u, v)$ for each path between a pair of nodes u and v, and a matrix Π holding the predecessor labels $\pi_{u,v}$ for the reconstruction of a max capacity path connecting u and v. This is beneficial in case of an online algorithm, where edges are generated successively, as updates take place in two matrices instead of n different tree structures, that contain specific edges weight.

Despite a concrete implementation as single source or all-pairs algorithm, we use the label correction idea to develop an online algorithm for the computation of maximum capacity trees. The algorithm maintains a forest at any time. As with shortest path trees, the trees contain maximum capacity paths. Initially, we start with a forest of trivial trees consisting of only a single node each. There are no edges and weights are strictly nonnegative, hence $mc(u, v) = 0$ for all $(u, v) \in V^2$. We add edges (co-occurrences) successively. Whenever an edge (u, v) with weight w is added, the following cases may occur:

(i) there is already a tree edge (u, v) with $mc(u, v) < w$: set $mc(u, v) := w$,

(ii) there is no tree edge (u, v) yet, u and v are part of different trees: connect the two trees by inserting (u, v) and set $mc(u, v) := w$,

(iii) there is no tree edge (u, v) yet, u and v are part of the same tree: inserting (u, v) would generate a cycle. In order to avoid that, follow the path from u to v and determine the lowest capacity weight edge(s) on this path: if w is lower, leave everything as is, otherwise remove the lowest capacity weight edge (in case there are more than one, choose one arbitrarily), and insert (u, v) instead.

Finally, we have to update the matrices according to the above operation: update predecessor labels $\pi_{u,v}$ in case of (ii) and (iii), and update the capacities $mc(u, v)$ in all three cases. The runtime complexity of an update operation is bounded by $\mathcal{O}(n^2)$.

The determination of the item(s) to recommend connected to an item u by paths of maximum capacity amounts to looking up the maximum in one column or row, respectively, of the matrix. This amounts to $\mathcal{O}(n)$. Determining the $n-1$ recommendations to all other nodes in decreasing order of their connecting maximum capacity paths amounts to sorting that column or row in decreasing order by their capacities. This amounts to $\mathcal{O}(n \log n)$. Note that the tree-based variant can be implemented for arbitrary, i.e. real-valued edge capacities.

4.3   Discussion

Using bi-criterion capacities as in [17] favors shorter paths; hence closer items are ranked higher. However, all items in the connected components are still reachable. In that sense, the bi-criterion approach ranges in between purely neighborhood-based and our maximum capacity-based approaches. Consider the following example:

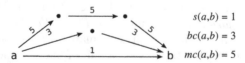

A simple neighborhood-based approach will simply connect the nodes a and b by their connecting edge and leads to a score of one. The bi-criterion algorithm however enumerates all paths between a and b and decides for the aggregated score of three as the capacity is weighted by the length of the path. Finally, maximum capacity also enumerates all paths from a to b but chooses the maximum of the three capacities as the resulting score.

Note that the two maximum capacity-based algorithms described in Sect. 4 tackle the problem differently, but produce the same results. Due to lack of space, we leave this textual statement without formal proof as the algorithmic invariants are easy to verify. In the empirical evaluation, we compare both in terms of their complexities but focus on the tree-based approach when we study performance.

5   Empirical Evaluation

5.1   Time and Space Complexity

To compare the complexities of the proposed algorithms in time and space, we train the buckets (MCb) and the tree-based (MCt) algorithms on a synthetic dataset made of 21k items and 50k transactions. The experiment consists of sequentially reading and processing/storing the data. Except for the first transaction, the maximum capacity of each transaction is computed on its arrival to update the buckets or trees. For comparison, we include as a baseline the cost of only building and reading the adjacency matrix A.

Figure 1 shows the results for varying training set sizes. The upper left subfigure shows the linear growth of edges in the size of the data. The bottom left sub-figure indicates that all three algorithms learn at the similar pace. This result is not surprising as all three algorithms have to learn the adjacency matrix. However, it is interesting to see that updating the buckets or the trees is negligible compared to only adjacencies.

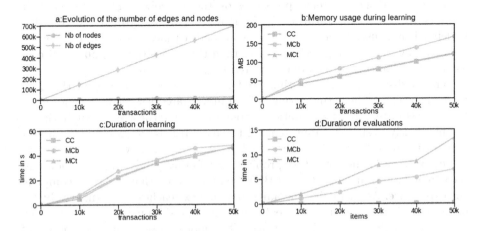

Fig. 1. Runtime comparisons

On the other hand, the bottom right sub-figure shows that the data structure is very important for the capacities. The co-occurrence baseline is extremely fast as it simply retrieves coefficients from the matrix. By contrast, the tree structure proves very costly when it comes to retrieve elements. The tree structure has to build the path to the root at least once, even if the two nodes are in the same connected component (or on the same tree). This may be overcome by using a matrix holding all maximum capacities between all pairs of nodes such as in the Floyd-Warshall algorithm. Then, evaluations take constant time whereas the complexity of updates remains unchanged. As capacities are monotonously increasing, two $n \times n$ matrices are sufficient, one for the maximum capacities between each pair of nodes, and one for the predecessors.

A drawback of the buckets-based approach is the amount of buckets. There are as many of them as there are different weights. The consequence for the memory usage can be observed in the upper right sub-figure. It should be noted that for both maximum capacity algorithms, the adjacency matrix is built along the buckets or trees. However, it is not necessary to compute the capacities themselves. In a production system, the adjacency matrix can be discarded once the learning has been done. Hence, the actual memory usage for a recommender system that is based on one of the two propagation algorithms would be the difference of the respective curve and the baseline. This implies that the tree-based method is in fact very efficient.

5.2   Precision and Incertitude on Cold-Start

We compare co-occurrence (CC), cosine (CS), the Bi-Criterion Shortest Path (BCSP) approach by [17] and two variants of maximum capacity (MC) and (MC+dist). The latter aims at breaking similarity blocks by sorting items in a block relatively to the average distance of the maximum capacity paths. Note that as we use the tree-based algorithm, these distances are side products.

We evaluate the different approaches on the MovieLens 1M dataset [8]. It contains over 1 million ratings of 3952 movies made by 6040 users. A rating is defined by a userID, a movieID, a score and a timestamp. The ratings are binarized by thresholding scores greater than three (positive examples). Scores smaller or equal than three are considered negative examples.

The cold-start problem is simulated by reading and processing the data chronologically. If the actual rating is for a movie rated less than 20 times more but at least once, a recommendation is computed using the average similarity to the previously positively rated items of the user. If it is the user's ir the item's first rating, it is skipped. The threshold of 20 is chosen as we are interested in the early stage of the cold start problem. For fairness, only the first thousand recommendations are reported, as BCSP requires more than a day to complete the experience. At this point the adjacency matrix reaches approximatively 1% of sparsity. The experience is repeated six times by skipping respectively none, the 2k, 4k, 6k, 8k and 10k first ratings. The reported results are the average of the six iterations.

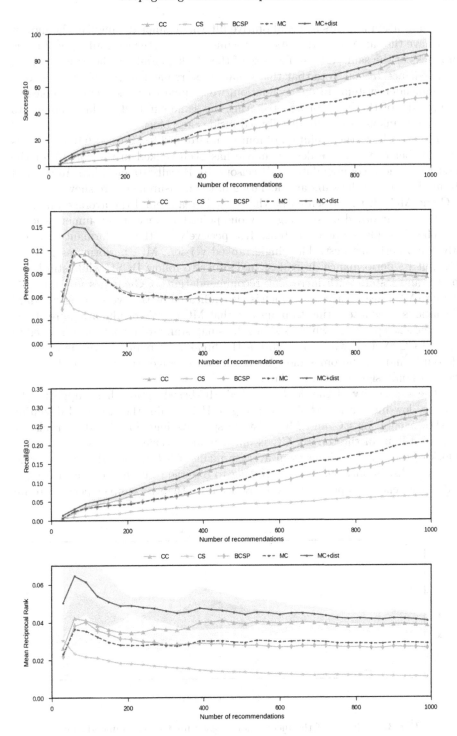

Fig. 2. Standard metrics.

A limitation appears as collaborative filtering cannot distinguish the movies that have the same similarity. As a consequence, the returned ranking will made of blocks of the same values. The size of the block containing the expected item is called *incertitude*. Note that this situation is frequent in this early stage of a recommender system. In our evaluation, we assume that the item is ranked in the middle of the block of items sharing the same similarity. This amounts to treating items as randomly distributed inside each block.

Figure 2 shows the evolution of four standard metrics: Success@10 defined as the number of times the desired movie has been ranked in the top 10 for the first thousand recommendations, Precison@10, Recall@10 and Mean Reciprocal Rank. For clarity the standard deviation of the measurement are shown only for CC and MC+dist represented by the shaded area around the average lines. All curves are smoothed by showing only one point for every 30 recommendations.

The four plots are consistent. Irrespectively of the performance metric, MC+dist performs best. The single ranked version, MC, performs as good as CC but its performance drops fast and starts to follow BCSP while still being better and faster. With increasing recommendations, CC catches up and stays close to MC+dist on average, which is also indicated by the overlapping standard deviations. It is interesting to point out that MC+dist's results are more stable over the six repetitions which is shown by small standard deviation compared to that of CC. Not shown in the figure is the break-even point where the two lines decouple and CC becomes more successful on average. However the difference becomes only significant much later.

The superiority of the double ranked MC-based approach is supported by its very low incertitude as shown in Fig. 3. Here again, the standard deviation is shown only for CC and MC+dist. Despite its high likelihood to rank the expected item in the top 10, CC is much more *uncertain* than MC+dist. The block of the expected item is on average made of 315 items, while the average for MC+dist is only 39. It is interesting to observe that the double ranking of MC+dist render its performance more accurate than its simpler peer, in terms

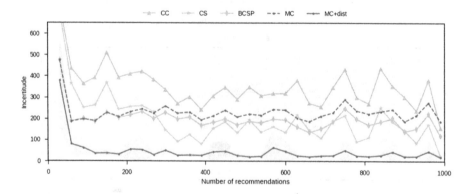

Fig. 3. Evolution of the incertitude of each model's recommendation.

of precision and ambiguity of the recommendation. Note that this improvement comes almost for free. The MC+dist is also particularly more consistent over the six folds of the experiment, as the standard deviation is again much smaller than that of CC.

6 Conclusion

We cast the problem of recommendation as a propagation problem in an item graph using network flow theory and proposed two efficient online algorithms, a bucket and tree-based one. Empirically, the two algorithms effectively leverage sparse data at enterprise level scales. Our approaches distinguish themselves in cold-start scenarios, in term of precisions and quality of their recommendations. Future work will study the relation with T-transitive closures.

Acknowledgments. This research has been funded in parts by the German Federal Ministry of Education and Science BMBF under grant QQM/01LSA1503C and the Brazilian CAPES Foundations and a grant from CNPq.

References

1. Aiolli, F.: Efficient top-n recommendation for very large scale binary rated datasets. In: Proceedings of the 7th ACM Conference on Recommender Systems, pp. 273–280. ACM (2013)
2. De Baets, B., De Meyer, H.: On the existence and construction of t-transitive closures. Inf. Sci. **152**, 167–179 (2003)
3. Dijkstra, E.W.: A note on two problems in connexion with graphs. Numerische mathematik **1**(1), 269–271 (1959)
4. Gantner, Z., Drumond, L., Freudenthaler, C., Rendle, S., Schmidt-Thieme, L.: Learning attribute-to-feature mappings for cold-start recommendations. In: Proceedings of the 2010 IEEE International Conference on Data Mining, ICDM 2010, pp. 176–185. IEEE Computer Society, Washington, DC (2010)
5. Gemulla, R., Nijkamp, E., Haas, P.J., Sismanis, Y.: Large-scale matrix factorization with distributed stochastic gradient descent. In: Proceedings of the 17th ACM SIGKDD International Conference on Knowledge Discovery and Data Mining (2011)
6. Gori, M., Pucci, A., Roma, V., Siena, I.: ItemRank: a random-walk based scoring algorithm for recommender engines. IJCAI **7**, 2766–2771 (2007)
7. Hansen, P.: Bicriterion path problems. In: Fandel, G., Gal, T. (eds.) Multiple Criteria Decision Making Theory and Application: Proceedings of the Third Conference, pp. 109–127. Springer, Heidelberg (1980). doi:10.1007/978-3-642-48782-8_9
8. Harper, F.M., Konstan, J.A.: The movielens datasets: history and context. ACM Trans. Interact. Intell. Syst. (TiiS) **5**(4), 19 (2016)
9. Henig, M.I.: The shortest path problem with two objective functions. Eur. J. Oper. Res. **25**(2), 281–291 (1986)
10. Hofmann, T.: Probabilistic latent semantic analysis. In: Proceedings of Uncertainty in Artificial Intelligence (1999)
11. Hu, T.C.: Letter to the editor-the maximum capacity route problem. Oper. Res. **9**(6), 898–900 (1961)

12. Hu, Y., Koren, Y., Volinsky, C.: Collaborative filtering for implicit feedback datasets. In: Proceedings of the 8th IEEE International Conference on Data Mining (2008)
13. Kang, U., Bilenko, M., Zhou, D., Faloutsos, C.: Axiomatic analysis of co-occurrence similarity functions. Technical report CMU-CS-12-102, School of Computer Science, Carnegie Mellon University (2012)
14. Koren, Y.: Factorization meets the neighborhood: a multifaceted collaborative filtering model. In: Proceedings of the 14th ACM SIGKDD International Conference on Knowledge Discovery and Data Mining, pp. 426–434. ACM (2008)
15. Koren, Y.: Factor in the neighbors: scalable and accurate collaborative filtering. ACM Trans. Knowl. Disc. Data (TKDD) **4**(1), 1 (2010)
16. Li, M., Dias, B., El-Deredy, W., Lisboa, P.J.G.: A probabilistic model for item-based recommender systems. In: Proceedings of the ACM Conference on Recommender Systems (2007)
17. Malucelli, F., Cremonesi, P., Rostami, B.: An application of bicriterion shortest paths to collaborative filtering. In: Proceedings of the Federated Conference on Computer Science and Information Systems (FedCSIS) (2012)
18. Pollack, M.: Letter to the editor-the maximum capacity through a network. Oper. Res. **8**(5), 733–736 (1960)
19. Popescul, A., Ungar, L., Pennock, D.M., Lawrence, S.: Probabilistic models for unified collaborative and content-based recommendation in sparse-data environments. In: Proceedings of the Conference on Uncertainity in Artificial Intelligence (2001)
20. Raith, A., Ehrgott, M.: A comparison of solution strategies for biobjective shortest path problems. Comput. Oper. Res. **36**(4), 1299–1331 (2009)
21. Rendle, S., Schmidt-Thieme, L.: Online-updating regularized kernel matrix factorization models for large-scale recommender systems. In: Proceedings of the ACM Conference on Recommender Systems (2008)
22. Sarwar, B., Karypis, G., Konstan, J., Riedl, J.: Application of dimensionality reduction in recommender system-a case study. Technical report, DTIC Document (2000)
23. Sarwar, B., Karypis, G., Konstan, J., Riedl, J.: Item-based collaborative filtering recommendation algorithms. In: Proceedings of the International World Wide Web Conference (2010)
24. Schein, A.I., Popescul, A., Ungar, L.H., Pennock, D.M.: Methods and metrics for cold-start recommendations. In: Proceedings of the Annual International ACM SIGIR Conference on Research and Development in Information Retrieval (2002)
25. Simas, T., Rocha, L.M.: Semi-metric networks for recommender systems. In: Proceedings of the 2012 IEEE/WIC/ACM International Joint Conferences on Web Intelligence and Intelligent Agent Technology, vol. 03, pp. 175–179. IEEE Computer Society (2012)
26. Skriver, A.J., Andersen, K.A.: A label correcting approach for solving bicriterion shortest-path problems. Comput. Oper. Res. **27**(6), 507–524 (2000)
27. Wang, J., Sarwar, B., Sundaresan, N.: Utilizing related products for post-purchase recommendation in e-commerce. In: Proceedings of the Fifth ACM Conference on Recommender Systems, pp. 329–332. ACM (2011)
28. Wartena, C., Brussee, R., Wibbels, M.: Using tag co-occurrence for recommendation. In: Proceedings of the International Conference on Intelligent Systems Design and Applications (2009)

Preventing Groundings and Handling Evidence in the Lifted Junction Tree Algorithm

Tanya Braun$^{(\boxtimes)}$ and Ralf Möller

Institute of Information Systems, Universität zu Lübeck, Lübeck, Germany
{braun,moeller}@ifis.uni-luebeck.de

Abstract. For inference in probabilistic formalisms with first-order constructs, lifted variable elimination (LVE) is one of the standard approaches for single queries. To handle multiple queries efficiently, the lifted junction tree algorithm (LJT) uses a specific representation of a first-order knowledge base and LVE in its computations. Unfortunately, LJT induces unnecessary groundings in cases where the standard LVE algorithm, GC-FOVE, has a fully lifted run. Additionally, LJT does not handle evidence explicitly. We extend LJT (i) to identify and prevent unnecessary *groundings* and (ii) to effectively handle *evidence* in a lifted manner. Given multiple queries, e.g., in machine learning applications, our extension computes answers faster than LJT and GC-FOVE.

Keywords: Probabilistic logical models · Reasoning · Lifting

1 Introduction

AI research and application areas such as machine learning (ML) need efficient inference algorithms. Modeling realistic scenarios results in large probabilistic knowledge bases (KBs) that require reasoning about sets of individuals. Lifting uses symmetries in a KB, also called model, to speed up reasoning with known objects. We study the problem of reasoning in large KBs with symmetries for answering multiple queries, a common scenario in ML. Answering queries reduces to computing marginal distributions. We aim to enhance the efficiency of these computations exploiting that a model remains constant under multiple queries.

In [3], we introduce a lifted junction tree algorithm (LJT) for multiple queries on models with first-order constructs. The algorithm combines the junction tree algorithm [12] and lifted variable elimination (LVE) [18]. LJT currently does not provide a lifted run for all models that have a lifted solution in LVE, requiring unnecessary groundings. This paper contributes the following: First, we identify when LJT induces unnecessary *groundings*. Second, we add a *fusion* step that aims at preventing these groundings for models with a lifted solution in LVE. Third, we add efficient *evidence* handling.

LJT imposes some static overhead for building a first-order junction tree (FO jtree) and for propagating knowledge in this tree. The fusion step slightly adds to the static overhead in exchange for faster knowledge propagation. Evidence

© Springer International Publishing AG 2017
G. Kern-Isberner et al. (Eds.): KI 2017, LNAI 10505, pp. 85–98, 2017.
DOI: 10.1007/978-3-319-67190-1_7

handling does not affect FO jtree construction but inherently affects knowledge distribution and query answering. We significantly speed up runtime compared to LJT and LVE. Overall, we handle multiple queries more efficiently than existing approaches tailored for handling single queries.

The remainder of this paper is structured as follows: First, we look at related work on exact inference and lifting. Next, we introduce basic notations and recap LJT. Then, we present conditions for groundings and our extensions regarding fusion and evidence. A short evaluation shows the potential of our approach. Last, we give a conclusion and provide future work.

2   Related Work

For single queries given some evidence, researchers have sped up runtimes for inference significantly over the last two decades. For propositional formalisms, VE decomposes a model into subproblems to evaluate them in an efficient order [21]. We can represent such a decomposition using a dtree [6]. LVE, also called first-order VE (FOVE), first introduced in [14] and expanded in [13,15], exploits symmetries at a global level. LVE saves computations by reusing intermediate results for isomorphic subproblems. Its current standard form GC-FOVE generalizes counting and decouples lifting from constraint handling [18].

For multiple queries in a propositional setting, Lauritzen and Spiegelhalter [12] present jtrees along with a reasoning algorithm that uses a message passing scheme, known as probability propagation (PP). Well known PP schemes include [11,16] trading off runtime and storage differently. The connection between jtrees and VE lies in a dtree representing a VE: The clusters of a dtree form a jtree [7]. Taghipour *et al.* [19] introduce first-order dtrees (FO dtrees) and perform a theoretical analysis of lifted inference using the clusters of an FO dtree.

Many researchers apply lifting to various settings, e.g., continuous or dynamic KBs [5,20], logic programming [2], or theorem proving [10]. For example, van den Broeck [4] lifts weighted model counting and knowledge compilation. Lifted belief propagation combines PP and lifting, often using lifted representations [1,9,17], allowing for approximate inference. Das *et al.* [8] use graph data bases storing compiled models for scalability. To the best of our knowledge, none of them focus on multiple queries or changing evidence.

In [3], we lift jtrees introducing FO jtrees. Our reasoning algorithm induces additional groundings and does not handle evidence effectively. We widen its scope with our extensions regarding fusion and evidence.

3   Preliminaries

This section introduces basic notations, provides an overview of LVE and recaps LJT along with FO jtrees based on [3,18].

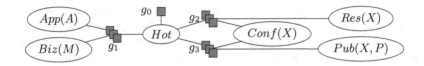

Fig. 1. Parfactor graph for G_{ex}

3.1 Parameterized Models

Parameterized models compactly represent models with first-order constructs. We first denote basic building blocks for constructing more complex structures.

Definition 1. *Let* **L** *be a set of logical variable names (logvars),* Φ *a set of factor names, and* **R** *a set of random variable names (randvars). A parameterized randvar (PRV)* $R(L_1, \ldots, L_n), n \geq 0$, *is a syntactical construct of a randvar* $R \in \mathbf{R}$, *combined with logvars* $L_1, \ldots, L_n \in \mathbf{L}$ *to represent a set of randvars. Domain* $\mathcal{D}(L)$ *refers to the values a logvar* L *can take and* $range(A)$ *to the values a PRV* A *can take. A* constraint $(\mathbf{X}, C_{\mathbf{X}})$ *is a tuple of a sequence of logvars* $\mathbf{X} = (X_1, \ldots, X_n)$ *and a set* $C_{\mathbf{X}} \subseteq \times_{i=1}^n \mathcal{D}(X_i)$ *restricting logvars to certain values. Symbol* $\top$ *marks that no restrictions apply and may be omitted.*

Parametric factor (parfactor) g *has a function mapping inputs to real values. We specify* g *with* $\forall \mathbf{X} : \phi(\mathcal{A}) \mid C$. $\mathbf{X}$ *is a set of logvars that* g *generalizes over.* $\mathcal{A} = (A_1, \ldots, A_n)$ *is a sequence of PRVs, each PRV built from* **R** *and possibly* **L**. *We omit* $(\forall \mathbf{X} :)$ *if* $\mathbf{X} = logvars(\mathcal{A})$. C *is a constraint on* $\mathbf{X}$. $\phi : \times_{i=1}^n range(A_i) \mapsto \mathbb{R}^+$ *is a potential function with name* $\phi \in \Phi$. ϕ *is identical for all randvars represented by the logvars in* $\mathcal{A}$ *w.r.t.* C. *A full specification of* ϕ *includes values for each combination of input values. A set of parfactors forms a model* $G := \{g_i\}_{i=1}^n$ *representing the probability distribution* $P_G = \frac{1}{Z} \prod_{f \in gr(G)} \phi_f(\mathcal{A}_f)$. *Term* $gr(G)$ *denotes a set of instances with all logvars in* G *grounded.*

The terms $logvars(P)$ and $randvars(P)$ denote the logvars and randvars in input P, e.g., a parfactor or model. We specify model G_{ex} for publications on some topic. We model that the topic may be hot, serves business markets and application areas, people do research, attend conferences, and publish in publications.

Example 1. Let $\mathbf{L} = \{A, M, P, X\}$, $\Phi = \{\phi_0, \phi_1, \phi_2, \phi_3\}$, and $\mathbf{R} = \{Hot, Biz, App, Res, Conf, Pub\}$. We build five binary PRVs with $n > 0$ and one with $n = 0$: Hot, $Biz(M)$, $App(A)$, $Conf(X)$, $Res(X)$, $Pub(X, P)$. The model reads $G_{ex} = \{g_0, g_1, g_2, g_3\}$ where $g_0 = \phi_0(Hot)$, $g_1 = \phi_1(Hot, App(A), Biz(M)) \mid C_1$, $g_2 = \phi_2(Hot, Conf(X), Res(X)) \mid C_2$, and $g_3 = \phi_3(Hot, Conf(X), Pub(X, P)) \mid C_3$. We omit concrete functions for ϕ_0 to ϕ_3. We exemplarily define constraint $C_3 = ((P, X), C_{(P,X)})$. Let $\mathcal{D}(P) = \{p_1, p_2\}$ and $\mathcal{D}(X) = \{alice, eve, bob\}$. We define $C_{(W,X)}$ as $\{(p_1, eve), (p_1, bob), (p_2, alice), (p_2, eve)\}$. ϕ_3 applies to all tuples in C_3. Figure 1 depicts G_{ex} as a graph with six variable nodes for the PRVs and four factor nodes for g_0 to g_3 with edges to the PRVs involved.

The semantics of a model is given by grounding w.r.t. constraints and building a full joint distribution. Query answering (QA) asks for a probability distribution of a randvar w.r.t. a model's joint distribution and fixed events (evidence). A grounded PRV Q and a set of events $\mathbf{E}$ (grounded PRVs with values) build a query $P(Q|\mathbf{E})$. For G_{ex}, $P(pub(eve, p_1)|conf(eve))$ forms a query. Next, we look at QA algorithms seeking to avoid grounding and building a joint distribution.

3.2   Lifted Variable Elimination

LVE employs two main techniques for QA, (i) decomposition into isomorphic subproblems and (ii) counting of domain values leading to a certain range value. The first one refers to lifted summing out. The idea is to compute VE for one case and exponentiate the result for isomorphic instances. The second one exploits that all randvars of a PRV A evaluate to $range(A)$, forming a histogram by counting for each $v \in range(A)$ how many instances of $gr(A)$ evaluate to v.

Definition 2. $\#_{X \in C}[P(\mathbf{X})]$ denotes a counting randvar (CRV) with PRV $P(\mathbf{X})$ and constraint C, where $logvars(\mathbf{X}) = \{X\}$. Its range is the space of possible histograms. If $\{X\} \subset logvars(\mathbf{X})$, the CRV is a parameterized CRV (PCRV) representing a set of CRVs. Since counting binds logvar X, $logvars(\#_{X \in C}[P(\mathbf{X})]) = \mathbf{X} \setminus \{X\}$. We count-convert a logvar X in a parfactor $g = \mathbf{L} : \phi(\mathcal{A})|C$ by turning a PRV $A_i \in \mathcal{A}, X \in logvars(A_i)$, into a CRV A_i'. In the new parfactor g', the input for A_i' is a histogram h. Let $h(a_i)$ denote the count of a_i in h. Then, $\phi'(\ldots, a_{i-1}, h, a_{i+1}, \ldots)$ maps to $\prod_{a_i \in range(A_i)} \phi(\ldots, a_{i-1}, a_i, a_{i+1}, \ldots)^{h(a_i)}$.

For both techniques, preconditions exist, see [18]. E.g., to sum out PRV A from parfactor g, $logvars(A) = logvars(g)$. To count-convert logvar X in g, only one input in g contains X. Let us apply LVE to parfactor $g_1 \in G_{ex}$.

Example 2. In $g_1 = \phi_1(Hot, App(A), Biz(M))|C_1$, we cannot sum out any PRV as neither includes both logvars. To sum out $App(a)$ of some a in the propositional case, we would multiply all factors that include $App(a)$ into a factor with inputs Hot, $App(a)$, and $Biz(m_1), \ldots Biz(m_n)$ for each market in C_1. All $Biz(m_i)$ lead to true or false, making $Biz(M)$ a CRV. We rewrite $Biz(M)$ into $\#_M[Biz(M)]$ and g_1 into $g_1' = \phi'(Hot, App(A), \#_M[Biz(M)])|C_1$. The CRV refers to histograms that specify for each $v \in range(Biz(M))$ how many grounded PRVs evaluate to v. The mappings $(h, a, true) \mapsto x$ and $(h, a, false) \mapsto y$ in ϕ become $(h, a, [n_1, n_2]) \mapsto x^{n_1} y^{n_2}$ in ϕ'. We can now sum out $App(A)$.

Evidence shows symmetries as well, exhibiting the same value for n ground randvars of a PRV. Evidence parfactor $\phi_E(P(\mathbf{X}))|C_E$ holds evidence for PRV $P(\mathbf{X})$. Potential function ϕ_E and constraint C_E encode the observed values and randvars. For each evidence parfactor g_E, LVE tests each parfactor $g \in G$ if $C_E \cap C \neq \emptyset$. If true, it splits g for lifted absorption: We add a duplicate g' and restrict C to tuples where a component receives evidence through g_E and C' to tuples unaffected by evidence. Then, g absorbs g_E, eliminating P in g.

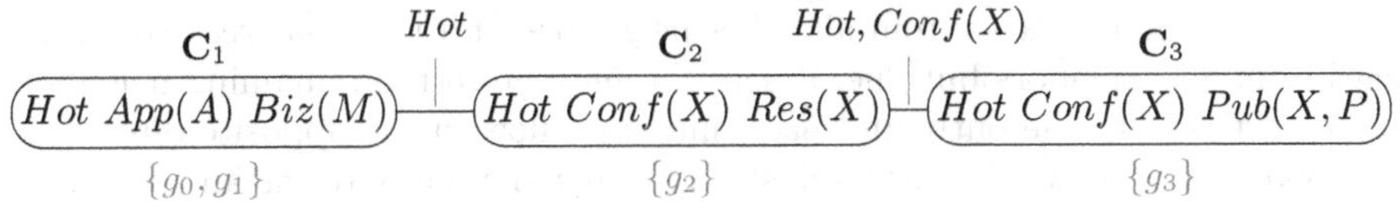

$$\mathbf{C}_1 \qquad\qquad Hot \qquad\qquad \mathbf{C}_2 \qquad\qquad Hot, Conf(X) \qquad\qquad \mathbf{C}_3$$

$$\boxed{Hot\ App(A)\ Biz(M)}\!-\!\boxed{Hot\ Conf(X)\ Res(X)}\!-\!\boxed{Hot\ Conf(X)\ Pub(X,P)}$$

$$\{g_0, g_1\} \qquad\qquad\qquad \{g_2\} \qquad\qquad\qquad \{g_3\}$$

Fig. 2. FO jtree for G_{ex} (local parcluster models in gray)

Example 3. We observe that $Conf(x_1), \ldots, Conf(x_{10})$ are true. In evidence parfactor $g_E = \phi_E(Conf(X))|C_E$, C_E restricts X to $x_1, \ldots, x_{10}$. $\phi_E(true) = 1$ and $\phi_E(false) = 0$. g_E affects g_2 and g_3. After splitting, g_2 and g_3 absorb g_E.

3.3   Lifted Junction Tree Algorithm

LJT builds an FO jtree for faster QA. We first define a parameterized cluster (parcluster) and FO jtrees, analogous to propositional jtrees, before diving into the algorithm. Compared to [3], we assign a set of parfactors F, i.e., a local model, to a parcluster instead of one parfactor due to evidence splitting.

Definition 3. *A parcluster* $\mathbf{C}$ *is denoted by* $\mathbf{C} := \forall \mathbf{L} : \mathcal{A} \mid C$ *where* $\mathbf{L}$ *is a set of logvars and* $\mathcal{A}$ *is a set of PRVs with* $logvars(\mathcal{A}) \subseteq \mathbf{L}$. *We omit* $(\forall \mathbf{L} :)$ *if* $\mathbf{L} = logvars(\mathcal{A})$. *Constraint* C *puts limitations on* $\mathbf{L}$. *Each parcluster has a possibly empty set of parfactors* F *assigned. A parfactor* $g_{\mathbf{C}} = \phi(\mathcal{A}_\phi)|C_\phi$ *assigned to* $\mathbf{C}$ *fulfills (i)* $\mathcal{A}_\phi \subseteq \mathcal{A}$, *(ii)* $logvars(\mathcal{A}_\phi) \subseteq \mathbf{L}$, *and (iii)* $C_\phi \subseteq C$.

Definition 4. *An FO jtree for a model* G *is a pair* $(\mathcal{J}, f_{\mathbf{C}})$ *where* $\mathcal{J}$ *is a cycle-free graph and* $f_{\mathbf{C}}$ *is a function mapping each node* i *in* $\mathcal{J}$ *to a label* $\mathbf{C}_i$ *called a parcluster. An FO jtree must satisfy three properties: (i) A parcluster* $\mathbf{C}_i$ *is a set of PRVs from* G. *(ii) For every parfactor* $g = \phi(\mathcal{A})|C$ *in* G, $\mathcal{A}$ *appears in some* $\mathbf{C}_i$. *(iii) If a PRV from* G *appears in* $\mathbf{C}_i$ *and* $\mathbf{C}_j$, *it must appear in every parcluster on the path between nodes* i *and* j *in* $\mathcal{J}$. *Set* $\mathbf{S}_{ij}$, *called* separator *of edge* i—j *in* $\mathcal{J}$, *contains the shared randvars of* $\mathbf{C}_i$ *and* $\mathbf{C}_j$.

By way of construction, LJT assigns each parfactor in G to exactly one parcluster in $(\mathcal{J}, f_{\mathbf{C}})$, by adding them to local models F_i at nodes i.

Example 4. For G_{ex}, Fig. 2 shows its FO jtree with three parclusters, $\mathbf{C}_1 = \forall A, M : \{Hot, App(A), Biz(M)\}|\top$, $\mathbf{C}_2 = \forall X : \{Hot, Conf(X), Res(X)\}|\top$, and $\mathbf{C}_3 = \forall X, P : \{Hot, Conf(X), Pub(X, P)\}|\top$. Separators are $\mathbf{S}_{12} = \mathbf{S}_{21} = \{Hot\}$ and $\mathbf{S}_{23} = \mathbf{S}_{32} = \{Hot, Conf(X)\}$. Each parcluster has one or two parfactors in its local model (g_0 could have been assigned to any of them).

LJT answers a set of queries $\mathbf{Q}$ given a model G and evidence $\mathbf{E}$. The main workflow is: (i) Construct an FO jtree for G. (ii) Enter $\mathbf{E}$. (iii) Pass messages. (iv) Compute answers for $\mathbf{Q}$. For construction, see [3]. Message passing spreads information among nodes. Two passes propagating information from peripheral to inner nodes and back suffice [12]. A *message* m_{ij} from node i to node j is a parfactor with the PRVs in $\mathbf{S}_{ij}$ as inputs. To compute m_{ij}, we sum out $\mathcal{A}_i \setminus \mathbf{S}_{ij}$

from F_i and the messages from all other neighbors. If a node has received messages from all neighbors but one, it sends a message to the remaining neighbor (inbound pass). In the outbound pass, messages flow in the opposite direction. To answer a query, we take a parcluster covering the query terms and sum out all non-query terms in its model and received messages.

Example 5. In the FO jtree in Fig. 2, messages flow from nodes 1 and 3 to node 2 and back with the corresponding separators as inputs. E.g., messages between nodes 1 and 2 have the argument Hot. For m_{12}, we sum out $App(A)$ and $Biz(M)$ from F_1. For m_{21}, we sum out $Conf(X)$ and $Res(X)$ from F_2 and message m_{32} from node 3. After message passing, we can answer, e.g., query $P(Conf(x_1))$ at node 3 by summing out Hot and $Pub(X, P)$ from $F_3 \cup \{m_{23}\}$.

4   Algorithm-Induced Groundings

A lifted solution to a query given a model means that we compute an answer without grounding a part of the model. Not all models have a lifted solution as LVE requires certain conditions to hold to be applicable. Computing a solution to queries based on these models involves groundings with any exact lifted inference algorithm. But additionally to inherent groundings, LJT may induce unnecessary groundings during message passing as the separators may impede a reasonable elimination order. Grounding a logvar is expensive and, during message passing, may propagate through all nodes, forcing even more groundings in a worst case. This section examines when algorithm-induced groundings occur and derives conditions for messages that allow lifted solutions if possible.

Within this section, we use examples displayed in Fig. 3. Each example is a node with two PRVs in its parcluster and an edge with a separator consisting of one of the PRVs. The local model has one parfactor with both PRVs as inputs. We use the labels $\mathbf{L} = \{X, Y, Z\}$ and $\mathbf{R} = \{P, Q, R\}$ to build PRVs.

Informally, LJT does not induce groundings due to message calculations if it can sum out the PRVs in a separator last. Figure 3a shows an example without groundings. The parcluster contains $P(X)$ and $Q(X, Y)$. For the message, we have to eliminate $Q(X, Y)$ from the local parfactor. $Q(X, Y)$ fulfills all preconditions for lifted summing out. We can sum out $P(X)$ last. No groundings occur.

Formally, for message m_{ij} from node i to j with parcluster $\mathbf{C}_i = \mathcal{A}_i | C_i$, local model F_i, and separator $\mathbf{S}_{ij}$, we eliminate the parcluster PRVs not part of the separator, i.e., $\mathbf{E}_{ij} := \mathcal{A}_i \setminus \mathbf{S}_{ij}$, from the local model and all messages received from other nodes than j, i.e., $F' := F_i \cup \{m_{il}\}_{l \neq j}$. To eliminate $E \in \mathbf{E}_{ij}$ by lifted summing out from F', we replace all parfactors $g \in F'$ that include E with a parfactor $g^E = \phi(\mathcal{A}^E) | C^E$ that is the lifted product of these parfactors g. Let $\mathbf{S}_{ij}^E := \mathbf{S}_{ij} \cap \mathcal{A}^E$ be the set of randvars in the separator that occur in g^E. For lifted message calculation, it necessarily has to hold $\forall S \in \mathbf{S}_{ij}^E$,

$$logvars(S) \subseteq logvars(E). \tag{1}$$

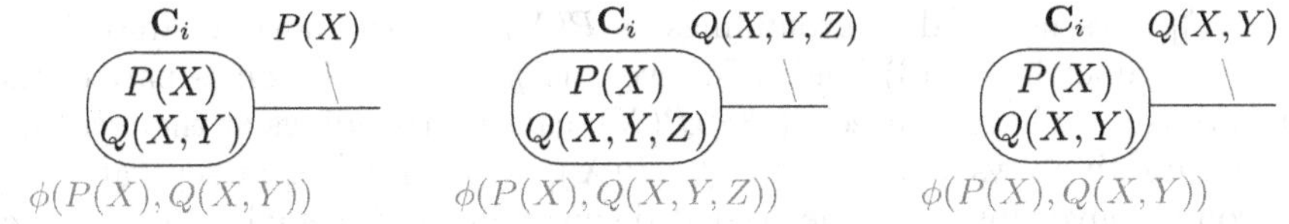

(a) No groundings   (b) Groundings   (c) $\#_Y[Q(X,Y)]$

Fig. 3. Conceptual examples with liftable and non-liftable message calculation

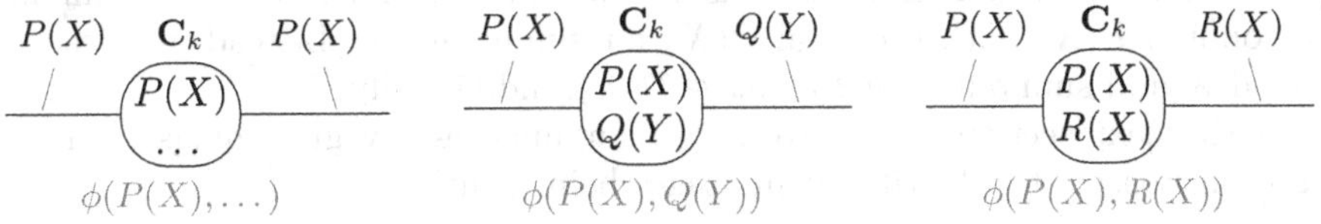

(a) No groundings at $\mathbf{C}_k$ (b) No groundings at $\mathbf{C}_k$ (c) Groundings at $\mathbf{C}_k$

Fig. 4. Conceptual examples with $\#_X[P(X)]$ in incoming message

Otherwise, E does not include all logvars in g^E. We may induce Eq. (1) for a particular S by count conversion if S has an additional, count-convertible logvar:

$$logvars(S) \setminus logvars(E) = \{L\}, L \text{ count-convertible in } g^E. \qquad (2)$$

If Eq. (2) holds, we count-convert L, yielding a (P)CRV in m_{ij}, else, we ground.

Figure 3b shows a parcluster with $E = P(X)$ and $S = Q(X,Y,Z)$ where we ground. As $logvars(Q(X,Y,Z)) \not\subseteq logvars(P(X))$ and $Q(X,Y,Z)$ has two logvars not in $P(X)$, Eqs. (1) and (2) do not hold. We can count-convert Y (or Z), still leaving us with Z (or Y) to ground. In Fig. 3c, the separator PRV, $Q(X,Y)$, has one logvar, Y, more than $P(X)$. Y is count-convertible so Eq. (2) holds. We count-convert Y, building $\#_Y[Q(X,Y)]$. Now, X is the only logvar and we sum out $P(X)$. The same holds if P has more logvars, e.g., $P(X,Z)$. Y would not be count-convertible if the parcluster and parfactor contain, for instance, a PRV $R(Y)$ as Y appears in two PRVs, leading to a grounding of Y.

Count conversion of a logvar L may prevent groundings at node i but the (P)CRV of the affected PRV S may cause problems at node j. As S appears in F_j, we have S present as a PRV and a (P)CRV. If we do not need to sum out S or if L is count-convertible in g^S, the (P)CRV does not lead to groundings. But if we have to eliminate S and L is not count-convertible, we need to ground all occurrences of the counted logvar in the affected parfactors. Hence, count conversion only helps in preventing a grounding if all following messages can handle the resulting (P)CRV. Formally, for each node k receiving S as a (P)CRV with counted logvar L, it has to hold for each neighbor n of k that

$$S \in \mathbf{S}_{kn} \vee L \text{ count-convertible in } g^S \qquad (3)$$

Let us look at some examples for clarification. Figure 4 shows example nodes as in Fig. 3 with another edge and $\#_X[P(X)]$ in an incoming message. In Fig. 4a,

$\#_X[P(X)]$ does not lead to groundings as $P(X)$ is in the next separator, i.e., the first disjunct in Eq. (3) holds. However, as $\#_X[P(X)]$ becomes part of the next message, we have to check if $\#_X[P(X)]$ causes groundings at the receiving node. Figure 4b shows a case where $\#_X[P(X)]$ is not in the next separator but X is count-convertible, i.e., the second disjunct in Eq. (3) holds. As an aside, to actually sum out $\#_X[P(X)]$, we need to count-convert logvar Y in $Q(Y)$. But that conversion is not due to $\#_X[P(X)]$. In Fig. 4c, neither disjunct holds for $P(X)$. $P(X)$ is not in the separator and X is not count-convertible as X appears in $R(X)$ as well. Because X is not count-convertible, we cannot combine the counted $P(X)$ with the local $P(X)$ for summing out. Instead, we need to ground X and sum out each $P(x)$, $x \in \mathcal{D}(X)$, individually.

In the next section, we derive a test for unnecessary groundings at nodes based on Eqs. (1) to (3) without messages being sent.

5   Extended Lifted Junction Tree Algorithm

We extend LJT to prevent unnecessary groundings by adding a *fusion* step and to fully support evidence in an efficient manner.

5.1   Fusion: Preventing Groundings

The main idea of fusion is to merge nodes if message calculation needs groundings. We first set up a grounding test. Then, we present fusion using the test to decide mergings. Last, we analyze the effects on data structure and workload.

Test for Groundings. Checking message m_{ij}, PRV E to eliminate, and separator PRV S, the test strings together Eqs. (1) to (3). Testing E only needs $\mathcal{A}^E$ of g^E, making it easier to build. But, we need to track changes from quasi-eliminating E for the next PRV E'. Our test runs before message passing. Since we do not have the actual messages for F', we assume that a message covers the separator. This slight over-approximation may result in a larger $\mathcal{A}^E$ which may lead to more PRVs in $\mathbf{S}_{ij}^E$ that have to fulfill Eqs. (1) to (3). Thus, our test may identify a grounding that does not occur. The test outcomes for S given m_{ij} and E are:

> Eq. (1) holds $\rightarrow$ No groundings. Check next S.
> Eq. (1) does not hold $\rightarrow$ Check Eq. (2).
> Eq. (2) holds $\rightarrow$ Check Eq. (3) for each node receiving S.
> Eq. (2) does not hold $\rightarrow$ Groundings.
> Eq. (3) holds $\rightarrow$ No groundings. Check next S.
> Eq. (3) does not hold $\rightarrow$ Groundings.

Extension. We use the test to decide if we merge two nodes. Merging nodes i and j means building their union in terms of parclusters and neighbors. Formally, the union of parclusters $\mathbf{C}_i$ and $\mathbf{C}_j$, denoted by $\mathbf{C}_i \cup \mathbf{C}_j$, is given by $gr(\mathbf{C}_i) \cup gr(\mathbf{C}_j)$.

Exploiting that parclusters have certain properties by way of construction, we need not ground but can build the union component-wise. For the local models, we build $F_i \cup F_j$. Regarding graph structure, the merged node k with parcluster $\mathbf{C}_k = \mathbf{C}_i \cup \mathbf{C}_j$ takes over all neighbors from i and j.

Algorithm 1 shows pseudo code for fusion combining the grounding test with merging given an FO jtree J. For each node i in J, we merge i with a neighboring node j until Eqs. (1) to (3) hold if applicable. Algorithm 2 shows LJT with the new step in line 3 after construction. The other steps remain the same.

Theorem 1. *FusedLJT is sound, i.e., produces the same result as LJT.*

Proof sketch. The proof relies on LJT being sound. Fusion alters an underlying FO jtree with merging, preserving the FO jtree properties. Given LJT is sound, LJT works with a valid FO jtree after fusion and produces sound results.

FusedLJT does not induce any unnecessary groundings. As the grounding test over-approximates, we may merge two nodes whose messages do not need groundings. But, no node remains that grounds due to message calculation.

We add a parameter α to encode how many steps our grounding test should follow. If $\alpha = 0$, we do not execute the fusion step. If $\alpha = 1$, we only check Eq. (1) at a node i. It saves work on checking Eqs. (2) and (3) concerning (P)CRVs which may inhibit smaller local models for faster query answering. If $\alpha = 2$, we additionally check Eq. (2) and move on to the next PRV in $\mathbf{S}_{ij}^E$ if it holds. If $\alpha = 3$, we also check Eq. (3) at j. With $\alpha > 3$, we check Eq. (3) at all nodes receiving a (P)CRV with a path length of $\alpha - 3$ starting from j.

Effects. We look at the effects of fusion on LJT in terms of data structure and workload. Regarding data structure, effects can range from no change to a collapse into one node. Without a change, we add work for all checks without any merging (no or only model-inherent groundings). Collapsing into one node with the input model in its local model is a worst case scenario: We add overhead for construction and fusion without a payoff as query answering compares to LVE.

Regarding workload, fusion adds to it for checking Eqs. (1) to (3). At a node i, most work occurs if Eq. (1) does not hold for each neighbor j, PRV $E \in \mathbf{E}_{ij}$, and PRV $S \in \mathbf{S}_{ij}^E$. Then, we check for each S that Eq. (2) holds and for each neighbor at nodes k reached through j receiving S that Eq. (3) holds. Let c_1, c_2, and c_3 denote the workload of checking Eqs. (1) to (3), respectively. Let d_k denote the number of neighbors at a node k. Then, a workload amounts of

---

Algorithm 1. Fusion of FO jtree J to prevent groundings

1: **function** FUSE(FO jtree J)
2:     **for** node i in J **do**
3:         **while** $\exists$ node $j \in neighbors(i), E \in \mathbf{E}_{ij}, S \in \mathbf{S}_{ij}^E$: (Eq. (1) does not hold $\wedge$ (Eq. (2) does not hold $\vee$ Eq. (3) does not hold)) **do**
4:             MERGE(i, j)

Algorithm 2. Extended Lifted Junction Tree Algorithm

1: **function** FUSEDLJT(Model G, Queries Q, Evidence E)
2:      FO jtree $J =$ FO-JTREE(G)
3:      FUSE(J)
4:      ENTEREVIDENCE(J,E)
5:      PASSMESSAGES(J)
6:      GETANSWERS(J,Q)

$$T^{Fusion}(\mathcal{J}) = \sum_i \sum_j |\mathbf{E}_{ij}| \cdot |\mathbf{S}_{ij}^E| \cdot \left(c_1 + c_2 + \sum_k (d_k - 1) \cdot c_3 \right) \qquad (4)$$

where i covers the nodes in $\mathcal{J}$, j the neighbors of i, and k the nodes reached through j. If $\alpha = 0$, we do not add work, save for an if-condition check. If $\alpha = 1$ or 2, Eq. (4) ends after c_1 or c_2. With increasing α, we reach more nodes k.

In a worst case, we have the most checks if $\mathbf{E}_{ij}$ and $\mathbf{S}_{ij}$ have the same size, i.e., $\frac{1}{2}|\mathcal{A}_i|$. We replace $\mathcal{A}_i$ with $\mathcal{A}^{max}$ denoting the largest parcluster, meaning the one with the most PRVs. As we cover each edge twice checking each neighbor j of each node i, we rewrite $\sum_i \sum_j$ with $2 \cdot |E|$, E being the set of edges in $\mathcal{J}$. We reformulate $\sum_k$ as $|E| - 1$ since we may cover each edge except i—j. Combined, we have a complexity of $O(|E|^2 \cdot |\mathcal{A}^{max}|^2)$.

5.2 Evidence Handling

This section formalizes evidence handling, a central feature of any inference algorithm. Though we look at evidence in general, we have to keep in mind that computing conditional probabilities, i.e., marginals given evidence, is not liftable unless evidence consists of PRVs with at most one logvar [4].

Extension. Entering evidence includes formalizing when we add evidence, how we distribute it, and how we absorb it. We add an evidence parfactor g_E with constraint C_E to local model F_i at node i with constraint C_i in its parcluster iff

$$C_i \cap C_E \neq \emptyset \qquad (5)$$

Unlike LVE, we avoid testing all parfactors in G using the third FO jtree property. The property states that if a PRV appears in parclusters $\mathbf{C}_i$ and $\mathbf{C}_j$, it must appear in every parcluster on the path between nodes i and j. To distribute g_E, we find a first node with a parcluster that meets Eq. (5) and add g_E. If adding g_E at a node i, we add g_E to each neighboring node j if C_i projected onto the PRVs in separator $\mathbf{S}_{ij}$ fulfills Eq. (5). After distributing all evidence, we split the parfactors in the local models accordingly and use lifted absorption. (We store the original model for new evidence.)

In the following example, we add the evidence from Example 3 ($Conf(X)$ is true for 10 people) to the FO jtree of G_{ex}.

Example 6. $Conf(X)$ appears in parclusters $\mathbf{C}_2$ and $\mathbf{C}_3$. For lifted absorption in $\mathbf{C}_2$, we split the parfactor in F_2 into $g_2 = \phi_2(Hot, Conf(X), Res(X))|(C_2 \setminus C_E)$ and $g_2' = \phi_2(Hot, Conf(X), Res(X))|C_E$. g_2' absorbs g_E by dropping the values where $\neg conf(X)$ and removing $Conf(X)$ from its arguments. F_2 is now $\{g_2, g_2' = \phi_2(Hot, Conf(X))|C_E\}$. Absorbing g_E in $\mathbf{C}_3$ proceeds analogously.

With new evidence, LJT enters evidence and passes messages again. We can save work on both if evidence changes only incrementally: We only enter changed evidence. After entering evidence, leaf nodes calculate a new message if evidence changed. Without a change, an empty message is sent. Inner nodes calculate a message if their own evidence changed or a non-empty message arrived from any neighbor. Otherwise, they send an empty message.

Theorem 2. *Evidence handling in LJT is sound, i.e., is equivalent to handling evidence in the ground version.*

Proof sketch. The proof relies on the LVE operations, specifically lifted absorption and splitting, and LJT to be sound. Since lifted absorption drops the affected PRVs, we enter evidence at each node that includes evidence randvars. With a correct split and absorption in the local model of a node, the node absorbs evidence correctly. Given LJT is sound, all following computations are sound.

Effects. Evidence has an effect on message passing and query answering since the local models change with absorption of evidence. The effect is inherent to handling evidence. Message passing starts after lifted absorption. In case evidence affects sender and receiver, i.e., the evidence PRVs are part of the separator, the message covers those PRVs without evidence since the part with evidence is already absorbed at both parclusters. In case evidence only affects the sender but $logvars(\mathbf{S}_{ij}) \cap logvars(g_E) \neq \emptyset$, the message consists of two parts, one for the part without evidence and one for the part with evidence as F_i is shattered w.r.t. C_E splitting up all occurrences of $logvars(g_E)$. In all other cases, evidence is hidden from the other nodes through summing out.

Entering evidence means checking Eq. (5) for each evidence parfactor $g_E \in \mathbf{E}$ at each node and each parfactor in a local model absorbing g_E in a worst case scenario, leading to a worst case complexity of $O(|N| \cdot |\mathbf{E}| \cdot |F^{max}|)$, N denoting the set of nodes in $\mathcal{J}$ and F^{max} the largest local model. With more evidence, the size of intermediate results decreases and consequently, runtimes fall.

If a change in evidence leads to changes in all nodes, a full message passing run is necessary. With changes only in one part of the model, we save calculating inbound messages from the unchanged part and outbound messages distributing the information from the unchanged part to the remaining model.

6   Empirical Evaluation

We have implemented a prototype of the LJT extended with fusion and evidence handling, named `exfojt`. Taghipour provides a baseline implementation

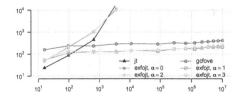
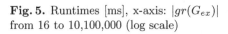
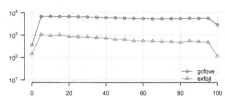

Fig. 5. Runtimes [ms], x-axis: $|gr(G_{ex})|$ from 16 to 10,100,000 (log scale)

Fig. 6. Runtimes [ms] (log scale), x-axis: evidence from 0% to 100%

of GC-FOVE including its operators (available at https://dtai.cs.kuleuven.be/software/gcfove), named `gcfove` in this test. We include the `gcfove` operators in `exfojt`. We test our implementation against `gcfove`.

We have also implemented a propositional junction tree algorithm as a reference point, named `jt`. `jt` requires substantially more time and memory and therefore, is not part of the discussion. We compare runtimes for inference summed up over queries answered, averaged over several executions per setup.

Fusion. We use a variation of G_{ex} as input whose FO jtree has four nodes and requires groundings with $\alpha = 0$ and $\alpha = 2$. If $\alpha = 1$, its FO jtree has two nodes with five PRVs in its largest parcluster after fusion. If $\alpha = 3$, its FO jtree has three nodes with four PRVs in its largest parcluster after fusion. The probability entries are random. We query each PRV once with random groundings.

Figure 5 shows runtimes with increasing domain sizes for `jt` (filled triangle), `gcfove` (circle), and `exfojt` with $\alpha \in \{0, 1, 2, 3\}$ (squares). There is no strong difference noticeable for varying α and the depth of its checks in terms of runtime with this limited example. Between construction and message passing, the fusion step does not add significantly to the overhead.

The runs of `exfojt` with groundings (filled squares) have a runtime worse than the runtime of `jt` for small domains. Runtimes for `exfojt` without groundings (empty squares) and `gcfove` do not have the steep increase in runtime with larger domains. `exfojt` ($\alpha = 1, \alpha = 3$) needs 30 to 60% of the time `gcfove` needs which it trades off with memory. It requires 1.06 to 1.16 times the memory of `gcfove`. The decrease in runtime is mirrored in the number of LVE operations performed, independent of the size of the grounded model: `exfojt` ($\alpha = 1$) performs 170 operations (181 with $\alpha = 3$). `gcfove` performs 368 operations.

Evidence. We use G_{ex} as input with random probability entries and set $\alpha = 0$. We enter evidence on all PRVs except *Hot* and *Pub*(*X*, *P*) ranging from 0% to 100% in 5% steps. We query each PRV once and *Pub*(*X*, *P*) twice with random groundings. We fix the domain sizes, yielding $|gr(G_{ex})| = 111,000$.

Figure 6 shows runtimes with increasing evidence coverage. On all evidence settings, `exfojt` (triangles) outperforms `gcfove` (circles). Entering evidence increases runtimes since handling evidence costs time. With more evidence, runtimes decrease for both programs as a larger part of the model is fixed with evidence. Apart from the settings with 0% and 100% evidence, `exfojt` needs 8 to 16% of the time `gcfove` needs. In terms of VE operations, `exfojt` needs 128 operations (including message passing) against 475 by `gcfove`. `exfojt` trades off runtimes with memory. It requires 1.2 to 1.4 times the memory of `gcfove`.

With its static overhead, `exfojt` outperforms `gcfove` with the second query at 0% evidence. In all other cases, `exfojt` is faster with the first query.

In summary, spending effort on building an FO jtree and passing messages pays off. Even with little evidence, `exfojt` runs faster after the first query.

7 Conclusion

We present extensions to LJT to answer multiple queries efficiently in the presence of symmetries in a model. We identify when LJT induces unnecessary groundings during message passing. To remedy this effect, we add a step to LJT that merges parclusters. Additionally, we formalize how LJT handles evidence. We speed up runtimes significantly, especially with evidence, for answering multiple queries compared to the current version of LJT and GC-FOVE.

We currently work on adapting LJT to incrementally changing knowledge bases. Other interesting algorithm features include parallelization, construction using hypergraph partitioning, and different message passing strategies as well as using local symmetries. Additionally, we look into areas of application to see its performance on real-life scenarios.

References

1. Ahmadi, B., Kersting, K., Mladenov, M., Natarajan, S.: Exploiting symmetries for scaling loopy belief propagation and relational training. In: Machine Learning, vol. 92, pp. 91–132. Kluwer Academic Publishers, Hingham (2013)
2. Bellodi, E., Lamma, E., Riguzzi, F., Santos Costa, V., Zese, R.: Lifted variable elimination for probabilistic logic programming. Theory Pract. Logic Program. 14(4–5), 681–695 (2014). Cambridge University Press, Cambridge
3. Braun, T., Möller, R.: Lifted junction tree algorithm. In: Friedrich, G., Helmert, M., Wotawa, F. (eds.) KI 2016. LNCS, vol. 9904, pp. 30–42. Springer, Cham (2016). doi:10.1007/978-3-319-46073-4_3
4. Van den Broeck, G.: Lifted Inference and Learning in Statistical Relational Models. Ph.D. Thesis, KU Leuven (2013)
5. Choi, J., Amir, E., Hill, D.J.: Lifted inference for relational continuous models. In: Proceedings of the 26th Conference on Artificial Intelligence. The AAAI Press, Menlo Park (2012)
6. Darwiche, A.: Recursive conditioning. In: Artificial Intelligence, vol. 2, pp. 4–41. Elsevier Science Publishers, Essex (2001)
7. Darwiche, A.: Modeling and Reasoning with Bayesian Networks. Cambridge University Press, Cambridge (2009)
8. Das, M., Wu, Y., Khot, T., Kersting, K., Natarajan, S.: Scaling lifted probabilistic inference and learning via graph databases. In: Proceedings of the SIAM International Conference on Data Mining, pp. 738–746. Society for Industrial and Applied Mathematics, Philadelphia (2016)

9. Gogate, V., Domingos, P.: Exploiting logical structure in lifted probabilistic inference. In: Working Note of the Workshop on Statistical Relational Artificial Intelligence at the 24th Conference on Artificial Intelligence. The AAAI Press, Menlo Park (2010)

10. Gogate, V., Domingos, P.: Probabilistic theorem proving. In: Proceedings of the 27th Conference on Uncertainty in Artificial Intelligence, pp. 256–265. AUAI Press, Arlington (2011)

11. Jensen, F.V., Lauritzen, S.L., Oleson, K.G.: Bayesian updating in recursive graphical models by local computations. In: Computational Statistics Quarterly, vol. 4, pp. 269–282. Physica-Verlag, Vienna (1990)

12. Lauritzen, S.L., Spiegelhalter, D.J.: Local computations with probabilities on graphical structures and their application to expert systems. J. Roy. Stat. Soc.: Ser. B (Stat. Methodol.) **50**, 157–224 (1988). Wiley-Blackwell, Oxford

13. Milch, B., Zettlemoyer, L.S., Kersting, K., Haimes, M., Pack Kaelbling, L.: Lifted probabilistic inference with counting formulas. In: Proceedings of the 23rd Conference on Artificial Intelligence, pp. 1062–1068. The AAAI Press, Menlo Park (2008)

14. Poole, D.: First-order probabilistic inference. In: Proceedings of the 18th International Joint Conference on Artificial Intelligence, pp. 985–991. Morgan Kaufman Publishers Inc., San Francisco (2003)

15. de Salvo Braz, R.: Lifted First-Order Probabilistic Inference. Ph.D. Thesis, University of Illinois at Urbana-Champaign (2007)

16. Shafer, G.R., Shenoy, P.P.: Probability propagation. Ann. Math. Artif. Intell. **2**, 327–351 (1989). Springer, Heidelberg

17. Singla, P., Domingos, P.: Lifted first-order belief propagation. In: Proceedings of the 23rd Conference on Artificial Intelligence, pp. 1094–1099. The AAAI Press, Menlo Park (2008)

18. Taghipour, N.: Lifted Probabilistic Inference by Variable Elimination. Ph.D. Thesis, KU Leuven (2013)

19. Taghipour, N., Davis, J., Blockeel, H.: First-order decomposition trees. In: Advances in Neural Information Processing Systems 26, pp. 1052–1060. Curran Associates, Red Hook (2013)

20. Vlasselaer, J., Meert, W., van den Broeck, G., de Raedt, L.: Exploiting local and repeated structure in dynamic baysian networks. In: Artificial Intelligence, vol. 232, pp. 43–53. Elsevier, Amsterdam (2016)

21. Zhang, N.L., Poole, D.: A simple approach to bayesian network computations. In: Proceedings of the 10th Canadian Conference on Artificial Intelligence, pp. 171–178. Morgan Kaufman Publishers, San Francisco (1994)

Improving the Cache-Efficiency of Shortest Path Search

Stefan Edelkamp[(✉)]

King's College London, London, UK
edelkamp@tzi.de

Abstract. Flood-filling algorithms as used for coloring images and shadow casting show that improved locality greatly increases the cache performance and, in turn, reduces the running time of an algorithm. In this paper we look at Dijkstra's method to compute the shortest paths for example to generate pattern databases. As cache-improving contributions, we propose edge-cost factorization and flood-filling the memory layout of the graph. We conduct experiments in commercial game maps and compare the new priority queues with advanced heap implementations as well as and with alternative bucket implementations.

1 Introduction

For finding shortest paths in a graph $G = (V, E, w)$ Dijkstra's algorithm [6] is the apparent implementation option, as for a consistent heuristic h, where $w(u, v) \geq h(u) - h(v)$ for all edges (u, v), the A* algorithm [16] is equivalent to Dijkstra's method applied to a compiled graph; the heuristic h reweights edges $e = (u, v)$ to map the original graph $G = (V, E, w)$ setting $w'(u, v) = w(u, v) + h(v) - h(u)$ to $G = (V, E, w')$.

In this paper we solve the single-source *all-target* shortest paths problem where the search does not terminate at a goal. In this setting, lower-bound heuristics are not helpful, as they only modify the ordering of nodes visits. Hence, even in the presence of search heuristics, improvements to Dijkstra's original method remain essential.

The all-target shortest paths problem usually arises in the inverse graph, with directed edges reversed. For example, in an abstract graph the goal distances from every node are used to precompute heuristic estimate tables called *pattern databases* [4], effective in both AI search [20], and AI planning [8].

Speed-up techniques accelerate on-line *one-pair* shortest paths queries, including containers, edge flags etc. [14,30], which also determine all-target shortest paths in the precomputation stage. The running time for finding all-target shortest paths also crucially affects the applicability of multi-goal motion planning [23]. Last but not least, computing all shortest paths from/to a distinguished set of map nodes is a necessity in vehicle routing systems to compress large maps. This generates distance tables, serving as inputs for variants of the traveling salesman problem [15].

© Springer International Publishing AG 2017
G. Kern-Isberner et al. (Eds.): KI 2017, LNAI 10505, pp. 99–113, 2017.
DOI: 10.1007/978-3-319-67190-1_8

In modern computers with a hierarchy of caches, localizing the search can be effective: the retrieval time for the next nodes can decrease considerably if they are already present in a cache, rather than located in main memory. We introduce and analyze data structures that exploit either the limited set of available cost values, or the graph memory layout to prefer a cache-friendly exploration. For the former we propose an algorithm that operates on a matrix of cost buckets, and for the latter we study a *flood-fill* algorithm for shortest path search. Such traversal order different to Dijkstra's algorithm may lead to reopening of nodes. The hope is that by fewer cache misses the search becomes faster and compensates for this additional work.

The paper is structured as follows. We start with Dijkstra's algorithm and then turn to general priority queues. Next, we study bucket-based implementations, especially ones that can deal with large edge weights. The technical core besides the comparison of a larger body of state-of-the-art priority queues on an agreed benchmark are the analyses of the correctness of the flood-fill algorithm and of the efficiency of the factorized priority queue representation. We run the algorithms on commercial games maps.

2   Dijkstra's Algorithm

Finding shortest paths in a directed and weighted graph $G = (V, E, w)$ with $E \subseteq V \times V$ and $w : V \to \mathbf{R}^+$ is essential to many areas of computer science. While for general graphs (assuming an adjacency list representation) the input is of size $O(|E| + |V|)$, in planar graphs by the virtue of Euler's formula we have $|E| = O(|V|)$, so that the input (and the output) have size $O(|V|)$.

It is an open question if there is a shortest path algorithm for that is linear in the size of a general graph. For special graph classes, like planar graphs [19] and undirected graphs with integer or IEEE floating point weights [29], the problem has been theoretically solved, with the results for directed graphs continuously improving [25]. The algorithms, however, are involved: for planar graphs, graph separators are recursively applied, while for undirected graphs with integer weights, heaps that are efficient only for very large values of $|V|$ have been proposed. Essentially, the proper choice of a data structure for shortest path search remains challenging.

One implementation for shortest path search uses a bitvector for tagging elements to be *open* (visited). While for dense graph this option imposes an acceptable overhead, for sparse graphs with limited branching, finding the next open node can be costly. The priority queue itself has to provide the usual operations *is-empty, insert, find-min, decrease-key,* and *extract-min*.

3   General Priority Queues

With binary heaps, Fibonacci heaps, and pairing heaps we look at general priority queues that can be used to solve the shortest paths problem in any directed graph with totally-ordered cost function. They are general in the sense that they are supporting the full set of priority queue operations, including a *delete* and a *decrease-key* (Fibonacci and pairing heaps also provide an efficient *meld*) operation. This flexibility of the priority queue, however, comes at a price, as these operations require maintaining *handles* to nodes, given that nodes are continously moved within the priority queue data structure.

Our implementation takes additional node labels (unlabeled, labeled or scanned) to avoid redundant work [3]. It assumes the merging of graph and queue nodes. This *joint node representation* includes: the state label, a linked list of graph edges; the element for storing the distances; the heap priority information for the node; and the pointers for linking the elements in the heap. An edge is a pair of a successor node ID and according weight (cost/distance). In some graphs the joint node representation was more important than the type of the data structure [3]. One reason was to avoid memory allocation, another was that efforts for maintaining handles were removed.

For general priority queues in a precomputation stage, the grid is scanned once and compiled into a graph with nodes for the cells and edges for the links connecting cells.

3.1   Binary Heaps

The first structure we look at is a binary heap, as independently suggested by Floyd and Williams in the context of the *Heapsort* algorithm [11,31]. As all operations are logarithmic, in total at most $O((|E| + |V|) \log_2 |V|)$ time is spent for finding the shortest paths with a priority queue based on binary heaps; $|V|$ *delete-min* and at most $|E|$ *decrease-key* operations are executed in Dijkstra's algorithm.

We have also implemented *k-ary heaps* for $k > 2$ that have a smaller height but a larger node branching factor. This leads to a better cache performance (for $k = 4$ about half as many cache misses [22]). When deleting the minimum at each branch one has to find the smallest of the elements stored at its children. This minimum finding requires $k - 1$ element comparisons and one more comparison is needed to determine whether or not we can stop the traversal. Since the height of a k-ary heap of size n is $h(n, k) = \lceil \log_k(kn - n + 1) \rceil$ (the height of a single node being 1), insertion involves at most $h(n + 1, k) - 1$ element comparisons and minimum extraction at most $k \times (h(n, k) - 1)$ element comparisons. There is an interesting trade-off between the cost of these two operations: By making k larger, insertion becomes faster but delete-min becomes slower. But even for the best trade-off $k = 4$ the runtime improvements wrt binary heaps were small (see also [26] for a study on addressable priority queues), so that as the baseline, in the experiments we, therefore, stick to binary heaps.

3.2   Fibonacci Heaps

Fibonacci heaps are doubly-linked root lists of heap-ordered trees. They have been characterized as a *lazy-meld version of a binomial queue*, which itself is an extension to binomial trees. A *binomial tree* B_n, in turn, is a tree of height

n with 2^n nodes in total (and i nodes at depth i) and consists of two trees B_{n-1}. Binomial queues are unions of heap-ordered binomial trees. Tree B_i is represented in queue Q if the ith bit in the binary representation of size $|Q|$ is set.

Several trees of rank i may be represented in one Fibonacci heap. *Consolidation* traverses the linear list and merges trees of the same rank so that each rank becomes unique. The priority queue operations of extracting the minimum and decreasing the key of a node in a Fibonacci heap result in $O(|E| + |V| \log_2 |V|)$ worst-case time for finding shortest paths [13]. This efficiency is mainly due to the amortized constant time for *decrease-key*. There are priority queues with worst-case constant *decrease-key* operations [2,7], but for basic edge cost data types these structures are less performant. Moreover, there are recent suggestions to simplify the implementation of Fibonacci heaps. We implemented several Fibonacci heap variants and chose one that was at least as good as the recent implementation refinement in [18].

3.3   Pairing Heaps

A pairing heap is a heap-ordered (not necessarily binary) self-adjusting tree. The basic operation is *pairing*, which combines two pairing heaps by attaching the root with the larger key to the other root as its leftmost child. For two pairing heaps with respective root values l_1 and l_2, *pairing* inserts the first as the leftmost subtree of the second if $l_1 > l_2$, and otherwise inserts the second into the first as its leftmost subtree.

Pairing takes constant time and the minimum is found at the root. In a multiway tree representation realizing the priority queue operations is simple. Insertion pairs the new node with the root of heap; *decrease-key* splits the node and its subtree from the heap (if the node is not the root), decreases the key, and then pairs it with the root of the heap; *delete* splits the node to be deleted and its subtree, performs a *delete-min* on the subtree, and pairs the resulting tree with the root of the heap. Minimum deletion itself removes and returns the root, and then, in pairs, pairs the remaining trees. Then, the remaining trees from right to left are incrementally paired,

Since the multiple-child representation is difficult to maintain, the child-sibling binary tree representation for pairing heaps is used, in which siblings are connected as follows. The left link of a node accesses its first child, and the right link of a node accesses its next sibling, so that the value of a node does not exceed the values of the nodes in its left subtree. The time analysis for pairing heaps [12], e.g., with two-phase root consolidation is involved. Nonetheless, empirical work [27] shows strong evidence that pairing heaps perform well in practice.

4   Bucket-Based Priority Queues

There are priority queue data structures that exploit the data type of the keys. While for general priority queues we only imposed a total order, for bucket-based structures we usually require integer keys with a maximum edge weight $C = \max_{e \in E} w(e)$. As we aim at general weight functions, we scaled and truncated real-valued distance values like $\sqrt{2}$. Due to this approximation of floating-point data considerably large integer edges costs are generated (based on the Taylor expansion, there are fractional representation of $\sqrt{2}$ with a small error, with the constant denominator to be compiled away). The worst-case time performance for a one-level bucket representation of the priority queue [5] is $O(C \cdot |V| + |E|)$, as we might have $C - 1$ empty buckets in between two non-empty ones. For a constant value C, the shortest paths algorithm based on buckets has optimal complexity, but for the cost values we consider, the performance degrades quickly.

Most shortest paths algorithms based on buckets assume a *monotone* cost function, that is the cost of each successor node is larger than the one of the current one. This leads to *addressable* priority queues that only need to support *push* (aka *insert*), *top* (aka *find-min*) and *pop* (aka *delete-min*). The reason for buckets to work is that while a node might be reached and stored more than once with different cost values, it will be expanded first with optimal cost. We maintain traversal information such as distance or visitedness in tables, and assume to have access to the information if a cell is free or occupied. We choose pairs of distance and grid location to be stored in the priority queue.

4.1 Radix Heaps

Let C be the maximum weight of all edges. One-level buckets are arrays of of lists size C that contain the nodes to be expanded. There are multi-level bucket representations that decrease the influence on C to $\sqrt{C}$ and below. To decrease the effect on C further, radix heaps have been proposed with an amortized worst-case complexity of $O(1)$ for delete-min and decrease-key and $O(\log_2 C)$ for the insert operation [1].

A *radix heap* [1] maintains a list of $\lceil \log_2(C + 1) \rceil + 1$ buckets of sizes 1, 1, 2, 4, 8, 16, etc. Elements in the buckets are doubly-linked. The main difference to layered buckets is the use buckets of exponentially increasing sizes. Therefore, only $O(\log_2 C)$ buckets are needed. This leads to an $O(|V| \log_2 C + |E|)$ time shortest path algorithm. There are further theoretical improvements like a combination of radix with Fibonacci heaps [1] but for our domain, we consider $\log_2 C$ to be sufficiently small.

When assuming that the maximum edge weight is a constant independent of the size of the graph, the radix heap implementation for Dijsktra's algorithm is a linear-time algorithm. However, as $\sqrt{2}$ is infinitisimal, choosing a small C is not immediate.

4.2 Bucket Maps

To bypass this dependency on C completely a *map* of buckets can be used, e.g., maintained in the form of a search tree (as done in STL). This way only buckets that are non-empty are stored and inspected for expansion.

The access time, however, increases to the logarithm of number of all buckets currently stored in the queue. In the unlikely case, each bucket contains at most one element. In principle, bucket maps work not only for integer but also for floating-point data and even real-valued data, as long as there is a toatal ordering. As the buckets are ordered and considered along costs we call the bucket-map algorithm *cost*.

4.3   Factorized Heaps

In octile grids with Euclidean distances, every path has cost $k \cdot 1 + l \cdot \sqrt{2}$ for some integer values $k, l \geq 0$ (both k and l are smaller than any upper bound L of the length of the optimal path). This can be exploited to label the following table of buckets.

k, l	0	1	2	3	4	$\cdots$
0	$0 + 0 \cdot \sqrt{2}$	$0 + \sqrt{2}$	$0 + 2 \cdot \sqrt{2}$	$0 + 3 \cdot \sqrt{2}$	$0 + 4 \cdot \sqrt{2}$	$\cdots$
1	$1 + 0 \cdot \sqrt{2}$	$1 + \sqrt{2}$	$1 + 2 \cdot \sqrt{2}$	$1 + 3 \cdot \sqrt{2}$	$1 + 4 \cdot \sqrt{2}$	$\cdots$
2	$2 + 0 \cdot \sqrt{2}$	$2 + \sqrt{2}$	$2 + 2 \cdot \sqrt{2}$	$2 + 3 \cdot \sqrt{2}$	$2 + 4 \cdot \sqrt{2}$	$\cdots$
3	$3 + 0 \cdot \sqrt{2}$	$3 + \sqrt{2}$	$3 + 2 \cdot \sqrt{2}$	$3 + 3 \cdot \sqrt{2}$	$3 + 4 \cdot \sqrt{2}$	$\cdots$
4	$4 + 0 \cdot \sqrt{2}$	$4 + \sqrt{2}$	$4 + 2 \cdot \sqrt{2}$	$4 + 3 \cdot \sqrt{2}$	$4 + 4 \cdot \sqrt{2}$	$\cdots$
5	$5 + 0 \cdot \sqrt{2}$	$5 + \sqrt{2}$	$5 + 2 \cdot \sqrt{2}$	$5 + 3 \cdot \sqrt{2}$	$5 + 4 \cdot \sqrt{2}$	$\cdots$
$\vdots$	$\vdots$	$\vdots$	$\vdots$	$\vdots$	$\vdots$	$\ddots$

By processing the labels in this table we precompute an index that is used for addressing the buckets during the search. The order of buckets has to warrant increasing cost, so we sort the table entries. In the worst case L is linear in $|V|$, e.g., in a grid with a singleton path from start to goal in the form of a spiral. In practice, however, L will be much smaller; in search practice we can safely assume $L^2 = O(|V|)$. The order of expanding nodes within a bucket can be chosen freely and, thus, a natural bucket scan makes the algorithm cache oblivious.

As a side product, we can remove buckets that are no longer needed, which improves the memory profile of the algorithm. Moreover, by assuming an exact sorting of the bucket labels, the algorithm does not rely on infinitisimal numbers and works with arbitrary precision. In octile grids that we will look at, *cutting corners* is not allowed.

Determining the ordering of indices reduces to sorting, and with a standard sorting algorithm it takes $L^2 \log_2 L^2 = O(|V| \log_2 |V|)$ time to sort the numbers labeling the buckets in the worst case. With *multiway-merging* (or k-way merging) [17] the complexity reduces to $L^2 \log_2 L = O(|V| \cdot \log_2(\sqrt{|V|}))$, which is an acceptable off-line effort, as for any given L the work to compute the index is done only once.

Theorem 1 (Complexity Factorized Shortest Paths Search). *If $L^2 = O(|V|)$, in an octile grid Algorithm 1 requires time $O(|V|)$.*

```
procedure factorize(start, indices)
global ← 0
for 0 ≤ i < X, 0 ≤ j < Y :
 |   vis[i][j] ← 0
pq[0].append(start)
s ← 1, n ← 0
while true :
 |   for 0 ≤ i < |pq[n]| :
 |    |   (x, y) ← pq[n][i]
 |    |   s ← s − 1
 |    |   if not vis[x, y] :
 |    |    |   vis[x, y] ← 1
 |    |    |   if not vis[x + 1][y] and not obs[x + 1][y] :
 |    |    |    |   pq[MaxLength + n].append((x + 1, y))
 |    |    |    |   s ← s + 1
 |    |    |   [...]
 |    |    |   if not vis[x + 1][y − 1] and not obs[x + 1][y − 1] and (not obs[x][y −
 |    |    |   1] or not obs[x + 1][y]) :
 |    |    |    |   pq[1 + n].append((x + 1, y − 1))
 |    |    |    |   s ← s + 1
 |    |   [...]
 |   pq[n] ← ∅
 |   if s = 0 :
 |    |   break
 |   do:
 |    |   global ← global + 1
 |    |   n ← indices[global]
 |   while pq[n] = ∅
```

Algorithm 1. Code for factorized shortest paths search.

Proof. After precomputation, Dijkstra's algorithm as shown in Fig. 1 takes $O(|V| + K)$ time, where K is the number of buckets found empty during the search. All operations in the outer while loop are constant-time, the additional efforts in the *do-while* loop for pushing the pointers are $O(K)$. As $K \leq L^2$ and $L^2 = O(|V|)$ we achieve an optimal linear runtime complexity for Dijkstra's algorithm.

One may also set a bit in a vector in case of insertion in the corresponding bucket, so that finding the first non-empty bucket is a leading zero count (native on modern processors). The factorized shortest path algorithm is *localized* in the sense that states in one bucket residing next to each other in memory are expanded one after the other. There is only a small number of buckets into which successors are inserted.

5   Cache-Efficient Layout

The layout of the nodes to be visited can result in drastic changes to the performance. For example in 2D image manipulating software, filling areas in a new color is usually addressed with *flood-filling* that strictly prefers the y- to the

x-direction [24]. In a memory layout neighboring cells are preferred to be visited subsequent to each other.

A related sweep-line exploration of a state space has been seen in the more general context of external-memory model checking [10,21]. The algorithm defines a progress measure and initiates several scans over the search space.

5.1 Flood-Filling

For cache-efficient shortest-path search, the algorithmic considerations are more challenging than for coloring and breadth-first search. In the literature we found only one proposal to refine shortest path search via flood-filling [23]. The main idea is the following: when traversing the grid row-wise when encounting an obstacle, the cells above or below the current one are enqueued. A new scan for them is invoked only if at that time it offers a possible cost improvement.

As with Dijkstra's algorithm the approach initializes every entry in the distance map with infinity and the current position with 0. The algorithm maintains a queue of cells from which to scan, beginning with the starting position. From each cell, the algorithm scans the distance map first to the left and then to the right. For each scanned cell, a tentative distance is computed by a one-step lookahed.

This way, nodes may be reconsidered more than once for improvement. It is not difficult to see that the strategy may lead to a quadratic number of reopenings. In this work, we show that the suggested implementation in Fig. 2 fails to find shortest paths. If one is not willing to sacrifice optimality for an increase in speed, we design an optimal algorithm at the cost of further reopenings. In the following we call a node with coordinates (i, j) settled if $minDist(i, j) = dist[i, j]$.

In our setting, the algorithm has to compute the optimal goal distances for all nodes in the grid. However, as said, there are cases, in which the flood-fill algorithm fails.

Theorem 2 (Flood-Fill Shortest Paths Search). *Algorithm 2 (without improvements) does not necessarily compute the optimal solution cost at each node.*

Proof. We show that the problem exists even in 4-way grids and with uniform instead of Euclidian weights. We prove the result by providing a counter-example. One problem of the Algorithm 2 is settling a node that is still to be reopened, as a settled node with $minDist(i, j) = dist[i, j]$ terminates the scanning process. Take the example in Table 1 of a small grid fragment (X denotes a blocked cell), where we have enqueued but not updated the value at cell (c), reaching it on a better path via cell (d). Before deleting cell (c) from the queue and initiating the scan from right to left, we come from the other side via cell (e) and reach cell (b) with a worse value than the one at cell (d). While scanning from left to right, cell (c) will settle, even though it is pending in the queue. Now, when extracting cell (c) from the queue it already has the value updated, which in turn limits other cells from participating in the new information. For example

procedure MinDist(x, y)
$d \leftarrow \infty$
if $dist[x-1, y] \geq 0$ **and** $d > dist[x-1, y] + w((x-1, y), (x, y))$:
| $d \leftarrow dist[x-1, y] + w((x-1, y), (x, y))$
if $dist[x-1, y-1] \geq 0$ **and** $d > dist[x-1, y-1] + w((x-1, y-1), (x, y))$:
| $d \leftarrow dist[x-1, y-1] + w((x-1, y-1), (x, y))$
[...]
return d

procedure better(x, y)
return $dist[x, y] > \max\{MinDist(x, y), 0\}$

procedure scan(x, y, γ)
$i \leftarrow y + \gamma$
$d \leftarrow MinDist(x, i)$
while $dist[x, i] \leq d$:
| $dist[x, i] \leftarrow d$
| **if not** $vis(x-1, i)$ **and** better$(x-1, i)$ **and not** better$(x-1, i-\gamma)$:
| | open.push$((x-1, i))$ $vis(x-1, i) \leftarrow 1$
| **if not** $vis(x+1, i)$ **and** better$(x+1, i)$ **and not** better$(x+1, i-\gamma)$:
| | open.push$((x+1, i))$ $vis(x+1, i) \leftarrow 1$
| $i \leftarrow i + \gamma$

procedure floodfill$(start)$
for $0 \leq i < X, 0 \leq j < Y - 1$:
| $dist[i, j] \leftarrow obs[i, j]? - \infty : \infty$
open.push$(start)$
$dist[start] \leftarrow 0$
$vis[start] \leftarrow 1$
while $open \neq \emptyset$:
| $(x, y) \leftarrow$ open.pop$()$
| $vis[start] \leftarrow 0$
| **if** $(s = start)$ **or** better(x, y) :
| | **if** $s \neq start$:
| | | $dist[x, y] \leftarrow MinDist(x, y)$
| | **if not** $vis(x-1, y)$ **and** better$(x-1, y)$:
| | | open.push$((x-1, y))$; $vis(x-1, y) \leftarrow 1$
| | **if not** $vis(x+1, y)$ **and** better$(x+1, y)$:
| | | open.push$((x+1, y))$; $vis(x+1, y) \leftarrow 1$
| | scan$(x, y, -1)$
| | scan$(x, y, +1)$

Algorithm 2. Flood-fill shortest paths search (improvements colored in red).

having (a)–(e) equal to $\infty, \infty, \infty, 1, 3$ yields $5, 4, 2, 1, 3$ instead of the optimum value sequence $4, 3, 2, 1, 3$.

Hence, we prevent nodes from modification if they are currently contained in the queue. However, in octile grids diagonal reachable cells not in the queue can also settle and block scanning, like cell (b) due to an improvement encountered

Table 1. Counterexample and corresponding queue content with invoked scans (*
denoting the settlement of nodes).

X	X	(e)	X	X
X	(a)	(b)	(c)	X
X	X	X	(d)	X

1. (e)*	(d)*	scan(e)
2. (d)*	(b)	scan(d)
3. (b)	(c)	scan(b)

in cell (d). As the minimum distance at cell (b) will not change in the scan started in cell (c) the scan stops and will not update cell (a). Therefore, as a fix we additionally continue scans even if intermediate nodes in a scan are settled. This leads to the improved implementation of the flood-fill (hightlighted in red in Algorithm 2).

Precise conditions, on whether or not the traversal order in a *localized algorithm* retains optimal solutions have been derived by [9]. In the classical case if $G = (V, E, w)$ is a positively weighted graph and $dist$ be the tentative distance for the true shortest path value δ in Dijkstra's original algorithm. We have the invariance that at the time a node u is selected (and about to be expanded), we have $dist(u) = \delta(s, u)$. This way we change the exploration order and allow reopening of nodes [9].

Lemma 1 (Reopening). *Let $G = (V, E, w)$ be a weighted graph, $p = (s = v_0, ..., v_n = t)$ be a least-cost path from the start node s to any selected goal node t, and dist be the tentative value of the shortest paths in an shortest path algorithm that allows reopening. At each selection of a node u from open, we have the following invariance: (I) Unless t is closed with $dist(t) = \delta(s, t)$, (a) there is a node v_i in open such that $dist(v_i) = \delta(s, v_i)$, and (b) no $j > i$ exists such that v_j is closed with $dist(v_j) = \delta(s, v_j)$.*

Here, we do not have an explicit list of closed noded. To avoid duplicates in the open list, in Algorithm 2 (with its improvements) nodes in open are marked visited. Expanded nodes are closed, if they are not in open. With the change from strict inequality to inequality we avoid case (b), and obtain the following result.

Theorem 3 (Optimality Floodfill). *Algorithm 2 (with improvements) computes the optimal solution cost at each node.*

Proof. As the edge costs are strictly positive the values at each node monotonically rise, so that shortest paths have no cycles. Hence, the length of all optimal paths are bounded by the size of the node set. In our case of all-target search, we do not have a specific goal t but invariance (Ia), holds for all selections of t. It says that for all nodes t eventually we have $dist(t) = \delta(s, t)$. The problematic case of a settled node with $dist(v_j) = \delta(s, v_j)$ for which $j > i$ exists has been bypassed changing comparator $<$ to $\leq$ in procedure scan.

6   Experiments

For the evaluation we used a single core of a desktop PC (Ubuntu 14.04 LTS (64 Bit), Intel Core i7-4500U, 1.8 GHz, 16 GB; L1 cache: 32 K, L2 cache: 256 K, L3 cache: 3072 K). We considered two sets of problems.

6.1   Game Graphs

For game graphs, we took all the maps from the GPPC-15 benchmark repository [28]. While the task lists include many *s*-to-*t* queries, we removed the goals *t* and concentrated on the efforts needed for computing shortest paths in a complete state-space enumeration.

There are several possible starting locations. The performance measured in Figs. 1 and 2 is the CPU time for the solving the first instance, in which the initial cell was not blocked (by the additional frame cells).

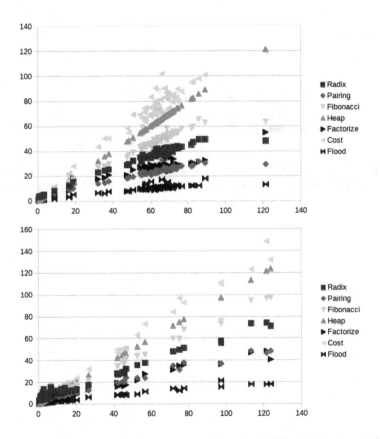

Fig. 1. Time in ms for SSSP search in the game maps of Baldur's Gate II and Starcraft (left to right) using scatter plots wrt the performance of SSSP search with binary heaps.

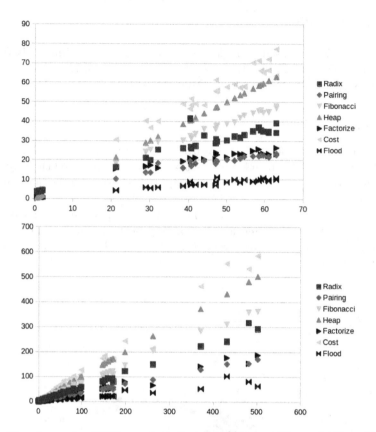

Fig. 2. Time in ms for SSSP search in the game maps of Warcraft III and Dragon Age (left to right) using scatter plots wrt the performance of SSSP search with binary heaps.

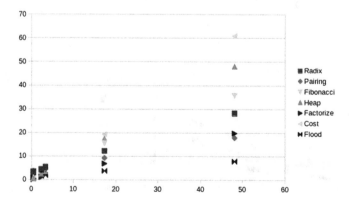

Fig. 3. Time in ms for SSSP search in random maps; in scatter plot wrt the search with binary heaps.

From the plots we can clearly identify that *improved flood-fill* is generally the fastest method despite its additional work for re-expanding nodes. Moreover, pairing heaps result in the fastest general single-source shortest paths method and perform equally well, if not better than the factorized priority queue data structures. Fibonacci beat binary heaps, and the cost-based exploration maintaining an STL map performs worst.

6.2 Random Graphs

Next, we took random maps from the GPPC-15 benchmark repositorium. Note that for a random number of obstacles, where each grid cell is marked *occupied* with parameterized probability $p \in \{10\%, 20\%, 30\%, 40\%\}$, for larger values of p the grid quickly becomes disconnected. In Fig. 3 we again measured the time of the first instance for which the initial cell was not blocked. The general performance picture on the relative quality of the different shortest-path algorithms, however, remained roughly the same.

7   Conclusion

Shortest path search is essential in all almost areas of computer science, and the flood-fill algorithm provides an interesting example for a cache-efficient implementation. The experiments in moderately-sized game maps show that this strategy pays off: we obtain a roughly six-fold speed-up of flood-filling wrt a binary heaps, and about halving the runtime wrt pairing heaps and a related contribution of factorizing total cost.

Localization of the search is of crucial importantance to reduce the access to disk and to remove communication overhead between processes [9]. Cache-efficient shortest-path search, thus, completes the picture by showing that careful designs of search algorithms that improve locality within main memory are effective. Moreover, general priority queues can be as efficient and sometimes even outperform solutions specialized for integer keys or grids, so that extensions of the flood-fill shortest-path algorithms to other graph layouts are exiting research avenues for the future.

References

1. Ahuja, R.K., Mehlhorn, K., Orlin, J.B., Tarjan, R.E.: Faster algorithms for the shortest path problem. J. ACM **37**(2), 213–223 (1990)
2. Brodal, G.S.: Worst-case efficient priority queues. In: ACM-SIAM Symposium on Discrete Algorithms, pp. 52–58 (1996)
3. Bruun, A., Edelkamp, S., Katajainen, J., Rasmussen, J.: Policy-based benchmarking of weak heaps and their relatives. In: Festa, P. (ed.) SEA 2010. LNCS, vol. 6049, pp. 424–435. Springer, Heidelberg (2010). doi:10.1007/978-3-642-13193-6_36
4. Culberson, J.C., Schaeffer, J.: Pattern databases. Comput. Intell. **14**(4), 318–334 (1998)

5. Dial, R.B.: Shortest-path forest with topological ordering. Commun. ACM **12**(11), 632–633 (1969)
6. Dijkstra, E.W.: A note on two problems in connexion with graphs. Numer. Math. **1**, 269–271 (1959)
7. Driscoll, J.R., Gabow, H.N., Shrairman, R., Tarjan, R.E.: Relaxed heaps: an alternative to Fibonacci heaps with applications to parallel computation. Commun. ACM **31**(11), 1343–1354 (1988)
8. Edelkamp, S.: Planning with pattern databases. In: ECP, pp. 13–24 (2001)
9. Edelkamp, S., Schrödl, S.: Localizing A*. In: AAAI, pp. 885–890 (2000)
10. Evangelista, S., Kristensen, L.M.: A sweep-line method for Büchi automata-based model checking. Fundam. Inform. **131**(1), 27–53 (2014)
11. Floyd, R.W.: Algorithm 245: treesort 3. Commun. ACM **7**(12), 701 (1964)
12. Fredman, M.L., Sedgewick, R., Sleator, D.D., Tarjan, R.E.: The pairing heap: a new form of self-adjusting heap. Algorithmica **1**(1), 111–129 (1986)
13. Fredman, M.L., Tarjan, R.E.: Fibonacci heaps and their uses in improved network optimization algorithm. J. ACM **34**(3), 596–615 (1987)
14. Geisberger, R., Schieferdecker, D.: Heuristic contraction hierarchies with approximation guarantee. In: SOCS, pp. 31–38 (2010)
15. Ghiani, G., Guerriero, F., Laporte, G., Musmanno, R.: Real-time vehicle routing: solution concepts, algorithms and parallel computing strategies. Eur. J. Oper. Res. **151**, 1–11 (2003)
16. Hart, P.E., Nilsson, N.J., Raphael, B.: A formal basis for heuristic determination of minimum path cost. IEEE Trans. Syst. Sci. Cybern. **4**, 100–107 (1968)
17. Horowitz, E., Sahni, S., Anderson-Freed, S.: Fundamentals of Data Structures in C, 2nd edn. Silicon Press, Summit (2007)
18. Kaplan, H., Tarjan, R.E., Zwick, U.: Fibonacci heaps revisited, pp. 187–205 (2014). arXiv:1407.5750v1
19. Klein, P., Rao, S., Rauch, M., Subramanian, S.: Faster shortest-path algorithms for planar graphs. J. Comput. Syst. Sci. **55**(1), 3–23 (1997)
20. Korf, R.E.: Finding optimal solutions to Rubik's Cube using pattern databases. In: AAAI, pp. 700–705 (1997)
21. Kristensen, L., Mailund, T.: Path finding with the sweep-line method using external storage. In: ICFEM, pp. 319–337 (2003)
22. LaMarca, A., Ladner, R.E.: The influence of caches on the performance of sorting. J. Algorithms **31**(1), 66–104 (1999)
23. Liebana, D.P., Powley, E.J., Whitehouse, D., Rohlfshagen, P., Samothrakis, S., Cowling, P.I., Lucas, S.M.: Solving the physical traveling salesman problem: tree search and macro actions. IEEE Trans. Comput. Intell. AI Games **6**(1), 31–45 (2014)
24. Lieberman, H.: How to color in a coloring book. SIGGRAPH Comput. Graph. **12**(3), 111–116 (1978)
25. Otte, M.: On solving floating point SSSP using an integer priority queue. CoRR, abs/1606.00726 (2016)
26. Sanders, P.: Fast priority queues for cached memory. ACM J. Exp. Algorithmics **5**, 7 (2000)
27. Stasko, J.T., Vitter, J.S.: Pairing heaps: experiments and analysis. Commun. ACM **30**(3), 234–249 (1987)
28. Sturtevant, N.R.: The grid-based path planning competition. AI Mag. **35**(3), 66–69 (2014)

29. Thorup, M.: Undirected single-source shortest paths with positive integer weights in linear time. J. ACM **46**, 362–394 (1999)
30. Wagner, D., Willhalm, T.: Geometric speed-up techniques for finding shortest paths in large sparse graphs. In: Battista, G., Zwick, U. (eds.) ESA 2003. LNCS, vol. 2832, pp. 776–787. Springer, Heidelberg (2003). doi:10.1007/978-3-540-39658-1_69
31. Williams, J.W.J.: Algorithm 232: heapsort. Commun. ACM **7**(6), 347–348 (1964)

Automating Emendations of the Ontological Argument in Intensional Higher-Order Modal Logic

David Fuenmayor[1(✉)] and Christoph Benzmüller[1,2(✉)]

[1] Freie Universität Berlin, Berlin, Germany
davfuenmayor@gmail.com, c.benzmueller@fu-berlin.de
[2] University of Luxembourg, Esch-sur-Alzette, Luxembourg
http://christoph-benzmueller.de

Abstract. A shallow semantic embedding of an intensional higher-order modal logic (IHOML) in Isabelle/HOL is presented. IHOML draws on Montague/Gallin intensional logics and has been introduced by Melvin Fitting in his textbook *Types, Tableaus and Gödel's God* in order to discuss his emendation of Gödel's ontological argument for the existence of God. Utilizing IHOML, the most interesting parts of Fitting's textbook are formalized, automated and verified in the Isabelle/HOL proof assistant. A particular focus thereby is on three variants of the ontological argument which avoid the modal collapse, which is a strongly criticized side-effect in Gödel's resp. Scott's original work.

Keywords: Automated theorem proving · Computational metaphysics · Higher-order logic · Intensional logic · Isabelle · Modal logic · Ontological argument · Semantic embedding

1 Introduction

The first part of this paper introduces a shallow semantic embedding of an intensional higher-order modal logic (IHOML) in classical higher-order logic (Isabelle/HOL[1]). IHOML, as introduced by Fitting [15], is a modification of the intensional logic originally developed by Montague and later expanded by Gallin [18] by building upon Church's type theory and Kripke's possible-world semantics. Our approach builds on previous work on the semantic embedding of multimodal logics with quantification [6], which we expand here to allow for actualist quantification, intensional terms and their related operations. From an AI perspective we contribute a highly flexible framework for automated reasoning in intensional and modal logic. IHOML, which has not been automated before,

---

[1] In this paper we work with the Isabelle/HOL proof assistant [22], which explains the chosen abbreviation. Generally, however, the work presented here can be mapped to any other system implementing Church's simple type theory [13].

© Springer International Publishing AG 2017
G. Kern-Isberner et al. (Eds.): KI 2017, LNAI 10505, pp. 114–127, 2017.
DOI: 10.1007/978-3-319-67190-1_9

has several applications, e.g. towards the deep semantic analysis of natural language rational arguments as envisioned in the new DFG Schwerpunktprogramm RATIO (SPP 1999).

In the second part, we present an exemplary, non-trivial application of this reasoning infrastructure: A study on *computational metaphysics*[2], the computer-formalization and critical assessment of Gödel's [19] (resp. Dana Scott's [25]) modern variant of the ontological argument and two of its proposed emendations as discussed in [15]. Gödel's ontological argument is amongst the most discussed formal proofs in modern literature. Several authors (e.g. [2,3,11,15,20]) have proposed emendations with the aim of retaining its essential result (the necessary existence of God) while at the same time avoiding the *modal collapse* (whatever is the case is so necessarily) [26,27]. The modal collapse is an undesirable side-effect of the axioms postulated by Gödel (resp. Scott). It essentially states that there are no contingent truths and everything is determined.

Related work[3] has formalized several of these variants on the computer and verified or falsified them. For example, Gödel's axiom's system has been shown inconsistent [9,10], while Scott's version has been verified [8]. Further experiments, contributing amongst others to the clarification of a related debate regarding the redundancy of some axioms in Anderson's emendation, are presented and discussed in [7]. The enabling technique in these case studies has been shallow semantic embeddings of *extensional* higher-order modal logics in classical higher-order logic (see [4,6] and the references therein).[4]

In contrast to the related work, Fitting's variant is based on *intensional* higher-order modal logic. Our experiments confirm that Fitting's argument, as presented in his textbook [15], is valid and that it avoids the modal collapse as intended. Due to lack of space, we refer the reader to our (computer-verified) paper [17] for further results. That paper has been written directly in the Isabelle/HOL proof assistant and requires some familiarity with this system and with Fitting's textbook.

The work presented here originates from the *Computational Metaphysics* lecture course held at the FU Berlin in Summer 2016 [28].

2   Embedding of Intensional Higher-Order Modal Logic

2.1   Type Declarations

Since IHOML and Isabelle/HOL are both typed languages, we introduce a type-mapping between them. We follow as closely as possible the syntax given by

---

[2] This term was originally coined by Fitelson and Zalta in [14] and describes an emerging, interdisciplinary field aiming at the rigorous formalization and deep logical assessment of philosophical arguments in an automated reasoning environment.

[3] More loosely related work studied Anselm's older, non-modal version of the ontological argument directly in Prover9 [23] and PVS [24].

[4] In contrast to deep semantic embeddings, where the embedded logic is presented as an abstract datatype, our shallow semantic embeddings avoid inductive definitions and maximize the reuse of logical operations from the meta-level. In particular, tedious new binding mechanisms are avoided in our approach.

Fitting ([15] p. 86), according to which, for any extensional type τ, $\uparrow\tau$ becomes its corresponding intensional type. For instance, a set of (red) objects has the extensional type $\langle e \rangle$, whereas the concept 'red' has intensional type $\uparrow\langle e \rangle$.

typedecl e — type for entities
typedecl w — type for possible worlds
type-synonym $wo = (w{\Rightarrow}bool)$ — type for world-dependent formulas

Aliases for some common complex types (predicates and relations).

type-synonym $ie=(w{\Rightarrow}e)$ ($\uparrow e$) — individual concepts (map worlds to objects)
type-synonym $se=(e{\Rightarrow}bool)$ ($\langle e \rangle$) — (extensional) sets
type-synonym $ise=(e{\Rightarrow}wo)$ ($\uparrow\langle e \rangle$) — (intensional predicative) concepts
type-synonym $sise=(\uparrow\langle e\rangle{\Rightarrow}bool)$ ($\langle\uparrow\langle e\rangle\rangle$) — sets of concepts
type-synonym $isise=(\uparrow\langle e\rangle{\Rightarrow}wo)$ ($\uparrow\langle\uparrow\langle e\rangle\rangle$) — 2-order concepts
type-synonym $see=(e{\Rightarrow}e{\Rightarrow}bool)$ ($\langle e,e\rangle$) — (extensional) relations
type-synonym $isee=(e{\Rightarrow}e{\Rightarrow}wo)$ ($\uparrow\langle e,e\rangle$) — (intensional) relational concepts

2.2 Logical Constants as Truth-Sets

We embed modal operators as sets of worlds satisfying a corresponding formula.

abbreviation $mand::wo{\Rightarrow}wo{\Rightarrow}wo$ (**infix**$\wedge$) **where** $\varphi\wedge\psi \equiv \lambda w.\ (\varphi\ w)\wedge(\psi\ w)$
abbreviation $mor::wo{\Rightarrow}wo{\Rightarrow}wo$ (**infix**$\vee$) **where** $\varphi\vee\psi \equiv \lambda w.\ (\varphi\ w)\vee(\psi\ w)$
abbreviation $mimp::wo{\Rightarrow}wo{\Rightarrow}wo$ (**infix**$\rightarrow$) **where** $\varphi\rightarrow\psi \equiv \lambda w.\ (\varphi\ w)\longrightarrow(\psi\ w)$
abbreviation $mequ::wo{\Rightarrow}wo{\Rightarrow}wo$ (**infix**$\leftrightarrow$) **where** $\varphi\leftrightarrow\psi \equiv \lambda w.\ (\varphi\ w)\longleftrightarrow(\psi\ w)$
abbreviation $mnot::wo{\Rightarrow}wo$ ($\neg$-) **where** $\neg\varphi \equiv \lambda w.\ \neg(\varphi\ w)$
abbreviation $mnegpred::\uparrow\langle e\rangle{\Rightarrow}\uparrow\langle e\rangle$ ($\rightarrow$-) **where** $\rightarrow\Phi \equiv \lambda x.\lambda w.\ \neg(\Phi\ x\ w)$

Possibilist quantifiers are embedded as follows.[5]

abbreviation $mforall::('t{\Rightarrow}wo){\Rightarrow}wo$ ($\forall$) **where** $\forall\Phi \equiv \lambda w.\forall x.\ (\Phi\ x\ w)$
abbreviation $mexists::('t{\Rightarrow}wo){\Rightarrow}wo$ ($\exists$) **where** $\exists\Phi \equiv \lambda w.\exists x.\ (\Phi\ x\ w)$

The *actualizedAt* predicate is used to additionally embed *actualist* quantifiers by restricting the domain of quantification at every possible world. This standard technique has been referred to as *existence relativization* ([16], p. 106), highlighting the fact that this predicate can be seen as a kind of meta-logical 'existence predicate' telling us which individuals *actually* exist at a given world. This meta-logical concept does not appear in our object language.

consts $Actualized::\uparrow\langle e\rangle$ (**infix** $actualizedAt$)
abbreviation $mforallAct::\uparrow\langle\uparrow\langle e\rangle\rangle$ ($\forall^A$) — actualist variants use superscript
  where $\forall^A\Phi \equiv \lambda w.\forall x.\ (x\ actualizedAt\ w)\longrightarrow(\Phi\ x\ w)$
abbreviation $mexistsAct::\uparrow\langle\uparrow\langle e\rangle\rangle$ ($\exists^A$)
  where $\exists^A\Phi \equiv \lambda w.\exists x.\ (x\ actualizedAt\ w)\wedge(\Phi\ x\ w)$

Frame's accessibility relation and modal operators.

---

[5] Possibilist and actualist quantification can be seen as the semantic counterparts of the concepts of possibilism and actualism in the metaphysics of modality. They relate to natural-language expressions such as 'there is', 'exists', 'is actual', etc.

consts $aRel::w{\Rightarrow}w{\Rightarrow}bool$ (**infix** r)
abbreviation $mbox :: wo{\Rightarrow}wo$ ($\square$-) **where** $\square\varphi \equiv \lambda w.\forall v.\ (w\ r\ v){\longrightarrow}(\varphi\ v)$
abbreviation $mdia :: wo{\Rightarrow}wo$ ($\Diamond$-) **where** $\Diamond\varphi \equiv \lambda w.\exists v.\ (w\ r\ v){\wedge}(\varphi\ v)$

2.3 Equality

abbreviation $meq::\ 't{\Rightarrow}'t{\Rightarrow}wo$ (**infix** $\approx$) — standard equality (for all types)
    where $x \approx y \equiv \lambda w.\ x = y$
abbreviation $meqC::\ \uparrow\langle\uparrow e,\uparrow e\rangle$ (**infix** $\approx^C$) — equality for individual concepts
    where $x \approx^C y \equiv \lambda w.\ \forall v.\ (x\ v) = (y\ v)$
abbreviation $meqL::\ \uparrow\langle e,e\rangle$ (**infix** $\approx^L$) — Leibniz equality for individuals
    where $x \approx^L y \equiv \lambda w.\ \forall \varphi.\ (\varphi\ x\ w){\longrightarrow}(\varphi\ y\ w)$

2.4 *Extension-of* Operator

According to Fitting's semantics ([15], pp. 92–94), $\downarrow$ is an unary operator applying only to intensional terms. A term of the form $\downarrow\alpha$ designates the extension of the intensional object designated by α, at some *given* world. For instance, suppose we take possible worlds as persons, we can therefore think of the concept 'red' as a function that maps each person to the set of objects that person classifies as red (its extension). We can further state that the intensional term r of type $\uparrow\langle e\rangle$ designates the concept 'red'. As can be seen, intensional terms in IHOML designate functions on possible worlds and they always do it *rigidly*. We will sometimes refer to an intensional object explicitly as 'rigid', implying that its (rigidly) designated function has the same extension in all possible worlds.[6]

Terms of the form $\downarrow\alpha$ are called *relativized* (extensional) terms; they are always derived from intensional terms and their type is extensional (in the color example $\downarrow r$ would be of type $\langle e\rangle$). Relativized terms may vary their denotation from world to world of a model, because the *extension of* an intensional term can change from world to world, i.e. they are non-rigid.

In our Isabelle/HOL embedding, we had to follow a slightly different approach; we model $\downarrow$ as a predicate applying to formulas of the form $\Phi(\downarrow\alpha_1\ldots\alpha_n)$. For instance, the formula $Q(\downarrow a_1)^w$ (evaluated at world w) is modeled as $\downarrow(Q,a_1)^w$, or $(Q\downarrow a_1)^w$ using infix notation, which gets further translated into $Q(a_1(w))^w$.

(a) Predicate φ takes as argument a relativized term derived from an (intensional) individual concept of type $\uparrow e$.

  abbreviation $extIndArg::\uparrow\langle e\rangle{\Rightarrow}\uparrow e{\Rightarrow}wo$ (**infix** $\downarrow$) **where** $\varphi \downarrow c \equiv \lambda w.\ \varphi\ (c\ w)\ w$

(b) A variant of (a) for terms derived from predicates (types of form $\uparrow\langle t\rangle$).

  abbreviation $extPredArg::(('t{\Rightarrow}bool){\Rightarrow}wo){\Rightarrow}('t{\Rightarrow}wo){\Rightarrow}wo$ (**infix** $\downarrow$)
    where $\varphi \downarrow P \equiv \lambda w.\ \varphi\ (\lambda x.\ P\ x\ w)\ w$

---

[6] The notion of *rigid designation* was introduced by Kripke in [21], where he discusses its many interesting ramifications in logic and the philosophy of language.

2.5 Verifying the Embedding

The above definitions introduce modal logic K with possibilist and actualist quantifiers, as evidenced by the following tests.[7]

> **abbreviation** $valid::wo \Rightarrow bool$ ($\lfloor$-$\rfloor$) **where** $\lfloor \psi \rfloor \equiv \forall w.(\psi\ w)$ — modal validity
> **lemma** K: $\lfloor(\Box(\varphi \to \psi)) \to (\Box\varphi \to \Box\psi)\rfloor$ **by** $simp$ — verifying K principle
> **lemma** NEC: $\lfloor\varphi\rfloor \Longrightarrow \lfloor\Box\varphi\rfloor$ **by** $simp$ — verifying $necessitation$ rule

Local consequence implies global consequence (not the other way round).[8]

> **lemma** $localImpGlobalCons$: $\lfloor\varphi \to \xi\rfloor \Longrightarrow \lfloor\varphi\rfloor \longrightarrow \lfloor\xi\rfloor$ **by** $simp$
> **lemma** $\lfloor\varphi\rfloor \longrightarrow \lfloor\xi\rfloor \Longrightarrow \lfloor\varphi \to \xi\rfloor$ **nitpick oops** — countersatisfiable

(Converse-)Barcan formulas are satisfied for possibilist, but not for actualist, quantification.

> **lemma** $\lfloor(\forall x.\Box(\varphi\ x)) \to \Box(\forall x.(\varphi\ x))\rfloor$ **by** $simp$
> **lemma** $\lfloor\Box(\forall x.(\varphi\ x)) \to (\forall x.\Box(\varphi\ x))\rfloor$ **by** $simp$
> **lemma** $\lfloor(\forall^A x.\Box(\varphi\ x)) \to \Box(\forall^A x.(\varphi\ x))\rfloor$ **nitpick oops** — countersatisfiable
> **lemma** $\lfloor\Box(\forall^A x.(\varphi\ x)) \to (\forall^A x.\Box(\varphi\ x))\rfloor$ **nitpick oops** — countersatisfiable

β-redex is valid for non-relativized (intensional or extensional) terms.

> **lemma** $\lfloor(\lambda\alpha.\ \varphi\ \alpha)\ (\tau::\uparrow e) \leftrightarrow (\varphi\ \tau)\rfloor$ **by** $simp$
> **lemma** $\lfloor(\lambda\alpha.\ \varphi\ \alpha)\ (\tau::e) \leftrightarrow (\varphi\ \tau)\rfloor$ **by** $simp$
> **lemma** $\lfloor(\lambda\alpha.\ \Box\varphi\ \alpha)\ (\tau::\uparrow e) \leftrightarrow (\Box\varphi\ \tau)\rfloor$ **by** $simp$
> **lemma** $\lfloor(\lambda\alpha.\ \Box\varphi\ \alpha)\ (\tau::e) \leftrightarrow (\Box\varphi\ \tau)\rfloor$ **by** $simp$

β-redex is valid for relativized terms as long as no modal operators occur.

> **lemma** $\lfloor(\lambda\alpha.\ \varphi\ \alpha)\ {\downarrow}(\tau::\uparrow e) \leftrightarrow (\varphi\ {\downarrow}\tau)\rfloor$ **by** $simp$
> **lemma** $\lfloor(\lambda\alpha.\ \Box\varphi\ \alpha)\ {\downarrow}(\tau::\uparrow e) \leftrightarrow (\Box\varphi\ {\downarrow}\tau)\rfloor$ **nitpick oops** — countersatisfiable

Modal collapse is countersatisfiable.

> **lemma** $\lfloor\varphi \to \Box\varphi\rfloor$ **nitpick oops** — countersatisfiable

2.6 Stability, Rigid Designation, *De Dicto* and *De Re*

Intensional terms are trivially rigid. This predicate tests whether an intensional predicate is 'rigid' in the sense of denoting a world-independent function.

> **abbreviation** $rigid::('t \Rightarrow wo) \Rightarrow wo$ **where** $rigid\ \tau \equiv (\lambda\beta.\ \Box((\lambda z.\ \beta{\approx}z)\ {\downarrow}\tau))\ {\downarrow}\tau$

---

[7] We prove theorems in Isabelle by using the keyword 'by' followed by the name of a proof method. Some methods used here are: $simp$ (term rewriting), $blast$ (tableaus), $meson$ (model elimination), $metis$ (ordered resolution and paramodulation), $auto$ (classical reasoning and term rewriting) and $force$ (exhaustive search trying different tools). In our computer-formalization and assessment of Fitting's textbook [17], we provide further evidence that our embedded logic works as intended by verifying the book's theorems and examples.

[8] We utilize here (counter-)model finder $Nitpick$ [12] for the first time. For the conjectured lemma, $Nitpick$ finds a countermodel (not shown here), i.e. a model satisfying all the axioms which falsifies the given formula.

Following definitions are called 'stability conditions' by Fitting ([15], p. 124).

abbreviation $stabilityA::('t{\Rightarrow}wo){\Rightarrow}wo$ **where** $stabilityA\ \tau \equiv \forall\alpha.\ (\tau\ \alpha) \to \Box(\tau\ \alpha)$
abbreviation $stabilityB::('t{\Rightarrow}wo){\Rightarrow}wo$ **where** $stabilityB\ \tau \equiv \forall\alpha.\ \Diamond(\tau\ \alpha) \to (\tau\ \alpha)$

We prove them equivalent in *S5* logic (using *Sahlqvist correspondence*).

lemma *equivalence aRel* $\implies \lfloor stabilityA\ (\tau::\uparrow\langle e\rangle)\rfloor \longrightarrow \lfloor stabilityB\ \tau\rfloor$ **by** *blast*
lemma *equivalence aRel* $\implies \lfloor stabilityB\ (\tau::\uparrow\langle e\rangle)\rfloor \longrightarrow \lfloor stabilityA\ \tau\rfloor$ **by** *blast*

A term is 'rigid' if and only if it satisfies the stability conditions.

lemma $\lfloor rigid\ (\tau::\uparrow\langle e\rangle)\rfloor \longleftrightarrow \lfloor(stabilityA\ \tau \wedge stabilityB\ \tau)\rfloor$ **by** *meson*
lemma $\lfloor rigid\ (\tau::\uparrow\langle\uparrow e\rangle)\rfloor \longleftrightarrow \lfloor(stabilityA\ \tau \wedge stabilityB\ \tau)\rfloor$ **by** *meson*

De re is equivalent to *de dicto* for non-relativized terms.[9]

lemma $\lfloor\forall\alpha.\ ((\lambda\beta.\ \Box(\alpha\ \beta))\ (\tau::\langle e\rangle)) \leftrightarrow \Box((\lambda\beta.\ (\alpha\ \beta))\ \tau)\rfloor$ **by** *simp*
lemma $\lfloor\forall\alpha.\ ((\lambda\beta.\ \Box(\alpha\ \beta))\ (\tau::\uparrow\langle e\rangle)) \leftrightarrow \Box((\lambda\beta.\ (\alpha\ \beta))\ \tau)\rfloor$ **by** *simp*

De re is not equivalent to *de dicto* for relativized terms.

lemma $\lfloor\forall\alpha.\ ((\lambda\beta.\ \Box(\alpha\ \beta))\ \downarrow(\tau::\uparrow\langle e\rangle)) \leftrightarrow \Box((\lambda\beta.\ (\alpha\ \beta))\ \downarrow\tau)\rfloor$
nitpick[*card e=1, card w=2*] **oops** — countersatisfiable

2.7 Useful Definitions for the Axiomatization of Further Logics

The best-known normal logics (*K4, K5, KB, K45, KB5, D, D4, D5, D45, ...*) can be obtained by combinations of the following axioms:

abbreviation T **where** $T \equiv \forall\varphi.\ \Box\varphi \to \varphi$
abbreviation B **where** $B \equiv \forall\varphi.\ \varphi \to \Box\Diamond\varphi$
abbreviation D **where** $D \equiv \forall\varphi.\ \Box\varphi \to \Diamond\varphi$
abbreviation IV **where** $IV \equiv \forall\varphi.\ \Box\varphi \to \Box\Box\varphi$
abbreviation V **where** $V \equiv \forall\varphi.\ \Diamond\varphi \to \Box\Diamond\varphi$

Instead of postulating combinations of the above axioms we make use of the well-known *Sahlqvist correspondence*, which links axioms to constraints on a model's accessibility relation. We show that reflexivity, symmetry, seriality, transitivity and euclideanness imply axioms T, B, D, IV, V respectively.[10]

lemma *reflexive aRel* $\implies \lfloor T\rfloor$ **by** *blast*
lemma *symmetric aRel* $\implies \lfloor B\rfloor$ **by** *blast*
lemma *serial aRel* $\implies \lfloor D\rfloor$ **by** *blast*
lemma *transitive aRel* $\implies \lfloor IV\rfloor$ **by** *blast*
lemma *euclidean aRel* $\implies \lfloor V\rfloor$ **by** *blast*
lemma *preorder aRel* $\implies \lfloor T\rfloor \wedge \lfloor IV\rfloor$ **by** *blast* — S4: reflexive + transitive
lemma *equivalence aRel* $\implies \lfloor T\rfloor \wedge \lfloor V\rfloor$ **by** *blast* — S5: preorder + symmetric

---

[9] The *de dicto/de re* distinction is used regularly in the philosophy of language for disambiguation of sentences involving intensional contexts.

[10] Implication can also be proven in the reverse direction (which is not needed for our purposes). Using these definitions, we can derive axioms for the most common modal logics (see also [5]). Thereby we are free to use either the semantic constraints or the related *Sahlqvist* axioms. Here we provide both versions. In what follows we use the semantic constraints for improved performance.

3   Gödel's Ontological Argument

3.1   Part I - God's Existence Is Possible

Gödel's particular version of the argument is a direct descendant of that of Leibniz, which in turn derives from one of Descartes. His argument relies on proving *(T1) 'Positive properties are possibly instantiated'*, which together with *(T2) 'God is a positive property'* directly implies the conclusion. In order to prove *T1*, Gödel assumes *(A2) 'Any property entailed by a positive property is positive'*. As we will see, the success of this argumentation depends on how we formalize our notion of entailment.

> **abbreviation** *Entails*::↑⟨↑⟨e⟩,↑⟨e⟩⟩ (**infix**⇒) **where** $X \Rightarrow Y \equiv \Box(\forall^A z.\ X z \rightarrow Y z)$
> **lemma** $\lfloor (\lambda x\ w.\ x \neq x) \Rightarrow \chi \rfloor$ **by** *simp* — an impossible property entails anything
> **lemma** $\lfloor \neg(\varphi \Rightarrow \chi) \rightarrow \Diamond \exists^A \varphi \rfloor$ **by** *auto* — possible instantiation of φ implicit

The definition of property entailment introduced by Gödel can be criticized on the grounds that it lacks some notion of relevance and is therefore exposed to the paradoxes of material implication. In particular, when we assert that property A does not entail property B, we implicitly assume that A is possibly instantiated. Conversely, an impossible property (like being a round square) entails any property (like being a triangle). It is precisely by virtue of these paradoxes that Gödel manages to prove *T1*.[11]

> **consts** *Positiveness*::↑⟨↑⟨e⟩⟩ (𝒫) — positiveness applies to intensional predicates
> **abbreviation** *Existence*::↑⟨e⟩ (E!) — object-language existence predicate
>   **where** $E!\ x \equiv \lambda w.\ (\exists^A y.\ y \approx x)\ w$

Gödel's axioms for the first part essentially say that (A1) either a property or its negation must be positive, (A2) positive properties are closed under entailment and (A3) also closed under conjunction.

> **abbreviation** *appliesToPositiveProps*::↑⟨↑⟨↑⟨e⟩⟩⟩ (*pos*) **where**
> $pos\ Z \equiv \forall X.\ Z X \rightarrow \mathcal{P} X$
> **abbreviation** *intersectionOf*::↑⟨↑⟨e⟩,↑⟨↑⟨e⟩⟩⟩ (*intersec*) **where**
> $intersec\ X Z \equiv \Box(\forall x.(X x \leftrightarrow (\forall Y.\ (Z Y) \rightarrow (Y x))))$
> **axiomatization where**
> *A1a*: $\lfloor \forall X.\ \mathcal{P}\ (\rightarrow X) \rightarrow \neg(\mathcal{P} X) \rfloor$ **and**
> *A1b*: $\lfloor \forall X.\ \neg(\mathcal{P} X) \rightarrow \mathcal{P}\ (\rightarrow X) \rfloor$ **and**
> *A2*: $\lfloor \forall X Y.(\mathcal{P} X \wedge (X \Rightarrow Y)) \rightarrow \mathcal{P} Y \rfloor$ **and**
> *A3*: $\lfloor \forall Z X.\ (pos\ Z \wedge intersec\ X Z) \rightarrow \mathcal{P} X \rfloor$

> **lemma** *True* **nitpick**[*satisfy*] **oops**   — model found: axioms are consistent
> **lemma** $\lfloor D \rfloor$ **using** *A1a A1b A2* **by** *blast* — D axiom is implicitly assumed

Positive properties are possibly instantiated.

---

[11] To prove T1, the fact is used that positive properties cannot *entail* negative ones (A2), from which the possible instantiation of positive properties follows. A computer-formalization of Leibniz's theory of concepts can be found in [1], where the notion of *concept containment* in contrast to ordinary *property entailment* is discussed.

theorem $T1$: $\lfloor \forall X.\ \mathcal{P}\ X \to \Diamond \exists^A X \rfloor$ **using** $A1a\ A2$ **by** *blast*

Being Godlike is defined as having all (and only) positive properties.

abbreviation $God{::}{\uparrow}\langle e \rangle$ (G) **where** $G \equiv (\lambda x.\ \forall Y.\ \mathcal{P}\ Y \to Y\ x)$
abbreviation $God\text{-}star{::}{\uparrow}\langle e \rangle$ $(G*)$ **where** $G* \equiv (\lambda x.\ \forall Y.\ \mathcal{P}\ Y \leftrightarrow Y\ x)$
lemma $GodDefsAreEquivalent$: $\lfloor \forall x.\ G\ x \leftrightarrow G*\ x \rfloor$ **using** $A1b$ **by** *force*

While Leibniz provides an informal proof for the compatibility of all perfections, Gödel postulates this as $A3$ (the conjunction of *any* collection of positive properties is positive), which is a third-order axiom. As shown below, the only use of $A3$ is to prove that being Godlike is positive ($T2$). Dana Scott, apparently noting this, proposed taking it directly as an axiom (see [15], p. 152).[12]

theorem $T2$: $\lfloor \mathcal{P}\ G \rfloor$ **proof** –
{ **fix** w
  have 1: $((pos\ \mathcal{P}) \wedge (intersec\ G\ \mathcal{P}))\ w$ **by** *simp*
  have $(\forall Z\ X.\ (pos\ Z \wedge intersec\ X\ Z) \to \mathcal{P}\ X)\ w$ **using** $A3$ **by** $(rule\ allE)$
  hence $(((pos\ \mathcal{P}) \wedge (intersec\ G\ \mathcal{P})) \to \mathcal{P}\ G)\ w$ **using** $allE$ **by** $(rule\ allE)$
  hence $((pos\ \mathcal{P} \wedge intersec\ G\ \mathcal{P})\ w) \longrightarrow \mathcal{P}\ G\ w$ **by** *simp*
  hence $\mathcal{P}\ G\ w$ **using** 1 **by** $(rule\ mp)$
} **thus** $?thesis$ **by** $(rule\ allI)$
qed

Conclusion for the first part: Possibly God exists.

theorem $T3$: $\lfloor \Diamond \exists^A G \rfloor$ **using** $T1\ T2$ **by** *simp*

3.2   Part II - God's Existence Is Necessary, if Possible

We show here that some additional (philosophically controversial) assumptions are needed to prove the argument's conclusion, including an *essentialist* premise and the *S5* axioms. (Gödel's resp. Scott's original version works in *extensional* HOML already for modal logic B [8,9]). Further derived results like monotheism and absence of free will are also discussed.

axiomatization where $A4a$: $\lfloor \forall X.\ \mathcal{P}\ X \to \Box(\mathcal{P}\ X) \rfloor$

$A4b$ was originally assumed by Gödel as an axiom. We can now prove it.

lemma $A4b$: $\lfloor \forall X.\ \neg(\mathcal{P}\ X) \to \Box\neg(\mathcal{P}\ X) \rfloor$ **using** $A1a\ A1b\ A4a$ **by** *blast*
lemma $True$ **nitpick**$[satisfy]$ **oops** — model found: all axioms A1-4 consistent

Axiom $A4a$ and its consequence $A4b$ together imply that $\mathcal{P}$ satisfies Fitting's *stability conditions* ([15], p. 124). This means $\mathcal{P}$ designates rigidly. Note that this makes for an *essentialist* assumption which may be considered controversial by some philosophers: every property considered positive in our world (e.g. honesty) is necessarily so.

lemma $\lfloor rigid\ \mathcal{P} \rfloor$ **using** $A4a\ A4b$ **by** *blast*

---

[12] We provide a proof in Isabelle/Isar, a language specifically tailored for writing proofs that are both computer- and human-readable. We refer the reader to [17] for other proofs not shown in this article.

Gödel defines a particular notion of essence. Y is an essence of x iff Y *entails* every other property x possesses.[13]

abbreviation *Essence*::↑⟨↑⟨e⟩,e⟩ ($\mathcal{E}$) **where** $\mathcal{E}\ Y\ x \equiv Y\ x \wedge (\forall Z.\ Z\ x \to Y \Rrightarrow Z)$
abbreviation *beingIdenticalTo*::e⇒↑⟨e⟩ (*id*) **where** $id\ x \equiv (\lambda y.\ y \approx x)$

Being Godlike is an essential property.

lemma *GodIsEssential*: $\lfloor \forall x.\ G\ x \to (\mathcal{E}\ G\ x) \rfloor$ **using** *A1b A4a* **by** *metis*

Something can have only *one* essence.

lemma $\lfloor \forall X\ Y\ z.\ (\mathcal{E}\ X\ z \wedge \mathcal{E}\ Y\ z) \to (X \Rrightarrow Y) \rfloor$ **by** *meson*

An essential property offers a complete characterization of an individual.

lemma *EssencesCharacterizeCompletely*: $\lfloor \forall X\ Y.\ \mathcal{E}\ X\ y \to (X \Rrightarrow (id\ y)) \rfloor$
proof (*rule ccontr*) — Isar proof by contradiction not shown here

Gödel introduces a particular notion of *necessary existence* as the property something has, provided any essence of it is necessarily instantiated.

abbreviation *necessaryExistencePredicate*::↑⟨e⟩ (*NE*)
where $NE\ x \equiv (\lambda w.\ (\forall Y.\ \mathcal{E}\ Y\ x \to \Box \exists^A\ Y)\ w)$

axiomatization where *A5*: $\lfloor \mathcal{P}\ NE \rfloor$ — necessary existence is a positive property
lemma *True* **nitpick**[*satisfy*] **oops** — model found: so far all axioms consistent

(Possibilist) existence of God implies its necessary (actualist) existence.

theorem *T4*: $\lfloor \exists\ G \to \Box \exists^A\ G \rfloor$ **proof** – – not shown

We postulate the *S5* axioms (via *Sahlqvist correspondence*) separately, in order to get more detailed information about their relevance in the proofs below.

axiomatization where
ax-T: *reflexive aRel* **and** *ax-B*: *symmetric aRel* **and** *ax-IV*: *transitive aRel*

lemma *True* **nitpick**[*satisfy*] **oops** — model found: axioms still consistent

Possible existence of God implies its necessary (actualist) existence (note that we only rely on axioms *B* and *IV*).

theorem *T5*: $\lfloor \Diamond \exists\ G \rfloor \longrightarrow \lfloor \Box \exists^A\ G \rfloor$ **proof** – – not shown
theorem *GodExistsNecessarily*: $\lfloor \Box \exists^A\ G \rfloor$ **using** *T3 T5* **by** *metis*
lemma *GodExistenceIsValid*: $\lfloor \exists^A\ G \rfloor$ **using** *GodExistsNecessarily ax-T* **by** *auto*

Monotheism for non-normal models (using Leibniz equality) follows directly from God having all and only positive properties, but the proof for normal models is trickier. We need to consider previous results ([15], p. 162).

lemma *Monotheism-LeibnizEq*: $\lfloor \forall x.\ G* \ x \to (\forall y.\ G* \ y \to x \approx^L y) \rfloor$ **by** *meson*
lemma *Monotheism-normal*: $\lfloor \exists x.\forall y.\ G\ y \leftrightarrow x \approx y \rfloor$ **proof** – – not shown

Fitting [15] also discusses the objection raised by Sobel [27], who argues that Gödel's axiom system is too strong since it implies that whatever is the case is so

---

[13] Essence is defined here (and in Fitting's variant) in the version of Scott; Gödel's original version leads to the inconsistency reported in [9,10].

necessarily: the modal system collapses. In the context of our S5 axioms, we can formalize Sobel's argument and prove modal collapse valid ([15], pp. 163–164).

lemma *useful*: $(\forall x.\ \varphi\ x \longrightarrow \psi) \implies ((\exists x.\ \varphi\ x) \longrightarrow \psi)$ **by** *simp*
lemma *ModalCollapse*: $\lfloor \forall \varPhi.\ \varPhi \to \Box\varPhi \rfloor$ **proof** –
{ **fix** w
    { **fix** Q
    have $(\forall x.\ G\ x \to (\mathcal{E}\ G\ x))\ w$ **using** *GodIsEssential* **by** (*rule allE*)
    hence $\forall x.\ G\ x\ w \longrightarrow (Q \to \Box(\forall^A z.\ G\ z \to Q))\ w$ **by** *force*
    hence 1: $(\exists x.\ G\ x\ w) \longrightarrow ((Q \to \Box(\forall^A z.\ G\ z \to Q))\ w)$ **by** (*rule useful*)
    have $\exists x.\ G\ x\ w$ **using** *GodExistenceIsValid* **by** *auto*
    from 1 *this* **have** $(Q \to \Box(\forall^A z.\ G\ z \to Q))\ w$ **by** (*rule mp*)
    hence $(Q \to \Box((\exists^A z.\ G\ z) \to Q))\ w$ **using** *useful* **by** *blast*
    hence $(Q \to (\Box(\exists^A z.\ G\ z) \to \Box Q))\ w$ **by** *simp*
    hence $(Q \to \Box Q)\ w$ **using** *GodExistsNecessarily* **by** *simp*
    } **hence** $(\forall \varPhi.\ \varPhi \to \Box\ \varPhi)\ w$ **by** (*rule allI*)
} **thus** *?thesis* **by** (*rule allI*)
qed

4   Fitting's Variant

In this section we consider Fitting's solution to the objections raised in his discussion of Gödel's Argument ([15], pp. 164–169), especially the problem of modal collapse, which has been metaphysically interpreted as implying a rejection of free will. In Gödel's variant, positiveness and essence were thought of as predicates applying to *intensional* properties and correspondingly formalized using intensional types for their arguments ($\uparrow\langle\uparrow\langle e\rangle\rangle$ and $\uparrow\langle\uparrow\langle e\rangle, e\rangle$ respectively). In this variant, Fitting chooses to reformulate these definitions using *extensional* types ($\uparrow\langle\langle e\rangle\rangle$ and $\uparrow\langle\langle e\rangle, e\rangle$) instead, and makes the corresponding adjustments to the rest of the argument (to ensure type correctness). This has some philosophical repercussions; e.g. while we could say before that honesty (as concept) was a positive property, now we can only talk of its extension at some world and say of some group of people that they are honest (necessarily honest, in fact, because $\mathcal{P}$ has also been proven 'rigid' in this variant).[14]

consts *Positiveness*::$\uparrow\langle\langle e\rangle\rangle$ ($\mathcal{P}$)
abbreviation *Entails*::$\uparrow\langle\langle e\rangle,\langle e\rangle\rangle$ (**infix**$\Rightarrow$) **where** $X \Rightarrow Y \equiv \Box(\forall^A z.\ (\!| X\ z |\!) \to (\!| Y\ z |\!))$
abbreviation *Essence*::$\uparrow\langle\langle e\rangle, e\rangle$ ($\mathcal{E}$) **where** $\mathcal{E}\ Y\ x \equiv (\!| Y\ x |\!) \wedge (\forall Z.(\!| Z\ x |\!) \to (Y \Rightarrow Z))$

Axioms and theorems remain essentially the same. Particularly (T2) $\lfloor \mathcal{P}\ \downarrow G \rfloor$ and (A5) $\lfloor \mathcal{P}\ \downarrow NE \rfloor$ work with *relativized* extensional terms now.

theorem *T1*: $\lfloor \forall X::\langle e\rangle.\ \mathcal{P}\ X \to \Diamond(\exists^A z.\ (\!| X\ z |\!)) \rfloor$ **using** *A1a A2* **by** *blast*
theorem *T3deRe*: $\lfloor (\lambda X.\ \Diamond\exists^A\ X)\ \downarrow G \rfloor$ **using** *T1 T2* **by** *simp*
lemma *GodIsEssential*: $\lfloor \forall x.\ G\ x \to ((\mathcal{E}\ \downarrow_1 G)\ x) \rfloor$ **using** *A1b* **by** *metis*

---

[14] In what follows, the '$(\!|$-$|\!)$' parentheses are used to convert an extensional object into its 'rigid' intensional counterpart (e.g. $(\!|\varphi|\!) \equiv \lambda w.\ \varphi$).

The following theorem could be formalized in two variants[15] (drawing on the *de re/de dicto* distinction). We prove both of them valid and show how the argument splits, culminating in two non-equivalent versions of the conclusion, both of which are proven valid.

lemma *T4v1*: $\lfloor \exists \downarrow G \to \Box \exists^A \downarrow G \rfloor$ **proof** – — not shown
lemma *T4v2*: $\lfloor \exists \downarrow G \to ((\lambda X. \Box \exists^A X) \downarrow G) \rfloor$ **using** *A4a T4v1* **by** *metis*

In contrast to Gödel's version (as presented by Fitting), the following theorems can be proven in logic K (the $S5$ axioms are no longer needed).

lemma *T5v1*:$\lfloor \Diamond \exists \downarrow G \rfloor \longrightarrow \lfloor \Box \exists^A \downarrow G \rfloor$ **using** *T4v1 T3deRe* **by** *metis*
lemma *T5v2*:$\lfloor (\lambda X. \Diamond \exists^A X) \downarrow G \rfloor \longrightarrow \lfloor (\lambda X. \Box \exists^A X) \downarrow G \rfloor$ **using** *T4v2* **by** *blast*

Necessary Existence of God (*de dicto* and *de re* readings).

lemma *GodNecExists-deDicto*: $\lfloor \Box \exists^A \downarrow G \rfloor$ **using** *T3deRe T4v1* **by** *blast*
lemma *GodNecExists-deRe*: $\lfloor (\lambda X. \Box \exists^A X) \downarrow G \rfloor$ **using** *T3deRe T5v2* **by** *blast*

Modal collapse is countersatisfiable even in $S5$. Note that countermodels with a cardinality of *one* for the domain of individuals are found by *Nitpick* (the countermodel shown in Fitting's book has cardinality of *two*).

lemma *equivalence aRel*$\Longrightarrow \lfloor \forall \Phi. \Phi \to \Box \Phi \rfloor$ **nitpick**[*card e=1, card w=2*] **oops**

5   Anderson's Variant

In this section, we verify Anderson's emendation of Gödel's argument [3], as presented by Fitting ([15], pp. 169–171). In the previous variants there were no 'indifferent' properties, either a property or its negation had to be positive. Anderson makes room for 'indifferent' properties by dropping axiom *A1b* ($\lfloor \forall X. \neg(\mathcal{P} X) \to \mathcal{P} (\neg X) \rfloor$). As a consequence, he changes the following definitions to ensure argument's validity.

abbreviation *God*::$\uparrow\langle e \rangle$ (*G*) **where** $G \equiv \lambda x. \forall Y. (\mathcal{P} Y) \leftrightarrow \Box(Y x)$
abbreviation *Essence*::$\uparrow\langle\uparrow\langle e\rangle,e\rangle$ (*$\mathcal{E}$*) **where** $\mathcal{E} Y x \equiv (\forall Z. \Box(Z x) \leftrightarrow Y \Rightarrow Z)$

There is now the requirement that a Godlike being must have positive properties *necessarily*. For the definition of essence, Scott's addition [25], that the essence of an object actually applies to the object, is dropped. A necessity operator has been introduced instead.[16]

The rest of the argument is essentially similar to Gödel's (also in $S5$ logic).

theorem *T1*: $\lfloor \forall X. \mathcal{P} X \to \Diamond \exists^A X \rfloor$ **using** *A1a A2* **by** *blast*
theorem *T3*: $\lfloor \Diamond \exists^A G \rfloor$ **using** *T1 T2* **by** *simp*

If g is Godlike, the property of being Godlike is its essence.[17]

---

[15] Fitting's original treatment in [15] left several details unspecified and we had to fill in the gaps by choosing appropriate formalization variants (see [17] for details).

[16] Gödel's original axioms (without Scott's addition) are proven inconsistent in [9].

[17] This theorem's proof could be completely automatized for Gödel's and Fitting's variants. For Anderson's version however, we had to reproduce in Isabelle/HOL the original natural-language proof given by Anderson (see [3], Theorem 2*, p. 296).

theorem *GodIsEssential*: $\lfloor \forall x.\ G\ x \rightarrow (\mathcal{E}\ G\ x) \rfloor$ **proof** − — not shown

The necessary existence of God follows from its possible existence.

theorem *T5*: $\lfloor \Diamond \exists\ G \rfloor \longrightarrow \lfloor \Box \exists^A\ G \rfloor$ **proof** − — not shown

The conclusion could be proven (with one fewer axiom, though more complex definitions) and *Nitpick* is able to find a countermodel for the *modal collapse*.

lemma *GodExistsNecessarily*: $\lfloor \Box \exists^A\ G \rfloor$ **using** *T3 T5* **by** *metis*
lemma *ModalCollapse*: $\lfloor \forall \varPhi.\ \varPhi \rightarrow \Box \varPhi \rfloor$ **nitpick oops** — countersatisfiable

6 Conclusion

We presented a shallow semantic embedding in Isabelle/HOL for an intensional higher-order modal logic (a successor of Montague/Gallin intensional logics) and employed this logic to formalize and verify three different variants of the ontological argument: the first one by Gödel himself (resp. Scott), the second one by Fitting and the last one by Anderson.

By employing our embedding of IHOML in Isabelle/HOL, we could not only verify Fitting's results, but also guarantee consistency of axioms. Moreover, for many theorems we could prove stronger versions and find better countermodels (i.e. with smaller cardinality) than the ones presented by Fitting. Another interesting aspect was the possibility to explore the implications of alternative formalizations of axioms and theorems which shed light on interesting philosophical issues concerning entailment, essentialism and free will.

The latest developments in automated theorem proving, in combination with the embedding approach, allow us to engage in much better experimentation during the formalization and assessment of arguments than ever before. The potential reduction (of several orders of magnitude) in the time needed for proving or disproving theorems (compared to pen-and-paper proofs), results in almost real-time feedback about the suitability of our speculations. The practical benefits of computer-supported argumentation go beyond mere quantitative aspects (easier, faster and more reliable proofs). The advantages are also qualitative, since a significantly different approach to argumentation is fostered: We can now work iteratively (by trial-and-error) on an argument by making gradual adjustments to its definitions, axioms and theorems. This allows us to continuously expose and revise the assumptions we indirectly commit ourselves to every time we opt for some particular formalization.

References

1. Alama, J., Oppenheimer, P.E., Zalta, E.N.: Automating Leibniz's theory of concepts. In: Felty, A.P., Middeldorp, A. (eds.) CADE 2015. LNCS, vol. 9195, pp. 73–97. Springer, Cham (2015). doi:10.1007/978-3-319-21401-6_4
2. Anderson, A., Gettings, M.: Gödel ontological proof revisited. In: Hajek, P. (ed.) Gödel 1996: Logical Foundations of Mathematics, Computer Science, and Physics. Lecture Notes in Logic, vol. 6, pp. 167–172. Springer (2001)

3. Anderson, C.: Some emendations of Gödel's ontological proof. Faith Philos. **7**(3), 291–303 (1990)
4. Benzmüller, C.: Universal reasoning, rational argumentation and human-machine interaction. arXiv (2017). http://arxiv.org/abs/1703.09620
5. Benzmüller, C., Claus, M., Sultana, N.: Systematic verification of the modal logic cube in Isabelle/HOL. In: Kaliszyk, C., Paskevich, A. (eds.) PxTP 2015, EPTCS, Berlin, Germany, vol. 186, pp. 27–41 (2015)
6. Benzmüller, C., Paulson, L.: Quantified multimodal logics in simple type theory. Logica Univers. (Special Issue on Multimodal Logics) **7**(1), 7–20 (2013)
7. Benzmüller, C., Weber, L., Woltzenlogel-Paleo, B.: Computer-assisted analysis of the Anderson-Hájek controversy. Logica Univers. **11**(1), 139–151 (2017)
8. Benzmüller, C., Woltzenlogel Paleo, B.: Automating Gödel's ontological proof of God's existence with higher-order automated theorem provers. In: Schaub, T., Friedrich, G., O'Sullivan, B. (eds.) ECAI 2014. Frontiers in Artificial Intelligence and Applications, vol. 263, pp. 93–98. IOS Press (2014)
9. Benzmüller, C., Woltzenlogel Paleo, B.: The inconsistency in Gödel's ontological argument: a success story for AI in metaphysics. In: IJCAI 2016 (2016)
10. Benzmüller, C., Woltzenlogel Paleo, B.: An object-logic explanation for the inconsistency in Gödel's ontological theory (extended abstract). In: Helmert, M., Wotawa, F. (eds.) KI 2016: Advances in Artificial Intelligence. LNAI, vol. 9904, pp. 205–244. Springer, Berlin (2016)
11. Bjørdal, F.: Understanding Gödel's ontological argument. In: Childers, T. (ed.) The Logica Yearbook 1998. Filosofia (1999)
12. Blanchette, J.C., Nipkow, T.: Nitpick: a counterexample generator for higher-order logic based on a relational model finder. In: Kaufmann, M., Paulson, L.C. (eds.) ITP 2010. LNCS, vol. 6172, pp. 131–146. Springer, Heidelberg (2010). doi:10.1007/978-3-642-14052-5_11
13. Church, A.: A formulation of the simple theory of types. J. Symbol. Logic **5**, 56–68 (1940)
14. Fitelson, B., Zalta, E.N.: Steps toward a computational metaphysics. J. Philos. Logic **36**(2), 227–247 (2007)
15. Fitting, M.: Types, Tableaus and Gödel's God. Kluwer, Dordrecht (2002)
16. Fitting, M., Mendelsohn, R.: First-Order Modal Logic. Synthese Library, vol. 277. Kluwer, Dordrecht (1998)
17. Fuenmayor, D., Benzmüller, C.: Types, Tableaus and Gödel's God in Isabelle/HOL. Archive of Formal Proofs (2017). Formally verified with Isabelle/HOL
18. Gallin, D.: Intensional and Higher-Order Modal Logic. N.-Holland, Amsterdam (1975)
19. Gödel, K.: Appx. A: notes in Kurt Gödel's hand. In: [27], pp. 144–145 (2004)
20. Hájek, P.: A new small emendation of Gödel's ontological proof. Studia Logica **71**(2), 149–164 (2002)
21. Kripke, S.: Naming and Necessity. Harvard University Press, Cambridge (1980)
22. Nipkow, T., Wenzel, M., Paulson, L.C. (eds.): Isabelle/HOL — A Proof Assistant for Higher-Order Logic. LNCS, vol. 2283. Springer, Heidelberg (2002)
23. Oppenheimera, P., Zalta, E.: A computationally-discovered simplification of the ontological argument. Australas. J. Philos. **89**(2), 333–349 (2011)
24. Rushby, J.: The ontological argument in PVS. In: Proceedings of CAV Workshop "Fun With Formal Methods", St. Petersburg, Russia (2013)
25. Scott, D.: Appx.B: notes in Dana Scott's hand. In: [27], pp. 145–146 (2004)
26. Sobel, J.: Gödel's ontological proof. In: On Being and Saying. Essays for Richard Cartwright, pp. 241–261. MIT Press (1987)

27. Sobel, J.: Logic and Theism: Arguments for and Against Beliefs in God. Cambridge U. Press, Cambridge (2004)
28. Wisniewski, M., Steen, A., Benzmüller, C.: Einsatz von Theorembeweisern in der Lehre. In: Schwill, A., Lucke, U. (eds.) Hochschuldidaktik der Informatik: 7. Fachtagung des GI-Fachbereichs Informatik und Ausbildung/Didaktik der Informatik, 13–14 September 2016 an der Universität Potsdam, Commentarii informaticae didacticae (CID), Potsdam, Germany (2016)

Real-Time Public Transport Delay Prediction for Situation-Aware Routing

Lukas Heppe and Thomas Liebig[✉]

Computer Science VIII: Artificial Intelligence Unit,
TU Dortmund University, Dortmund, Germany
{lukas.heppe,thomas.liebig}@tu-dortmund.de
http://www-ai.cs.uni-dortmund.de/

Abstract. Situation-aware route planning gathers increasing interest. The proliferation of various sensor technologies in smart cities allows the incorporation of real-time data and its predictions in the trip planning process. We present a system for individual multi-modal trip planning that incorporates predictions of future public transport delays in routing. Future delay times are computed by a Spatio-Temporal-Random-Field based on a stream of current vehicle positions. The conditioning of spatial regression on intermediate predictions of a discrete probabilistic graphical model allows to incorporate historical data, streamed online data and a rich dependency structure at the same time. We demonstrate the system with a real-world use-case at Warsaw city, Poland.

1 Introduction

With the emergence of smart cities, trip computation received increased attention. While conventional trip computation algorithms minimize a static cost function and provide an optimal route for an unlikely stationary traffic situation with constant costs. Traffic situations are not stationary but vary over time, e.g. at rush hour commuters cause traffic jams at streets which are almost empty at night. The integration of various sensor systems (e.g. crowdsourcing, video cameras, automatic traffic loops, [20]) in the smart city ecosystem enables incorporation of real-time measurements in intelligent traffic systems, and their predictions [21].

In this work, we target, for the first time, the question how to incorporate predictions of delays in the public transport network in multi-modal trip planning. In result, we aim to obtain a smart trip planner that supports citizens of a smart city to make informed decisions on their transit route. The possible benefits for the informed travelers are:

1. A smart decision among different modes of transportation,
2. a smart choice among different transit routes,
3. an informed decision among different initial walking directions, or
4. different transit stops.

© Springer International Publishing AG 2017
G. Kern-Isberner et al. (Eds.): KI 2017, LNAI 10505, pp. 128–141, 2017.
DOI: 10.1007/978-3-319-67190-1_10

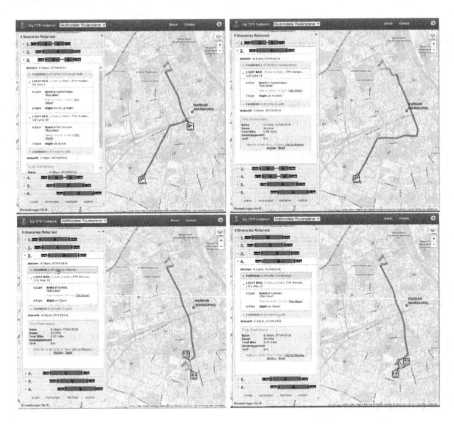

Fig. 1. Exemplified trips for same start and goal. Top: different tram lines are suggested, bottom: different initial walking direction is suggested. Best viewed in color. (Color figure online)

We exemplify points two and three next in Warsaw, the capital of Poland, for different representative cases, see Fig. 1. In the two subfigures on the top same origin destination pairs lead to different transit suggestions. Different initial walking directions are suggested in the lower subfigures of Fig. 1.

As seen in previous examples, the prediction of delay supports planning of situation-aware trips in advance (not just when travelling). This enables a smart decision for the very first step and even enables decision to start a trip earlier or later (depending on expected transfer reachability). Imagine for example, dining with your friends in the suburbs of your city. On your return, our trip planner provides you with the information that the required transfer in the city centre (from the tram in the suburbs to your means of transportation) is likely not to be reached (Note that we incorporate predictions based on the current situation in contrast to existing planners that incorporate just current information). Based on this information, you may stay longer with your friends instead of useless waiting outside at the tram station.

Our approach towards this situation-aware trip planner detects current and past delays of transit vehicles based on a comparison of their live GPS streams with the scheduled arrival times. Of course, other sensor technology e.g. Bluetooth would have been also possible [13,23], but with stationary sensors you easily get problems of sensor placement [16] and a stream of GPS data from the vehicles is available in the city of Warsaw. The detected delays are used to estimate future delays by a probabilistic graphical model. These real-time predictions are incorporated in route computations generated with OpenTripPlanner an open source trip planning tool. The data, our approach bases on, are

- the street network,
- public transport schedules and
- a real-time stream of the current vehicle positions.

We perform our experiments in Warsaw, Poland, and use open data provided via open geospatial consortium standardized protocols and interfaces.

Our paper is structured as follows. Section 2 reviews current state-of-the-art for routing algorithms and positions our work. Afterwards, we present the real-time architecture of our approach that uses predictions-as-a-service. In Sect. 4 we present the application of an existing Spatio-Temporal-Random-Field (STRF) model to the real-time tram delay prediction task. In Sect. 5 we highlight the application of our approach and discuss future directions for improvement in the closing Sect. 6.

2   Related Work

The task to plan a route from one start location to a target location is called trip planning, when multiple means of transportation (also called 'travel modes') are involved this becomes multi-modal trip planning. The integration of transportation systems with personal constraints, residential and city services systems can offer real promise for implementing an intelligent transportation infrastructure that can efficiently address issues beyond congestion, resiliency and safety. Trip planning operates on a graph representation of the road and transit network the so-called traffic network G consisting of vertices V (e.g. junctions) and connecting edges E (e.g. streets). A cost function maps each edge to a positive number that denotes how much it would 'cost' to travel the corresponding segment. The cost function needs to be homogeneous throughout the traffic network, but can be defined in several ways, such that it holds the most important aspects: for example length of the segment, travel time, or comfortableness. With a given start and end location in the traffic network, trip planning searches the path that connects start and goal and minimizes the cost.

Several algorithms exist to compute this minimizing path. Dijkstra [5] proposes a best-first traversal of the graph where the candidates for traversal are hold in a priority-queue. In the slightly modified version of the algorithm A* [9] the order in the priority-queue for the traversal not only depends on the cumulated costs to reach a vertex in the graph but also on the expected costs to reach the goal from this vertex. Bound by Minkowski's inequality, whereas $||x + y||_p \leq ||x||_p + ||y||_p$ (known as triangle inequality for $p = 2$), A* prunes the search space in comparison to Dijkstra's Algorithm. A sound heuristic for the remaining cost estimation is the geographical distance that is always lower than the road-based distance. In multi-modal trip planning multiple of these traffic networks G (one for each mode) are linked together at locations where it is possible to switch from one mode to another (transfer vertices). Multi-modal trip planning requires a consistent cost function which is applicable to all parts of the traffic network and thus to all modes of transportation.

In case of static cost functions contraction hierarchies [7] are a data structure that speeds-up the A* algorithm and enables trip calculation in large traffic networks at European scale. Instead of searching the shortest path directly within the traffic network, contraction hierarchies reduce the search space to the most important ones. In a preprocessing step these important segments are identified (based on the topology) and the network is extended by edges between these important links.

For transit networks, Transfer Pattern [1] provides a speed-up heuristic. Transfer Pattern exploit that a transit network consists of central locations (hubs as major airports or train stations) where most people from a particular region have to change the means of transportation. These (multi-modal) routing heuristics are great for trip computation in embedded devices, and according to [2] they provide sufficient accuracy in case of dynamic cost functions (based on estimations and predictions of traffic). However, dynamic transfer patterns [14] incorporate also unexpected novel transfers that were enabled by the delay itself.

In this work, we focus on the incorporation of dynamic cost estimates in multi-modal trip planning. Thus, we combine a real-time prediction of delay in transit networks with the trip computation. Previous works introduce already the incorporation of traffic predictions in vehicular path finding. E.g. the work in [15] proposes situation-aware routing with real-time predictions. Their method bases on a spatio-temporal graphical model that provides estimates for future traffic values based on current and past observations. These spatio-temporal estimates serve as cost function for routing and traffic jams were avoided. The work in [19] uses Conditional Random Fields for future traffic prediction, but lacks the inclusion in the trip planning application.

In contrast to vehicular traffic, trams and trains can not overtake, and vehicles in transit networks wait for each others (e.g. connecting trains), this causes delays to propagate differently than vehicular traffic jams. In addition, two modes of transportation may share the same physical resource (e.g. buses or trams riding on vehicular street). Thus, two forms of delays in transit networks are distinguished in literature: 1) a vehicle is late due to own reasons, and 2) other vehicles are late caused by the former [18].

Several models for transit delays are reported in literature. The work in [4] assumes independence. In contrast, [8] allows delays to cumulate. Sophisticated models incorporate dependencies among the vehicles into the delay [11]. In the trip planning application it is a crucial requirement to the prediction model to provide real-time predictions. Thus, we highlight two recent works on delay prediction and delay recognition: [6] applies queueing theory and assumes delays to aggregate, [24] detects delays and unexpected vehicle movement in real-time from the GPS traces.

In contrast, our approach will be a probabilistic one, where similar to the approach in [6] the delay of a vehicle at the stops in a trip depends on its predecessors and the delay event that a vehicle is delayed is detected directly from its GPS stream [24] using spatio-temporal constraints, in the experiments section we compare our approach to [6].

3   Architecture

Our proposed system comprises two layers (1) a real-time event detection layer that processes the incoming GPS data stream of the transit vehicles (detection of delay events and estimation of future delays), and (2) an asynchronous trip planning layer which is triggered by user-generated trip queries and incorporates current predictions[1].

In the event detection layer, every single GPS data is processed and current delays of the vehicles are detected, furthermore this information is used to update (in real-time) predictions of the expected delay for the whole day. The survey in [22] provides a list of possible spatio-temporal event detection and pattern matching frameworks depending on the required expressiveness of the spatio-temporal pattern. We decide to use a streams framework and pose spatio-temporal constraints as real-time operators to the stream of GPS data points.

The asynchronous trip planning layer incorporates the predictions as a service and utilizes them for multi-modal trip computations. In result, we obtain situation-aware routes. Similar to [15], we base our trip planning on the Open-TripPlanner (OTP) implementation. This open source routing software provides interfaces for inclusion of transit schedules (in the commonly used General Transit Feed Specification (GTFS) standard[2]) and OpenStreetMap (see Fig. 2).

3.1   OpenTripPlanner

OpenTripPlanner (OTP) is an open source initiative for multi-modal route computation. The traffic network for route computation is generated using open data from OpenStreetMap and public transport schedules (in the widely used Google Transit Feed Standard protocol). Thus, OpenTripPlanner is an open source trip planner that connects to open data and provides route calculation capabilities for multiple modes of transportation (e.g. walking, transit) and their combinations.

---

[1] Our source code and the required virtual machine are publicly available as vagrant box at https://bitbucket.org/tliebig/developvm.

[2] https://developers.google.com/transit/gtfs/.

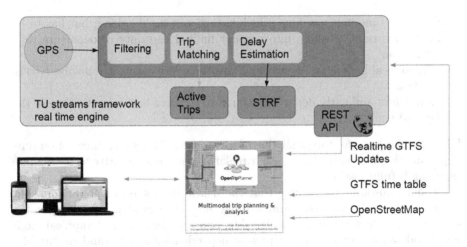

Fig. 2. Architecture of our proposed trip planner system. The real-time processing of the GPS streams detects delays of the vehicles, assigns them to trips and estimates real-time predictions of future delays. By a REST server these delays are handed in GTFS-realtime format to the OpenTripPlanner server. The user triggers a trip query with his/her browser and during trip computation real-time predictions are incorporated. Best viewed in color. (Color figure online)

3.2 Streams Framework

We use TU streams framework as real-time engine [3]. It contains basic real-time machine learning algorithms and provides any-time predictions-as-a-service functionality. Furthermore it seamlessly compiles to Apache Kafka or Flink and thus can be integrated in state-of-the-art distributed real-time architectures.

The steps for delay estimation from the GPS stream of the transit vehicle locations are:

- Data cleaning: Removal of duplicates and noisy GPS recordings.
- Plausibility Test: Test whether the recorded GPS location is plausible given previous recordings.
- Trip Matching: Match the position of the vehicle to a trip and line of the transit graph.
- Delay Estimation: Estimate current delay of the vehicles using the assigned trip and line information, and matching it to the schedule.
- Delay Prediction: Compute estimates of future delays given the training data and past and current delay.

The latter predictions are served to OpenTripPlanner in GTFS realtime format via a Representational State Transfer (REST) webserver interface.

4   Tram Delay Prediction with STRF

The preliminary analysis of tram location data compared with schedule data, confirms the findings of [17], namely that:

– departure time not matching schedule time can be identified, but has to be analysed carefully, taking into account limited certainty of departure time estimation,
– still, noticeable number of early and late departure events can be observed in the data,
– tram delays and early departures significantly vary based on the time of the day and tram line.

This provides basis for the prediction of tram delays. Moreover, since not on time departures happen, situation-aware trip planning as an alternative to static route planning is fully justified.

In our approach, we assume that the delays do not occur at random, but follow a stochastic process. Thus, we may introduce random variables for the delay of a particular line, particular ride, and specific station. Graphical models provide an intuitive way to represent dependencies among random variables in a network structure. Thus, we model the (previously in real-time detected) tram delay by a probabilistic graphical model. Some of its random variables are related, these relations are noted by edges. In this probabilistic graphical model, we may apply observations as evidence and use loopy belief propagation to gain an estimate of the maximum a-posteriori probability. In our model, we differentiate the random variables in time and space: spatially we connect the random variables along a trip of a tram with edges, temporally we introduce one layer of this spatial structure for every ride of the line and connect edges to adjacent stations. Thus one vertex in the graph holds the delay of the corresponding ride at the corresponding stop, and one layer in the spatio-temporal random field represents the delay of one ride. The so built spatio-temporal random field not only uses discrete space and time but also discrete random variables. We distinguish these five states:

1. more than 5 min too early
2. 1 to five minutes too early
3. in time
4. 1 to 4 min belated
5. more than 4 min belated

When a tram passes a stop, the time of the delay is detected, and the corresponding node is set to its observed value. Afterwards, the maxprod-algorithm is applied to estimate a maximum a-posteriori (MAP) configuration.

In order to model the delay of the public transit vehicles as measured by the GPS stream, a Spatio-Temporal Random Field is constructed. The intuition behind STRF is based on sequential probabilistic graphical models, also known as linear chains, which are popular in the natural language processing community. There, consecutive words or corresponding word features are connected to a sequence of labels that reflects an underlying domain of interest like entities or part of speech tags. If a sensor network, represented by a spatial graph $G_0 = (V_0, E_0)$, is considered that generates measurements over space and time, it is appealing to identify the joint measurement of all sensors with a single word in a sentence and connect those structures to form a temporal chain $G_1 - G_2 - \cdots - G_T$. Each part $G_t = (V_t, E_t)$ of the temporal chain replicates the given spatial graph G_0, which represents the underlying physical placement of sensors, i.e., the spatial structure of random variables that does not change over time. The parts are connected by a set of spatio-temporal edges $E_{t-1;t} \subset V_{t-1} \times V_t$ for $t = 2, \dots, T$ and $E_{0;1} = \emptyset$, that represent dependencies between adjacent snapshot graphs G_{t-1} and G_t, assuming a Markov property among snapshots, so that $E_{t;t+h} = \emptyset$ whenever $h > 1$ for any t. The resulting spatio-temporal graph G, consists of the snapshot graphs G_t stacked in order for time frames $t = 1, 2, \dots, T$ and the temporal edges connecting them: $G := (V, E)$ for $V := \cup_{t=1}^{T} V_t$ and $E := \cup_{t=1}^{T} \{E_t \cup E_{t-1;t}\}$.

Finally, G is used to induce a generative probabilistic graphical model that allows us to predict (an approximation to) each random variables MAP state as well as the corresponding marginal probabilities. The full joint probability mass function is given by

$$p_{\boldsymbol{\theta}}(\boldsymbol{X} = \boldsymbol{x}) = \frac{1}{\Psi(\boldsymbol{\theta})} \prod_{v \in V} \psi_v(\boldsymbol{x}) \prod_{(v,w) \in E} \psi_{(v,w)}(\boldsymbol{x}).$$

Here, $\boldsymbol{X}$ represents the random state of all sensors at all T points in time and $\boldsymbol{x}$ is a particular assignment to $\boldsymbol{X}$. It is assumed that each sensor emits a discrete value from a finite set $\mathcal{X}$. By construction, a single vertex v corresponds to a single stop s at a fixed point in time t. The potential function of an STRF has a special form that obeys the smooth temporal dynamics inherent in spatio-temporal data.

$$\psi_v(\boldsymbol{x}) = \psi_{s(t)}(\boldsymbol{x}) = \exp \left\langle \sum_{i=1}^{t} \frac{1}{t - i + 1} \boldsymbol{Z}_{s,i}, \phi_{s(t)}(\boldsymbol{x}) \right\rangle$$

The STRF is therefore parametrized by the vectors $\boldsymbol{Z}_{s,i}$ that store one weight for each of the $|\mathcal{X}|$ possible values for each stop s and point in time $1 \leq i \leq T$. The function $\phi_{s(t)}$ generates an indicator vector that contains exactly one 1 at the position of the state that is assigned to stop s at time t in $\boldsymbol{x}$ and zero otherwise. For a given data set, the parameters $\boldsymbol{Z}$ are fitted by regularized maximum-likelihood estimation.

As soon as the parameters are learned from the data, predictions can be computed via MAP estimation,

$$\hat{\boldsymbol{x}} = \arg \max_{\boldsymbol{x}_{V \setminus U} \in \mathcal{X}} p_{\boldsymbol{\theta}}(\boldsymbol{x}_{V \setminus U} \mid \boldsymbol{x}_U), \tag{1}$$

where $U \subset V$ is a set of spatio-temporal vertices with known values. The nodes in U are termed observed nodes. Notice that $U = \emptyset$ is a perfectly valid choice that yields the most probable state for each node, given no observed nodes. To compute this quantity, the sum-product algorithm [12] is applied, often referred to as loopy belief propagation (LBP). Although LBP computes only approximate marginals and therefore MAP estimation by LBP may not be perfect [10], it suffices our purpose.

5   Experiments

In our experiments, we use real-time GPS traces of trams in Warsaw, Poland[3], and predict current tram delays. The street network, we use, originates from OpenStreetMap, the tram schedule (in standardized GTFS format) was generated manually. As stated in previous section, we build one STRF model for every line, the stations of one trip form the spatial graph and each trip generates a temporal extrusion of the graph. Thus, a random variable is generated for the delay of a tram at every stop. The dependencies among these variables are modeled as stated in previous section. The data was trained with data recorded from June 13th till June 17th.

We apply the model to data on July 4th, 2016. In Fig. 3, we plot an example query without incorporation of our real-time predictions and, beneath, with a proposed trip. The figure highlights that our approach utilizes the prediction-as-a-service and suggests trips with different tram lines or initial walking directions based on predicted delays.

A comparison of our method with the queuing model presented in [6] for line 15 can be seen in Tables 1 and 2. As can be seen, the related approach performs worse in four of five classes, highest improvement of our method is in class two. Only in class three our method performs slightly worse.

The poor performance in the delay prediction task of both methods seems to highlight some challenges with the data we used. Possible problem could be that the tram schedule originates from a different period than the GPS data and the schedule is outdated. If so, there should be a systematic at which time and space our method performs well and worse and it should not be at random.

Therefore, we utilize the visual approach presented in [17] and inspect in more detail the accuracy of our predictions in Fig. 4. Every line corresponds to one trip and every column to one stop. The vertical axis denotes the line per day and the horizontal axis the stop per trip. The patterns that are visual in the figure, e.g. high accuracy in the beginning of the day or at the end of a trip, justify our assumption that the model accuracy does not change arbitrary but depends on the schedule. Incorporation of up-to-date tram schedules is, thus, a major point for future work.

---

[3] Data was provided via https://api.um.warszawa.pl.

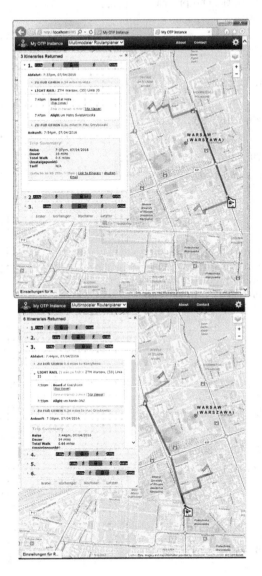

Fig. 3. Results for same start and goal. Top: without incorporation of real-time predictions, Bottom: Real-time predictions are incorporated and suggested trip avoids line 33. Best viewed in color. (Color figure online)

Table 1. Confusion matrix of the prediction results for line 15 using our approach. Horizontally predicted classes (P) vertically True classes (T). In the end precision (Prec.) and recall (Rec.).

T	P					
	1	2	3	4	5	Prec.
1	601	188	40	0	20	0.71
2	40	979	385	5	30	0.68
3	462	948	3307	40	803	0.59
4	180	128	320	197	432	0.15
5	426	252	479	120	1510	0.54
Rec.	0.35	0.39	0.72	0.54	0.54	

Table 2. Confusion matrix of the prediction results for line 15 using queueing approach by [6]. Horizontally predicted classes (P) vertically True classes (T). In the end precision (Prec.) and recall (Rec.).

T	P					
	1	2	3	4	5	Prec.
1	721	9	476	1	57	0.57
2	8	28	55	0	1	0.3
3	768	69	6608	43	508	0.82
4	1	6	43	5	2	0.09
5	93	3	771	0	350	0.29
Rec.	0.45	0.24	0.83	0.1	0.38	

●	0 − 25%
●	26 − 50%
●	51 − 65%
○	65 − 80%
●	80 − 100%

Legend for accuracy plot in Figure 4.

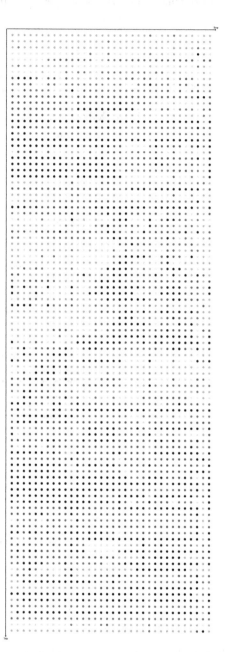

Fig. 4. Accuracy per random variable in the STRF for line 15. Depicts horizontally stop per trip and vertically trip per day, compare [17]. Find the legend next to the figure. Best viewed in color. (Color figure online)

6   Discussion

In this work we presented a novel approach to incorporate real-time delay predictions in a multi-modal trip planner. The achieved model incorporates the predictions and generates situation-aware trips which allow for informed travel plan decisions within a smart city. These decisions can be a situation-aware initial walking direction, a situation-aware transfer from one line to another, or a different tram connection. We highlighted usability of our approach in the city of Warsaw, Poland. For real-world application the dynamic multi-modal routing has to become more efficient to handle thousands of route queries a day. A possible solution would be the incorporation of dynamic transfer pattern [2]. We studied this direction in [14]. Another important task is the combination with other modes of transportation and their predictions: vehicular traffic jams, availability of bike rentals or parking lots. In this direction it will be important to analyse how the modes of transportation interact with each others, e.g. a tram or bus is stuck in a vehicular traffic jam.

Acknowledgements. This research received funding under the Horizon 2020 programme, grant number 688380 VaVeL - Variety, Veracity, VaLue: Handling the Multiplicity of Urban Sensors. We gratefully thank Nico Piatkowski for supply of his STRF library, support and discussion.

References

1. Bast, H., Delling, D., Goldberg, A., Müller-Hannemann, M., Pajor, T., Sanders, P., Wagner, D., Werneck, R.F.: Route planning in transportation networks (2015). arXiv:1504.05140
2. Bast, H., Sternisko, J., Storandt, S.: Delay-robustness of transfer patterns in public transportation route planning. In: ATMOS-13th Workshop on Algorithmic Approaches for Transportation Modelling, Optimization, and Systems-2013, vol. 33, pp. 42–54. Schloss Dagstuhl-Leibniz-Zentrum für Informatik (2013)
3. Bockermann, C., Blom, H.: The streams framework. Techical report 5, TU Dortmund University, December 2012. http://jwall.org/streams/tr.pdf. Accessed 28 Nov 2013
4. Dibbelt, J., Pajor, T., Strasser, B., Wagner, D.: Intriguingly simple and fast transit routing. In: Bonifaci, V., Demetrescu, C., Marchetti-Spaccamela, A. (eds.) SEA 2013. LNCS, vol. 7933, pp. 43–54. Springer, Heidelberg (2013). doi:10.1007/978-3-642-38527-8_6
5. Dijkstra, E.W.: A note on two problems in connexion with graphs. Numer. Math. 1(1), 269–271 (1959)
6. Gal, A., Mandelbaum, A., Schnitzler, F., Senderovich, A., Weidlich, M.: Traveling time prediction in scheduled transportation with journey segments. Inf. Syst. **64**, 266–280 (2015)
7. Geisberger, R., Sanders, P., Schultes, D., Delling, D.: Contraction hierarchies: faster and simpler hierarchical routing in road networks. In: McGeoch, C.C. (ed.) WEA 2008. LNCS, vol. 5038, pp. 319–333. Springer, Heidelberg (2008). doi:10.1007/978-3-540-68552-4_24

8. Goerigk, M., Knoth, M., Müller-Hannemann, M., Schmidt, M., Schöbel, A.: The price of robustness in timetable information. In: OASIcs-OpenAccess Series in Informatics, vol. 20. Schloss Dagstuhl-Leibniz-Zentrum für Informatik (2011)

9. Hart, P.E., Nilsson, N.J., Raphael, B.: A formal basis for the heuristic determination of minimum cost paths. IEEE Trans. Syst. Sci. Cybern. **4**(2), 100–107 (1968)

10. Heinemann, U., Globerson, A.: What cannot be learned with Bethe approximations. In: Proceedings of the 27th Conference on Uncertainty in Artificial Intelligence, Barcelona, Spain (2011)

11. Higgins, A., Kozan, E.: Modeling train delays in urban networks. Transp. Sci. **32**(4), 346–357 (1998)

12. Kschischang, F.R., Frey, B.J., Loeliger, H.A.: Factor graphs and the sum-product algorithm. IEEE Trans. Inf. Theor. **47**(2), 498–519 (2001)

13. Liebig, T., Kemloh Wagoum, A.U.: Modelling microscopic pedestrian mobility using bluetooth. In: ICAART, pp. 270–275. SciTePress (2012)

14. Liebig, T., Peter, S., Grzenda, M., Junosza-Szaniawski, K.: Dynamic transfer patterns for fast multi-modal route planning. In: Bregt, A., Sarjakoski, T., van Lammeren, R., Rip, F. (eds.) GIScience 2017. LNGC, pp. 223–236. Springer, Cham (2017). doi:10.1007/978-3-319-56759-4_13

15. Liebig, T., Piatkowski, N., Bockermann, C., Morik, K.: Dynamic route planning with real-time traffic predictions. Inf. Syst. **64**, 258–265 (2017). http://www.sciencedirect.com/science/article/pii/S0306437916000181

16. Liebig, T., Xu, Z., May, M.: Incorporating mobility patterns in pedestrian quantity estimation and sensor placement. In: Nin, J., Villatoro, D. (eds.) CitiSens 2012. LNCS, vol. 7685, pp. 67–80. Springer, Heidelberg (2013). doi:10.1007/978-3-642-36074-9_7

17. Mazimpaka, J.D., Timpf, S.: A visual and computational analysis approach for exploring significant locations and time periods along a bus route. In: Proceedings of the 9th ACM SIGSPATIAL International Workshop on Computational Transportation Science, pp. 43–48. ACM (2016)

18. Müller-Hannemann, M., Schnee, M.: Efficient timetable information in the presence of delays. In: Ahuja, R.K., Möhring, R.H., Zaroliagis, C.D. (eds.) Robust and Online Large-Scale Optimization. LNCS, vol. 5868, pp. 249–272. Springer, Heidelberg (2009). doi:10.1007/978-3-642-05465-5_10

19. Niu, X., Zhu, Y., Cao, Q., Zhang, X., Xie, W., Zheng, K.: An online-traffic-prediction based route finding mechanism for smart city. Int. J. Distrib. Sens. Netw. **2015**, 18 (2015)

20. Schnitzler, F., et al.: Heterogeneous stream processing and crowdsourcing for traffic monitoring: highlights. In: Calders, T., Esposito, F., Hüllermeier, E., Meo, R. (eds.) ECML PKDD 2014. LNCS, vol. 8726, pp. 520–523. Springer, Heidelberg (2014). doi:10.1007/978-3-662-44845-8_49

21. Schnitzler, F., Liebig, T., Mannor, S., Souto, G., Bothe, S., Stange, H.: Heterogeneous stream processing for disaster detection and alarming. In: IEEE International Conference on Big Data, pp. 914–923. IEEE Press (2014)

22. Souto, G., Liebig, T.: On event detection from spatial time series for urban traffic applications. In: Michaelis, S., Piatkowski, N., Stolpe, M. (eds.) Solving Large Scale Learning Tasks. Challenges and Algorithms. LNCS, vol. 9580, pp. 221–233. Springer, Cham (2016). doi:10.1007/978-3-319-41706-6_11

23. Utsch, P., Liebig, T.: Monitoring microscopic pedestrian mobility using bluetooth. In: 2012 8th International Conference on Intelligent Environments (IE), pp. 173–177. IEEE (2012)

24. Zygouras, N., Zacheilas, N., Kalogeraki, V., Kinane, D., Gunopulos, D.: Insights on a scalable and dynamic traffic management system. In: EDBT, pp. 653–664 (2015)

Online Multi-object Tracking-by-Clustering for Intelligent Transportation System with Neuromorphic Vision Sensor

Gereon Hinz[1], Guang Chen[1(✉)], Muhammad Aafaque[4], Florian Röhrbein[2],
Jörg Conradt[3], Zhenshan Bing[2], Zhongnan Qu[2], Walter Stechele[4],
and Alois Knoll[2]

[1] fortiss GmbH, An-Institut Technische Universität München, Munich, Germany
guang@in.tum.de
[2] Robotics and Embedded Systems,
Technische Universität München, Munich, Germany
[3] Neuroscientific System Theory group,
Technische Universität München, Munich, Germany
[4] Integrated Systems, Technische Universität München, Munich, Germany

Abstract. Instead of wastefully sending entire images at fixed frame rates, neuromorphic vision sensors only transmits the local pixel-level changes caused by movement in a scene *at the time they occur*. This results in a stream of events, with a latency in the order of *micro*-seconds. While these sensors offer tremendous advantages in terms of latency and bandwidth, they require new, adapted approaches to computer vision, due to their unique event-based pixel-level output. In this contribution, we propose an online multi-target tracking system utilizing for neuromorphic vision sensors, which is the first neuromorphic vision system in intelligent transportation systems. In order to track moving targets, a fast and simple object detection algorithm using clustering techniques is developed. To make full use of the low latency, we integrate an online tracking-by-clustering system running at a high frame rate, which far exceeds the real-time capabilities of traditional frame based industry cameras. The performance of the system is evaluated using real world dynamic vision sensor data of a highway bridge scenario. We hope that our attempt will motivate further research on neuromorphic vision sensors for intelligent transportation systems.

Keywords: Neuromorphic vision · Dynamic vision sensor, Multi-object tracking · Intelligent transportation system · Clustering

1 Introduction

In the past decade, computer vision research has been devoted to classical, frame-based cameras. Such cameras have been widely used in intelligent transportation systems [7]. To identify the shortcomings of state-of-the-art approaches, researchers have created standardized vision benchmarks and developed new

© Springer International Publishing AG 2017
G. Kern-Isberner et al. (Eds.): KI 2017, LNAI 10505, pp. 142–154, 2017.
DOI: 10.1007/978-3-319-67190-1_11

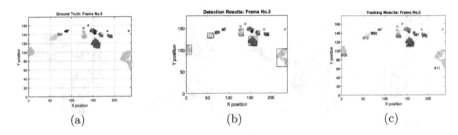

Fig. 1. The results of our tracking-by-clustering system. (a) the labeled event data. (b) the object hypotheses generated by clustering algorithm. (c) the tracking results with tracker ID. One color per object. (Best viewed in color).

approaches to overcome the challenges posed by these standard datasets [12]. This has greatly contributed to the rapid development in many application areas, such as autonomous driving or traffic monitoring. However, we note that new sensing technologies have received insufficient attention and still offer significant potential for improvements of intelligent transportation systems (Fig. 1).

In this paper, we present an approach to intelligent transportation systems (ITS) based on neuromorphic vision sensors [15], which are event-based sensors inspired by biological vision that use silicon retinas. Traditionally, ITS use conventional vision sensors for perception tasks and consequently have to cope with well known challenges, such as the limited real-time performance and substantial computational costs. The key problem is that conventional cameras see the world as a series of frames, which contain enormous amounts of redundant information, wasting memory access, energy, computational power and time. In contrast, neuromorphic vision sensors only transmit local pixel-level changes caused by movement in a scene *at the time of occurrence* and provide an information rich stream of events with a latency in the order of *micro*-seconds. Apart from the latency, requirements for data storage and computational resources are drastically reduced due to the sparse nature of the event stream. Another excellent property of neuromorphic vision sensors is their high dynamic range of 120 dB. In combination, these properties of neuromorphic vision sensors enable entirely new designs of intelligent systems, profiting from extremely low latency and high-dynamic range.

This paper tackles the mentioned challenges of traditional vision tasks from the sensing perspective. We take advantage of the unique properties of neuromorphic vision sensors and propose an online multi-target tracking-by-clustering system as the first case study on neuromoprhic vision sensor based intelligent infrastructure in ITS. In conventional camera systems, object detection is carried out with the help of methods like appearance feature extraction based on learning methods. These methods are considered to be computationally demanding [13]. Moreover, in order to get good detection performance, large amounts of labeled data are required for the training and learning process. Also, dedicated hardware such as GPUs is desired during the training and prediction stages.

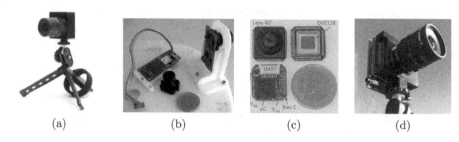

(a)	(b)	(c)	(d)

Fig. 2. Different versions of DVS sensors: (a) Dynamic Vision Sensor 128 (DVS128). (b) Embedded Dynamic Vision Sensor (eDVS). (c) Miniature Embedded Dynamic Vision Sensor (meDVS). (d) Dynamic and Active Pixel Vision Sensor (DAVIS)

In contrast, we develop a simple and efficient multi-object detection algorithm using clustering algorithms. An online multi-object tracking-by-clustering system is built based on the detection hypothesis. The tracking system runs at an average rate of 250–300 Hz, which far exceeds the real time performance of conventional cameras. We test our tracking-by-clustering method with real world dynamic vision sensor data of a highway bridge scenario. We provide a detailed analysis of our experimental results, point out the limitations of this work, and provide insight for future work (Fig. 2).

2   Neuromorphic Vision Sensor

We provide a short description of different versions of the neuromorphic vision sensor in this section. The purpose is to encourage researchers who are not familiar with neuromorphic vision sensor to explore the potential applications in the intelligent system.

Dynamic Vision Sensor. Comparing to conventional frame-based camera which transmitted complete images at fixed latency (typically 30 ms to 100 ms), the dynamic vision sensor [15] emitted events individually and asynchronously at the time they occur. Events are time-stamped in the latency of micro-second. A single event is a tuple (x, y, t, p), where x, y are the pixel coordinates of the event in 2D space, t is the time-stamp of the event and $p = 1$ is the polarity of the event, which is the sign of the brightness change (increasing or decreasing).

Embedded Dynamic Vision Sensor. For embedded systems in mobile robotics such as unmanned aerial vehicle, an USB interface to transmit raw events is not desirable, nor is a desktop PC for event processing acceptable. For this purpose, a small embedded DVS (eDVS) is developed consisted of a DVS chip and a compact 64 MHz 32bit micro-controller directly connecting to the DVS chip.

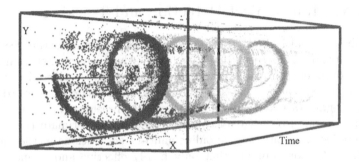

Fig. 3. Visualization of the event stream from DVS which is facing a rotating scene. It generates a spiral-like structure in space-time. Events are represented by colorful dots, from red (far in time) to blue (close in time). Event polarity is not displayed. Noise is visible by isolated points. This figure is adapted from [11]

Miniature Embedded Dynamic Vision Sensor. The miniaturized version of the eDVS(meDVS) has minimum size (18 cm × 18 cm) and lightest weight (2.2 g) of DVS so far [6]. The typical power consumption is 300 mW. The strengths of meDVS make it desirable to any applications on the limited storage, bandwidth, and low latency of the on-board embedded system of the intelligent system (Fig. 3).

Dynamic and Active Pixel Vision Sensor. In this paper we use a new neuromorphic vision sensor which is named the Dynamic and Active Pixel Vision Sensor (DAVIS) [3]. The model DAVIS240 camera has a higher resolution of 240 × 180, higher dynamic range, lower power consumption and allows a concurrent readout of global shutter image frames, which are captured using the same photodiodes as for the DVS event generation. In this work, we only use the event data (Fig. 4).

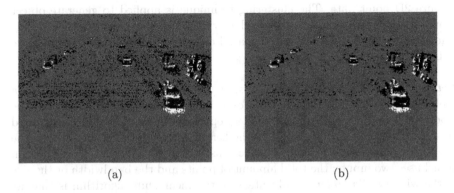

(a)   (b)

Fig. 4. Background activity filter: (a) Events collected in 20 ms time interval prior to filtering (b) Events collected in 20 ms time interval after filtering.

3   Online Multi Object Detection and Tracking

We describe our multi object tracking-by-clustering system in this section. In contrast to traditional object detection approaches, we generate our object hypotheses directly from the measurements with a classic clustering method. The advantage is that we can skip the background modeling step (dynamic foreground segmentation) as most of the events transmitted by the dynamic vision sensor result from dynamic objects. In order to estimate the states of the actual objects, we integrate an online multi-target tracking method into our system [1,4]. It is our opinion that only highly effective and online tracking methodology can take full advantage of neuromorphic vision cameras. We utilize a single hypothesis tracking methodology with standard Kalman filter and frame-by-frame data association using the Hungarian method [1,4].

3.1   Vehicle Detection by Clustering Algorithm

Neuromorphic vision sensors transmit only dynamic information in the form of sparse streams of asynchronous time-stamped events [13]. In this paper, we accumulate event data for different time intervals (10 ms, 20 ms, 30 ms), and cluster event data reflecting objects together, which fits very well with classic clustering methods. Prior to generating object hypotheses, we perform a background activity filter step to filter out noise from the events produced by the sensor. For every new transmitted event, our filter checks the activity that occurred in an area surrounding the event location. If there is no new activity (nothing within a difference of δT time), the event is filtered out. We then evaluate two standard clustering algorithms, named Mean-Shift [5] and DBSCAN [9] with our event data.

Detection. As neuromorphic sensors only transmit relative light intensity changes for each pixel, we cannot utilize methods which use appearance features, such as color and texture as input. In this work, we consider event data as pure 2D point data. The clustering technique is applied to generate object proposals. We evaluate two classic clustering methods: mean-shift clustering (Mean-Shift) [5] and density based spatial clustering of applications with noise (DBSCAN) [9].

Detection by Mean-Shift: The mean-shift algorithm considers the input as a probability density function and the objective of the algorithm is to find the modes of this function [5]. These modes represent the centers of the discovered clusters. The input points are fed to the kernel density estimation and then the gradient ascent method is applied to the density estimate. The density estimation kernel uses two inputs: the total amount of points and the bandwidth or the size of the window. The main disadvantage of the mean-shift algorithm is that its iterative nature and density estimation make it slower than some alternative other clustering algorithms. Figure 5a shows the mean-shift clustering results,

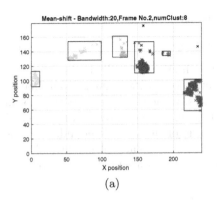 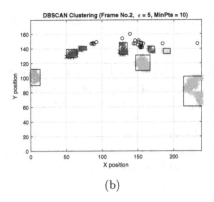

(a)   (b)

Fig. 5. Detection-by-clustering results: (a) Mean-Shift clustering applied to the events data accumulated at 20 ms time interval (b) DBSCAN clustering applied to the events data accumulated at 20 ms time interval

with a chosen bandwidth of 20. The mean-shift algorithm successfully detected six clusters.

Detection by DBSCAN: DBSCAN uses density based spatial clustering for applications with noise. For each point, the associated density is calculated by counting the number of points in a search area of specified radius, ϵ, around the point. The points with density higher than the specified threshold value, MinPts, are classified as core points while the rest are classified as non-core points. Those non-core points are also classified as noise points. The main advantages of DBSCAN is that it can find the clusters of arbitrary shapes [8]. Figure 5b shows a DBSCAN clustering result. The search radius, ϵ, is chosen as 5 and the density, MinPts, is chosen as 10. Seven clusters including noise events have been detected.

By comparing the results depicted in Fig. 5, we choose DBSCAN as our detection method due to its low-complexity, hence fast execution time and robust nature. In Fig. 5a, it can be observed that while some false detections occur, in Fig. 5b the DBSCAN shows promising results along with the indication of noise.

3.2   Online Multi-target Tracking

Our online multi-target tracking is a highly effective, simple and standard method which is widely explored in traditional camera based multi object tracking [1,4]. We utilize a single hypothesis tracking methodology with standard Kalman filter and frame-by-frame data association using Hungarian method [1,4]. As the event data have no texture information, we use the bounding box overlap as an simple association metric for the data association problem.

State Estimation. As a very general tracking scenario, we have no calibration of the DAVIS sensor and no ego-motion information available. For each target in our tracking scenario, its state is modelled as:

$$\mathbf{x} = [u, v, s, r, \dot{u}, \dot{v}, \dot{s}]^T \tag{1}$$

which contains the bounding box center of each cluster (u, v), the aspect ratios (r), and the area scale (s), and their respective velocities in image coordinates. We approximate the frame level displacements of each detected object with an independent linear constant velocity model. (u, v, s, r) are direct observations of the detected object state which the aspect ratio of the target's bounding box is considered as a constant value. The velocity components are solved optimally via a Kalman filter framework when the target state is updated by a new associated detected cluster.

Data Association. In oder to assign detected clusters to existing targets, each target's geometry and image coordinates are estimated by predicting its new state in the current frame. The cost matrix for each detected cluster and each existing target is calculated as the intersection over union distance (IOU). The Hungarian algorithm is used to optimally solve the assignment problem. We also define a minimum IOU to reject assignments where the detected cluster to target cluster overlap is less than the threshold.

Track Handling. When a new cluster enters into the camera field of view or when an existing target leaves the camera view, target identities get updated, either by adding new IDs or by according deletion. We apply the same strategy as presented in [1]. To add new IDs, we consider any detected cluster in the current frame which has an overlap with the existence of untracked clusters in previous frames. The covariance of the velocity component is initiated to large values to reflect the uncertainty as the velocity is unobserved. Instead of solving for detection for tracking in a global assignment problem, we choose an early deletion of lost targets policy. This prevents unbounded growth of the number of trackers. Trackers are terminated if targets are not detected for $Tlost$ frames. We set the $Tlost$ to 1 concerning with frame-by-frame tracking.

4   Experiments

We evaluate the performance of our tracking-by-detection implementation on testing sequences. Data are recorded in a typical highway bridge scenario where the DAVIS sensor is attached to the bridge and faces the highway. We annotate the recorded data by using the annotation software VitBAT [2]. As the first work of multi-target tracking based on neuromorphic vision sensor, we are not able to compare to state-of-the-art tracking algorithms. Instead, we provide our evaluation results as a baseline tracker for future neuromorphic vision based multi-object tracking methods. Additionally, we study the effects of different parameters of the DBSCAN algorithm on the performance of object detection in event data, and of different tracking parameters on the performance of the multi-object tracking results.

4.1   Metrics

For performance evaluation, we follow the current evaluation protocols for visual object detection and multi-object tracking. Although these protocols are designed for frame-based vision sensor, they are still suitable for quantitative evaluation of our tracking method. In this work, we accumulate events to frames in different time intervals. The detection and tracking results are in sampled accumulated events frames which are the same with frame-based vision sensor.

The evaluation metrics for object detection is defined in [10]:

- Rcll($\uparrow$): Recall is defined as the proportion of all positive examples
- Prcn($\uparrow$): Precision is the proportion of all examples which are from the positive class
- FAR($\downarrow$): number of false alarms per frame

It is worth to note that the precision/recall curve is widely used for detection evaluation. Since our detection result from clustering method has no probability score, we are not able to provide the mean precision to summarise the shape of the precision/recall curve.

The evaluation metrics for multi-object tracking is defined in [14], which is also the standard MOT challenge metrics.

- MOTA($\uparrow$): multiple object tracking accuracy
- MOTP($\uparrow$): multiple object tracking precision
- MT($\uparrow$): number of mostly tracked trajectory
- PT($\uparrow$): number of partially tracked trajectory
- ML($\downarrow$): number of mostly lost trajectory
- FP($\downarrow$): number of false detection
- FN($\downarrow$): number of missed detection
- IDsw($\downarrow$): number of times an ID switched
- FR($\downarrow$): number of fragmentations

Evaluation measures with $\uparrow$, higher scores donote better performance. Evaluation measures with $\downarrow$, lower scores denote better performance. Evaluation codes were downloaded from MOT Challenge official website[1].

4.2   Performance Evaluation

We report the detection and tracking performance of our approach in this section. First, we analyze the impact of a key parameter of the DBSCAN algorithm on the detection performance: ϵ, the search area radius (when calculating the associated density by counting the number of points in that area). We then study the impact of different sample intervals and detection results on the tracking performance.

---

[1] https://motchallenge.net.

Detection. We assess the detection performance by clustering approach in terms of the metrics of recall, precision and false alarms per frame. Evaluation was carried out using three different time intervals 10 ms, 20 ms, 30 ms and four search radii 3, 4, 5, 6. The results of our detection evaluation are shown in Table 1. As a result, detection performance improves with increasing search radius ϵ at time interval 10 ms, while a decrease of detection performance occurs for increasing search radius at time intervals 20 ms, 30 ms. A possible explanation is that for the time interval 10 ms there are less events per frame than for the time intervals 20 ms, 30 ms. We can also see from the Table 1 that there is a large increase of *Recall* from time interval 10 ms to time interval 20 ms. Also the maximum value of *Recall* for the time intervals 20 ms and 30 ms is above 58%, which shows that our detection by clustering method works better with more events per frame and with a small search radius. The results indicate that the detection performance is highly dependent on the number of events during the accumulated time. This points out an alternative way of accumulating a constant number of events instead of constant time intervals may increase the robustness of our detection by clustering approach.

Table 1. The detection performance of DBSCAN algorithm on our neuromorphic data with different time intervals and search area radius. We choose the recall (Rec), precision (Prec) and false alarms (Fal) per frame as our evaluation metrics which are widely used by traditional camera based object detection tasks (best viewed in color).

Tis	$\epsilon = 3$			$\epsilon = 4$			$\epsilon = 5$			$\epsilon = 6$		
	Rec	Prec	Fal	Rec	Prec	Fal	Rec	Prec	Fal	Rec	Prec	Fal
10 ms	24.7%	56.6%	1.27	40.6%	78.6%	0.74	46.2%	82.9%	0.64	46.7%	83.0%	0.64
20 ms	59.3%	79.2%	1.05	59.3%	78.6%	1.08	54.7%	74.1%	1.28	50.8%	70.2%	1.44
30 ms	58.0%	82.5%	0.82	54.0%	77.8%	1.03	48.7%	71.7%	1.29	41.5%	65.5%	1.47

Tracking. Figure 6 shows the detection and tracking results in sampled accumulated events data frames. From the tracking performance evaluations in Table 2, MOTA and MOTP are increasing in line with the density radius ϵ at the time interval 10 ms. The number of mostly tracked trajectory (MT) is less than 10. One possible reason is that there are less events at each time-stamp which result in worse detection performance. As the tracking component is highly dependent on the detection results, the number of times an ID switched is pretty large due to the inconsistent detection results. The maximum value of MOTA and MOTP are 44.6% and 70.9% at time interval 30 ms. There is a clear trend toward better performance when increase the time intervals with a small density radius. From the overall tracking performance evaluation results in Table 3, the maximum value of MOTA and MOTP are 34.8% and 70.5% at time interval 20 ms and 30 ms respectively. The MT of 20 ms time interval is 96 which is much better than others. The best tracking performance in Table 3 goes to the time interval 20 ms. As a frame-by-frame based tracking approach, it is not surprising that we

Table 2. The tracking performance using different detection results. We studied the impact of time intervals from 10 ms to 40 ms and ϵ from 1 to 12. Due to space limitations, we only present part of results in this table.

Tis	ϵ	MOTA↑	MOTP↑	MT↑	PT↑	ML↓	FP ↓	FN↓	IDs↓	FR↓
10 ms	3	5.1%	63.9%	0	56	51	5756	22910	196	1494
10 ms	4	29.0%	67.2%	4	70	33	3357	18051	184	1501
10 ms	5	36.2%	69.2%	8	**79**	20	**2891**	16369	**146**	1302
10 ms	6	36.7%	69.8%	9	77	21	2911	**16196**	151	**1097**
20 ms	3	43.1%	69.5%	**26**	72	**9**	2374	**6182**	95	542
20 ms	4	42.6%	70.4%	22	71	14	2451	6189	**91**	470
20 ms	5	35.0%	70.2%	18	71	18	2905	6893	92	444
20 ms	6	28.6%	70.0%	16	67	24	3276	7482	93	**433**
30 ms	3	**44.6%**	70.7%	20	75	12	**1247**	**4255**	110	299
30 ms	4	37.5%	**70.9%**	14	77	16	1563	4656	103	265
30 ms	5	28.5%	70.4%	12	69	26	1950	5190	**94**	265
30 ms	6	23.7%	70.3%	9	69	29	2067	5559	99	**263**

Table 3. The overall tracking performance across different detection results within the same time interval.

Tis	MOTA↑	MOTP↑	MT↑	PT↑	ML↓	FP ↓	FN↓	IDs↓	FR↓
10 ms	28.3%	68.5%	30	**358**	147	18094	90029	805	6432
20 ms	**34.8%**	70%	**96**	346	**93**	14410	34707	**458**	2294
30 ms	30.6%	**70.5%**	60	359	116	9044	25576	493	1361

get large number of false detection, missed detection, ID switch and fragmentations. One possible way to decrease the number of missed detection, ID switch and fragmentations is that by replacing the simple association metric *IOU* in this paper to a more informed metric including motion information, it is able to track objects through longer periods of occlusions and disappearances.

Runtime. The detection experiment was performed on a Intel Core™i5-2410M CPU with 2.30 GHz quad core processor and 4.00 GB of RAM. The average runtime by the DBSCAN algorithm for 10 ms, 20 ms and 30 ms time intervals, is 51.99 ms, 394.4 ms, and 887.8 ms respectively. The increasing computation time is due to the increased number of events in the density search area, ϵ, and hence calculating more distances. By increasing the ϵ in the same time interval, 10 ms for example, the computation time is also increasing. As our DBSCAN algorithm is implemented in MATLAB without speed optimization, it is still a reasonable result. For the tracking component, we are able to achieve 317 *FPS*, 286 *FPS* and 284 *PFS* for the time intervals 10 ms, 20 ms and 30 ms respectively. Apart

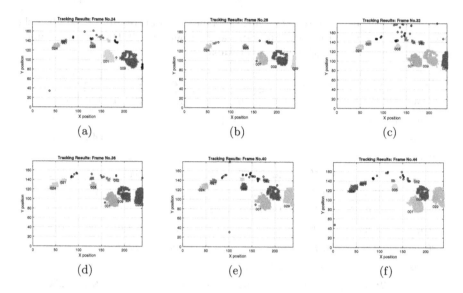

Fig. 6. Tracking reulsts from Frame 24 to Frame 44. Colorful clusters correspond to object hypotheses. It is easy to see that almost each object hypothesis is associated a tracker with a unique ID. There are also small size clusters which are not tracked very well (different colors are only used for visualization). (Color figure online)

from its simplicity, the tracker also combines the two desirable properties, speed and precision.

4.3　Limitation

As the first attempt of introducing neuromorphic vision sensor in ITS, we think that our work is still on its very early stage. Our method is not optimized for the top performance on multi object detection and tracking, but rather keep it as simple and efficient as possible and provide an initial analysis as well as a baseline for future work in this direction. It is also important to note that in order to take full usage of event data, completely new neuromorphic vision algorithms are required instead of extending existing methods from computer vision.

5　Conclusion

The introduction of neuromorphic vision sensor in this paper opens a promising opportunity for a new type of sensing ability in intelligent transportation system. The sparse stream of event data from the sensor captures only motion and salient information which is perfect for the intelligent infrastructure systems. The proposed event-based online multiple target tracking-by-detection system is strikingly simple algorithm while it achieves good detection and tracking performance with respect to runtime requirement. To the best of our knowledge, the presented system is the first application of neuromorphic vision sensor on ITS which makes it well suited as a baseline, allowing for new researcher to work on intersection of the neuroscience and intelligent system. As a baseline we would like see new approaches to improving the detection and tracking performance. As our experiment highlight the importance of detection results, future work will investigate other clustering algorithm as well as feature learning methods such as convolutional neural network for event-based object representation and detection.

Acknowledgments. The research leading to these results has received funding from the European Unions Horizon 2020 Research and Innovation Program under Grant Agreement No. 720270 (HBP SGA1).

References

1. Bewley, A., Ge, Z., Ott, L., Ramos, F., Upcroft, B.: Simple online and realtime tracking. CoRR (2016). http://arxiv.org/abs/1602.00763
2. Biresaw, T.A., Nawaz, T., Ferryman, J., Dell, A.I.: Vitbat: Video tracking and behavior annotation tool. In: 2016 13th IEEE International Conference on Advanced Video and Signal Based Surveillance (AVSS). pp. 295–301 (August 2016)
3. Brandli, C., Berner, R., Yang, M., Liu, S.C., Delbruck, T.: A 240 × 180 130 db 3 μs latency global shutter spatiotemporal vision sensor. IEEE J. Solid-State Circuits **49**(10), 2333–2341 (2014)
4. Chen, G., Zhang, F., Clarke, D., Knoll, A.: Learning to track multi-target online by boosting and scene layout. In: 2013 12th International Conference on Machine Learning and Applications, vol. 1, pp. 197–202 (December 2013)
5. Comaniciu, D., Meer, P.: Mean shift: a robust approach toward feature space analysis. IEEE Trans. Pattern Anal. Mach. Intell. **24**(5), 603–619 (2002)
6. Conradt, J.: On-board real-time optic-flow for miniature event-based vision sensors. In: 2015 IEEE International Conference on Robotics and Biomimetics, ROBIO, pp. 1858–1863 (2015). http://dx.doi.org/10.1109/ROBIO.2015.7419043
7. Datondji, S.R.E., Dupuis, Y., Subirats, P., Vasseur, P.: A survey of vision-based traffic monitoring of road intersections. IEEE Trans. Intell. Transport. Syst. **17**(10), 2681–2698 (2016)
8. Ertöz, L., Steinbach, M., Kumar, V.: Finding clusters of different sizes, shapes, and densities in noisy, high dimensional data. In: Proceedings of Second SIAM International Conference on Data Mining (2003)
9. Ester, M., Kriegel, H.P., Sander, J., Xu, X.: A density-based algorithm for discovering clusters a density-based algorithm for discovering clusters in large spatial databases with noise. In: Proceedings of the Second International Conference on Knowledge Discovery and Data Mining, KDD 1996, pp. 226–231. AAAI Press (1996). http://dl.acm.org/citation.cfm?id=3001460.3001507
10. Everingham, M., Van Gool, L., Williams, C.K.I., Winn, J., Zisserman, A.: The pascal visual object classes (voc) challenge. Int. J. Comput. Vis. **88**(2), 303–338 (2010)
11. Gallego, G., Lund, J.E.A., Mueggler, E., Rebecq, H., Delbrück, T., Scaramuzza, D.: Event-based, 6-dof camera tracking for high-speed applications. CoRR (2016). http://arxiv.org/abs/1607.03468

12. Geiger, A., Lenz, P., Urtasun, R.: Are we ready for autonomous driving? the kitti vision benchmark suite. In: 2012 IEEE Conference on Computer Vision and Pattern Recognition. pp. 3354–3361 (June 2012)
13. Lagorce, X., Meyer, C., Ieng, S.H., Filliat, D., Benosman, R.: Asynchronous event-based multikernel algorithm for high-speed visual features tracking. IEEE Trans. Neural Netw. Learn. Syst. **26**(8), 1710–1720 (2015)
14. Leal-Taixé, L., Milan, A., Reid, I.D., Roth, S., Schindler, K.: Motchallenge 2015: Towards a benchmark for multi-target tracking. CoRR (2015). http://arxiv.org/abs/1504.01942
15. Lichtsteiner, P., Posch, C., Delbruck, T.: A 128 × 128 120 db 15 μs latency asynchronous temporal contrast vision sensor. IEEE J. Solid-State Circuits **43**(2), 566–576 (2008)

A Generalization of Probabilistic Argumentation with Dempster-Shafer Theory

Nguyen Duy Hung[(✉)]

Sirindhorn International Institute of Technology, Pathum Thani, Thailand
hung.nd.siit@gmail.com

Abstract. One of the first (and key) steps in analyzing an argumentative exchange is to reconstruct complete arguments from utterances which may carry just enthymemes. In this paper, using legal argument from analogy, we argue that in this reconstruction process interpreters may have to deal with a kind of uncertainty that can be appropriately represented in Dempster-Shafer (DS) theory rather than classical probability theory. Hence we generalize and relax existing frameworks of Probabilistic Argumentation (PAF), which are currently based on classical probability theory, by what we refer to as DS-based Argumentation framework (DSAF). Concretely, we first define a DSAF form and semantics by generalizing existing PAF form and semantics. We then present a method to translate existing proof procedures for standard Abstract Argumentation into DSAF inference procedures. Finally we provide a Prolog-based implementation of the resulted DSAF inference procedures.

Keywords: Argumentation · Dempster-Shafer theory · Inference procedures

1 Introduction

An Abstract Argumentation framework (AF [4]) is a pair (Arg, Att) where Arg is a set of arguments, $Att \subseteq Arg \times Arg$ is a set of attacks. The semantics of AF rests on a crisp notion of argument acceptability, namely an argument X is acceptable wrt a set S of arguments iff S attacks every argument attacking X. For example, wrt the AF framework in Fig. 1(a)[1], B is acceptable wrt $\{B\}$ while A_1 is acceptable wrt none. AF has been used to unify different reasoning formalisms in AI, and also extended in several directions. Notably, Probabilistic Argumentation (PAF) [5,7,8,10,12,20] extends AF with classical probability theory. Under the distribution semantics, a PAF framework is equivalent to a probabilistic distribution of AF frameworks representing different "possible worlds". The probability that an argument X is acceptable is obtained by marginalizing the joint probability distribution of possible worlds and the acceptability of X.

In real life people may not fully express their arguments for various reasons even in areas where complete arguments are desired, e.g. the area of law.

---

[1] Conventionally, arguments are shown as nodes and attacks as directed edges.

© Springer International Publishing AG 2017
G. Kern-Isberner et al. (Eds.): KI 2017, LNAI 10505, pp. 155–169, 2017.
DOI: 10.1007/978-3-319-67190-1_12

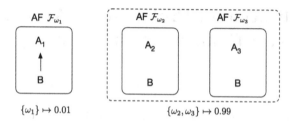

Fig. 1. Abstract Argumentation frameworks

Hence one of the first (and key) steps in analyzing an argumentative exchange is to reconstruct complete arguments from utterances which may carry just enthymemes. In this process interpreters may have to deal with a kind of uncertainty that can be appropriately represented in Dempster-Shafer (DS) theory [3,15] rather than classical probability theory. To illustrate, in this paper we use the analysis of Posner [13], a distinguished legal thinker, about Adam v. New Jersey Steamboat. As summarized by Fig. 1 (detailed later), Posner gives three "possible worlds" of the judge's argumentation represented by AF frameworks $\mathcal{F}_{\omega_1}, \mathcal{F}_{\omega_2}$ and $\mathcal{F}_{\omega_3}$. He considers $\mathcal{F}_{\omega_1}$ very unlikely but does not compare the other two frameworks. In DS terminology, Posner assigns a "mass" close to 0 to $\mathcal{F}_{\omega_1}$ and a mass close to 1 to the set $\{\mathcal{F}_{\omega_2}, \mathcal{F}_{\omega_3}\}$. Note that Posner did not (and, in fact, did not want to) assign masses to $\mathcal{F}_{\omega_2}$ and $\mathcal{F}_{\omega_3}$ individually. Had he done so his analysis could have been represented in PAF, which requires probabilities to be assigned to possible worlds individually.

To address the above limitation of PAF, in this paper we develop a generalization of AF using Dempster-Shafer theory, which we refer to as a DS-based Argumentation framework (DSAF). Concretely, we first define a form and semantics for DSAF by mathematically generalizing the existing PAF form and semantics, especially from the PAF proposal in [5]. It turns out that DSAF also generalizes AF in an elegant and mathematical way, and this provides us a basis to then develop a method to automatically translate existing AF proof procedures into DSAF inference procedures. The resulted DSAF inference procedures are implemented using Prolog (download link: http://ict.siit.tu.ac.th/~hung/dsafengine).

To the best of our knowledge, though there are many existing proposals to combine DST and argumentation theory (e.g. [2,9,11,14,16,17]), none of them mathematically generalize PAF (and AF) like ours does (details in the paper body). To stress, again, that this generalization helps us translate AF proof procedures into DSAF inference procedures. We also believe that it allows DSAF to take for granted other results from AF. Note that since PAF is a subclass of DSAF, our DSAF inference procedures can also be used to compute PAF, for which the current literature contains only the procedure for PAF grounded semantics of Thang [18]. The literature has no inference procedures for DSAF.

To close this introduction, let's remark that in this paper we motivate DSAF by a reconstruction task of legal argument from analogy but one can easily imagine different applications for DSAF. For example, a recommendation system predicting the rating that a specific user would give to a product may start with a model of a generic user (represented by an AF framework). It then extends this model to take into account, for example, the specific user's preference profile, to construct a personalized model. There are various reasons demanding that the personalized model be a DSAF framework rather than an AF or PAF framework: the uncertainty about the user's preference profile is given by a DST mass function rather than a probability function; one user's preference profile gives rise to a set of indistinguishable models rather a single model, etc.

The rest of the paper is structured as follows: Sect. 2 presents the background; Sect. 3 presents our model of DSAF; Sect. 4 presents an application of DSAF in reconstructing legal argument from analogy; Sect. 5 abstractly presents our DSAF inference procedures, whose procedural form is given in an online appendix[2]; Sect. 6 presents related work and concludes.

2   Background

2.1   Argumentation

An Abstract Argumentation (AF) framework is a pair (Arg, Att) where Arg is a set of arguments, $Att \subseteq Arg \times Arg$ and $(A, B) \in Att$ means that A attacks B [4]. $S \subseteq Arg$ attacks $A \in Arg$ iff $(B, A) \in Att$ for some $B \in S$. S defends A (aka A is acceptable wrt to S) iff S attacks every argument attacking A. S is *conflict-free* iff S does not attack itself; *admissible* iff S is conflict-free and defends each argument in S; *complete* iff S is admissible and contains all arguments that S defends; a *preferred* extension iff S is a maximal (wrt set inclusion) complete set; the *grounded* extension iff S is the least complete set. An argument A is accepted under semantics *sem*, denoted AF $\mathcal{F} \vdash_{sem} A$, iff A is in a *sem* extension. In this paper, we restrict ourselves to *sem* $\in \{pr, gr\}$[3].

AF has been used to unify different reasoning formalisms in AI, and also extended in several directions to address its shortcomings. Notably, Probabilistic Argumentation models [5,7,8,10,12,20] extends AF with classical probability theory. One of the most early and abstract among these is the model of [5] defined as a triple $(\mathcal{F}, \mathcal{W}, P)$ where $\mathcal{F} = (Arg, Att)$ is a standard AF framework, $\mathcal{W}$ is a set of possible worlds such that each $\omega \in \mathcal{W}$ defines a subset of arguments $Arg_\omega \subseteq Arg$, and $P : \mathcal{W} \to [0, 1]$ is a probability distribution over $\mathcal{W}$ (i.e. $\sum_{\omega \in \mathcal{W}} P(\omega) = 1$). The probability that an argument A is acceptable under a

---

[2] http://ict.siit.tu.ac.th/~hung/dsafengine/appendix.pdf.
[3] **Preferred/grounded.**

semantics *sem* is obtained by marginalizing the joint probability distribution of possible worlds and the acceptability of A^4. Concretely,

$$Prob_{sem}(A) = \sum_{\omega \in W} P(\omega).P(\mathcal{F}_\omega \vdash_{sem} A \mid \omega) = \sum_{\omega \in W: \mathcal{F}_\omega \vdash_{sem} A} P(\omega)$$

where $\mathcal{F}_\omega$ denotes the AF framework $(Arg_\omega, Att \cap (Arg_\omega \times Arg_\omega))$.

2.2   AF Proof Procedures

Many proof procedures for AF have been developed, mostly by simulating disputes between two fictitious parties. For example, in [19], to determine whether AF $\mathcal{F} \vdash_{pr} A$, the authors simulate disputes where a proponent starts by putting forward A, then alternates with an opponent in attacking each other's previous arguments. Formally a dispute is represented by a dispute derivation in which a state is a tuple $t_i = \langle P_i, O_i, SP_i, SO_i \rangle$. $P_i \subseteq Arg$ is a set of arguments presented by the proponent that have not been defended by the proponent. $SP_i \subseteq Arg$ is the set of all arguments presented by the proponent. $O_i \subseteq Arg$ is a set of opponent's arguments against arguments presented by the proponent in previous steps that are not counter-attacked yet by the proponent. SO_i contains opponent's arguments that have been counter-attacked by the proponent.

Definition 1. *Given a selection function, a dispute derivation for an argument A is a sequence $\langle P_0, O_0, SP_0, SO_0 \rangle, \ldots, \langle P_n, O_n, SP_n, SO_n \rangle$ where:*

1. *P_i, O_i, SP_i, and SO_i are argument sets.*
2. *$\langle P_0, O_0, SP_0, SO_0 \rangle = \langle \{A\}, \emptyset, \{A\}, \{\} \rangle$ and $P_n = O_n = \emptyset$.*
3. *Let B be the argument selected at step i from either P_i or O_i.*
   (a) *If $B \in P_i$ and $Attack_B \cap SP_i = \emptyset^5$ then*
       $$P_{i+1} = P_i \setminus \{B\} \qquad O_{i+1} = O_i \cup (Attack_B \setminus SO_i)$$
       $$SP_{i+1} = SP_i \qquad SO_{i+1} = SO_i$$
   (b) *If $B \in O_i$ then there exists some argument $C \in Attack_B \setminus (SO_i \cup O_i)$ such that*
       $$P_{i+1} = P_i \cup \{C\} \text{ if } C \notin SP_i, \text{ otherwise } P_{i+1} = P_i$$
       $$O_{i+1} = O_i \setminus Attacked_C$$
       $$SP_{i+1} = SP_i \cup \{C\} \qquad SO_{i+1} = SO_i \cup (Attacked_C \cap O_i)$$

The intuition behind the above definition is as follows.

---

[4] As discussed in [6], not all PAF proposals adopt this distribution semantics. For example the PAF proposals of [7,8,20] define their semantics in terms of some *rational conditions* on Probabilistic Distribution Function (PDF) $f : Arg \to [0,1]$, for $f(A)$ to represent some value of argument A, which may not relate to the acceptability of A. In fact $f(A)$ has been given diverse interpretations, from the truth of A, the reliability of A, the probability of A being effective, the belief degree put into A, to whatever measure that can be attached to A as an argument [7].

[5] For $X \in Arg$, $Attack_X \triangleq \{Y \in Arg \mid (Y, X) \in Att\}$ and $Attacked_X \triangleq \{Y \in Arg \mid (X, Y) \in Att\}$.

- Rule 3(a):
  - $Attack_B \cap SP_i = \emptyset$: the proponent could not attack his own arguments.
  - $O_{i+1} = O_i \cup (Attack_B \setminus SO_i)$ excludes arguments belonging to SO_i from O_{i+1}, thus every opponent's argument is counterattacked only once.
- Rule 3(b):
  - $C \in Attack_B \setminus (SO_i \cup O_i)$: the proponent to select an argument among possibly many arguments in $Attack_B$ to counter-attack B but the selected argument should not have been deployed by the opponent.
  - $O_{i+1} = O_i \setminus Attacked_C$: the proponent does not need to counterattack those arguments in O_i that are attacked by C.

For illustration, a dispute derivation for argument B_2 in AF $\mathcal{F} = (Arg, Att)$ with $Arg = \{A, B_1, B_2\}$ and $Att = \{(A, B_1), (B_1, B_2), (B_2, B_1)\}$ is given below.

i	P_i	O_i	SP_i	SO_i	Rule (of Definition 1) used	Remark
0	$\{B_2\}$	$\{\}$	$\{B_2\}$	$\{\}$	rule 2	Proponent starts dispute
1	$\{\}$	$\{B_1\}$	$\{B_2\}$	$\{\}$	rule 3.a	Opponent attacks B_2 by B_1
2	$\{\}$	$\{\}$	$\{B_2\}$	$\{B_1\}$	rule 3.b	Proponent repeats B_2

As shown in [19], dispute derivations represent sound and complete proofs for the preferred semantics because: (1) if $\langle P_0, O_0, SP_0, SO_0 \rangle \ldots \langle P_n, O_n, SP_n, SO_n \rangle$ is a dispute derivation for argument A, then SP_n is admissible and contains A; (2) if an argument A belongs to an admissible set S of arguments in a finitary argumentation framework, then for any selection function there is a dispute derivation for A, whose component SP_n of the final tuple is a subset of S.

2.3   Dempster-Shafer Theory (DST)

The key elements making up DST [3,15] are mass, belief and plausibility, and combination rules. A mass function m over a *frame of discernment* (FoD) Θ consisting of mutually exclusive and exhaustive hypotheses is such that $m : 2^\Theta \rightarrow [0,1]$ and $\sum_{X \subseteq \Theta} m(X) = 1$. A subset $X \subseteq \Theta$ is called a *focal* element if $m(X) > 0$. Belief function and plausibility function, which also have signature $2^\Theta \rightarrow [0,1]$, are derived from m as follows: $Bl(X) = \sum_{Y \subseteq X, Y \neq \emptyset} m(Y)$ and $Pl(X) = \sum_{X \cap Y \neq \emptyset} m(Y)$. DST is said to subsume and relax Bayesian probability theory because it does not require X in $m(X)$ to be a singleton set.

3   DS-Based Argumentation Frameworks

In this section we present an extension of AF using Dempster-Shafer theory instead of classical probability theory, as follows.

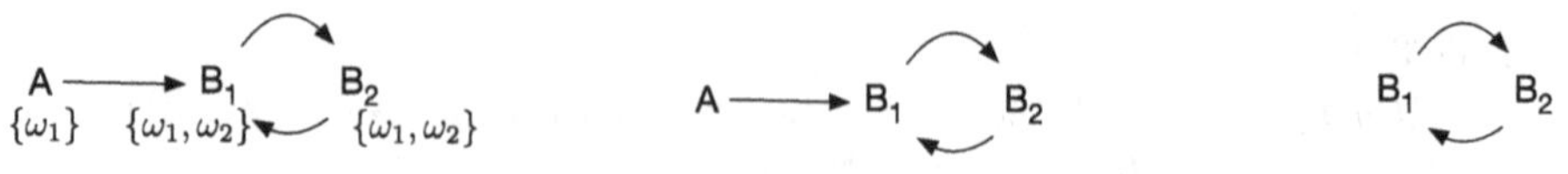

(a) DASF   (b) AF $\mathcal{F}_{\omega_1}$ (c) AF $\mathcal{F}_{\omega_2}$

Fig. 2. A DSAF framework

Definition 2. *A DS-based Argumentation framework (DSAF) is a triple* $(\mathcal{F}, \mathcal{W}, m)$ *where* $\mathcal{F} = (Arg, Att)$ *is an AF framework,* $\mathcal{W}$ *is a set of possible worlds such that each* $\omega \in \mathcal{W}$ *defines a subset of arguments* $Arg_\omega \subseteq Arg$, *and* $m : 2^{\mathcal{W}} \to [0, 1]$ *is a mass function on FoD* $\mathcal{W}$.

We can graphically show a DSAF framework $\mathcal{D} = (\mathcal{F}, \mathcal{W}, m)$ by annotating each node $A \in Arg$ of the graph of $\mathcal{F}$ with the set of possible worlds in which A occurs, i.e. $\{\omega \in \mathcal{W} \mid A \in Arg_\omega\}$. *From now on, we refer to this set by* $W(A)$. *Also let* $\mathcal{F}_\omega$ *denote AF framework* $(Arg_\omega, Att \cap (Arg_\omega \times Arg_\omega))$.

Example 1. Figure 2 graphically shows DSAF $\mathcal{D} = (\mathcal{F}, \mathcal{W}, m)$ where

- $\mathcal{F} = \{Arg, Att\}$ with $Arg = \{A, B_1, B_2\}$ and $Att = \{(A, B_1), (B_1, B_2), (B_2, B_1)\}$.
- $\mathcal{W} = \{\omega_1, \omega_2\}$ with $Arg_{\omega_1} = \{A, B_1, B_2\}$ and $Arg_{\omega_2} = \{B_1, B_2\}$.
- $m = \{\{\omega_1\} \mapsto 0.1; \{\omega_2\} \mapsto 0.2; \{\omega_1, \omega_2\} \mapsto 0.7\}$.

Definition 3. *The semantics of DSAF framework* $\mathcal{D} = (\mathcal{F}, \mathcal{W}, m)$ *is defined by two functions*

$$Bl_{sem}(A) = \sum_{Y \subseteq W_{sem}(A), Y \neq \emptyset} m(Y) \ and \ Pl_{sem}(A) = \sum_{Y \cap W_{sem}(A) \neq \emptyset} m(Y)$$

where $W_{sem}(A) \subseteq \{\omega \in \mathcal{W} \mid \mathcal{F}_\omega \vdash_{sem} A\}$[6].

Example 2. Continue Example 1, it is easy to see that $W_{pr}(B_1) = \{\omega_2\}$; $W_{pr}(B_2) = \{\omega_1, \omega_2\}$; $W_{gr}(B_1) = \emptyset$ and $W_{gr}(B_2) = \{\omega_1\}$, and hence

- $Bl_{pr}(B_1) = \sum_{Y \subseteq \{\omega_2\}} m(Y) = m(\{\omega_2\}) = 0.2$ and $Pl_{pr}(B_1) = \sum_{Y \cap \{\omega_2\} \neq \emptyset}$ $m(Y) = m(\{\omega_2\}) + m(\{\omega_1, \omega_2\}) = 0.9$
- $Bl_{pr}(B_2) = \sum_{Y \subseteq \{\omega_1, \omega_2\}} m(Y) = 1$ and $Pl_{pr}(B_2) = \sum_{Y \cap \{\omega_1, \omega_2\} \neq \emptyset} m(Y) = 1$
- $Bl_{gr}(B_1) = \sum_{Y \subseteq \emptyset} m(Y) = 0$ and $Pl_{gr}(B_1) = \sum_{Y \cap \emptyset \neq \emptyset} m(Y) = 0$
- $Bl_{gr}(B_2) = \sum_{Y \subseteq \{\omega_1\}} m(Y) = m(\{\omega_1\}) = 0.1$ and $Pl_{gr}(B_2) = \sum_{Y \cap \{\omega_1\} \neq \emptyset} m(Y) = m(\{\omega_1\}) + m(\{\omega_1, \omega_2\}) = 0.8$

---

[6] Note that $W_{sem}(A) \subseteq W(A)$.

It is easy to see that

Lemma 1. $0 \leq Bl_{sem}(A) \leq Pl_{sem}(A) \leq 1$.

Lemma 2. *DSAF subsumes PAF.*

Proof. Any PAF $\mathcal{P} = (\mathcal{F}, \mathcal{W}, P)$ can be represented by a DSAF $\mathcal{D} = (\mathcal{F}, \mathcal{W}, m)$ where each focal element of m is a singleton set $\{\omega\}$ for some $\omega \in \mathcal{W}$ with $m(\{\omega\}) = P(\omega)$. $Prob_{sem}(A)$ defined by $\mathcal{P}$ equals $Bl_{sem}(A)$ and $Pl_{sem}(A)$ defined by $\mathcal{D}$.

4   Application: Reconstructing Argument from Analogy

In real life people do not often fully express their arguments for various reasons even in areas where complete arguments are desired like the area of law. For example, consider Adam v. New Jersey Steamboat (151 N.Y. 163, 168) where the issue was whether the Steamboat owed passenger Adam who had occupied a stateroom the same very high duty of care that as courts had held in previous cases an innkeeper owes its guests, or the lower duty of care that as courts had held in another case a railroad owes its passengers [13]. Judge O' Brien analogized the steamboat company to the innkeeper (calling the steamboat "a floating inn"), rather than the railroad, and held therefore that the steamboat company owed the higher duty of care to Adam and so was liable for the loss of Adam's 160$ by an intruder. The relevant portion of judge O' Brien decision is

> ...*The defendant has, therefore, been held liable as an insurer against the loss which one of its passengers.... The relations that exist between a steamboat company and its passengers, who have procured staterooms for their comfort during the journey, differ in no essential respect from those that exist between the innkeeper and his guests...*

So according to judge O' Brien, the similarity between innkeepers and steamboat operators as providers of sleeping accommodations for travelers makes the rule that governs innkeepers a candidate for a rule to govern steamboat operators. But what is "the innkeeper's rule"? Unfortunately it is not stated in judge O' Brien's argument, which is hence better seen as an enthymeme as follows.

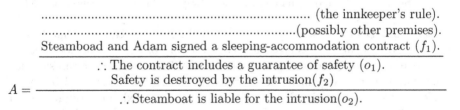

According to many legal experts, common view embraced in any legal system is that in deciding a case, a judge needs to search for a rule that might cover it

[1,13]. The many gaps in the law coupled with the judges' duty to decide cases whether or not there is a clear governing rule, force the judges to legislate. But unlike the members of real legislatures, judges do not have the full democratic legitimacy of a legislature. Hence they tend to reply on information that can be gleaned from the previous cases and to emphasize the continuity between those cases and the current case. By describing the decision in the current case as the product of "analogy" to decisions in previous cases, they can often get away with not stating a rule at all, leaving it to later judges or to academics to make explicit the rule that is implicit in or can explain the line of cases. Multiples interpretations for the same rule are usual. For example, for Porner [13] the Innkeeper's rule might be:

– A contract for sleeping accommodation must include a safety guarantee (r_1).
– A contract for sleeping accommodation includes a guarantee of safety unless it is made impossible by an act of God or the public enemies (r_2).
– A business that provides sleeping accommodations to its customers must take as much care to protect them as is feasible (r_3).

These three rules result in three different reconstructions of argument A:

$$A_1 = \cfrac{\cfrac{\cfrac{r_1}{f_1}}{\therefore o_1}\; f_2}{\therefore o_2} \qquad A_2 = \cfrac{\cfrac{\cfrac{r_2\; f_3}{f_1}}{\therefore o_1}\; f_2}{\therefore o_2} \qquad A_3 = \cfrac{\cfrac{\cfrac{r_3\; f_4}{f_1}}{\therefore o_1}\; f_2}{\therefore o_2}$$

where f_3, f_4 stand for "Neither act of God nor the public enemies causes the incident" and "It is feasible for Steamboat to safeguard its sleeper's belongings."

An interpreter could do further analysis to see which reconstructions are more possible than the others. For example, on the basis that r_1 is too broad since it would require the railroad to extend the same high level of care to its sleeping-berth customers, Posner considers A_1 nearly impossible. This analysis can be modeled by bringing in the following argument B to attack A_1.

$$B = \frac{\text{Railroad and Customer signed a sleeping-accommodation contract.}}{\therefore \text{Sleeping-accommodation contract not always includes a guarantee of safety.}}$$
Railroad is not liable for the loss of Customer's belongings.

Note that B does not attack A_2 and A_3. In fact, we can say that Posner considers both A_2 and A_3 as possible reconstructions of A. Since he does not say which one between r_2 and r_3 better represents Innkeeper's rule, we can say that he has no opinion as to which one between A_2 and A_3 reconstructs A better[7].

Now, let's try to model Posner's full analysis using existing argumentation frameworks. The AF framework $\mathcal{F}_{\omega_1}$ in Fig. 1(a) represents Posner's first "possible world" of O' Brien's decision making. Posner's second and third possible

---

[7] Other legal academics give different reconstructions of A, e.g. Brewer [1].

worlds are represented by AF frameworks $\mathcal{F}_{\omega_2}$ and $\mathcal{F}_{\omega_3}$ respectively. Unfortunately we can not say that Posner's analysis is fully represented by three possible worlds because Posner also assigns "masses" to them: namely a mass close to to 0 to $\mathcal{F}_{\omega_1}$ and a total mass close to 1 to the set $\{\mathcal{F}_{\omega_2}, \mathcal{F}_{\omega_3}\}$. So Posner's analysis can be represented by a DSAF framework $\mathcal{D} = (\mathcal{F}, \mathcal{W}, m)$ where $\mathcal{F} = (Arg, Att)$ with $Arg = \{A_1, A_2, A_3, B\}$ and $Att = \{(B, A_1)\}$; $\mathcal{W} = \{\omega_1, \omega_2, \omega_3\}$; and $m = \{\{\omega_1\} \mapsto 0.01; \{\omega_2, \omega_3\} \mapsto 0.99\}$. Note that Posner did not assign masses to $\mathcal{F}_{\omega_2}$ and $\mathcal{F}_{\omega_3}$ individually.

Finally, one might ask why Posner did not assign masses to $\mathcal{F}_{\omega_2}$ and $\mathcal{F}_{\omega_3}$ individually. We believe that, on one hand, he does not want to do so to avoid possible overstatements. On the other hand, for the purpose of understanding or explaining the judge's decision, he does not need to do so. This is because his current analysis already reveals that $Bl_{sem}(A) \sim 1$, and because $Prob_{sem}(A) \geq Bl_{sem}(A)$, it must be that $Prob_{sem}(A) > 0.5$. In general judges decide a civil case using the standard of proof that the plaintiff wins if the claim is more probable than not (aka, a preponderance of the evidence). Hence with the current analysis, Posner already understands the judge's decision, though he does not know the actual value of $Prob_{sem}(A)$ inside the judge's mind.

5   DSAF Inference Procedures

Inference procedures for DSAF compute $Bl_{sem}(A)$ and/or $Pl_{sem}(A)$ for a given an argument A wrt a DSAF framework[8]. This section aims at automatically deriving such procedures from AF proof procedures, which are supposedly given[9]. To motivate our methodology, let us consider a naive approach below.

Data: An argument A and DSAF $\mathcal{D} = (\mathcal{F}, \mathcal{W}, m)$; a AF proof procedure for
semantics *sem*
Result: $Bl_{sem}(A)$
/* Compute $W_{sem}(A) = \{\omega \in \mathcal{W} \mid \mathcal{F}_\omega \vdash_{sem} A\}$*/
$W_{sem}(A) = \{\}$;
foreach $\omega \in \mathcal{W}$ **do**
    /* invoke AF proof procedure*/
    if $\mathcal{F}_\omega \vdash_{sem} A$ **then**
      | $W_{sem}(A) = W_{sem}(A) \cup \{\omega\}$;
    end
end
$result = 0$;
foreach *non-empty focal element Y of m* **do**
    if $Y \subseteq W_{sem}(A)$ **then**
      | $result = result + m(Y)$;
    end
end
return *result*;

---

[8] In this section we always refer to an arbitrary but fixed DSAF framework $\mathcal{D} = (\mathcal{F}, \mathcal{W}, m)$ with $\mathcal{F} = (Arg, Att)$ if not explicitly stated otherwise.

[9] Because of the lack of space, we present only the computation of $Bl_{sem}(A)$. Note that our Prolog-based implementation can compute both $Bl_{pr}(A)$ and $Pl_{pr}(A)$.

The major advantage of the above approach is that it does not need to make any surgery to a given AF proof procedure. However, since AF proof procedure is invoked afresh for different possible worlds (at the test **if** $\mathcal{F}_w \vdash_{sem} A$), the common parts of different dispute derivations (for convenience, let's call them partial dispute derivations) are repeatedly constructed. To address the above problem, common partial dispute derivations need to be reused among possible worlds. This can be done by annotating each partial dispute derivation with a set of focal elements[10] of m where the partial derivation is valid for each possible world of such a focal element. To avoid any surgery to given AF proof procedures (so that the approach can be fully automated), the annotations should not be incorporated into dispute derivation states. However, we can assume that these states are readable and so are state transitions. Thus we define a function $Follow_{\mathcal{F}}(\_, \_)$ which can be considered as the "API" that AF proof procedures provide.

Definition 4. *Let $\mathcal{F}$ be an AF framework. For a dispute derivation state t and a selection function sl, $Follow_{\mathcal{F}}(t, sl)$ denotes the set of states that can immediately follow t in a dispute derivation using sl.*

The implementation of $Follow_{\mathcal{F}}(t, sl)$ is up to AF proof procedures and DSAF inference procedures should not be concerned with that. DSAF inference procedures call $Follow_{\mathcal{F}}(t, sl)$, examine each returned state $t' \in Follow_{\mathcal{F}}(t, sl)$ and probably also the cause of state transition $t \to t'$. In the following definition which describes our DSAF inference procedures abstractly, we use notation $t \xrightarrow[\mathcal{P}:C]{\mathcal{O}:B} t'$ to say that state transition $t \to t'$ is caused by the proponent's movement of argument C to attacks opponent's argument B.

Definition 5. *Given a selection function, a **foci derivation** for an argument A is a sequence $T_0, T_1, \ldots, T_n$ where*

1. *T_i is a set of pairs of the form $(t, \mathcal{X})$ where t is a dispute derivation state and $\mathcal{X} \subseteq 2^{\mathcal{W}}$.*
2. *At each step i, a pair $(t, \mathcal{X})$ is selected from T_i, and $T_{i+1} = T_i \setminus \{(t, \mathcal{X})\} \cup \Delta T$ where*
   (a) *If $\mathcal{X} = \emptyset$ then $\Delta T = \emptyset$,*
   (b) *Otherwise, an argument B is selected from the P or O component of t, and*
      i. *If $B \in P$ then $\Delta T = \{(t', \mathcal{X})\}$ if there is $t' \in Follow_{\mathcal{F}}(t, sl)$[11] otherwise $\Delta T = \emptyset$.*
      ii. *If $B \in O$ then $\Delta T = \{(\langle P, O \setminus \{B\}, SP, SO \rangle, \{X \in \mathcal{X} \mid X \cap W(B) = \emptyset\})\} \cup \{(t', \{X \in \mathcal{X} \mid X \subseteq W(C)\}) \mid t' \in Follow_{\mathcal{F}}(t, sl) \text{ and } t \xrightarrow[\mathcal{P}:C]{\mathcal{O}:B} t'\}.*

---

[10] Recall that $X \in 2^{\mathcal{W}}$ is a focal element of m iff $m(X) > 0$.
[11] In this case $Follow_{\mathcal{F}}(t, sl)$ is a singleton set.

The intuition behind Definition 5 is as follows.

- Rule 1: Each dispute derivation state t is annotated with a set $\mathcal{X}$ of focal elements where for each $X \in \mathcal{X}$, the current partial dispute derivation (which ends with state t) is still valid wrt each possible world $\omega \in X$.
- Rule 2(a): the current partial dispute derivation is abandoned because there is no focal element $X \in \mathcal{X}$ such that it is valid wrt each possible world $\omega \in X$.
- Rule 2(b).i: the current partial dispute derivation is extended by state transition $t \rightarrow t'$.
- Rule 2(b).ii: the current partial dispute derivation is extended by either ways:
  - by state transition $t \xrightarrow[\mathcal{P}:C]{\mathcal{O}:B} t'$: Here the proponent is moving argument C and hence a focal element $X \in \mathcal{X}$ is removed if argument C does not occur in some possible world $\omega \in X$.
  - by keeping only focal elements $X \in \mathcal{X}$ where argument B (which is moved by the opponent) does not occur in any $\omega \in X$.

Our DSAF inference procedures are defined abstractly as follows.

Definition 6. *A foci derivation d for an argument A is a foci derivation $T_0, T_1, \ldots, T_n$ where $T_0 = \{(\langle\{A\}, \emptyset, \{A\}, \emptyset\rangle, \mathcal{X}_A)\}$ with $\mathcal{X}_A = \{X \mid X$ is a focal element and $X \subseteq W(A)\}$, and T_n consists of only pairs of the form $(\langle\emptyset, \emptyset, \_, \_\rangle, \_)$. The set of foci derived by d is $\bigcup\limits_{(\_,\mathcal{X})\in T_n} \mathcal{X}$.*

The following theorem says that our DSAF inference procedures are correct whenever given AF proof procedures are sound and complete. For the lack of space, we omit the proof.

Theorem 1. *Assume the soundness and completeness of dispute derivations for AF semantics sem. If $\mathcal{W}_d$ is the set of foci derived by a foci derivation d for an argument A, then $Bl_{sem}(A) = \sum\limits_{Y \in \mathcal{W}_d} m(Y)$.*

In the following, we demonstrate a Prolog-based implementation of our DSAF inference procedures. As illustrated by code Listing 1.1, users need to specify DSAF frameworks using a tiny syntax: `arg(.,[.])` declares, for each argument A, the set of possible worlds $W(A)$ containing A; `att(.,.)` declares an attack between two arguments; and `m([.],.)` assigns masses to sets of possible words.

Listing 1.1. The specification of the DSAF in Example 2

```
arg(a, [w1]).
arg(b1, [w1,w2]).
arg(b2, [w1,w2]).
att(a,b1).
att(b1,b2).
att(b2,b1).

m([w1],0.1).
m([w2],0.2).
m([w1,w2],0.7).
```

Note that a DSAF specification is a valid Prolog program. The screen shot in Fig. 3 shows how users could load the specification in code Listing 1.1, then call our DSAF procedures to compute $Bl_{pr}(.)$ and $Pl_{pr}(.)$, using Prolog queries `blpr/1` and `plpr/1` respectively.

```
                        implementation — swipl — 73×19

For help, use ?- help(Topic). or ?- apropos(Word).

?- ['./dsafengine.pl'].
true.

?- ['./test/dsex.pl'].
true.

?- blpr(b1).
0.2
derived set of foci:[[w2]]
true .

?- plpr(b1).
0.8999999999999999
derived set of foci:[[w2],[w1,w2]]
true .
```

Fig. 3. Sample invocations of DSAF procedures

6   Conclusions and Related Work

Abstract Argumentation (AF [4]) has been used to unify different reasoning formalisms in AI, and also extended in several directions to address its shortcomings. Recently several authors combine AF with classical probability theory to propose different Probabilistic Argumentation frameworks (PAF). In this paper, using legal argument from analogy, we argue that interpreters of real-life arguments may have to deal with a kind of uncertainty that can be appropriately represented in Dempster-Shafer (DS) theory rather than the classical probability theory. Hence we develop an extension of AF using Dempster-Shafer theory, which we refer to as DS-based Argumentation framework (DSAF). Concretely, we first define a DSAF form and semantics by generalizing the existing PAF form and semantics. We then develop a method to translate existing proof procedures for standard Abstract Argumentation into DSAF inference procedures. Finally, we give a Prolog-based implementation of the resulted DSAF inference procedures. Note that since PAF is a subclass of DSAF, our DSAF inference procedures can also be used to compute PAF, for which the current literature contains only the procedure for PAF grounded semantics of Thang [18].

The results in this paper came out much easily since we define DSAF as a mathematical generalization of PAF and AF. To the best of our knowledge, though there are many existing proposals to combine DST and argumentation theory, none of them mathematically generalize PAF (and even AF) truly. Notably, in [2,16] the authors combine DST with deductive reasoning, which is a too simple form of argumentation because it does not allow attacks. In

[9] Kohlas, Berzati and Haenni show how to associate probability mass with formula and compute measures-like belief degrees of the reasoning with these formula. However, arguments in [9] are restricted to conjunctions of literals. In [11] Oren, Norman and Preece present argumentation semantics for subjective logic equiped with measures from DST. In [17], Tang et al. shows how DST measures associated with logical sentences and rules can be used to derive DST measures of arguments constructed from such elements. However the authors do not introduce any argumentation semantics for such a system of arguments. Recently, Samet et al. in [14] introduces a so-called evidential argumentation framework (EvAF) $(\mathcal{F}, M)$ where $\mathcal{F}$ is a standard AF framework and M is a set of mass functions each of which is associated with an individual argument in $\mathcal{F}$. Under Samet et al's interpretation, each argument A in an EvAF $(\mathcal{F}, M)$ has a set of alternatives Θ_A, and hence the mass function $m_A \in M$ represents the uncertainty regarding which alternative in Θ_A actually occurs. For example, EvAF $(\mathcal{F}, M)$ with $\mathcal{F} = (\{A, B\}, \{(A, B)\})$; $M = \{m_A, m_B\}$; $\Theta_A = \{A_1, A_2\}$, $\Theta_B = \{B_1\}$; $m_A = \{\{A_1\} \mapsto 0.5; \{A_2\} \mapsto 0.5\}$; and $m_B = \{\{B_1\} \mapsto 1.0\}$ represents an argumentative context with an argument A attacking an argument B; and while A has two equal alternatives, B has only one. The semantics of EvAF are defined by coercing EvAF into AF. As a result, EvAF does not generalize PAF in anyway. Moreover, because AF can not handle DST measures, the coercion of EvAF into AF may give counter-intuitive results. For example, weirdly enough, B is accepted in the above sample EvAF. This is because this EvAF is coerced into two AF frameworks (the authors call them "belief scenario graphs"), namely $\mathcal{F}_1 = (\{A_1, B_1\}, \{\})$ and $\mathcal{F}_1 = (\{A_2, B_1\}, \{\})$. Note that in these belief scenario graphs, A_1, A_2 do not attack B_1 because for the authors, an attack (X_i, Y_j) (where $X_i \in \Theta_X$, $Y_j \in \Theta_Y$ and X attacks Y according to $\mathcal{F}$) materializes only if $Bl(X_i) \geq Bl(Y_j)$ and $Pl(X_i) \geq Pl(Y_j)$, where Bl and Pl are computed from m_X and m_Y (see Sect. 3). So in the above sample EvAF, $Pl(B_1) = Bl(B_1) = 1$ and hence neither A_1 nor A_2 can attack B_1. Note that this argumentative context can be represented by a DSAF framework with $m(\omega_1) = m(\omega_2) = 0.5$ shown below. Under our DSAF semantics, $Bl_{sem}(B_1) = Pl_{sem}(B_1) = 0$, which faithfully reflects our expectation that B is totally unacceptable.

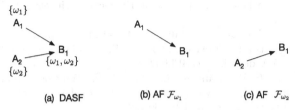

(a) DASF   (b) AF $\mathcal{F}_{\omega_1}$ (c) AF $\mathcal{F}_{\omega_2}$

Acknowledgment. This work was partially funded by: (1) Center of Excellence in Intelligent Informatics, Speech and Language Technology and Service Innovation (CILS), Thammasat University; and (2) Intelligent Informatics and Service Innovation (IISI), SIIT, Thammasat University.

References

1. Brewer, S.: Exemplary reasoning: semantics, pragmatics, and the rational force of legal argument by analogy. Harv. Law Rev. **109**, 923–1028 (1996)
2. Chatalic, P., Dubois, D., Prade, H.: An approach to approximate reasoning based on the dempster rule of combination. Int. J. Expert Syst. **1**(1), 67–85 (1987)
3. Dempster, A.P.: Upper and lower probabilities induced by a multivalued mapping. In: Yager, R.R., Liu, L. (eds.) Classic Works of the Dempster-Shafer Theory of Belief Functions. STUDFUZZ, vol. 219, pp. 57–72. Springer, Heidelberg (2008). doi:10.1007/978-3-540-44792-4_3
4. Dung, P.M.: On the acceptability of arguments and its fundamental role in non-monotonic reasoning, logic programming and n-person games. Artif. Intell. **77**(2), 321–357 (1995)
5. Phan, M.D., Phan, M.T.: Towards (probabilistic) argumentation for jury-based dispute resolution. In: COMMA 2010, pp. 171–182 (2010)
6. Fazzinga, B., Flesca, S., Parisi, F.: On the complexity of probabilistic abstract argumentation frameworks. ACM Trans. Comput. Logic **16**(3), 22:1–22:39 (2015)
7. Gabbay, D.M., Rodrigues, O.: Probabilistic argumentation. An Equational Approach. CoRR (2015)
8. Hunter, A.: A probabilistic approach to modelling uncertain logical arguments. Int. J. Approximate Reasoning **54**(1), 47–81 (2013)
9. Kohlas, J., Berzati, D., Haenni, R.: Probabilistic argumentation systems and abduction. Ann. Math. Artif. Intell. **34**(1), 177–195 (2002)
10. Li, H., Oren, N., Norman, T.J.: Probabilistic argumentation frameworks. In: Modgil, S., Oren, N., Toni, F. (eds.) TAFA 2011. LNCS, vol. 7132, pp. 1–16. Springer, Heidelberg (2012). doi:10.1007/978-3-642-29184-5_1
11. Oren, N., Norman, T.J., Preece, A.: Subjective logic and arguing with evidence. Artif. Intell. **171**(10), 838–854 (2007)
12. Polberg, S., Doder, D.: Probabilistic abstract dialectical frameworks. In: Fermé, E., Leite, J. (eds.) JELIA 2014. LNCS, vol. 8761, pp. 591–599. Springer, Cham (2014). doi:10.1007/978-3-319-11558-0_42
13. Posner, R.A.: Reasoning by analogy. Cornell L. Rev. **91**, 761–774 (2006)
14. Samet, A., Raddaoui, B., Dao, T.-T., Hadjali, A.: Argumentation framework based on evidence theory. In: Carvalho, J.P., Lesot, M.-J., Kaymak, U., Vieira, S., Bouchon-Meunier, B., Yager, R.R. (eds.) IPMU 2016. CCIS, vol. 611, pp. 253–264. Springer, Cham (2016). doi:10.1007/978-3-319-40581-0_21
15. Shafer, G.: A Mathematical Theory of Evidence. Princeton University Press, Princeton (1976)
16. Smets, P.: Probability of deductibility and belief functions. In: Clarke, M., Kruse, R., Moral, S. (eds.) ECSQARU 1993. LNCS, vol. 747, pp. 332–340. Springer, Heidelberg (1993). doi:10.1007/BFb0028218
17. Tang, Y., Hang, C.-W., Parsons, S., Singh, M.P.: Towards argumentation with symbolic Dempster-Shafer evidence. In: Computational Models of Argument - Proceedings of COMMA 2012, pp. 462–469 (2012)

18. Thang, P.M.: Dialectical proof procedures for probabilistic abstract argumentation. In: Baldoni, M., Chopra, A.K., Son, T.C., Hirayama, K., Torroni, P. (eds.) PRIMA 2016. LNCS (LNAI), vol. 9862, pp. 397–406. Springer, Cham (2016). doi:10.1007/ 978-3-319-44832-9_27

19. Thang, P.M., Dung, P.M., Hung, N.D.: Toward a common framework for dialectical proof procedure in abstract argumentation. J. Logic Comput. **19**, 1071–1109 (2009)

20. Thimm, M.: A probabilistic semantics for abstract argumentation. In: ECAI, vol. 242, pp. 750–755. ISO Press (2012)

Evolving Kernel PCA Pipelines
with Evolution Strategies

Oliver Kramer[(✉)]

Computational Intelligence Group, Department of Computer Science,
University of Oldenburg, Oldenburg, Germany
`oliver.kramer@uni-oldenburg.de`

Abstract. This paper introduces an evolutionary tuning approach for
a pipeline of preprocessing methods and kernel principal component
analysis (PCA) employing evolution strategies (ES). A simple (1+1)-
ES adapts the imputation method, various preprocessing steps like normalization and standardization, and optimizes the parameters of kernel
PCA. A small experimental study on a benchmark data set with missing
values demonstrates that the evolutionary kernel PCA pipeline can be
tuned with relatively few optimization steps, which makes evolutionary
tuning applicable to scenarios with very large data sets.

Keywords: Dimension reduction · Evolutionary machine learning ·
Machine learning pipelines · Kernel PCA

1 Introduction

Large and diverse data sets increase the demand for fast and flexible adaptations
of machine learning pipelines. Such pipelines comprise numerous preprocessing
steps like imputation of missing values, normalization and standardization, selection of a dimension reduction technique, and the choice of parameters. Finding
proper settings for such a machine learning pipeline is a combinatorial optimization problem and often induces a large solution space. The choice of methods
and their parameterization have a significant impact on the learning result.

The objective of this paper is to demonstrate that even simple ES allow
a fast adaptation of machine learning pipelines for kernel PCA [10] comprising preprocessing steps and kernel optimization like kernel bandwidths of radial
basis function kernels and degrees of polynomial kernels. The pipeline optimization process will be demonstrated experimentally on incomplete data sets with
randomly missing values. The paper is structured as follows. Section 2 gives a
short introduction to kernel PCA. Related work is presented in Sect. 3. Section 4
introduces the evolutionary kernel PCA pipeline optimization process, which is
experimentally analyzed in Sect. 5. Conclusions are drawn in Sect. 6.

© Springer International Publishing AG 2017
G. Kern-Isberner et al. (Eds.): KI 2017, LNAI 10505, pp. 170–177, 2017.
DOI: 10.1007/978-3-319-67190-1_13

2   Kernel PCA

In machine learning we often face the problem of processing high-dimensional patterns. The intrinsic structure of the data is often much lower than the pattern dimensionality. For example, the intrinsic structure of objects on photos is lower than the dimensionality of the color and pixel space of a raw image. To handle this problem, dimension reduction methods seek low-dimensional representations $\hat{\mathbf{x}}_i \in \mathbb{R}^q$ with $i = 1, \ldots, N$ of high-dimensional patterns $\mathbf{x}_i \in \mathbb{R}^d$ with $q < d$ without losing essential information. Such essential information may be neighborhoods of patterns as well as distances between patterns.

PCA [3] computes a basis transformation with an estimate of the covariance matrix C of the patterns $\mathbf{x}_1, \ldots, \mathbf{x}_N$ with $\sum_{i=1}^{N} \mathbf{x}_i = 0$ with $C = 1/N \sum_{i=1}^{N} \mathbf{x}_i \mathbf{x}_i^T$. The orthogonal projections onto the eigenvectors are the principal components. Schölkopf et al. [10] generalize PCA for handling nonlinear data by mapping the data into a feature space F with a kernel function $\phi : \mathbb{R}^N \to F$. The following depiction is a short introduction based on [10]. Also for the kernel version of PCA the data mapped to F is assumed to be centered $\sum_{i=1}^{N} \phi(\mathbf{x}_i) = 0$. For computation of the feature space variant of the covariance matrix

$$\hat{C} = 1/N \sum_{i=1}^{N} \phi(\mathbf{x}_i)\phi(\mathbf{x}_i)^T, \tag{1}$$

eigenvalues $\lambda \geq 0$ and eigenvectors $\mathbf{V} \in F \setminus \{0\}$ have to be found that satisfy $\lambda \mathbf{V} = \hat{C}\mathbf{V}$. After substitution the eigenvectors can be expressed with coefficients $\alpha_1, \ldots, \alpha_N$ such that $\mathbf{V} = \sum_{i=1}^{N} \alpha_i \phi(\mathbf{x})_i$. With kernel matrix $K_{ij} = (\phi(\mathbf{x}_i) \cdot \phi(\mathbf{x}_j))$ it holds $N\lambda K\alpha = K^2\alpha$ with $\alpha = (\alpha_1, \ldots, \alpha_N)^T$. For solutions of this equation, the eigenvalue problem $N\lambda\alpha = K\alpha$ can be solved. After normalization of solutions α^k by normalizing vectors in F corresponding to $1 = \alpha^k \cdot K\alpha^k$, the projections of the mapping of a pattern $\phi\mathbf{x}$ onto the eigenvectors $\mathbf{V}^k$ are achieved by

$$\mathbf{V}^k \cdot \phi(\mathbf{x}) = \sum_{i=1}^{N} \alpha_i^k (\phi(\mathbf{x}_i) \cdot \phi(\mathbf{x})). \tag{2}$$

The mapping $\phi(\mathbf{x}_i)$ does not have to be computed explicitly, but the dot product is sufficient, commonly known as kernel trick.

The kernel functions we use for the kernel PCA pipeline are the linear kernel $k(\mathbf{x}_i, \mathbf{x}_j) = \mathbf{x}_i^T \mathbf{x}_j$, the polynomial kernel $k(\mathbf{x}_i, \mathbf{x}_j) = (\mathbf{x}_i^T \mathbf{x}_j + c)^r$ of degree r with $c \in \mathbb{R}$, the radial basis function (RBF) kernel

$$k(\mathbf{x}_i, \mathbf{x}_j) = \exp(-\|\mathbf{x}_i - \mathbf{x}_j\|^2/(2\gamma^2)), \tag{3}$$

with kernel bandwidth γ, the sigmoid kernel $k(\mathbf{x}_i, \mathbf{x}_j) = \tanh(\mathbf{x}_i + \mathbf{x}_j + c)$ with $c \in \mathbb{R}$, and the cosine kernel $(\mathbf{x}_i \cdot \mathbf{x}_j^T)/(\|\mathbf{x}_i\| \cdot \|\mathbf{x}_j\|)$. Their parameters will be evolved with the (1+1)-ES as part of the pipeline tuning process.

3   Related Work

From the analysis of related work on evolutionary search in unsupervised learning, we derive a short taxonomy, see Fig. 1. It divides the related work into three branches: (1) evolutionary tuning of dimension reduction parameters, (2) evolving unsupervised learning pipelines, e.g., order and configuration of the pipeline steps, and (3) primary learning approaches, where the ES is the main solver of the primary machine learning optimization problem. The evolutionary kernel PCA pipeline approach introduced in this work belongs to the second branch.

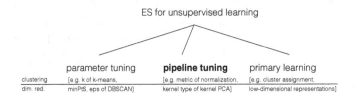

Fig. 1. Taxonomy of ES in unsupervised learning with examples for objective variables targeting clustering (upper row) and dimension reduction (lower row).

Evolutionary methods have proven well in tuning unsupervised methods like clustering. For example in [4], the parameters of DBSCAN are optimized with differential evolution. Further, evolutionary algorithms have been applied to subspace clustering problems [5]. For optimization of supervised machine learning parameters Bayesian optimization is a common approach, e.g., presented for latent Dirichlet allocation, structured support vector machines, and convolutional neural networks in [11]. Evolutionary tuning of kernels for support vector machines has been conducted in [2].

Few work has been introduced for the automatic evolution of machine learning pipelines. Olson *et al.* [8] proposed an evolvable machine learning pipeline called tree-based pipeline optimization tool (TPOT) for supervised learning based on SCIKIT-LEARN [9] with tree-based genetic programming. The approach does not allow the employment of dimension reduction measures.

The primary optimization problem can be solved by evolutionary techniques. For example, evolutionary clustering aims at finding clusters in data with evolutionary algorithms [1]. An unsupervised regression variant for dimension reduction has been introduced that alternates gradient descent and iterative evolutionary embeddings [7].

Kernel PCA has originally been introduced by Schölkopf *et al.* [10]. It has successfully been applied to many domains, e.g. in [6]. Sun *et al.* [12] evolved kernel parameters of kernel PCA with evolutionary algorithms for fault diagnosis applications.

4 Pipeline Evolution

The dimension reduction pipeline employed in this work comprises the three steps imputation, preprocessing, and dimension reduction. The imputation step is based on the SCIKIT-LEARN [9] method preprocessing.Imputer. It imputes all occurrences of missing values. The pipeline optimization process can choose among three possibilities, i.e., imputation based on the mean, the median, or the most frequent value of each dimension for all patterns. The output of the imputation step is a complete pattern set without missing values.

As next step the imputed patterns are forwarded to the preprocessing step, which has the task of transforming patterns to be more suitable for the dimension reduction process. Similar to the imputation step, the preprocessing methods are based on the SCIKIT-LEARN class preprocessing, and use the ScaleStandardScaler() with or without mean centering before scaling, the MinMaxScaler() with intervals $[0, 1], [-1, 1], [0, 100], [-100, 100]$, the RobustScaler(), and the Normalizer() with l1-norm, l2-norm, and max-norm.

The last step is the kernel PCA step, which can be parameterized with a linear kernel, a polynomial kernel, an RBF kernel, a sigmoid kernel, and a cosine kernel. For the polynomial kernel the degree of freedom can be a discrete value from the interval $[2, 20]$ with the term $c \in \mathbb{R}$ taking values from $10^{-20}, 10^{-19}$ to 10^{20}. The same settings are possible for the sigmoid kernel, while the RBF kernel bandwidth settings range in the same interval.

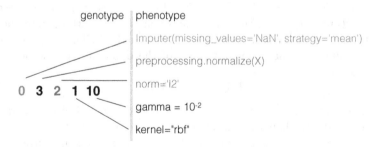

Fig. 2. Exemplary illustration of genotype-phenotype mapping of the dimension reduction pipeline. The vector of integers encodes the choice of imputation method, of preprocessing variant with parameterization, of kernel type, and its parameter.

To examine, if evolutionary search is a powerful tool for the pipeline tuning task, we restrict the budget of fitness evaluations to less than 0.2% of the solution space size. The overall number of method and parameter choices is 26,460 and we only allow 50 pipeline evaluations, which may be a reasonable scenario in case of large data sets or computationally restricted domains.

The chromosome that represents the dimension reduction pipeline is a vector $\mathbf{z} \in \mathbb{Z}^n$ of n integers. Each gene z_i encodes the choice of a method or its parameterization. The chromosome is translated into an SCIKIT-LEARN machine learning pipeline. Figure 2 illustrates this genotype-phenotype mapping. In this example, the imputer employs the mean-method for reconstructing missing values, normalization is based on the l2-norm, and kernel PCA uses an RBF-kernel with bandwidth $\gamma = 10^{-2}$.

For optimization of the dimension reduction pipeline, a (1+1)-ES is used, see Algorithm 1. Based on solution $\mathbf{z}$ the ES generates an offspring solution $\mathbf{z}' \in \mathbb{Z}^n$ in each generation with random resetting. Each gene z_i is mutated with rate $\sigma = 1/n$ by randomly drawing a new integer from the interval $[0, l_i - 1]$, where l_i is the number of possible settings for the i-th pipeline part. The initial solution is drawn in the same way.

Algorithm 1. $(1 + 1)$-ES with random resetting

1: choose $\mathbf{z}$ with $z_i \in [0, l_i - 1]$ uniformly at random
2: **repeat**
3:     produce $\mathbf{z}'$ from $\mathbf{z}$ with random resetting and probability $1/n$
4:     replace $\mathbf{z}$ with $\mathbf{z}'$ if $f(\mathbf{z}') \leq f(\mathbf{z})$
5: **until** termination condition

The Shepard-Kruskal index is a reasonable measure for evaluating the dimension reduction result. In the evolutionary optimization process, it defines the objective function. Shepard-Kruskal measures the maintenance of distances in the low dimensional space. Let $\mathbf{D}$ be the distance matrix in data space and $\hat{\mathbf{D}}$ be the distance matrix in the low-dimensional space. Both contain the pairwise Euclidean distances and are considered as normalized. The Shepard-Kruskal measure is defined as the Frobenius norm of the differences of the normalized distance matrixes

$$E_{sk} = \|\mathbf{D} - \hat{\mathbf{D}}\|_F^2. \tag{4}$$

A low Shepard-Kruskal measure is preferable. For example, if distances are completely preserved, the Shepard-Kruskal measure is zero. Further dimension reduction measures exclusively concentrate on the maintenance of neighborhoods, e.g., the co-ranking matrix measure, and can easily replace E_{sk} in our approach.

5   Experiments

In this section we analyze the dimension reduction pipeline evolution experimentally on a small set of benchmark problems. The analysis is based on the data sets *Digits*, *Friedman*, a *Wind* data set, and a set comprising image segmentation features, each with $N = 500$ incomplete patterns employing two missing rates. The missing values[1] are randomly generated with uniform distribution and missing rate m. Table 1 shows the outcome of the experimental results of fifty (1+1)-ES runs optimizing the Shepard-Kruskal measure E_{sk}. The table shows

---

[1] type `numpy.nan` in PYTHON.

Table 1. Experimental analysis of the evolving kernel PCA pipeline approach on the four benchmark data sets. The figures show the best, mean, standard deviations, and worst results for E_{sk} of 50 (1+1)-ES runs, each with 50 fitness function evaluations. PCA serves as reference method. Bold values indicate the most successful runs.

Data	m	Best	mean $\pm$ dev	Worst	PCA
Digits	0.1	**132.90**	136.17 $\pm$ 2.84	140.60	138.39
	0.25	**137.33**	143.49 $\pm$ 5.47	151.21	138.39
Friedman	0.1	**286.35**	309.37 $\pm$ 13.13	322.77	324.94
	0.25	**315.76**	316.68 $\pm$ 0.82	317.94	317.45
Wind	0.1	43.67	45.16 $\pm$ 2.53	50.16	**31.78**
	0.25	59.11	72.94 $\pm$ 8.45	81.75	**31.78**
Image	0.1	**33.87**	41.07 $\pm$ 8.85	53.55	40.08
	0.25	**25.75**	43.19 $\pm$ 24.38	88.28	40.08

the best, mean, standard deviations, and the worst results of the runs. For comparison, a simple PCA is conducted on the complete data sets without missing values. The target dimensionality is $q = 2$.

The results show that the (1+1)-ES pipeline evolution achieves significantly better results than standard PCA despite the fact that the latter is based on the data set with complete patterns and no missing values. Only in case of the *Wind* data set, standard PCA outperforms the evolved pipeline, which may be due to a significant influence of the incomplete patterns. The mean, standard deviations, and worst values show that the results are quite stable. Most E_{sk} values are better for low missing rates.

Figure 3 visualizes the fitness developments of the evolutionary runs on *Digits*, *Friedman*, and the *Image* data set with missing rate $m = 0.1$. The plots show the developments of the mean, best, and worst fitness values of 50 runs at each generation for the complete evolutionary runs. The fitness developments on the *Digits* data set differ at the beginning. When the optimization process finds an adequate method constellation, the fitness improves fast and converges to similar

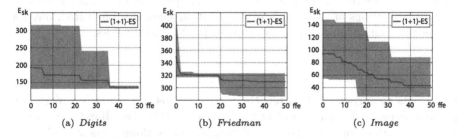

(a) *Digits*　　　　　　　(b) *Friedman*　　　　　　　(c) *Image*

Fig. 3. Fitness developments of the evolutionary kernel PCA pipeline process on *Digits*, *Friedman*, and the *Image* data set with missing rate $m = 0.1$.

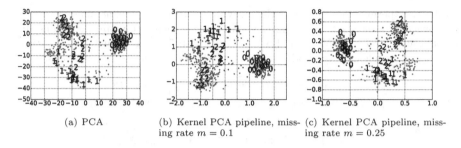

(a) PCA   (b) Kernel PCA pipeline, miss-   (c) Kernel PCA pipeline, miss-
                         ing rate $m = 0.1$ ing rate $m = 0.25$

Fig. 4. Visualization of exemplary embeddings of PCA on the complete *Digits* data set and two kernel PCA pipelines evolved on the incomplete *Digits* data set with missing rates $m = 0.1$ and $m = 0.25$.

values. On *Friedman*, the first part of the optimization process is converging fast, while the second part shows different behaviors in different runs. Different runs vary significantly on the *Image* data set.

Figure 4 visualizes the final embeddings that result from the dimension reduction processes. PCA achieves a Shephard-Kruskal measure of $E_{sk} = 122.67$ in this run, which is outperformed by both kernel PCA pipelines for the missing rates $m = 0.1$ with $E_{sk} = 118.93$ and $m = 0.25$ with $E_{sk} = 115.93$. The plots show that all settings lead to reasonable embeddings without significant differences between the complete and the incomplete data sets. Moreover, the two evolved pipeline results are rotated variants of the PCA embedding.

6   Conclusions

Machine learning pipelines become more and more complex because of numerous preprocessing steps. Further, each step requires the specification of numerous parameters. The overall optimization problem induces a particularly large space of pipeline variants. In this paper, we demonstrate how ES can be used to evolve kernel PCA pipelines for dimension reduction. The analysis concentrates on incomplete data sets comprising the steps imputation, preprocessing, and kernel tuning. A simple (1+1)-ES achieves satisfying tuning results, in particular when considering the large size of the solution space. With a small budget of only 50 evaluations at most 0.2% of the solution space can be visited, but yet the resulting embedding shows excellent Shepard-Kruskal values.

A   Data Sets

UCI Digits comprises handwritten *Digits* with $d = 64$. *Friedman* is a regression problem generated with SCIKIT-LEARN and $d = 500$. The *Wind* data set is based on spatio-temporal time series data from the National Renewable Energy Laboratory (NREL) comprising 11 three MW turbines for three years in a 10-minute resolution, resulting in $d = 11$ dimensions. The *Image* data set contains image segmentation data with $d = 19$ dimensions.

References

1. Das, S., Abraham, A., Konar, A.: Automatic clustering using an improved differential evolution algorithm. IEEE Trans. Syst. Man Cybern. Part A **38**(1), 218–237 (2008)
2. Friedrichs, F., Igel, C.: Evolutionary tuning of multiple SVM parameters. Neurocomputing **64**, 107–117 (2005)
3. Jolliffe, I.: Principal Component Analysis. Springer Series in Statistics. Springer, New York (1986)
4. Karami, A., Johansson, R.: Choosing DBSCAN parameters automatically using differential evolution. Int. J. Comput. Appl. **91**(7), 1–11 (2014)
5. Kramer, O.: Hybrid manifold clustering with evolutionary tuning. In: Mora, A.M., Squillero, G. (eds.) EvoApplications 2015. LNCS, vol. 9028, pp. 481–490. Springer, Cham (2015). doi:10.1007/978-3-319-16549-3_39
6. Kwok, J.T., Mak, B., Ho, S.K.: Eigenvoice speaker adaptation via composite kernel PCA. In: Neural Information Processing Systems (NIPS), pp. 1401–1408 (2003)
7. Lückehe, D., Kramer, O.: Alternating optimization of unsupervised regression with evolutionary embeddings. In: Mora, A.M., Squillero, G. (eds.) EvoApplications 2015. LNCS, vol. 9028, pp. 471–480. Springer, Cham (2015). doi:10.1007/978-3-319-16549-3_38
8. Olson, R.S., Bartley, N., Urbanowicz, R.J., Moore, J.H.: Evaluation of a tree-based pipeline optimization tool for automating data science. In: Genetic and Evolutionary Computation Conference (GECCO), pp. 485–492 (2016)
9. Pedregosa, F., Varoquaux, G., Gramfort, A., Michel, V., Thirion, B., Grisel, O., Blondel, M., Prettenhofer, P., Weiss, R., Dubourg, V., Vanderplas, J., Passos, A., Cournapeau, D., Brucher, M., Perrot, M., Duchesnay, E.: Scikit-learn: machine learning in Python. J. Mach. Learn. Res. **12**, 2825–2830 (2011)
10. Schölkopf, B., Smola, A., Müller, K.-R.: Nonlinear component analysis as a kernel eigenvalue problem. Neural Comput. **10**(5), 1299–1319 (1998)
11. Snoek, J., Larochelle, H., Adams, R.P.: Practical bayesian optimization of machine learning algorithms. In: Neural Information Processing Systems (NIPS), pp. 2960–2968 (2012)
12. Sun, R., Tsung, F., Qu, L.: Integrating KPCA with an improved evolutionary algorithm for knowledge discovery in fault diagnosis. In: Leung, K.S., Chan, L.-W., Meng, H. (eds.) IDEAL 2000. LNCS, vol. 1983, pp. 174–179. Springer, Heidelberg (2000). doi:10.1007/3-540-44491-2_26

An Experimental Study of Dimensionality Reduction Methods

Almuth Meier$^{(\boxtimes)}$ and Oliver Kramer

Computational Intelligence Group, Department of Computing Science,
University of Oldenburg, Oldenburg, Germany
{almuth.meier,oliver.kramer}@uni-oldenburg.de

Abstract. Dimensionality reduction (DR) lowers the dimensionality of a high-dimensional data set by reducing the number of features for each pattern. The importance of DR techniques for data analysis and visualization led to the development of a large diversity of DR methods. The lack of comprehensive comparative studies makes it difficult to choose the best DR methods for a particular task based on known strengths and weaknesses. To close the gap, this paper presents an extensive experimental study comparing 29 DR methods on 13 artificial and real-world data sets. The performance assessment of the study is based on six quantitative metrics. According to our benchmark and evaluation scheme, the methods mMDS, GPLVM, and PCA turn out to outperform their competitors, although exceptions are revealed for special cases.

Keywords: Dimensionality reduction · Manifold learning · Feature extraction

1 Introduction

High-dimensional data appear in many applications, but are demanding in different ways. High dimensionalities not only challenge storage and network throughput technologies, but also complicate data analysis tasks. For humans, data with a dimensionality larger than three are difficult to understand since no intuitive visualization is possible. Even if machine learning techniques are employed to extract important information from the data, e. g., by clustering or classification, a high dimensionality is impeding as it requires a large training data set (curse of dimensionality) and extends the runtime.

DR computes a mapping $\mathbf{F} : \mathbb{R}^d \to \mathbb{R}^q$ from a d-dimensional data space to a q-dimensional latent space with $q < d$. Each data point (pattern) from the original data set is mapped to a latent point with only q features. In other words, each pattern is embedded into latent space leading to an embedding (manifold) of the whole data set. The dimensionality q of the latent space (intrinsic dimensionality) is often not determined by the DR methods, but has to be estimated with separate techniques, e. g., maximum likelihood [27]. Instead of an estimation, the user can adapt the intrinsic dimensionality to his needs. For example,

© Springer International Publishing AG 2017
G. Kern-Isberner et al. (Eds.): KI 2017, LNAI 10505, pp. 178–192, 2017.
DOI: 10.1007/978-3-319-67190-1_14

an intrinsic dimensionality less or equal three is often chosen if DR is used to visualize data.

The way of computing mapping **F** significantly differs among the DR methods. Unlike feature selection, feature extraction methods generate completely new dimensions, which are combinations of the old ones and are therefore not directly interpretable. Our study exclusively concentrates on feature extraction methods. We include parametric methods that explicitly learn **F** and its parameters, and that are able to embed new unknown patterns. But we also concentrate on non-parametric DR methods that directly map high-dimensional patterns to latent points and thus modeling **F**. The study also comprises numerous convex and non-convex techniques. Convex methods use convex objective functions that guarantee to find the corresponding optimum, while non-convex methods might yield better mappings, in particular for non-linear data, but do not guarantee to find the best solution of their objective function. Furthermore, the methods can be grouped into families which apply similar mathematical concepts.

Due to the fact that new DR methods are often compared only against older established DR methods, like PCA [18,37], Isomap [47] or LLE [40], but not against newer ones, overall quality differences are not transparent. In most existing studies only few data sets and few quantitative measures are used deteriorating the understanding, why methods have specific strengths and weaknesses. These reasons hamper a reasonable performance evaluation of DR methods for defined applications and motivate the comparative study this paper presents.

This work is structured as follows: We review existing comparative studies in Sect. 2 and explain the setup of our experiments in Sect. 3. Afterwards, we evaluate the outcomes of our experiments in Sect. 4. A summary concludes this paper in Sect. 5.

2   Current Comparative Studies

In the current literature, various contributions giving an overview of DR techniques exist, e. g., [10,25]. They describe method design and applied mathematical concepts, but do not include empirical comparisons. Therefore, they do not give insights into differences between the methods regarding practical usage.

Other contributions, e. g., by Gisbrecht and Hammer [12], investigate the suitability of DR methods for visualization tasks. They embed high-dimensional data sets with different DR methods, visualize the resulting manifolds and assess the embedding quality with one quantitative measure. Nevertheless, these comparisons are not satisfactory as data sets, method diversity and metrics run too short.

The most extensive quantitative study is presented by van der Maaten et al. [33]. Newer methods like UNN [20], EE [5] or t-SNE [32] are not included. Mysling et al. [35] conduct a quantitative comparison that examines the dependence of four DR methods on data set properties, like data density and noise, in terms of a classification and a regression error. Also Yeh et al. [52] present a limited comparison with three DR methods on one data set with respect to one metric that assesses the methods' suitability as pre-processing techniques before clustering. Furthermore, some studies exist that compare DR methods solely for specific applications, e.g., by Niskanen and Silvén [36].

3   Experimental Setup

Our experimental study comprises 29 DR methods, 13 data sets, and six metrics. On each data set, each DR method is executed repeatedly, each time with a separate parameter setting like grid search. Due to the non-deterministic behavior of some DR methods, each of these executions is run 25 times. Only for methods with an extensive runtime only 3 repetitions are conducted. The metrics are computed for each run and are averaged over the 25 repetitions. For each DR method we aggregate one value per data set and metric, i.e., the best one the DR method has achieved among all parameter settings.

3.1   DR Methods

We selected the DR methods in our study with the objective to include at least one method from each family of unsupervised feature extraction methods (Fig. 1). The convex DR methods are based on an eigenvalue (or spectral) decomposition. They can be subdivided according to whether the eigenvalue decomposition is performed for a sparse or full matrix. Within both categories the DR methods employ different mathematical techniques. Kernels make DR methods capture non-linear structures in the data. Neighborhood graphs are used to set up a distance matrix containing the similarities of neighbored patterns, which are often measured in terms of Euclidean distances. DR methods use the distance matrix, but can only embed patterns belonging to the largest sub-graph. Since our evaluation requires an embedding for all patterns we embed the remaining patterns with a so called out-of-sample extension implemented by van der Maaten [31].

Concepts used by non-convex methods are unsupervised regression, neural networks, and probabilistic approaches. Regression methods optimize the latent points so that the patterns reconstructed from the latent points by k-nearest neighbors (kNN) regression differ as little as possible from the original patterns. In case of so called autoencoders, neural networks for DR have an odd number of layers and the middle layer of neurons represents the latent point belonging to the input pattern. During the training procedure the weights are optimized so that the output of the network, i.e., the reconstructed pattern, is similar to the input, i.e., the original pattern.

Probabilistic DR methods can also be divided into different families: methods based on the latent variable model (LVM), techniques employing a mixture model and methods that use probabilities as a measure for the similarity of patterns and latent points. Methods based on the LVM assume that the features of the observed patterns are random variables underlying a common probability distribution, which actually is based on a smaller set of unobservable random

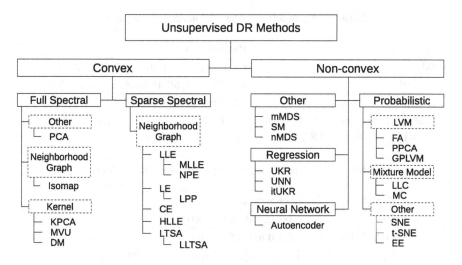

Fig. 1. A taxonomy of employed unsupervised DR methods, based on [33]

variables, so called latent variables. The values of the latent variables are the latent points. They are optimized along with the parameters of the probability distribution to maximize the likelihood for observing the patterns. A mixture model is an aggregation of multiple density estimators to one larger estimator. Its parameters and the latent points are optimized similar to the optimization procedure of the LVM.

This experimental study is based on the following methods, which we also arranged in a taxonomy (Fig. 1): CE (Conformal Eigenmaps) [44], DM (Diffusion Maps) [6,7], EE (Elastic Embedding), FA (Factor Analysis) [45], GPLVM (Gaussian Process LVM) [24], HLLE (Hessian LLE) [9], Isomap (Isometric Feature Mapping), itUKR (iterative UKR) [29], KPCA (Kernel PCA) [43], LE (Laplacian Eigenmaps) [3], LLC (Locally Linear Coordination) [46], LLE (Locally Linear Embedding), LLTSA (Linear LTSA) [53], LPP (Locality Preserving Projections) [14], LTSA (Local Tangent Space Alignment) [54], MC (Manifold Charting) [4], MDS (Multidimensional Scaling), MLLE (Modified LLE) [55], mMDS (metric MDS) [48], MVU (Maximum Variance Unfolding) [50,51], nMDS (nonmetric MDS) [23], NPE (Neighborhood Preserving Embedding) [13], PCA (Principal Component Analysis), PPCA (Probabilistic PCA) [39], SM (Sammon Mapping) [41], SNE (Stochastic Neighbor Embedding) [16], t-SNE (t-Distributed SNE), UKR (Unsupervised Kernel Regression) [34], and UNN (Unsupervised Nearest Neighbors). The autoencoder was proposed in [8,17].

We use the following implementations: SCIKIT-LEARN [38] for mMDS, nMDS, MLLE and HLLE, MATLAB code by Vladymyrov and Carreira-Perpiñán for EE according to [49], MATLAB toolbox by Klanke [19] for UKR, self-implementation of UNN in PYTHON in accordance with Kramer [21, Sect. 4.1], PYTHON code for itUKR from its author and the MATLAB toolbox by van der Maaten [31] for all other methods.

Table 1. Parameter ranges of convex DR methods

Technique	Parameter ranges
DM	$t \in \{1, 10, 30, 50, 70, 90\}, \sigma \in \{0.2, 1.0, 5.0\}$
LE, LPP	$k \in \{5, 9, 13, 50, 100\}, \sigma \in \{0.2, 1.0, 5.0\}$
KPCA	$i \in \{100, 200, 300, 400, 500\}$
Isomap, MVU, LLE, MLLE, NPE, CE, HLLE, LTSA, LLTSA	$k \in \{5, 7, 9, 11, 13, 15, 50, 100\}$

Table 2. Parameter ranges of non-convex DR methods

Technique	Parameter ranges
PPCA	$i \in \{100, 200, 300, 400, 500\}$
GPLVM	$\sigma \in \{0.2, 0.5, 1.0, 2.5, 5.0\}$
LLC	$k \in \{5, 13, 100\}, a \in \{2, 9, 20\}, i \in \{200, 400\}$
MC	$a \in \{2, 7, 12, 20\}, i \in \{200, 400\}$
SNE, t-SNE	$p \in \{5, 10, 15, 20, 25, 30, 35, 40, 45, 50\}$
EE	$h \in \{0.01, 0.1, 0.0, 10.0, 100.0\}, p \in \{5, 25, 50\}$
UKR	$kernel \in \{\text{Gaussian}, \text{Quartic}, \text{Triweight}\}$
UNN	$k \in \{5, 10, 20, 40\}, \kappa \in \{10, 30, 50\}$
itUKR	$\kappa \in \{30, 50, 70\}, bandwidth \in \{10, 20, 30, 40, 50\}$
Autoenc	$\lambda \in \{0.0, 0.2, 0.5, 1.0, 1.5, 2.5, 5.0\}$

The parameter settings we employ are listed in Tables 1 and 2; methods without parameters are not included. For a description of the parameters we refer to the documentation of the respective implementation. We executed each method for each parameter value combination except the autoencoder. Due to an extensive runtime we ran the autoencoder on the data sets CNS and ORL (Sect. 3.3) only with setting $\lambda = 0.0$. We chose value 0.0 since a larger λ often led to NaN metric values on other data sets because latent points were mapped nearly to the same point.

3.2   Metrics

No single criterion for DR methods exists, since the information to be preserved depends on the data set and the purpose of the DR task. Therefore, we assess the methods' quality with different metrics. On the one hand, we measure the topology preservation in terms of neighborhood preservation (ENX), distance preservation (EKS) and structure preservation in general (DSRE, E1NN, CRR). On the other hand, we measure the DR methods' ability for preceding a classification or regression task in terms of information preservation (EKNN, CRR). These metrics seem to be reasonable as it is assumed that most important information of a data set is encoded in its spacial properties. We adapt some metrics so that all metrics are error measures, i. e., lower values represent better qualities.

The ENX measure becomes better the more latent points belonging to neighbored patterns are neighbors, i. e. the more neighborhoods are preserved. It is based on the co-ranking matrix $\mathbf{Q}$ [26]. Following Lueks et al. [30], we adapt ENX to

$$\text{ENX}(k) = 1 - \frac{1}{nk} \sum_{i=1}^{k} \sum_{j=1}^{k} q_{ij}, \tag{1}$$

where q_{ij} is an entry of $\mathbf{Q}$, variable n is the number of patterns or latent points and k is the neighborhood size.

EKS [22] is the objective function of the MDS variants and is computed from the squared Frobenius norm of the distance of the normalized distance matrices of patterns ($\mathbf{D_P}$) and latent points ($\mathbf{D_L}$):

$$\text{EKS} = \|\mathbf{D_P} - \mathbf{D_L}\|_F^2. \tag{2}$$

The distance matrices are normalized by dividing each value by the largest value of the respective matrix. A small EKS indicates similar distances between latent points and their corresponding patterns.

The DSRE [20] measures how well the patterns can be reconstructed from the latent points by applying the kNN regression model $\mathbf{f_L}$ with

$$\mathbf{f_L} : \mathbb{R}^q \rightarrow \mathbb{R}^d, \ \mathbf{f_L}(\mathbf{l}) = \frac{1}{k} \sum_{i \in \mathcal{N}_k(\mathbf{l}, \mathbf{L})} \mathbf{p}_i. \tag{3}$$

Let $\mathbf{P} \in \mathbb{R}^{n \times d}$ denote a pattern matrix, $\mathbf{L} \in \mathbb{R}^{n \times q}$ the corresponding matrix of latent points, $\mathbf{p}_i \in \mathbb{R}^d$ the ith pattern and $\mathbf{l} \in \mathbb{R}^q$ a latent point. The set $\mathcal{N}_k(\mathbf{l}, \mathbf{L})$ contains the indices of the k latent points from $\mathbf{L}$ that are most similar to $\mathbf{l}$. Then the DSRE is defined as

$$\text{DSRE}(\mathbf{L}, k) = \|\mathbf{P} - \mathbf{f_L}(\mathbf{L})\|_F^2, \tag{4}$$

where $\mathbf{f_L}(\mathbf{L}) \in \mathbb{R}^{n \times d}$ is a matrix containing the reconstructions of all patterns. A good DSRE is attained if latent points of neighbored patterns are neighbored.

E1NN [42] measures the overlapping of points with labels from different classes in the data and the latent space. In a w. r. t. E1NN optimal DR process latent points from different classes are clearly separated. This could be desired e. g. for visualization tasks. E1NN counts the number l^- of latent points whose next neighbor has a label from a different class and divides it by p^-, which is analogously defined for patterns:

$$\text{E1NN} = \frac{l^-}{p^-}. \tag{5}$$

An E1NN larger than one indicates a worse structure of the manifold compared to the data space.

CRR [36] calculates the ratio of the number of falsely classified latent points and the number of falsely classified patterns. EKNN [22] is the counterpart of CRR for regression. It is the ratio of the regression error of the latent space and the regression error of the data space. CRR and EKNN use the kNN classification and regression model, respectively. They are useful to examine whether a classification or regression task, respectively, would be more successful on the original or reduced data set.

CRR and E1NN are only applicable to data sets with discrete labels, EKNN only to data sets with continuous labels, whereas ENX, DSRE and EKS are suitable for all data sets. We set the metrics' parameter k, representing the neighborhood size, to 15. Based on the results of Lee and Verleysen [26] this seems to be a reasonable compromise between fluctuating metric values for a very small k and smooth values for a large k.

3.3   Data Sets

We apply the DR methods to five artificial and eight real-world data sets. The artificial data sets come from the comparative study of van der Maaten et al. [33]. Swiss roll, Broken swiss roll, Helix and Twin peaks are shown in Fig. 2, HD is a 10-dimensional data set with a 5-dimensional manifold. They have known manifolds and are generated with the MATLAB toolbox by van der Maaten [31].

The real-world data sets stem from different domains and employ different dimensionalities. In Table 3, their properties are listed. The intrinsic dimensionalities are estimated with the maximum likelihood estimator implementation by van der Maaten [31]. For the MNIST data set, only the GMST estimator from the same toolbox computed a reasonable dimensionality. For the experiments we randomly select 300 patterns from each data set, except for Iris and CNS since they contain less patterns.

Table 3. Properties of real-world data sets

Data set	Dim.	Intrins. dim.	Label type	#Classes	Description
Iris [38]	4	3	Discrete	3	Plant properties of iris flowers
Boston [38]	13	2	Contin.	-	House properties
Digits [38]	64	17	Discrete	10	Pictures of handwritten digits
RCT [28]	386	28	Contin.	-	CT pictures of different persons
MNIST [28]	784	2	Discrete	10	Pictures of handwritten digits
HIVA [2]	1617	15	Discrete	2	Properties of drugs
CNS [15]	7130	30	Discrete	2	Gene data of tumor patients
ORL [1]	10304	7	Discrete	40	Faces of different persons

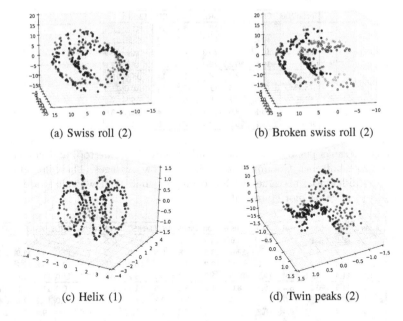

Fig. 2. Artificial data sets and intrinsic dimensionalities. Colors represent labels.

4   Experimental Results

Before the actual evaluation, we examine the statistical significance of the differences between the DR methods. We conduct one Friedman test per metric leading to statistically significant p values (ENX: 4.25e−28, EKS: 1.65e−43, DSRE: 4.57e−66, E1NN: 1.94e−36, CRR: 7.58e−36). For EKNN, no test can be conducted since EKNN requires data sets with continuous labels but only two such data sets are included in our study. For the analysis of the metric values we perform two steps. First, we rank the methods and analyze their rank differences. Second, we compute quality differences that give better insight into the methods' performance. In both steps we compare the methods' performance with respect to both the metrics and the data sets.

4.1   Analysis of Rank Differences

Each DR technique is separately assigned to a rank so that each technique T employs a rank $R_T(D, M)$ for each data set D and metric M. For a more manageable comparison, we average the ranks of each technique in two ways, i.e., over all data sets resulting in one average rank per metric $\varnothing_{R_T}(M)$ and over all metrics resulting in one average rank per data set $\varnothing_{R_T}(D)$. Figures 3 and 4 show the average ranks for the convex and non-convex methods with the best

Technique	ENX	EKS	DSRE	E1NN	CRR	EKNN	∅
PCA	10.8	7.0	12.0	16.9	15.4	11.5	12.3
Isomap	12.8	9.2	13.7	9.7	8.3	15.5	11.4
MLLE	10.8	15.9	10.3	10.9	7.6	10.5	10.9
LE	10.8	15.2	13.4	6.5	7.5	16.5	11.6
mMDS	7.4	2.7	8.2	11.5	14.1	14.5	11.1
GPLVM	10.8	6.6	11.4	15.3	14.7	10.0	11.5
t-SNE	4.9	17.2	8.2	5.4	6.1	5.5	7.8
EE	5.1	8.5	7.1	4.2	4.0	11.5	6.6
UKR	12.2	15.9	3.0	9.0	6.5	1.5	8.0

Fig. 3. Average ranks per metric for best-ranked convex (at the top) and non-convex methods (at the bottom). Column ∅ contains the row averages. The color gradient visualizes the differences of values within columns: small (yellow) values are better than large (red) ones. (Color figure online)

Technique	Swiss	Broken	Helix	Twin	HD	Iris	Boston	Digits	RCT	MNIST	HIVA	CNS	ORL	∅(a.)	∅(r.)	Diff.
PCA	21.4	20.6	23.0	11.2	12.4	5.6	15.3	4.2	3.8	18.6	7.8	6.2	7.0	17.7	8.6	9.2
Isomap	8.6	4.8	9.6	6.6	18.4	12.0	13.3	14.8	9.0	14.0	8.0	7.0	17.0	9.6	11.9	2.3
MLLE	10.6	6.4	8.4	12.4	11.0	17.2	10.3	7.6	17.5	10.2	7.2	14.8	13.2	9.8	12.2	2.5
LE	8.2	11.4	8.2	12.8	17.2	16.2	21.0	8.4	9.3	5.2	6.6	10.4	11.0	11.6	11.0	0.6
mMDS	9.0	11.6	20.2	5.4	8.6	8.0	11.3	5.2	4.8	11.2	5.2	6.4	6.0	11.0	7.3	3.7
GPLVM	21.0	20.2	23.0	11.0	11.0	5.6	14.5	3.8	3.3	17.4	4.6	6.2	7.0	17.2	7.8	9.4
t-SNE	6.2	5.4	7.0	9.4	18.8	11.2	6.8	9.6	7.5	1.8	11.8	6.8	7.0	9.4	7.8	1.6
EE	6.0	4.6	4.0	10.8	9.2	6.8	8.5	5.0	11.5	2.8	4.2	5.2	1.8	6.9	5.7	1.2
UKR	5.8	7.0	7.8	13.4	21.4	16.4	8.8	7.6	8.3	2.8	6.6	7.2	6.2	11.1	8.0	3.1

Fig. 4. Average ranks per data set for best-ranked convex (at the top) and non-convex methods (at the bottom). Data sets are separated into artificial (left) and real-world ones (right). Columns ∅(a.) and ∅(r.) contain the row averages for artificial and real-world data sets, respectively. The differences between both are listed in the last column.

average rank among all methods (i. e. with best value in column ∅ of Fig. 3), which were able to embed all data sets.[1]

Considering the average ranks per metric (Fig. 3), in particular EE, t-SNE and UKR achieve promising results, while no method performs best w. r. t. all metrics. Taking into account the average ranks per data set (Fig. 4), it can be observed that the presented methods (except Isomap and MLLE) perform better on real-world data sets, due to lower values in column ∅(r.) than in ∅(a.). Furthermore, on real-world data sets clearly better results of non-convex methods in contrast to convex methods can be observed. However, PCA is nearly as good as other non-convex methods.

---

[1]   MVU, CE, NPE, LPP, HLLE, LLTSA (convex) and SM, FA, MC (non-convex) were not able to embed up to six real-world data sets due to, e. g., not computable eigenvalue problems, extensive runtime (more than four weeks) or too few patterns.

4.2   Analysis of Quality Differences

To compare the methods' quality differences, based on the percentage of the maximum accuracy employed by Fernández-Delgado et al. [11] we compute for each DR technique T the percentage of the minimum error (PME) per metric M with

$$\text{PME}_T(M) = \frac{1}{13} \sum_{D \in \{\text{Swiss roll},...,\text{ORL}\}} \frac{\text{value for } M \text{ achieved by } T \text{ on } D}{M^* \text{ on } D}$$

and equivalently per data set D with

$$\text{PME}_T(D) = \frac{1}{6} \sum_{M \in \{\text{ENX},...,\text{EKNN}\}} \frac{\text{value for } M \text{ achieved by } T \text{ on } D}{M^* \text{ on } D},$$

where M^* is the best (minimum) value for metric M that any DR technique has achieved on data set D. For example, $\text{PME}_{\text{PCA}}(\text{ENX}) = 2.0$ denotes that the ENX values of PCA are on average two times worse than the best ENX value of any DR method. For each DR method only the data sets are included into the average for the PME measure, which the method was able to embed. This may unfairly improve the PME values of failing methods since their missing metric values for the respective data sets do not influence their PME values, whereas the possibly poor metric values of other methods deteriorate their PME values.

In the left part of Fig. 5 the nine best PME values per metric and the corresponding DR techniques are listed. It is notable that the differences of the PME values are approximately equal among the metrics except for EKS. This has two reasons. First, SM and mMDS are unfairly preferred since the EKS is their objective function. Second, the methods' absolute values for EKS differ stronger than their values for other metrics, in particular on real-word data sets. Hence, the PME values of DR techniques with failed embedding attempts are improved especially regarding the EKS. Averaging the PME values over all metrics and ignoring the failing methods, e. g., SM, CE and MVU (Sect. 4.1), shows that mMDS, GPLVM and PCA are by far the best DR methods (Fig. 5, middle part). This is surprising since mMDS and PCA belong to the earliest DR methods.

Comparing the results of the rank and the PME analysis regarding the metrics it can be observed that the methods with best ranks (EE, t-SNE, UKR) surprisingly do not always have best PME values. This is mainly caused by the poor quality of their embeddings regarding the EKS. Averaging the PME values without EKS (Fig. 5, right part) again leads to t-SNE, EE and UKR as best methods. Interestingly Isomap, MLLE and LE are among the best-ranked methods despite their poor average PME values (Fig. 5, middle part).

At last we analyze the PME values per data set. Figure 6 contains the PME values for the best convex and non-convex methods according to their average PME values listed in the middle part of Fig. 5. The symbols ### signify a failed embedding attempt; reasons for them are given in Sect. 4.1. We observe that all best convex and non-convex methods have a better average PME value

Technique	ENX	Technique	EKS	Technique	DSRE	Technique	E1NN	Technique	CRR	Technique	EKNN		Technique	Ø		Technique	Ø w/o EKS
SM	1.8	SM	1.1	UKR	1.2	t-SNE	1.3	Isomap	1.6	MVU	1.0		mMDS	2.4		t-SNE	1.6
mMDS	1.9	mMDS	1.3	t-SNE	1.4	UKR	2.1	UKR	1.6	UKR	1.0		SM	2.5		EE	1.9
PCA	2.0	CE	1.5	EE	1.7	EE	2.7	EE	1.6	SM	1.1		CE	2.7		UKR	2.1
GPLVM	2.0	MVU	1.6	itUKR	2.1	LE	3.0	t-SNE	1.7	NPE	1.1		MVU	2.8		LE	2.5
MVU	2.1	GPLVM	3.2	UNN	2.3	itUKR	3.3	LE	2.0	GPLVM	1.1		GPLVM	2.8		mMDS	2.6
CE	2.1	PCA	3.2	LE	2.6	Isomap	3.8	itUKR	2.0	PCA	1.1		PCA	2.8		Isomap	2.6
t-SNE	2.4	LLTSA	15.7	MLLE	2.7	MLLE	3.9	MLLE	2.1	HLLE	1.1		LLTSA	6.1		itUKR	2.7
EE	2.5	FA	76.8	SNE	2.7	DM	3.9	DM	2.1	SNE	1.1		Isomap	15.1		GPLVM	2.7
HLLE	2.8	Isomap	77.3	mMDS	2.9	LTSA	4.0	HLLE	2.1	CE	1.1		FA	15.9		PCA	2.8

Fig. 5. PME values per metric in ascending order (left part), average PME per method (middle part), and average PME without values for EKS (right part). Smaller (yellow) values are better, convex methods are highlighted blue. (Color figure online)

Technique	Swiss	Broken	Helix	Twin	HD	Iris	Boston	Digits	RCT	MNIST	HIVA	CNS	ORL	Ø(a.)	Ø(r.)	Diff.
PCA	2.9	3.0	12.8	2.5	1.5	1.3	1.7	1.5	4.2	2.0	1.8	2.9	1.9	4.5	2.2	2.4
MVU	2.5	3.0	11.3	2.1	1.4	1.3	1.8	###	###	1.7	###	###	2.0	4.0	1.7	2.3
CE	2.5	2.8	11.6	1.9	1.4	1.3	1.7	###	###	1.6	###	###	1.7	4.1	1.6	2.5
mMDS	2.1	2.6	12.1	1.6	1.2	1.5	1.4	1.6	1.9	1.7	1.4	1.3	1.8	3.9	1.6	2.3
SM	2.2	2.5	12.9	1.8	1.1	###	1.4	1.2	1.1	1.8	1.3	###	1.7	4.1	1.4	2.7
GPLVM	2.9	3.0	12.8	2.5	1.4	1.3	1.7	1.5	4.1	2.0	1.7	2.9	1.9	4.5	2.1	2.4

Fig. 6. PME values per data set for methods with best average PME (Fig. 5, middle part)

on real-world than on artificial data sets (Fig. 6, columns $\varnothing(r.)$ and $\varnothing(a.)$). This observation is consistent with the results from the rank analysis, albeit no differences between convex and non-convex methods can be observed. The suitability for practical usage of the methods listed in Fig. 6 is emphasized by the finding that all other methods except LLTSA perform much worse on real-world than on artificial data sets. In general, the PME values per data set have to be interpreted critically because they are strongly influenced by the EKS due to the large differences between best and worse EKS values among the DR methods. This strong influence not necessarily reflects the actual importance of the EKS as quality measure, which may depend on the application purpose.

In summary, mMDS, GPLVM and PCA score well in both evaluation parts. EE, t-SNE and UKR only perform well regarding the ranks, but do not have satisfying PME values due to their poor EKS values. In contrast, there are some methods (SM, CE, MVU) that seem to be quite good but fail on some real-world data sets.

5   Summary

In this paper we present a quantitative experimental study that assesses the quality of 29 DR methods on 13 artificial and real-world data sets with six metrics. It goes beyond previous comparisons by employing more and newer methods from all families of unsupervised feature extraction methods using a larger number of data sets and examining a variety of quality properties.

Based on our analysis mMDS, GPLVM and PCA are the overall best DR methods. However, depending on which metrics actually are reasonable quality measures for a specific application, other methods may be better choices, like e. g., EE, t-SNE, and UKR if distance preservation is negligible. Depending on the data set the experimental results of this paper may guide the choice of methods in real applications.

Of course, our findings can only be generalized to a certain extend due to the no free lunch theorem. But as an extensive experimental analysis is often impossible due to time and cost constraints, we recommend to choose a reasonable subset of DR methods based on our results, to perform an own evaluation and to select the best among these methods for performing the final DR task. According to the application, suitable metrics should be chosen for the analysis. For example, in a pipeline with classification, CRR and EKNN are appropriate test candidates as they assess information preservation.

Future work may concentrate on an extension and update of the experimental analysis w. r. t. the set of benchmark methods, problems, and test metrics.

References

1. The database of faces. http://www.cl.cam.ac.uk/research/dtg/attarchive/facedatabase.html
2. World congress on computational intelligence (WCCI) performance prediction challenge (2006). http://www.modelselect.inf.ethz.ch/datasets.php
3. Belkin, M., Niyogi, P.: Laplacian eigenmaps for dimensionality reduction and data representation. Neural Comput. 15(6), 1373–1396 (2003)
4. Brand, M.: Charting a manifold. In: Advances in Neural Information Processing Systems (NIPS), pp. 985–992. MIT Press (2003)
5. Carreira-Perpiñán, M.Á.: The elastic embedding algorithm for dimensionality reduction. In: International Conference on Machine Learning (ICML), pp. 167–174 (2010)
6. Coifman, R.R., Lafon, S., Lee, A.B., Maggioni, M., Nadler, B., Warner, F., Zucker, S.W.: Geometric diffusions as a tool for harmonic analysis and structure definition of data: diffusion maps. Natl. Acad. Sci. U. S. A. (PNAS) 102(21), 7426–7431 (2005)
7. Coifman, R.R., Lafon, S.: Diffusion maps. Appl. Comput. Harmon. Anal. 21(1), 5–30 (2006)
8. DeMers, D., Cottrell, G.W.: Non-linear dimensionality reduction. In: Hanson, S.J., Cowan, J., Giles, L. (eds.) Advances in Neural Information Processing Systems (NIPS), pp. 580–587. Morgan-Kaufmann, San Mateo (1992)
9. Donoho, D.L., Grimes, C.: Hessian eigenmaps: locally linear embedding techniques for high-dimensional data. Natl. Acad. Sci. U. S. A. (PNAS) 100(10), 5591–5596 (2003)
10. Dzemyda, G., Kurasova, O., Žilinskas, J.: Multidimensional Data Visualization: Methods and Applications. Springer, New York (2013)
11. Fernández-Delgado, M., Cernadas, E., Barro, S., Amorim, D.: Do we need hundreds of classifiers to solve real world classification problems? J. Mach. Learn. Res. (JMLR) 15(1), 3133–3181 (2014)

12. Gisbrecht, A., Hammer, B.: Data visualization by nonlinear dimensionality reduction. Wiley Interdiscip. Rev. Data Min. Knowl. Discov. **5**(2), 51–73 (2015)

13. He, X., Cai, D., Yan, S., Zhang, H.J.: Neighborhood preserving embedding. In: International Conference on Computer Vision (ICCV), pp. 1208–1213 (2005)

14. He, X., Niyogi, P.: Locality preserving projections. In: Advances in Neural Information Processing Systems (NIPS), pp. 153–160. MIT Press (2004)

15. Henschel, S., Hoyer, P.O., Ong, C.S., Sonnenburg, S., Braun, M.L.: Machine learning data set repository. http://mldata.org/repository/data/viewslug/central-nervous-system/

16. Hinton, G.E., Roweis, S.T.: Stochastic neighbor embedding. In: Advances in Neural Information Processing Systems (NIPS), pp. 857–864. MIT Press (2002)

17. Hinton, G.E., Salakhutdinov, R.R.: Reducing the dimensionality of data with neural networks. Science **313**(5786), 504–507 (2006)

18. Hotelling, H.: Analysis of a complex of statistical variables into principal components. J. Educ. Psychol. **24**(6), 417 (1933)

19. Klanke, S.: http://www.sklanke.de/

20. Kramer, O.: Dimensionality Reduction with Unsupervised Nearest Neighbors. Springer, Heidelberg (2013)

21. Kramer, O.: Unsupervised nearest neighbor regression for dimensionality reduction. Springer Soft Comput. **19**(6), 1647–1661 (2015)

22. Kramer, O.: Machine Learning for Evolution Strategies. Springer, Heidelberg (2016)

23. Kruskal, J.B.: Nonmetric multidimensional scaling: a numerical method. Psychometrika **29**(2), 115–129 (1964)

24. Lawrence, N.D.: Gaussian process latent variable models for visualisation of high dimensional data. In: Thrun, S., Saul, L., Schölkopf, B. (eds.) Advances in Neural Information Processing Systems (NIPS), pp. 329–336. MIT Press, Cambridge (2003)

25. Lee, J.A., Verleysen, M.: Nonlinear Dimensionality Reduction. Springer, New York (2007)

26. Lee, J.A., Verleysen, M.: Quality assessment of dimensionality reduction: rank-based criteria. Neurocomputing **72**(7), 1431–1443 (2009)

27. Levina, E., Bickel, P.J.: Maximum likelihood estimation of intrinsic dimension. In: Saul, L.K., Weiss, Y., Bottou, L. (eds.) Advances in Neural Information Processing Systems (NIPS), pp. 777–784. MIT Press, Cambridge (2005)

28. Lichman, M.: UCI machine learning repository. http://archive.ics.uci.edu/ml

29. Lückehe, D., Kramer, O.: Leaving local optima in unsupervised kernel regression. In: Wermter, S., Weber, C., Duch, W., Honkela, T., Koprinkova-Hristova, P., Magg, S., Palm, G., Villa, A.E.P. (eds.) ICANN 2014. LNCS, vol. 8681, pp. 137–144. Springer, Cham (2014). doi:10.1007/978-3-319-11179-7_18

30. Lueks, W., Mokbel, B., Biehl, M., Hammer, B.: How to evaluate dimensionality reduction? - Improving the co-ranking matrix. CoRR abs/1110.3917 (2011)

31. van der Maaten, L.: Matlab toolbox for dimensionality reduction. https://lvdmaaten.github.io/drtoolbox/

32. van der Maaten, L., Hinton, G.: Visualizing data using t-SNE. J. Mach. Learn. Res. (JMLR) **9**(2579–2605), 85 (2008)

33. van der Maaten, L., Postma, E., van den Herik, H.: Dimensionality reduction: A comparative review. Technical report TiCC-TR 2009-005, Tilburg University (2009)

34. Meinicke, P., Klanke, S., Memisevic, R., Ritter, H.: Principal surfaces from unsupervised kernel regression. IEEE Trans. Pattern Anal. Mach. Intell. (TPAMI) **27**(9), 1379–1391 (2005)
35. Mysling, P., Hauberg, S., Pedersen, K.S.: An empirical study on the performance of spectral manifold learning techniques. In: Honkela, T., Duch, W., Girolami, M., Kaski, S. (eds.) ICANN 2011. LNCS, vol. 6791, pp. 347–354. Springer, Heidelberg (2011). doi:10.1007/978-3-642-21735-7_43
36. Niskanen, M., Silvén, O.: Comparison of dimensionality reduction methods for wood surface inspection. In: Quality Control by Artificial Vision, pp. 178–188 (2003)
37. Pearson, K.: On lines and planes of closest fit to systems of points in space. Lond. Edinb. Dublin Philos. Mag. J. Sci. **2**(11), 559–572 (1901)
38. Pedregosa, F., Varoquaux, G., Gramfort, A., Michel, V., Thirion, B., Grisel, O., Blondel, M., Prettenhofer, P., Weiss, R., Dubourg, V., Vanderplas, J., Passos, A., Cournapeau, D., Brucher, M., Perrot, M., Duchesnay, E.: Scikit-learn: machine learning in Python. J. Mach. Learn. Res. (JMLR) **12**, 2825–2830 (2011)
39. Roweis, S.T.: EM algorithms for PCA and SPCA. In: Advances in Neural Information Processing Systems (NIPS), pp. 626–632. MIT Press (1997)
40. Roweis, S.T., Saul, L.K.: Nonlinear dimensionality reduction by locally linear embedding. Science **290**(5500), 2323–2326 (2000)
41. Sammon, J.W.: A nonlinear mapping for data structure analysis. IEEE Trans. Comput. **18**(5), 401–409 (1969)
42. Sanguinetti, G.: Dimensionality reduction of clustered data sets. IEEE Trans. Pattern Anal. Mach. Intell. (TPAMI) **30**(3), 535–540 (2008)
43. Schölkopf, B., Smola, A., Müller, K.R.: Nonlinear component analysis as a kernel eigenvalue problem. Neural Comput. **10**(5), 1299–1319 (1998)
44. Sha, F., Saul, L.K.: Analysis and extension of spectral methods for nonlinear dimensionality reduction. In: International Conference on Machine learning (ICML), pp. 784–791 (2005)
45. Spearman, C.: "General Intelligence", objectively determined and measured. Am. J. Psychol. **15**(2), 201–292 (1904)
46. Teh, Y.W., Roweis, S.T.: Automatic alignment of local representations. In: Advances in Neural Information Processing Systems (NIPS), pp. 865–872. MIT Press (2002)
47. Tenenbaum, J.B., De Silva, V., Langford, J.C.: A global geometric framework for nonlinear dimensionality reduction. Science **290**(5500), 2319–2323 (2000)
48. Torgerson, W.S.: Multidimensional scaling: I. theory and method. Psychometrika **17**(4), 401–419 (1952)
49. Vladymyrov, M., Carreira-Perpiñán, M.Á.: Partial-hessian strategies for fast learning of nonlinear embeddings. In: International Conference on Machine Learning (ICML), pp. 345–352 (2012)
50. Weinberger, K.Q., Saul, L.K.: Unsupervised learning of image manifolds by semidefinite programming. In: Computer Vision and Pattern Recognition (CVPR), pp. 988–995 (2004)
51. Weinberger, K.Q., Sha, F., Saul, L.K.: Learning a kernel matrix for nonlinear dimensionality reduction. In: International Conference on Machine Learning (ICML), pp. 839–846 (2004)
52. Yeh, M.C., Lee, I.H., Wu, G., Wu, Y., Chang, E.Y.: Manifold learning, a promised land or work in progress?. In: International Conference on Multimedia and Expo (ICME). IEEE (2005)

53. Zhang, T., Yang, J., Zhao, D., Ge, X.: Linear local tangent space alignment and application to face recognition. Neurocomputing **70**(7), 1547–1553 (2007)
54. Zhang, Z.Y., Zha, H.Y.: Principal manifolds and nonlinear dimensionality reduction via tangent space alignment. J. Shanghai Univ. (Engl. Ed.) **8**(4), 406–424 (2004)
55. Zhang, Z., Wang, J.: MLLE: modified locally linear embedding using multiple weights. In: Advances in Neural Information Processing Systems (NIPS), pp. 1593–1600. MIT Press (2006)

Planning with Independent Task Networks

Felix Mohr$^{(\boxtimes)}$, Theo Lettmann, and Eyke Hüllermeier

Department of Computer Science, Paderborn University, Paderborn, Germany
{felix.mohr,lettmann,eyke}@upb.de

Abstract. Task networks are a powerful tool for AI planning. Classical approaches like forward STN planning and SHOP typically devise non-deterministic algorithms that can be operationalized using classical graph search techniques such as A*. For two reasons, however, this strategy is sometimes inefficient. First, identical tasks might be resolved several times within the search process, i.e., the same subproblem is solved repeatedly instead of being reused. Second, large parts of the search space might be redundant if some of the objects in the planning domain are substitutable.

In this paper, we present an extension of simple task networks that avoid these problems and enable a much more efficient planning process. Our main innovation is the creation of new constants during planning combined with AND-OR-graph search. To demonstrate the advantages of these techniques, we present a case study in the field of automated service composition, in which search space reductions of several magnitudes can be achieved.

1 Introduction

Hierarchical planning is an established and powerful technique for AI planning [1,3,13]. One interesting application of hierarchical planning is automated service composition, which is the task to compose a new software artifact from existing ones [8,15,19]. However, there are settings in which standard hierarchical planning, even when looking like a natural approach, turns out to be infeasible.

As an illustration, we consider the example of *nested dichotomies*, a technique for polychotomous classification in machine learning [5]. A nested dichotomy (ND) is a binary tree, in which every node n is labeled with a set $c(n) \subseteq \mathcal{Y}$ of *classes* $\mathcal{Y}$, such that the root is labeled with $\mathcal{Y}$, and $c(n) = c(n_1) \dot\cup c(n_2)$ for every inner node n with successors n_1 and n_2. Figure 1 shows two example dichotomies for the case of four classes. An object to be classified is submitted to the root and, at every inner node, sent to one of the successors by the binary classifier associated with that node; the class assigned is then given by the leaf node reached in the end. Since different NDs give rise to different sets of binary classification problems, the overall performance is strongly influenced by the tree topology. Considering an ND as a "classification service", hierarchical planning appears to be a natural approach for its configuration: starting at the root, the splits are configured iteratively until every leaf node is labeled with exactly one class.

G. Kern-Isberner et al. (Eds.): KI 2017, LNAI 10505, pp. 193–206, 2017.
DOI: 10.1007/978-3-319-67190-1_15

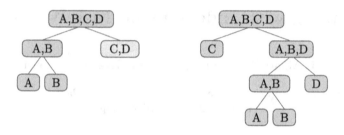

Fig. 1. A partial and a complete ND for four classes.

The first problem with classical hierarchical planning is that, when enumerating different NDs, the same subsolutions are computed several times. For example, both NDs in Fig. 1 contain the node A, B, which is refined twice by a classical planner. The second problem is that each node of the ND is represented by a planning constant, but the constants actually have no specific meaning. For example, we need 7 constants, say $v_1, ..., v_7$, for the nodes of the right ND of Fig. 1. It does not matter which of the nodes is represented by which constant, but a classical planner tries all combinations, which yields an enormous and unnecessary search space explosion.

We propose planning with independent task networks (ITN) to overcome these problems (Sect. 2). The main novelties are the on-the-fly creation of planning constants and the reuse of subsolutions through the notion of AND-OR-graph search. In a case study, we show that this can yield search space reductions of several orders of magnitude (Sect. 3). The case study also sheds light onto a class of planning problems rarely considered in the planning community, e.g., the typical competitions, namely the one of automated service composition. While most frequently considered planning problems may not exhibit the discussed property of independent tasks, it *is* a common (sometimes essential) property in every recursive program. Drawing attention to this class of planning problems is, hence, another aim of the paper.

2   Independent Task Network Planning

We introduce our method in four steps. The first two subsections explain the formal basis of planning in general and hierarchical planning, respectively. We then describe the core elements of ITN planning and the ITN algorithm. Finally, we address some important aspects of the ITN that enable additional search space reductions.

2.1   Basic Elements of Planning

As for any planning formalism, our basis is a logic language $\mathcal{L}$ and planning operators that are defined in terms of $\mathcal{L}$. The language $\mathcal{L}$ has function-free first-order logic capacities, i.e., it defines an infinite set of variable names, constant names, predicate names, and quantifiers and connectors to build formulas. An *operator* is a tuple $\langle name_o, pre_o, post_o \rangle$ where $name_o$ is a name and pre_o and $post_o$ are formulas from $\mathcal{L}$ that constitute preconditions and postconditions, respectively.

The postconditions $post_o$ are often restricted to be literal sets, like in STRIPS. We relax this assumption a bit and allow conditional postconditions, i.e., $post_o$ is of the form $\bigwedge \alpha \to \beta$ where α is a formula from $\mathcal{L}$ and β is a set of literals.

A plan is a sequence of ground operations. As usual, we use the term *ground* to say that all variables have been replaced by terms that only consist of constants. That is, an operation is ground if all variables in the precondition and postcondition have been substituted by terms from $\mathcal{L}$ that only contain constants. Ground operators are also called *actions*; we write pre_a and $post_a$ for its precondition and postcondition, respectively.

The semantic of actions is that they modify the state in which they are applied. A *state* is a set of ground positive literals. Working under the closed world assumption, we assume that every ground literal not explicitly contained in a state is false. An action a is *applicable* in state s iff $s \models_{cwa} pre_a$. The *successor state* s' induced by this application is s if a is not applicable in s and $(s \cup add) \setminus del$ otherwise; here, add and del contain all the positive and negative literals, respectively, that are in a conditional postcondition of a whose condition is true in s.

2.2   Simple Task Networks

A simple task network (STN) is a partially ordered set T of tasks [7]. A task $t(v_0, ..., v_n)$ is a name together with a list of parameters, which are variables or constants from $\mathcal{L}$. A task named by an operator is called *primitive*, otherwise it is *complex*. A task whose parameters are constants is ground.

We are interested in deriving a plan from a task network. Intuitively, we can refine (and ground) complex tasks iteratively until we reach a task network that only consists of ground primitive tasks, i.e., a set of partially ordered actions. While primitive tasks can be realized canonically by a single operation, complex tasks need to be decomposed by *methods*. A method $m = \langle name_m, task_m, pre_m, T_m \rangle$ consists of its name, the (non-primitive) task $task_m$ it refines, a logic formula $pre_m \in \mathcal{L}$ that constitutes a precondition, and a task network T_m that realizes the decomposition. Replacing complex tasks by the network specified in the methods we use to decompose them, we iteratively *derive* new task networks until we obtain one with ground primitive tasks (actions) only.

The definition of a simple task network planning problem is then straight forward. Given an initial state s_0 and a task network T_0, the planning problem is to derive a plan from T_0 that is applicable in s_0. A simple task network planning problem is then a tuple $\langle s_0, T_0, O, M \rangle$, where O and M are finite sets of operators and methods, respectively.

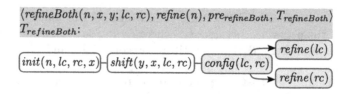

Fig. 2. The task network that refines node n of a partial nested dichotomy.

Note that the definition of a method usually contains more variables than the task it refines. That is, it makes use of objects that are not directly relevant for formulating the task, yet relevant to solve it in the spirit of the respective method.

2.3   Independent Task Networks: General Idea

We propose independent task networks (ITNs), which are an extension of STNs, with the purpose to enable an efficient decomposition of independent subproblems. The core feature of ITNs is that tasks may be labeled as *independent* to assert that each of its refinements is compatible with every refinement of non-preceding tasks. More formally, let T be a task network with $t \in T$ marked as independent, and let $T' \subset T \setminus \{t\}$ be the tasks in T that are no predecessors of t. Then for every state s on which we decompose T, and for which plans π and π' can be derived from $\{t\}$ and T', respectively, such that $\pi.\pi'$ is applicable in s, *every* derivable plan π'' of $\{t\}$ applicable in s must be combinable with π' such that $\pi''.\pi'$ is applicable in s. In other words, the choice of the first partial plan π'' does not affect the applicability of the second partial plan π'.

As an example, consider the task network in Fig. 2. This is the task network belonging to the method that refines a non-terminal node of a partial dichotomy by splitting it up into two *new* child nodes. The first two tasks in the network are primitive, i.e., they can be realized by single actions, and the last three tasks are complex. The tasks $init(n, lc, rc, x)$, $shift(y, x, lc, rc)$, and $config(lc, rc)$ create the child nodes lc and rc of n and define their labels; the exact formalization is given below in Sect. 3.2. The tasks $refine(lc)$ and $refine(rc)$ mark a refinement of those child nodes, i.e., they are independent since their solutions are independent of each other. *Every* plan derived for $refine(lc)$ can be combined with *every* plan derived for $refine(rc)$.

The need to manually define whether or not a task is independent of the others has its root in the difficulty to define complete conditions of independence that can be checked automatically. Indeed, it is easy to specify sufficient conditions, e.g., based on the task names. For example, we can syntactically check whether two tasks must be independent if all methods and operators reachable from them have disjoint preconditions and effects respectively. However, this specific rule is too strict in general, and we expect that deciding independence in general is undecidable. On the other hand, in particular when the planning algorithm simulates a recursive execution tree—like in our nested dichotomy problem but also, the expert easily sees that the tasks are independent.

Algorithm 1. IFD(s, T, O, M)

1   **if** $T = \emptyset$ **then return** the emply plan $U \leftarrow \{t \mid t \in T, t$ has no non-recursive predecessor in $T\}$

2   **if** $U = \emptyset$ **then**

3   choose any $u \in T$ that has no predecessor in T

4   **if** u *is a primitive task* **then**

5         $active \leftarrow \{(a, \sigma) \mid a$ is a ground instance of an

6   operator in O, σ is a substitution such that

7             $name_a = \sigma(t_u)$, and a is applicable to $s\}$

8   **if** $active = \emptyset$ **then return** failure choose any $(a, \sigma) \in active$

            $\pi \leftarrow IFD(\gamma(s, a), \sigma(T \setminus \{u\}), O, M)$

9   **if** $\pi = failure$ **then return** failure **else** return $a.\pi$

10   **else**

11         $active \leftarrow \{(m, \sigma) \mid a$ is a ground instance of a

12   method in M, σ is a substitution such that

13             $name_m = \sigma(t_u)$, and m is applicable to $s\}$

14   **if** $active = \emptyset$ **then return** failure choose any $(m, \sigma) \in active$

15   **return** $IFD(s, \sigma(T_m), O, M)$

16   **end**

17 **else**

18      $\forall u \in U : \pi_u = IFD(s, \{u\}, O, M)\}$

19      $\pi_{T-U} \leftarrow IFD(s, T \setminus U, O, M)$

20   **return** $\pi_{u_1} ... \pi_{u_n} . \pi_{T-U}$

21 **end**

The non-deterministic independent forward decomposition (IFD) algorithm is shown in Algorithm 1. In fact, the part for $U = \emptyset$ is *equal* to the partial forward decomposition algorithm (PFD) [7, p. 243] except that the recursive call is IFD and not PFD. So the important points are the computation of the relevant recursive tasks U in the beginning (line 1), and the final else-branch where those tasks are resolved (lines 16–19). Note that there is no choice point in the last branch, because all of the tasks must be solved—no decision is required. The independent tasks are solved in isolation and the solution of the remaining problem is appended to the concatenation of subsolutions of the independent tasks. It is easy to show that the routine is sound and complete; we omit the proofs of these formal properties due to space limitations.

A deterministic implementation of the above algorithm can be devised by an AND-OR-graph search such as general best first (GBF). As usual, the choice points (non-deterministic choices) constitute OR-nodes in such a graph. While PFD induces a simple OR-graph, the last branch of RFD induces an AND-node with one successor for each $u \in U$ and one for $T \setminus U$. Note that the child nodes here are partially ordered: there is no order among the child nodes for $u \in U$, but all of them are ordered previously to the node for $T \setminus U$.

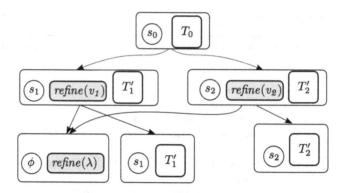

Fig. 3. Context functions help identify search graph nodes.

2.4   A Look at the Details

While the RFD algorithm is already sufficient to solve subproblems independently, we allow for three more features that are important to actually achieve an efficiency improvement in the planning process. These features are *constant creation*, *context functions*, and *lonely methods*.

First, we allow operators (and methods) to introduce new constants. Intuitively, the connection to independent tasks is that those tasks constitute subproblems, which are *derived* from the current one. In Fig. 2, for example, refining the child nodes lc and rc are subproblems we derived from n. Since lc and rc are only relevant for this specific task, it is reasonable that they are created only for this purpose and known only within this method instead of being taken from a previously defined object storage. In the algorithm, this becomes relevant when active methods and actions are determined. Here, substitutions map output parameters not to constants of the state s but to globally unique new constants from $\mathcal{L}$.

Second, ITNs allow one to equip tasks with context functions that enable the identification of equal subproblems *during the search process*. We face the problem that we may create independently solvable identical tasks that cannot be recognized as such. For example, the nested dichotomies in Fig. 1 both contain the node labeled A, B. Covering both dichotomies in the course of plan derivation, we would encounter a task $refine(v_1)$ for some state s_1 and $refine(v_2)$ for some state s_2, where v_1 and v_2 are different constants both encoding the refinement of A, B. That is, the subproblems $refine(v_1)$ and $refine(v_2)$ are identical, but $s_1 \neq s_2$ and $v_1 \neq v_2$ prevent us from detecting this equality. A context function $\phi_t : S \to S \times \Lambda$ overcomes this problem by assigning a state s a pair (s', λ), where $s' \subseteq s$ is a reduction of the state s, such that a plan derived from $\{t\}$ is applicable in s' iff it is applicable in s, and $\lambda \in \Lambda$ is a bijective mapping of constants in s' to constants in $\mathcal{L}$, i.e., a renaming of constants. In the above example, we would have $\lambda(v_1) = AB = \lambda(v_2)$, where AB is a constant, and the

states are reduced to the literals really relevant to the subproblems such that
$\phi_{refine(v_1)}(s_1) = \phi_{refine(v_2)}(s_2)$.

Incorporating context functions in the search algorithm simply means to change the recursive call for the tasks $u \in U$ in the lower else-branch to $RFD(\phi(s), \{\lambda(u)\}, O, M)$. Figure 3 shows how this allows for the identification of nodes in the search space.

Third, methods may be declared as *lonely* in order to denote that the possible derivations of the resulting task network do not depend on the choices of the parameters. This is important for methods that only check some property while not affecting the state. For example, we may want to check that a node n is labeled with exactly one class. We achieve this by (i) choosing one class in the label of n, removing it, and (ii) checking whether the node label is then empty. If n would be labeled with several classes, the emptiness check (ii) would fail *independently* of which class we chose. Hence, we only need one representative of the labels of n to check the condition, i.e., only one instance of that method is required.

Just like simple task networks, ITNs induce a specific planning routine. It is common sense that simple task networks can only be reasonably solved through forward planning [7]. For ITNs, this is particularly true due to the context functions, which can not be evaluated until the state of invocation is known. Typically, this is only the case if the task network is resolved in a forward fashion.

3   Case Study: Configuration of Dichotomies

The improvements that can be achieved by ITN planning (in the settings where it applies) obviously depend on the concrete problem at hand. Here, we focus on the problem of ND configuration already presented in the introduction. For this example, we demonstrate a tremendous reduction of the search space (fully effective if AND-OR-graph search can reasonably be applied). Prior to proceeding, let us again emphasize that the approach is by no means restricted to this problem, but applies to other configuration problems (e.g., the configuration of deep neural networks) in very much the same way. All implementations are available for public[1].

3.1   Nested Dichotomies

As already explained, nested dichotomies reduce a polychotomous classification problem to a set of binary problems (that are presumably easier to solve). To this end, the set of classes is recursively partitioned into subsets, and for each such partition, a classifier is trained on a given set of training data. The criterion to be optimized is the overall prediction accuracy (percentage of correctly classified items), which depends on the quality of the binary classifiers, and therefore on the topology of the ND. Given a dichotomy, the accuracy can be estimated by training the required binary classifiers and applying the ND to suitable test data.

---

[1] Sources are available at http://www.felixmohr.de/en/research/crc901/itn.

Since training and evaluation are not relevant here, we ignore these steps in our case study; instead, we focus on searching the space of nested dichotomies (topologies). This already constitutes a challenging planning problem. It has been shown that for n classes, there are $(2n-3)!!$ nested dichotomies [5], where $!!$ is the double factorial (and *not* taking the factorial twice). Hence, for 10 classes, there are 34,459,425 many nested dichotomies—certainly too many for picking one by hand.

3.2   Problem Formalization

We now explain how the configuration of such NDs can be encoded as a hierarchical planning problem. The formalization makes sure that each ND is constructed exactly once. Besides the standard elements, it requires universal quantifiers, conditional postconditions whose conditions may be 2-CNFs, and *outputs*, which are separated by a semicolon. We need five operators, which will correspond to primitive tasks:

1. $init(n, x; lc, rc)$
   Pre: $in(x, n)$
   Post: $\bigwedge$
   $\quad true \rightarrow in(x, rc) \wedge bst(x, rc) \wedge sst(x, rc)$
   $\quad \forall x_n : in(x_n, n) \wedge x_n \neq x \rightarrow in(x_n, lc)$
   $\quad \forall x_2, x_o : x \neq x_2 \wedge in(x_2, n) \wedge$
   $\qquad sst(x, n) \wedge (\neg in(x_o, n) \vee x_o > x_2) \rightarrow sst(x_2, lc)$
   $\quad \forall x_s : sst(x_s, n) \wedge x_s \neq x \rightarrow sst(x, lc)$
2. $shift(y, x, lc, rc)$
   Pre: $in(x, l) \wedge bst(y, r)$
   Post: $in(x, r) \wedge bst(x, r) \wedge \neg in(x, l) \wedge \neg bst(y, r)$
3. $close(l, lw, r, rw)$
   Pre: $in(lw, l) \wedge in(rw, r)$
   Post: $\emptyset$

Intuitively, the idea behind these operators is to split up the labels of a node until every leaf node is labeled with a single class. A node is refined by creating two child nodes (via the $init$ operator), where initially all classes except one (x) of the parent are in the left child. Then, we can use the $shift$ operator to move single classes from the left to the right child. The predicates bst and smt are used to memorize the biggest and smallest elements of nodes, which is necessary to avoid mirroring NDs, i.e. one separating A, B from C, D and the other C, D from A, B The $close$ operator is used to guarantee the existence of at least one class in each of the children, which are the "witnesses" lw an rw.

We need two tasks with five methods to complete the specification. The first task is $refine(n)$, which means that the classes of node n shall be split up somehow. The second task is $config(l, r)$, which means that classes are to be moved from the left to the right child of some node. In the following, lonely methods are annotated with an asterisk, and independent tasks are underlined. There are three methods for $refine(n)$:

1. $finalSplit^*(n, x, y; lc, rc)$
     Pre: $in(x, n) \wedge in(y, n) \wedge y > x \wedge \forall z : in(z, n) \rightarrow z = x \vee z = y$
     Task Network:
     $init(n, lc, rc, y)$
2. $isolatingSplit(n, x; lc, rc)$
     Pre: $in(x, n)$
     Task Network:
     $init(n, lc, rc, y) \rightarrow \underline{refine(lc)}$
3. $doubleSplit(n, x, y; lc, rc)$
     Pre: $in(x, n) \wedge in(y, n) \wedge y > x \wedge \neg sst(x, n)$
     Task Network:
     $init(n, lc, rc, y) \rightarrow shift(y, x, lc, rc) \rightarrow config(lc, rc) \rightarrow \underline{refine(lc)} \rightarrow \underline{refine(rc)}$

There are two methods for $config(l, r)$, which are

1. $shiftElementAndConfigure(l, r, x, y)$
     Pre: $in(x, l) \wedge bst(y, r) \wedge x > y$
     Task Network: $shift(x, y, l, r) \rightarrow config(l, r)$
2. $closeSetup^*(l, lw, r, rw)$
     Pre: $in(lw, l) \wedge in(rw, r)$
     Task Network: $close(l, lw, r, rw)$

The initial task network is then simply $\{refine(root)\}$ where the initial state s_0 defines root and the ordering of classes. That is, $s_0 = \varphi(C) \wedge \bigwedge_{x \in C} in(x, root)$ where C is the set of classes and φ maps C to an arbitrary explicit total order of items of C, e.g., the lexicographical order. The latter one is important to maintain the bst and sst predicates.

3.3 Results

The evaluation is a mixture of experiments and *rough* bound estimates. On the one hand, it is non-trivial to calculate the exact search space sizes for a problem. Moreover, since the results cannot be immediately generalized, this calculation is not worth the effort. On the other hand, since we only want to demonstrate the general effects, namely orders of magnitudes of search space reduction, accurate values only distract from the key message. For the same reason we omit the proofs for the bounds. In fact, we determined better bounds than the ones we report here, but these are complicated to compute, which is not justified in light of the limitations imposed by the setup and space.

The results are summarized in Fig. 4. In cases where the number could not be computed algorithmically, values with an asterisk were estimated based on expansion models. We now discuss the results in detail.

The Baseline: Standard STN/PFD Planning. We can easily modify the above encoding to make it fit to standard STN planning. Since standard planning cannot create new objects, we must define a set of objects for the nodes of the dichotomy already in the initial state. Every nested dichotomy for k classes has $2k - 1$ many nodes, one of which is the root, so the initial state of the problem must define the root node object and $2k - 2$ additional node objects. The methods and operators that create objects are redefined in the sense that the outputs are now inputs. An auxiliary predicate $inuse(x)$, which is initially true for the root node and false for the other node objects, is required to be false in the preconditions of the "creating" methods and operator, and it is set to true in the postcondition of the creating operators. In addition, we add $lc \neq rc$ to the preconditions in order to make sure that the two "created" objects are distinct. Such a problem can then be fed to an implementation of PFD [7]; since we are interested in the total search space size, we used a simple breadth first search.

In principle, a more efficient encoding is possible for STN planning. When using alternative effects with universal quantifiers, we could simulate the constant generation process. However, these are not supported by common hierarchical planners, and such an encoding would also require a neat implementation of the planner in order to avoid an explosion of the node expansion time. Besides, this option is limited to cases where we already know the number of required constants, which is not the case in many scenarios, e.g., the configuration of a deep neural network.

The search space growth under this encoding renders the search process hopeless. One can show that the number of nodes induced for an OR-graph by PFD planning is at least $(2k - 3)!!^k$, where k is the number of classes.

The extreme search space explosion is caused by an unnecessary redundancy in the set of found solutions. This is because different node objects are used to carry out the same operation. For example, a node n_i is split into children (n_{i+1}, n_{i+2}), (n_{i+1}, n_{i+3}), ..., (n_{i+1}, n_l), ..., (n_{l-1}, n_l), even though only one of those would be sufficient. This is avoided by creating new constants, which are built exactly for that single refinement purpose. This problem was discussed previously in the context of automated service composition [9]. As a consequence, PFD produces 2, 72, and 17 280 solution nodes for $k = 2, 3$, and 4, respectively, although there are actually only 1, 3, and 15 distinct solutions.

Improvement by Creating Constants. Now consider the case that we still stick to an OR-graph search like PFD but allow the creation of new objects. That is, the encoding is as specified above, except that we apply PFD instead of the RFD algorithm introduced in Sect. 2.3. In the following, we call this strategy PFD + OC.

In comparison to the naive approach of a standard STN encoding, the search space size already looks much more feasible. For values of $k = 2, ..., 10$, the values are contained in the second column of the table in Fig. 4. Clearly, the search space is still quite huge, i.e., still grows exponentially in the number of classes, but the order of magnitude is much less. More precisely, we can safely upper bound the search space size by $c \cdot k \cdot (2k - 3)!!$, where k is the number of classes and c is a small constant. By the above lower bound for naive search, this implies that the search space size is smaller by a factor of at least $(\frac{2k-3!!}{c \cdot k})^{k-1} > (2k - 3!!)^{k-2}$. This enormous gap can be observed in Fig. 4 between the green and the red line.

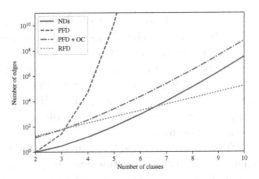

# classes	PFD	PFD + OC	RFD
2	1	15	18
3	27	59	64
4	56 625	349	202
5	1.3E+10*	2 694	625
6	7.1E+17*	26 000	1 935
7	1.3E+28*	301 833	5 988
8	1.1E+41*	4 094 241	18 456
9	5.8E+56*	42 788 697*	56 563
10	2.4E+75*	660 099 747*	172 381

(a) Number of edges   (b) Number of dichotomies/edges.

Fig. 4. Search space sizes for the three models measured in terms of the number of edges, which corresponds to the number of nodes for STN. Values with asterisk were obtained by estimates, since the model exceeded the machine resources. (Color figure online)

Improvement by ITN Planning. Let us now consider the savings achieved by ITN planning. That is, we apply the RFD algorithm to the problem description as given above.

The result is again a dramatic search space reduction. The search space growth is still exponential but significantly less than in the case of STN planning with object creation. We can lower bound the search space size of PFD + OC by $k \cdot (2k - 3)!! \gg 10^{k-2}$ and upper bound the search space size of ITN planning by 3^{k+1}. These bounds imply that the search space size of PFD + OC is at least 3^{k-2} times higher than the search space size induced by running an AND-OR-graph search on the graph imposed by the RFD algorithm. In other words, for deriving NDs, the search space of PFD + OC is exponentially larger than the one of ITN planning.

Another important (though maybe typical) observation one can make by comparing the two blue lines in Fig. 4 is that the number of edges in ITN planning grows *slower* than the number of *solutions*. This is because the solutions are implicitly stored in the *sub-graphs* of the search space, so we actually need less nodes and edges to cover all solutions than in the other approaches. The impact of such an efficient representation can be quite paramount. For example, for the case of NDs it is often said that one cannot consider all NDs [5], which is a reasonable assertion at first sight given their tremendous number. Of course, there are limits. However, with an admissible and sufficiently informative heuristic for solution bases, we can actually (implicitly) consider all NDs even for sizes that significantly exceed the possibilities of OR-graphs.

3.4 Discussion

The case study of ND configuration impressively shows the potential benefits of ITN planning with respect to the search space size. In fact, the improvements are so obvious that no further discussion is needed. Instead, we dedicate the remaining space to the discussion of some more subtle aspects.

For example, a reduction of the search space does not immediately imply better solutions. First, in spite of all savings, we usually cannot construct the complete search graph. Instead, we still need to rely on heuristic search to explore promising parts of the search space. If these heuristics are good enough, it may happen that we find comparable solutions, or even the optimal ones, within a given time bound.

Second, an important requirement for successful AND-OR-graph search is that the quality of a solution can be aggregated from its partial solutions. If this is not directly possible, AND-OR-graph search may even deliver *worse* results than a simple best-first search, which has a complete solution base available in every node, no matter the search space size. However, at least for the shift from classical STN planning to STN planning with object creation, we *can* be certain that solution qualities will be at least as good and often better. Any heuristic we can apply for the classical STN planning version, we can also apply for the one with object creation. More precisely, for each node n of the search space of the object creation version, there is a *set* $N(n)$ of actually equivalent nodes in the search space of the classical problem formulation that are very likely to be *all* expanded before any solution is found.

To summarize, an ITN planning encoding does significantly decrease the search space size regardless of whether the search takes place in an OR-graph or an AND-OR-graph. Compared to the use of a classical encoding, this enables a much more efficient search. In this regard, AND-OR-graph search is even better than OR-graph search, but this approach assumes that solution quality can be aggregated from partial solutions.

4   Related Work

We are not the first in pointing out the necessity to create new constants during planning. In particular, for web service composition [10], the positive effect of allowing the introduction of new objects on the search space size was already discussed in [9]. In fact, such a technique was even incorporated earlier into a forward planning, [17], backward planning [12], and partial ordered planning [11]. However, we are not aware that constant creation has been used in hierarchical planning.

Constant creation can be simulated with effects that allow for negation, universal quantifiers, and implications. However, the only planners allowing universal quantifiers we are aware of, which are SIPE-2 [18], SHOP2 [13], and SIADEX [2], have no support for conditional effects; SHOP2 and SIADEX do not even support negations in the effects [6]. But in many cases, we have no canonical upper bound for these constants anyway. While we do have one in our example, in others, like configuring a deep neural network, there is no such bound for the number of layers.

A recent survey [6] categorizes HTN planning methods and discusses expressiveness of HTN planning languages and their impact on parallelizability. Currently, the most popular approach to implement HTN planning is depth first search in an OR-graph, which is adopted for instance by SIPE-2 [18], UCMP [3], SHOP2 [13], and SIADEX [2]. We are not aware of any other hierarchical planning algorithm that applies AND-OR-graph search.

The idea of reusing subsolutions has been addressed through the notion of "task sharing". Task sharing identifies common sub-tasks for sharing within a plan [16]. In [1] the HTN formalism is compared to a unified version of Hierarchical Goal Network (HGN) [14] and task sharing. However, task sharing only reuses subsolutions *within* a plan but does not use this knowledge within plan search, e.g., by organizing the search space like ITN.

5   Conclusion

We have introduced independent network planning as an alternative to classical hierarchical planning methods such as STN planning. While we do not claim that the required property of independent tasks is satisfied in planning problems frequently considered in the competitions (which it is probably not), we have shown at the example of nested dichotomy configuration that there *are* relevant practical problems where the conditions apply and where the search space size is decreased by several orders of magnitude. Nested dichotomies are not a pathological case: Since the core idea is to reuse computation results, we assume that ITN planning plays a role similar to dynamic programming, which makes it a key technology in automated service composition problem.

Our current work is focused on the use of ITN planning for automated machine learning [4], i.e., the automated configuration of data processing and model induction pipelines for learning predictive models from data. While our example of nested dichotomies originates from this domain, it constitutes only a first step and small share in this endeavor.

Acknowledgements. This work was supported by the German Research Foundation (DFG) within the Collaborative Research Center "On-The-Fly Computing" (SFB 901).

References

1. Alford, R., Shivashankar, V., Roberts, M., Frank, J., Aha, D.W.: Hierarchical planning: relating task and goal decomposition with task sharing. In: Proceedings of IJCAI, pp. 3022–3029 (2016)
2. Castillo, L., Fdez-Olivares, J., García-Pérez, Ó., Palao, F.: Temporal enhancements of an HTN planner. In: Marín, R., Onaindía, E., Bugarín, A., Santos, J. (eds.) CAEPIA 2005. LNCS, vol. 4177, pp. 429–438. Springer, Heidelberg (2006). doi:10. 1007/11881216_45
3. Erol, K., Hendler, J.A., Nau, D.S.: UMCP: a sound and complete procedure for hierarchical task-network planning. In: Proceedings of the Second International Conference on Artificial Intelligence Planning Systems, University of Chicago, Chicago, Illinois, USA, pp. 249–254, 13–15 June 1994

4. Feurer, M., Klein, A., Eggensperger, K., Springenberg, J., Blum, M., Hutter, F.: Efficient and robust automated machine learning. In: Advances in Neural Information Processing Systems, pp. 2962–2970 (2015)
5. Frank, E., Kramer, S.: Ensembles of nested dichotomies for multi-class problems. In: Proceedings of the Twenty-First International Conference on Machine Learning (ICML 2004), Banff, Alberta, Canada, 4–8 July 2004
6. Georgievski, I., Aiello, M.: HTN planning: overview, comparison, and beyond. Artif. Intell. **222**, 124–156 (2015)
7. Ghallab, M., Nau, D.S., Traverso, P.: Automated Planning - Theory and Practice. Elsevier, Amsterdam (2004)
8. Klusch, M., Gerber, A., Schmidt, M.: Semantic web service composition planning with OWLS-XPlan. In: Proceedings of the 1st International AAAI Fall Symposium on Agents and the Semantic Web, pp. 55–62 (2005)
9. Mohr, F.: Issues of automated software composition in AI planning. In: ACM/IEEE International Conference on Automated Software Engineering, ASE 2014, Vasteras, Sweden, pp. 895–898, 15–19 September 2014
10. Mohr, F.: Automated Software and Service Composition - A Survey and Evaluating Review. Springer Briefs in Computer Science. Springer, Heidelberg (2016). doi:10.1007/978-3-319-34168-2
11. Mohr, F.: Towards automated service composition under quality constraints. Ph.D. thesis, Paderborn University (2017)
12. Mohr, F., Jungmann, A., Kleine Büning, H.: Automated online service composition. In: 2015 IEEE International Conference on Services Computing, SCC, pp. 57–64 (2015)
13. Nau, D.S., Au, T., Ilghami, O., Kuter, U., Murdock, J.W., Wu, D., Yaman, F.: SHOP2: an HTN planning system. J. Artif. Intell. Res. (JAIR) **20**, 379–404 (2003)
14. Shivashankar, V., Kuter, U., Nau, D.S., Alford, R.: A hierarchical goal-based formalism and algorithm for single-agent planning. In: Proceedings of AAMAS, pp. 981–988 (2012)
15. Sirin, E., Parsia, B., Wu, D., Hendler, J.A., Nau, D.S.: HTN planning for web service composition using SHOP2. J. Web Semant. **1**(4), 377–396 (2004)
16. Smith, D.E., Frank, J., Cushing, W.: The ANML language. In: Proceedings of KEPS (2008)
17. Weber, I.M.: Semantic Methods for Execution-level Business Process Modeling: Modeling Support Through Process Verification and Service Composition. LNBIP, vol. 40. Springer, Heidelberg (2009). doi:10.1007/978-3-642-05085-5
18. Wilkins, D.E.: Can AI planners solve practical problems? Comput. Intell. **6**(4), 232–246 (1990)
19. Wu, D., Parsia, B., Sirin, E., Hendler, J., Nau, D.: Automating DAML-S web services composition using SHOP2. In: Fensel, D., Sycara, K., Mylopoulos, J. (eds.) ISWC 2003. LNCS, vol. 2870, pp. 195–210. Springer, Heidelberg (2003). doi:10.1007/978-3-540-39718-2_13

Complexity-Aware Generation of Workflows by Process-Oriented Case-Based Reasoning

Gilbert Müller$^{(\boxtimes)}$ and Ralph Bergmann

Business Information Systems II, University of Trier, 54286 Trier, Germany
{muellerg,bergmann}@uni-trier.de
http://www.wi2.uni-trier.de

Abstract. One of the biggest challenges in business process management is the creation of appropriate and efficient workflows. This asks for intelligent, knowledge-based systems that assist domain experts in this endeavor. In this paper we investigate workflow creation by applying Process-Oriented Case-Based Reasoning (POCBR). We introduce POCBR and describe how it can be applied to the experience-based generation of workflows by retrieval and adaptation of available best-practice workflow models. While existing approaches have already demonstrated their feasibility in principle, the generated workflows are not optimized with respect to complexity requirements. However, there is a high interest in workflows with a low complexity, e.g., to ensure the appropriate enactment as well as the understandability of the workflow. The main contribution of this paper is thus a novel approach to consider the workflow complexity during the workflow generation. Therefore, a complexity measure for workflows is proposed and integrated into the retrieval and adaptation process. An experimental evaluation with real cooking recipes clearly demonstrates the benefits of the described approach.

Keywords: Case-based reasoning · Process-Oriented Case-Based Reasoning · Workflow complexity · Workflow adaptation

1 Introduction

Business process management is a well-established discipline that deals with the identification, modeling, analysis, improvement, and implementation of business processes [1]. Workflow management is a specific area of business process management that aims at "the automation of a business process, in whole or part, during which documents, information or tasks are passed from one participant to another for action, according to a set of procedural rules" [39]. In the recent years, the use of workflows has significantly expanded from the original domain of business processes towards new areas such as e-science [36], information integration [14], private activities [12], and even cooking [28]. One of the biggest challenges in the application of workflows today arises from the fact that workflows must be constructed or adapted more frequently [1,11,32]. This asks for intelligent, knowledge-based systems that assist domain experts in the creation

© Springer International Publishing AG 2017
G. Kern-Isberner et al. (Eds.): KI 2017, LNAI 10505, pp. 207–221, 2017.
DOI: 10.1007/978-3-319-67190-1_16

or adaptation of workflows. Such systems must be able to represent and reason with knowledge about workflows and workflows elements, such as task, and data items.

In our research we address this problem by the application of Process-Oriented Case-Based Reasoning (POCBR) [25], which deals with the integration of Case-Based Reasoning (CBR) with process-oriented research areas like workflow management. POCBR aims at providing experience-based support for the automatic extraction [10], generation [20], execution [4], monitoring, and optimization [26,35] of workflows. We use POCBR to support the construction of workflows by reuse of already available workflows. Workflows are retrieved [6] and subsequently adapted [27,29,30] to new purposes and circumstances. More precisely, a case base (or repository) of successful workflows reflecting best-practices in a domain is the core of such a POCBR approach. Users can query the repository with a specification of important properties of the workflow s/he wants to create in order to retrieve potentially reusable workflows. Using adaptation methods from CBR, workflows can be automatically adapted to better match the user's requirements.

While existing approaches have already demonstrated their feasibility in principle, the generated workflows are not optimized with respect to complexity requirements. However, complex workflows are more difficult to understand and to maintain, which may also result in a higher error-proneness of the workflow model [9]. Furthermore, the enactment of workflow models must not exceed the skills of the workflow participants or given time restrictions. In this paper, we address this issue by proposing a novel approach for the complexity-aware generation of workflows. Therefore, we introduce a measure for workflow complexity that can be used to asses created workflows automatically. Then, we adjust the POCBR methods for retrieval and adaptation such that this measure is considered during workflow creation. The proposed approach is fully implemented and demonstrated in the domain of cooking using workflows describing real cooking recipes. The complexity-aware creation of cooking workflows thus leads to new recipes which are easy to prepare.

The remainder of this paper is organized as follows: The next section presents the foundations of POCBR and our approaches for retrieval and adaptation. Then, we introduce a complexity measure for workflows and explain how the POCBR approaches can be adjusted to consider this measure. Finally, we present an experimental evaluation of the described approach.

2   Process-Oriented Case-Based Reasoning

Case-Based Reasoning is a problem solving paradigm built upon a rule of thumb suggesting that "similar problems tend to have similar solutions" [2,16,34]. The core of every case-based problem solver is a case base, which is a collection of memorized experience, called cases. The R^4-CBR cycle proposed by Aamodt and Plaza [2] consists of the four CBR phases retrieve, reuse, revise, and retain, which are performed sequentially when a new problem (also called new case or query) must be solved [22].

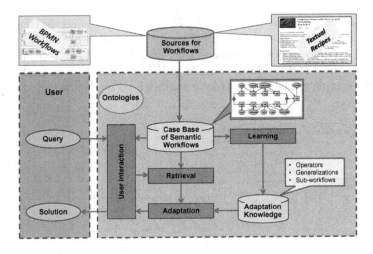

Fig. 1. POCBR architecture

In POCBR a case is usually a workflow or process description expressing procedural experiential knowledge. Most basically, POCBR aims at generating new workflows or processes by retrieval and reuse of existing ones. The overall architecture the POCBR approach we follow is illustrated in Fig. 1. First, a case base (or repository) of semantic workflows is constructed by selecting appropriate best-practice workflows from existing sources. The workflows in this case base can be reused, i.e., for a particular problem situation a suitable process represented as workflow can be suggested. This is primarily achieved by retrieving the best matching workflow from the repository. If required, the workflow is automatically adapted according to the requirements and restriction in the particular scenario. In the following of this section, we will summarize our related research in the field of POCBR.

2.1 Semantic Workflows

In order to formalize procedural experience, we employed *semantic workflows* [6] as case representation. Broadly speaking, a workflow consists of a set of *activities* (also called *tasks*) combined with *control-flow structures* like sequences, parallel (AND) or alternative (XOR) branches, as well as repeated execution (LOOP). In addition, tasks exchange certain *data items*, which can also be of physical matter. Tasks, data items, and relationships between the two of them form the *dataflow*. For the example application domain of cooking, a workflow describes the preparation steps required and ingredients used in order to prepare a particular dish. Here, the tasks represent the cooking steps and the data items refer to the ingredients being processed.

We consider workflows represented as a graph $W = (N, E)$ consisting of nodes $N = N^T \cup N^D \cup N^C$ and edges $E = E^C \cup E^D$. Nodes represent *tasks* N^T, *data nodes* N^D, or *control-flow nodes* N^C. The execution order of tasks is defined by *control-flow edges* $E^C \subseteq (N^T \cup N^C) \times (N^T \cup N^C)$ and the consumption or production of data nodes is specified by *dataflow edges* $E^D \subseteq (N^T \times N^D) \cup (N^D \times N^T)$. Furthermore, we enforce that each task $t \in N^T$ consumes ($\exists d \in N^D : (d,t) \in E^D$) and produces (i.e., $\exists d \in N^D : (t,d) \in E^D$) at least one data node. An example workflow graph for a sandwich recipe is illustrated in Fig. 2.

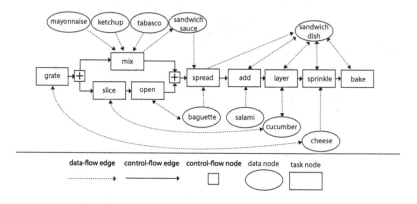

Fig. 2. Example of a block-oriented cooking workflow

To support retrieval and adaptation of workflows, the individual workflow elements are annotated with ontological information resulting in a *semantic workflow* [6]. We use a taxonomy of data items and a taxonomy of tasks to define the relevant aspects of their semantics and in particular as a means for similarity assessment. A taxonomy organizes the involved terms in a generalization/specialization hierarchy. In particular, an inner node represents a generalized term that stands for the set of more specific terms below it. An example data item taxonomy in the cooking domain is given in Fig. 3 organizing cooking ingredients. For example, the generalized term *vegetarian* stands for the set {*potatoes, rice, noodles, . . .*}. Inner nodes in generalized workflows represent that an arbitrary ingredient from the set of its specializations can be chosen.

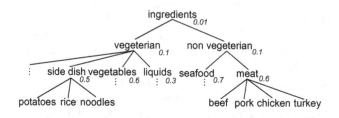

Fig. 3. Example of an ingredient taxonomy

2.2 Similarity-Based Workflow Retrieval

We developed a semantic similarity measure for workflows that enables the similarity assessment of a case workflow W_c w.r.t. a query workflow W_q [6], i.e., $sim(W_c, W_q)$. Each query workflow element $x_q \in W_q$ is mapped by the function $m : W_q \rightarrow W_c$ to an element of the case workflow $x_c \in W_c$, i.e., $x_c = m(x_q)$. The mapping is used to estimate the similarity between the two workflow elements utilizing the taxonomy, i.e., $sim(x_q, x_c)$. The similarity of tasks or data items reflects the closeness in the taxonomy and further regards the level of the taxonomic elements. In general, the similarity is defined by the attached similarity value of the least common ancestor, e.g., $sim(beef, pork) = 0.6$ (see Fig. 3). If a more general query element such as $meat$ is compared with a specific element below it, such as $pork$, the similarity value is 1. This ensures that if the query asks for a recipe containing $meat$, any recipe workflow containing any kind of $meat$ is considered highly similar. All the similarity values of the mappings are then aggregated to estimate an overall workflow similarity.

To capture user requirements for a workflow to be generated, we employ POQL (Query Language for Process-Oriented Case-Based Reasoning) [31]. It allows to represent a query q consisting of desired and undesired data items and/or tasks of the workflow to be constructed. Let $q_d = \{x_1, \ldots, x_n\}$ be a set of desired data items or tasks and $q_u = \{y_1, \ldots, y_n\}$ be a set of undesired data items or tasks. A query q is defined as $(x_1 \wedge \ldots \wedge x_2) \wedge \neg y_1 \wedge \ldots \wedge \neg y_n$. POQL also enables the specification of generalized terms, i.e., if a vegetarian dish is desired, this can be defined by $\neg meat$. The query q is then used to guide retrieval, i.e., to search for a workflow which at best contains all desired elements but no undesired element. Based on the query q the not matching elements can be identified, enabling to determine the elements to be deleted or added to the retrieved workflow during the subsequent adaptation stage. The query fulfillment for a query q and a workflow W is defined as the similarity between the desired tasks/data items and the workflow W and the number of undesired tasks/data items not contained in W according to the semantic similarity measure in relation to the size of the query:

$$QF(q, W) = \frac{\sum_{x \in q_d} sim(x, m(x)) + |\{y \in q_u | sim(y, m(y)) \neq 1\}|}{|q_d| + |q_u|} \quad (1)$$

Consequently, similar desired data items or tasks increase the query fulfillment, while matching undesired data items or tasks reduce the query fulfillment between the POQL query and the workflow.

2.3 Automatic Workflow Adaptation

We aim at supporting the users in situations in which the best matching workflow from the case base does not sufficiently fulfill the query. This requires that the workflow is automatically adapted according to the restrictions and requirements specified in the query, i.e., workflow elements or fragments are added or deleted according to the particular needs.

For that purpose, we developed several domain-independent workflow adaptation methods which we now briefly describe (for a more detailed description of these methods we refer to our previous work [27–30]). Since such adaptation methods usually require a significant amount of domain-specific adaptation knowledge, we additionally developed new methods that allow to automatically learn the required adaptation knowledge from the workflow repository. Hence, we distinguish between a learning phase of adaptation knowledge and a problem solving phase in which for a given query the best matching workflow is adapted such that it matches the particular problem scenario at best (see Fig. 1). The developed adaptation methods can mostly be classified into *transformational adaptation, compositional adaptation* and *adaptation by generalization* [22].

Transformational Adaptation. The *operator-based adaptation* [30] is a *transformational adaptation* method in which the individual transformation steps are performed by so called *workflow adaptation operators*. They are denoted in a STRIPS-like manner. An operator consists of two workflow sub-graphs we call *streamlets*: a DELETE-streamlet specifies a workflow fragment to be deleted from the workflow and an ADD-streamlet represents a workflow fragment to be added to the workflow. The overall adaptation is implemented as a search process that aims at incrementally modifying the workflow with the goal to increase the query fulfillment (see formula 1). The required workflow adaptation operators can be learned from the workflow repository by analyzing pairs of highly similar workflows (selected by using a similarity threshold). For each pair, the difference is determined and workflow operators are generated, whose ADD and DELETE-streamlets basically cover those differences. Roughly speaking, the generated operators thus transform one workflow of the pair into the other one.

Compositional Adaptation. The developed method for *compositional adaptation* is based on the idea that each workflow can be decomposed into meaningful sub-workflows called *workflow streams* [27]. This decomposition is based on the fact that the final workflow output is quite often achieved by producing partial outputs that are somehow combined to create the final workflow output. Such workflow streams can be automatically discovered from the workflow repository in the learning phase. Workflow streams represent valuable adaptation knowledge, which are used as "chunks" that can be used as replacement during compositional adaptation. More precisely, a workflow stream can be replaced by a stream learned from another workflow that produces the same partial output but in a different manner, i.e., with other task or data items. Workflow streams can only be replaced, if their data nodes indicate that they represent the same kind of sub-process. This ensures that replacing an arbitrary stream does not violate the syntactic correctness of the workflow. Compositional adaptation is also implemented as a search process that aims to increase query fulfillment, but it replaces larger portions of a workflow than transformational adaptation.

Adaptation by Generalization and Specialization of Workflows. Finally, *generalization and specialization* was investigated as a third adaptation approach [29]. A *generalized workflow* is structurally identical to the base workflow but the semantic descriptions of task and data items are generalized. We generalize a workflow by considering a set of similar workflows as training samples and employ the taxonomy as generalization hierarchy from which generalized semantic descriptions are selected. The computed generalized cases are then stored as a generalized workflow repository. During problem solving, adaptation is performed by specializing a previously generalized workflow in a manner such that query fulfillment is maximized.

Integration of Adaptation Methods. The three approaches can be integrated to form a hybrid adaptation approach that combines the three adaptation capabilities [28]. This integration involves the actual adaptation process as well as the learning phase.

First of all, during the learning phase, adaptation operators and workflow streams can be learned not only from the available specific workflows, but also from workflows resulting from generalization. Thus, we first apply generalization to the workflows in the case base and then we learn adaptation operators and workflow streams from the generalized workflows. The learned knowledge can then be used when adapting generalized workflows retrieved from the generalized case base.

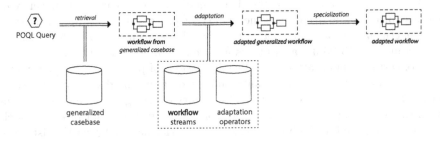

Fig. 4. Integration of adaptation approaches

The adaptation process itself then uses the three adaptation methods in combination (see Fig. 4). First, similarity-based retrieval selects the best matching workflow from the generalized case base of semantic workflows. Then, compositional adaptation is applied. Thereby, entire sub-workflows (e.g., the preparation of the *sandwich sauce*) are replaced by matching learned sub-workflows (e.g., other *sauces*) from other workflows. Next, adaptation is performed by applying adaptation operators, which result in additional modifications of the workflows (e.g., the ingredient *tomato* is replaced by *mushrooms*). Finally, the workflows are specialized (if necessary) by replacing single generalized data items or tasks by means of the specified taxonomy (e.g. the generalized ingredient *meat* is replaced by *chicken*).

In all approaches, the adaptation of the workflow is performed by chaining several adaptation steps $w \xrightarrow{\alpha_1} w_1 \xrightarrow{\alpha_2} \ldots \xrightarrow{\alpha_n} w_n = w'$, which iteratively transforms the retrieved workflow w towards an adapted workflow w'. This process solves an optimization problem aiming at maximizing the query fulfillment (as specified in formula 1). This optimization process is implemented as a heuristic search procedure with the goal to achieve an adapted workflow with the highest query fulfillment possible. In the domain of cooking, this integrated adaptation process aims at adding missing desired ingredients/preparation steps and at removing undesired contained ingredients/preparation steps specified in the query.

3   Complexity Assessment of Workflows

We now summarize related work on workflow complexity and then introduce a novel criterion for the retrieval and adaptation process that considers the complexity of workflows in addition to the query fulfillment. Thus, retrieval and adaptation become complexity-aware by optimizing the constructed workflow also in this regard.

3.1   Business Process Complexity

In business process literature, several assessment approaches exist that aim at measuring process quality. Existing quality models [21] propose quality attributes, criteria, and predicates. They relate to the efficacy and efficiency of business processes and measure the quality of process design, implementation, and enactment. In addition, *quality metrics* have been proposed for business process models [13,23,37] as a means for the systematic and automated assessment of certain quality attributes. The discussions of process model quality also involves complexity as an important issue. Several authors discuss process complexity from the perspective of pragmatic quality referring to the understandability of the process model [24,33]. Various complexity measures for process models have been proposed in the literature. A study performed by Latva-Koivisto [18], for example, suggests the use of graph complexity measures (e.g., *coefficient network complexity* or a *complexity index*). Furthermore, various approaches assess the complexity of business processes based on established measures in software development [7,8,19]. For example, Cardoso et al. [9] present complexity measures that include the number of activities or control-flow elements, consider the complexity induced by control-flow nodes, or the complexity resulting from the dataflow. As an alternative approach, Vanderfeesten et al. [38] introduce the cross-connectivity metric considering the connectivity strength between process elements. For process models based on petri nets (referred to as workflow nets) Lassen and Van der Aalst [17] presented several complexity metrics. However, despite the large number of different complexity measures, no standard approach for assessing the complexity of workflows currently exists.

3.2 Complexity-Aware Query Fulfillment

In order to consider complexity during the construction process, a new complexity-aware criterion is required. In this work, we consider the complexity of a workflow W as a generic function $complexity(W) \rightarrow [0,1]$ that assigns a high value to workflows with a high complexity and a lower value to less complex workflows.

$$QF_{complexity}(q, W) = \alpha \cdot QF(q, W) + (1 - \alpha) \cdot (1 - complexity(W)) \quad (2)$$

Based on this complexity function, we define a new complexity-aware query fulfilment measure $QF_{complexity}(q, W) \rightarrow [0,1]$ (see Eq. 2). Both criteria are weighted by a parameter $\alpha \in [0,1]$. The complexity-aware query fulfilment measure replaces the original measure specified in formula 1. It is used during the retrieval process to select the best matching workflow from the case base and during the hybrid adaptation process. Thus, it aims at optimizing the constructed workflow also with regard to complexity. Please note that this results in a multi-objective optimization problem and thus the adaptation may not be able to maximize the query fulfillment and to reduce the complexity of the workflow at the same time.

3.3 Complexity Measure

Due to the various approaches and perspectives to measure workflow complexity presented in the literature, we assume that the complexity of a workflow is not determined by a single feature, but is composed of several criteria. We introduce a new complexity function $complexity(W) \rightarrow [0,1]$ that covers five different indicators for determining the complexity of a workflow (see Table 1).

Table 1. Complexity criteria

Critera description	Criteria measure
Number of data nodes	$\dfrac{|N^D|}{max\{|N_1^D|,...,|N_n^D|\}}$
Number of control-flow elements	$\dfrac{|N^T \cup N^C|}{max\{|N_1^T \cup N_1^C|,...,|N_n^T \cup N_n^C|\}}$
Complexity of dataflow	$1 - \dfrac{2 \cdot |N^T|}{|E^D|}$
Complexity of tasks	$\dfrac{\sum\limits_{t \in N^T} taskComplexity(t)}{|N^T|}$
Lead time	$\dfrac{leadTime(W)}{max\{leadTime(W_1),...,leadTime(W_n)\}}$

The first two criteria measure basic complexity properties, i.e., the *number of control-flow elements* (task and control-flow nodes) as well as the *number of data nodes* in the workflow $W = (N, E)$. Both measures are normalized by the highest amount of control-flow elements or data nodes contained in a workflow from the case base. Consequently, workflows with more data nodes or more control-flow elements are assumed to be more complex. Furthermore, the *complexity of tasks* as well as the *complexity of dataflow* represent two additional complexity criteria. The complexity measure for the *dataflow* considers the average amount of data nodes consumed and produced by the tasks, which assigns a high complexity value to those workflows in which the tasks N^T consume and produce a large amount of data nodes[1] E^D. For computing the *complexity of tasks*, which determine the required skill level for executing the task [21], each task t in the taxonomy is annotated by an estimated task complexity value $taskComplexity(t) \in [0,1]$. The criterion is defined as the average complexity of the tasks in the workflow W. Finally, the total time to execute a particular workflow (also referred to as *lead time* [15]) is also considered as an indicator for the workflow complexity. Therefor, each task t in the taxonomy is annotated by an approximated throughput time $throughputTime(t) \in \mathbb{N}$. The throughput time [15] measures the execution time of a task t as the elapsed time between finishing the previous task and finishing the particular task t. The *lead time* for a workflow W is then heuristically measured by aggregating the throughput times of the tasks. We denote $maxPath(W) \subseteq N^T$ as those tasks that are part of the longest sequence path with regard to highest total throughput time from start to end node. The overall lead time is then computed by adding up the single throughput times of the tasks in $maxPath(W)$, i.e., $leadTime(W) = \sum_{t \in maxPath(W)} throughputTime(t)$. To assess the corresponding complexity, this value is normalized in relation to the workflows from the repository as defined in Table 1. The overall complexity measure $complexity(W)$ of a workflow W is then defined as the arithmetic mean of these five complexity criteria.

3.4   Complexity in the Cooking Domain

As our evaluation is performed in the cooking domain, we will now briefly describe the implications of the domain-independent complexity measure described in the previous section on cooking recipes. In the cooking domain, the complexity of workflows basically determines the difficulty of preparation. Due to several reasons, amateur chefs may search for easy-to-prepare cooking recipes with a low complexity. Thus, the complexity-aware generation of cooking workflows is a highly relevant application field.

We assume that also in cooking the complexity is composed by various criteria that are mostly reflected by the introduced complexity measure. Thus, we measure the *number of preparation steps* (number of control-flow nodes) and *number of ingredients* (number of data nodes) as two basic complexity criteria. Furthermore, the complexity of dataflow determines the *complexity of the preparation*, assuming that recipes in which each preparation step consumes and produces a high amount of ingredients is more complex. The application of task complexity in the cooking domain measures the *complexity of preparation steps*.

---

[1] Please note that each task in a workflow consumes and produces at least one data node, respectively.

For instance, the preparation step *blanche* is more complex than the preparation step *mix*. The lead time denotes the duration time of preparation, which is another indicator for the preparation complexity. The preparation step *mix*, for example, is considered as short, while *baking* results in a longer preparation time.

4   Experimental Evaluation

We implemented the described approach for complexity-aware workflow generation by extending our generic POCBR system CAKE [5]. Using CAKE, we also developed an application in the cooking domain, called CookingCAKE [28], which uses a workflow repository of 61 sandwich recipe workflows manually modelled from various Internet sources (e.g., sandwich recipes on WikiTaaable [3][2]). The resulting workflows are purely sequential, thus no control-flow nodes occur. The employed taxonomies of preparation steps and ingredients are based on the WikiTaaable ontology and were manually annotated with similarity, preparation time, and task complexity values.

A running prototype of the complexity-aware workflow generation in CookingCAKE is available under http://cookingCAKE.wi2.uni-trier.de/complexity. The query of CookingCAKE involves desired and undesired ingredients as well as desired and undesired preparation steps. An example query could ask to generate a *salmon* and *cherry tomato* recipe without using any kind of *cheese*. CookingCAKE then selects the best matching workflow from the repository and subsequently adapts it according to the novel criterion $QF_{complexity}(q, W)$. Thus, the system tries to maximize the query fulfilment on the one hand and on the other hand aims at reducing the complexity of the workflow to generate an appropriate easy-to-prepare recipe for an amateur chef.

To evaluate the complexity-aware approach for workflow construction in the cooking domain, we performed several leave-one-out experiments. We generated 61 queries automatically as follows: for each workflow W in the repository, a corresponding query was constructed by selecting the most similar workflow W' from the repository and by determining the difference between the two workflows. The constructed query considers workflow elements as desired that are only contained in the workflow W and considers the elements only contained in workflow W' as undesired. At most 4 randomly selected ingredients and 2 preparation steps are determined as desired or undesired respectively. For each query we executed the described POCBR approach to generate an appropriate workflow, while the workflow from which the query was derived was temporarily removed from the repository. We performed this experiment with the standard approach, applying only the query fulfillment criterion as well as with the complexity-aware approach. For the complexity-aware recipe construction we chose the parameter $\alpha = 0.5$ to consider the query fulfillment and the complexity in equal shares. For both approaches, we measured the query fulfillment, the complexity, and the

---

[2] http://wikitaaable.loria.fr.

Table 2. Evaluation results: average values over all queries

	Query fulfillment	Complexity	Combined	Computation time
Standard retrieval	0.83	0.43	0.70	1.15 s
Standard adaption	0.92	0.48	0.72	18.73 s
Complexity-aware retrieval	0.75	0.28	0.74	1.42 s
Complexity-aware adaption	0.87	0.29	0.79	9.49 s

combined complexity-aware criterion of the retrieved as well as of the adapted workflow.

The evaluation results illustrated in Table 2 clearly demonstrate several benefits of the presented approach. First of all, the experiments confirm our previous experimental evaluations of the adaptation methods [27, 29, 30] by showing that they lead to a significant increase in query fulfillment (from 0.83 to 0.92 for the standard approach and from 0.75 to 0.87 for the complexity-aware approach). For the domain of cooking this means that cooking recipes are generated that are close to the users requirements. Second, the impact of the proposed complexity-aware query fulfillment approach is clearly visible. During retrieval, less complex workflows are selected as starting point for adaptation. In both approaches adaptation tends to increase the workflow complexity in favor of query fulfillment. However, altogether with the complexity-aware approach, the complexity of the generated workflow is significantly reduced (−40%), while the query fulfillment itself is only slightly decreased (−5%). Furthermore, the overall computation time is significantly decreased[3].

5   Conclusions and Future Work

This paper presents a new approach to consider workflow complexity during the automatic generation of workflows in a case-based manner. The complexity measure is composed of several criteria including the number of tasks and data items, the complexity of the tasks and the dataflow as well as the lead time. We demonstrated the benefits of the presented approach in an experimental study in the domain of cooking based on real cooking recipes and ontologies.

In future work, the complexity assessment will be extended and evaluated by considering various other complexity and quality measures (see Sect. 3.1). So far, we demonstrated our methods primarily in the domain of cooking. Thus, we further aim at broadening the experimental basis by exploring existing workflow and business process model repository collections. In particular, we will investigate the field of scientific text mining workflows in more detail.

Acknowledgements. This work was funded by the German Research Foundation (DFG), project number BE 1373/3-3.

---

[3] The adaptation time depends on the size of the workflow, which is usually smaller, if a less complex workflow is retrieved.

References

1. van der Aalst, W.M.: Business process management: a comprehensive survey. ISRN Softw. Eng. **2013** (2013)
2. Aamodt, A., Plaza, E.: Case-based reasoning: foundational issues, methodological variations, and system approaches. AI Commun. **7**(1), 39–59 (1994)
3. Badra, F., Bendaoud, R., Bentebibel, R., Champin, P., Cojan, J., Cordier, A., Desprès, S., Jean-Daubias, S., Lieber, J., Meilender, T., Mille, A., Nauer, E., Napoli, A., Toussaint, Y.: TAAABLE: text mining, ontology engineering, and hierarchical classification for textual case-based cooking. In: Schaaf, M. (ed.) ECCBR 2008, Workshop Proceedings, pp. 219–228 (2008)
4. Bergmann, R., Freßmann, A., Maximini, K., Maximini, R., Sauer, T.: Case-based support for collaborative business. In: Roth-Berghofer, T.R., Göker, M.H., Güvenir, H.A. (eds.) ECCBR 2006. LNCS (LNAI), vol. 4106, pp. 519–533. Springer, Heidelberg (2006). doi:10.1007/11805816_38
5. Bergmann, R., Gessinger, S., Görg, S., Müller, G.: The collaborative agile knowledge engine CAKE. In: Goggins, S.P., Jahnke, I., McDonald, D.W., Bjørn, P. (eds.) Proceedings of the 18th International Conference on Supporting Group Work, Sanibel Island, FL, USA, 09–12 November 2014, pp. 281–284. ACM (2014). http://doi.acm.org/10.1145/2660398.2663771
6. Bergmann, R., Gil, Y.: Similarity assessment and efficient retrieval of semantic workfows. Inf. Syst. **40**, 115–127 (2014)
7. Cardoso, J.: About the data-flow complexity of web processes. In: 6th International Workshop on Business Process Modeling, Development, and Support: Business Processes and Support Systems: Design for Flexibility, pp. 67–74 (2005)
8. Cardoso, J.S.: Business process control-flow complexity: metric, evaluation, and validation. Int. J. Web Service Res. **5**(2), 49–76 (2008). http://dx.doi.org/10.4018/jwsr.2008040103
9. Cardoso, J., Mendling, J., Neumann, G., Reijers, H.A.: A discourse on complexity of process models. In: Eder, J., Dustdar, S. (eds.) BPM 2006. LNCS, vol. 4103, pp. 117–128. Springer, Heidelberg (2006). doi:10.1007/11837862_13
10. Dufour-Lussier, V., Ber, F.L., Lieber, J., Nauer, E.: Automatic case acquisition from texts for process-oriented case-based reasoning. Inf. Syst. **40**, 153–167 (2014)
11. Fleischmann, A., Schmidt, W., Stary, C., Augl, M.: Agiles Prozessmanagement mittels Subjektorientierung. HMD Praxis der Wirtschaftsinformatik **50**(2), 64–76 (2013)
12. Görg, S., Bergmann, R.: Social workflows - vision and potential study. Inf. Syst. **50**, 1–19 (2015)
13. Heravizadeh, M., Mendling, J., Rosemann, M.: Dimensions of business processes quality (QoBP). In: Ardagna, D., Mecella, M., Yang, J. (eds.) BPM 2008. LNBIP, vol. 17, pp. 80–91. Springer, Heidelberg (2009). doi:10.1007/978-3-642-00328-8_8
14. Hung, P., Chiu, D.: Developing workflow-based information integration (WII) with exception support in a web services environment. In: Proceedings of the 37th Annual Hawaii International Conference on System Sciences, p. 10 (2004)
15. Jansen-Vullers, M., Loosschilder, M., Kleingeld, P., Reijers, H.: Performance measures to evaluate the impact of best practices. In: Proceedings of Workshops and Doctoral Consortium of CAiSE 2007 (BPMDS workshop), vol. 1, pp. 359–368. Tapir Academic Press, Trondheim (2007)
16. Kolodner, J.: Case Based Reasoning. Morgan Kaufmann, San Mateo (1993)

17. Lassen, K.B., van der Aalst, W.M.P.: Complexity metrics for workflow nets. Inf. Softw. Technol. **51**(3), 610–626 (2009). http://dx.doi.org/10.1016/j.infsof.2008.08.005

18. Latva-Koivisto, A.M.: Finding a complexity measure for business process models. Helsinki University of Technology, Systems Analysis Laboratory (2001)

19. Laue, R., Gruhn, V.: Complexity metrics for business process models. In: BIS. LNI, vol. 85, pp. 1–12. GI (2006)

20. Leake, D.B., Wilson, D.C.: Combining CBR with interactive knowledge acquisition, manipulation and reuse. In: Althoff, K.-D., Bergmann, R., Branting, L.K. (eds.) ICCBR 1999. LNCS, vol. 1650, pp. 203–217. Springer, Heidelberg (1999). doi:10.1007/3-540-48508-2_15

21. Lohrmann, M., Reichert, M.: Understanding business process quality. In: Glykas, M. (ed.) Business Process Management - Theory and Applications. SCI, vol. 444, pp. 41–73. Springer, Heidelberg (2013). doi:10.1007/978-3-642-28409-0_2

22. Lopez Mantaras, R., McSherry, D., Bridge, D., Leake, D., Smyth, B., Craw, S., Faltings, B., Maher, M.L., Cox, M.T., Forbus, K., Keane, M., Aamodt, A., Watson, I.: Retrieval, reuse, revision and retention in case-based reasoning. Knowl. Eng. Rev. **20**(03), 215–240 (2005)

23. Mendling, J.: Metrics for Process Models: Empirical Foundations of Verification, Error Prediction, and Guidelines for Correctness. LNBIP, vol. 6. Springer, Heidelberg (2008)

24. Mendling, J., Reijers, H.A., van der Aalst, W.M.P.: Seven process modeling guidelines (7PMG). Inf. Softw. Technol. **52**(2), 127–136 (2010). http://dx.doi.org/10.1016/j.infsof.2009.08.004

25. Minor, M., Montani, S., Recio-García, J.A.: Process-oriented case-based reasoning. Inf. Syst. **40**, 103–105 (2014)

26. Montani, S., Leonardi, G.: Retrieval and clustering for supporting business process adjustment and analysis. Inf. Syst. **40**, 128–141 (2014)

27. Müller, G., Bergmann, R.: Workflow streams: a means for compositional adaptation in process-oriented CBR. In: Lamontagne, L., Plaza, E. (eds.) ICCBR 2014. LNCS, vol. 8765, pp. 315–329. Springer, Cham (2014). doi:10.1007/978-3-319-11209-1_23

28. Müller, G., Bergmann, R.: CookingCAKE: a framework for the adaptation of cooking recipes represented as workflows. In: Kendall-Morwick, J. (ed.) Workshop Proceedings from ICCBR 2015, Frankfurt, Germany, 28–30 September 2015. CEUR Workshop Proceedings, vol. 1520, pp. 221–232. CEUR-WS.org (2015)

29. Müller, G., Bergmann, R.: Generalization of workflows in process-oriented case-based reasoning. In: Proceedings of FLAIRS 2015, pp. 391–396. AAAI Press, Hollywood (Florida) (2015)

30. Müller, G., Bergmann, R.: Learning and applying adaptation operators in process-oriented case-based reasoning. In: Hüllermeier, E., Minor, M. (eds.) ICCBR 2015. LNCS (LNAI), vol. 9343, pp. 259–274. Springer, Cham (2015). doi:10.1007/978-3-319-24586-7_18

31. Müller, G., Bergmann, R.: POQL: a new query language for process-oriented case-based reasoning. In: Bergmann, R., Görg, S., Müller, G. (eds.) Proceedings of the LWA 2015 Workshops: KDML, FGWM, IR, and FGDB, Trier, Germany, 7–9 October 2015. CEUR Workshop Proceedings, vol. 1458, pp. 247–255. CEUR-WS.org (2015)

32. Reichert, M., Weber, B.: Enabling Flexibility in Process-aware Information Systems: Challenges, Methods, Technologies. Springer, Heidelberg (2012)

33. Reijers, H.A., Mendling, J., Recker, J.: Business process quality management. In: vom Brocke, J., Rosemann, M. (eds.) Handbook on Business Process Management 1. IHIS, pp. 167–185. Springer, Heidelberg (2015). doi:10.1007/978-3-642-45100-3_8

34. Richter, M.M., Weber, R.O.: Case-Based Reasoning - A Textbook. Springer, Berlin (2013)

35. Sauer, T., Maximini, K.: Using workflow context for automated enactment state tracking. In: Minor, M. (ed.) Workshop Proceedings: ECCBR 2006, Workshop: Case-based Reasoning and Context Awareness, pp. 300–314. Universität Trier (2006)

36. Taylor, I.J., Deelman, E., Gannon, D.B.: Workflows for e-Science. Springer, London (2007)

37. Vanderfeesten, I., Cardoso, J., Mendling, J., Reijers, H.A., Van der Aalst, W.: Quality metrics for business process models. BPM Workflow Handbook 144, 179–190 (2007)

38. Vanderfeesten, I., Reijers, H.A., Mendling, J., Aalst, W.M.P., Cardoso, J.: On a quest for good process models: the cross-connectivity metric. In: Bellahsène, Z., Léonard, M. (eds.) CAiSE 2008. LNCS, vol. 5074, pp. 480–494. Springer, Heidelberg (2008). doi:10.1007/978-3-540-69534-9_36

39. Workflow Management Coalition: Workflow management coalition glossary & terminology (1999)

LiMa: Sequential Lifted Marginal Filtering on Multiset State Descriptions

Max Schröder[(✉)], Stefan Lüdtke, Sebastian Bader, Frank Krüger, and Thomas Kirste

Mobile Multimedia Information Systems Group, Institute of Computer Science, University of Rostock, 18051 Rostock, Germany
{max.schroeder,stefan.luedtke2,sebastian.bader,frank.krueger2, thomas.kirste}@uni-rostock.de

Abstract. Maintaining the a-posteriori distribution of categorical states given a sequence of noisy and ambiguous observations, e.g. sensor data, can lead to situations where one observation can correspond to a large number of different states. We call these states *symmetrical* as they cannot be distinguished given the observation. Considering each of them during the inference is computationally infeasible, even for small scenarios. However, the number of situations (called *hypotheses*) can be reduced by abstracting from particular ones and representing all symmetrical in a single abstract state. We propose a novel Bayesian Filtering algorithm that performs this abstraction. The algorithm that we call *Lifted Marginal Filtering* (LiMa) is inspired by Lifted Inference and combines techniques known from Computational State Space Models and Multiset Rewriting Systems to perform efficient sequential inference on a parametric multiset state description. We demonstrate that our approach is working by comparing LiMa with conventional filtering.

1 Introduction

Maintaining the a-posteriori distribution of categorical states given a sequence of noisy and ambiguous observations, e.g. sensor data, can lead to situations where one observation can correspond to a large number of different states. For example, when tracking persons based on anonymous presence sensors, we do not know which concrete person corresponds to which observation (track) [9,11,25]. We call such persons (more general entities) *observation equivalent*, i.e. they cannot be distinguished, based on the current observation. Thus, the number of states that need to be considered can grow very large, even for small scenarios. For example, when tracking the location and movement of 6 persons in 10 rooms, there are already 10^6 possible states. Even though this is a theoretical number of states, also the states that actually need to be tracked and cannot be precluded given the observation (also called *hypotheses*) is large. Thus, inference quickly becomes infeasible for real-world sized domains due to the combinatorial explosion with respect to the number of hypotheses that need to be tracked.

Several approaches exists that try to exploit such *symmetries*. Approaches that abstract from the identity of the entities [11,16] cannot be used, because

© Springer International Publishing AG 2017
G. Kern-Isberner et al. (Eds.): KI 2017, LNAI 10505, pp. 222–235, 2017.
DOI: 10.1007/978-3-319-67190-1_17

identifying observations might reveal the correspondence between some of the tracks and some of the identities. Additionally, in order to answer application specific questions, we might need the identity of entities. Such scenarios require an inference algorithm that can represent observation equivalent entities as a group, thus compactly representing states that are different but cannot be distinguished given the sensor data. However, this approach must also be able to break symmetries, i.e. split groups, when indicated by observations. Recently, Lifted Inference [12,18,23] showed that inference in graphical models can be performed on a first-order level, by reasoning over equivalent random variables as a group. However, none of these approaches allows to *recursively* compute the a-posteriori distribution, which is necessary when the complete observation sequence is not known in advance such as when using real world sensor data.

We propose a novel filtering algorithm that can compactly represent symmetrical states. It employs a multiset state representation that allows to group observation equivalent entities. This abstract state representation is embedded in the Bayesian Filtering framework in order to recursively compute the a-posteriori state distribution. For this purpose, the next belief state according to a transition model is *predicted* followed by an *update* of the probabilities according to an observation model that takes the current observation into account. This allows us to reason over them as a group, leading to a more compact belief state and a much more efficient filtering algorithm. To exemplify our approach, we will use the following office scenario [22] as a running example throughout the paper:

Example 1 (Office scenario). Up to six agents are in an office building with five rooms and a hall connecting the rooms. There are also two coffee machines and ten coffee capsules in a storage. Agents can walk between the rooms and take a capsule from the storage, respectively, replenish the coffee machine. If a capsule is inserted in the coffee machine, agents can take a coffee. All rooms contain presence sensors that detect if at least one agent is present. Our goal is to track the current state (positions of agents, items the agents are carrying as well as the number of capsules left and the state of the coffee machine etc.) based on sequences of presence sensor data.

The agents in this scenario are observation equivalent, as they cannot be distinguished given the presence sensor data. Although this scenario is a specific instance, the underlying problem is more general and can be found in many similar scenarios involving multiple observation equivalent entities acting in parallel. Note that this scenario requires modeling of entities along with their properties and thus cannot be solved by considering the number of entities only.

In Sect. 2, we introduce basic concepts that lay the foundations for our novel inference approach. The inference approach itself is described in Sect. 3. Section 4 evaluates the inference mechanism and Sect. 5 presents connections to other methods and related work. We finish this paper with our conclusion and a description of our future work in Sect. 6.

2   Preliminaries

In the following, we will give a brief overview of two concepts our approach is based on. Computational State Space Models allow Bayesian Filtering in a state space described by precondition-effect actions. Multiset Rewriting Systems offer a formalism for compactly representing states with multiple equivalent entities.

Computational State Space Models (CSSMs) allow the knowledge-based construction of state spaces for Bayesian Filtering. They are for instance used for human behavior and goal recognition [2,19]. The transition model is described by a computable function by means of preconditions and effects. This allows the compact representation of potentially infinite state spaces by avoiding explicit state enumeration. Standard methods for Bayesian Filtering (e.g. Particle Filtering) is used to estimate the most likely state sequence.

CSSMs allow to handle large, even infinite, state spaces [17]. However, CSSMs perform inference in grounded state spaces (i.e. concrete values are assigned to all state variables). For representing observation equivalent states, this means the approach needs to track all of the different observation equivalent states individually, leading to a combinatorial explosion.

Multiset Rewriting Systems (MRSs) are an established formalism for modeling systems with many equal objects. They are for instance used to model chemical reactions happening in a solution [4] or cell interactions [5]. The state of such a system is described as a multiset of *entities*, where each entity is an instance of one of finitely many *species*. The reactions between entities are modeled as *multiset rewriting rules* that have preconditions (a multiset of entities that are consumed by the reaction) and effects (a multiset of entities that are created by the reaction). Under the probabilistic maximally parallel semantics [3], a maximal set of applicable rules (a compound rule) is applied in parallel. Each rule is assigned a *rate*, which defines the probability of a compound rule.

We are interested in MRS because they allow an abstract representation of states with multiple, equivalent entities. However, Bayesian Filtering algorithms for MRSs that incorporate observations have not yet been devised.

3   LiMa: Lifted Marginal Filtering

In the following, we present our approach that performs Bayesian Filtering using a multiset-based state representation. Our concept of Bayesian Filtering in state spaces described by precondition-effect actions is based on CSSMs (cf. Sect. 2). The state space representation is inspired by MRSs, which enable a compact representation of multiple equivalent states.

This section aims at giving a comprehensive overview of our *Lifted Marginal Filtering* approach. The next section is concerned with the question how states can be formalized in an abstract manner to represent multiple observation equivalent situations (Sect. 3.1). Section 3.2 extends this abstract representation to be capable of expressing uncertainty. The efficient manipulation of this uncertain abstract representation regarding a model of the system's dynamics is introduced in Sect. 3.3. Section 3.4 describes how observations can be taken into account to perform a complete Bayesian Filtering cycle. As Bayesian Filtering is used to answer application specific questions, in particular questions about the activity of the entities, we discuss how this can be performed in LiMa in Sect. 3.5.

3.1   Abstract State Description

Similar to MRS, we model a state as a multiset of entities with certain properties, e.g. objects or persons, that are part of a situation. Such entities often have many properties in common, but some properties with different values. For example, two persons may both be at the same location and both holding nothing in their hands, but having different names. In MRSs, these two persons are considered a different species. Thus, inference in MRS with many entities that are not exactly equal leads to a combinatorial explosion in the number of species. This combinatorial explosion can be avoided by extending the multiset representation to be able to group entities that are similar, but not equal.

For this purpose, our state space representation separates the *structure* of the entities from the actual property values of these entities, allowing us to group entities with similar structure, but different property values. While the number as well as the structure of entities is maintained in what we call a *state formula*, the possibly uncertain property values are maintained in the *context*. The context contains *representations* of densities[1] encoding the uncertainty respectively certainty over the entity properties. It is connected to the structure via *density labels*. Our inference algorithm manipulates the structure (the state formula), as well as these representations. Below, we introduce the concepts of entities, state formulae and contexts in detail including examples referring to the office scenario (Sect. 1).

An entity is a finite map of property names (called *slots*) to *density labels*. These density labels are used as a "name" for the possibly uncertain property values in the form of density representations that are later defined in the context.

Example 2. Let $\mathcal{E}$ be an entity that models agents with three slots Location, Holds and Name, with $\mathcal{E}$(Location) $=$ "$LHall$", $\mathcal{E}$(Holds) $=$ "$LNil$" and $\mathcal{E}$(Name) $=$ "$LNames$". We represent the entity as $\mathcal{E} = \langle$Location: "$LHall$", Holds: "$LNil$", Name: "$LNames$"$\rangle$.

Multiple entities involved within a scenario are encoded using multisets[2] such that multiple similar entities are grouped together: Let $\mathcal{E} := \{\mathcal{E}_1, \mathcal{E}_2, \ldots, \mathcal{E}_n\}$ be entities and let $i_1, \ldots, i_n$ be natural numbers. A state formula over $\mathcal{E}$ is defined as a multiset over $\mathcal{E}$. We use $[\![\, i_1\mathcal{E}_1, i_2\mathcal{E}_2, \ldots, i_n\mathcal{E}_n \,]\!]$ to represent multisets of entities with corresponding cardinalities.

---

[1] We use the term *density* to refer to densities over continuous domains as well as probability distributions over finite domains.

[2] A multiset over some set S is defined as a partial map from S to $\mathbb{N}$. We use $[\![\, n_1s_1, n_2s_s, n_3s_3 \,]\!]$ to denote the multiset containing s_1, s_2 and s_3 with the corresponding cardinalities. We use $\mathcal{M}(S)$ to refer to the set of all multisets over S.

Example 3. The situation in which 5 agents are located in the hall and another agent is located in room A can be represented as a state formula ϕ as follows:

$$\phi = [\![\, 5\langle\text{Location: } ``LHall", \text{Holds: } ``LNil", \text{Name: } ``LNames"\rangle,$$
$$1\langle\text{Location: } ``LRoomA", \text{Holds: } ``LNil", \text{Name: } ``LNames"\rangle\,]\!]$$

After modeling the structure as well as the number of entities, the actual property values are to be defined. The state formula is connected to the corresponding context that encodes the actual property values via density labels: A *context* is a finite map from density labels to density representations.

Below, we assume that, given a representation r of a density function d, there exists an algorithm SPLIT, which accepts r and a value v as input and returns a representation r' of a density d' that is the result of removing v from d. We furthermore assume an algorithm LIKELIHOOD, which accepts r and a value v as input and returns the likelihood of v with respect to d. For example, let $r = \mathcal{U}(a, b, c)$ represent a finite urn containing the items a, b and c, then SPLIT(r, a) must return the representation of an urn containing b and c, and LIKELIHOOD(r, v) will give $1/3$ for each item.

A context γ is called *valid* wrt. a given state formula ϕ, if and only if for all density labels occurring in ϕ there exists a density representation in γ and all density representations occurring in γ are referenced within ϕ. Furthermore, every density function d encoded in the context γ must be able to be split using SPLIT at least as many times as the sum of the cardinalities of the entities referencing this density. As an example, a context that connects "$LNames$" to an urn with three values only is not valid for the state formula as in Example 3, because the density is referenced six times.

In the example below, we use $\delta(x)$ to represent a density function which is non-zero for x only (i.e. we use $\delta(x)$ to refer to Dirac delta for continuous domains and the Kronecker delta for finite domains), we call $\delta(x)$ to be a *singleton distribution*. Note that singleton distributions cannot be split according to SPLIT and instead returns the same distribution. $\mathcal{U}$ is used to represent a finite urn as described above. Note that when using the $\delta(x)$ density, we might draw x multiple times compared to $\mathcal{U}(x)$.

Example 4. Let two contexts γ_1 and γ_2 be defined as follows and let ϕ be the state formula as in Example 3, then γ_1 is not valid whereas γ_2 is valid for ϕ.

$$\gamma_1 = \{ \text{``}LHall" \mapsto \delta(hall), \text{``}LNil" \mapsto \delta(nil), \text{``}LNames" \mapsto \mathcal{U}(a, \ldots, f) \}$$
$$\gamma_2 = \gamma_1 \cup \{ \text{``}LRoomA" \mapsto \delta(roomA) \}.$$

Below we assume all contexts to be valid contexts. A pair $\phi\gamma$ of state formula ϕ and valid context γ is called a *lifted state*. Note that by using this representation we assume all densities in the context to be independent from each other.

Example 5. The two situations (a) six agents are in the hall, and (b) five are in the hall and the sixth is in room A can be modeled as lifted state s_1 and s_2 as follows:

$$s_1 = [\![\, 6\langle \text{Location: } \text{``}LHall\text{''}, \text{Holds: } \text{``}LNil\text{''}, \text{Name: } \text{``}LNames\text{''}\rangle \,]\!]_{\gamma_1}$$
$$s_2 = [\![\, 5\langle \text{Location: } \text{``}LHall\text{''}, \text{Holds: } \text{``}LNil\text{''}, \text{Name: } \text{``}LNames\text{''}\rangle,$$
$$1\langle \text{Location: } \text{``}LRoomA\text{''}, \text{Holds: } \text{``}LNil\text{''}, \text{Name: } \text{``}LNames\text{''}\rangle \,]\!]_{\gamma_2}$$

Note that representing s_2 in conventional grounded approaches would require to track at least six different hypotheses, namely agent a, b, c, d, e, or f being in room A. In our formalization, however, these situations are encoded using the single hypothesis s_2.

This formalism allows to represent multiple observation equivalent states as a single lifted state. Note that additional to the connection of MRS this representation employs Rao-Blackwellization: Some aspects of the state are described explicitly (via the state formula), while some aspects have a parametric representation (via the context).

3.2 Handling Uncertainty over Lifted States

Lifted states enable the modeling of groups of situations, i.e. groups of conventional states. However, as there are several sources of noise (observations, non-deterministic actions, ...), we will consider not just a single lifted state, but a probability distribution over lifted states as CSSMs maintain a probability distribution over grounded states. We call this probability distribution *lifted belief state*.

Before introducing it in detail, we define the concepts of *grounded states*: A ground state is a lifted state if and only if its context consists of singleton distributions only. Ground states correspond to the states used in conventional Bayesian Filtering: Each ground state represents a specific situation, while a lifted state in general represents a set of situations. We call this set of situations *state instances*, i.e. the state instances are the set of ground states that are subsumed under a lifted state. Note that this set is infinite if one of the underlying densities has an infinite domain.

A probability distribution over lifted states, called *lifted belief state*, thus specifies a probability distribution over sets of grounded states. We will use *lifted belief states* to represent the current set of hypotheses while tracking activities based on noisy observations.

Example 6. Let $S = \{s_1, s_2\}$ with s_1 and s_2 be as given in Example 5. Let $b(s_1) = 0.75$ and $b(s_2) = 0.25$. Then b is a belief state over S. Below we will use the following notation to describe belief states: $b = \{0.75 \times s_1, 0.25 \times s_2\}$. b describes the situations in which with probability 0.75 all six agents are in the hall, and with probability 0.25 one of them is in room A.

3.3 Abstract State Dynamics

After describing how states can be modeled in an abstract manner (cf. lifted states) and how uncertainty about the actual state can be represented (cf. lifted belief state), in this section, we describe how the dynamics of the system is modeled and how the representation is manipulated efficiently. This corresponds to the predict step of Bayesian Filtering. We call the function that maps a lifted belief state to a successor lifted belief state the *transition model*.

We use precondition-effect actions to model the dynamics of the system. The transition model is a parallel execution of multiple actions that are all applicable in the current state, similar to MRSs.

An action maps a set of entities satisfying the precondition (specific slots and slot values) to a new set of entities. These new entities are obtained by removing entities, by creating new ones, or by modifying entities (updating slot values, removing slots or adding slots). Before defining actions, we introduce a notion of slot and entity constraints:

Slot constraints check if a single value satisfies a condition. That is, slot constraints are Boolean functions of slot values indicating whether the condition is satisfied. We denote such functions as $sc := \lambda v \mapsto v \equiv v_{\text{test}}$. v is the property value to be evaluated and $v \equiv v_{\text{test}}$ is a Boolean expression of the property value, e.g. a test for (in)equality wrt. a given value, or set membership of simply the constant function *true* and *false*.

Multiple slot constraints then are combined in an *entity constraint* that maps slot names on slot constraints. Thus, an entity satisfies an entity constraint if: (1) the entity possesses all slots that are connected to a slot constraint, and (2) all slot constraints are satisfied. Note that considering the corresponding context may be necessary to decide on the satisfaction of slot constraints.

Example 7. Let $sc_h := (\lambda v \mapsto v \equiv hall)$ be the slot constraint testing if the given slot value v is identical to the value '*hall*', $sc_\top := (\lambda v \mapsto \top)$ be the slot constraint used to ensure the presence of a given slot. Then $ec_1 = \{$Location $\mapsto sc_h\}$ is an entity constraint, satisfied by all entities and corresponding contexts with a slot Location whose value is *hall*, and $ec_2 = \{$Name $\mapsto sc_\top\}$ is satisfied by all entities which posses the slot Name.

As mentioned above, actions can modify the set of entities. A function transforming an entity into a new one is called *entity update function*. Possible entity update functions include the addition of new slots, the update of slot values or the removal of slots. These operations always include the modification of the corresponding context γ. However, for ease of understanding, we omit to mention that the context has always to be updated accordingly. I.e. given an entity $\mathcal{E}$, we use $\mathcal{E}\{s \mapsto v\}$ to refer to the entity which results by setting the slot s to the value v (i.e., addition or update of s), and we use $\mathcal{E}\{-s\}$ to refer to the entity obtained by removing slot s.

The effects of an action are specified by an *effect function* mapping a tuple of entities to a multiset of entities. This multiset can contain new entities, and entities resulting from performing entity update functions on the original entities. An *action schema* is the specification of an action, consisting of (1) a name, (2) a sequence of entity constraints π (preconditions), and (3) an effect function ϵ.

Example 8. For ec_1 as in Example 7, the schema ('H2A', $[ec_1], (\mathcal{E}) \mapsto [\![1\mathcal{E}\{$Location $\mapsto RoomA\}]\!])$ captures the movement from the hall to room A.

An action is applicable in a given lifted state if and only if the state contains entities which satisfy the actions preconditions. However, if a lifted state contains an entity possessing all slots required by the entity constraint but with a non-singleton distribution in one of these slots, we cannot decide whether the entity satisfies the precondition. In this case, we split the corresponding lifted state into two lifted states: One where the precondition is satisfied, and one which contains all other grounded states that are instances of the original lifted states. Note the similarity to splitting in Lifted Inference [18]. These splits also involve the modification of the context as the densities encoding the uncertainty regarding the preconditions will be split (using SPLIT) into two densities to remove the uncertainty. This does not necessarily require a complete grounding of the state, but only as far as needed to decide on the preconditions.

Example 9. Let $act = (\text{'H2A'}, \pi_{act}, (\mathcal{E}) \mapsto [\![1\mathcal{E}\{\text{Location} \mapsto RoomA\}]\!])$ be an action schema, and $\pi_{act} = [\{\text{Location} \mapsto sc_h, \text{Name} \mapsto sc_a\}]$ be the corresponding precondition. Let $sc_h := (\lambda v \mapsto v \equiv hall)$ and $sc_a = (\lambda v \mapsto v \equiv a)$ be the corresponding slot constraints. Then, act encodes the move action from the hall to room A performed by the agent named a. Considering the lifted state s_2 as in Example 5, there is no entity that already satisfies the action's preconditions. However, there is an entity in s_2 that is more general so that a modified version of this entity would satisfy the preconditions π_{act}. Thus, the lifted state can be split according to this entity on slot Name into the two lifted states: (1) a is at room A and the other agents are in the hall (satisfying the preconditions), and (2) a is at the hall, one of the other agents is in room A and the remaining are in the hall, too (not satisfying the preconditions). These splits include the modification of the context: the urn representation $\mathcal{U}(a, \ldots, f)$ will be converted into $\mathcal{U}(b, \ldots, f)$ and another density representation $\delta(a)$ will be inserted.

Splits, thus, can be used to ensure satisfaction of preconditions of an action schema. An action schema a together with a sequence of entities e satisfying the precondition is called an *action instance*. The entities in e are consumed while applying the action and replaced by the effect. I.e., the resulting state can *in principle* be computed by $s' = s \setminus e \cup \epsilon(e)$. Unfortunately, this would require the state s to be grounded. As described below it is also possible to compute the resulting state in a lifted manner. Before, we introduce the concept of maximal compound actions that encode the idea of maximally parallel actions in MRSs: A multiset of action instances is called *maximal compound action* (short: compound action) with respect to a lifted state if no further action instance can be added to the set so that the compound action can still be applied in the lifted state. Note that a compound action is applicable only if there is no entity referenced in two action instances.

Given a state formula ϕ, we can compute the successor states as follows:

1. Compute the set of maximal compound actions C
2. For each $c \in C$: (a) Compute the resulting splits, and (b) Compute the successor state s_c,
3. Merge the resulting successor states.

Predicting the successor states by a set of maximal compound actions might result in a set of lifted states that can be merged or pruned to reduce the number of hypotheses. A simple form of merging is summing probabilities of equal lifted states, as there might be multiple compound actions resulting in the same lifted state. Furthermore, multiple similar states can be merged by combining their entities so that the corresponding slot values are joined (exact or approximate). However, in this paper, we only perform simple merging by summing probabilities of equal lifted states.

3.4   Observation Model

In the previous section, we described state transitions based on actions. This corresponds to the *predict* step in Bayesian Filtering. In this section, we describe how the *update* step is realized in LiMa. This means, we want to manipulate the belief state, by use of an observation.

An observation is simply a condition on a property value, similar to a precondition of an action. The observation model OM takes a lifted belief state and the current observation to calculate a list of new states with updated probabilities for every lifted state of the belief state. I.e., the probabilities of the lifted states were weighted according to the current observation. For this purpose, the observation model splits each lifted state in the belief state on the observation and keeps only those lifted states that are consistent with the observation. The probabilities are then normalized to get a new valid belief state. Note that this procedure can easily be used for uncertain observations.

Example 10. For s_1 as in Example 5, let b_1 be a belief state with $b_1(s_1) = 1$. Observing $o = [\{\textsf{Location} \mapsto sc_h, \textsf{Name} \mapsto sc_a\}]$ with sc_h and sc_a as in Example 9, we get $OM(o, s_1) = \{1 \times s_1'\}$ with

$$s_1' = [\![\, 5\langle \textsf{Location: } "LHall", \textsf{Holds: } "LNil", \textsf{Name: } "LNames'"\rangle$$
$$1\langle \textsf{Location: } "LHall", \textsf{Holds: } "LNil", \textsf{Name: } "LNameA"\rangle \,]\!]$$
$$\{ "LHall" \mapsto \delta(hall), "LNil" \mapsto \delta(nil), "LNames'" \mapsto \mathcal{U}(b, \ldots, f), "LNameA" \mapsto \delta(a) \}$$

After multiplying this with the probabilities in b_1 and normalizing it (both trivial in this example), we get $b_1' = \{1 \times s_1'\}$ as new belief state for observing o in b_1.

3.5   Reasoning over Lifted States

The predict and update steps (described in Sects. 3.3 and 3.4) together define a complete Bayesian Filtering cycle. As we aim at answering application specific questions during the inference, we need to be able to reason about the lifted belief state after every predict-update-cycle.

Example 11. Considering the lifted belief state in Example 6, the question we want to answer is "Where is a?". I.e. we want to calculate the distribution of values of the Location slot for entities with the Name being a. For this purpose,

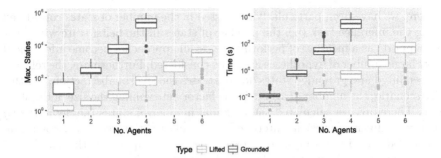

Fig. 1. Maximum number of (lifted) states during inference (left) and inference time (right) for grounded inference and Lifted Inference with LiMa. For the grounded inference, the scenarios with 5 and 6 agents could not be calculated due to the high computational effort. Note the log scale on the y axis.

every lifted state in the lifted belief state needs to be evaluated against this question. In our example, both lifted states s_1 and s_2 contain only entities with slot **Name** mapping to the density $\mathcal{U}(a, \ldots, f)$. I.e. agent a is involved in any of those more general entities and thus the corresponding lifted states need to be split to decide on the position of a:

(s_1) Splitting the entity in s_1 on **Name** with value a results in a single lifted state as the only possible **Location** for a is the *hall*. Thus, the probability of agent a being at the hall in s_1 is 1.0 resp. 0.75 (weighted by the probability of s_1).

(s_2) There are 2 entities in s_2 with **Name** mapping to a density that includes agent a. A split on the name of agent a results in two possible lifted states: (a) a is at the hall, or (b) a is at room A. Whereas the first lifted state represents 5 grounded states, the second represents only one. Thus, a is at the *hall* with a probability of $\frac{5}{6}$ and at *roomA* with a probability of $\frac{1}{6}$. These need to be weighted by the probability of the lifted state s_2.

Summing up the particular probability gives a probability that agent a is at the hall of 0.95833 and that the agent is at room A of 0.04167. Note that this split is for answering the application specific questions only. However, the un-split lifted states will be used for the further inference.

4 Evaluation

In the following, our approach is compared with a conventional Bayesian Filtering algorithm based on grounded states. As benchmark, we use the office dataset [21] that is described as office scenario in Sect. 1. It includes 720 observation sequences (120 for each number of agents between one and six) for which we perform activity recognition using both approaches.

Here, we have been particularly interested in the number of states considered during the inference task (i.e. the number of states in the belief state with non-zero support) as a measure of performance, as all approaches become infeasible if a very large number of hypotheses has to be considered. Furthermore, the relation between lifted and grounded states demonstrates the level of abstraction. For this office scenario, the number of agents is the factor determining the size of the state space. Therefore, we calculated the maximal number of states (i.e. hypotheses) maintained during Bayesian Filtering for each observation sequence. For LiMa, we counted the lifted states, and for the grounded approach the number of grounded states are considered. The results are shown in the left part of Fig. 1. Note the log scale on the y axis.

The maximum number of states visited during Bayesian Filtering grows exponentially for both inference algorithms. However, for LiMa, the number of states is several orders of magnitude smaller than for the grounded state representation. Thus, LiMa successfully exploits observation equivalence by reducing the large number of grounded states to a much smaller number of lifted states. In fact, for the grounded state representation, Bayesian Filtering has been infeasible for problems with 5 or 6 agents due to the large number of states. Furthermore, considering the overall time necessary for each inference task, LiMa also performs several orders of magnitude faster than the grounded approach (see right part of Fig. 1).

5   Related Work

There are several other approaches that perform efficient probabilistic inference or Bayesian Filtering on an abstract (e.g. logical) representation. A prominent approach concerned with inference in relational graphical models is known as Lifted Inference. The general idea is to exploit symmetries in the model, e.g. in cases where many objects with similar properties and relationships are present. We refer to [13,15] for a more thorough overview. Opposed to LiMa, these methods do not explicitly support sequential inference in dynamic domains, i.e. Bayesian Filtering consisting of a predict-update cycle. The approach presented in [1] efficiently evaluates multiple Lifted Inference queries on the same network, but is not concerned with *dynamic* models, where random variables depends on random variables from previous time slices. Lifted Inference algorithms for dynamic models have also been devised [10], but this approach lacks an efficient way to preserve the lifted representation over time. Furthermore, it performs *approximate* inference, while LiMa is exact.

Ideas from Lifted Inference have also been used in the Relational Kalman Filter [7,8]. This approach is similar to LiMa in the sense that it performs lifted Bayesian Filtering. That is, a compact representation of the belief state is maintained by grouping equivalent variables, and reasoning over them is performed "in bulk". However, the approach can only be used for gaussian linear models, like the standard Kalman filter.

First-Order Markov Decision Processes (FOMDPs) [6,20] employ first-order logic to represent states of a Markov Decision Process. The task performed in these formalisms is *lifted planning*, i.e. obtaining an abstract policy (that is independent of specific domain objects), given a goal. The algorithmic ideas used in this context decision-theoretic regression are different from Bayesian Filtering applied by LiMa. However, there is a certain relationship between Lifted Inference and FOMDPs that has recently been discussed in [14].

6 Conclusion and Future Work

In this work, we presented a modeling formalism for abstract states that encodes multiple grounded states in a Bayesian Filtering context. Our approach that we call *Lifted Marginal Filtering* (LiMa) combines ideas of Computational State Space Models (CSSMs) and Multiset Rewriting Systems (MRS) to overcome the combinatorial explosion in grounded inference approaches. Our abstraction is based on *observation equivalence*, i.e. we reason over groups of situations that cannot be distinguished given the observations. Such groups (*lifted states*) are represented as a multiset of structure descriptions (entities) along with a *context* that describes the corresponding (possibly uncertain) values that can be inserted into that structure in the form of density functions. The transition model of LiMa is represented by precondition-effect actions similar to CSSMs that are combined to *compound actions* representing a maximally parallel application of such simple actions which is similar in MRS. We showed that applying actions and observations may require *splitting* of lifted states as in Lifted Inference, and derived a Bayesian Filtering algorithm that is capable of this representation and computes prediction and update in the lifted domain. To answer application specific questions, we demonstrated how to reason over lifted states. We expect that in many scenarios, these answers can often be computed without completely grounding and thus exploiting the lifted representation.

For an office scenario that suffers from a combinatorial explosion in the state space size, we showed that the state space size as well as the inference time is several orders of magnitude smaller than for the corresponding grounded inference.

Our approach can be extended in several ways. We will investigate the definition of a smoothing and MAP algorithm for the state representation. Furthermore, we plan to model time-dependency of state transitions, similar to Hidden Semi-Markov Models. Approximation is another interesting aspect: In some domains, *identifying* observations may lead to many splits, so that the algorithm actually resorts to grounded inference. This problem has been addressed before in Lifted Inference [24] by grouping states that are only approximately equal. In our case, this corresponds to approximate merging, which we plan to investigate in the future. A further aspect is to investigate which continuous densities can be used in the context, i.e. for which densities appropriate splitting functions can be defined that result in a compact representation of the split densities.

References

1. Ahmadi, B., Kersting, K., Sanner, S.: Multi-evidence lifted message passing, with application to pagerank and the kalman filter. In: Proceedings-International Joint Conference on Artificial Intelligence, p. 1152 (2011)
2. Baker, C.L., Saxe, R., Tenenbaum, J.B.: Action understanding as inverse planning. Cognition **113**(3), 329–349 (2009)
3. Barbuti, R., Levi, F., Milazzo, P., Scatena, G.: Maximally parallel probabilistic semantics for multiset rewriting. Fundam. Inform. **112**(1), 1–17 (2011)
4. Berry, G., Boudol, G.: The chemical abstract machine. In: POPL, pp. 81–94. ACM, San Francisco(1990)
5. Bistarelli, S., Cervesato, I., Lenzini, G., Marangoni, R., Martinelli, F.: On representing biological systems through multiset rewriting. In: Moreno-Díaz, R., Pichler, F. (eds.) EUROCAST 2003. LNCS, vol. 2809, pp. 415–426. Springer, Heidelberg (2003). doi:10.1007/978-3-540-45210-2_38
6. Boutilier, C., Reiter, R., Price, B.: Symbolic dynamic programming for first-order MDPs. In: Proceedings of the Seventeenth International Joint Conference on Artificial Intelligence, vol. 1, pp. 690–700 (2001)
7. Choi, J., Amir, E., Xu, T., Valocchi, A.J.: Learning relational kalman filtering. In: Proceedings of the Twenty-Ninth AAAI Conference on Artificial Intelligence, pp. 2539–2546 (2015)
8. Choi, J., Hill, D.J., Amir, E.: Lifted inference for relational continuous models. In: Proceedings of the Twenty-Sixth Conference on Uncertainty in Artificial Intelligence, UAI 2010, pp. 126–134. AUAI Press (2010)
9. Fox, V., Hightower, J., Liao, L., Schulz, D., Borriello, G.: Bayesian filtering for location estimation. IEEE Pervasive Comput. **2**(3), 24–33 (2003)
10. Geier, T., Biundo, S.: Approximate online inference for dynamic Markov logic networks. In: 23rd IEEE International Conference on Tools with Artificial Intelligence, pp. 764–768. IEEE (2011)
11. Huang, J., Guestrin, C., Jiang, X., Guibas, L.: Exploiting probabilistic independence for permutations. In: AISTATS, Clearwater, USA, pp. 248–255 (2009)
12. Kersting, K., Ahmadi, B., Natarajan, S.: Counting belief propagation. In: UAI, Montreal, Canada, pp. 277–284 (2009)
13. Kersting, K.: Lifted probabilistic inference. In: 20th European Conference on Artificial Intelligence, ECAI 2012. Frontiers in Artificial Intelligence and Applications, vol. 242. IOS Press (2012)
14. Khardon, R., Sanner, S.: Stochastic planning and lifted inference. arXiv preprint arXiv:1701.01048 (2017)
15. Kimmig, A., Mihalkova, L., Getoor, L.: Lifted graphical models: a survey. Mach. Learn. **99**, 1–45 (2015)
16. Kondor, R., Howard, A., Jebara, T.: Multi-object tracking with representations of the symmetric group. In: AISTATS, vol. 2, pp. 211–218 (2007)
17. Krüger, F., Nyolt, M., Yordanova, K., Hein, A., Kirste, T.: Computational state space models for activity and intention recognition. A feasibility study. PLOS ONE **9**(11), e109381 (2014)
18. Poole, D.: First-order probabilistic inference. In: IJCAI, pp. 985–991 (2003)
19. Ramírez, M., Geffner, H.: Goal recognition over POMDPs: inferring the intention of a POMDP agent. In: Proceedings of the Twenty-Second International Joint Conference on Artificial Intelligence, pp. 2009–2014, July 2011

20. Sanner, S., Boutilier, C.: Practical solution techniques for first-order MDPs. Artif. Intell. **173**, 748–788 (2009)

21. Schröder, M., Lüdtke, S., Bader, S., Krüger, F., Kirste, T.: An office scenario dataset for benchmarking observation-equivalent entities (2016). http://dx.doi.org/10.18453/rosdok_id00000138

22. Schröder, M., Lüdtke, S., Bader, S., Krüger, F., Kirste, T.: Abstracting from observation-equivalent entities in human behavior modeling. In: AAAI Workshop: Plan, Activity, and Intent Recognition, February 2017

23. Van Den Broeck, G., Taghipour, N., Meert, W., Davis, J., De Raedt, L.: Lifted probabilistic inference by first-order knowledge compilation. In: IJCAI, pp. 2178–2185 (2011)

24. Venugopal, D., Gogate, V.: Evidence-based clustering for scalable inference in Markov logic. In: Calders, T., Esposito, F., Hüllermeier, E., Meo, R. (eds.) ECML PKDD 2014. LNCS, vol. 8726, pp. 258–273. Springer, Heidelberg (2014). doi:10.1007/978-3-662-44845-8_17

25. Wilson, D.H., Atkeson, C.: Simultaneous tracking and activity recognition (STAR) using many anonymous, binary sensors. In: Gellersen, H.-W., Want, R., Schmidt, A. (eds.) Pervasive 2005. LNCS, vol. 3468, pp. 62–79. Springer, Heidelberg (2005). doi:10.1007/11428572_5

A Priori Advantages of Meta-Induction and the No Free Lunch Theorem: A Contradiction?

Gerhard Schurz[✉] and Paul Thorn

DCLPS, Heinrich Heine University Düsseldorf, Düsseldorf, Germany
`schurz@phil.hhu.de`

Abstract. Recently a new account to the problem of induction has been developed [1], based on a priori advantages of regret-weighted meta-induction (RW) in online learning [2]. The claimed a priori advantages seem to contradict the no free lunch (NFL) theorem, which asserts that relative to a state-uniform prior distribution (SUPD) over possible worlds all (non-clairvoyant) prediction methods have the same expected predictive success. In this paper we propose a solution to this problem based on four novel results:

- RW enjoys free lunches, i.e., its predictive long-run success dominates that of other prediction strategies.
- Yet the NFL theorem applies to online prediction tasks provided the prior distribution is a SUPD.
- The SUPD is maximally induction-hostile and assigns a probability of zero to all possible worlds in which RW enjoys free lunches. This dissolves the apparent conflict with the NFL.
- The a priori advantages of RW can be demonstrated even under the assumption of a SUPD. Further advantages become apparent when a frequency-uniform distribution is considered.

Keywords: Problem of induction · No free lunch theorem · Online prediction under expert advice · Regret-weighted meta-induction

1 Introduction: The NFL Theorem and Hume's Problem of Induction

How can inductive inferences be rationally justified, in the sense of being reliable or at least preferable to non-inductive inferences? This is the problem of induction raised by the philosopher David Hume 250 years ago. Hume showed that all standard methods of justification fail when applied to the task of justifying induction. He concluded that induction has no rational justification at all.

The no free lunch theorem (NFL) expresses a deepening of Hume's inductive skepticism. In this paper we consider the NFL theorem in application to

This work was supported by the DFG (Deutsche Forschungsgemeinschaft), SPP 1516. For valuable help we are indebted to Ronald Ortner.

G. Kern-Isberner et al. (Eds.): KI 2017, LNAI 10505, pp. 236–248, 2017.
DOI: 10.1007/978-3-319-67190-1_18

online prediction tasks. A number of variants of the NFL theorem have been formulated (cf. [3–7]); the most general formulation is found in [8]. Wolpert's NFL theorem comes in a weak and a strong version. Since the strong version rests on unrealistic assumptions about the loss function, we focus in this paper on the weak NFL theorem. It says that the probabilistically expected success of any (non-clairvoyant) prediction method is equal to the expected success of random guessing or any other prediction method, provided one assumes (a) a *state-uniform* prior probability distribution (abbreviated SUPD) i.e., one that is uniform over all possible event sequences, and (b) a *weakly homogeneous* loss function (see below).

Does the NFL theorem undermine the project of learning theory? A standard defense of learning theorists against the NFL challenge maintains that one should not compute the expected success of learning strategies by means of a SUPD. Rather one should compute expected success using the (conjectured) *actual* distribution of the possible states of our environment, and 'according to our evidence' the latter distribution is clearly not uniform.[1] We argue that this line of defense against the NFL challenge does not work, because our beliefs about the actual distribution of possible states of our environment are themselves based on an inductive inference. Thus, this argument commits the *fallacy of circularity*. A general argument demonstrating the unacceptability of circular justifications runs as follows: If we accept the inductive justification of induction ("inductions were successful in the past, whence, by induction, they will be successful in the future"), then – on pain of inconsistency – we must also accept the anti-inductive justification of anti-induction ("anti-inductions were not successful in the past, whence by anti-induction they will be successful in the future").

For a robust defense of inductive learning methods against the NFL challenge a better argument is needed; one that does not presuppose what must be proved. Recently, a non-circular response to the problem of induction has been proposed, based on a priori advantages of regret-based meta-induction (in short: RW) in online learning. In Sects. 2 and 3 these results are presented and confronted with a version of the weak NFL theorem that applies to iterated prediction tasks in online learning. Thereafter the apparent contradiction is analyzed and dissolved, from the long-run (Sect. 4) and short-run perspectives (Sect. 5). Our analysis leads to four novel results that are summarized in the conclusion (Sect. 6).

2   Regret-Based Meta-Induction

In the area of *regret-based learning*, theoretical results concerning the vanishing long-run regrets of certain meta-strategies of prediction have been developed that hold universally, i.e., for strictly all possible event sequences, independently from any assumed probability distribution [2]. Although labeled as "online learning under expert advice" these results characterize the performance of strategies of *meta-learning*, inasmuch as a forecaster which we call the "meta-inductivist"

---

[1]   Cf. [6, Sect. 4] and [7, Sect. 3], citing statements from a 1994 e-mail discussion.

tracks the past success rates of accessible prediction methods ("experts") and utilizes that information in constructing an improved prediction strategy. Since the meta-inductivist predicts future events based on past success rates, short-run regrets (compared to the best method) are unavoidable. However, in the long run the regret-weighted meta-inductivist is guaranteed to predict at least as accurately as the best accessible prediction method, even in circumstances of non-convergent success rates of the independent methods. A standard label for this property is "Hannan-consistency" [2, p. 70]. Schurz and Thorn [9] argue that it is preferable to call this property *access-optimality*, because

- it expresses a long-run optimality result restricted to *accessible* methods, and
- this label is in line with standard game-theoretical terminology of "optimality" and "dominance"; results concerning *access-dominance* are stated below.

The proposed solution to the problem of induction developed in [1,10] works as follows: The meta-strategy RW has an 'a priori' justification, because in the long run it is recommendable in every possible environment to apply this meta-strategy on top of all prediction methods accessible to the epistemic agent. Following [1] we explicate this result within the framework of prediction games.

Definition 1 (Prediction game). *A prediction game is a pair $((e), \Pi)$ consisting of:*

(1) An infinite sequence $(e) := (e_1, e_2, \ldots)$ of events e_n coded by real numbers between 0 and 1, possibly rounded according to a finite accuracy. In what follows $\mathcal{V} \subseteq [0, 1]$ denotes the value space of possible events $e_n \in \mathcal{V}$. Each time n corresponds to one round of the game.

(2) A finite set of prediction methods (or 'players') $\Pi = \{O_1, \ldots, O_m, M_1, \ldots, M_k\}$ whose task, in each round n, is to predict the next event e_{n+1} of the event sequence. Methods are of two sorts, independent 'object-level' methods $O_1, \ldots, O_m$ (algorithms or experts) who base their predictions on the observed events, and dependent 'meta-level' methods $M_1, \ldots, M_k$ who base their predictions on those of the independent methods in dependence on their success (this is meant by the O_i's 'being accessible' to the M_j's).

An example of (e) could be a sequence of daily weather conditions. In what follows the variable 'X' ranges over arbitrary prediction methods. We use the following notions:

- $p_n(X)$ is the prediction of method X *for* time n delivered *at* time $n - 1$.
- The distance of the prediction p_n from the event e_n is measured by a normalized loss function, $\ell(p_n, e_n) \in [0, 1]$.
- The *natural* loss-function is defined as the absolute distance between prediction and event, $|p_n - e_n|$. The theoretical results below apply to a much larger class, namely to all loss functions that are *convex* in the argument p_n.
- $s(p_n, e_n) := 1 - \ell(p_n, e_n)$ is the *score* obtained by prediction p_n of event e_n.
- $abs_n(X) := \sum_{i=1}^{n} s(p_i(X), e_i)$ is the *absolute success* achieved by method X until time n.

- $suc_n(X) := abs_n(X)/n$ is the *success rate* of method X at time n.
- $maxsuc_n$ is the maximal success rate of the independent methods at time n.

The simplest meta-inductive strategy is *Imitate-the-best*, abbreviated ITB, which, in each round n, imitates the prediction of the independent method with maximal success at time n. ITB fails to be universally access-optimal: Its success rate breaks down when it imitates *adversarial* methods, who return inaccurate predictions as soon as their predictions are imitated by ITB [1, Sect. 4].

The strategy of *regret-weighted meta-induction* comes in several versions. Its simplest version is abbreviated as RW and defined as follows (where $O_1, \ldots, O_m$ are the independent methods of the prediction game):

Definition 2 (Regret-weighted meta-induction)

(i) *The absolute regret of RW with respect to independent method O_i at time n is defined as $Reg_n(O_i) := abs_n(O_i) - abs_n(RW)$ and the relative regret as $reg_n(O_i) := Reg_n(O_i)/n$.*

(ii) *Where $w_n(O_i) := max(Reg_n(O_i), 0)$, the predictions of RW are defined as*

$$p_{n+1}(RW) := \frac{\sum_{i=1}^{m} w_n(O_i) \cdot p_{n+1}(O_i)}{\sum_{i=1}^{m} w_n(O_i)}$$

as long as $n > 0$ and the denominator is positive; else $p_{n+1}(RW) = 0.5$

RW is identical with the polynomially weighted forecaster F_p described in [2, p. 12] with parameter p set to 2.

Theorem 1 (Universal access-optimality of RW). (Cesa-Bianchi and Lugosi 2006, Corollary 2.1)

For every prediction game $((e), \Pi)$ with $RW \in \Pi$ the following holds:

(1.1) (Short run:) $(\forall n \geq 1)\ suc_n(RW) \geq maxsuc_n - \sqrt{\frac{m}{n}}$.

(1.2) (Long-run:) $limsup_{n \to \infty}(maxsuc_n - suc_n(RW)) = 0$.

In the short run, RW may suffer from a possible regret. According to Theorem 1, RW's relative regret is upper-bounded by $\sqrt{\frac{m}{n}}$ and converges to zero when n grows large, or it oscillates endlessly but with a limsup converging to zero.

An improvement of RW is possible with help of so-called exponential weights. The weights of exponential regret-based meta-induction, abbreviated ERW, are defined as: $w_n(X) := e^{\sqrt{(8 \cdot ln(m)/n)} \cdot Reg_n(X)}$. If ERW's predictions are defined as in Definition 2(ii) but with help of exponential weights, then one can prove that ERW's short-run regret is upper-bounded by $1.77 \cdot \sqrt{ln(m)/n}$ [2, Theorem 2.3]. This is a significant improvement, but in regard to the NFL theorem the difference between RW and ERW is negligible: their long-run advantage is identical and their performance difference in the simulations presented in Sect. 5 turned out to be minor. Therefore we concentrate our investigation on RW.

Even if the events are binary, RW's predictions are real-valued, because proper weighted averages of 0 s and 1 s are real-valued. Thus the predictions are assumed to be elements of a value space $\mathcal{V}_p \subseteq [0,1]$ that may extend the space of event values: $\mathcal{V}$ $(\mathcal{V} \subseteq \mathcal{V}_p)$.

What stands in apparent conflict with the NFL theorem is not the access-optimality of RW but rather its *access-dominance*, that is, the fact that RW performs at least as well and sometimes better than other accessible methods. By definition, a meta-method M *dominates* another method X (in the long run) iff (i) there is no prediction game $((e), \Pi)$ with $\{X, M\} \subseteq \Pi$ and $limsup_{n \to \infty}(suc_n(X) - suc_n(M)) > 0$, but there is a prediction game $((e)', \Pi')$ with $\{X, M\} \subseteq \Pi'$ and $limsup_{n \to \infty}(suc_n(M) - suc_n(X)) > 0$; this implies that X is not access-optimal. Theorem 1 asserts the access-optimality but not the dominance of regret-based meta-induction. Since there are other methods, different from RW, that are likewise long-run optimal (such as ERW mentioned above), RW cannot be universally access-dominant. However, the following restricted dominance result for RW can be derived from Theorem 1.

Theorem 2 (access-dominance for RW)

(2.1) *RW dominates every accessible prediction method X (in the long run) that is not universally access-optimal.*

(2.2) *Not universally access-optimal in the long run are (a) all independent (non-clairvoyant) methods, and (b) among meta-strategies, for example, (b1) all one-favorite methods (who at each time point imitate the prediction of one independent method) and (b2) success-weighting, which identifies weights with success rates (also called "Franklin's rule" [11, p. 83]).*

Proof. Theorem (2.1) is an immediate consequence of Theorem 1 and the definitions of "access-optimality" and "-dominance".

Proof of Theorem (2.2)(a): Let O be an independent method and (e') an O-adversarial event sequence defined as follows: $e'_1 = 0.5$, and $e'_{n+1} = 1$ if $pred_{n+1}(O) < 0.5$; else $e'_{n+1} = 0$. The predictions of the perfect (e')-forecaster O' are identified with the so-defined sequence, i.e., $p_n(O') = e'_n$. In the prediction game $((e'), \{O, O', RW\})$ the success rate of O can never exceed $1/2$, that of O' is always 1 and that of RW converges to 1 (by Theorem 1). So O is not universally access-optimal.

The proof of Theorem (2.2)(b1) is found in [1, Sect. 4] and that of (2.2)(b2) in [9, Sect. 7].   □

Theorem $(2.1 + 2)$ entails that in the long run there are "free lunches" for regret-based meta-induction in the sense that there are prediction methods X and event sequences (e) for which RW's long run success is strictly greater than that of X without there being any 'compensating' event sequences (e') in which RW's long-run success is smaller than that of X. This apparent conflict with the NFL folklore is investigated in the next sections.

3   NFL Theorems for Prediction Games

It is not straightforward to apply the NFL theorems to regret-based online learning. First of all, the RW account is more general than the NFL framework as the results of the former account hold even if clairvoyant methods are admitted – these are prediction functions that may have future events as input. However, regret-based meta-induction should not only be attractive for those who consider paranormal worlds as possible. Thus in what follows we take the *non-clairvoyance* assumption of the NFL theorems [8, p. 1380] as granted.

Two further possible hindrances of applying the NFL framework to regret-based online learning are treated as follows:

- Regret-based learning is defined for meta-strategies, while the NFL framework applies to arbitrary prediction methods (defined as computable functions from past event sequences into the next event). But every finite combination of a *fixed* set of independent prediction methods is itself a defined prediction method. Thus the NFL framework equally applies to prediction meta-strategies, given that they are applied to an (arbitrary but) fixed set of independent methods. This assumption will be made in the following.
- Online learning consists of a (possibly infinite) *iteration* of one-shot learning tasks in which the test item of round n is added to the training set of round $n+1$. For this reason the NFL theorems are only applicable if one assumes a SUPD (see below).

The strong version of Wolpert's NFL theorem presupposes that the loss function is *homogeneous* [8, p. 1349], which means by definition that for every possible loss value c, the number of possible event values $e \in \mathcal{V}$ for which a given prediction leads to a loss of c is the same for all possible predictions. This requirement is overly strong; it is satisfied for prediction games with binary events and the zero-one loss function $loss_{1-0}$, which has only two possible loss values: $loss_{1-0}(p, e) = 0$ if $p = e$ and $loss_{1-0}(p, e) = 1$ if $p \neq e$. As soon as real-valued predictions are allowed, a reasonable loss function will assign a loss different from 0 or 1 to predictions different from 0 or 1. Such a loss function is no longer homogeneous. So the strong NFL theorem does not apply to RW or any other real-valued prediction method. Note that real-valued predictions not only make sense in application to real-valued events but also to binary or discrete events, by predicting their conjectured probabilities. Only a weak version of the NFL theorem holds for prediction games with binary events and real-valued predictions, provided the loss function is weakly homogeneous:

Definition 3 (Weakly homogeneous loss function). [2] *A loss function is weakly homogeneous iff for each possible prediction the sum of losses over all possible events is the same, or formally, iff $\forall p \in \mathcal{V}_p$: $\sum_{e \in \mathcal{V}} \ell(p, e) = c^\star$ (where $c^\star$ is a constant).*

For binary games with real-valued predictions and natural loss function the condition of Definition 3 is satisfied, since for every prediction $p \in [0, 1]$, $\ell(p, 1) + \ell(p, 0) = 1 - p + p = 1$. Under this assumption the following weak NFL theorem holds for the probabilistic expectation value (Exp_P) of the success rate of a

---

[2] [8] mentions the weak no free lunch theorem in a small paragraph on p. 1354; for our purpose this NFL theorem is the most important one.

prediction method X, where "(e_{1-n})" abbreviates "$(e_1, \ldots, e_n)$" and $\mathcal{V}(C) = \{\ell(p, e) : p \in \mathcal{V}_p, e \in \mathcal{V}\}$ is the set of possible loss values:

Theorem 3 (Weak NFL theorem for prediction games). *Given a state-uniform P-distribution over the space of event sequences with r possible event values and a weakly homogeneous loss function, the following holds for every (non-clairvoyant) prediction method X and $n \geq 0$:*

The expectation value of X's success rate after an arbitrary number of rounds is $1 - \frac{c^*}{r}$, or formally, $Exp_P(suc_n(X)) := \sum_{c \in \mathcal{V}(C)} c \cdot P(suc_n(X) = c) = 1 - \frac{c^*}{r}$.

Proof. First we prove the following.

Lemma: For every prediction method X, the expectation value of X's loss in the prediction of the 'next' event equals c^*/r, conditional on every possible sequence of 'past' events, or formally:

$$Exp_P(\ell(p_{n+1}, e_{n+1}) \mid (e_{1-n})) := \sum_{c \in \mathcal{V}(C)} c \cdot P(\ell(p_{n+1}, e_{n+1}) = c \mid (e_{1-n})) = c^*/r.$$

Proof of lemma: As in [8] we allow that prediction methods are probabilistic, i.e., deliver predictions conditional on past events with certain probabilities $P(p_{n+1} \mid (e_{1-n}))$. First we compute the conditional probability of a particular loss value c. By probability theory it holds for all $n \geq 0$:

$P(\ell(p_{n+1}, e_{n+1}) = c \mid (e_{1-n})) = \sum_{p_{n+1} \in V_p} \sum_{e_{n+1} \in V} \delta(\ell(p_{n+1}, e_{n+1}), c) \cdot P(p_{n+1}, e_{n+1}) \mid (e_{1-n}))$, where "$\delta$" is the Kronecker symbol. By probability theory we obtain $= \sum_{p_{n+1} \in V_p} \sum_{e_{n+1} \in V} \delta(\ell(p_{n+1}, e_{n+1}), c) \cdot P(p_{n+1} \mid (e_{1-n}), e_{n+1}) \cdot P(e_{n+1} \mid (e_{1-n}))$, which gives us by non-clairvoyance $= \sum_{p_{n+1} \in V_p} \sum_{e_{n+1} \in V} \delta(\ell(p_{n+1}, e_{n+1}), c) \cdot P(p_{n+1} \mid (e_{1-n})) \cdot P(e_{n+1} \mid (e_{1-n}))$, and by rearranging terms $= \sum_{p_{n+1} \in V_p} P(p_{n+1} \mid (e_{1-n})) \cdot \sum_{e_{n+1} \in V} \delta(\ell(p_{n+1}, e_{n+1}), c) \cdot P(e_{n+1} \mid (e_{1-n}))$, and finally by the state-uniformity of P (*) $= \sum_{p_{n+1} \in V_p} P(p_{n+1} \mid (e_{1-n})) \cdot (1/r) \cdot \sum_{e_{n+1} \in V} \delta(\ell(p_{n+1}, e_{n+1}), c)$. Next we compute the expectation value: $Exp_P(\ell(p_{n+1}, e_{n+1}) \mid (e_{1-n})) := \sum_{c \in \mathcal{V}(C)} c \cdot P(\ell(p_{n+1}, e_{n+1}) = c \mid (e_{1-n}))$ from which we get by the result in line (*) $= \sum_{c \in \mathcal{V}(C)} c \cdot \sum_{p_{n+1} \in V_p} P(p_{n+1} \mid (e_{1-n})) \cdot (1/r) \cdot \sum_{e_{n+1} \in V} \delta(\ell(p_{n+1}, e_{n+1}), c)$ and by rearranging terms $= \sum_{p_{n+1} \in V_p} P(p_{n+1} \mid (e_{1-n})) \cdot (1/r) \cdot \sum_{c \in \mathcal{V}(C)} c \cdot \sum_{e_{n+1} \in V} \delta(\ell(p_{n+1}, e_{n+1}), c)$.

Note that "$\sum_{c \in \mathcal{V}(C)} c \cdot \sum_{e_{n+1} \in V} \delta(\ell(p_{n+1}, e_{n+1}), c)$" is nothing but the sum of p_{n+1}'s loss values for all possible events, i.e., $\sum_{e_{n+1} \in V} \ell(p_{n+1}, e_{n+1})$. So, by the weak homogeneity of the loss function, we continue as follows: $= \sum_{p_{n+1} \in V_p} P(p_{n+1} \mid (e_{1-n})) \cdot (1/r) \cdot c^* = c^*/r$ (since $\sum_{p_{n+1} \in V_p} P(p_{n+1} \mid (e_{1-n})) = 1$). *(End of proof of lemma.)*

The expectation value of X's success rate is the expectation value of the sum of X's scores divided by n. Since the result of the lemma holds for every round n, the additivity of expectation values ($Exp_P(X_1 + X_2) = Exp_P(X_1) + Exp_P(X_2)$) entails that $Exp_P(suc_n(X)) = n \cdot (1 - (c^*/r))/n = 1 - (c^*/r)$. $\qquad\square$

The SUPD is a *necessary* condition of the application of the NFL theorem to prediction games, because its proof presupposes that the P-distribution over $\mathcal{V}$ is uniform *conditional* on every possible past sequence. There are generalizations of NFL theorems for one-shot learning procedures to certain non-uniform P-distributions [6], but they are not valid for prediction games.

For prediction games with real-valued events, convex loss functions are not even weakly homogeneous, although certain restricted NFL theorems can be demonstrated [12]. However, in this paper we focus on prediction games with *binary* events, to which the weak NFL theorem applies, because here the apparent conflict of this theorem with RW's access-dominance is most vivid.

4   Meta-Induction and NFL: The Long-Run Perspective

Is there a contradiction between the weak NFL theorem and the existence of free lunches for RW meta-induction? In regard to the *long run* perspective our answer can be summarized as follows: No, the contradiction is only apparent. According to Theorem 2 (Sect. 2) there are RW-accessible methods whose long-run success rate is strictly smaller than that of RW in some world states and never greater than that of RW in any world state. Let us call these methods X_{inf} (for "inferior"). Nevertheless the state-uniform expectation values of the success rates of RW and X_{inf} are equal, because the state-uniform distribution that Wolpert assumes assigns a probability of zero to all worlds in which RW dominates X_{inf}; so these worlds do not affect the probabilistic expectation value.

Wolpert seems to assume that the state-uniform prior distribution is epistemically privileged. Reasonable doubts can be raised here, inasmuch as a well-known result in probability theory tells us that the state-uniform distribution is the most induction-hostile prior distribution one can imagine:

Theorem 4 (Induction-hostile uniformity). [13, pp. 564–566], [14, pp. 64–66]: *Assume the probability density distribution D_P is uniform over the space of all infinite binary event sequences $\{0,1\}^\omega$. Then $P(e_{n+1} = 1 \mid (e_{1-n})) = 1/2$, for every possible next event e_{n+1} and sequence of past events (e_{1-n}). Thus P satisfies the properties of a random IID-distribution over $\{0,1\}$, whence inductive learning from experience is impossible.*

Theorem 4 implies that a proponent of a state-uniform distribution believes with probability 1 that the event sequence to be predicted is an IID random sequence, i.e., (a) it consists of mutually independent events with a limiting frequency of 0.5, and (b) it is non-computable. Condition (a) follows from Theorem 4 and condition (b) from the fact that there are uncountably many sequences, but only countably many computable ones. However, the sequences for which a non-clairvoyant prediction method can be better than random guessing are precisely those that do not fall into the intersection of classes (a) or (b). Summarizing, according to a state-uniform prior distribution we are a priori certain that the world is completely irregular so that no inductive or other intelligent prediction method can have more than random success.

If every sequence $(e) \in \{0,1\}^\omega$ is represented by a real number $r \in [0,1]$ in binary representation, then the state-uniform *density* distribution D_P is uniform over the interval $[0,1]$. Yet, if the same density is distributed over the space of statistical hypotheses H_r, asserting that the limiting frequency of 1s in (e) is r (for $r \in [0,1]$), it becomes maximally dogmatic, being concentrated over the point $r = 1/2$: $D(H_q) = 0$ for $q \neq r$ and $D(H_q) = \infty$ for $q = r$.

According to a second well-known result in probability theory, a prior distribution that is not state-uniform but *frequency-uniform*, i.e., uniform over all possible frequency limits $r \in [0,1]$ of binary sequences, is highly induction-friendly. Such a distribution validates Laplace's rule of induction, $P(e_{n+1} = 1 \mid freq_n(1) = \frac{k}{n}) = \frac{k+1}{n+2}$. Solomonoff [15, Sect. 4.1] has proved that a distribution is frequency-uniform iff the probability it assigns to sequences decreases exponentially with their algorithmic complexity.

Which prior distributions are more 'natural', state-uniform ones or frequency-uniform ones? In our eyes, this question has no objective answer. It is a great advantage of the optimality of meta-induction that it holds regardless of any assumed prior probability distribution. For a frequency-uniform prior distribution the probability of world-states in which meta-induction dominates random guessing in the long run is one. For a state-uniform prior the probability of world-states in which meta-induction dominates random guessing in the long run is zero. Nevertheless there are (uncountably) many such world-states and we should certainly not exclude these induction-friendly world-states from the start by assigning a probability of zero to them. This consideration gives us the following minimal acceptance criterion for prior distributions: They should assign a positive (even if small) probability to those world-states in which access-dominant prediction methods enjoy their free lunches.

5   Meta-Induction and NFL: The Short-Run Perspective

For finite sequences, the strict dominance of RW fails since the advantage of RW meta-induction comes at a certain regret. Is meta-induction still advantageous over the space of all short-run sequences? This question is addressed in this section.

Table 1 presents the result of a simulation of all possible binary prediction games with a length of 20 rounds. The considered independent methods are

- majority-induction "M-I", predicting the event that so far has been in the majority, or formally, $p_{n+1}(\text{M-I}) = 1/0.5/0$ iff $freq_n(1) > / = / < 0.5$,
- majority anti-induction "M-AI", predicting the opposite of M-I, i.e., $p_{n+1}(\text{M-AI}) = 1/0.5/0$ iff $freq_n(1) < / = / > 0.5$, and
- averaging "Av", which always predicts the average of all possible event values, which is 0.5 in binary games.

The considered meta-inductive strategies are RW and, for sake of comparison, ITB.

Table 1 displays the frequencies of sequences for which the absolute success of a prediction method (based on the natural loss function) lies in a particular interval, as specified at the left margin. Success intervals are arranged symmetrically around the average value 10. As expected, the weak NFL theorem applies: in accordance with it one sees on the bottom line that the state-uniform average success is the same for all five methods. Nevertheless the frequencies of sequences for which these methods reach certain success levels are remarkably different.

The success frequencies of M-I and M-AI are different for different success intervals, because M-I has its highest success in very regular sequences (e.g., 1111...) with high frequencies of 1s or of 0s, in which ties of so far observed frequencies are rare, while M-AI has its highest success in oscillating sequences (e.g., 1010...) in which ties of so far observed frequencies are frequent. This brings a score of 0.5 more often to M-AI than M-I. As a result, M-I's success can climb higher than M-AI's success, though the frequency of such cases is small. In compensation, the number of sequences in which M-AI does only little better than average is higher than the corresponding number of sequences for M-I. Observe the mirror-symmetric distribution of sequences over M-I's and M-AI's success intervals, following from the fact that for any given sequence $\text{abs}_{20}(\text{M-I})$ $= 1 - \text{abs}_{20}(\text{M-AI})$.

In contrast, Av always predicts 0.5 and earns a sum-of-scores of 10 in all possible worlds. The meta-inductive methods ITB and RW reach the top successes that object-induction (M-I) achieves in highly regular worlds, although in a diminished way due to their short run regrets. The advantage of RW is that it manages to avoid low success rates: following from its near access-optimality RW's success is in every possible sequence close to the maximal success in this sequence; so RW cannot fall much behind Av's success rate which is 0.5 (10 of 20 points) in all sequences. In contrast, M-I has a poor performance, and ITB and M-AI an even worse performance, in some sequences.

Similar tendencies can also be observed in other settings. Increasing the number of rounds has the effect that the frequency of sequences with high or low success rates steadily decreases, as explained in the previous section.

Based on these results we obtain a justification of object-induction and meta-induction even *within* the induction-hostile perspective of a state-uniform prior distribution for *binary short-run* sequences. What counts are two things: (a) To reach high success in those environments which allow for non-accidentally high success by their intrinsic regularities. This is what independent inductive methods do. (b) To protect oneself against high losses (compared to average success) in induction-hostile environments. This is what cautious methods such as Av do. The advantage of RW meta-induction is that it combines *both*: reaching high success rates where it is possible and avoiding high losses. Thus RW achieves 'the best of both worlds'. This, however, comes at the cost of a certain short-run regret.

The preceding version of a justification of meta-induction works within the most induction-hostile prior distribution – a SUPD. If one switches to a frequency-uniform prior distribution, one thereby adopts an induction-friendly perspective. This result is displayed in Table 2 for a simulation of all possible

Table 1. Meta-induction and no-free-lunch for binary-event games. Cells show percentage of possible binary sequences with 20 rounds, for which the five methods M-I, M-AI, Av, ITB and RW have reached certain intervals of absolute successes (left margin).

		M-I	M-AI	Av	ITB	RW
	[0,1)	0	0.0002	0	0	0
	[1,2)	0	0.003	0	0.0004	0
	[2,3)	0	0.029	0	0.008	0
	[3,4)	0	0.159	0	0.077	0
	[4,5)	0	0.618	0	0.394	0
	[5,6)	0.537	1.824	0	1.412	0
	[6,7)	3.540	4.254	0	3.708	0
	[7,8)	9.579	8.035	0	7.555	0
	[8,9)	15.622	12.476	0	12.966	36.491
	[9,10)	18.346	16.065	0	18.238	23.472
Absolute success intervals	10	8.910	8.910	100	9.848	0
	(10,11]	16.065	18.346	0	17.642	14.835
	(11,12]	12.476	15.622	0	14.213	11.880
	(12,13]	8.035	9.579	0	8.155	7.469
	(13,14]	4.254	3.540	0	3.558	3.595
	(14,15]	1.824	0.537	0	1.486	1.513
	(15,16]	0.618	0	0	0.555	0.560
	(16,17]	0.159	0	0	0.152	0.153
	(17,18]	0.029	0	0	0.029	0.029
	(18,19]	0.003	0	0	0.003	0.003
	(19,20]	0.0002	0	0	0.0002	0.0002
State-uniform average success		10	10	10	10	10

sequences of length 20 applied to the methods of Table 1. In Table 2 the left margin displays intervals for the possible frequencies of 1s in the 20-round sequences and the cells display the achieved (average) absolute successes of the methods for sequences whose frequencies lie in these intervals.

Note that the more decentered a frequency interval, the lower is its corresponding entropy. M-I is most successful in all frequency intervals that are not close to the center. It is only in the interval [0.4,0.6] – which, of course, contains many more individual sequences than the other intervals – that Av performs better than M-I. However, Av's mean success in this interval is worse than the mean success of the anti-inductive method M-AI, which performs badly in the decentral intervals. Again, the meta-inductive methods combine both features: in the central interval they don't lose much compared to Av, while in the decentral intervals their mean success rate comes close to that of M-I and beats

Table 2. Meta-induction for binary events from the perspective of frequency-uniform distributions. Cells show (average) absolute successes of the five methods M-I, M-AI, Av, ITB and RW, for binary sequences with 20 rounds, in dependence of their event-frequencies (left margin).

		M-I	M-AI	Av	ITB	RW
	[0,0.1]	17,5	2,5	10	17,12	17,14
	[0.1,0.2]	15,4898	4,5102	10	14,7254	14,7103
	[0.2,0.3]	13,4314	6,56857	10	12,2263	12,1212
	[0.3,0.4]	11,2313	8,76873	10	9,81723	9,90422
Frequency intervals	[0.4,0.5]	8,82824	11,1718	10	9,80868	9,77248
	[0.5,0.6]	8,82824	11,1718	10	9,80868	9,77248
	[0.6,0.7]	11,2313	8,76873	10	9,81723	9,90422
	[0.7,0.8]	13,4314	6,56857	10	12,2263	12,1212
	[0.8,0.9]	15,4898	4,5102	10	14,7254	14,7103
	[0.9,1]	17,5	2,5	10	17,12	17,14
Average for frequency uniform distribution		13.30	6.70	10	12.74	12.73

that of Av and M-AI. As expected, the frequency-uniform expectation values of the absolute success is much higher for inductive than for non-inductive methods; M-I has the lead, closely followed by ITB and RW.

6 Conclusion

In this paper we applied the (weak) no free lunch (NFL) theorem to regret-based meta-induction (RW) in the framework of prediction games. The challenge of the NFL theorem cannot be 'solved' by arguing that expected successes should be computed relative to the 'actual' (instead of some prior) distribution, because this idea is viciously circular. A more robust defense is possible based on an a priori result concerning the access-dominance of RW. Since this dominance result implies the existence of free lunches for RW it seems to contradict the NFL theorem. This conflict was dissolved based on four core result:

(1) A weak NFL theorem can be proved for prediction games (with binary events and natural loss function) under the assumption of a SUPD (a state-uniform probability distribution). A SUPD is maximally induction-hostile. In contrast, a frequency-uniform distribution is induction-friendly. Either sort of prior distribution is subjective and biased.

(2) Concerning success in the long run, the meta-inductive prediction strategy RW enjoys free lunches compared to all prediction methods that are not access-optimal (and most prediction methods aren't). However, the SUPD underlying the NFL theorem assigns a probability of zero to the class of all event sequences in which RW dominates other methods. This dissolves the apparent conflict with the NFL within the long-run perspective.

(3) Concerning success in the short run, the following short-run advantage of RW can be demonstrated even under the induction-hostile perspective of an SUPD: What counts is (a) to reach high success rates in regular (low-entropy) environments, which is what independent inductive methods do, and (b) to protect against high losses, compared to average success, in irregular (high-entropy) environments, which is what cautious "averaging" methods do. RW meta-induction combines both advantages, at the cost of a small short-run regret.

(4) If one assumes a frequency-uniform prior, then (meta-) inductive prediction strategies outperform non-inductive methods for all event sequences whose entropy is not close-to-maximal.

References

1. Schurz, G.: The meta-inductivist's winning strategy in the prediction game: a new approach to Hume's problem. Philos. Sci. **75**, 278–305 (2008)
2. Cesa-Bianchi, N., Lugosi, G.: Prediction, Learning, and Games. Cambridge University Press, Cambridge (2006)
3. Wolpert, D., Macready, W.: No free lunch theorems for search. Technical report SFI-TR-95-02-010, Santa Fe Institute (1995)
4. Wolpert, D.: On the connection between in-sample testing and generalization error. Complex Syst. **6**, 47–94 (1992)
5. Schaffer, C.: A conservation law for generalization performance. In: Machine Learning (Proceedings of ICML 1994), pp. 259–265. Morgan Kaufmann, Burlington (1994)
6. Rao, R., Gordon, D., Spears, W.: For every generalization action, is there really an equal and opposite reaction? In: Machine Learning (Proceedings of ICML 1995), pp. 471–479. Morgan Kaufmann, Burlington (1994)
7. Giraud-Carrier, C., Provost, F.: Toward a justification of meta-learning: is the no free lunch theorem a show-stopper? In: Proceedings of the ICML-2005 Workshop on Meta-learning, pp. 12–19 (2006)
8. Wolpert, D.: The lack of a priori distinctions between learning algorithms. Neural Comput. **8**, 1341–1390 (1996)
9. Schurz, G., Thorn, P.: The revenge of ecological rationality: strategy-selection by meta-induction. Minds Mach. **26**(1), 31–59 (2016)
10. Schurz, G.: Meta-induction is an optimal prediction strategy. In: Proceedings of the 18th Annual Belgian-Dutch Conference on Machine Learning, pp. 66–74. University of Tilburg (2009)
11. Gigerenzer, G., Todd, P.M., the ABC Research Group. (eds.): Simple Heuristics That Make Us Smart. Oxford University Press, Dordrecht (1999)
12. Schurz, G.: The Optimality of Meta-induction. A New Approach to Hume's Problem. Book manuscript (2017)
13. Carnap, R.: Logical Foundations of Probability, 2nd edn. University of Chicago Press, Chicago (1962)
14. Howson, C., Urbach, P.: Scientific Reasoning: The Bayesian Approach, 2nd edn. Open Court, Chicago (1996)
15. Solomonoff, R.: A formal theory of inductive inference. Inf. Control **7**(1–22), 224–254 (1964)

Dynamic Map Update of Non-static Facility Logistics Environment with a Multi-robot System

Nayabrasul Shaik[1]([⊠]), Thomas Liebig[1], Christopher Kirsch[2],
and Heinrich Müller[1]

[1] TU Dortmund University, Dortmund, Germany
{nayabrasul.shaik,thomas.liebig,heinrich.mueller}@tu-dortmund.de
[2] Fraunhofer Institute for Material Flow and Logistics, Dortmund, Germany
Christopher.Kirsch@iml.fraunhofer.de

Abstract. Autonomous robots need to perceive and represent their environments and act accordingly. Using simultaneous localization and mapping (SLAM) methods, robots can build maps of the environment which are efficient for localization and path planning as long as the environment remains unchanged. However, facility logistics environments are not static because pallets and other obstacles are stored temporarily.

This paper proposes a novel solution for updating maps of changing environments (i.e. environments with low-dynamic or semi-static objects) in real-time with multiple robots. Each robot is equipped with a laser range sensor and runs localization to estimate its position. Each robot senses the change in the environment with respect to a current map, initially built with a SLAM method, and constructs a temporary map which will be merged into the current map using localization information and line features of the map. This procedure enables the creation of long-term mapping robot systems for facility logistics.

1 Introduction

For autonomous navigation, robots need a representation of the operating environment. Maps of static environments can be built using simultaneous localization and mapping (SLAM) methods. Maps built with SLAM work well for localization and path panning as long as the environment remains static [9]. But most of the environments are not static due to changes during day-to-day operations. These changes can be due to *high-dynamic objects* or *low-dynamic objects*. Objects whose location change can be observed in the robot's field of view, e.g. humans or other moving vehicles are high-dynamic objects. Objects like pallets and stationary vehicles, which are stationary in the robot's field of view, are low-dynamic objects [26,31]. Low-dynamic objects are also termed *semi-static objects* [25]. Considering changes in the environment due to the low-dynamic objects can improve the localization capabilities of the robot system [25] and improve path planning of large robot teams [17] as well as the coordination of

© Springer International Publishing AG 2017
G. Kern-Isberner et al. (Eds.): KI 2017, LNAI 10505, pp. 249–261, 2017.
DOI: 10.1007/978-3-319-67190-1_19

a multi-robot system. If the up-to-date map could be combined with a coordination algorithm (e.g. Multi-Agent-System), fixed routes could be changed and optimized for changes in the environment. A very crucial part is the reduction of "reactive behaviours". If the robots of the multi-robot system can share the information about dynamic or semi-static objects, the efforts of obstacle avoidance could be reduced. This could save costs and time in logistic environments because the robots can always drive the faster path which is coordinated with all robots and planned according to the latest environment information. Hence coordinated path planning with updated environment information could reduce waiting time and guarantees the achievement of transports [22,23].

The mapping of dynamic obstacles is therefore a major step towards life-long robot navigation. The scope of this work is (1) to detect the low-dynamic objects and (2) to update the representation of the environment in long-term operation of multi-robot system.

The following terminology is used throughout the paper:

– *Static Map:* Map built initially by a standard SLAM algorithm. It contains static features of the environment like walls and fixed machinery which never changes. Its line features will be used by the approach for alignment.
– *Temporary Map:* Maps built by each robot upon detecting changes.
– *Current Map:* Map updated so far by merging temporary maps. With each sensor update every robot checks for changes in the environment in comparison to the current map. Initially, the current map is the same as the static map.

The paper is organized as follows. In the next section related work is presented. The succeeding section describes the approach and explains the method for calculating divergence and line-based map merging. Real-world results are presented in Sect. 5 followed by conclusions and future work.

2 Related Work

In case of building a static map of an unknown environment with a single robot system, many SLAM methods are described in literature. Most of those methods are based on the Extended Kalman Filter (EKF) [12] and the Rao-Blackwellised particle filter [27]. Cooperative Simultaneous Localization and Mapping (C-SLAM) methods are used in case of multi-robot systems [13]. Particle filters are also extended to handle multi-robot SLAM [14].

Handling changes in the environment for life-long navigation of robots is currently a major research topic [4]. Meyer-Delius et al. [25] used temporary maps for localisation in a semi-static environment. Their approach maintains temporary maps in a KD-tree and uses the corresponding map when observations are not consistent with the static map. Temporary maps are created when the fraction of range measurements in the current observation, which is not consistent with the current map (called *outlier ratio*), exceeds a predefined threshold, and when no existing temporary map explains the current observations. Temporary maps are discarded when the average outlier ratio is high. Jensen et al. [15] employed the shape information of objects and visibility criteria to update changes in a semi-static environment. Both [15,25] are for the case of a single robot system. In [10], each robot maintains a global map and senses changes in the environment based on divergence of short term and long term likelihoods. Upon detecting a change, a temporary map is built. Temporary maps are merged into the global map using rigid transformation. The calculation of the transformation bases on the Hough spectrum [11]. The resulting map is dispatched to the other robots, and each robot updates its map based on this information. Kleiner et al. [17] used occupancy grid maps with Hidden Markov Models (HMM) to detect changes with a large team of robots in real-time to compute an optimal road map.

Various direct and indirect map merging algorithms [20] find transformations between maps (that are built by individual robots) using relative positions, and common areas. Carpin et al. [11] find the transformation between maps based on Hough transform, X-spectrum and Y-spectrum. Lakaemper et al. [19] used shape similarity to merge maps with polygonal curves.

Many autonomous guided vehicle systems are present for intra-logistics in warehouses for material flow and order fulfillment. Kiva systems use the mobile robot drivepod shown in Fig. 1(a) [3] which uses cameras for navigation to read bar codes placed on the floor. The KARIS system, shown in Fig. 1(b) [30], uses grid map based Monte Carlo localization for autonomous navigation. Grenzebach's G-Pro vehicles, see Fig. 1(c) [1], use induction loops in the floor for navigation. Fraunhofer IML's Cellular Transport System [16] replaces conveyor systems by a swarm of Cellular Transport Vehicles, shown in Fig. 1(d), with transport capabilities for material handling.

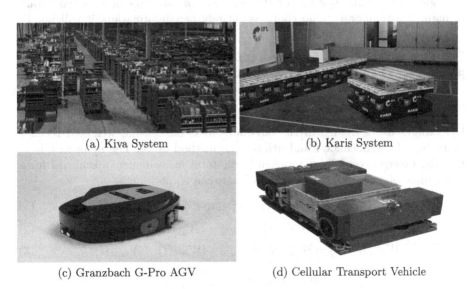

(a) Kiva System

(b) Karis System

(c) Granzbach G-Pro AGV

(d) Cellular Transport Vehicle

Fig. 1. Robots in warehouse logistics

3   Approach

In the approach proposed in this paper each robot detects changes in the environment and builds a temporary map. The temporary maps are merged into the current map. An initial map of the environment is built with a standard SLAM algorithm which contains only static parts of the environment (i.e. walls and fixed installations). This map will be called *static map* in the following.

Each robot is equipped with a laser range sensor and runs the localization to estimate its position. Sensor observations and the estimated position are used to detect changes in the environment with respect to the given *current map* (at first, the initial current map equals the static map). Upon detecting a change in the environment, the robot can start and stop building a *temporary map* which will be merged into the current map. Figure 2 shows an outline of the approach. In this context a robot can either be in *free state* in which it did not detect any change, or a robot can be in *building temporary map* state in which the robot detected a change and is building a temporary map. Afterwards, merging of the temporary map and the current map is done using line features from the static parts of the environment. The updated current map will be used for further detection of changes.

3.1   Assumptions

The approach makes the following assumptions for reliable map merging:

- The localization uncertainty is not very high. Otherwise matching of corresponding lines will be difficult.
- The environment has enough line features. This is mostly common in indoor environments.
- Enough static line features of the environment are present in a temporary map. If a temporary map contains entirely new information, it will not be possible to do line matching.

The three main blocks of the approach, *Detecting/sensing change, Building temporary maps, Map merging*, are described in the following subsections.

3.2   Detecting/Sensing Change

Detecting/sensing change in the environment is done using weighted recency averaging of the likelihood and utilizes the method of [9]. The main idea is to find the divergence of short-term and long-term measurement likelihood for a given tuple of an estimated pose x_t, a laser scan Z_t and a map m:

$$W_{avg}(t) = p(z_t|x_t, m), \tag{1}$$

$$W_{slow}(t+1) = W_{slow}(t) + \alpha_{slow} * (W_{avg}(t) - w_{slow}(t)), \tag{2}$$

$$W_{fast}(t+1) = W_{fast}(t) + \alpha_{fast} * (W_{avg}(t) - W_{fast}(t)), \tag{3}$$

$$d(t) = max(0, 1 - \frac{W_{fast}(t)}{W_{slow}(t)}). \tag{4}$$

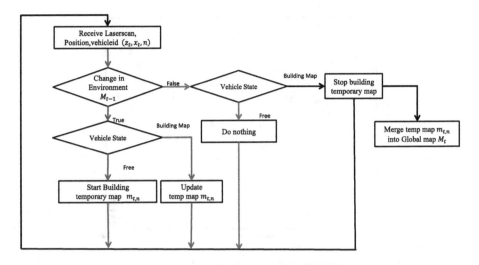

Fig. 2. Outline of the approach

- If $d(t) > 0$ start building a temporary map.
- If $d(t) \leq 0$ stop building the temporary map and merge it with the current map.

$\alpha_{slow}, \alpha_{fast}$ are decay parameters such that $0 \leq \alpha_{slow} \ll \alpha_{fast}$ and Eq. (1) represents a laser sensor model based on beam range finder model [29] to find the probability p of the observation Z_t being at the location x_t given the map m. Figure 3 shows the evolution of the divergence $d(t)$, α_{slow}, α_{fast}, α_{avg} for a period of about five minutes navigation through a changing environment. Besides changes in the environment also a rotation of the robot can cause a change in the divergence which may trigger the creation of a temporary map even if there is no change in the environment. This is mitigated by not updating the divergence during rotation of the robot which can be seen in the plot as constant values.

3.3 Building Temporary Maps

Temporary maps were built using the Hector SLAM [2] package available in *Robot Operating System* (ROS) [7]. Hector SLAM builds the occupancy grid based on scan matching by aligning the end points of current laser scan beams with the map learned so far using a Gauss-Newton approach. A multi-resolution map representation is used to address the problem of local minima [18]. Examples of temporary maps can be seen in Figs. 4(b) and 5(c).

3.4 Fusion/Merging Temporary Map

The goal of the merging process is to align and merge the temporary maps with the current map. In this step an obstacle which is temporarily mapped will be

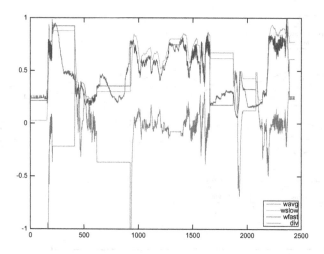

Fig. 3. Evaluation of divergence, $w_{avg}(t)$, $w_{fast}(t)$, $w_{slow}(t)$

added to the map or subtracted by its removal. To align the maps, localization information and line features are used. Initially, the temporary map is transformed into a static map coordinate system, utilizing the first robot location from which the construction of the temporary map started. Depending on the localization method, the accuracy of the estimated position varies. The effect of an uncertainty in the localization position can be seen in Fig. 4(c). Ideally, if the estimated position, obtained by localization, is accurate, the temporary map should align with the current map perfectly. To adjust misalignments of these maps, occurring due to the uncertainty in estimated position, line features from the static environment are used. The correcting transformation $T\{dx, dy, d\theta\}$ is calculated sequentially, i.e. initially a correction in angle $d\theta$ is found. Afterwards, the vertical displacement dy and the horizontal displacement dx are calculated [28].

Line segments from the static map and the temporary map are extracted using the Hough transform [6]. Due to the width of the edges and noise in the sensor readings the same edge can provide various lines. This set of line segments is preprocessed so that each edge is represented by a single line segment. Extracted lines can be seen in Fig. 4(c), green and red line segments correspond to static and temporary maps, respectively. Afterwards, matching line segments in pairs are determined. Each line segment is represented by Hesse Normal Form which contains the normal distance from the origin r and the angle between the normal and the horizontal axis θ. A pair of lines is defined by the normal distance $(r_m - r_n)$ and angular difference $(\theta_m - \theta_n)$. For a given pair of line segments in the temporary map $\{l_{tm}, l_{tn}\}$, all the matching pairs of line segments in the static map are found. All the lines in the static map are candidates for matching line segments. For both segments in the temporary pair, a normal is drawn from the mid point. In turn, the nearest line segment from the candidate line segments

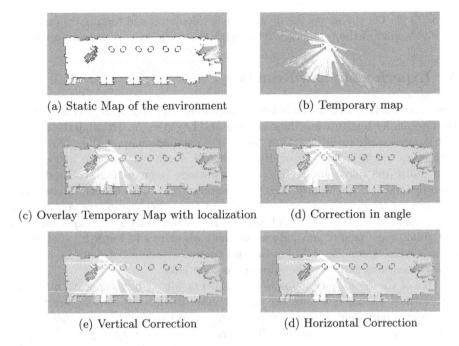

(a) Static Map of the environment   (b) Temporary map

(c) Overlay Temporary Map with localization   (d) Correction in angle

(e) Vertical Correction   (d) Horizontal Correction

Fig. 4. Exemplification of the proposed map merging steps using line segments. (Color figure online)

of the matched static pair is found. The nearest lines are matching lines if the nearest line segment pair is matched with temporary pair.

Correction in angle $d\theta$ is the mean value of the angle differences between the matched line segments weighted by the length of the temporary line. The vertical displacement dy is the normal distance between the matching line segments after rotating temporary line segments with correction angle $d\theta$.

Before calculating the horizontal displacement dx, the temporary map is transformed with the previously calculated correction in angle $d\theta$, see Fig. 4(d), and the vertical displacement dy (Fig. 4(e)). The horizontal displacement is calculated by finding maximum matching horizontal displacement i.e. the displacement which corresponds to the maximum matching of grid cells in the static map and transformed temporary map.

4   Implementation

The approach has been implemented on Cellular Transport System (CTS) vehicles (Fig. 1(d)) [16]. Each vehicle is equipped with a *Sick* safety laser sensor and runs landmark-based Monte Carlo localization to estimate its position. The server runs Ubuntu 14.04 with ROS Indigo. Each vehicle sends its estimated position (x_t) and the corresponding laser reading (Z_t) to the server through

ZeroMQ [8]. On the server the divergence is calculated and temporary maps are built. Merging of the temporary maps with the static map is done on server.

5   Experiments and Results

The approach has been tested in the LivingLab for Cellular Transport Systems at the Fraunhofer Institute for Material Flow and Logistics [5]. The dimension of the testing area is about 60 m × 18 m. Initially a complete map of the environment with static parts is built using Hector SLAM which can be seen in Fig. 5(a). This static map contains walls, picking stations (seen as ellipses) and other fixed installations (one on the right and another one far to the left). Later, two pallets were placed in the environment and few other stationary robots were also present along the horizontal wall at the bottom during the experiment. A test robot was made to navigate along the path shown in Fig. 5(b) at speed of 0.5 m/s which takes about 5 min. In this experiment, the robot detected changes at four locations and corresponding maps were built.

One of the temporary maps is shown in Fig. 5(c). The temporary maps are transformed and merged into the current map. Figure 5(d) shows correction of temporary map overlaid onto current map. The two pallets were successfully detected and updated in the map after merging the temporary maps, cf. Fig. 5(e). In addition, added stationary robots can be seen along the horizontal wall at the bottom (Fig. 6).

Next, the performance of map matching has been investigated in detail. Two cases are distinguished: (1) addition of obstacles and (2) removal. The robot speed is equal in both cases. For each case three temporary maps are presented

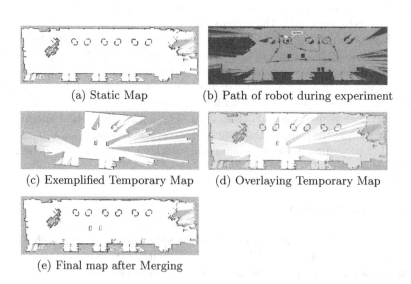

(a) Static Map   (b) Path of robot during experiment

(c) Exemplified Temporary Map   (d) Overlaying Temporary Map

(e) Final map after Merging

Fig. 5. Results of map updating

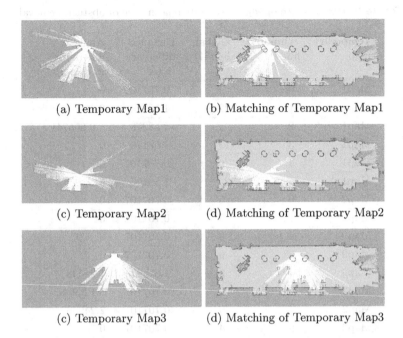

(a) Temporary Map1   (b) Matching of Temporary Map1

(c) Temporary Map2   (d) Matching of Temporary Map2

(c) Temporary Map3   (d) Matching of Temporary Map3

Fig. 6. Evaluation of line matching for temporary maps in case of obstacle addition. Lines from both the static and the temporary map are numbered and shown in green, and red, respectively. Additionally lines from the temporary map after using corrected transformation are shown in blue. Best viewed in color. (Color figure online)

Table 1. Performance of edge-wise matching in case of obstacle addition.

Temporary map	Temporary line ID	Global line ID	Distance difference in px	Angle difference in degrees
Map1	0	2	0.707107	0
Map1	1	12	0.707107	0
Map1	2	9	0.707107	0
Map1	3	2	0.689639	−1.20035
Map1	4	0	1.6094	2.24936
Map2	0	2	2.54951	0
Map2	2	2	0.695382	−0.925865
Map2	3	12	0.707107	0
Map2	4	9	0.707107	1.20035
Map2	5	2	1.58114	0
Map3	0	8	2.54951	0
Map3	1	4	0.695382	0
Map3	2	8	0.707107	0
Map3	3	5	0.707107	0
Map3	6	17	1.58114	3.08052
Map3	8	11	0.707107	0.605741
Map3	9	2	1.58114	0

Table 2. Performance of edge-wise matching in case of obstacle removal.

Temporary map	Temporary line ID	Global line ID	Distance difference in px	Angle difference in degrees
Map1	0	2	0.707107	0
Map1	1	22	1.58114	0
Map1	2	2	1.58378	−0.605741
Map1	3	12	1.58114	0
Map1	4	9	0.707107	0
Map1	5	22	1.58114	0
Map2	0	0	0.707107	0
Map2	1	0	0.707107	0
Map2	2	0	0.707107	0
Map2	3	0	0.707107	0
Map2	4	0	1.57597	1.21538
Map2	5	0	0.707107	−1.83647
Map2	7	0	0.707107	2.24936
Map2	8	4	0.707107	0
Map2	9	11	1.4301	−1.25872
Map2	11	0	1.58114	0
Map2	14	0	1.58114	0
Map2	17	0	0.707107	0
Map3	1	2	0.707107	0
Map3	2	8	0.707107	0
Map3	3	0	1.63474	4.13334
Map3	4	4	0.707107	0
Map3	5	8	0.707107	0
Map3	6	0	0.695467	−1.03391
Map3	7	2	52.5024	0
Map3	9	22	1.59199	−1.93029
Map3	11	2	0.707107	2.81821
Map3	12	8	1.58114	0
Map3	13	5	1.59479	−2.3415

and the edge-wise matching errors are highlighted. The resulting maps for case one (addition of obstacle) are shown in Fig. 7 (Tables 1 and 2).

Results from the two datasets above show that the approach has produced consistent occupancy grid maps which represent the map changes. Also from the evaluation calculations, the distance difference between matched lines in almost

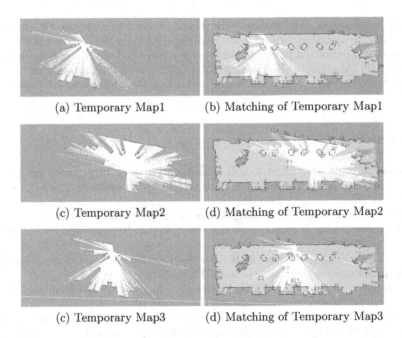

(a) Temporary Map1   (b) Matching of Temporary Map1

(c) Temporary Map2   (d) Matching of Temporary Map2

(c) Temporary Map3   (d) Matching of Temporary Map3

Fig. 7. Evaluation of line matching for temporary maps in case of obstacle removal. Lines from both static and temporary map are numbered and shown in green, and red, respectively. Additionally lines from temporary map after using corrected transformation are shown in blue. Best viewed in color. (Color figure online)

all the cases was less than 1 or 2 pixels. This error can occur due to the noise from the laser measurements or due to the approximation of lines from Hough transformation. Also the angle difference between matched lines was zero in most cases and maximum difference obtained was less than 5 degrees.

6   Conclusion and Future Work

We proposed a method for updating the environment map for long term operation of a multi-robot system. Therefore, we utilized line features to merge grid maps. Our experiments demonstrate practicability of the approach. The method can be applied easily in a multi-robot environment. Next steps will be, besides improvement of the approach, to perform qualitative evaluations in more complex and realistic scenarios for longer durations. The mapping of dynamic obstacles is a major step towards life-long navigation. In future, related path planning, collision avoidance and congestion avoidance problems will also be studied. The fusion with stationary sensors (e.g. Bluetooth [21,24]) directs to autonomous vehicle problems, where Car/to/Infrastructure communication is an active research topic.

Acknowledgements. The authors were partially funded by Deutsche Forschungsgemeinschaft (DFG) within the Collaborative Research Center SFB 876, project B2 (the study was also performed in collaboration with project B4) and the European Union Horizon 2020 Programme (Horizon2020/2014–2020), under grant agreement number 688380 "VaVeL: Variety, Veracity, VaLue: Handling the Multiplicity of Urban Sensors".

References

1. Grenzebach maschinenbau GmbH, Hamlar, Germany. http://www.grenzebach. com/index.php/eng/technology/logistic_solutions/agv_solutions/g_pro. Accessed 03 May 2015
2. Hector SLAM. http://wiki.ros.org/hector_slam. Accessed 07 Apr 2015
3. Kivasystems. http://www.kivasystems.com/solutions/system-overview/. Accessed 03 May 2015
4. Lifenav - reliable lifelong navigation for mobile robots. http://lifenav.informatik. uni-freiburg.de/index.html. Accessed 03 May 2015
5. Livinglab zellulare transportsysteme. http://www.iml.fraunhofer.de/en/ researchhallslaboratories/zft-halle.html. Accessed 10 Apr 2015
6. OpenCV HoughLinesP. http://docs.opencv.org/modules/imgproc/doc/feature_ detection.html?highlight=houghlinesp#houghlinesp. Accessed 12 Apr 2015
7. Robot operating system. http://www.ros.org/about-ros/. Accessed 07 Apr 2015
8. ZeroMQ. http://www.zeromq.org. Accessed 07 Apr 2015
9. Abrate, F., Bona, B., Indri, M., Rosa, S., Tibaldi, F.: Map updating in dynamic environments. In: ISR/ROBOTIK 2010, pp. 1–8 (2010)
10. Abrate, F., Bona, B., Indri, M., Rosa, S., Tibaldi, F.: Multi-robot map updating in dynamic environments. In: Martinoli, A., Mondada, F., Correll, N., Mermoud, G., Egerstedt, M., Hsieh, M.A., Parker, L.E., Støy, K. (eds.) Distributed Autonomous Robotic Systems, vol. 83, pp. 147–160. Springer, Heidelberg (2010). doi:10.1007/ 978-3-642-32723-0
11. Carpin, S.: Fast and accurate map merging for multi-robot systems. Auton. Robots **25**(3), 305–316 (2008)
12. Durrant-Whyte, H., Bailey, T.: Simultaneous localization and mapping: Part I. IEEE Robot. Autom. Mag. **13**(2), 99–110 (2006)
13. Fenwick, J.W., Newman, P.M., Leonard, J.J.: Cooperative concurrent mapping and localization, pp. 1810–1817 (2002)
14. Howard, A.: Multi-robot simultaneous localization and mapping using particle filters. Int. J. Robot. Res. **25**(12), 1243–1256 (2006)
15. Jensen, B., Ramel, G., Siegwart, R.: Detecting semi-static objects with a laser scanner. In: Dillmann, R., Wörn, H., Gockel, T. (eds.) Autonome Mobile Systeme 2003. Informatik aktuell, pp. 21–31. Springer, Heidelberg (2003). doi:10.1007/ 978-3-642-18986-9_3
16. Kamagaew, A., Stenzel, J., Nettstrater, A., ten Hompel, M.: Concept of cellular transport systems in facility logistics. In: 2011 5th International Conference on Automation, Robotics and Applications (ICARA), pp. 40–45, December 2011
17. Kleiner, A., Sun, D., Meyer-Delius, D.: ARMO: adaptive road map optimization for large robot teams. In: 2011 IEEE/RSJ International Conference on Intelligent Robots and Systems (IROS), pp. 3276–3282, September 2011

18. Kohlbrecher, S., Meyer, J., von Stryk, O., Klingauf, U.: A flexible and scalable SLAM system with full 3D motion estimation. In: Proceedings of the IEEE International Symposium on Safety, Security and Rescue Robotics (SSRR). IEEE, November 2011

19. Lakaemper, R., Latecki, L., Wolter, D.: Incremental multi-robot mapping. In: 2005 IEEE/RSJ International Conference on Intelligent Robots and Systems (IROS 2005), pp. 3846–3851, August 2005

20. Lee, H.C., Lee, S.H., Lee, T.S., Kim, D.J., Lee, B.H.: A survey of map merging techniques for cooperative-SLAM. In: 2012 9th International Conference on Ubiquitous Robots and Ambient Intelligence (URAI), pp. 285–287, November 2012

21. Liebig, T., Kemloh Wagoum, A.U.: Modelling microscopic pedestrian mobility using bluetooth. In: ICAART, pp. 270–275. SciTePress (2012)

22. Liebig, T., Piatkowski, N., Bockermann, C., Morik, K.: Dynamic route planning with real-time traffic predictions. Inf. Syst. **64**, 258–265 (2017). http://www.sciencedirect.com/science/article/pii/S0306437916000181

23. Liebig, T., Sotzny, M.: On avoiding traffic jams with dynamic self-organizing trip planning. In: Clementini, E., Donnelly, M., Yuan, M., Kray, C., Fogliaroni, P., Ballatore, A. (eds.) Proceedings of the 13th International Conference on Spatial Information Theory, COSIT 2017, L'Aquila, Italy, 4–8 September 2017 (2017, accepted)

24. Liebig, T., Xu, Z., May, M.: Incorporating mobility patterns in pedestrian quantity estimation and sensor placement. In: Nin, J., Villatoro, D. (eds.) CitiSens 2012. LNCS, vol. 7685, pp. 67–80. Springer, Heidelberg (2013). doi:10.1007/978-3-642-36074-9_7

25. Meyer-Delius, D., Hess, J.M., Grisetti, G., Burgard, W.: Temporary maps for robust localization in semi-static environments. In: IROS, pp. 5750–5755. IEEE (2010)

26. Mitsou, N., Tzafestas, C.: Temporal occupancy grid for mobile robot dynamic environment mapping. In: Mediterranean Conference on Control Automation, MED 2007, pp. 1–8, June 2007

27. Montemerlo, M., Thrun, S., Koller, D., Wegbreit, B.: FastSLAM: a factored solution to the simultaneous localization and mapping problem. In: Proceedings of the AAAI National Conference on Artificial Intelligence, pp. 593–598. AAAI (2002)

28. Nguyen, V., Harati, A., Tomatis, N., Martinelli, A., Siegwart, R.: Orthogonal SLAM: a step toward lightweight indoor autonomous navigation. In: None (2006)

29. Thrun, S., Burgard, W., Fox, D.: Probabilistic Robotics. Intelligent Robotics and Autonomous Agents. MIT Press, Cambridge (2005)

30. Trenkle, A., Seibold, Z., Stoll, T.: Safety requirements and safety functions for decentralized controlled autonomous systems. In: 2013 XXIV International Symposium on Information, Communication and Automation Technologies (ICAT), pp. 1–6, October 2013

31. Walcott, A.N.: Long-term robot mapping in dynamic environments. Ph.D. thesis, Cambridge, MA, USA, aAI0823852 (2011)

Similarity and Contrast on Conceptual Spaces for Pertinent Description Generation

Giovanni Sileno[1,2]([✉]), Isabelle Bloch[1], Jamal Atif[2], and Jean-Louis Dessalles[1]

[1] LTCI, Télécom ParisTech, Université Paris-Saclay, Paris, France
`giovanni.sileno@telecom-paristech.fr`
[2] Université Paris-Dauphine, PSL Research University,
CNRS, UMR 7243, LAMSADE, 75016 Paris, France

Abstract. Within the general objective of conceiving a cognitive architecture for image interpretation able to generate outputs relevant to several target user profiles, the paper elaborates on a set of operations that should be provided by a cognitive space to guarantee the generation of relevant descriptions. First, it attempts to define a working definition of contrast operation. Then, revisiting well-known results in cognitive studies, it sketches a definition of similarity based on contrast, distinguished from the metric defined on the conceptual space.

Keywords: Similarity · Contrast · Conceptual spaces · Relevance · Description generation · Triangle inequality · Asymmetry · Diagnosticity effect

1 Introduction

Similarity, for its fundamental role in human reasoning, occupies a central role in cognitive science. In general, it is modeled as a function of a context-dependent distance (e.g. [1]). On the other hand, most machine learning methods rely on adequate metrics to perform comparisons between inputs; certain methods even attempt to achieve (pseudo-)metric learning. This convergence towards geometric models is not without problems. First, there exist many empirical studies, starting from the famous work of Tversky [2], that show that similarity in human judgment does not satisfy fundamental metric axioms. Secondly, a good part of *reasoning* operations performed by artificial devices still relies on symbolic means (e.g. ontologies expressed in description logics), that do not have a direct geometric interpretation. Attempts to fill these gaps exist, for instance by enriching the metric model of similarity with additional elements to align it with the empirical results (e.g. [3]), or by approaching the logical structures used in artificial reasoning via geometrical notions (e.g. [4]).

This work attempts to follow an alternative path. On the one hand, we continue along the tradition of works on psychological spaces, and precisely, we build upon the theory of *conceptual spaces* [5,6], acknowledging a third cognitive level, between symbolic and associationistic, where conceptual entities are

© Springer International Publishing AG 2017
G. Kern-Isberner et al. (Eds.): KI 2017, LNAI 10505, pp. 262–275, 2017.
DOI: 10.1007/978-3-319-67190-1_20

geometric representations. In our general research project, we aim to introduce conceptual spaces as a sort of *middle-ware* for image interpretation applications. Here, assuming that conceptual spaces exist, we focus on operations required for generating *relevant descriptions*, i.e. *pertinent characterizations* of a given input. We sketch a technical solution satisfying properties of predication observed in direct experiences. As a result of this proposal, we argue that the mismatches between geometric and empirical properties of similarity might not be a consequence of the space *per se* but of neglecting part of the mechanisms behind description generation.

The paper unveils its arguments incrementally. We first give a brief overview of the theory of conceptual spaces [5,6] and of a recent variation [7], focusing on pertinent predication. We then sketch the infrastructure required for generating relevant descriptions starting from simple examples of predication, but which are already problematic for semantic approaches relying on set theory. From this base, we present an alternative definition of similarity, that predicts results observed in empirical studies (asymmetry of similarity judgments, non satisfaction of the triangle inequality, diagnosticity effect). A note on further developments ends the paper.

2   Conceptual Spaces and Predication

2.1   Overview on Conceptual Spaces

According to Gärdenfors' theory of *conceptual spaces* [5,6], the meaning of words can be faithfully represented as convex regions in a high-dimensional geometric space, in which dimensions correspond to cognitively primitive features. Technically, conceptual spaces are usually modeled as vector spaces (e.g. [8–10]). An object of the conceptual space is characterized by several *qualities* or attributes:

$$(q_1, q_2, \ldots, q_n), \forall i : q_i \in Q_i$$

where Q_i are sets of possible values for each quality q_i. Quality dimensions correspond to the ways in which two *stimuli* can be considered to be similar or different, usually according to an ordering relation of the *stimulus*. In general, the Q_i are modeled as *concrete domains* on $\mathbb{R}, \mathbb{R}^2, \ldots, \mathbb{N}, \mathbb{N}^2$, etc. but proposals exist to process nominal domains (e.g. [11,12]). So far, we used the term domain in the mathematical sense. However, in works on conceptual spaces—in agreement with the cognitive psychology literature—the term *domain* identifies a set of *integral dimensions*, i.e. dimensions that cannot be separated perceptually (e.g. for humans, the color dimensions *hue-luminosity-saturation*). A conceptual space consists therefore of:

$$C = D_1 \times D_2 \times \ldots \times D_m$$

where each D_i is a domain. As each D_i consists of a set of qualities, the resulting structure is hierarchical. According to its proponents, this infrastructure enables the distinction between *objects*, i.e. points of the space (used to represent *exemplars* and *prototypes*, i.e. *exemplar-based* and *prototypical* bodies of knowledge [11]), and *concepts*, defined as regions of the space.

To guarantee betweenness among *similar* elements, *natural properties* correspond to *convex regions* in a domain [5]. A concept is a combination of properties, typically across multiple domains (linguistically, properties are usually expressed as adjective-like attributes, while concepts as nouns or verbs). Prototypes emerge as centroids of those convex regions (properties or concepts); at the same time, the division of conceptual spaces in regions can be seen as the result of a competition between prototypes, that might be captured by *Voronoï tessellations*, useful for *categorization* applications; technically, existing implementations exploit e.g. *region connection calculus* (RCC) [8], or polytope structures [13].

Evidently, there is a strong affinity between the representation based on features used in machine learning and the idea of conceptual spaces. For instance, *word embeddings* techniques also represent the meaning of words as points on a high-dimensional Euclidean space; however, conceptual spaces offer two advantages: first, working with regions and not only with similarity, they provide an intuitive way to process subsumption, overlap and typicality; second, dimensions of conceptual spaces have (or should have) a direct relation to a domain, while word embeddings dimensions are essentially meaningless.[1]

2.2 Predication and Relevance

The theory of conceptual spaces assumes a generally working association between regions and linguistic marks. For this insistence on *lexical meaning*, the proposal can be seen as an extension of the symbolic approach. A recent alternative proposal [7] considers instead that predicates are the result of *contrast* operations made *on the fly* between conceptual objects, following principles of relevance. In essence, contrast is a "difference" operator (denoted with $-$) between the vectors pointing to the exemplar (O) and to the prototype (P):

$$C = O - P$$

Being the outcome C a vector, with (theoretically) the same dimensionality of the conceptual space, it may be a conceptual object as well. However, this vector should not be interpreted extensionally, but rather as a conceptual *force* or *modifier*; we will name these objects *contrastors*.

The proposal carries interesting innovations. First, whereas practically all other works rely on a global distance, it does not necessarily require a *holistic* perspective on all available dimensions. Second, it does not have to refer to average lexical meanings emerging from usage, but it is computed contingently with C and P grounded on the agent's own experience.[2] Third, working with

---

[1] Jameel and Schockaert [14] show that a NLP architecture based on conceptual spaces yields better results than word-embeddings and knowledge-graph embedding.

[2] The negotiation of the specific symbols associated to C and P (*anchoring*), here assumed as given, remains deferred at social level.

contrast would allow to overlook the convexity constraint, requiring in principle only access to the representational level of points. For these reasons, we take it as a starting point for our investigation. In the following, we start working out an implementation of contrast, missing in the original paper [7].

3   Experiments for the Specification of Contrast

3.1   First Example: *"red dog"*

In predicate logic, the expression "red dog" is usually written as an x such that $Red(x) \land Dog(x)$, that, in the set-theoretic semantics, refers to an entity included both in the set of dogs and in the set of red entities. However, a red dog is not red as would be a red face, nor as would be a red book; in the usual labeling of colors it looks actually rather brown. Being red—semantically— might depend on the type of object on which the predicate applies. Accepting this, we suppose that the description of an object is constructed in at least two steps: first, an association to the nearest prototype (categorization), and then the extraction of the characteristic features by contrast. In this work, we bypass the prototype association, assuming it as given (machine learning algorithms have been proven successful in this respect). We focus only on the contrastive component of predication. In our example, *"this dog" exemplar* contrasted with the *"dog" prototype* should return a *"red" contrastor*.

For simplicity, we consider dogs as defined merely by their colors. We have taken the RGB colors of 9 common furs of dogs from the Internet, and converted them in HLS dimensions (*hue, luminosity, saturation*), in accordance with the conceptual space literature. Other color spaces, such as CIELAB or CIELUV can even better match visual perception, and first experiments confirm that the proposed approach applies in these spaces as well. For the sake of the argument, we continue with HLS. The statistical properties of the set are:[3]

`mean: [ 0.10  0.52  0.46 ], std dev: [ 0.02  0.22  0.27 ]`

Simplifying, we could take the mean as a prototype of color of a dog. This computation is transparent or at least less sensible to frequency effects; we are not averaging on actual populations of dogs, but on breeds. Figure 1 shows the selected points and the centroid, including points from the HLS spectrum with a plausible label association, e.g. "red" to $(0, 0.5, 1)$.

Let us consider a dog exemplar that would go under the "red sable" label. As a first step, we see contrast as *vectorial difference* of exemplar and prototype:[4]

`[ 0.07  0.24  0.92 ] - [ 0.10  0.52  0.46 ] = [ -0.16 -0.28  0.45 ]`

---

[3] Hue is an angular dimension, so the calculation of mean and standard deviation follows *circular* (also known as *directional*) *statistics* methods.

[4] Given two angles a and b, we have computed $a - b$ as the angle of the vectorial difference of the two normalized vectors corresponding to the input angles, which is equivalent to the circular mean of a and $b + \pi$.

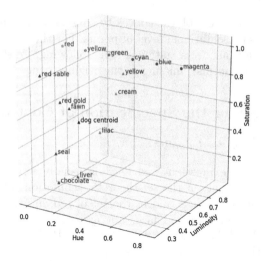

Fig. 1. Colors of dog furs and standard colors (with labels), on HLS dimensions. (Color figure online)

As the contrastor aims to capture the distinctive characteristics of the subject entity (e.g. this dog), with respect to a reference entity (e.g. the dog prototype), it lies, as a vector, in the same space as the two conceptual objects. The operation in itself however gives no evident clue on how to compare the outcome with, for instance, a previously acquired contrastor.

Let us consider now a red book. Assuming that practically all colors are possible for a book cover, each quality dimension can be modeled under a uniform distribution. When normalized, their standard deviation is $1/\sqrt{12} \approx 0.29$.[5] We may then define an *empirical principle of relevant dimension*: the more the standard deviation along a normalized quality dimension approaches 0.29 the less we expect that quality to be relevant to form the prototype. In the extreme case, we should not take it to define the centroid. Applying roughly the principle on the dog case, the only pertinent dimension for the prototype is hue.

Now, the standard mathematical tool for vectorial spaces requires that points have a value for all coordinates. However, conceptual spaces have potentially infinite dimensions, and points may have undefined dimensions. To enable the possibility to operate with any point, we introduce a *void value* ∗ when a certain dimension is not applicable.[6]

We want to identify a method to generate, from this representation, that our dog is a red dog, and that our book is a red book. For the book, being the prototypical book color void, the color characterization mirrors the color specification given by the sensory module, i.e. there is no contextualizing effect

---

[5] $\mu = 1/2$, Var $= E[(X - \mu)^2] = \int_0^1 (x - 1/2)^2 dx = 1/12$.
[6] In a similar spirit, Aisbett and Gibbon [15] introduce the idea of *distinguishing point*.

due to the prototype.[7] In formula, we have that:

$$(.., a, ..) - (.., *, ..) = (.., a, ..)$$

The color spectrum serves as a source of contrastors. In the case of dogs, we expect instead a contextualizing effect. Assuming that contrastors have prototypes as well, we require a method to compute to which category the contrastor we computed falls upon, in order to enable a reuse of this category in different contexts (e.g. red dog, red book, red face). In clustering algorithms (see e.g. [16]) the comparison between two numeric points is done using *distance measures* (usually Euclidean, Manhattan or Chebychev), or functions such as *cosine similarity, Pearson correlation measure* etc. In *typicality-based clustering* (e.g. [17]), it relies on a *typicality degree* computed using a *internal resemblance* (with other members of the cluster) and an *external dissimilarity* (with members of other clusters).

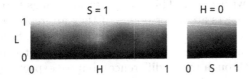

Fig. 2. *Hue, luminosity, saturation* (HLS) color spectrum. (Color figure online)

For the aim of this paper, we do not need to decide a clustering algorithm (i.e. a prototype formation mechanism), nor to settle upon how a contrastor should be associated to its prototype (i.e. a categorization mechanism).[8] In the following, we will denote the category/prototype association with the symbol '⤳'. For instance, in our red dog example, we have: $(0.07, 0.24, 0.92) - (0.10, *, *) = (-0.16, 0.24, 0.92)$ ⤳ *red*. In effect, looking at the HLS spectrum (Fig. 2), the contrastor calculated for our dog exemplar is still in the gravitation of red but on the opposite side of brown and yellow.[9]

3.2   Second Example: "*a above b*"

Imagine we have two objects, a and b, one above the other. In predicate logic their relationship might be written as $above(a, b)$, that, from a logical point of

---

[7] This contextualization can be interpreted as informational *compression*. When a prototype cannot be formed for a quality (because e.g. exemplars exhibit a uniform distribution with respect to that dimension), the sensory input cannot be compressed.

[8] As exemplars and contrastors are vectors of the same space, it is plausible to hypothesize that they share similar prototyping/categorization mechanisms.

[9] The fact that the contrastor is capturing magenta can be explained by an incomplete parametrization of additional semantic aspects (concerning e.g. the actual conceptual space on which contrast is applied).

view, would be the inverse of $below(b, a)$. From a natural language point of view, however, considering a an apple and b a table, we observe it is much more natural to say "the apple is on the table" rather than "the table is below the apple". We hypothesize therefore that contrast is at stake, selecting the relation most pertinent to the situation.

Objects are extended: they occupy a certain space, that may be described as a solid shape, with a center and a rotation angle, or, when captured in images, by pixels. Intuitively, directional relations should be computed by this spatial information. Applying the principle of contrast here, we should have that a contrasted with b should return an *"above" contrastor*.

Simplifying, let us reduce objects to points. Considering their positions specified in e.g. a 2D space, we have that $(a_x, a_y) - (b_x, b_y)$ is actually a seen from b, or, equivalently, as if the origin of the space has been moved to b. Defining the *above* contrastor prototype as a vector $(0, u)$, with u positive number, and similarly *below* $(0, -u)$, *right* $(u, 0)$, *left* $(-u, 0)$, it seems we might utilize the same principle of the previous example. For instance, $(2, 4) - (1.5, 2) = (-0.5, 2) \rightsquigarrow above$ (and a bit of *left*), with $u = 2$. This interpretation brings two questions to the foreground. First, objects are never points: if they are represented as such, it is because they have been discretized at a certain granularity. Second, vectors have an intrinsic metric unit, which, mathematically, is inherited by the contrastor (when constructed through vector difference), but we expect e.g. *above* to be the same relation when applied to macro or to micro-objects. Leaving the study of such normalization mechanism to future research, we focus on the first problem.

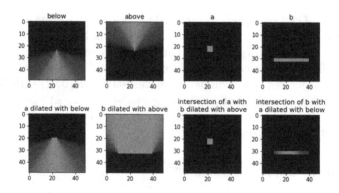

Fig. 3. Computing directional relationships using morphological dilation [18].

We consider an existing method [18] used in image processing to compute directional relative positions of visual entities (e.g. of biomedical images). The method exploits *mathematical morphology* operators—namely *fuzzy dilation*— to create an adequate *fuzzy landscape* (a fuzzy region) from a model of the directional relationship, and the position and shape of a reference object. The *strength* of the relation between the target and the reference is quantified via a normalized degree of intersection of the target object with the fuzzy landscape region (please refer to [18] for technical details). We have reported in Fig. 3 an example similar to the "the apple is on the table" case. The strength of *b below a* results to be inferior to *a above b*, basically because the "below a" region, seen through the "b" mask, contains gray pixels, while the opposite is not true.

Interpreting the previous operations at a higher level, we can draw interesting observations. The method enables the comparison of two descriptions, but it does not primarily make any reference to a contrast between two entities. The strength of the directional relationship is computed via its *realization* in the image space. The structuring element stands as a model of the region *above* of a *point element* located at the origin; it corresponds to the reification of all possible answers to the question "Is this point above the origin?" The dilation operation contextualizes these answers using the reference *b*; it is as if the binary relation $above(a, b)$ is reduced to a unary form: $above\_b(a)$. The subject entity *a* is then taken into account in the computation of the degree of intersection: how much *a*'s extension *falls within* the virtual entity *above_b*. If we consider multiple virtual entities as *right_of_b* etc. we are recreating a problem similar to the categorization/prototype association, but where the categories have been created on the fly and concern the image space around the reference. Rather than performing a direct *contrast* between two objects ($a - b \rightsquigarrow above$), here it seems we are exploiting the dual operation *merge* ($a \rightsquigarrow b + above$).[10] In effect, this mapping works also in the previous example, i.e. we are able to map *this_dog − prototype_dog $\rightsquigarrow$ red* to *this_dog $\rightsquigarrow$ prototype_dog + red*.

This intuition sheds light on how $\rightsquigarrow$ may operate. The right operand specifies the final result (the category or the nearest prototype to which the contrastor is associated); but to achieve it, several possible candidates, distributed over the conceptual space, have to be adequately compared to the left operand. If the left and right operands can be processed as points, cluster association methods will do. If they are regions, we will need to assess the *overlap* over the candidate regions, using analytical (as the intersection degree) or also random (e.g. Monte Carlo) methods. These candidate regions might need to be realized (i.e. contextualized with a reference) when they are not directly available, which is an operation computationally expensive. In future work, we will investigate how to remap the merge operations to the left part of the contrast equation.

4   Similarity

In this section we build upon the previous analysis to define *similarity*. We will start from presenting two reference models of similarity judgment presented in cognitive science, widely used in many applications (particularly Tversky's model); we will then introduce our model of similarity as double contrast, and evaluate it with empirical results reviewed in the literature.

---

[10] This interpretation is still compatible with the contrast formula, as, in effect, we are implicitly assuming that *a* has not a prototypical position.

4.1   Similarity as Feature Matching

A rich tradition of psychological and cognitive studies on similarity starts from working with sets of *features* associated with objects.[11] In a well-known paper, Tversky [2] argued that similarity cannot be modeled as a distance, because many empirical experiences shows that similarity judgments does not satisfy three geometric axioms:

- *minimality*: $d(a, b) \geq d(a, a) = 0$; respondents identify another object similar to the object more often than an object to itself;
- *symmetry*: $d(a, b) = d(b, a)$; for instance, "Tel Aviv is like New York" is not the same as "New York is like Tel Aviv";
- *triangle inequality*: $d(a, b) + d(b, c) \geq d(a, c)$; for instance, Russia and Cuba are (were) similar as political systems, Cuba and Jamaica are similar geographically, but Russia and Jamaica do not share anything.

Besides, Tversky [2] observes another relevant phenomenon:

- *diagnosticity effect*: the result of similarity judgment changes when the list of possible alternative changes. For instance, participants are asked for the country most similar to Austria to be decided amongst Hungary, Poland (at those times both communist countries), and Sweden; most responses indicate Sweden. If Norway is added to the list, however, responders turn to Hungary.

Given certain assumptions, Tversky proves that similarity can be expressed with what he calls the *contrast model* (A is a set of features of a, B of b):

$$S(a, b) = \theta f(A \cap B) - \alpha f(A \setminus B) - \beta f(B \setminus A)$$

where S is the *similarity scale*, f a non-negative scale, and θ, α and β positive parameters. If $\alpha > \beta$, the model creates the asymmetry between subject a and reference b, explaining the observed lack of symmetry in similarity judgments. This account is also compatible with an observed *imperfect* complementarity of similarity and dissimilarity (*difference*, in Tversky's terms).

4.2   Similarity with Density Effects

Soon after Tversky's proposal, Krumhansl [3] presented an alternative model to explain the same phenomena, attempting to recover the geometrical hypothesis. She starts from the problem of minimality axiom, observing that in experiments problems increase when the subject point has many neighbors, i.e. when it is

---

[11] It is worth observing that such collections are the result of a preliminary extraction and compilation by some modeler. Approaches based on conceptual spaces, although certain implementations may be in practice very similar to feature-based works (e.g. by considering nominal dimensions), in principle insist on direct, perceptual grounds of quality dimensions.

more prototypical. She then considers similarity as a function both of an *inter-point distance*, and of a *spatial density* of stimuli points:

$$d'(a,b) = d(a,b) + \alpha\delta(a) + \beta\delta(b)$$

where δ is a density function. The similarity function is then suggested to be a composition of this distance with a monotonically decreasing function. Like Tversky, she suggests that the difference between similarity and dissimilarity in empirical tests may be due to different factors α, β or to difference in density between subject and referent points.

4.3   Similarity as Double Contrast

So far, we have not defined similarity in our account. For calculating contrast, we have used distances inherent to the integral dimensions. These distances may in effect be interpreted as quantities of how much two stimuli are *dissimilar*, but, because these two stimuli should belong to the same domain (e.g. color, image space), they cannot refer to (multi-dimensional) concepts. Similarity, instead, operates at level of concepts. This is evident in metaphors, i.e. expressions like "my love is as deep as the ocean", "he is like a lion". For this reason, we start from sketching a general template for metaphor generation.

For simplicity, let us consider a sentence like "he is strong". Following the red dog example, this predicate should result from the operation:

$$this\_person - prototype\_person \rightsquigarrow strong, ...$$

Saying instead "he is like a lion", we are performing a double operation: we are matching one or more characteristic properties of that person with one or more characteristic properties of the concept of lion.

$$this\_person - prototype\_person \rightsquigarrow X, ...$$
$$prototype\_lion - prototype\_animal \rightsquigarrow X, ...$$

However, whereas the contrastor category X is recognized as the same in the contrasts, the two contrastors have plausibly different intensities. The *asymmetry* between the subject and the referent can be seen as a consequence of the relative intensities of the contrastors (cf. *above* vs *below*). We can generalize this idea:

Proposition 1 (Comparison Ground). *A comparison ground between two conceptual objects holds when the contrasts with their prototypes results into two contrastors falling upon the same category, but possibly with different intensities. The natural reference is the object whose contrastor has greater intensity.*

The suspension dots in these equations are meant to show that in principle many contrastors could be generated, related to different domains. For instance, lion's distinguishing features are being strong, living in the savannah, etc. Why we match the strength dimension rather than the position? A *descriptive criterion* may be because in common-sense there are few animals as strong as lions, but there are plausibly many other animals that live in the savannah. This criterion is related to the empirical principle of relevance.

Tversky's **asymmetry** examples, e.g. "Tel Aviv is like New York", can be interpreted following the metaphor's template. This sentence means that one or more distinctive characteristic of New York are used as modifiers for defining Tel Aviv. To decide whether it is nightlife, cosmopolitanism or green areas we may use the descriptive criterion to compute the distinctiveness of certain features. Saying the opposite ("New York is like Tel Aviv") would mean to activate Tel Aviv's more distinctive characteristics.

For the **triangle inequality**, suppose the concept of country is defined by political and geographical dimensions. A sentence like "Cuba is similar to Russia", without defining the dimensions of the comparison, follows a scheme similar to the metaphor case, but in this case, the two objects belong to the same category. The double contrast works in the Cuba–Russia case (for the matching on the political dimension) and in the Jamaica–Cuba case (for the matching on the geographical dimension), but it does not work in the Jamaica–Russia case, as it is not able to find a common comparison ground.

To explain the **diagnosticity effect**, we hypothesize that respondents construct a rough estimate of the group. Rather than a real prototype, we are dealing here with a temporary construct, bringing to the foreground the *relative* distinctive features of the given individuals. For the sake of the argument, let us consider a simplified model of Tversky's test (*political index* 1 means communist country; *position* approximates the position on a map of the centers of the countries). Averaging these values, we can construct a sort of virtual prototype of the group, with and without Norway:

	political_index	position (x, y)
Austria	0	1, 0
Hungary	1	2, 0
Poland	1	2, 1
Sweden	0	1, 4
Norway	0	0, 4
Group prototype without Norway	0.5	1.5, 1.25
Group prototype with Norway	0.4	1.2, 1.8

Following the double contrast formula, in order to decide which country in the group is most similar to Austria, we have first to contrast the Austria object with the virtual prototype, and then apply the same operation to the other countries to form a compatible *comparison ground*. In the group without Norway, we need to specify Austria's political dimension, as the group is split perfectly in two; for the spatial dimension, Austria is more central in the group, so geography is a bit less pertinent dimension to describe the country. Sweden is selected as the most similar country to Austria because the comparison ground lies on the political index. In the group with Norway, it is more common not to be a communist country (so the political dimension becomes a bit less pertinent), whereas the center goes further North: the geographical dimension becomes more pertinent. For this internal change, Hungary is selected as more similar to Austria.

The search for a satisfactory comparison ground can also explain the experiences in which the **minimality axiom** is not satisfied. The original tests were about recognizing, given a Morse code, the most similar code in a list of codes, including the input one [3]. According to our model, when the input is far from the group prototype it is more difficult to find a reference with which to form a comparison ground: the respondent will correctly identify the same element as the best response to the task. When the input is near to the prototype, another entity may be *satisfactorily* similar to stop the search.

Comparison. Although the models presented by Tversky [2] and Krumhansl [3] might yield as well predictions aligned with these experiences, they require the specification of adequate parameters and, more importantly, the manual selection of features (potentially infinite). Consider two objects that are almost the same, save for a detail that make them crucially different in pertinence to a task: Tversky's contrast model would lead to implausible results, as the weight of common features would outnumber that of distinct features. On the other hand, proposals as that of Krumhansl's have the problem of defining a coherent global distance amongst features. In principle, our proposal is not concerned by these problems: we have not used any parameters; if the conceptual spaces have been correctly constructed, they are grounded to perceptive spaces and respecting the conceptual hierarchies; contrast and similarity are computed without relying on global distances.

5 Conclusion and Further Developments

The paper presents a novel account of contrast and similarity operations to be performed on conceptual spaces. Contrast relies on distances computed along integral dimensions (belonging to independent cognitive domains), capturing dissimilarities between entities on given scales of stimuli. Similarity judgments are modeled instead as double contrasts forming a *comparison ground*, where the distinctive characteristics of a reference are used as contrastors. To our knowledge, such sequential, multi-layered nature of similarity has not been hypothesized before in the literature. The dimensions of psychological spaces, even in the theory of conceptual spaces, are usually elicited via *multi-dimensional scaling* (MDS) techniques applied on people's similarity judgments, presupposing the existence of underlying metrics to be captured by features expressed in a verbal form. These approaches and similar dimensional reduction techniques used in machine learning conflate two aspects of similarity, respectively of perceptual and contrastively analogical nature, that our proposal attempts to distinguish.

Future work is required to complete our specification of contrast: additional semantic parameters, the analytical relationship with merge, and a definition operating on regions.[12] Prototypes were processed here merely as points; how-

---

[12] As the merge operation (+) seems to be captured by *dilation*, we are currently investigating methods to capture contrast (−) considering the dual morphological operator *erosion*: first experiments look promising.

ever, the empirical principle of relevance presented here relies on standard deviation, and for that, it works with a neighborhood of the mean, representative of an underlying group or population. The principle was applied in a binary fashion: either the prototype has no effect on the exemplar, or the prototype counts at par with the exemplar. The next step would be to specify a graded solution, taking into account some regional information of prototypes, captured by standard deviation or other means. We expect the problem has points of contact with the contrast on regions. Parallel to this work, we need to study the interaction of possible definitions of contrast with dependent qualities, to take into account semantically redundant information.

Finally, this work focused on the descriptive aspect of predicate generation, but relevance is not only a matter of best description. At higher level, additional factors play a role, as e.g. the rarity or the emotional response associated to the situation to be described. Understanding how this interplay works will be crucial for generating truly pertinent descriptions.

References

1. Nosofsky, R.: Similarity scaling and cognitive process models. Annu. Rev. Psychol. **43**(1), 25–53 (1992)
2. Tversky, A.: Features of similarity. Am. Psychol. (1977)
3. Krumhansl, C.L.: Concerning the applicability of geometric models to similarity data: The interrelationship between similarity and spatial density. Psychol. Rev. **85**(5), 445–463 (1978)
4. Distel, F., Bloch, I., Atif, J.: Concept dissimilarity based on tree edit distance and morphological dilation. In: 21st European Conference on Artificial Intelligence (ECAI) (2014)
5. Gärdenfors, P.: Conceptual Spaces: The Geometry of Thought. Institute of Technology, Massachusetts (2000)
6. Gärdenfors, P.: The Geometry of Meaning: Semantics Based on Conceptual Spaces. MIT Press, Cambridge (2014)
7. Dessalles, J.-L.: From conceptual spaces to predicates. In: Zenker, F., Gärdenfors, P. (eds.) Applications of Conceptual Spaces. SL, vol. 359, pp. 17–31. Springer, Cham (2015). doi:10.1007/978-3-319-15021-5_2
8. Gärdenfors, P., Williams, M.A.: Reasoning about categories in conceptual spaces. In: IJCAI International Joint Conference on Artificial Intelligence, pp. 385–392 (2001)
9. Raubal, M.: Formalizing conceptual spaces. Formal ontol. Inf. Syst. **114**, 153–164 (2004)
10. Adams, B., Raubal, M.: A metric conceptual space algebra. In: Hornsby, K.S., Claramunt, C., Denis, M., Ligozat, G. (eds.) COSIT 2009. LNCS, vol. 5756, pp. 51–68. Springer, Heidelberg (2009). doi:10.1007/978-3-642-03832-7_4
11. Lieto, A., Radicioni, D.P., Rho, V.: A common-sense conceptual categorization system integrating heterogeneous proxytypes and the dual process of reasoning. In: IJCAI International Joint Conference on Artificial Intelligence, pp. 875–881 (2015)
12. Lewis, M., Lawry, J.: Hierarchical conceptual spaces for concept combination. Artif. Intell. **237**, 204–227 (2016)

13. Adams, B., Raubal, M.: Conceptual Space Markup Language (CSML): Towards the cognitive Semantic Web. In: 2009 IEEE International Conference on Semantic Computing ICSC, pp. 253–260 (2009)
14. Jameel, S., Schockaert, S.: Entity embeddings with conceptual subspaces as a basis for plausible reasoning. In: European Conference on Artificial Intelligence, pp. 1353–1361 (2016)
15. Aisbett, J., Gibbon, G.: A general formulation of conceptual spaces as a meso level representation. Artif. Intell. **133**(1–2), 189–232 (2001)
16. Rokach, L., Maimon, O.: Clustering methods. In: The Data Mining and Knowledge Discovery Handbook, p. 32 (2010)
17. Lesot, M.J.: Typicality-based clustering. Int. J. Inf. Technol. Intell. Comput. **1**(2), 279–292 (2005)
18. Bloch, I.: Spatial reasoning under imprecision using fuzzy set theory, formal logics and mathematical morphology. Int. J. Approx. Reason. **41**(2), 77–95 (2006)

Technical Communications

Alarm Management on a Liquid Bulk Terminal

Bram Aerts, Kylian Van Dessel, and Joost Vennekens[✉]

Department of Computer Science, KU Leuven,
Campus De Nayer, Sint-katelijne-waver, Belgium
joost.vennekens@kuleuven.be

Abstract. This paper reports on a research project to use Artificial Intelligence (AI) technology to reduce the alarm handling workload of control room operators in a terminal in the harbour of Antwerp. Several characteristics of this terminal preclude the use of standard methods, such as root cause analysis. Therefore, we focused attention on the process engineers and developed a system to help these engineers reduce the number of alarms that occur. It consists of two components: one to identify interesting alarms and another to analyse them. For both components, user-friendly visualisations were developed.

1 Introduction

This paper presents work conducted together the company *Agidens* on alarm management for a liquid bulk terminal in the harbour of Antwerp, Belgium. This terminal handles various fluids and gasses. These typically arrive by ship, are transferred on-site tanks, and are later transferred again to trucks, trains or barges. This is done by a complex network of pipelines, valves and pumps.

The terminal is monitored by operators in a control room, who ensure that scheduled tasks are executed as planned. E.g., when a new transfer needs to be started, the operators are responsible for establishing a route between the two endpoints (e.g., from tank to loading station) by opening and closing the appropriate valves. Because of the dangerous products, safety is very important. The installation contains numerous sensors that raise alarms as soon as parameters leave the expected operating conditions. Handling these alarms is a significant part of the workload of the control room operators. Moreover, significant expertise is required to distinguish important alarms from irrelevant ones.

The main goal of this project was to investigate the use of AI technology to improve the alarm handling workload of the operators. Before going into more detail, we discuss some relevant properties of the terminal.

Discontinuous operations. Activity on the terminal consists of different processes, which are typically rather short-lived, lasting at the most a few hours. Moreover, each of these processes (i.e., transfer operations between two end-points) is almost unique, in the sense that even when they share a common origin and

---

Work supported by the Flemish Agency for Innovation by Science and Technology (R&D project IWT140876).

G. Kern-Isberner et al. (Eds.): KI 2017, LNAI 10505, pp. 279–285, 2017.
DOI: 10.1007/978-3-319-67190-1_21

destination, the route between them may be different, as may the product that is being transferred, its temperature or its level in the tank.

Changing circumstances. The terminal is continuously undergoing maintenance and expansion. From one day to the next, the layout of the terminal may therefore be different. Moreover, normal operations are sometimes halted in order to perform these tasks, which may in itself cause a flurry of alarms.

No complete terminal model. Information about the terminal is spread out over different databases. During the project, we investigated whether it would be possible to integrate these databases into a single coherent model. However, the companies involved decided against this, because of the prohibitive cost of constructing such a model and of keeping it up-to-date.

Infrequent and diverse alarms. Roughly 20000 different alarms can be generated in the terminal. Obviously, many of these occur very infrequently.

2   Related Work

It is widely recognised that, in a complex modern industrial environment, the task of operators is growing ever more complex, and that technological support is needed to keep this manageable [5]. Several opportunities exist for Artificial Intelligence technology to play a role in solving this problem.

Many approaches focus on providing real-time advice to the operator about a specific alarm, e.g., by means of a root cause analysis [8]. This kind of functionality typically requires detailed knowledge about the layout of the industrial system that is being monitored [7]. Because, in our case, information about the layout of the terminal is not available, these methods are not applicable for us.

A different approach is to reduce the number of alarms shown to the operators, e.g., by filtering them according to specific rules [4,6,9]. In the course of this project, we extensively discussed this possibility with the operators. However, because of the dangerous nature of the chemicals handled in the terminal, no sufficiently safe policy for hiding alarms could be determined.

3   Project Goals

There are several ways in which the workload of operators might be reduced. Initially, the project considered providing online advice to the operators, to help them handle alarms more quickly. However, this approach was abandoned for a number of reasons. First, in order to give specific advice for a concrete situation, the present condition of the terminal needs to be known. While the status of individual components is known, the lack of a complete model of the terminal means that it is unknown how these components relate to each other. Because of this lack of knowledge, it would be difficult to achieve a high degree of accuracy in the operator advice provided by the system. Second, a closer inspection revealed that the operators typically do not spend a lot of time handling individual alarms.

Since their main focus is on completing the tasks at hand, they typically simply retry the operation, reroute around a damaged component and/or call maintenance. To significantly affect their workload, it is more important to reduce the *number* of alarms that occur in the first place, rather than the *time* spent on each alarm. Third, because of the dangerous products being handled, it is not desirable to actually hide alarms from the operators: the final decision should always be in the hands of a human operator.

For these reasons, we decided not to focus directly on the operators themselves, but to focus instead on the terminal's process engineers. By helping them to better understand which alarms are occurring and why, we can enable these engineers to improve the processes on the terminal, thereby indirectly also reducing the number of alarms that the operators have to deal with.

4   Identifying Interesting Alarms

As a first step towards helping the process engineer reduce the number of alarms, we attempt to identify alarms that are interesting for him to take a closer look at. Discussions with the engineers revealed that two parameters are important for this. First, of course the number of occurrences of an alarm is important: analysing alarms that occur very rarely is probably not a good investment of the engineer's time. Second, our system could create the most added value for the engineers by alerting them to alarms that are lingering in the background. An alarm that occurs repeatedly during a single shift will be reported by the operator and so the process engineer will already be aware of it. However, an alarm that occurs, e.g., only a few times each week, might go unnoticed.

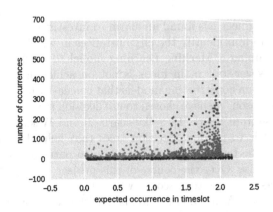

Fig. 1. Visualisation of alarm occurrences (Color figure online)

Based on these two parameters, we developed the visualisation shown in Fig. 1. In this scatter plot, the Y-axis plots the number of occurrences of the alarm. The X-axis attempts to capture the degree to which this is a "lingering

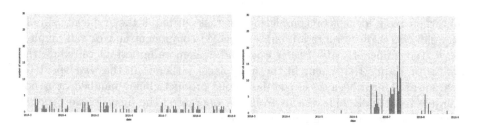

Fig. 2. An alarm with low Poisson λ (left) and one with high λ (right)

alarm". To this end, we fit a Poisson distribution to the occurrence graph of the alarm. Figure 2 shows an example of an alarm for which the parameter λ of the best-fit Poisson distribution is low and one for which it is high. Those with low λ are the kind of "lingering" alarms in which the process engineers are interested.

We define four different areas in the graph: (1) alarms occurring less than once a month (shown in green in Fig. 1); (2) alarms occurring more than once a day (red); (3) other alarms with λ parameter below average, i.e., "lingering" (yellow); (4) other alarms with λ parameter above average (orange).

Our system allows the engineers to construct such graphs for different selections of alarms, by applying various kinds of filtering and grouping operations. In addition, there is also the possibility of constructing a difference-graph for two different selections. This allows to easily detect, e.g., alarms that occur more frequently in a certain time period or in a specific subsystem.

5   Automated Analysis of Alarms

Once the process engineer has found an alarm to investigate further, our system will attempt to help him identify the circumstances in which this alarm occurs. It does this by training a Machine Learning model to predict the occurrence of this alarm. However, our main focus is not on achieving a high prediction accuracy, but rather on constructing models that can easily be interpreted by the engineer. For this reason, we have chosen to use decision tree learning algorithms, in particular, those from Spark [1], Scikit-learn [2] and Weka [3].

Our main goal is to produce decision trees that help the process engineer analyse alarms on the terminal, by alerting him to patterns that he might not have noticed otherwise. Over the course of this project, we closely collaborated with the engineers in order to discover which kind of decision trees are best suited for this purpose. A first observation is that the depth of the tree is crucial: branches of more than three nodes were very difficult for the process engineer to interpret. A second observation is that the engineers are mainly interested in nodes with a large positive bias (i.e., with a greater ratio of covered positive to covered negative examples than the root node). Combining these two observations, the most interpretable trees can be achieved by minimizing the depth of positive leafs.

When discussing the learned decision trees with the process engineers, it became apparent that they still found these hard to interpret. In addition, they were often distracted by less relevant parts of the trees. In an attempt to make the trees easier to interpret, we developed a visualisation with the following features. The thickness of an edge from parent P to child C is proportional to the fraction of positive examples covered by P that is still covered by C. When reading the tree from top to bottom, this allows to easily keep track of in which branches most of the alarms occur. The thickness of a node's border is proportional to the sum of the impurity gains of all the different appearances in the tree of the feature used in this node's decision. This makes it easy to see at a glance which features are most relevant for predicting the occurrence of the alarm, even when these features get used in different parts of the tree. Finally, nodes that cover more than a given number of positive examples are highlighted (Fig. 3).

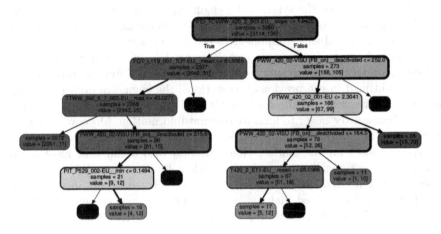

Fig. 3. Visualisation of a decision tree

In addition to these visualisations, we also allow the user to hide parts of the tree, in order not to be distracted by less relevant parts. In particular, it is possible to: (1) hide nodes that cover fewer positive examples than a given threshold; and (2) hide subtrees of nodes whose ratio of covered positive to covered negative examples is outside a specified range.

Even with these visualisations, the engineers continued to find it hard to locate the information they were most interested in (i.e., in which circumstances does the alarm typically occur) and to interpret the information in the tree. Therefore, we also developed an alternative representation, in which a branch of the tree is represented as a rule, in the following format:

The alarm occurred in 73 out of 88 cases in which:
   – the last half hour the value of $sensor_1$ increased by more than 1.9;
   – the value of $sensor_2$ lies between 2.3 and 2.9.
This describes 53% of the 136 occurrences of this alarm.

Such a rule is constructed by iterating over all decisions in the branch. We convert all branches to rules and list them in descending order of number of covered alarms, so that the most interesting rules appear first.

A problem with this method arises when multiple highly correlated features contribute to an alarm: a decision tree will typically contain only one of these, while the process engineer would like to see them all. For this reason, we also allow the user to train an entire *random forest* of multiple decision trees. In the presence of highly correlated features, the randomness of the forest will make different trees use a different feature from the correlated set. We then generate rules for the most interesting branches in this entire random forest.

6   Results

Our system has been tested out in collaboration with the process engineers. For the first component of the system, the engineers found that the statistics and visualisations indeed enabled them to identify interesting "lingering" alarms. They therefore judged this component to provide a relevant added value.

The second component was more challenging. For our initial prototypes, the engineers found it difficult to interpret the decision trees. After the improvements that were outlined in the previous two sections, the engineers eventually had a more positive reaction. In the final prototype that we delivered, the engineers found it significantly easier to identify relevant information. Moreover, they also agreed that the information in the trees was typically indeed indicative of the underlying causes for the alarms. However, they also found that most of this information was typically either already evident to them from their own experience, or that it would have been easily obtained by manually inspecting the logs. They therefore judged that the system did not provide enough added value to warrant its being integrated into their production environment.

7   Conclusions

This paper reports on a research project in collaboration with the company *Agidens* and an oil tanking terminal in the harbour of Antwerp, Belgium. Our goal was to investigate the use of Artificial Intelligence technology to reduce the workload of control room operators. Several characteristics of this terminal make it impossible or undesirable to apply standard methods, such as decision support by means of root cause analysis, or rule-based alarm reduction.

Therefore, we focused attention on the process engineers, in order to help them reduce the number of alarms that occur. We developed a system consisting of two components: the first visualises the alarms with the goal of allowing the process engineers to identify lingering alarms that may be beneficial to investigate; the second applies decision tree/forest learning methods in order to detect patterns that might help the process engineers figure out the general causes for certain kinds of alarms. For this purpose, interpretability of the learned models is crucial. We therefore developed different visualisations of the models.

When evaluating the prototype of the system, the engineers saw a clear benefit in the first component. The second component was found to be usable and to produce relevant results, but provided only limited added value.

References

1. spark.apache.org/mllib/
2. http://scikit-learn.org/
3. http://www.cs.waikato.ac.nz/ml/weka/spark.apache.org/mllib
4. Ahnlund, J., Bergquist, T., Spaanenburg, L.: Rule-based reduction of alarm signals in industrial control. J. Intell. Fuzzy Syst. **14**(2), 73–84 (2003)
5. Dubois, L., Fort, J.-M., Mack, P., Ryckaert, L.: Advanced logic for alarm and event processing: Methods to reduce cognitive load for control room operators. IFAC Proc. Vol. **43**(13), 158–163 (2010)
6. Gogos, C., Alefragis, P., Housos, E.: Sensor enabled rule based alarm system for the agricultural industry. In 12th IEEE conference on Emerging Technologies & Factory Automation, pp. 912–915 (2007)
7. Thambirajah, J., Benabbas, L., Bauer, M., Thornhill, N.F.: Cause-and-effect analysis in chemical processes utilizing XML, plant connectivity and quantitative process history. Comput. Chem. Eng. **33**(2), 503–512 (2009)
8. Wang, K., Xu, J., Zhu, D.: Online root-cause analysis of alarms in discrete Bayesian networks with known structures. In: Proceeding of the 11th World Congress on Intelligent Control and Automation (2014)
9. Yu, M., Yashio, H., Kikukawa, J., Joo, N.: Rule based intelligent alarm management system for digital surveillance system. US Patent 7,352,279 (2008)

Action Model Acquisition Using Sequential Pattern Mining

Ankuj Arora[✉], Humbert Fiorino, Damien Pellier, and Sylvie Pesty

Univ. Grenoble Alpes, CNRS, Grenoble INP, LIG, 38000 Grenoble, France
{ankuj.arora,humbert.fiorino,damien.pellier,
sylvie.pesty}@univ-grenoble-alpes.fr

Abstract. This paper presents an approach to learn the agents' action model (action blueprints orchestrating transitions of the system state) from plan execution sequences. It does so by representing intra-action and inter-action dependencies in the form of a maximum satisfiability problem (MAX-SAT), and solving it with a MAX-SAT solver to reconstruct the underlying action model. Unlike previous MAX-SAT driven approaches, our chosen dependencies exploit the relationship between consecutive actions, rendering more accurately learnt models in the end.

1 Introduction

In the planning community, intelligent agents require an action model to plan and solve real world problems. It is, however, becoming increasingly cumbersome to codify this model, and is more efficient to learn these action blueprints from plan execution sequences. This learning provides an opportunity for the evolution of the model towards a version more consistent and adapted to its environment, augmenting the possibility of success of the plans. Our approach, called SRM-Learn (**S**equential **R**ules-based **M**odel **Learn**er), uses alternating state-action representations as input to learn an action model as the output. It proceeds as follows: it represents a set of intra-action and inter-action dependencies in the form of constraints of a weighted maximum satisfiability problem. This problem is then solved with the help of a MAX-SAT solver, the solved constraints being used to reconstruct the underlying action model. This paper is divided into the following sections: we present some related work in Sect. 2, and define our learning problem in Sect. 3. We then detail our approach in Sect. 4, and present our empirical evaluations in Sect. 5. We conclude the paper with some perspectives and future work in Sect. 6.

2 Related Work

Learning action models in the field of Automated Planning (AP) has a considerable history. Some prominently used machine learning (ML) techniques to learn action models include: inductive techniques (e.g. PELA [7]), reinforcement learning techniques (e.g. LOPE [6]) and so on. More specific to our case,

© Springer International Publishing AG 2017
G. Kern-Isberner et al. (Eds.): KI 2017, LNAI 10505, pp. 286–292, 2017.
DOI: 10.1007/978-3-319-67190-1_22

various approaches have used the MAX-SAT framework to learn deterministic actions (e.g. ARMS [10]), macro-actions [12], models in Hierarchical Task Networks (HTNs) [11] and so on. In particular, our approach is on the same lines of ARMS, which also generates intra-action and inter-action constraints (mined with the Apriori algorithm [1]). As compared to ARMS, we hypothesize and experimentally demonstrate that short term dependencies among consecutively executing action pairs are a stronger indicator of correlation between actions, leading to improved learning.

3   Preliminaries and Problem Formulation

We begin by providing some definitions of key concepts. *Predicates* are properties that constitute the world state and actions. Here, each action $a \in A$ where $A = \{a_1, a_2, \ldots, a_n\}$, n being the maximum number of actions in the domain. An *action model* m is the blueprint of all the domain-applicable actions, each action defined as an aggregation of: (i) the action name (with zero or more typed variables as parameters), and (ii) predicates in the form of preconditions (*pre* list i.e. predicates whose satisfaction determines the applicability of the action) and effects (*add* and del list i.e. predicates added and deleted respectively from the current world state by action execution). A *plan* is a sequence of actions $\pi = [a_1, a_2, \ldots, a_n]$ that drives the system from the initial state to a goal state. Each such sequence consisting of (i) the initial state of the world, (ii) alternating action and state representations, and (iii) a desired goal state; constitutes a *trace* of a *trace set* T. A *sequential rule* $a_x \rightarrow a_y$ is a relationship between two actions $a_x, a_y \in A$ such that if a_x occurs in a sequence, then a_y will occur successively in the same sequence. Two measures are defined for sequential rules, these are (i) $support\,(a_x \rightarrow a_y) = |a_x \rightarrow a_y|/|T|$, and (ii) $confidence\,(a_x \rightarrow a_y) = |a_x \rightarrow a_y|/|a_x|$. Given the aforementioned information, our learning problem is as follows: given a set of plan traces T, the objective is to learn the underlying action model m which best explains the observed plan traces. AP uses a certain number of domains from the International Planning Competition (IPC), out of which we use the *gripper* domain to illustrate SRM-Learn (see Fig. 1). In this domain, the task of the robot is to move an object from one room to another, the principal domain actions being *move, pick* and *drop*.

4   Approach

Our approach is divided into three phases (see Fig. 2) which are elaborated in the forthcoming subsections.

4.1   Annotation and Generalization

Firstly, each trace is taken one by one, and each action as well as each predicate from the initial, goal and intermediate states is scanned to substitute the

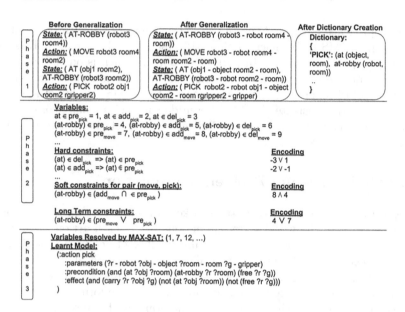

	Before Generalization	After Generalization	After Dictionary Creation

P h a s e 1	**State:** (AT-ROBBY (robot3 room4))
	Action: (MOVE robot3 room4 room2)
	State: (AT (obj1 room2), AT-ROBBY (robot3 room2))
	Action: (PICK robot2 obj1 room2 rgripper2)
		State: (AT-ROBBY (robot3 - robot room4 - room))
		Action: (MOVE robot3 - robot room4 - room room2 - room)
		State: (AT (obj1 - object room2 - room), AT-ROBBY (robot3 - robot room2 - room))
		Action: (PICK robot2 - robot obj1 - object room2 - room rgripper2 - gripper)
			Dictionary:
			{
			'PICK': (at (object, room), at-robby (robot, room))
			..
			}

$$P h a s e 2$$

Variables:
$at \in pre_{pick} = 1$, $at \in add_{pick} = 2$, $at \in del_{pick} = 3$
$(at\text{-}robby) \in pre_{pick} = 4$, $(at\text{-}robby) \in add_{pick} = 5$, $(at\text{-}robby) \in del_{pick} = 6$
$(at\text{-}robby) \in pre_{move} = 7$, $(at\text{-}robby) \in add_{move} = 8$, $(at\text{-}robby) \in del_{move} = 9$
...

Hard constraints:	**Encoding**
$(at) \in del_{pick} => (at) \in pre_{pick}$	-3 ∨ 1
$(at) \in add_{pick} => (at) \notin pre_{pick}$	-2 ∨ -1
...	

Soft constraints for pair (move, pick):	**Encoding**
$(at\text{-}robby) \in (add_{move} \cap \in pre_{pick})$	8 ∧ 4

Long Term constraints:	**Encoding**
$(at\text{-}robby) \in (pre_{move} \lor pre_{pick})$	4 ∨ 7

P h a s e 3

Variables Resolved by MAX-SAT: (1, 7, 12, ...)
Learnt Model:
  (:action pick
    :parameters (?r - robot ?obj - object ?room - room ?g - gripper)
    :precondition (and (at ?obj ?room) (at-robby ?r ?room) (free ?r ?g))
    :effect (and (carry ?r ?obj ?g) (not (at ?obj ?room)) (not (free ?r ?g)))
)

Fig. 1. Illustration of our learning problem. The learnt action model is written in PDDL (Planning Domain Description Language) [9] and conforms to the semantics of STRIPS [3].

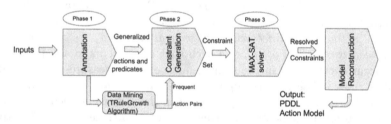

Fig. 2. Approach phases of SRMLearn

instantiated parameters with corresponding variable types, producing generalized actions and predicates. We then associate each action with its relevant predicates, where a predicate is said to be relevant to an action if they share the same variable types. The set of relevant predicates to an action $a_i \in A$ can be denoted as $relPre_{a_i}$. With generalized actions and predicates, a candidate action dictionary is built for the actions, where the key is the name of the action a_i and the value is a list of all relevant predicates to that action $relPre_{a_i}$ (see Fig. 1).

4.2 Constraint Generation

In this phase, we account for certain intra-action hard constraints and inter-action soft constraints.

Hard Constraints. In order to satisfy the semantics defined in Sect. 3, each action in A must satisfy certain *intra-action constraints*. Thus, for each action $a_i \in [a_1, a_2, \ldots, a_n]$ and each relevant predicate $p \in relPre_{a_i}$: (i) p cannot be in the *add* list and the *del* list for the same action, and (ii) p cannot be in the *add* list and the *pre* list for the same action.

Soft Constraints. The soft constraints among the actions may be short-term or long-term.

Short-Term Constraints. We hypothesize that if a sequential pair of actions appears frequently in the traces, there must be a reason for their frequent co-existence. We thus employ an algorithm called TRuleGrowth [4,5] used for mining sequential rules common to several sequences that appear in a trace set. Given (1) a trace set T, and (2) two user-specified thresholds, namely *support* and *confidence* as input, TRuleGrowth outputs all sequential rules having a support and confidence higher than *support* and *confidence* respectively. Starting with 20 traces, we consistently double the number of traces till we reach 200. In the process, we identify frequent sequential rules (action pairs) which consistently maintain the *confidence* and *support* over an increasing number of traces. These frequent pairs can be suspected to share a "semantic" relationship among themselves. These relationships are quantified by the ARMS [10] system, and serve as heuristics to explain the frequent co-existence of these actions. These heuristics produce good results in the case of the ARMS system, which serves as incentive for re-using them. More precisely, if there is an action pair $(a_i, a_j), 0 \le i < j \le (n-1)$ where n is the total number of actions in the plan; and pre_i, add_i and del_i represent a_i's *pre*, *add* and *del* list, respectively:

- A predicate p such that $(p \in relPre_{a_i}, p \in relPre_{a_j})$ added by the first action $(p \in add_i)$, which serves as a prerequisite for the second action a_j $(p \in pre_j)$, cannot be deleted by the first action a_i.
- A relevant predicate p $(p \in relPre_{a_i}, p \in relPre_{a_j})$ added by the first action a_i also appears in the *pre* list of the second action a_j.
- A predicate p that is deleted by the first action a_i is added by the second action a_j.
- The above plan constraints can be combined into one constraint and restated as: $\exists p((p \in (pre_i \cap pre_j) \wedge p \notin (del_i)) \vee (p \in (add_i \cap pre_j)) \vee (p \in (del_i \cap add_j)))$.

Long-Term Constraints. We introduce this set of constraints to explore the relationships between a chain of actions constituting a plan.

- If a predicate p is observed to be true for the last action a_n of a plan sequence and p is a relevant predicate to $a_1, \ldots, a_i, \ldots, a_n$ where $0 \le i < n$, then the predicate p must exist in the *add* list of a_i. This can be expressed as $p \in add_{a_1} \vee add_{a_2} \vee \ldots \vee add_{a_{n-1}}$.
- Predicates constituting the initial state of the plan are preconditions of the first executed action in the plan [10].

– If a predicate p is observed to be true in the intermediate states right before an action a_k of a plan sequence, and p is a relevant predicate to $a_{k+1}, \ldots, a_n$, then the predicate p must serve as a precursor to these following actions. This can be expressed as $p \in (pre_{a_{k+1}} \lor pre_{a_{k+2}} \lor \ldots \lor pre_{a_n})$.

5   Evaluation

We evaluate the accuracy of SPMSAT. For this, we construct a CNF formula consisting of a conjunction of the hard and soft constraints generated in Phase 2, each associated with a specific weight. The weights of the hard constraints and the long term constraints are "hyperparameters" which must be continuously tweaked and fine tuned to obtain the most accurate model. The weight of the short term constraints are equivalent to the support of the rules which are associated with the frequent action pairs obtained with the TRuleGrowth algorithm. The support is chosen because it is an indicator of the frequency of the action pair over the entire trace set. This CNF formula is then fed to a weighted MAX-SAT solver which finds a truth assignment that maximizes the total weight of the satisfied constraints, thus producing as output the constraints which evaluate to true. The true constraints are used to reconstruct the entire model, termed as the empirical model. This model is compared with artificial models which are considered as the ground truth. Let $diffpre_{a_i}$ represent the syntactic difference in pre lists of action a_i in the ground truth model and the empirical model. Each time the pre list of the ideal model presents a predicate which is not in the pre list of the empirical model, the count $diffpre_{a_i}$ is incremented by one. Similarly, each time the pre list of the empirical model presents a predicate which is not in the pre list of the ideal model, the count $diffpre_{a_i}$ is incremented by one. Similar counts are estimated for the add and del lists as $diffadd_{a_i}$ and $diffdel_{a_i}$ respectively. This total count is then divided by the number of relevant constraints for that particular action $relCons_{a_i}$ to obtain the cumulative error per action. This error is summed up for every action and averaged over the number of actions of the model to obtain an average error E for the entire model.

The cumulative error for the model is thus represented by:

$$E = \frac{1}{n} \sum_{i=1}^{n} \frac{diffPre_{a_i} + diffAdd_{a_i} + diffDel_{a_i}}{relCons_{a_i}} \tag{1}$$

We evaluate the performance of SRMLearn with our implementation of ARMS over five domains as follows: for each of the domains, we set the number of traces as (20, 50, 100, 200), generate and solve constraints with the help of two SAT solvers ([2,8]), and calculate the cumulative error for SRMLearn and ARMS. It should be noted that the key difference between SRMLearn and ARMS lies in SRMLearn's additional *long term constraints* and chosen data mining algorithm (TRuleGrowth). The evaluation domains include *depots, parking, mprime, gripper* and *satellite* and are represented in the Figs. 3, 4, 5, 6 and 7.

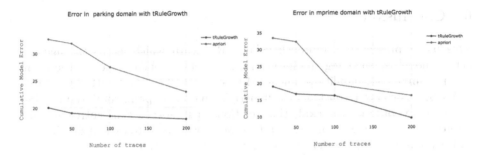

Fig. 3. Error comparison in *parking* domain

Fig. 4. Error comparison in *mprime* domain

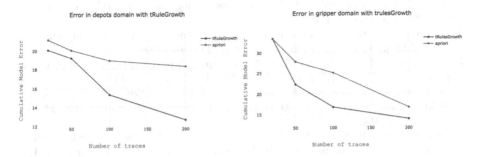

Fig. 5. Error comparison in *depots* domain

Fig. 6. Error comparison in *gripper* domain

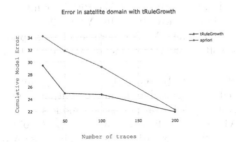

Fig. 7. Error comparison in *satellite* domain

As can be seen, the error percentages with SRMLearn are lower than with ARMS, indicating that frequent sequential action pairs mined with the TRule-Growth algorithm demonstrate a stronger correlation than those mined with the Apriori algorithm.

6 Conclusion

This paper presents an approach called SRMLearn which learns the agents' action model by encoding the inter and intra-action dependencies in the form of a maximum satisfiability problem (MAX-SAT) and solves it with a weighted MAX-SAT solver to reconstruct the underlying model. Experimental results reinforce our hypothesis that exploiting relationships between consecutive actions improves the learning accuracy. In future work, we intend to extend SRMLearn to learn temporal action models comprising durative actions.

References

1. Agrawal, R., Srikant, R.: Fast algorithms for mining association rules. In: VLDB, vol. 1215, pp. 487–499 (1994)
2. Borchers, B., Furman, J.: A two-phase exact algorithm for MAX-SAT and weighted MAX-SAT problems. J. Comb. Optim. **2**(4), 299–306 (1998)
3. Fikes, R.E., Nilsson, N.J.: STRIPS: A new approach to the application of theorem proving to problem solving. Artif. Intell. **2**(3–4), 189–208 (1971)
4. Fournier-Viger, P., Gomariz, A., Gueniche, T., Soltani, A., Wu, C.W., Tseng, V.S.: SPMF: a Java open-source pattern mining library. J. Mach. Learn. Res. **15**(1), 3389–3393 (2014)
5. Fournier-Viger, P., Wu, C.-W., Tseng, V.S., Nkambou, R.: Mining sequential rules common to several sequences with the window size constraint. In: Kosseim, L., Inkpen, D. (eds.) AI 2012. LNCS, vol. 7310, pp. 299–304. Springer, Heidelberg (2012). doi:10.1007/978-3-642-30353-1_27
6. García-Martínez, R., Borrajo, D.: An integrated approach of learning, planning, and execution. J. Intell. Rob. Syst. **29**(1), 47–78 (2000)
7. Jiménez, S., Fernández, F., Borrajo, D.: The PELA architecture: integrating planning and learning to improve execution. In: AAAI (2008)
8. Kautz, H.A., Selman, B., Jiang, Y.: A general stochastic approach to solving problems with hard and soft constraints. Satisfiability Probl. Theor. Appl. **35**, 573–586 (1996)
9. McDermott, D., Ghallab, M., Howe, A., Knoblock, C., Ram, A., Veloso, M., Weld, D., Wilkins, D.: PDDL-the planning domain definition language (1998)
10. Yang, Q., Wu, K., Jiang, Y.: Learning action models from plan examples using weighted MAX-SAT. Artif. Intell. **171**(2–3), 107–143 (2007)
11. Yoon, S., Kambhampati, S.: Towards model-lite planning: A proposal for learning & planning with incomplete domain models. In: ICAPS Workshop on Artificial Intelligence Planning and Learning (2007)
12. Zhuo, H.H., Nguyen, T.A., Kambhampati, S.: Refining incomplete planning domain models through plan traces. In: IJCAI, pp. 2451–2458, August 2013

Steering Plot Through Personality and Affect: An Extended BDI Model of Fictional Characters

Leonid Berov[(⊠)]

University of Osnabrück, 49078 Osnabrück, Germany
lberov@uos.de

Abstract. The present paper identifies an important narrative framework that has not yet been employed to implement computational story telling systems. Grounded in this theory, it suggests to use a BDI architecture extended with a personality-based affective appraisal component to model fictional characters. A proof of concept is shown to be capable of generating the plot of a folk tale. This example is used to explore the system's parameters and the plot-space that is spanned by them.

Keywords: Computational storytelling · Multi-agent systems · BDI · Narratology · Fictional characters

1 Introduction

The ability to invent stories is a distinctly human, creative act [1], so its computational modelling lies in the scope of the AI research program. Computational storytelling is the study of algorithms that are capable of automatically generating fictional narratives, and academic systems have been more or less continuously researched for the last 40 years [2].

When analysed from a narratological perspectives, many systems implement a functionalist view on fictional character grounded in structuralist narratology [3]. That is, they treat characters as interchangeable action-sources mainly defined over their function for the plot (e.g. hero, helper or opponent) [4]—a view that subjugates character to plot. The functionalist view is challenged by some post-classical narratologies that describe characters as distinct elements of a fictional world, having internal states that cause the characters' choice of action [5–7]. From such a perspective, plot emerges from character's actions, instead of the actions being dictated by the plot. While some storytelling systems that subjugate plot to character have been put forward [8,9], to the best of my knowledge none have been related to the respective narratological research. Since it is my conviction that computational models can greatly benefit from the rigorous analysis performed by narratologists, the present paper proposes a new character-centric representational formalism for stories, grounded in two particularly promising post-classical theories: Marie-Laure Ryan's approach [5], which describes fictional characters, and how plot emerges from their actions, in terms of a possible worlds framework; and Alan Palmer's [7] extension, which outlines

© Springer International Publishing AG 2017
G. Kern-Isberner et al. (Eds.): KI 2017, LNAI 10505, pp. 293–299, 2017.
DOI: 10.1007/978-3-319-67190-1_23

in great detail narrative phenomena resulting from the functioning of fictional minds. The present paper argues that a Multi-Agent Simulation (MAS), operating over a Belief-Desire-Intention (BDI) architecture [10,11] extended with a personality-based affective appraisal system [12], offers itself for a computational modelling of such a narrative framework.

It should be noted that by doing that the paper will focus on modelling narrative phenomena and not on the process of a creatively generating new narratives. The reason for this is the assumption that the process of generating stories will become easier once a rich representational formalisms for stories themselves is in place. For this to be the case, the representation should address two questions: (1) which parameters affect the course of the story, and (2) how can the quality of a particular story be measured. Hence, a first evaluation of the resulting system is performed by showing how it can be used to to generate the plot of the folk tale "The Little Red Hen"[1], and by investigating what effect changes in parameter values have.

2   Narratological Background

Two principle components of a narrative can be distinguished. Plot is the "content plane": a causally ordered series of events, potentially happening in parallel at multiple locations (what is told). Discourse is the "expression plane": the linear representation of events in a text, using stylistic devices like flash-backs, flash-forwards and point of view (how it is told) [13]. Most computational storytelling research has been focused on plot [14], a trend which I will follow.

Possible Worlds Framework: Ryan [5,15] describes narratives as spanning a narrative universe that consists of a factual domain created by the narrator: the Textual Actual World (TAW); and a set of modal ('private') worlds created by the fictional characters.

The TAW "is a succession of different states and events which together form a history. [...] TAW also comprises a set of general laws that determine the range of possible future developments [...]" [5].

The modal domains are epistemic, axiological and deontic representations of TAW by each character: their knowledge, wishes and obligations. The Knowledge (K) World contains all propositions regarding a character's beliefs about the narrative universe: the TAW or other character's private worlds. While K-Worlds can be incomplete or conflicting regarding the narrative universe, for a character they form their subjective, complete reality. The Wish (W) World "capture[s] how a character would like the [TAW] to be" [15], it contains propositions she wants to be true (or false), like an undesired state or a desired event. W worlds can be inconsistent when a character's wishes are mutually exclusive, or conflicting with the narrative universe when propositions in TAW have a different truth value than desired. The Obligation (O) World of a character is "[...] a system of

---

[1] http://www.home.uni-osnabrueck.de/leberov/little_red_hen.htm.

commitments and prohibitions defined by social rules and moral principles" [5]. It contains propositions that have to be true (the obligatory) or false (the pro-hibited) and can again be conflicting with the state of the narrative universe or inconsistent with itself.

Characters are "individuals whose actions, experience, and destiny form the central concern of narrative fiction" [15]. They select one of the not-actualized propositions in their O or W Worlds (a goal) and formulate a plan, based on their K-World, in order to change its truth value in TAW. Thus, fictional characters in Ryan's framework are fully constituted through their inner states, and the plans they formulate depending on these states. Their actions result in state changes in TAW and by that create the plot.

Fictional Minds and Actions: Following the theory so far, characters should always take the same actions if they have the same beliefs, wishes and obligations. However, e.g. in "The Little Red Hen" one character chooses to act upon a wish, while another acts upon an obligation although both are in the same situation.

Based on cognitive science theories about real minds Palmer [7] discusses how fictional minds are reconstructed from discourse, and by that creates a teleological model of these minds that can be used to address the above problem on a plot level. Like Ryan he points out that physical actions have a mental side rooted in beliefs and desires, but also notes two other significant phenomena: One is that different action tendencies can be a result of differences in personality, while the other is that the reasoning necessary for any type of mind functioning causes emotions, which in turn affect the selection of goals and by that also a character's actions. Palmer also points out that emotion and personality are tightly interconnected because the latter provide tendencies not only in action but also in affect.

With these insights at hand the problem above can be addressed by attribut-ing different personalities to the characters of "The Little Red Hen" and observ-ing that their planning strategy takes into account action tendencies based on these personalities and on affect. The resulting framework is not only practi-cal, but also a reasonable synthesis because, as Palmer himself points out, his approach is an extension of Ryan's work, especially on embedded narratives.

3   Implementation of a Character Architecture

There are several reasons for implementing the outlined narrative framework using a BDI [11] approach. First, a strong conceptual overlap exists, since both are rooted in possible worlds semantics [10] and explicitly model beliefs, inten-tions and plans. Second, modelling fictional characters as rational agents and TAW as environment allows plot to emerge from the interaction of agents with each other and the environment. Third, the BDI architecture allows for a bal-ancing between reactive and goal-directed behavior which makes it possible to model the results of conflict through plan failures and re-planing. For the present implementation the `Jason` BDI framework was selected due to its active development and further useful features like speech-acts and strong negation. It is grounded in an (extended) BDI-logic as per Rao and Georgeff and uses procedural reasoning techniques [16].

The structural properties of characters are modelled as follows. The K World of a character is represented through an agent's belief base. Incompleteness and (partial) incorrectness are supported using the open-word assumption and by allowing agent's beliefs to be incorrect, for instance due to an unreliable perception-function. A W World can be represented through its set of desires. This allows modelling inconsistent W Worlds, since the set of desires that have not yet been selected as intentions can contain conflicting propositions. The O World can be represented using a combination of beliefs and desires: the belief that the agent is expected to change the truth value of a proposition, and the corresponding desire to change it. Since the set of desires can be inconsistent, such a solution does not preclude a representation of conflicts between W and O Worlds. The adoption of a goal and selection of a plan to achieve it are performed by the BDI interpreter [11].

The standard BDI reasoning cycle can be extended with an affective component grounded in the Five Factor Model of personality [17], as proposed by Alfonso [12]. This means adding several steps to the reasoning algorithm, which perform affective appraisal of internal and external events using emotions from the OCC catalogue [18]. This emotions are aggregated into a multi-dimensional mood vector that represents the agent's medium-term affective state. Personality is used to determine the agent's default mood and influences the mood update function. The present approach implements the control loop proposed by Alfonso (see [12], Fig. 3) in three regards: (1) it changes the function that is responsible for selecting intentions from desires, to take into account personality instead of mood 11: $I \leftarrow filter(B, D, I, P)$, (2) it adds the current mood as a source of new desires 7: $D \leftarrow get\_options(B, I, M)$ and (3) it keeps track of the agents that caused a mood (its targets) via the targets of emotions.

Such an architecture is sufficient to address the phenomena explicitly mentioned in Sect. 2. However, to model "The Little Red Hen" one additional phenomenon needs to be addressed: communication. To model a direct information exchange between agents, `Jason`'s speech-act formalisation [16] is employed. In particular, the system implements the semantics of several speech act types: `(un)tell`, `(un)achieve`, `(un)tellHow`, `ask(One|All|How)`, which are all asynchronous apart from `ask`. This set was extended with a synchronous version of `achieve` in order to enable the communicative organization of collaborative action. The reception of a speech act generates an internal event, which is processed in the usual way.

4   Evaluation

For evaluation purposes a limited version of the character architecture was implemented to model a set of fictional characters from whose interactions the plot of the well known folk tale "The Little Red Hen" can emerge. The tale was selected because it involves all of the relevant phenomena, without requiring an elaborate environment modeling.

The environment model is implemented in Java and provides methods for all agent actions: plant/1, tend/1, harvest/1, grind/1 and bake/1, as well as a default farming/0 action and a no-op relax/0 action. Executing the farming action several times lets the diligent agent find a grain of wheat, which is added to its inventory. The environment maintains the current state of the wheat as well as the agent's inventories, which are accessible to the agents through perceptions. Owners of an item have access to an eat/1 action, which removes the (edible) target item from their inventory, and a share/2 action, which cornucopiously puts a copy of the target item in the patients inventory.

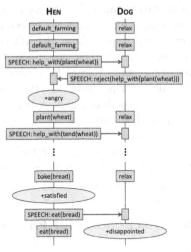

Fig. 1. Extract from the plot diagram created by an execution of the implemented system. Depicts actions performed, and inner events experienced, by agents (excluding beliefs for brevity).

The characters are modeled using four agents operating on the above architecture, with access to the same plan library and initial belief base. The personality of the hen is high on the conscientiousness (C), neuroticism (N) and extraversion (E) traits, while being medium on agreeableness (A). The personalities of the cat, pig and cow are low on the C and A traits.

All agents have the obligation to perform farming work, however this is selected as an intention only by agents with a sufficiently high C trait. Finding a wheat grain activates the desire to produce bread, for which an appropriate plan exists in the library. This plan includes the execution of several actions, which are noted as laborious in the belief base. Agents high on the E trait have a meta desire to request help from other agents using a synchronous achieve speech act, before executing laborious tasks alone. Such a request can be either accepted or rejected by the receiver, based on its A trait. The former case elicits a gratitude emotion when appraised by the sender, while the latter case elicits anger [19]. If the mood of an agent is strongly negative on the pleasure dimension, high on the arousal dimension and has targets, this activates a desire to punish the targets. One of the possible plans for punishment can be triggered when the agent is in possession of an edible item, in which case it uses an achieve speech act to tell the targets to perform the eat(Edible) action, but does not share the edible, which makes the action impossible for the receivers, and results in a disappointment emotion.

Unsurprisingly, executing the MAS generates the intended plot (see Fig. 1). More interestingly, however, the system allows the user to explore[2] a plot-space by modifying the characters' personalities: (1) If the **hen**'s C trait is low, she prefers to **relax** and no plot emerges. (2) If her N trait is low her mood stabilizes faster and she does not develop a punishment desire. (3) If her E trait is low she does never request help, doesn't get rejected and hence develops no punishment desire. (4) In the last two cases, if also her A trait is high, the positive emotions resulting from a successful creation of bread lead to a mood high on the pleasure dimension, which activates the desire to share bread with all other agents. (5) If another agent has a high A trait it complies with the help requests and doesn't get punished. (6) If at least two others have a high A trait, the **hen**'s positive emotions outweigh the negative ones, and she shares bread with all other agents.

It is worth noting that the last case results in an interesting plot where a lazy freeloader benefits from a benevolent society—a moral directly opposed to the one of the original tale.

5   Discussion and Future Work

Two narrative theories presented above argue that fictional characters can be modeled based on the following narrative phenomena: beliefs, wishes, obligations, personality, affect and planning. Plot is taken to be a secondary phenomenon that emerges from character actions and environment happenings. Taking these observations, the present paper suggests a BDI architecture extended with a personality-based affective appraisal system to model fictional characters. It shows that the resulting system is capable of generating the plot of a folk tale. The main parameters of the system so far are the five personality traits of each agent, which span a plot-space that includes at least six alternative plots. By that it illustrates how plot generation can be steered through personality in a simulative system, while also generating the narrative phenomenon of affect.

The presented system needs to be able to model a broad range of narratives. For that the character architecture needs to be extended to cover further narrative phenomena: Ryan highlights the importance of reasoning about other agents reasoning processes, in order to capture (double) deception. Palmer highlights the importance of a nuanced representation of social interactions. Furthermore, Ryan's work includes a theory of plot-quality based on embedded narratives— unrealized plans and counterfactual propositions in characters' private worlds. Thus, the next important step in the development of the proposed system is to implement a plot-quality measure based on internal data generated by the agent's reasoning cycle. By doing that the proposed story model would define a set of parameters that control plot generation as well as a quality measure to evaluate particular instances of plot, and could thus prove a useful representational formalism for computational storytelling systems.

---

[2] The exploration was performed by hand because the parameter space is fairly small: 4 characters with 4 relevant 3-valued personality traits. However, nothing precludes an automatic approach to generate all permutations for a bigger use case.

Acknowledgements. The author is grateful for support for this work provided by an Alexander von Humboldt Ph.D. fellowship funded by an Anneliese Maier-Forschungspreis awarded to Mark Turner.

References

1. Dessalles, J.L.: Why We Talk: The Evolutionary Origins of Language. Oxford University Press, New York (2007)
2. Gervás, P.: Computational approaches to storytelling and creativity. AI Mag. **30**(3), 49–62 (2009)
3. Cavazza, M., Pizzi, D.: Narratology for interactive storytelling: a critical introduction. In: Göbel, S., Malkewitz, R., Iurgel, I. (eds.) TIDSE 2006. LNCS, vol. 4326, pp. 72–83. Springer, Heidelberg (2006). doi:10.1007/11944577_7
4. Jannidis, F.: Character. In: Hühn, P., Meister, J.C., Pier, J., Schmid, W. (eds.) The Living Handbook of Narratology. Hamburg University, Hamburg (2013)
5. Ryan, M.L.: Possible Worlds, Artificial Intelligence, and Narrative Theory. Indiana University Press, Bloomington (1991)
6. Fludernik, M.: Towards a 'Natural' Narratology. Routledge London, London (1996)
7. Palmer, A.: Fictional Minds. University of Nebraska Press, Lincoln (2004)
8. Meehan, J.R.: Tale-spin, an interactive program that writes stories. In: Proceedings of the 5th International Joint Conference on Artificial Intelligence, pp. 91–98 (1977)
9. Swartjes, I.M.T., Theune, M.: The virtual storyteller: story generation by simulation. In: Proceedings of the 20th Belgian-Netherlands Conference on Artificial Intelligence (2008)
10. Rao, A.S., Georgeff, M.P.: Modeling rational agents within a BDI-Architecture. In: Proceedings of the International Conference on Principles of Knowlegde Representation and Reasoning, pp. 473–484 (1991)
11. Rao, A.S., Georgeff, M.P.: BDI agents: from theory to practice. In: Proceedings of the 1st International Conference of Multiagent Systems, pp. 312–319 (1995)
12. Alfonso, B., Vivancos, E., Botti, V.J.: An open architecture for affective traits in a BDI agent. In: Proceedings of the 6th International Conference on Evolutionary Computation Theory and Applications, Rome, Italy, pp. 320–325 (2014)
13. Prince, G.: A Dictionary of Narratology. University of Nebraska Press, Lincoln (2003)
14. Harmon, S., Jhala, A.: Revisiting computational models of creative storytelling based on imaginative recall. In: Schoenau-Fog, H., Bruni, L.E., Louchart, S., Baceviciute, S. (eds.) ICIDS 2015. LNCS, vol. 9445, pp. 170–178. Springer, Cham (2015). doi:10.1007/978-3-319-27036-4_16
15. Ryan, M.L.: Possible worlds. In: Hühn, P., Meister, J.C., Pier, J., Schmid, W. (eds.) The Living Handbook of Narratology. Hamburg University, Hamburg (2013)
16. Bordini, R.H., Hübner, J.F., Wooldridge, M.: Programming Multi-agent Systems in AgentSpeak Using Jason, vol. 8. John Wiley & Sons, New York (2007)
17. McCrae, R.R., John, O.P.: An introduction to the five-factor model and its applications. J. Pers. **60**(2), 175–215 (1992)
18. Ortony, A., Clore, G.L., Collins, A.: The Cognitive Structure of Emotions. Cambridge University Press, Cambridge (1990)
19. Gebhard, P.: ALMA: a layered model of affect. In: Proceedings of the Fourth International Joint Conference on Autonomous Agents and Multiagent Systems, pp. 29–36. ACM (2005)

Ontological Modelling of a Psychiatric Clinical Practice Guideline

Daniel Gorín[1], Malte Meyn[1], Alexander Naumann[2], Miriam Polzer[1],
Ulrich Rabenstein[1], and Lutz Schröder[1(✉)]

[1] Friedrich-Alexander-Universität Erlangen-Nürnberg, Erlangen, Germany
lutz.schroeder@fau.de
[2] Psychiatrische Klinik Lüneburg, Lüneburg, Germany

Abstract. Clinical practice guidelines (CPGs) serve to transfer results
from evidence-based medicine into clinical practice. There is growing
interest in clinical decision support systems (CDSS) implementing the
guideline recommendations; research on such systems typically considers combinations of workflow languages with knowledge representation
formalisms. Here, we report on experience with an OWL-based proof-
of-concept implementation of parts of the German S3 guideline for
schizophrenia. From the information-technological point of view, the
salient feature of our implementation is that it represents the CPG
entirely as a logic-based ontology, without resorting, e.g., to rule-based
action formalisms or hard-wired workflows to capture clinical pathways.
Our current goal is to establish that such an implementation is feasible;
long-range benefits we expect from the approach are modularity of CPG
implementation, ease of maintenance, and logical unity.

1 Introduction

Clinical practice guidelines (CPGs) are consensus documents intended to
improve the quality of the treatment of specific diseases following the paradigm
of evidence-based medicine. In the current work, we develop a methodology for
the ontology-centered implementation of CPGs that represents the guideline
content uniformly in terms of a description-logic based ontology, rather than
having separate expressive means for actions, e.g. a rule base as in [9] or a dedicated workflow formalism as in many guideline languages (Sect. 5). We present a
proof-of-concept stage CPG-based clinical decision support system (CDSS) for
schizophrenia implemented following this methodology, formalizing parts of the
German S3 (i.e. high-evidence) guideline for schizophrenia [5]. Envisaging our
framework to evolve into a generic Clinical Guideline Module, currently instantiated to ICD10 diagnostic code F20 (Schizophrenia), we call the arising tool
CGM/F20. Long-term advantages we expect from a purely ontological approach
include logical coherence, higher flexibility than achievable by hard-wired workflows, and ease of maintenance. We do emphasize that our preliminary results
do not yet justify any claim that these benefits will actually be realized; the purpose of the current work is to explore how far a purely declarative logic-based

© Springer International Publishing AG 2017
G. Kern-Isberner et al. (Eds.): KI 2017, LNAI 10505, pp. 300–308, 2017.
DOI: 10.1007/978-3-319-67190-1_24

implementation of a CPG is possible in principle. The schizophrenia guideline is particularly suitable as a case study, being given largely as a collection of recommendations on good clinical practice rather than as a set of definite clinical algorithms.

2 An Assistant for the Diagnosis and Treatment of Schizophrenia

We briefly describe the envisaged use of CGM/F20[1]. The tool consists of two parts, a generic clinical guideline module, CGM, and a formalization of (portions of) the *Schizophrenia Guideline* of the German Association of Psychiatry, Psychotherapy and Psychosomatics (DGPPN) [5]. The tool is not currently integrated into a real HIS, and instead implements basic patient data management itself in a fairly naive way to enable the intended proof of concept.

Recommendations are based on the medical record of a patient, represented as a time-ordered sequence of events such as symptoms reported, diagnoses made, test results, therapeutic measures etc. To see how this works, let us assume that a patient has been recently admitted and it is clear that he has been hearing hallucinatory voices commenting on his behaviour for a prolonged time. Because of additional symptomatology and patient background, he is considered possibly HIV positive. The DGPPN-SG stipulates [5, pp. 31–32]:

> *A diagnosis of schizophrenia requires at least one* unmistakable *symptom from Groups 1 to 4 (or two, if they are less certain), or at least two symptoms from Groups 5 to 8. These symptoms have to be constantly present for a month or longer.*

(Translated from the original German, like all further guideline quotes; our emphasis.) So let us assume that the patient's EHR already contains the abovementioned information that he "unmistakably" hears commenting voices. Since according to the DGPPN-SG, this is a symptom in Group 3, the system should recommend the diagnosis of schizophrenia. In fact, the system mentions "acute schizophrenia" as a possible diagnosis, but indicates that the recommendation cannot yet be made definite due to missing information. This follows from the guideline, which not only lists exceptional cases under which the diagnosis should not be made [5, p. 32]:

> *One should not diagnose schizophrenia in the presence of an unmistakable brain disorder or while the patient is intoxicated or undergoing detoxification.*

but also dictates a differential diagnosis to rule out alternative psychotic disorders. In addition to the putative diagnosis, the system recommends a *measure*, namely to perform a test for HIV; this again follows from the guideline:

---

[1] CGM/F20 is open source, and available at http://www8.cs.fau.de/research/cgm.

In case of a corresponding suspicion, an HIV test [...] should be performed.

At this point the physician could, e.g., immediately dismiss "detoxification" as a possibility, and then order blood tests and a brain scan to rule out the remaining obstacles to the diagnosis. If the patient's medical record were then updated with negative results for all tests, the other scenarios would vanish and the system would then actually recommend the diagnosis of acute schizophrenia.

We stress that this would be just a recommendation, that is, the diagnosis would not be automatically issued by the system. So assume the physician agrees with this diagnosis and records it in the system. The DGPPN-SG will now recommend a pharmacotherapy, but only once the informed consent of the the patient is recorded, as specified in the guideline [5, p. 43].

3   Implementation Challenges

We discuss challenges met in the implementation of the guideline (with solutions described in Sect. 4), and pinpoint aspects that make an ontology-based approach fit particularly well, but also ones were it becomes apparent that the current state of the art in description logics could be improved.

Partial knowledge. Unlike database systems, the system should follow the *open world assumption* as used in logic-based ontology languages; e.g. a condition being unmentioned in a patient's health record should be not conflated with absence of the condition.

Defaults and exceptions. In Sect. 2 we saw a guideline excerpt formulated in *default case/exceptional case* style: The CPG recommends to diagnose schizophrenia when sufficiently many symptoms from a given list are present, but then lists *exceptions* to this rule, such as not to issue the diagnosis if the patient has a brain disorder. Under the open world assumption, just incorporating absence of exceptions as a condition into the general rule would not yield the expected results: For instance, as we cannot yet dismiss the possibility of a brain disorder at the time the patient with commenting voices in Sect. 2 is admitted, the system would then simply not recommend a diagnosis of schizophrenia, without further comment. It is thus crucial to distinguish between default actions and exceptions when formalizing a guideline. On the other hand, the intended behaviour is not quite the same as in standard default reasoning paradigms, which in the example would presumably simply recommend diagnosing schizophrenia without further comment, unless a brain disorder is *known* to be present. In contrast, our system would indicate to the physician that schizophrenia is a likely diagnosis but explicitly hold off on a recommendation until exceptional conditions are known to be absent.

Epistemic queries. The user interaction with the system should depend on whether certain facts regarding a patient are *known* or not; e.g. the system should not ask questions whose answer is already in the patient record, or pursue possible diagnoses that are already known to be ruled out. A full treatment of such situations requires a query language with an epistemic operator [11], not currently supported by mature OWL reasoners. We deal with this issue by letting the tool launch appropriate ontological queries to check whether certain facts are known, and then recombine queries, in particular *negatively.*

Dismissing possible exceptions. Exceptions may rest on complex logical combinations of facts (e.g., a medication can be counterindicated by a combination of conditions); dismissing such an exception as a whole amounts to negating a complex concept, so having an expressive logic with unrestricted negation helps.

Judicious information gathering. Recommendations of the schizophrenia guideline sometimes depend on symptoms being "unmistakable" (*eindeutig*), and the system needs to query the physician accordingly. On the other hand, the system should not issue such a query for other symptoms (such as 'high fever').

Temporal relations. The guideline needs information about the temporal order and duration of certain events, and moreover has concepts of a *current phase* and *previous phases* of the disease.

4   The CGM/F20 Ontology

The CGM/F20 ontology consists of two static OWL ontologies, one for a general modelling of time and one for the actual guideline content (once additional CPGs are covered in future extensions, the latter will split into a generic and a disease-specific part). Additionally, each patient is modelled as a separate dynamic ontology that extends the static ontologies with assertional knowledge modelling the patient data; it is generated at admission and is continuously updated by the system as the clinical process progresses.

Time. As the guideline only needs fairly large-scale temporal concepts, we opt for modelling a highly abstracted temporal ontology from scratch (partly using SWRL) rather than import more fine-granular (clinical) temporal ontologies such as CNTRO [18]. Our time ontology is based on the central concept of *event*. Events may have a beginning, an end, and a duration, and may belong to a *session*. We use sessions as logical time units, ending with the release of the patient. One phenomenon creating the need for sessions is that many guideline statements (e.g. on specific laboratory tests and on efficiency and side effects of medications) depend on schizophrenia manifesting itself *for the first time*. An attempt to model this condition by saying that the patient was not diagnosed with schizophrenia in the past will clearly fail, as the relevant guideline recommendations will then be blocked from the moment the patient is diagnosed with schizophrenia. Our solution is to formulate the condition in terms of sessions – we require that the patient has not been diagnosed with schizophrenia in any previous session.

Overall Design of the Guideline Model. Unsurprisingly, the guideline model revolves around the concepts of Symptom, Diagnosis, Measure, and Patient. Additionally, there is a class TherapyGoal modelling abstract overall goals of the therapy that are not refined to concrete therapeutic measures in the guideline. The recommendations of the guideline are implemented in terms of named classes of patients (those to which the recommendation applies), the *recommendation classes*. These concepts are linked with the time ontology; in particular, symptoms, diagnoses and measures are events in the sense of the time ontology, and always belong to a session.

One important point to think about in designing an ontology is what individuals one imagines as potential members of a given class. For instance, we regard classes of symptoms and measures as inhabited by concrete instances attached to a given person over a given time period, e.g. 'the delusions experienced by patient X in the past three weeks'. To avoid conceptual pitfalls as pointed out in [15], not all inhabitants of such classes are required to exist in the real world – e.g. a therapeutic measure might just be recommended or currently planned. How far such entities are real or just putative is determined by their relationship to other individuals.

Recommendations are implemented in terms of object properties linking measures with patients, and governed by definitions of recommendation classes. There are three types of such properties: recommendations, non-recommendations (e.g. for diagnoses already issued in the past), and counter-recommendations (explicit discouragements). As indicated in Sect. 3, we need to emulate a form of default reasoning. To this end, recommendation classes may, via annotations, be associated with preconditions, expressed by *precondition classes*. This enables us to assign patients to a recommendation class although we yet do not know whether they fulfill these additional preconditions, and then confirm the recommendation once the preconditions are checked.

Annotations are used to configure the behaviour of the tool, in particular the query mechanism and the user interface. Besides for preconditions, we use annotations to trigger queries for additional qualifications of symptoms such as unmistakability; to link to the guideline text; and to mark preconditions that the physician is allowed to summarily dismiss without justification.

Reasoning. The reasoning service by means of which CGM/F20 arrives at recommendations is querying via SPARQL-DL formulas [17]. Ideally, one would want to query for classes C of diagnoses such that the patient at hand belongs to classes such as *hasRecommendedDiagnosis* **some** C; however, constructs of this type go beyond (the well-documented and stable part of) SPARQL-DL. As a workaround, we populate classes of measures and diagnoses with generic individuals, which we use in place of the class in the definition of recommendation classes. We then query for individuals that are, say, diagnoses, and are related to the patient at hand via *hasRecommendedDiagnosis*. For example, diagnostic recommendations for patient *John* are produced by the query

SELECT ?diagnosis **WHERE** {
    John schizophrenia:*hasRecommendedDiagnosis* ?diagnosis.
    FILTER NOT EXISTS {John schizophrenia:*hasNonRecommendedDiagnosis* ?diagnosis}.}

That is, we first query for recommended diagnoses and then filter out the non-recommended ones in our emulation of defeasible reasoning. In the example, if John has an unmistakable symptom from a certain list of symptoms, he will satisfy *hasRecommendedDiagnosis* R_Schizophrenia, but the diagnosis will not be recommended if that diagnosis has already been made, putting John also in the class *hasNonRecommendedDiagnosis* R_Schizophrenia, so that R_Schizophrenia is removed from the result of the query. Having thus established diagnoses to be explored, we next need to check the status of the preconditions before a diagnosis can be conclusively recommended. We thus query for all classes John belongs to, and then iterate over all preconditions of recommendation classes John belongs to and check their status: If the John belongs to the precondition class, its status is 'confirmed'; if he is in the negation of the precondition class, the status is 'excluded'; and otherwise 'unknown'.

Modularity. Currently we are only modelling a single CPG, but we provide an interface which should also fit for other guidelines. In a multi-guideline framework, one would put general-interest classes and object properties revolving around symptoms, diagnoses, therapy goals etc. into a master ontology and let ontologies for specific CPGs build on this ontology, using the same types of annotations. The tool would likely require only little adaptation, barring extensions necessary to cover new general phenomena not occurring in the schizophrenia guideline. In a multi-guideline framework, guidelines could and should refer to each other, e.g. for differential diagnoses. The logic-centered approach would then presumably play out its advantages quite visibly, as clinical pathways could be generated by combining logical axioms across different guidelines, avoiding the need for laborious manual integration of workflows.

5 Related Work

Our work is situated in the highly active area of clinical decision support. For systematic reviews of clinical decision support systems (CDSS) and guideline implementations, see [7,12]. Current CDSS are mostly focused on somatic diseases, one exception being the CompTMAP tool that implements a hard-wired medication protocol for depression [19]. A range of dedicated formalisms has been developed for the implementation of clinical practice guidelines; see [13] for an overview. A common denominator of these languages is that they focus on workflow descriptions fixing specific clinical paths, and use knowledge representation only at hardwired decision points in workflows. More recently, CDSS have emerged that are, like CGM/F20, based primarily on ontological representations, typically in OWL. One approach is to represent workflows explicitly by modelling states and transitions in OWL and SWRL [6,8,20]. Beyond this, ontologies have been used for patient classification in diabetes [9] and lung cancer [16], and for decision support in breast cancer follow-up [1], comorbidities in cardiology [2], pre-operative testing [4], and chemotherapy [3]. Out of these, it is probably [4] whose approach is most closely related to ours. The main differences between the CDSS described in [4] and CGM/F20 are on the one hand the fact that CGM/F20 deals with extended clinical processes and hence needs to consider temporal concepts, and on the other hand specific implementation challenges addressed in CGM/F20 that lead to extended use of DL querying in CGM/F20, cf. Sects. 3 and 4.

6   Conclusions and Future Work

We have explored an approach to CPG implementation that relies on representing the full content of the guideline, including procedural parts, as an OWL ontology. Our system CGM/F20 currently covers part of the German S3 guideline for schizophrenia. In its present state of development, CGM/F20 delivers recommendations for the next step in a clinical path (of course still leaving the actual decisions on diagnostic and therapeutic steps to the psychiatrist). The guideline content and, in particular, its appropriate interactive presentation to the user poses a number of specific challenges that are addressed in particular by the careful design of DL queries and intensive use of annotations.

As an immediate next step, still within the proof-of-concept stage, we will extend the tool to enable explicit look-ahead, i.e. to generate multi-step clinical pathways and replan these as the actual clinical process unfolds, possibly using OWL-S [10]. Moreover, we intend to substantiate our claim of genericity of our CPG implementation framework by formalizing additional guidelines, aiming especially for diseases whose diagnosis and treatment involve a vocabulary of concepts that intersects with those of schizophrenia. A point of particular interest is in-depth coverage of differential diagnoses. Interdisciplinary integration of guidelines will increase the need for connecting CPG ontologies with standard medical terminologies such as SNOMED CT or OpenGALEN [14].

References

1. Abidi, S., Abidi, S., Hussain, S., Shepherd, M.: Ontology-based modeling of clinical practice guidelines: A clinical decision support system for breast cancer follow-up interventions at primary care settings. In: MEDINFO 2007, pp. 845–849. IOS Press (2007)
2. Abidi, S., Cox, J., Abidi, S., Shepherd, M.: Using OWL ontologies for clinical guidelines based comorbid decision support. In: Hawaii International International Conference on Systems Science, HICSS 2012, pp. 3030–3038. IEEE Comp. Soc. (2012)

3. Beierle, C., Eisele, L., Kern-Isberner, G., Meyer, R.G., Nietzke, M.: Using ontological knowledge about active pharmaceutical ingredients for a decision support system in medical cancer therapy. In: Friedrich, G., Helmert, M., Wotawa, F. (eds.) KI 2016. LNCS, vol. 9904, pp. 119–125. Springer, Cham (2016). doi:10.1007/978-3-319-46073-4_9

4. Bouamrane, M.-M., Rector, A., Hurrell, M.: A hybrid architecture for a preoperative decision support system using a rule engine and a reasoner on a clinical ontology. In: Polleres, A., Swift, T. (eds.) RR 2009. LNCS, vol. 5837, pp. 242–253. Springer, Heidelberg (2009). doi:10.1007/978-3-642-05082-4_17

5. Deutsche Gesellschaft für Psychiatrie, Psychotherapie und Nervenheilkunde (ed.) Behandlungsleitlinie Schizophrenie. In: Gaebel, W., Falkai, P. (eds.) Steinkopff, Darmstadt (2006)

6. Doulaverakis, C., Koutkias, V., Antoniou, G., Kompatsiaris, I.: Applying SPARQL-based inference and ontologies for modelling and execution of clinical practice guidelines: a case study on hypertension management. In: Riaño, D., Lenz, R., Reichert, M. (eds.) KR4HC/ProHealth -2016. LNCS, vol. 10096, pp. 90–107. Springer, Cham (2017). doi:10.1007/978-3-319-55014-5_6

7. Garg, A., Adhikari, N., McDonald, H., Rosas-Arellano, M., Devereaux, P., Beyene, J., Sam, J., Haynes, R.: Effects of computerized clinical decision support systems on practitioner performance and patient outcomes: a systematic review. JAMA **293**, 1223–1238 (2005)

8. Jafarpour, B., Abidi, S.R., Abidi, S.S.R.: Exploiting semantic web technologies to develop OWL-based clinical practice guideline execution engines. IEEE J. Biomed. Health Inform. **20**, 388–398 (2016)

9. Kashyap, V., Morales, A., Hongsermeier, T.: On implementing clinical decision support: achieving scalability and maintainability by combining business rules and ontologies. In: AMIA Annual Symposium, vol. 2006, pp. 414–418. AMIA (2006)

10. Martin, D., Burstein, M., McDermott, D., McIlraith, S., Paolucci, M., Sycara, K., McGuinness, D., Sirin, E., Srinivasan, N.: Bringing semantics to web services with OWL-S. World Wide Web, WWW 2007 **10**, 243–277 (2007)

11. Mehdi, A., Rudolph, S., Grimm, S.: Epistemic querying of OWL knowledge bases. In: Antoniou, G., Grobelnik, M., Simperl, E., Parsia, B., Plexousakis, D., De Leenheer, P., Pan, J. (eds.) ESWC 2011. LNCS, vol. 6643, pp. 397–409. Springer, Heidelberg (2011). doi:10.1007/978-3-642-21034-1_27

12. Peleg, M.: Computer-interpretable clinical guidelines: a methodological review. J. Biomed. Inform. **46**, 44–763 (2013)

13. Peleg, M., Tu, S., Bury, J., Ciccarese, P., Fox, J., Greenes, R.A., Hall, R., Johnson, P., Jones, N., Kumar, A., Miksch, S., Quaglini, S., Seyfang, A., Shortliffe, E., Stefanelli, M.: Comparing computer-interpretable guideline models: a case-study approach. J. AMIA **10**, 52–68 (2003)

14. Rector, A., Rogers, J., Zanstra, P., van der Haring, E.: OpenGALEN: Open source medical terminology and tools. In: AMIA Annual Symposium, p. 982. AMIA (2003)

15. Schulz, S., Stenzhorn, H., Boeker, M., Smith, B.: Strengths and limitations of formal ontologies in the biomedical domain. Rev. Electron. Comun. Inf. Inov. Saude **3**, 31–45 (2009)

16. Sesen, M., Banares-Alcántara, R., Fox, J., Kadir, T., Brady, J.: Lung Cancer Assistant: an ontology-driven, online decision support prototype for lung cancer treatment selection. In: OWL: Experiences and Directions Workshop, OWLED 2012 (2012)

17. Sirin, E., Parsia, B.: SPARQL-DL: SPARQL query for OWL-DL. In: OWL: Experiences and Directions, OWLED 2007. CEUR Workshop Proceedings, vol. 258 (2007)
18. Tao, C., Wei, W., Solbrig, H., Savova, G., Chute, C.: CNTRO: A semantic web ontology for temporal relation inferencing in clinical narratives. In: Annual Sympposium on AMIA, pp. 787–791 (2010)
19. Trivedi, M., Kern, J., Grannemann, B., Altshuler, K., Sunderajan, P.: A computerized clinical decision support system as a means of implementing depression guidelines. Psych. Serv. **55**, 879–885 (2004)
20. Ye, Y., Jiang, Z., Diao, X., Yang, D., Du, G.: An ontology-based hierarchical semantic modeling approach to clinical pathway workflows. Comp. Bio. Med. **39**, 722–732 (2009)

A Logic Programming Approach
to Collaborative Autonomous Robotics

Binal Javia[✉] and Philipp Cimiano

Bielefeld University, Bielefeld, Germany
{bjavia,cimiano}@cit-ec.uni-bielefeld.de

Abstract. We consider scenarios in which robots need to collaboratively perform a task. Our focus is on scenarios where every robot has the same goal and performs autonomous decisions on which next step to do to reach the shared goal. The robots can synchronize by requesting each others' help. Our approach builds on a knowledge-based architecture in which robot goals and behaviour are encoded declaratively using logic programming, that is Prolog in our case. Each robot executes the same Prolog program and requests help from other robots to cooperatively solve some subtasks. In this paper we present the system architecture and a proof-of-concept scenario of tidying up an apartment. In this scenario a set of robots are working autonomously yet collaboratively to tidy up a simulated apartment by placing the scattered objects in their proper places.

Keywords: Collaborative robotics · Logical programming · Knowledge-based system

1 Introduction

In many scenarios and applications, the behaviour of different robots collaborating on a given task needs to be coordinated. This can be done via a central planning component that computes an overall plan and instructs each robot what to do in a particular time step. In such an approach, robots are not autonomous as they essentially follow instructions given by a central planning and synchronization component [1]. In contrast to this, we consider an approach in which the behaviour of robots working collaboratively on a common task can be coordinated in a decentralized fashion, leaving autonomy to every robot. In human-robot collaboration, several planning and action-related aspects must be implemented in collaborative task planning, human-aware navigation and joint manipulation [4], this also applies to multi robot collaboration. Our approach relies on declarative plans specified by means of a logic programming formalism, Prolog in our case. Each robot essentially executes the same plan and takes own decisions about which step to perform next. The behaviour of the different robots is coordinated by allowing them to exchange messages requesting each others' help. We instantiate this approach for a tidying up scenario

© Springer International Publishing AG 2017
G. Kern-Isberner et al. (Eds.): KI 2017, LNAI 10505, pp. 309–315, 2017.
DOI: 10.1007/978-3-319-67190-1_25

in which a set of robots need to collaborate on the task of putting all objects into their proper location. While many objects can be dealt with by each robot autonomously, some objects require joint handling (*e.g.* carrying) and thus synchronization between the robots. We perform experiments in a simulated world and report the rate of task completion averaged over a number of runs. The main novelty of the approach presented in this paper is that the robots work collaboratively, but are not coordinated centrally in contrast to other state-of-the-art approaches supporting robot collaboration [1]. This is important as it allows for autonomous but coordinated decision making and thus for more flexibility and allows to accommodate issues that could not be foreseen at planning time.

2   System Architecture and Implementation

This section gives an overview of the system architecture and software implementation used to realise the system architecture (see Fig. 1).

   The Knowledge Representation component acquires, stores and retrieves knowledge that is needed by the system. World knowledge comprises knowledge about everyday objects and their properties [5]. Such knowledge can be represented as an ontology [2] and can for instance be obtained from existing knowledge bases like OpenCyc [6] and RoboEarth [7]. Our ontology is encoded in the Web Ontology Language (OWL) and accessed via an OWL API implemented in KnowRob [8][1].

   A separate process running in parallel updates the *situational knowledge* base with the robot's current environment, creating an entry for each object detected with its unique object identifier and the timestamp. Object specific information such as type, color, location of the object and other relevant descriptive features are also stored in a database. We rely on a relational database, MySQL, in our current implementation. A set of Prolog predicates is implemented to access the situational knowledge base stored in MySQL using the SWI-Prolog-ODBC Interface.

   The Action Representation and Reasoning module implements a *client-server architecture* with a SWI-Prolog client and a Java server. An *action predicate* in Prolog represents an action that can be carried out by the robot. An *action plan predicate* consists of a sequence of action predicates. Each action predicate in the action plan predicate is executed sequentially with the ordering constraint that the next action predicate in the sequence is only executed if the previous action predicate was successful. For example, the action plan predicate *pick_and_place* is modeled as the head of a rule consisting of four premises: *reaching*, *picking*, *moving* and *placing* following [3]:

```
pick_and_place(R,O)  :-  reaching(R,O),picking(R,O),moving(R,O),
                         placing(R,O).
```

---

[1] http://knowrob.org/kb/knowrob.owl.

These premises correspond to the sequence of sub-actions that need to be carried out for the pick-and-place action to be successful. The action predicate *picking* is executed only when the previous action predicate *reaching* is successful, *i.e.* an object can be *picked* only after the robot hand has *reached* the object. Planning of concrete action executions takes place by generating ground Prolog plans as a result of Prolog resolution at runtime. In order to allow for action execution by the robot, Prolog sends HTTP requests to the Abstract Robot Control Module, specifying the action to be executed and the important parameters.

The *Robot Control Module* abstracts from specific robot platforms and is implemented as a Java server that receives HTTP requests from Prolog and invokes that robot controller method as specified in a mapping file that binds an action name (requested by Prolog client) to actual methods executable on a given robot platform.

The main predicate executed by each robot corresponds to the top goal of tidying up the apartment:

```
tidy_the_apt(R) :- getObjs(Objs),tidy_up(Objs,R).
```

where R is an identifier of the robot, and *Objs* is a list of objects returned by the predicate getObjs that are in the environment. The *tidy_up* predicate is then defined recursively and works through the list of objects:

```
tidy_up([O|T],R) :- tidy_obj(O,R),tidy_up(T,R).
```

The predicate that is responsible for tidying up a single object retrieves the prototypical location of the object (PLO), checks whether it does not match the current location and in this case moves the object to the prototypical location:

```
tidy_obj(O,R) :- getPLO(O,P), atLocation(P,L1), atLocation(O,L2),
                 wrongLocation(L1,L2), move_object(R,O,L1).
```

Before moving the object a set of pre-checks are performed *e.g.* such as whether the object requires a one-robot or a two-robot grasp to be moved. After moving the object, a set of post-checks are performed, *e.g.* to check whether the object is indeed placed in its proper storage location:

```
move_object(R,O,L) :- pre_checks(R,O,L),pick_and_place(R,O,L),
                      post_checks(R,O,L).
```

3   Example Scenario

As a proof-of-concept of our approach, we simulate the behaviour of the system in a simulated scenario of *tidying up an apartment*. In this scenario, a set of robots are working collaboratively to tidy up the apartment by putting away a certain number of objects that are lying around the apartment into their appropriate storage places. The proper storage location of an object is defined in

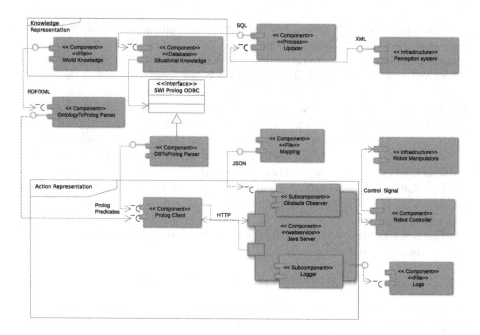

Fig. 1. UML component diagram of system architecture

the world knowledge by the predicate `getPLO`. A robot may randomly encounter a moving obstacle (moving human). The robots perform the tidy-up-apartment task by executing a series of pick-and-place tasks working independently and in coordination with the other robots. The robots synchronize with other robots by requesting their help via a messaging architecture implemented in our case through messages represented in the database.

Consider a virtual apartment with a kitchen, a bedroom, a bathroom and a living room (see Fig. 2). The virtual apartment is equipped with perception sensors such as cameras, motion sensors *etc.*, which can detect the location and properties of the objects lying around in the apartment as well as location and motion of the mobile robots moving around in the apartment. In our example scenario, we consider the following objects: an apple and a banana lying on the kitchen table which need to be stored within the fridge in the kitchen, a cup and a plate on the dining table which needs to be deposited in the cupboard in the kitchen. A toy scattered in the living room needs to be stored away in the bedroom. A laundry basket lying in the bedroom needs to be brought into the bathroom. As a special case, the basket requires two robots jointly lifting it so that it can be moved.

While our approach can accommodate any number of robots, we perform our simulations with two robots only. We assume that robots have a map of the apartment and the ability to localise and navigate from one room to another. The initial position of the objects and robots is generated randomly in each run of our simulation. While the location of storage locations (*e.g.* fridge, cupboard,

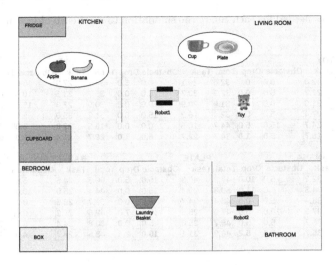

Fig. 2. Illustration of tidy up apartment scenario

box) as well as the apartment configuration can be adapted, it is fixed in our simulations. Errors are simulated randomly with a certain probability, such as a temporary/moving obstacle and the event of losing/dropping the object while moving it. The perception module is simulated by using a static snapshot that models the situation in terms of which objects are visible to the robot, their type as well as location. This static snapshot is loaded into the MySQL database.

We analyze the behaviour of the system in the following situations that occur while executing the aforementioned scenario:

1. **Errorless condition:** In this case no errors occur while picking up an object, moving it to the destination location and placing it there.
2. **Temporary Obstacle:** In this case a temporary/moving obstacle is detected in the path of the robot while moving to the destination location. The robot waits for a few seconds until the moving obstacle (moving human) is out of the way and then continues. We simulate an obstacle with a certain probability p_1.
3. **Lost Object:** In this case the object is lost/dropped while moving. The robot picks up the object from where it is dropped and then it continues. We simulate an object loss with a certain probability p_2.
4. **Two types of Grasps:** Depending on the object there are two types of grasps. The *one-robot grasp* is used for lighter and smaller objects which require only one robot to manipulate. The *two-robot grasp* is used for heavier and bigger objects which require the combined effort of two robots to manipulate.

As a proof of concept, Table 1 summarizes Task Execution Time (Task), Error Conditions (Obstacle, Drop object), Total Task Execution Time (Total) and Average Time (Average) over 5 simulations for each object. All times are measured in seconds.

Table 1. Times needed for each run of the simulation to store each object in the proper place

OBJECT	TOY				CUP				APPLE			
Simulation	Task	Obstacle	Drop	Total	Task	Obstacle	Drop	Total	Task	Obstacle	Drop	Total
1	32.0	0.0	0.0	32.0	29.1	0.0	5.0	34.1	27.9	10.0	0.0	37.9
2	27.3	5.0	0.0	32.3	30.7	5.0	0.0	35.7	33.5	10.0	0.0	43.5
3	31.9	0.0	0.0	31.9	20.9	10.0	0.0	30.9	27.8	15.0	3.0	45.8
4	27.4	5.0	0.0	32.4	16.2	15.0	0.0	31.2	35.0	5.0	0.0	40.0
5	24.7	15.0	5.0	44.7	16.5	0.0	0.0	16.5	32.8	5.0	0.0	37.8
Average	28.7	5.0	1.0	34.7	22.7	6.0	1.0	29.7	31.4	9.0	0.6	41.0

OBJECT	BANANA				PLATE				BASKET (two robot grasp)			
Simulation	Task	Obstacle	Drop	Total	Task	Obstacle	Drop	Total	Task	Obstacle	Drop	Total
1	32.2	5.0	10.0	47.2	40.3	15.0	5.0	60.3	24.5	5.0	0.0	29.5
2	34.3	5.0	11.0	50.3	29.4	15.0	0.0	44.4	25.0	10.0	0.0	35.0
3	38.4	5.0	0.0	43.4	34.7	5.0	0.0	39.7	25.5	0.0	7.0	32.5
4	37.9	10.0	0.0	47.9	25.5	10.0	7.0	42.5	24.2	0.0	0.0	24.2
5	35.7	5.0	5.0	45.7	25.8	5.0	0.0	30.8	24.4	5.0	0.0	29.4
Average	35.7	6.0	5.2	46.9	31.1	10.0	2.4	43.5	24.7	4.0	1.4	30.1

4 Discussion and Conclusion

In this paper, we have proposed a knowledge-based and logic programming based architecture that supports robots in collaborating to achieve a joint task while allowing them to maintain their autonomy in taking own decisions. This is in contrast to many state-of-the-art architectures in which the individual plans are fixed by a central planning component and then are only executed by the individual robots. This approach reduces flexibility of robots to adapt to changing conditions. Our robots all execute the same plan implemented as Prolog directives and they request each others' help when needed through a messaging system. In our simulated scenario, robots collaborate in tidying up an apartment with the goal of storing all objects into their proper place. While most objects can be carried individually, some objects require joint action taking to lift and move the object. Unforeseen problems such as interfering moving obstacles, dropping objects etc. are simulated with a certain probability. We have shown that our approach is robust to such unforeseen errors and all tasks could be accomplished within the same temporal range in spite of errors occurring. It shows also that the coordination of robots via the messaging system is effective as also the objects requiring joint lifting and moving were stored successfully. Future work includes the transfer and testing of the approach in a non-simulated environment.

Acknowledgements. The authors acknowledge funding from the Cluster of Excellence Cognitive Interaction Technology 'CITEC' (EXC 277), Bielefeld University.

References

1. Erdem, E., Aker, E., Patoglu, V.: Answer set programming for collaborative house-keeping robotics: representation, reasoning, and execution. Intell. Serv. Robot. **5**(4), 275–291 (2012). http://dx.doi.org/10.1007/s11370-012-0119-x
2. Gruber, T.R.: Toward principles for the design of ontologies used for knowledge sharing. Int. J. Hum. Comput. Stud. **43**(5–6), 907–928 (1995). http://dx.doi.org/10.1006/ijhc.1995.1081
3. Javia, B., Cimiano, P.: A knowledge-based architecture supporting declarative action representation for manipulation of everyday objects. In: Proceedings of the 3rd Workshop on Model-Driven Robot Software Engineering, MORSE 2016, pp. 40–46. ACM, New York (2016). http://doi.acm.org/10.1145/3022099.3022105
4. Kirsch, A., Kruse, T., Sisbot, E.A., Alami, R., Lawitzky, M., Brščić, D., Hirche, S., Basili, P., Glasauer, S.: Plan-based control of joint human-robot activities. Künstliche Intell. **24**(3), 223–231 (2010)
5. Lim, G.H., Suh, I.H., Suh, H.: Ontology-based unified robot knowledge for service robots in indoor environments. IEEE Trans. Syst. Man Cybern. Syst. Hum. **41**(3), 492–509 (2011)
6. Matuszek, C., Cabral, J., Witbrock, M., DeOliveira, J.: An introduction to the syntax and content of CYC. In: Proceedings of the AAAI Spring Symposium on Formalizing and Compiling Background Knowledge, pp. 44–49 (2006)
7. Riazuelo, L., Tenorth, M., Marco, D.D., Salas, M., Mösenlechner, L., Kunze, L., Beetz, M., Tardos, J.D., Montano, L., Montiel, J.M.M.: Roboearth web-enabled and knowledge-based active perception. In: Proceedings of the IROS Workshop on AI-based Robotics, Tokyo, Japan, 7th November 2013
8. Tenorth, M., Beetz, M.: KnowRob–A knowledge processing infrastructure for cognition-enabled robots. Int. J. Robot. Res. (IJRR) **32**(5), 566–590 (2013)

Parametrizing Cartesian Genetic Programming: An Empirical Study

Paul Kaufmann[1](✉) and Roman Kalkreuth[2]

[1] Department of Computer Science, Paderborn University, Paderborn, Germany
paul.kaufmann@gmail.com
[2] Department of Computer Science, University of Dortmund, Dortmund, Germany

Abstract. Since its introduction two decades ago, the way researchers parameterized and optimized Cartesian Genetic Programming (CGP) remained almost unchanged. In this work we investigate non-standard parameterizations and optimization algorithms for CGP. We show that the conventional way of using CGP, i.e. configuring it as a single line optimized by an (1+4) Evolutionary Strategies-style search scheme, is a very good choice but that rectangular CGP geometries and more elaborate metaheuristics, such as Simulated Annealing, can lead to faster convergence rates.

1 Introduction

Almost two decades ago Miller, Thompson, Kalganova, and Fogarty presented first publications on CGP—an encoding model inspired by the two-dimensional array of functional nodes connected by feed-forward wires of an Field Programmable Gate Array (FPGA) device [1,6]. CGP has multiple pivotal advantages:

- CGP comprises an inherent mechanism for the design of simple hierarchical functions. While in many optimization systems such a mechanism has to be implemented explicitly, in CGP multiple feed-forwards wires may originate from the same output of a functional node. This property can be very useful for the evolution of goal functions that may benefit from repetitive inner structures.
- The maximal size of encoded solutions is bound, saving CGP to some extent from "bloat" that is characteristic to Genetic Programming (GP).
- CGP offers an implicit way of propagating redundant information throughout the generations. This mechanism can be used as a source of randomness and a memory for evolutionary artifacts. Propagation and reuse of redundant information has been show beneficial for the convergence of CGP.
- CGP encodes a directed acyclic graph. This allows to evolve topologies. An example is the evolution of Artificial Neural Networks (ANNs) using CGP [7].
- CGP is simple. The implementation complexity in many programming languages is marginal relying on no special programming language properties like the ability to handle tree structures efficiently.

© Springer International Publishing AG 2017
G. Kern-Isberner et al. (Eds.): KI 2017, LNAI 10505, pp. 316–322, 2017.
DOI: 10.1007/978-3-319-67190-1_26

Along with the mentioned advantages, CGP suffers as a combinatorial representation model from the usual sources of epistasis. For instance, rewiring a single input of a functional node can change the overall transfer function dramatically. Additionally, the spatial arrangement of functional nodes on a two-dimensional grid introduces restrictions to the topology of the evolved solutions. Moving a functional node among the grid requires rearranging the genotype, if possible. Additionally, the connection set of an input of a node strongly depends on the location of the node on the grid. These dependencies implicitly impact on the evolvability and make it difficult to realize structural methods for CGP. For instance, a recombination operator needs to restructure large parts of a genotype to be able to swap functionally related substructures among candidate solutions [2,8]. A trial to free CGP from grid-induced epistasis was made in [3] by assigning each input and output of a node signatures. Best-fitting signatures were then used to clamp wires.

The first systematic investigation on an efficient optimization scheme for CGP was done by Miller 1999 in [5]. Miller employed a regular GA with a uniform recombination operator and a $(1 + \lambda)$ mutation-only search scheme. He configured CGP as a square grid of functional nodes with the maximal length of feed-forward wires of two. In 1999 it was already know that a "neutral selection" scheme that is preferring offspring individuals for propagating into the next generation if they are on par or better than the parent individual is highly beneficial for CGP. In a series of experiments Miller observed that the evolution of digital circuits using CGP can be solved better by local search-like approaches employing "neutral selection" than by GA.

In this work we address the question, whether the popular choice of $(1 + 4)$ search scheme in combination with single-line CGP genotype can be generalized. For this, we rely on an unbiased parameter tuning method to identify (i) well-performing parameterizations of CGP and (ii) efficient optimization schemes.

2   Experimental Setup

The first class of benchmark functions consists of Boolean adder, multiplier, and even parity functions. The set of 2-input Boolean functions that may be used as functional nodes in CGP genotypes is presented in Table 1. An experiment is stopped if a perfect solution has been found or the maximal number of fitness evaluations has been exceeded.

The second set of benchmark consists of twelve symbolic regression functions (Koza-2, -3, Nguyen-4 . . . -10, Keijzer-4, -6, Pagie-1). A training data set consists of c uniformly sampled from an interval $[a, b]$. The cost function is defined as the sum of absolute differences between functional values of the reference and evolved function at the data points of the according training set. An experiment is terminated if the cost function reaches a value below or equal 0.01 or the maximal number of fitness evaluations has been exceeded.

Table 1. Functional set and parameter space explored by iRace.

Benchmarks	Functional set
$(i, i, 1)$-add, (i, i)-mul	$a \wedge b$, $a \wedge \bar{b}$, $\bar{a} \wedge b$, $a \oplus b$, $a|b$
Even parity	$a \wedge b$, $a \wedge \bar{b}$, $\bar{a} \wedge b$, $a|b$, $a|\bar{b}$, $\bar{a}|b$
Koza	$+$, $-$, $*$, $/$, sin, cos, $\ln(|n|)$, e^n
Keijzer	$+$, $*$, n^{-1}, $-n$, $\sqrt{n}$

Optimization Algorithms

As the baseline method we select the (1+4) CGP The second and third algorithms are $(1 + \lambda)$ CGP and $(\mu + \lambda)$ CGP, where the number of offspring individuals λ and the number of parents μ are subject to optimization. For all CGPs schemes "neutral selection" has been realized. For optimizing Boolean circuits we have additionally selected SA with the following colling strategy:

$$A \leftarrow \frac{(T_{\text{start}} - T_{\text{end}})(N + 1)}{N}; \qquad B \leftarrow T_{\text{start}} - A; \qquad T_t \leftarrow \frac{A}{t + 1} + B.$$

Random sampling and random walk have also been investigated in preliminary experiments and sorted out because of inferior results.

Automatic Parameter Tuning: To detect good parameterizations, we are using the Iterated Race for Automatic Algorithm Configuration (iRace) package [4]. iRace was configured to execute 2000 trials for each of the tested algorithm-benchmark pairs.

iRace usually evolves multiple good-performing configurations for an algorithm-benchmark pair. To verify the results of iRace, we have computed for each configuration the median performance in 100 runs. We have then selected for each algorithm-benchmark pair the best performing configuration and report it in this paper.

3   Results

Evolution of Boolean circuits: The first observation that can be made is that the baseline (1+4) CGP on a single-line CGP is never a clear winner regarding the median number of fitness evaluations when evolving functionally correct Boolean circuits (c.f. Table 2). Except for the smallest benchmarks, the $(2, 2, 1)$-adder and the $(2, 2)$-multiplier, and for the 8-parity benchmark SA is always a clear winner. For the 8-parity benchmark SA is passed by $(\mu + \lambda)$ CGP only by roughly 2%. For larger benchmarks, like the $(3, 3, 1)$- and $(4, 4, 1)$-adder, $(3, 3)$-multiplier, and the parity benchmarks, the best performing algorithm is 1.3 to 3 times faster than the baseline (1+4) CGP. When looking at the CE metric, SA is the clear winner for all but the smallest and the $(3, 3, 1)$-adder benchmarks.

Table 2. Evaluation of CGP parameters for Boolean functions. Not optimized parameters are marked with an "–". The comparison prefers conventional (1+4) CGP, as iRace budget is set to 2000 for all configurations and challengers have more parameters to optimize. The results are measured in number of fitness evaluations. Best results are printed in *bold*. n_c and n_r - number of CGP columns and rows; m - mutation rate; T_{start} and T_{stop} - starting and stopping temperatures for SA. CE at $z = 99\%$.

goal function	algorithm	n_c	n_r	μ	λ	m[%]	T_{start}	T_{stop}	1Q	median	3Q	Comp. Effort	restart at eval.
(2,2,1) add	1+4 CGP	200	–	–	–	2.1112	–	–	14916	26532	49840	160753	91840
	1+λ CGP	100	200	–	3	0.3215	–	–	11316	18933	28797	89280	34350
	μ+λ CGP	200	50	1	1	0.3803	–	–	8114	**13129**	21723	**67860**	19849
	SA	200	2	–	–	1.8976	1299	0.0348	12242	20052	35411	109530	42284
(3,3,1) add	1+4 CGP	200	–	–	–	2.1512	–	–	113168	194120	326156	**689115**	689112
	1+λ CGP	150	1	–	3	1.9464	–	–	105789	178344	302211	929794	581961
	μ+λ CGP	100	4	1	3	0.8396	–	–	122460	190539	330936	1018919	451407
	SA	70	4	–	–	1.3706	4671	0.4366	88335	**149817**	246126	750368	621896
(4,4,1) add	1+4 CGP	200	–	–	–	1.2341	–	–	424924	697152	1182452	2830424	2404400
	1+λ CGP	300	2	–	2	0.6852	–	–	303080	501550	698950	2206982	1680482
	μ+λ CGP	100	4	1	1	0.6396	–	–	364545	545438	936699	2469195	2097544
	SA	150	3	–	–	0.6693	3610	0.6437	283038	**400832**	723341	**2034761**	1422236
(2,2) mul	1+4 CGP	100	–	–	–	2.9542	–	–	3452	5564	9136	28434	14864
	1+λ CGP	100	100	–	–	0.8680	–	·	2121	3417	5474	**16512**	9009
	μ+λ CGP	100	30	1	1	1.4332	–	–	2079	**3322**	5465	17349	7279
	SA	30	14	–	–	2.4941	58	0.0889	2661	4183	6801	21275	9959
(3,3) mul	1+4 CGP	2000	–	–	–	0.5008	–	–	274228	447220	722280	2103815	1787156
	1+λ CGP	200	20	–	2	0.2988	–	–	149824	288368	459822	1203021	1203020
	μ+λ CGP	150	30	1	2	0.2971	–	–	130250	224178	498888	1382722	361496
	SA	200	100	–	–	0.1622	3336	0.0870	84844	**148145**	356305	**949607**	169289
7-parity	1+4 CGP	300	–	–	–	1.2582	–	–	175628	271048	427788	1347746	645976
	1+λ CGP	300	8	–	2	0.7142	–	–	100408	186250	262668	762572	381284
	μ+λ CGP	300	2	1	2	0.9089	–	–	118996	186674	291118	696589	696588
	SA	150	8	–	–	0.7584	1528	0.2000	87773	**140463**	238599	**539214**	458054
8-parity	1+4 CGP	2000	–	–	–	0.9057	–	–	336420	461948	739504	2113156	1374636
	1+λ CGP	200	6	–	3	1.0381	–	–	310524	486894	798396	2408346	932859
	μ+λ CGP	300	6	1	1	0.5578	–	–	192417	**323192**	455204	1404562	702280
	SA	300	4	–	–	0.6733	417	0.3479	213877	329472	479532	**1196482**	1196482
9-parity	1+4 CGP	2000	–	–	–	0.8718	–	–	628536	1011220	1718660	5380705	1487336
	1+λ CGP	150	3	–	2	0.7050	–	–	617418	959194	1570728	2859287	2859286
	μ+λ CGP	300	3	1	1	0.8519	–	–	512420	755543	1239866	3073095	1774561
	SA	300	10	–	–	0.3784	2209	0.2907	392406	**579111**	910828	**2209561**	1876989

Sometimes, the best performing algorithm regarding the median number of fitness evaluations is not the winner regarding the CE. However, the differences in medians and CE values between the winner algorithm regarding the median and the winner algorithm regarding the CE are small to marginal.

Although we have showed for Boolean benchmarks that the conventional way of parameterizing CGP can always be outperformed, we would like to emphasize the following fact: Neither the best performing algorithm regarding the median nor the best algorithm regarding the CE metric can be in general considered dominant when it comes to the computational complexity of optimization and with it, time. The reason for this is the inaccurate assumption that the computational complexity of a fitness evaluation is constant among all CGP parameterizations. For example, $(\mu+\lambda)$ CGP is the best-performing algorithm regarding the median and CE metrics for the $(2, 2, 1)$-adder. However, despite worse median and CE values, $(1+4)$ CGP operating on a single-line CGP and SA evolve functionally correct adders in much shorter time. This is because the genotype sizes found by iRace are much smaller for the two algorithms than for the $(\mu + \lambda)$ CGP. But even having identical CGP geometries the functional evaluation complexity can vary greatly, as the number of active genes that are processed by the fitness evaluation procedure can be different.

Table 3. Evaluation of CGP parameters for symbolic regression functions. Not optimized parameters are marked with an "–". The comparison prefers conventional 1+4 CGP, as iRace budget is set to 2000 for all configurations and challengers have more parameters to optimize.

goal function	optimization algorithm	optimized parameters					best fitness quartiles			Success Rate
		n_c	n_r	μ	λ	$m[\%]$	1Q	2Q	3Q	
Koza-2	1 + 4 CGP	150	–	–	–	5	0.0095	0.0099	0.0325	0.65
	1 + λ CGP	150	3	–	128	2	0.0091	0.0098	0.0364	0.68
	$\mu + \lambda$ CGP	150	3	18	2048	10	0.0085	0.0099	0.0140	0.65
Koza-3	1 + 4 CGP	150	–	–	–	7	0.0104	0.0325	0.0328	0.21
	1 + λ CGP	120	10	–	16	2	0.0087	0.0099	0.0325	0.49
	$\mu + \lambda$ CGP	80	20	14	4096	5	0.0091	0.0100	0.0327	0.53
Nguyen-4	1 + 4 CGP	120	–	–	–	10	0.0120	0.0324	0.0487	0.21
	1 + λ CGP	40	8	–	64	15	0.0129	0.022	0.0395	0.06
	$\mu + \lambda$ CGP	60	6	18	2048	10	0.0101	0.0283	0.0498	0.24
Nguyen-5	1 + 4 CGP	60	–	–	–	7	0.0090	0.0100	0.0240	0.50
	1 + λ CGP	150	10	–	16	2	0.0099	0.0099	0.0229	0.50
	$\mu + \lambda$ CGP	150	20	22	4096	1	0.0085	0.0096	0.0100	0.77
Nguyen-6	1 + 4 CGP	100	–	–	–	2	0.0270	0.0382	0.0392	0.17
	1 + λ CGP	60	20	–	8	1	0.0091	0.0191	0.0381	0.44
	$\mu + \lambda$ CGP	80	14	–	4096	5	0.0100	0.0381	0.0407	0.25
Nguyen-7	1 + 4 CGP	200	–	–	–	7	0.0157	0.0262	0.0534	0.18
	1 + λ CGP	120	8	–	4096	7	0.0099	0.01866	0.0382	0.25
	$\mu + \lambda$ CGP	150	6	2	32	2	0.0116	0.0216	0.0288	0.20
Nguyen-8	1 + 4 CGP	150	–	–	–	15	0.0084	0.0111	0.0415	0.53
	1 + λ CGP	80	10	–	16	2	0.0072	0.0084	0.0098	0.85
	$\mu + \lambda$ CGP	150	6	2	32	2	0.0072	0.0088	0.0095	0.98
Nguyen-9	1 + 4 CGP	150	–	–	–	15	0.2475	0.4184	1.2077	0.00
	1 + λ CGP	200	4	–	16	7	0.2707	0.6189	1.0801	0.01
	$\mu + \lambda$ CGP	120	20	22	4096	15	0.5325	0.7245	1.0079	0.00
Nguyen-10	1 + 4 CGP	60	–	–	–	20	0.5728	0.9185	1.1150	0.01
	1 + λ CGP	120	10	–	4096	20	0.3718	0.5727	0.7346	0.01
	$\mu + \lambda$ CGP	150	20	8	4096	15	0.2975	0.4020	0.5921	0.00
Keijzer-4	1 + 4 CGP	22	–	–	–	5	3.6828	3.6828	3.6828	0.00
	1 + λ CGP	200	20	–	16	7	2.1038	2.3413	2.4953	0.00
	$\mu + \lambda$ CGP	120	20	22	1024	10	2.0837	2.2254	2.3484	0.00
Keijzer-6	1 + 4 CGP	100	–	–	–	2	0.3229	0.4883	0.6438	0.00
	1 + λ CGP	60	20	–	64	10	0.1538	0.2184	0.3445	0.00
	$\mu + \lambda$ CGP	200	20	6	256	10	0.0516	0.1008	0.2390	0.07
Pagie-1	1 + 4 CGP	150	–	–	–	20	31.5965	34.0846	35.2309	0.00
	1 + λ CGP	200	20	–	512	10	14.9535	21.4781	30.7461	0.00
	$\mu + \lambda$ CGP	200	20	14	256	15	14.7931	21.3225	30.1226	0.00

The second observation is that when tuning for λ or for λ and μ, small values are identified by iRace as beneficial. With this, HC and its close derivatives seem to work better for CGP when optimizing Boolean circuits.

In related work it was shown that the efficiency of (1+4) CGP on single-line CGP increases with rising n_c. This can be observed also in Table 2. However, the efficiency of CGP can be improved using rectangular grids and slightly different $(\mu+\lambda)$ CGP schemes as well as SA. This is our third observation for the evolution of Boolean functions.

Evolution of Symbolic Regression Functions: The first observation of Table 3 is that the regular (1+4) CGP can be outperformed always regarding approximation accuracy except for the Nguyen-8 benchmark. The second observation is that $(\mu + \lambda)$ CGP is very successful. Except for three benchmarks it is constantly better than all the other algorithms. For the symbolic regression we cannot observe increased efficiency for single-line CGP when increasing n_c. However, and this is our next observation, the number of offspring individuals is usually very large. This is similar to regular GP, where often large populations are used. Unlike to GP, the mutation operator in CGP is working on single individuals. CGP mutation and GP recombination are operators with very similar mechanisms and effects. It is an open question we want to investigate in future work: Assuming the intuition of the inner principle of GP is correct, i.e. parts of the goal solutions are randomly sampled initially and distributed among individuals of a large population, then the goal of GP is put this puzzle together correctly; Could GP also be solved effectively by a single-individual recombination (similar to CGP's mutation) and with smaller population sizes?

The last two findings in in Table 3 are: Similar to Boolean functions, rectangular CGP geometries are more efficient than single-line CGP and successful mutation rates are rather high, which is in contrast to prior findings suggesting to set the mutation rate as low as possible.

4   Conclusion and Future Work

In this paper, we proposed an empirical study investigating if the regular way CGP is parameterized and optimized in related work is good. The results are that, indeed, the single-line CGP with an (1+4) CGP scheme is good for Boolean benchmarks but that much better results can be achieved for Boolean and symbolic regression functions when using rectangular CGP grids and differently parameterized $(\mu + \lambda)$ CGP schemes as well as SA. Furthermore, we could observe that similar to GP, CGP greatly benefits from large exploration rates, i.e. large offspring populations and high mutation rates, when evolving symbolic regression functions. This behavior is surprising and requires further investigation. It is especially interesting, if the former results on inner CGP mechanisms, like "neutrality", are still valid.

Following recommendations can be drawn from our experiments.

- For simple Boolean functions (1+1) HC applied on CGP with 30 to 50 rows and 100 to 200 columns performs best.
- For complex Boolean functions SA applied on CGP with 3 to 10 rows and 30 to 300 columns performs best. Increasing the number of rows to 100 might help in case of heavy functions, such as the multiplication.
- For Boolean functions the best observed mutation rate interval is $[0.1, 1.6]\%$.
- For continuous functions CGP with 3 to 20 rows and 80 to 200 columns performs best.
- For continuous functions CGP with $\mu = 2 \ldots 22$ and $\lambda = 2048 \ldots 4096$ performs best. It is worth investigating $\lambda = 8 \ldots 32$ in cases where large λ values do not result in fast convergence.
- For continuous functions the mutation rate may vary from 1% to 15% with higher mutation rates being more successful for larger genotypes.

We will extend the benchmark set in our future work to more popular functions, like classification and image-processing tasks, and approach the questions regarding similarity of inner mechanisms to GP. Additionally we will try understand properly the ambivalent nature of CGP making it successful for combinatorial and continuous benchmarks.

References

1. Kalganova, T., Miller, J.F.: Evolutionary approach to design multiple-valued combinational circuits. In: Proceedings of International Conference on Applications of Computer Systems (ACS) (1997)
2. Kaufmann, P., Platzner, M.: Advanced techniques for the creation and propagation of modules in cartesian genetic programming. In: GECCO 2008: Proceedings of the 10th Annual Conference on Genetic and Evolutionary Computation, Atlanta, GA, USA, pp. 1219–1226. ACM, 12–16 July 2008
3. Lones, M.: Enzyme Genetic Programming. Ph.D. thesis, University of York (2003)
4. López-Ibáñez, M., Dubois-Lacoste, J., Cáceres, L.P., Birattari, M., Stützle, T.: The irace package: iterated racing for automatic algorithm configuration. Oper. Res. Perspect. **3**, 43–58 (2016)
5. Miller, J.F.: An Empirical Study of the Efficiency of Learning Boolean Functions Using a Cartesian Genetic Programming Approach. vol. 2, pp. 1135–1142. Morgan Kaufmann, Orlando (1999)
6. Miller, J.F., Thomson, P., Fogarty, T.: Designing Electronic Circuits Using Evolutionary Algorithms. Arithmetic Circuits: A Case Study (1997)
7. Turner, A.J., Miller, J.F.: The importance of topology evolution in neuroevolution: a case study using cartesian genetic programming of artificial neural networks. In: Bramer, M., Petridis, M. (eds.) Research and Development in Intelligent Systems XXX, pp. 213–226. Springer International Publishing, Cham (2013). doi:10.1007/978-3-319-02621-3_15
8. Walker, J.A., Miller, J.F.: Evolution and acquisition of modules in cartesian genetic programming. In: Keijzer, M., O'Reilly, U.-M., Lucas, S., Costa, E., Soule, T. (eds.) EuroGP 2004. LNCS, vol. 3003, pp. 187–197. Springer, Heidelberg (2004). doi:10.1007/978-3-540-24650-3_17

Gesture ToolBox: Touchless Human-Machine Interface Using Deep Learning

Elann Lesnes-Cuisiniez, Jesus Zegarra Flores[(⊠)],
and Jean-Pierre Radoux

Altran Research, Illkirch, France
{marine.cuisiniez, jesus.zegarraflores,
jeanpierre.radoux}@altran.com

Abstract. Human-Computer Interaction (HMI) is useful in sterile environments such as operating rooms (OR) where surgeons need to interact with images from scanners of organs on screens. Contamination issues may happen if the surgeon must touch a keyboard or the mouse. In order to reduce contamination and improve the interactions with the images without asking another team member, the Gesture ToolBox project, based on previous methods of Altran Research, has been proposed. Ten different signs from the LSF (French Sign Language) have been chosen as a way to interact with the images. In order to detect the signs, deep learning methods have been programmed using a pre-trained Convolutional Neural Network (VGG-16). A Kinect is used to detect the positions of the hand and classify gestures. The system allows the user to select, move, zoom in, or zoom out images from organs on the screen according to the recognised sign. Results with 11 subjects are used demonstrate this system in the laboratory. Future work will include tests in real situations in an operating room to obtain feedback from surgeons to improving the system.

Keywords: Human-Computer Interaction · Deep learning · Kinect

1 Introduction

Touchless Human-Machine Interface (HMI) is an interdisciplinary field with applications in robotics, computer gaming and sign-language interpretation. Moreover, touchless HMI is very useful in sterile environments such as in the operating rooms (OR) where surgeons need to interact with computers without introducing contamination issues. Most of the time, the joysticks, buttons, or touch screens are wrapped in a plastic and the surgeons need to change their gloves each time they have to use the computers. It is quite common for surgeons to ask colleagues or nurses, who are in another room to interact with the computers for moving images. This does not result in time delays only if colleagues are effectively available [1].

The aim of the Gesture ToolBox project is to propose a simple touchless Human-Machine Interface based on the surgeon's hand gesture recognition using deep learning methods. This investigation is based on previous work by the Altran Research Medic@ team [2] using other machine learning techniques and descriptors of the hand.

© Springer International Publishing AG 2017
G. Kern-Isberner et al. (Eds.): KI 2017, LNAI 10505, pp. 323–329, 2017.
DOI: 10.1007/978-3-319-67190-1_27

2   Related Work

Several projects explore the possibilities of the deep learning method or meeting the needs of the HMI for OR.

Touchless Human-Machine interfaces already exist for surgeons using different techniques. One of these is based on myoelectric signals (MES) [3], unfortunately, it needs electrodes or armbands which are not necessarily comfortable. In another project, L. Di Tomasso, et al. propose a Leap Motion device [4] as a human interface for neurosurgery. There are also solutions on the market for touchless interaction; for instance, the product "Fluid" produced by Therapixel [5]. This solution is based on a depth perception in addition to machine learning techniques that allows pointing one's fingers close to the screen in order to move images. On the other hand, the Gesture ToolBox solution is oriented to interact with cameras standing between one and four meters from the images to be interacted with.

Concerning the deep learning aspect, O. Koller, et al. use a CNN to recognise hand shapes as an example, the main subject of this paper is to combine a CNN and an iterative EM algorithm to train the CNN on a big dataset weakly labelled [6]. Another paper from Huang, et al. describes the research of finger key point's detection from a mobile camera [7]. Their system is robust to changing background, however it is available for only one finger which is not sufficient in the context of the Gesture ToolBox project. Two other projects use deep learning algorithms and the Kinect for hand segmentation and tracking [8] or sign language recognition [8, 9]. L. Pigou, et al. include the recognition of the body and descriptors [8]. In the method, presented in this paper, there is no hand feature extraction; this was a major part of the machine learning based method mentioned in [2].

3   Methodology

3.1   The Ten Hand Gestures

In order to test the hand gesture recognition, ten gestures were chosen (Fig. 1) from the French sign language (LSF). The algorithm has been trained with these particular gestures because of their simplicity (not causing additional fatigue to the surgeons).

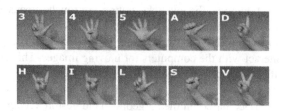

Fig. 1. Hand postures of the ten gestures

3.2   Gesture ToolBox System

Users stand in front of the Kinect and perform the defined gestures with their right hand in order to manipulate images on the screen in real time. The five main steps of the program (Fig. 2., on the left) are repeated in every frame. The upstream training phase of the neural network runs once. The code is flexible enough to recognise different signs without major modifications thanks to the ease of use of this deep learning approach.

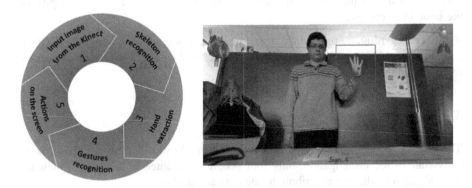

Fig. 2. Architecture of the gesture recognition system (left) and user interface (right)

Input Image from the Kinect and Skeleton Recognition. It uses the Microsoft Kinect for Windows V2. This device is able to track people and their skeleton (up to 25 skeletal joints of a maximum of 6 people) [10].

Hand Extraction and Gesture Recognition. Once the skeleton is identified by the Kinect (Fig. 2.), the position of the right hand is extracted for every frame; a picture centred on the entire right hand is obtained.

Before launching the program, two files which contain the structure and the weights of the neural network trained to classify the ten gestures, are loaded. The neural network is fed every extracted RGB picture and classifies the gesture. In order to reduce imprecisions, the result displayed is the most represented sign among the last five classifications.

Actions and User Interface. The detected gestures are used to select, move, zoom in or zoom out the images of the heart and the lungs on the screen. Future applications will include moving real medical images or specific 3D objects from the industry.

3.3   Deep Learning

The gesture recognition phase of the project is done by a convolutional neural network (CNN) adapted to the classification of pictures.

Data Acquisition. The project functions in real time dealing with pictures from videos. Data acquisition must be specific for each type of gesture in each type of environment (laboratory, very bright OR, etc.). For proof of concept, pictures were collected from eleven people with different skin colours in front of a metallic closet which provides a bicolour background. To simulate new pictures in order to increase the size of the dataset, a small random translation and rotation was applied.

Classification into ten classes is a supervised problem, consequently, a label was placed on the corresponding pictures. The final training dataset contains more than 2600 pictures for the ten classes with a quantity of between 220 and 320 pictures for each class. This remains a small dataset; as a consequence, much attention was given to the issue of overfitting.

Transfer Learning. A pre-trained neural network was used, in our case, the VGG-16 neural network [11] already trained on the ImageNet dataset [12] has been chosen and retrained with our training dataset.

4   Tests and Results

The tests are conducted having the same background as in the training phase. In the early state of the investigation, only four people contributed to these tests, including one subject who did not contribute to the data acquisition.

4.1   Confusion Matrix

The confusion matrix (Fig. 3.) provides the results of the 333 gestures done.

	3	4	5	A	D	H	I	L	S	V
3	20	0	0	0	0	0	0	1	1	0
4	0	34	1	0	0	0	1	1	0	4
5	3	0	39	1	0	0	0	0	0	0
A	0	0	0	39	0	0	0	2	2	0
D	0	0	0	0	26	0	0	1	0	3
H	0	0	0	0	4	26	2	0	1	3
I	0	0	0	0	2	2	18	2	1	0
L	4	0	0	1	0	0	0	26	0	0
S	0	0	0	2	4	0	0	1	29	0
V	2	0	0	0	2	0	0	0	1	21

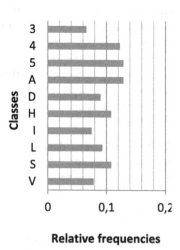

Fig. 3. Confusion matrix (left) and relative frequencies of the classes (right)

4.2   Evaluation

Thanks to the confusion matrix (M_{ij}), the precision, recall, and the f-score for each sign were obtained (Table 1).

Table 1. Precision, recall, and f-score

	Precision $\left(\frac{M_{ii}}{\sum_j M_{ji}}\right)$	Recall $\left(\frac{M_{ii}}{\sum_j M_{ij}}\right)$	f-score $\left(2 \times \frac{precision_i \times recall_i}{precision_i + recall_i}\right)$
3	69.0%	90.9%	78.4%
4	100.0%	82.9%	90.7%
5	97.5%	90.7%	94.0%
A	90.7%	90.7%	90.7%
D	68.4%	86.7%	76.5%
H	92.9%	72.2%	81.3%
I	85.7%	72.0%	78.3%
L	76.5%	83.9%	80.0%
S	82.9%	80.6%	81.7%
V	67.7%	80.8%	73.3%
mean	83.1%	83.1%	83.1%

5   Discussion

It is important to say that the program was deliberately given in difficult situations in order to test its limits: people very far from the Kinect, very close, far from centre, under a very strong light, with the right hand in front of the head or body. If the user is at a correct distance and without excessive light or lack of light, the program has fewer errors. Consequently, the authors would like to point out two main aspects.

5.1   Kinect's Limitations

These results do not take into account bad skeleton recognition from the Kinect. Sometimes, the Kinect is not able to detect the skeleton or distorts it. As a consequence, it does not place the right hand at the correct position. In such cases, the last known position of the right hand is used in order to extract the current hand position. In most of the cases, it is a good approximation because the user does not move his or her hand very abruptly. In other cases, the only solution is asking the person to move.

5.2   Errors

Three most common errors have been observed:

- The neural network is confused by two very similar signs. For instance, it confuses the "H" and "V" signs if the users have a small gap between their index finger and their middle finger (Fig. 4).

Fig. 4. Intended sign: "H", recognised sign: "V" (left), intended sign: "4", recognised sign: "V" (middle), intended sign: "D", recognised sign: "V" (right)

- The neural network does not "see" one or two finger(s). Sometimes, the neural network transforms "4" into "V" or "5" into "3. In the similar way, it transforms "H" into "D" (and sometimes, "H" into "I").
- The neural network "sees" one additional finger. Sometimes, it has been observed that it classifies a "D" into a "V" or the sign "L" into a "3" because it "adds" a finger near the others.

6   Conclusions and Future Work

In this paper, a deep learning solution for HMI was presented. The goal was not to prove that deep learning method obtains better results than other solutions, in particular classical machine learning methods, but to propose another way to process gestures. In a previous work done by Altran research, Belhaoua et al. [2], hand-crafted features were computed and decision trees were used for the classification. However, it might be interesting to mix the deep learning approaches and more classical methods of image processing or machine learning in order to overcome the Kinect's limitations and resolve the most commonly observed errors.

Tests in real conditions in operating rooms (OR) are now necessary in order to take into account the surgeons' feedback to improve the user interface to fill their requirements. The creation of an interface which allows them to register their own gestures in their particular environment and use them in the touchless interface is already implemented.

More data will be necessary in order to reduce the defect of overfitting. Future improvement may include the addition of the depth and infrared values provide by the Kinect to a neural network using transfer learning. To give more functionality to the surgeon, we may explore detecting both hands of the user using the mirror image of the right hand. Finally, we may consider the use of standard cameras.

References

1. O'Hara, K., et al.: Touchless interaction in surgery. Commun. ACM **57**(1), 70–77 (2014)
2. Belhaoua, A., Krebs, A., Radoux, J.-P.: Gesture-based interaction on surgical field using touchless technology. In: Conférence Reconnaissance de Formes et Intelligence Artificielle (2016)

3. Hettig, J., Mewes, A., Riabikin, O., Skalej, M., Preim, B., Hansen, C.: Exploration of 3D medical image data for interventional radiology using myoelectric gesture control. In: 7th Eurographics Workshop on Visual Computing for Biology and Medicine (2015)

4. Di Tommaso, L., Aubry, S., Godard, J., Katranji, H., Pauchot, J.: A new human machine interface in neurosurgery: The Leap Motion®. Technical note regarding a new touchless interface. Neuro-Chirurgie **62**(3), 178–181 (2016)

5. Therapixel Homepage. http://www.therapixel.com/. Accessed 3 May 2017

6. Koller, O., Ney, H., Bowden, R.: Deep hand: How to train a CNN on 1 million hand images when your data is continuous and weakly labelled. In: IEEE Conference on Computer Vision and Pattern Recognition (CVPR), Las Vegas, NV, USA, pp. 3793–3802, June 2016

7. Huang, Y., Liu, X., Jin, L., Zhang, X.: DeepFinger: A cascade convolutional neuron network approach to finger key point detection in egocentric vision with mobile camera. In: IEEE International Conference on Systems, Man and Cybernetics (SMC) (2015)

8. Pigou, L., Dieleman, S., Kindermans, P.-J., Schrauwen, B.: Sign language recognition using convolutional neural networks. In: Agapito, L., Bronstein, M.M., Rother, C. (eds.) ECCV 2014. LNCS, vol. 8925, pp. 572–578. Springer, Cham (2015). doi:10.1007/978-3-319-16178-5_40

9. Tang, A., Lu, K., Wang, Y., Huang, J., Li, H.: A real-time hand posture recognition system using deep neural networks. ACM Trans. Intell. Syst. Technol. **9**(4), Article 39 (2013). https://www.semanticscholar.org/paper/A-Real-Time-Hand-Posture-Recognition-System-Using-Tang-Lu/8c9f20348b2feb8762c327d5c0364bf64896a7fc. doi:10.1145/2735952

10. Developing with Kinect for Windows Homepage. https://developer.microsoft.com/en-us/windows/kinect/develop. Accessed 3 Jul 2017

11. Simonyan, K., Zisserman, A.: Very Deep Convolutional Networks for Large-Scale Image Recognition (2015). arXiv:1409.1556v3

12. ImageNet Homepage. http://www.image-net.org/. Accessed 3 Jul 2017

Analysis of Sound Localization Data Generated by the Extended *Mainzer Kindertisch*

Daniel Lückehe[1(✉)], Katharina Schmidt[2], Karsten Plotz[2], and Gabriele von Voigt[1]

[1] Computational Health Informatics (CHI),
Leibniz Universität Hannover, Hannover, Germany
lueckehe@chi.uni-hannover.de
[2] Institute of Hearing Technology and Audiology (IHA),
Jade University of Applied Sciences, Oldenburg, Germany

Abstract. In this paper, we analyze data generated by the extended *Mainzer Kindertisch* (ERKI setup). The setup uses five loudspeakers to generate 32 virtual sound sources which are ordered in an half circle. It is a new test setup in the medical field. The task for the test candidate is to locate sounds from different, randomly chosen directions. In our analysis, we apply data from test results of adults and of children and compare them. We show that the ERKI setup is applicable for sound localization and that the generated data contain various properties which can be explained by medical reasons. Further, we demonstrate the possibility to detect noticeable test results with data generated by the ERKI setup.

1 Introduction

Auditory localization is one of the most rudimentary and functionally aspects of human development. It aids orientation and can help to avoid dangerous situations, e.g., in traffic. The auditory localization also enables humans to communicate in noisy environments. Thus, it is a crucial aspect in everyday life. The perception of acoustic space is based on processing sounds with two ears and so, directional hearing is a characteristic of binaural way of hearing. The acoustic properties like signal intensity and arrival time are necessary for computing source locations. They depend on the different perception of the left and right ear. In clinical audiology, there is no standardized measuring method to evaluate the binaural localization ability in the free-field. The statement about the directional hearing is important for diagnostics, e.g., to determine *Central Auditory Processing Disorder*. Therefore, one objective of our project *Erfassung des Richtungshörens bei Kindern* (ERKI) is to upgrade a common diagnostic setup for audiology in Germany [8]. With this new setup that we refer to as ERKI setup, we measure the localization accuracy of adults and children [10] because there are no standard values for the auditory development from birth to adolescence [7]. The first test results are analyzed in this paper.

The paper is structured as follows. After the introduction, we present the ERKI setup including a description of the test runs and the employed data set.

G. Kern-Isberner et al. (Eds.): KI 2017, LNAI 10505, pp. 330–336, 2017.
DOI: 10.1007/978-3-319-67190-1_28

In Sect. 3, the basic properties of the data set are shown. In Sect. 4, approaches from the field of dimensionality reduction are employed. At the end of this paper, conclusions are drawn.

2 Extended *Mainzer Kindertisch*

The so called *Mainzer Kindertisch* is a typical pediatric diagnostic setup for auditory measurements. Employing the original measuring system with five or seven loudspeakers in a semicircular position, there is only low angular resolution of 30° or 45° between the loudspeakers. To archive a higher resolution, we modified the setup [8] and added virtual sound sources between two adjacent loudspeakers generated by loudspeaker level differences [9]. Figure 1 shows the test setup. It is based on the *Mainzer Kindertisch* according to DIN ISO 8253-3: speaker-distance of 1 m to the reference point, five loudspeakers with a resolution of 45°. We apply 37 reference angles – five real and 32 virtual sound sources. The sound sources are ordered in 5° steps from −90° to +90°. In the schematic of the setup, presented in Fig. 1(b), the acoustic cover is visualized by a dark gray, the control dial is shown in green, the LED-light strip is presented in blue, one example of a virtual sound source is visualized by red, and the loudspeakers are shown in orange. During the localization experiments, the sounds from the 37 angles are played in a randomized order. The result of the test candidate is recorded by the control dial and the LED-light strip gives a visual feedback. The feedback is possible with a resolution of 1°. Thereby, it is important that the test candidate looks forward to the mark of 0°. As the response time is about 400 ms, a stimuli of 300 ms is employed to avoid head movements during the stimulus. To avoid visual bias, the loudspeakers are hidden by a semicircular curtain. In this paper, our selected stimuli is a pink noise with a level of 65 dB SPL.

A perceived direction x for an angle α is denoted as x_α. The test result $\mathbf{x}$ of a complete test run is ordered as $\mathbf{x} = (x_{-90°}, x_{-85°}, \ldots, x_{90°})^T$. To get a perceived direction x_α of a test result $\mathbf{x}$, we define $x_\alpha = (\mathbf{x})_\alpha$. For a data set $\mathbf{X}$, it applies $\mathbf{X} = (\mathbf{x}_1, \mathbf{x}_2, \ldots, \mathbf{x}_n)$. In this paper, there are data sets for test results of adults $\mathbf{X}^a$ and of children $\mathbf{X}^c$ with $n = 58$ for both data sets. We also define a vector $\boldsymbol{\alpha}$ containing all angles, i.e., $\boldsymbol{\alpha} = (-90, -85, \ldots, 90)^T$. Thus, the errors of

(a) Test setup (Photo: P. Meyer).   (b) Schematic of the ERKI setup.

Fig. 1. The test setup. (Color figure online)

a test result $\mathbf{x}$ can be described as $\mathbf{x} - \boldsymbol{\alpha}$. We define $|\mathbf{x}| = (|x_{-90°}|, |x_{-85°}|, \ldots)^T$. As for each vector element in $|\mathbf{x}|$ the absolute value is computed, the absolute errors are $|\mathbf{x} - \boldsymbol{\alpha}|$.

3   Statistical Properties of the Data Set

In this section, we compute statistical properties of the data set and analyze them. In the first step, mean values and mean errors are presented. Then, we show the distribution of the errors.

In the first analysis, we compute the mean values $\overline{\mathbf{x}}$ of test results $\mathbf{x} \in \mathbf{X}$ with $\mathbf{X} = \mathbf{X}^a$ and $\mathbf{X} = \mathbf{X}^c$ and the standard deviations $\boldsymbol{\sigma}$. It applies $\overline{\mathbf{x}} = (\overline{x}_{-90°}, \overline{x}_{-85°}, \ldots)$ with $\overline{x}_\alpha = \frac{1}{m} \cdot \sum_{i=1}^{m}(\mathbf{x}_i)_\alpha$ for the $m = 37$ different angles in a data set $\mathbf{X}$. Figure 2 visualizes $\overline{\mathbf{x}}$ depending on $\boldsymbol{\alpha}$. Around the curves, the standard deviations $\boldsymbol{\sigma}$ are shown by a semi-transparent layer. As expected in both plots, a linear relation can be observed. In case of children, the standard deviations are larger. For adults, the standard deviations for angles around $0°$ are especially low.

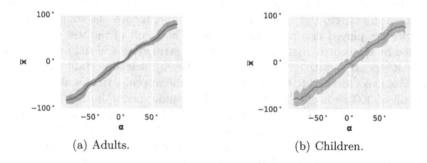

(a) Adults.   (b) Children.

Fig. 2. Visualization of mean results.

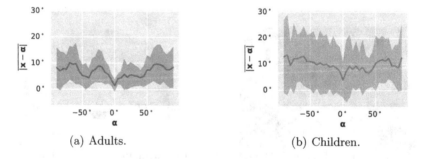

(a) Adults.   (b) Children.

Fig. 3. Visualization of mean differences.

To better recognize the differences between $\bar{\mathbf{x}}$ and $\boldsymbol{\alpha}$, Fig. 3 visualizes $\overline{|\mathbf{x} - \boldsymbol{\alpha}|}$ depending on $\boldsymbol{\alpha}$. Again, there are plots based on test results of adults and of children. The vector $\overline{|\mathbf{x} - \boldsymbol{\alpha}|}$ is computed like $\bar{\mathbf{x}}$ but with a substitution of $\mathbf{x}$ by $|\mathbf{x} - \boldsymbol{\alpha}|$. It is important to compute $\overline{|\mathbf{x} - \boldsymbol{\alpha}|}$ and not $|\bar{\mathbf{x}} - \boldsymbol{\alpha}|$ because for $\bar{\mathbf{x}}$, e.g., two errors with $-10°$ and $10°$ will be compensated to $0°$. When employing $\overline{|\mathbf{x} - \boldsymbol{\alpha}|}$, these two errors will be summarized to $20°$. In the plots, it can be observed that the errors for angles around $0°$ are smaller than for larger angles. This is due to the effect that humans can determine time and level differences between both ears especially well for sounds coming from $0°$ [12]. In particular, this effect can be recognized in the plot of test results of adults. The standard deviations of the errors of children are clearly larger than of adults.

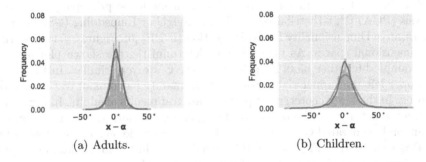

(a) Adults.   (b) Children.

Fig. 4. Distribution of the individual errors. (Color figure online)

In the next step, we present the distribution of the individual errors. The individual errors are the differences between the angle of the sound α and the chosen angle x_α by the test candidate. For the visualization, we consider all angles and all test results. Figure 4 shows the distribution – on the left side for adults and on the right side for children. In the background, the matching histogram can be seen. The curves in blue and green visualize kernel density estimates employing a Gaussian kernel. Additionally, we fitted a normal distribution, respectively a Gaussian distribution, to the data and plotted the normal distribution in an semi-transparent red. In Fig. 4, it can be observed that the distribution of the results of children is wider. Compared to the fitted normal distributions, both curves have similar properties: they are higher at $0°$ and at about $20°$ their values are smaller. Overall, the curves are similar to the fitted normal distributions.

4   Dimensionality Reduction on the Data Set

After basic properties of the data set are presented, we focus on methods from the field of dimensionality reduction to further evaluate the data set $\mathbf{X}^{ac}$ including all test results of $\mathbf{X}^a$ and $\mathbf{X}^c$. A test result $\mathbf{x}$ is a pattern located in a

37-dimensional space. We use dimensionality reduction [3,5] to embed the 37-dimensional patterns of the test results $\mathbf{x} \in \mathbf{X}^{ac}$ to a two-dimensional space $\mathcal{X}^q$. This two-dimensional space is visualized and offers additional information about the data set $\mathbf{X}^{ac}$. For the low-dimensional data set $\mathbf{X}^q$ in the low-dimensional space $\mathcal{X}^q$, it applies $\mathbf{X}^q = (\mathbf{x}_1^q, \mathbf{x}_2^q, \ldots, \mathbf{x}_n^q)$. So, $\mathbf{x}^q$ describes a low-dimensional pattern with $\mathbf{x}^q = (x_1^q, x_2^q)^T$ and $\mathbf{x}_1^q$ is the low-dimensional representation of the test result $\mathbf{x}_1$, while x_1^q is the first feature of the low-dimensional pattern. As every dimensionality reduction reduces the amount of data, the important question to find a matching low-dimensional representation is which information of the data are interesting. In general, dimensionality reduction methods are rated by their capability of maintaining neighborhoods and distances between the patterns [2,4]. To be able to choose a matching low-dimensional space, we employ three different dimensionality reduction methods: principal component analysis (PCA) [1], t-Distributed Stochastic Neighbor Embedding (t-SNE) [11], and iterative Dimensionality Photo-Projection (iDPP) [6]. Figure 5 visualizes the low-dimensional spaces. As t-SNE is non-deterministic, the shown plot is only one example but other plots computed by t-SNE are very similar. In Fig. 5(a), the upper left und upper right space contain mainly patterns of test results of children. In the lower center, most patterns are test results of adults. In Fig. 5(b), no clear structures can be observed. The patterns of both classes look similar to randomly generated Gaussian blobs. The low-dimensional space computed by iDPP is visualized in Fig. 5(c). In this visualization in the lower, left, and right part, there are mainly patterns of test results of children.

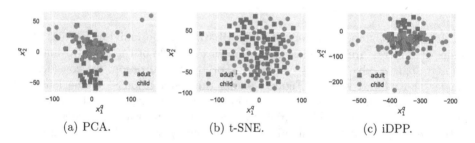

(a) PCA.   (b) t-SNE.   (c) iDPP.

Fig. 5. Visualization of low-dimensional spaces.

To choose the best matching low-dimensional space, we apply findings from preliminary experiments employing a decision tree: some patterns of test results of children can be separated easily but it is difficult to separate patterns of test results of adults from the data set $\mathbf{X}^{ac}$. This property is well represented by iDPP. In the low-dimensional space computed by PCA, a group of patterns of test results of adults can be separated easily. The low-dimensional space computed by t-SNE does not show any clear structures. Thus, we choose iDPP to deeper analyze the low-dimensional space.

Figure 6 visualizes the same space as Fig. 5(c) but some patterns $\mathbf{x}_i^q$ are visualized by the matching curve for $\mathbf{x}_i$. Due to clarity, not for all points the curves

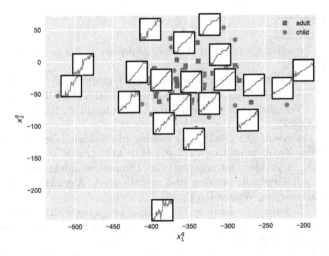

Fig. 6. Visualization of a low-dimensional space including tiny plots of the matching high-dimensional curves.

are visualized, i.e., i gets only few values from $1 \leq i \leq n$. It can be observed that in the center of the visualization, the curves are similar to a diagonal line. Additionally, it can be seen that the outliers are curves with clearly different developments. In the plot, all outliers are patterns of children. As the main purpose of the ERKI setup is to detect noticeable test results of children, this is important and indicates that the required information are within the data.

5   Conclusions

In this paper, we analyzed data generated by the ERKI setup. We showed that there is a strong correlation between angles and mean values of test results. This correlation is the basic requirement. If this demand is not met, the data would not be applicable. We can observe various properties in the data which can be explained by medical reasons, e.g., better localization results of angles if the angle is about $0°$. This emphasis the applicability of data generated by the ERKI setup. The findings made by applying dimensionality reduction methods indicate that the ERKI setup is able to detect noticeable test results of children. This is crucial as it is the main objective of the ERKI setup. In our future work, we plan to employ different algorithms from the field of anomaly detection to automatically detect noticeable test results.

Acknowledgments. We thank the Jade University of Applied Sciences for partly supporting this work with the PhD program *Jade2Pro*.

References

1. Jolliffe, I.: Principal Component Analysis. Springer series in statistics. Springer, New York (1986)
2. Kramer, O.: Dimensionality Reduction with Unsupervised Nearest Neighbors. Intelligent Systems Reference Library. Springer, Berlin Heidelberg (2013)
3. Lee, J.A., Verleysen, M.: Nonlinear Dimensionality Reduction. Springer, Heidelberg (2007)
4. Lee, J.A., Verleysen, M.: Quality assessment of dimensionality reduction: Rank-based criteria. Neurocomputing **72**(7–9), 1431–1443 (2009)
5. Lückehe, D.: Hybride Optimierung für Dimensionsreduktion: Unüberwachte Regression mit Gradientenabstieg und evolutionären Algorithmen. BestMasters, Springer Fachmedien, Wiesbaden (2015)
6. Lückehe, D., Oehmcke, S., Kramer, O.: Manifold learning with iterative dimensionality photo-projection. In: 2017 International Joint Conference on Neural Networks, IJCNN, pp. 2555–2561 (2017)
7. Moore, D.R., Cowan, J.A., Riley, A., Edmondson-Jones, M., Ferguson, M.A.: Development of auditory processing in 6- to 11-year-old children. Ear Hear. **32**, 269–285 (2011)
8. Plotz, K., Schmidt, K.: Lokalisation realer und virtueller Schallquellen mit einem automatisierten Erweiterungsmodul am Mainzer-Kindertisch- Entwicklung des ERKI-Verfahrens. Z Audiol **56**(1), 6–18 (2017)
9. Pulkki, V.: Virtual sound source positioning using vector base amplitude panning. J. Audio Eng. Soc. **45**(6), 456–466 (1997)
10. Schmidt, K., Plotz, K.: Lokalisation virtueller Schallquellen mit einem automatisierten Erweiterungsmodul am Mainzer Kindertisch - ERKI-. In: 5th European Pediatric Conference, Berlin (2016)
11. van der Maaten, L.: Accelerating t-sne using tree-based algorithms. J. Mach. Learn. Res. **15**(1), 3221–3245 (2014)
12. Wang, D., Brown, G.J.: Analysis, Computational Auditory Scene : Principles, Algorithms, and Applications. Wiley-IEEE Press, Hoboken (2006)

A Robust Number Parser
Based on Conditional Random Fields

Heiko Paulheim[✉]

Data and Web Science Group, University of Mannheim, Mannheim, Germany
heiko@informatik.uni-mannheim.de

Abstract. When processing information from unstructured sources, numbers have to be parsed in many cases to do useful reasoning on that information. However, since numbers can be expressed in different ways, a robust number parser that can cope with number representations in different shapes is required in those cases. In this paper, we show how to train such a parser based on Conditional Random Fields. As training data, we use pairs of Wikipedia infobox entries and numbers from public knowledge graphs. We show that it is possible to parse numbers at an accuracy of more than 90%.

Keywords: Number parsing · Number interpretation · Conditional Random Fields

1 Introduction

Number Parsing denotes the conversion of a string representation of a number into a binary representation which is processed as an actual number, such as an integer or a double value. For many systems in which subsequent processing of numeric information (e.g., in terms of comparisons and/or arithmetic operations) is required, number parsing is a necessary preprocessing step.

Since numbers can be represented in different formats (e.g., using different thousands and decimal separators), using blanks in between or not, using different characters for negation, etc., number parsing can be challenging if no prior knowledge about the format at hand exists. For example, the representation 1,000 can be interpreted as one thousand or one, depending on the interpretation of the comma character as a thousands or a decimal separator.

When processing data from the Web, there are quite a few use cases where number parsing is essential. Examples include:

- Information extraction. The creation of knowledge bases from Web resources, e.g., DBpedia from Wikipedia [5], requires the processing of numeric information in Wikipedia infoboxes.
- Question answering on the Web [7]. Questions including comparisons or arithmetics (e.g., *What is the largest lake in the United States?*) require processing of numeric information, and, hence, parsing the corresponding numeric information.

© Springer International Publishing AG 2017
G. Kern-Isberner et al. (Eds.): KI 2017, LNAI 10505, pp. 337–343, 2017.
DOI: 10.1007/978-3-319-67190-1_29

Hohwart

From Wikipedia, the free encyclopedia

Coordinates: 47°56'40.49"N 8°3'36.68"E

The **Hohwart** is a mountain near the village of Breitnau in the Black Forest in the German state of Baden-Wurttemberg. It is 1,123 metres high.

The Hohwart lies on an east-west ridge behind Breitnau. To the south the ridge slopes down over cattle pasture to the Breitnau bowl. To the north the slopes are wooded and descend towards the valley of the Griesdobelbach. The ridge continues northwest to the Otten (1040 m). Just over 1 km to the east is the Roßberg (1125 m) and 3 km to the east, across the Oberbach valley, is the highest mountain in Breitnau municipality: the Weißtannenhöhe (1190 m).

Hohwart

Fig. 1. Example from a Web page with numerical information. Source: https://en. wikipedia.org/wiki/Hohwart, accessed May 9th, 2017

– Information integration. Approaches such as InfoGather [14], Google Fusion Tables [2] or the Mannheim Search Join Engine [6] foresee the integration of data from different sources, usually tables on the Web, into a joint database. In order to create meaningful resources here, which allow for useful processing, numbers need to be parsed into a common format.

A challenge which is common to all those use cases is that numeric data on the Web comes in a large variety of formats. In the example depicted in Fig. 1, if an intelligent agent was to answer the question whether one of the mountains was higher or lower than another, interpreting the text would imply interpreting the numbers, which, even in this small snippet from just one single source, come in two different formats (with and without and thousands separator).

Despite the presence of those use cases and challenges, robust number parsing is still far from being solved. Many named entity recognition tools and benchmarks foresee the detection of number expressions [8], but without any further parsing of the number (i.e., they merely identify a substring of a larger string which contains a numerical expression).

This paper introduces a robust number parser for numeric data from the Web. It is based on a Conditional Random Field (CRF) [4] annotator which separates a string encoding numeric information into relevant parts, such as digits, thousands or decimal separators. Based on this annotation, the string can be interpreted as a number. We create a large number of training examples using numerical values from two Semantic Web knowledge graphs generated from Wikipedia – i.e., DBpedia and YAGO – and the corresponding raw strings from Wikipedia. An evaluation on a sample of tables from the Web shows that the overall accuracy of the approach exceeds 90%.

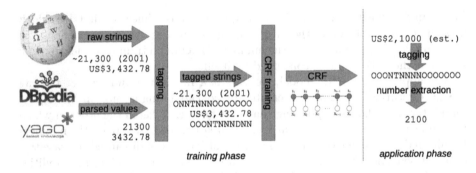

raw strings

~21,300 (2001)
US$3,432.78

parsed values

21300
3432.78

tagging

tagged strings

~21,300 (2001)
ONNTNNNOOOOOOO
US$3,432.78
OOONTNNNDNN

CRF training

CRF

US$2,1000 (est.)

tagging

OOONTNNNNOOOOOOO

number extraction

2100

training phase

application phase

Fig. 2. Overall depiction of the approach

2   Approach

Our approach takes pairs of a number and a string representation of that number as input, as depicted in Fig. 2. While we used raw text values from Wikipedia infoboxes, along with the corresponding numerical values found in the public knowledge graphs DBpedia [5] and YAGO [12] for training, our approach can, in general, be trained with any set of such pairs.

In a preparation step, the raw strings are tagged. The example tagger processes both the *characters* of the raw string and the *digits* of the number from left to right to create the training example, using the tags N (pre-decimal digit), P (post-decimal digit), D (decimal separator), T (thousands separator), and O (other). Each character of the string is processed as follows:

```
if the current character is the current digit of the number
  if the current digit is a pre-decimal digit
    tag with N
  else
    tag with P
  current digit <- next digit
else if the current digit is a -
  tag with M
  current digit <- next digit
else if the remaining number of pre-decimal digits is 0
  tag with D
else if the remaining number of pre-decimal digits is a multitude of 3
  tag with T
else
  tag with O
```

If there are digits left after the string has been processed, the whole example is a mismatch and discarded as a training example.

After the tagging is done, the tagged strings are used train a CRF model. We use LingPipe 4.1.2[1] as an implementation of Conditional Random Fields, and

---

[1] http://alias-i.com/lingpipe/.

the setup described in the tutorial[2]. This setup trains a linear chain CRF which uses the current token and the previous tag as features. As the only change to the example setup, we increased the number of maximum training cycles to make sure that the CRF training converged by itself.

For applying the CRF model, we pass it a raw string and inspect the tag sequence returned. A number is created by concatenating a – for an M tag, a . for a D tag, and the corresponding character for each N tag in the order in which they appear. Characters tagged as T and O are discarded. We create the numbers for all predicted sequences. If a number is not valid, it is discarded. In case two different sequences lead to the same number[3], the corresponding probabilities are added. The number with highest probability is returned.

3   Evaluation

We use two different datasets to create a large number of training examples, i.e., DBpedia [5] and YAGO [12], and we evaluate against a sample of HTML tables containing relational data, drawn from the *T2K* corpus [9,10].

We compare our approach to two baselines, i.e., the built-in floating point parser in Java[4], and the number parsing engine of the Mannheim Search Join Engine [6], a framework for searching and on-the-fly-integration of a large number of relational tables.

3.1   Datasets

DBpedia and YAGO are large-scale knowledge graphs, which are created from Wikipedia infoboxes using a set of mapping rules which map those infoboxes to a backing ontology. For number parsing, they use hard-coded number parsing rules. Since the original strings from the Wikipedia infoboxes are also available, we are able to collect pairs of a parsed number together with the original raw text from which it was extracted (given a certain amount of noise, as explicated below).

To evaluate our approach, we use (a) a hold-out set of 1,000 pairs from both the DBpedia and the YAGO dataset which is not used for training, and (b) a sample from the T2K corpus. The latter is a collection of relational Web tables extracted from the CommonCrawl[5]. Those tables are annotated, among others, with relations defined in the DBpedia ontology. From those, we sampled 1,000 non-empty table cells which are annotated with a number-valued relation according to the ontology.

For each parsing strategy, we compute the accuracy (where we count only deviations larger than 10^{-6} as errors, in order not to erroneously punishing rounding errors) and the root mean squared error (RMSE).

---

[2] http://alias-i.com/lingpipe/demos/tutorial/crf/read-me.html.
[3] This case may occur, e.g., if two sequences differ only in a T and an O.
[4] i.e., invoking `Double.parseDouble(s)` on a string s.
[5] https://commoncrawl.org.

For the hold-out sets as well as the T2K set, we hand-annotated 1,000 string values each with the correct number value. Note that although we have a parsed value for the DBpedia and YAGO sets, we re-created that value manually, since we do not rely on the internal parsing of the DBpedia and YAGO frameworks. Furthermore, this gives as an estimate of how good those parsing techniques work. This comparison yields that the DBpedia built-in parser has an accuracy of 0.734, while the YAGO built-in parser has an accuracy of 0.500. This confirms shortcomings in the accuracy of the processing of numeric expressions from Wikipedia also reported in other works [1,11,13].

3.2 Results

From both corpora, we take different sample sizes to train the CRF (i.e., 50, 500, 5,000, 50,000, and 500,000 instances), and also mixed samples (i.e., half from DBpedia, half from YAGO). The results are depicted in Table 1. We can observe that in all three cases, the mixed dataset with 500 training examples yields the best performing CRF. As expected, the CRFs trained on DBpedia and YAGO examples perform better than their counterpart on the respective holdout sets (although they are outperformed by the mixed variant, which is a bit surprising). The reason why the results constantly degrade when adding more than 500 examples is likely due to some overfitting effect.

It is also remarkable that the plain Java parser performs better in terms of RMSE in two out of three cases. The reason is that if it is capable of parsing a number, the result is usually always correct, otherwise it is not capable of parsing the number, in which case we treat the output as 0 for computing the RMSE, i.e., the absolute error is bound by the values in the dataset. In contrast, the CRF approach can also make predictions that are a few orders of magnitude away from the actual value (e.g., when erroneously concatenating a number and a year present in a string).

In terms of runtime, our approach is slower than the baselines: for parsing a single number, the Java API takes 0.008 ms per string, MSJE takes 0.0215, while our approach takes 0.247.[6] On the other hand, this means that even with our approach, 4,000 strings can be parsed per second, which is fast enough for most applications.[7]

3.3 Error Analysis

In addition to the quantitative analysis, we inspected the mistakes made by our approach manually. There are several main sources of errors: strings containing rare symbols adjacent to a number (such as rare currency symbols), negative numbers, and numbers that are expressed partly textually (e.g., 3.2 million). Negative numbers are very underrepresented in our training sets, thus, the CRF

---

[6] Runtimes on a commodity Windows laptop.

[7] The training of the CRF, however, can take up to several hours, but only needs to be performed once. An executable version with the best pre-trained CRF is available at http://bit.ly/2qRbwDq.

Table 1. Results on the T2K dataset and the holdout sets of DBpedia and YAGO

Dataset	T2K		DBpedia holdout		YAGO holdout	
Approach	Acc.	RMSE	Acc.	RMSE	Acc.	RMSE
Java	0.171	7.03E+09	0.223	**4.03E+09**	0.4055	**1.07E+07**
T2K/MSJE	0.2155	7.03E+09	0.3	4.24E+149	0.4495	1.69E+07
DBpedia50	0.82	8.74E+09	0.779	5.70E+09	0.936	1.52E+07
DBpedia500	0.923	2.12E+05	0.936	8.25E+09	0.963	1.52E+07
DBpedia5000	0.89	1.26E+06	0.932	8.25E+09	0.793	1.52E+07
DBpedia50000	0.853	3.77E+07	0.928	1.04E+10	0.73	1.52E+07
DBpedia500000	0.863	4.41E+06	0.928	6.29E+13	0.767	1.52E+07
YAGO50	0.823	9.94E+09	0.715	5.70E+09	0.939	1.52E+07
YAGO500	0.929	**1.84E+05**	0.927	5.70E+09	0.984	1.52E+07
YAGO5000	0.92	6.92E+05	0.901	8.25E+09	0.983	1.52E+07
YAGO50000	0.922	2.12E+05	0.911	1.42E+15	0.982	1.52E+07
YAGO500000	0.921	6.87E+05	0.906	1.04E+10	0.981	1.52E+07
Mix50	0.906	6.84E+05	0.891	5.70E+09	0.984	1.52E+07
Mix500	**0.933**	2.12E+05	**0.941**	8.25E+09	**0.986**	1.52E+07
Mix5000	0.922	2.12E+05	0.938	8.25E+09	0.984	1.52E+07
Mix50000	0.919	1.26E+06	0.932	8.25E+09	0.983	1.52E+07
Mix500000	0.918	8.65E+05	0.929	6.29E+13	0.983	1.52E+07

always predicts a very low probability for a negative number. Partly textual numbers cannot be handled by our approach, since it only tags digits and separators in a string. Extending the approach to semi-textual numbers is subject to future work.

4   Conclusion and Outlook

In this paper, we have presented a first approach to train a robust number parser using Conditional Random Fields. The parser was tested on different datasets, where it constantly yields more than 90% accuracy.

Current limitations are the presence of rare symbols. To overcome those, better and more diverse training sets are needed, although this is not trivial: in an experiment, resampling the dataset for an equal coverage of symbols using a Kennard Stone sample [3] did not bring any improvement here. Further challenges to be addressed include: methods are needed to cope with partly textual, partly numerical representations, such as 3 `million`, and the interpretation of units of measurement [11].

For use cases in which a *set* of numbers which are likely to be formatted equally (e.g., from one column in a table) are to be processed, it would also be interesting to adapt the approach in a way that it exploits those common patterns.

References

1. Fleischhacker, D., Paulheim, H., Bryl, V., Völker, J., Bizer, C.: Detecting errors in numerical linked data using cross-checked outlier detection. In: Mika, P., et al. (eds.) ISWC 2014. LNCS, vol. 8796, pp. 357–372. Springer, Cham (2014). doi:10. 1007/978-3-319-11964-9_23

2. Gonzalez, H., Halevy, A.Y., Jensen, C.S., Langen, A., Madhavan, J., Shapley, R., Shen, W., Goldberg-Kidon, J.: Google fusion tables: web-centered data management and collaboration. In: Proceedings of the 2010 ACM SIGMOD International Conference on Management of Data, pp. 1061–1066. ACM (2010)

3. Kennard, R.W., Stone, L.A.: Computer aided design of experiments. Technometrics **11**(1), 137–148 (1969). http://www.jstor.org/stable/1266770

4. Lafferty, J., McCallum, A., Pereira, F., et al.: Conditional random fields: probabilistic models for segmenting and labeling sequence data. In: Proceedings of the Eighteenth International Conference on Machine Learning, ICML, vol. 1, pp. 282–289 (2001)

5. Lehmann, J., Isele, R., Jakob, M., Jentzsch, A., Kontokostas, D., Mendes, P.N., Hellmann, S., Morsey, M., van Kleef, P., Auer, S., Bizer, C.: DBpedia - a large-scale, multilingual knowledge base extracted from Wikipedia. Semant. Web J. **6**(2), 167–195 (2013)

6. Lehmberg, O., Ritze, D., Ristoski, P., Meusel, R., Paulheim, H., Bizer, C.: The Mannheim search join engine. Web Semant. Sci. Serv. Agents World Wide Web **35**, 159–166 (2015)

7. Lopez, V., Uren, V., Sabou, M., Motta, E.: Is question answering fit for the semantic web?: a survey. Semant. Web **2**(2), 125–155 (2011)

8. Nadeau, D., Sekine, S.: A survey of named entity recognition and classification. Lingvisticae Investigationes **30**(1), 3–26 (2007)

9. Ritze, D., Lehmberg, O., Bizer, C.: Matching HTML tables to DBpedia. In: Proceedings of the 5th International Conference on Web Intelligence, Mining and Semantics, p. 10. ACM (2015)

10. Ritze, D., Lehmberg, O., Oulabi, Y., Bizer, C.: Profiling the potential of web tables for augmenting cross-domain knowledge bases. In: Proceedings of the 25th International Conference on World Wide Web, pp. 251–261. International World Wide Web Conferences Steering Committee (2016)

11. Subercaze, J.: Chaudron: extending DBpedia with measurement. In: Blomqvist, E., Maynard, D., Gangemi, A., Hoekstra, R., Hitzler, P., Hartig, O. (eds.) ESWC 2017. LNCS, vol. 10249, pp. 434–448. Springer, Cham (2017). doi:10.1007/ 978-3-319-58068-5_27

12. Suchanek, F.M., Kasneci, G., Weikum, G.: YAGO: a core of semantic knowledge unifying WordNet and Wikipedia. In: 16th International Conference on World Wide Web, pp. 697–706 (2007)

13. Wienand, D., Paulheim, H.: Detecting incorrect numerical data in DBpedia. In: Presutti, V., d'Amato, C., Gandon, F., d'Aquin, M., Staab, S., Tordai, A. (eds.) ESWC 2014. LNCS, vol. 8465, pp. 504–518. Springer, Cham (2014). doi:10.1007/ 978-3-319-07443-6_34

14. Yakout, M., Ganjam, K., Chakrabarti, K., Chaudhuri, S.: InfoGather: entity augmentation and attribute discovery by holistic matching with web tables. In: Proceedings of the 2012 ACM SIGMOD International Conference on Management of Data, pp. 97–108. ACM (2012)

From Natural Language Instructions
to Structured Robot Plans

Mihai Pomarlan$^{(\boxtimes)}$, Sebastian Koralewski, and Michael Beetz

Institute for Artificial Intelligence, Universität Bremen, Bremen, Germany
pomarlan@uni-bremen.de

Abstract. Research into knowledge acquisition for robotic agents has looked at interpreting natural language instructions meant for humans into robot-executable programs; however, the ambiguities of natural language remain a challenge for such "translations". In this paper, we look at a particular sort of ambiguity: the control flow structure of the program described by the natural language instruction. It is not always clear, when more conditional statements appear in a natural language instruction, which of the conditions are to be thought of as alternative options in the same test, and which belong to a code branch triggered by a previous conditional. We augment a system which uses probabilistic reasoning to identify the meaning of the words in a sentence with reasoning about action preconditions and effects in order to filter out non-sensical code structures. We test our system with sample instruction sheets inspired from analytical chemistry.

1 Motivation

A current topic of research is the acquisition of knowledge for robotic agents, aimed at enabling them to perform more complex manipulation tasks. One method, explored in previous work [1], is to mine "how to" resources, such as wikiHow, for recipes and instructions for various activities. The benefits of having robotic agents capable to understand natural language instructions are obvious. On one hand, sites like wikiHow already contain a wealth of information about many activities; on the other, it helps usability if a human can instruct a robot as they would another human.

However, the state of the art is still far from agents robustly capable of understanding natural language. Humans, relying on their already rich commonsense knowledge and experience, can tolerate much more ambiguity and underspecification in their communication than machines can. Work on resolving ambiguities and inferring missing information is ongoing [1,2], but has focused so far on instructions with a simple structure that can be represented as a sequence of steps with ambiguous parameters.

In this paper, we are concerned with instructions with more complex structures caused by the presence of (the natural language equivalent of) program flow controls such as conditionals and loops, which create ambiguities of structure.

© Springer International Publishing AG 2017
G. Kern-Isberner et al. (Eds.): KI 2017, LNAI 10505, pp. 344–351, 2017.
DOI: 10.1007/978-3-319-67190-1_30

pipette naoh analyte
if (color analyte brown) **then**
   say iron
else if (color analyte white) **then**
   pour naoh analyte
   if (color analyte clear) **then**
     say aluminum
   else if (color analyte white) **then**
     say magnesium
	pipette naoh analyte
	if (color analyte brown) **then**
	   say iron
	   if (color analyte white) **then**
	     pour naoh analyte
	     if (color analyte clear) **then**
	       say aluminum
	       if (color analyte white) **then**
	         say magnesium

Fig. 1. Two possible interpretations for the metal cation identification instruction

Consider the following text, describing a procedure to identify metal cations in a solution: *add three drops of NaOH to the solution. If a brown precipitate appears, say the solution contains Iron. If a white precipitate appears, add five mL of NaOH. If the precipitate disappears, say the solution contains Aluminum. If the precipitate remains, say the solution contains Magnesium.* Two possible ways to interpret this text into a program are given in Fig. 1, and there are other ways as well.

These two programs, though consistent with the operations enumerated in natural language, behave very differently. Nevertheless, a human can tell the second program is wrong, even without chemistry knowledge. The purpose of the procedure described in the example is to identify the metal ions in a solution. Once the ion has been identified, therefore the goal has been reached, the program should be over.

The example above suggests that at least some ambiguity in program structure can be resolved through knowledge of a task's goal, and/or its component actions in terms of preconditions and effects. It is this intuition we examine here.

2 Overview

We consider the problem of turning a text written in natural language into a simple structured program (a "code tree") that may contain simple statements, conditionals (if..else if..else..end if structures) and loops. Currently, we support arbitrarily complex conditionals, and loop-while/untils with one instruction in their body.

First, the natural language text is fed into a probabilistic inference system called PRAC [1] which is used to identify the meanings of words and coreference pronouns. PRAC uses Markov logic networks to represent a probability distribution on how various action requests are formulated; the networks are created from training on large text corpora. Interpreting a text is formalized as a probabilistic query: finding the most likely action(s) requested given the natural language text as evidence. This produces a list of so-called "action cores", action descriptions in terms of roles and values. Based on this list of action cores, the system produces a list of candidate code trees, which are then validated based on a STRIPS-like procedure that checks whether action preconditions are met at all points of the code tree. The STRIPS validation is used as a way to add more knowledge and help disambiguating between structures for the code trees.

3 Representing Actions and World States

We use disjunctive normal form expressions (dnf-expressions) to represent world states, action pre- and postconditions, and "ifconditions" (the conditions appearing in an if or loop statement). A "term" is a simple statement about the world state or its negation (for example, $(STATE\ switch\ on)$ and $(NOT\ (STATE\ switch\ on))$ are terms). A "clause" is a conjunction of terms. A dnf-expression is then a disjunction of clauses.

We say that a clause is consistent (with itself) when it doesn't contain both a term and its negation; we will thereafter assume all clauses we work with are self-consistent, except for postcondition clauses. We say two clauses are consistent if there is no term appearing in one clause that appears negated in the other. We say that clause A includes clause B if they are consistent and all terms appearing in B also appear in A. The **world state** is represented by a dnf-expression in which each clause is a possible world. The world state is updated during code tree validation, based on the postconditions of the actions in the code tree. We use open-world semantics: if something is not stated, in a possible world, to be true or false, then it is unknown in that world.

A **precondition** is represented by a dnf-expression. When validating an action in a code tree, we say that the action is valid if its precondition is known to be true in all worlds that are possible when the action is encountered in the code tree: for every possible world W, there exists a clause P in the precondition such that W includes P. If an action is invalid when it is encountered in the code tree, then this counts as an error and the code tree is considered invalid and rejected.

An **ifcondition** is represented by a dnf-expression. When checking an if or loop instruction in the code tree, we say that the instruction is meaningful if its ifcondition is consistent with at least one of the worlds possible when the instruction is met: there exists a possible world W, such that there exists a clause P in the ifcondition, such that W and P are consistent with each other. If there is no such possible world W, then this counts as a warning, which we currently treat as a reason to reject a code tree.

A **postcondition** is represented by what is syntactically a dnf-expression; this allows our actions to have several sets of possible effects, such as different reactions which may be observed between a known and an unknown reagent. However, we interpret a postcondition dnf differently from other expressions above. In particular, clauses are allowed to be inconsistent and their order matters. When performing an update on a possible world, terms about the world are added in the order in which they appear in the postcondition clause, and replace previous contradicting terms. For example, a postcondition branch $(AND\ (NOT\ (STATE\ s\ off))\ (NOT\ (STATE\ s\ on))\ (STATE\ s\ ?new))$ first makes sure the entity s will no longer be in either on or off states, and then puts entity s in state ?new (which can be, for example, on).

A **terminal condition** is a dnf expression we use to represent a goal state, after which no more statements are expected. A terminal condition is considered achieved if there is at least one possible world in which it holds: there is a possible world W, such that there is a clause P in the terminal condition, such that W includes P. The reason why we ask whether a satisfying possible world exists (rather than requiring the terminal condition to hold everywhere) is to guarantee that instructions achieving the terminal condition are the last executed in a code tree.

Note that while our code tree validation procedure is inspired by STRIPS, we go beyond it by using open-world semantics and actions with more sets of possible effects. This is important, since we aim for an approach usable in environments that are only partially known, and where the effects of actions are unpredictable.

4   Code Tree Generation and Validation

As our motivating example shows, knowledge about the basic actions in a program can help check that the program's structure makes sense. We chose a STRIPS representation for actions because it is easy to use. Note, we do not do STRIPS planning; we obtain candidate "plans" from interpreting the input natural language instruction, where a plan may not be just a sequence (as would be the case with STRIPS plans) but instead a structured program with branches and loops. A program is considered valid if the procedure described below comes to the conclusion that at every step of the program, preconditions for the current action to perform are met.

Our procedure is to generate all possible code trees from a list of action cores returned by PRAC, then discard from this list all code trees that produce errors (preconditions not met) or warnings (meaningless ifconditions). In the future, we will merge the validation and generation steps, for efficiency.

In order to validate a code tree, we first "unroll" all the loops present: a loop is replaced with an IF statement (with ifcondition being the negation of the loop termination condition), where the body of this IF is the body of the loop repeated twice, followed by an assertion of the loop's termination condition. Our STRIPS-like validation, which we will call cs-validation here, is defined as follows:

- sequences without control structures (branches or loops) are cs-valid if they are valid STRIPS sequences (no invalid actions, no action after terminal condition met)
- an IF and its branches are cs-valid if each branch is cs-valid, and if the ifcondition is meaningful (consistent with at least one possible world)
- sequences with control structures are valid if each of their elements are cs-valid

While the validation procedure traverses the code tree, it updates the world state based on postconditions and assertions about the world state. Postconditions and assertions are applied to all possible worlds at a point in a program (all

	"nested"	"sequential"	"else-if"

(if ifcondition-1)
(block-1)
(if ifcondition-2)
(block-2)
	if ifcondition-1 then
	block-1
	if ifcondition-2 then
	block-2
		if ifcondition-1 then
		block-1
		if ifcondition-2 then
		block-2
			if ifcondition-1 then
			block-1
			else if ifcondition-2 then
			block-2

Fig. 2. Converting a list of action cores (left) into possible code trees (right)

clauses in the world state dnf expression). Entering an IF branch also affects the world state: for instructions inside the IF body, only possible worlds consistent with its ifcondition are considered.

Our procedure takes as input: the code tree to validate; a domain description (action preconditions and effects); an initial world state; optionally, a terminal condition.

We will now look at structural ambiguities caused by conditionals. Figure 2 shows the three possible structures that are consistent with a list of action cores containing two conditional instructions (for conciseness, the action cores are simplified). More structures are possible in the sequential case: if more statements appear in block-1, there are several ways to split it into statements appearing in, and outside of the IF body, but for ease of exposition, we will focus here on these three cases.

We will refer to the postconditions of block-1 as the changes to the world state done by the postconditions of the actions in block-1, and by the selection of possible worlds made by ifcondition-1. Similarly, preconditions of block-2 will mean here both the preconditions of the actions in block-2, and ifcondition-2.

A "nested" structure can be unambiguously selected when the preconditions of block-2 depend on the postconditions of block-1 to be valid/meaningful. An "else-if" structure can be unambiguously selected when block-1 achieves the terminal condition, or the preconditions of block-2 would be invalidated by the postconditions of block-1. An "else-if" structure can also be explicitly invoked in natural language (for example by statements such as "otherwise, if") and we take this into account when generating candidate code trees: when it is clear from the language that a conditional appears as an ELSE-IF branch of some previous conditional, we mark it as such.

Currently, our approach does not have a way to unambiguously select the sequential case. If the preconditions of block-2 are unaffected by block-1, then both nested and sequential interpretations are still cs-valid; this will be shown in the evaluation, below.

5   Evaluation

To test cs-validation as a method to disambiguate code structures we have used several instruction sheets inspired by analytical chemistry. For page count reasons we don't include the action pre-/postconditions here, but these are available on request; they are currently hand-coded, but we will look at more autonomous ways to acquire them. For each instruction sheet, we generate a list of code trees, from which we then remove the code trees that generate errors or warnings during cs-validation. When more code trees remain in the list, we also look at the world state after each code tree is run.

An example instruction sheet is storage: *if the jar is sealed, put it into the fridge. If the jar is empty, then open the drawer. If the lid is there, take it and put it on the jar.* This results in 37 candidate code trees, out of which only the one corresponding to the correct interpretation survives cs-validation. In this case, cs-validation is able to uniquely select among the available options to arrange control structures, and it is able to do so despite the large number of candidates present.

Another example instruction sheet we use is base titration: *put a drop of alizarin into the test solution. Put drops of hydrogen chloride into the solution until it turns yellow. If the drop count is less than five, put two drops of litmus in the solution. If the solution turns red, put more drops of the NaOH in the solution until it turns blue.* There are three possible candidates generated for this instruction sheet, out of which two survive cs-validation (given in Fig. 3). These two candidates result in the same set of possible final world states, and both look like plausible interpretations.

```
pipette alyzarin analyte                 pipette alyzarin analyte
loop-until (color analyte yellow)        loop-until (color analyte yellow)
    pipette hcl analyte                      pipette hcl analyte
if (drop-count hcl small) then           if (drop-count hcl small) then
    pipette litmus analyte                   pipette litmus analyte
    if (color analyte red) then          if (color analyte red) then
        loop-until (color analyte blue)      loop-until (color analyte blue)
            pipette naoh analyte                 pipette naoh analyte
```

Fig. 3. CS-valid code trees for base titration

Another example instruction sheet is the metal cation identification, given in Sect. 1. In this case, 55 candidate code trees are generated from the instruction sheet, however only 2 survive cs-validation, which shows its power to prune the candidate set. The surviving code trees are shown in Fig. 4. This time however the two code trees do not result in the same set of possible final world states: only the correct plan would say nothing when the analyte contains neither iron, aluminum, or magnesium.

Ambiguities result when a nested and a sequential structure both survive cs-validation. For base titration this appears benign, but in general the code trees will not behave the same, and some further disambiguation (e.g. via questions to a human) is necessary. Still, cs-validation significantly reduces the number of candidates to disambiguate.

```
pipette naoh analyte
if (color analyte brown) then
    say iron
else if (color analyte white) then
    pour naoh analyte
    if (color analyte clear) then
        say aluminum
    else if (color analyte white) then
        say magnesium
```

```
pipette naoh analyte
if (color analyte brown) then
    say iron
else
    if (color analyte white) then
        pour naoh analyte
    if (color analyte clear) then
        say aluminum
    else if (color analyte white) then
        say magnesium
```

Fig. 4. CS-valid code trees for metal cation identification

6   Related Work

There has been substantial work in analyzing the meaning of conditionals in natural language [3,4]. Other work has tackled the ambiguity of sentiment analysis in conditionals [5]. We used an intensional interpretation [3], which matches the procedural one from computer programming: a conditioned action is performed iff its condition is true.

Extracting sequences of procedures (without branching) from text has been shown in [6]. Workflows that branch into parallel tracks that may recombine are extracted from text in [7] using a notion of "trace index". These workflows describe deterministic, possibly parallel actions in known environments. There are also natural language interpretation systems to enable dialog between humans and robotic agents [8–10]. However, they are intended for deterministic environments where the initial state is fully observable, and can handle only simple conditionals– a condition, an action, optionally an else with its action, with no nesting.

References

1. Nyga, D., Beetz, M.: Cloud-based probabilistic knowledge services for instruction interpretation. In: International Symposium of Robotics Research (ISRR), Italy, Sestri Levante (Genoa) (2015)
2. Misra, D.K., Sung, J., Lee, K., Saxena, A.: Tell me dave: context-sensitive grounding of natural language to manipulation instructions. In: Proceedings of Robotics: Science and Systems, Berkeley, USA, July 2014
3. Abbott, B.: Conditionals in English and fopl. In: Shu, D., Turner, K., (eds.) Contrasting Meanings in Languages of the East and West, pp. 579–606. Peter Lang, Oxford (2010)
4. Rothschild, D.: Conditionals and propositions in semantics. J. Philos. Logic 44(6), 781 (2015)
5. Narayanan, R., Liu, B., Choudhary, A.: Sentiment analysis of conditional sentences. In: Proceedings of the 2009 Conference on Empirical Methods in Natural Language Processing, vol. 1, pp. 180–189. Association for Computational Linguistics (2009)
6. Dufour-Lussier, V., Le Ber, F., Lieber, J., Nauer, E.: Automatic case acquisition from texts for process-oriented case-based reasoning. Inf. Syst. 40, 153–167 (2014)

7. Schumacher, P., Minor, M.: Extracting control-flow from text. In: IRI, pp. 203–210. IEEE (2014)
8. Bos, J., Oka, T.: A spoken language interface with a mobile robot. Artif. Life Robot. **11**(1), 42–47 (2007)
9. Misra, D.K., Tao, K., Liang, P., Saxena, A.: Environment-driven lexicon induction for high-level instructions. In: ACL (1), pp. 992–1002 (2015)
10. Eppe, M., Trott, S., Feldman, J.: Exploiting deep semantics and compositionality of natural language for human-robot-interaction. In: 2016 IEEE/RSJ International Conference on Intelligent Robots and Systems (IROS), pp. 731–738. IEEE (2016)

Opportunistic Planning with Recovery for Robot Safety

Bernhard Reiterer[(✉)] and Michael Hofbaur

ROBOTICS – Institute for Robotics and Mechatronics,
JOANNEUM RESEARCH Forschungsgesellschaft mbH,
Lakeside B08a, 9020 Klagenfurt, Austria
{bernhard.reiterer,michael.hofbaur}@joanneum.at
http://www.joanneum.at/robotics

Abstract. Emerging applications for various types of robots require them to operate autonomously in the vicinity of humans. Ensuring the safety of humans is a permanent requirement that must be upheld at all times. As tasks performed by robots are becoming more complex, adaptive planning components are required. Modern planning approaches do not contribute to a robot system's safety capabilities, which are thus limited to means like reduction of force and speed or halt of the robot. We argue that during a plan's execution there should be a backup plan that the robot system can fall back to as an alternative to halting. We present our approach of generating variations of plans by optional exploitation of opportunities, which extend the initially safe plan for extra value when the current safety situation allows it, while maintaining recovery policies to get back to the safe plan in the case of safety-related events.

Keywords: Automated planning · Collaborative robot · Opportunistic planning · Robot safety

1 Introduction

Modern applications for robots are posing considerable challenges for the capabilities of a robot system to determine the actions that it should take in order to fulfill its goals. Typical solutions involve planning components, which use the system's knowledge to search for action sequences that lead from the current state to a desired goal state. However, in real-world scenarios, the plan generated based upon abstract knowledge often cannot be followed due to external events and possible failures. The robot system is still required to achieve the posed goals rather than giving up or following a plan that has become pointless. Collaborative robots facilitate a wide range of applications by letting teams of humans and robots work together, utilizing each team member's individual

---

B. Reiterer—This research was partially funded by the Austrian Ministry for Transport, Innovation and Technology (BMVIT) within the framework of the sponsorship agreement formed for 2015–2018 under the project CollRob.

G. Kern-Isberner et al. (Eds.): KI 2017, LNAI 10505, pp. 352–358, 2017.
DOI: 10.1007/978-3-319-67190-1_31

strengths. Typically, physical contacts between humans and robots will often occur in such scenarios. With halts as the main means of dealing with contacts, the team's performance would plummet. Meanwhile, the problems that can be solved collaboratively tend to be more complex than traditional robot problems, boosting the need for powerful planning capabilities. In this paper we propose to meaningfully support safety in robot planning by following the concept of opportunistic planning, which we evolve in a way that also broadens its general applicability.

2   Opportunistic Planning for Fallback Plans

A robot system must possess the means to properly adapt to unexpected events. If these are related to safety, such as the appearance of a human in the robot's path, it is particularly desirable to provide a safe reaction after a minimal time span. The potential to offer such a feature is defined by combined qualities of the used planning approach and its implementation, the planning executive and the way it is joined with the planner, the planning domain, and the planning problem generation from current knowledge and sensor data. The planning executive should be able to quickly switch to what we call a *fallback plan*. The fallback plan is supposed to be significantly more useful than a plain halting of the robot.

We have examined planning approaches that may seem to be candidates for realizing fallback plans naturally. Considerations of algorithms that provide contingent plans [10], policies [8], or their common extreme form of universal plans [5], have not lead to consistent productive approaches supporting safety. Thus we moved the fallback plan functionality to the scope of the planning executive. This component's concept and integration into the overall architecture follow the approach shown in the ROSPlan framework [2].

Previous research has suggested to enrich the executive with the capability of exploiting opportunities [1,6] in order to fulfill additional non-mandatory goals for an increased overall value. An opportunity is a plan fragment or template thereof along with specifications of its use. Cashmore et al. [1] build this meta-data around an object type, meaning that the opportunity can be applied whenever such an object is encountered during execution.

Opportunistic planning is a candidate approach for realizing our fallback plan concept. In a nutshell, the safe fallback plan corresponds to the main plan, and opportunities are applied for optimizations or optional goals.

2.1   Example Scenario Opportunities

We are considering the scenario of a mobile manipulator that performs transportation or service tasks in an indoor location, which could be a factory or an office complex. We have identified the following types as a subset of the opportunities that the mobile manipulator can encounter in the example scenario:

Unsafe shortcut: There is a shorter connection between two points along the safe path, but it was not used in the safe path for a reason: It bears an inherent

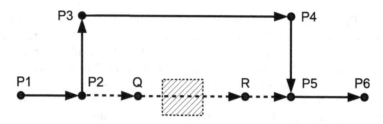

Fig. 1. The robot plans to move from waypoint P1 to P6. The safe path, marked by continuous arrows, traverses P2, P3, P4, and P5. There is a potential shortcut from P2 to P5, denoted by dashed arrows, but a part of it crosses a safety-critical section between waypoints Q and R.

increased safety risk. The shortcut crosses an area that is also frequented by humans. It is necessary to traverse this passage at a lower speed, if it can be crossed at all. Such an opportunity is sketched in Fig. 1.

Carry along: The robot knows the current location of an object that is not related to the current mission, and that it should rather be at a different location. The target location is near a point further down in the safe path.

Explore: The robot has detected that its surroundings differ from their representation in the used map, e.g., a production line or some furniture was moved, changing the abstract waypoint network.

Go faster: The opportunity consists of a modified copy of a sequence of movement actions from the main plan, with parameters that control the movement speed modified. The opportunity buys speed at the cost of safety at the action level, which is then mitigated on the overall planning level.

2.2 Planning with Opportunity Instantiation

One main challenge in opportunistic planning lies in enabling the switching of the execution from the main plan to an opportunity and back – which can be easily extended to a nested view, allowing for switching between opportunities. The previous work on planning with opportunities typically overcomes this challenge by building on certain characteristics of their scenario. In the domain of [1], the only elements that are relevant to both the main plan and to the opportunity are the robots' location, achieved utility, and the current time, which is treated as a simplification of costs in general. As their opportunities are considered to be of low probability – thus not foreseeable in the main plan – and high utility, they should always be executed if expected durations still allow for sufficient chance of completing the main plan. To perform the switching in either direction, it is enough to execute a "go to" action, potentially replacing one or multiple other such actions. In a similar way, [6] shows opportunities that are loops restoring their initial state (besides achieved soft goals and resources spent) at the end, consequently their execution can be inserted at certain states in the main plan's execution rather easily.

In order to increase the aptitude of opportunistic planning for a greater variety of domains and to make it support our safety concepts in particular, we apply a few modifications to the idea. We refrain from some of the spontaneity it bears in related work and in turn establish a certain level of preparedness.

The planning system knows a set of *opportunity templates* (OT), which represent the applicable opportunity types as listed above. Conceptually, an OT has the same components as a PDDL [3, 4, 7, 9] action – name, parameters, preconditions, effects, and duration if durative actions are used, plus a plan fragment, which consists of a list of parametrized actions just like the main plan. However, in contrast to a concrete plan, the fragment can contain variables that match the OT's parameters and are thus assigned values in the course of the decision for the opportunity's usage. An *opportunity instance* (OI) is a copy of an OT, with variables filled according to the foreseen execution of the OI.

Initially, the safe plan is generated by planning, using pessimistic assumptions for all safety-related variables. E.g., for any part of the working area that *may be* occupied by persons, the initial state for planning contains a fact denoting that it *is* currently occupied. This way, we assure that only safe actions are used in the plan. This pessimistic assumption is not applied to the evaluation of opportunity applicability, which is done in the next step.

Checking the main plan against the available OTs, for each state we obtain a set of candidate OIs. From our list above, this means for the "unsafe shortcut" OT that the plan is searched for pairs of waypoints connected via safe movements. The "carry along" OT is treated in a similar way: the plan is checked for movements connecting an object's current location with the place where it should be. Note that, while waypoints pose a handy example, other OTs may require considering different predicates of arbitrary semantics. Found tuples of waypoints are used to parametrize the OI, then it can be processed further:

1. Check if the OI's preconditions hold in its starting state.
2. Check if the OI's effects break any preconditions of actions of the main plan after the OI's finishing state. Depending on the domain definition, this may also consider action durations and resources spent in the OI.
3. Evaluate the utility against a OT-specific static or cost-dependent threshold.
4. Construct a recovery policy for the OI. This step is covered further below.

These steps can mostly be covered by utilizing or emulating the capabilities of the used planner, such as comparing sets of facts and computing the state that results from an action execution. If given in the domain, a metric in the terms of PDDL 2.1 [3] could be a measure for utility. But, as for other steps listed here, efficiency or easier feasibility may yield OT-specific hardcoded implementation to be a viable means, since a generic solution that understands OT descriptions is not yet available.

Failure of any of these processing steps cause the OI candidate to be dropped. Others are remembered in the OI map for the execution, keyed to the respective starting state. The actual execution of the OI is usually still tied to the later evaluation of not yet known facts, such as observation results along the way. Also, the preparation and maintenance of the OI map for the currently executed plan can be a recurring activity that the planning system performs in parallel, taking into account new knowledge from sensor readings. Basically, following the initial preparation of OIs – or even before its completion, the plan execution can start in a straight-forward manner, with the extra step of considering switching to a currently possible OI before triggering the execution of the current plan's next action.

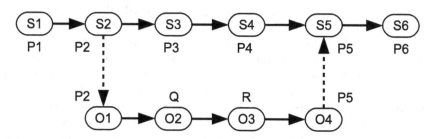

Fig. 2. Example of a safe plan with an added opportunity instance

Figure 2 shows an example of an "unsafe shortcut" OI added to the plan from the example in Fig. 1. On the top we see the plan for moving along the safe path (states S1, S2, ..., S6). The OI map includes the optional switching at S2 to the shortcut OI via states O1, O2, O3, and O4. From there the executive would switch back to S5, in which the robot is at the same location, P5.

3   Recovering from Failed Opportunities

To realize our safety requirements, an essential capability is the quick reaction to events that would make the continuation of an OI a significant safety risk.

The OI is enriched with a recovery policy, which maps each OI state to a recovery plan that leads to a state in the main plan. The recovery plan is a – usually short, potentially empty – list of action instances that is to be executed as the act of switching back from the opportunity to the main plan.

The construction of the recovery plan P_x must be performed for each state O_x of the opportunity. It follows these steps:

1. Trivial cases: If O_x is the first or last state of the OI, P_x is empty.
2. Find a plan P_0 from O_x to main plan state S_0, which is the main plan state from which the OI forked off. Verify that the remaining main plan still holds.
3. Find a plan P_f from O_x to main plan state S_f, which is the main plan state at which the OI is joined to main plan after successful execution. Verify that the remaining main plan still holds.
4. If neither P_0 nor P_f are found, discard the OI.
5. If both P_0 and P_f are found, compare them, e.g., based upon utility or resource consumption, and choose the better one as P_x.

In the example OI from Fig. 2, we obtain the following recovery policy: From O1, reach S2 via an empty plan. From O2, reach S2 via plan "go to P2". From O3, reach S5 via plan "go to P5". From O4, reach S5 via an empty plan.

It is important to use the same safety assumptions in the finding of recovery plans that were used for generating the main plan, so that only safe actions are used in recovery plans. In the example, this assures that the robot does not get a recovery plan from O2 telling it to move from waypoint Q to S5 with an unsafe traversal of the critical area between Q and R, but rather to return to P2.

The other main plan states after S_0 can also be considered as possible destinations in the construction of recovery plans. It makes sense to enable or disable this addition per OT. E.g., for a "carry along" OI, the recovery plan will contain a "drop" action – possibly wrapped with movement to and from predefined drop-off locations – from most OI states, and the destination state could be the corresponding main plan state with the closest matching waypoint.

In the case of a safety-related event, such as an impending collision, the immediate physical evasive reaction is beyond the responsibility of the planning system. However, it must be followed by an estimation of the current state. If it is a state in the OI's plan fragment, the recovery policy can be applied to switch back to the safe plan. The event or the reaction may have caused a deviation that led to the equivalent of a main plan state already, but it is also possible that the current state is an unforeseen one, in which case the system has to regress to conventional replanning to solve its mission with an up-to-date plan. The new plan can then be ameliorated by the application of opportunities.

4   Conclusion

In this paper we described our approach of using opportunistic planning to provide a safety-supporting planning component for collaborative robots. The scenario of a supportive mobile manipulator in a production space or similar shared working environment is used to illustrate the suitability of our contribution, which can just as well be transferred to different types of robots and domains. The main plan is generated for completing the current mission in a safe operation mode, while additional soft goals, including optimizations and shortcuts, are achieved by opportunities. Safety-related events occurring during the plan execution cause falling back to the always available safe plan rather than a potentially hazardous delay for replanning. Recovery plans are short or even empty and are also prepared before the opportunity's execution, thus always available when needed.

Our future work includes exploration of ways to process OTs with purely formal and generic methods, increasing expressive power and reducing the need for OT-specific implementation. There is also the need to underpin the aptitude of our approach by getting the implementation to a level that allows for comparison with alternatives, mainly conventional replanning.

References

1. Cashmore, M., Fox, M., Long, D., Magazzeni, D., Ridder, B.: Opportunistic planning for increased plan utility. In: Finzi, A., Karpas, E. (eds.) Proceedings of the 4th Workshop on Planning and Robotics at ICAPS 2016, London, UK, pp. 82–92 (2016)
2. Cashmore, M., Fox, M., Long, D., Magazzeni, D., Ridder, B., Carrera, A., Palomeras, N., Hurtós, N., Carreras, M.: ROSPlan: planning in the robot operating system. In: Proceedings of the 25th International Conference on Automated Planning and Scheduling (ICAPS 2015), Jerusalem, Israel, pp. 333–341. AAAI Press (2015)
3. Fox, M., Long, D.: PDDL2.1: an extension to PDDL for expressing temporal planning domains. J. Artif. Intell. Res. (JAIR) **20**, 61–124 (2003)
4. Gerevini, A.E., Haslum, P., Long, D., Saetti, A., Dimopoulos, Y.: Deterministic planning in the fifth international planning competition: PDDL3 and experimental evaluation of the planners. Artif. Intell. **173**(56), 619–668 (2009)
5. Ginsberg, M.L.: Universal planning: an (almost) universally bad idea. AI Mag. **10**(4), 40–44 (1989)
6. Gough, J., Fox, M., Long, D.: Plan execution under resource consumption uncertainty. In: Proceedings of the Workshop on Connecting Planning Theory with Practice at ICAPS 2004, Whistler, Canada, pp. 24–29 (2004)
7. Hoffmann, J., Edelkamp, S.: The deterministic part of IPC-4: an overview. J. Artif. Intell. Res. (JAIR) **24**, 519–579 (2005)
8. Kaelbling, L.P., Littman, M.L., Cassandra, A.R.: Planning and acting in partially observable stochastic domains. Artif. Intell. **101**(1), 99–134 (1998)
9. McDermott, D.V.: The 1998 AI planning systems competition. AI Mag. **21**(2), 35–55 (2000)
10. Pryor, L., Collins, G.: Planning for contingencies: a decision-based approach. J. Artif. Intell. Res. (JAIR) **4**, 287–339 (1996)

Towards Simulation-Based Role Optimization in Organizations

Lukas Reuter$^{(\boxtimes)}$, Jan Ole Berndt, and Ingo J. Timm

Business Informatics I, Trier University, Behringstraße 21, 54296 Trier, Germany
{reuter,berndt,itimm}@uni-trier.de

Abstract. The modern workplace is driven by a high amount of available information which can be observed in various domains, e.g., in Industry 4.0. Hence, the question arises: Which competences do actors need to build and efficient work environment? This paper proposes an simulation-based optimization approach to adapt role configurations for team work scenarios. The approach was tested using a multiagent-based job-shop-scheduling model to simulate the effects of various role configurations.

Keywords: Optimization · Multiagent-based simulation · Agent-based modeling · Team cognitions

1 Introduction

The modern workplace is driven by a high amount of available information [5]. This phenomenon can be observed in various domains, e.g., in Industry 4.0 or administration [8]. This poses a challenge for organizations to structure the information process in order to enable access to relevant information for employees. On the other hand, it is essential that employees have the required knowledge and competences to process this information. If these requisitions of a structured information flow and the employee's knowledge do not coincide, then negative effects like information overload can occur causing a delay in operation. Especially, when the employee's competences do not match their organizational roles. Therefore the key question arises: How can roles be optimized in order to build an efficient work environment? From an artificial intelligence perspective agent-based modeling and multiagent-based simulation have been successfully applied to the design and evaluation of novel approaches to flexible distributed task processing and cooperative problem-solving [2,11]. Hence, it is a suitable approach to model collaboration, e.g., in an Industry 4.0 context.

Towards this optimization issue, this paper presents a simulation based optimization concept for roles which simulates the effects of different role configurations. In order to model human actors, it is promising to integrate psychological findings about the effects of role configurations on human teams with formalization, modeling and simulation methods from distributed artificial intelligence. Moreover, to enable simulation based optimization it is essential that the role configurations for the simulation model are formalized and accessible for the

© Springer International Publishing AG 2017
G. Kern-Isberner et al. (Eds.): KI 2017, LNAI 10505, pp. 359–365, 2017.
DOI: 10.1007/978-3-319-67190-1_32

optimization algorithm. Hence, the developed model uses the well-known *Game Description Language - GDL* to formalize generic role descriptions, which then can be used to configure a team work scenario for multiagent-based simulations.

The optimization model is tested using a multiagent-based implementation of the *job-shop-scheduling (JSS)* problem, which models machines processing jobs. This facilitates the evaluation of team knowledge structures by transferring role configuration tasks to a formal optimization problem [14]. The roles in this JSS model are optimized using a simulated annealing approach which adjusts the overall process duration as an indicator for efficient role design. This approach provides a first step towards the development of a multiagent-based simulation as a method for designing and evaluating modern work processes in dynamic and complex environments (e.g., in Industry 4.0).

The remainder of this paper is structured as follows. The next Sect. 2 describes role formalization from a distributed artificial intelligence and a business psychological perspective. In Sect. 3 the role optimization approach is discussed which uses GDL as formalization for the role description, a multiagent-based JSS simulation to model team work processes and simulated annealing to optimize the role description for JSS. This model is tested and evaluated in Sect. 4.

2   Role Optimization in Teams: Foundations and Challenges

The representation and distribution of knowledge can be modeled and analyzed by use of *multiagent systems* (MAS) [17]. From a distributed artificial intelligence perspective, MAS apply decentralized solution strategies to complex computational problems [16]. MAS consists of software agents which autonomously fulfill different tasks and coordinate their distributed activities. These agents process knowledge in their decision-making and exchange it in their coordination efforts [17].

In business psychology, teams are collective information-processing systems [7]. Team members have qualifications required for their tasks, they can specialize of particular areas of expertise, or they share knowledge and information with each other [4]. These various approaches to the organization of team knowledge are known as team cognitions [10]. Team cognitions describe the structure in which knowledge important to team functioning is mentally organized, represented, and distributed within the team and allows team members to anticipate and execute actions [4]. Therefore, they are particularly suitable as a theoretical concept for describing, modeling, and analyzing knowledge configuration approaches in collaborative work processes. Team cognitions, as an emergent state, are be conceptualized as (1) shared team knowledge (generalization) or (2) distributed team knowledge (specialization) [4].

The problem of optimizing distributed problem-solving in MAS resembles the challenge of identifying and applying appropriate team cognitions among humans. Organizing roles and processes in team work plays an important role in artificial intelligence as well as business psychology. Researchers of both disciplines face the question of how knowledge should be shared or divided among team members to allow for optimal collaboration. Consequently, this paper adopts an interdisciplinary perspective in which the disciplines complement each other to cope with that challenge and to develop a common understanding of distributed work processes.

As a first step towards that vision, a formal setting for analyzing and simulating collaborative work processes is required. That setting must be capable of representing the spectrum of knowledge organization approaches between generalization and specialization. This will allow for comparing different team cognitions according to their performance in various task scenarios. To that end, the remainder of this paper proposes an optimization approach to find efficient role configurations for team work in a given scenario.

3   Formalizing and Optimizing Team Work Scenarios: A Job-Shop-Scheduling Approach

This chapter presents a simulation-based optimization approach of role configurations in the context of team work scenarios. The optimization itself is a search for valid team configurations and consists of four subcomponents *simulation, performance, adaptation and role description*, which have to be redefined for domain specific contexts. In Fig. 1 shows the interaction of each component.

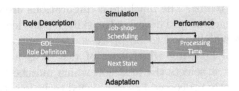

Fig. 1. Optimization approach for teamwork scenarios

From a business psychological perspective, roles define the capabilities and qualifications an employee has to process different kinds of tasks. In order to use multiagent-based simulation, one need to make role descriptions accessible for software agents, i.e., one need to formalize them. Hence, a role formalization is needed which enables agents to reason about their qualifications and capabilities. These requirements resembles aspects of descriptions in general game playing where agents try to solve games by a formalized description. The goal in this domain is to develop intelligent agents (general game player) which can reason about any games and their rules in a specific description [6]. In this domain the *game description language GDL* is commonly used [12]. The definition of GDL is written in Listing 1.1. GDL is universal and therefore a promising approach which can be tested in different applications ,e.g., role descriptions in organizations [13].

```
role (R)       defines a role R
init (F)       initial game state
true (F)       refers to facts about the current state
legal (R,M)    role R can do move M in the current position
does (R,M)     player R does move M
next (F)       refers to facts about the next game state
terminal       the current position is terminal
goal(R,N)      defines goal value for a role R
```

Listing 1.1. GDL definition [12]

In order to test the effects of different role configurations, a simulation which is able to model role descriptions in team work scenarios is needed. In [14] a multiagent-based approach which uses the well-known job-shop-scheduling problem to formalize team cognitions is successfully utilized. It simulates the effects of various role configurations in teams, e.g. generalist vs. specialist structures. Therefore, it is a first approach to test the efficiency of optimizing role descriptions in GDL.

The job-shop-scheduling problem is a well-established problem formalization in the area of production processes and describes the scheduling of jobs which consists of tasks to machines [1]. Similar to human teams, in which team members produce an output by processing information, the machines process tasks to finish jobs [1,3]. The scheduling itself is described as an assignment of tasks t_i to machines m_j, with the aim of optimizing the process efficiency which can be measured with the overall process time. The key requirement for this task allocation is knowing which jobs need to be done and which machines can process them. In fact, different machine configurations can be used to represent different role configurations in teams. The machine configurations are defined in the role description for each machine and describe the skills i.e. the legal moves a machine can make. The jobs which need to be processed are centrally accessible. Each machine is capable of knowing which sort of task it is able to process (task qualifications). Hence, it selects the next job which matches its task processing skills. If the job currently processed has unfinished tasks left, the machine pushes it back to job stock, which functions as pool of unfinished jobs.

```
role (machine1)
setSkill(machine1,task1) setSkill(machine1,task2) ...
legal(Machine, Task) ←—can_Process(Machine, Task) ...
```

Listing 1.2. Examplary role description in GDL

The JSS simulation model uses GDL role descriptions as input which includes the knowledge structure of its expertise and simulates the processing of a set of predefined jobs. A role definition for a single machine can be defined like the following example in Listing 1.2.

Since there are many possible role description combinations, it is not manageable to test each combination. Hence, it is essential to use an optimization algorithm. Simulated annealing is an optimization procedure which combines hill climbing and random walk. It is efficient and complete [9]. In order to successfully apply simulated annealing to the job-shop-scheduling problem it is necessary to define *configurations, cost function and neighborhood structure* [15]. A configuration is defined by the assignment of task processing skills to machines, i.e. the GDL role description. The overall configuration is described as the sum of role definitions of all agents.

$$Set\ of\ all\ Agents\ A : conf(A) = \sum_{i=1}^{n} role(a_i)\ \forall a_i \in A \qquad (1)$$

In order to optimize a certain role configuration it is essential to evaluate its fitness. Therefore, a performance component evaluates the computed output and defines a cost function. The cost function is given by the overall processing time. The basic assumption is that an efficient role description is faster than an inefficient one.

$$Set\ of\ all\ Jobs\ J : cost(J) = \sum_{i=1}^{n} processingTime(j_i)\ \forall j_i \in J \qquad (2)$$

The neighborhood structure is defined by the permutation of task processing skills. A neighbor of a role description is calculated by adding or removing one skill from one machine. The neighborhood for roles is defined as follows:

$$Role(a_2)\ is\ a\ neighbor\ of\ Role(a_1) \Leftrightarrow Role(a_2) \pm Task\ t = Role(a_1) \qquad (3)$$

4   Experiments and Results

In order to address various knowledge structures it is necessary to create tasks in different distributions. For example if the amount of tasks randomly distributed over all task classes, it would address a specialist knowledge structure [14]. The optimization approach is tested with binomial, normal and equal task distributions to address different role configurations. In Fig. 2 the results of an exemplary optimization run with ten different task classes is shown. The relative frequency describe how many machines are able to process a particular task class. It is relatively set to the amount of overall machines, which is ten in this scenario. In the task distribution chart the relative frequency shows how many task are from a particular task class.

In order to measure the efficiency of the optimization it is calculated from the relative difference of the process time of the initial start configuration and the optimized start configuration. The initial start configuration is set to a random role configuration. The binomial task distribution showed the highest optimization efficiency of 32,60%. The optimization in normal and equal task distributions was lower (14,68% and 16,61%). To measure the impact of random role configurations the sensitivity (standard deviation) for 20 simulation runs is computed with the difference of the process time of the start configuration and the optimized role configuration. The sensitivity is depending on the task distribution. The equal distributions shows the lowest sensitivity (0,258s). The normal (0,707s) and the binomial distribution (0,643s) are varying more in the optimization result.

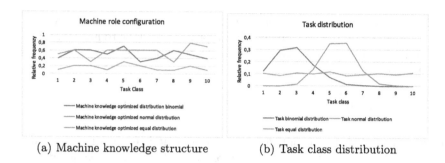

(a) Machine knowledge structure   (b) Task class distribution

Fig. 2. Role optimization result

5   Conclusions

This paper introduced a simulation-based optimization approach for role descriptions which uses the game description language to formalize role descriptions. In order to achieve this, psychological theory of team cognitions was integrated in agent-based modeling from artificial intelligence. The concept was tested using a multiagent-based job-shop-scheduling simulation to model the effects of different knowledge configurations. The simulation used role descriptions in GDL as an input. The role configurations are adapted using a simulated annealing optimization algorithm. An fictional setting is used which focuses on the effects of shared or divided knowledge as role configurations in teams. The computed results showed that simulated annealing can be successfully used to adapt role configurations in teams.

Overall, it is a first approach to formalize and optimize role configurations for artificial intelligence systems. However, work processes in reality have dependencies between them and require communication of the team members. Therefore, it would be necessary to integrate real data from experiments to evaluate this model for a practical use. Moreover, to simulate work processes a more sophisticated agent model is needed. A belief desire intention agent architecture is a promising extension to model the actors behavior and decision making more human.

Acknowledgments. The project *AdaptPRO: Adaptive Process and Role design in Organizations* (TI 548/-1) is funded by the German Research Foundation (DFG) within the Priority Program "Intentional Forgetting in Organizations" (SPP 1921).

References

1. Applegate, D., Cook, W.: A computational study of the job-shop scheduling problem. ORSA J. Comput. 3(2), 149–156 (1991)
2. Berndt, J.O., Herzog, O.: Efficient multiagent coordination in dynamic environments. In: Boissier, O., Bradshaw, J., Cao, L., Fischer, K., Hacid, M.S. (eds.) IEEE/WIC/ACM International Conferences on Web Intelligence and Intelligent Agent Technology (WI-IAT), pp. 188–195. IEEE Computer Society, Lyon (2011)

3. Blażewicz, J., Pesch, E., Sterna, M.: The disjunctive graph machine representation of the job shop scheduling problem. Eur. J. Oper. Res. **127**(2), 317–331 (2000)
4. Ellwart, T., Antoni, C.H.: Shared and distributed team cognition and information overload. Evidence and approaches for team adaptation. In: Marques, R.P.F., Batista, J.C.L. (eds.) Information and Communication Overload in the Digital Age, pp. 223–245. IGI Global, Hershey (2017). doi:10.4018/978-1-5225-2061-0.ch010
5. Eppler, M.J., Mengis, J.: The concept of information overload: a review of literature from organization science, accounting, marketing, MIS, and related disciplines. Inf. Soc. **20**, 325–344 (2004)
6. Genesereth, M., Love, N., Pell, B.: General game playing: overview of the AAAI competition. AI Mag. **26**(2), 62–72 (2005)
7. Hinsz, V.B., Tindale, R.S., Vollrath, D.A.: The emerging conceptualization of groups as information processors. Psychol. Bull. **121**(1), 43–64 (1997)
8. Kagermann, H., Wahlster, W., Helbig, J. (eds.): Recommendations for implementing the strategic initiative INDUSTRIE 4.0. Final report of the Industrie 4.0 Working Group. Industry-Sciemce Research Alliance; acatech - National Academy of Science and Engineering, Frankfurt (2013)
9. Russell, S., Norvig, P.: Artificial Intelligence: A Modern Approach. Prentice-Hall, Englewood Cliffs (1995)
10. Salas, E., Fiore, S.M., Letsky, M.P. (eds.): Theories of Team Cognition - Cross-Disciplinary Perspectives. Taylor & Francis Group, New York (2012)
11. Schuldt, A.: Multiagent Coordination Enabling Autonomous Logistics. Springer, Berlin (2011)
12. Thielscher, M.: A general game description language for incomplete information games. In: Proceedings of the Twenty-fourth AAAI Conference on Artificial Intelligence, vol. 10, pp. 994–999 (2010)
13. Thielscher, M.: The general game playing description language is universal. In: IJCAI Proceedings-International Joint Conference on Artificial Intelligence, vol. 22 (2011)
14. Timm, I.J., Berndt, J.O., Reuter, L., Ellwart, T., Antoni, C., Ulfert, A.S.: Towards multiagent-based simulation of knowledge management in teams. In: Leyer, M., Richter, A., Vodanovich, S. (eds.) Flexible Knowledge Practices and the Digital Workplace (FKPDW), Workshop Within the 9th Conference on Professional Knowledge Management, pp. 25–40. KIT, Karlsruhe (2017)
15. Van Laarhoven, P.J., Aarts, E.H., Lenstra, J.K.: Job shop scheduling by simulated annealing. Oper. Res. **40**(1), 113–125 (1992)
16. Weiss, G.: Multiagent Systems, 2nd edn. The MIT Press, Cambridge (2013)
17. Wooldridge, M.J., Jennings, N.R.: Towards a theory of cooperative problem solving. In: Perram, J.W., Müller, J.-P. (eds.) MAAMAW 1994. LNCS, vol. 1069, pp. 40–53. Springer, Heidelberg (1996). doi:10.1007/3-540-61157-6_20

One Knowledge Graph to Rule Them All? Analyzing the Differences Between DBpedia, YAGO, Wikidata & co.

Daniel Ringler and Heiko Paulheim[(✉)]

Data and Web Science Group, University of Mannheim, Mannheim, Germany
`heiko@informatik.uni-mannheim.de`

Abstract. Public Knowledge Graphs (KGs) on the Web are considered a valuable asset for developing intelligent applications. They contain general knowledge which can be used, e.g., for improving data analytics tools, text processing pipelines, or recommender systems. While the large players, e.g., DBpedia, YAGO, or Wikidata, are often considered similar in nature and coverage, there are, in fact, quite a few differences. In this paper, we quantify those differences, and identify the overlapping and the complementary parts of public KGs. From those considerations, we can conclude that the KGs are hardly interchangeable, and that each of them has its strenghts and weaknesses when it comes to applications in different domains.

1 Knowledge Graphs on the Web

The term "Knowledge Graph" was coined by Google when they introduced their knowledge graph as a backbone of a new Web search strategy in 2012, i.e., moving from pure text processing to a more symbolic representation of knowledge, using the slogan "things, not strings"[1].

Various public knowledge graphs are available on the Web, including DBpedia [3] and YAGO [9], both of which are created by extracting information from Wikipedia (the latter exploiting WordNet on top), the community edited Wikidata [10], which imports other datasets, e.g., from national libraries[2], as well as from the discontinued Freebase [7], the expert curated OpenCyc [4], and NELL [1], which exploits pattern-based knowledge extraction from a large Web corpus.

Although all these knowledge graphs contain a lot of valuable information, choosing one KG for building a specific application is not a straight forward task. Depending on the domain and task at hand, some KGs might be better suited than others. However, there are no guidelines or best practices on how to choose a knowledge graph which fits a given problem. Previous works mostly report global numbers, such as the overall size of knowledge graphs, such as [6],

---

[1] https://googleblog.blogspot.de/2012/05/introducing-knowledge-graph-things-not.html.

[2] https://www.wikidata.org/wiki/Wikidata:Data_donation.

ⓒ Springer International Publishing AG 2017
G. Kern-Isberner et al. (Eds.): KI 2017, LNAI 10505, pp. 366–372, 2017.
DOI: 10.1007/978-3-319-67190-1_33

and focus on other aspects, such as data quality [2]. The question which KG fits which purpose, however, has not been answered so far.

2   Overall Size and Shape of Knowledge Graphs

For the analysis in this paper, we focus on the public knowledge graphs DBpedia, YAGO, Wikidata, OpenCyc, and NELL.[3,4] For those five KGs, we used the most recent available versions at the time of this analysis, as shown in Table 1.

Table 1. Global properties of the knowledge graphs compared in this paper

Version	DBpedia	YAGO	Wikidata	OpenCyc	NELL
	2016-04	YAGO3	2016-08-01	2016-09-05	08m.995
# instances	5,109,890	5,130,031	17,581,152	118,125	1,974,297
# axioms	397,831,457	1,435,808,056	1,633,309,138	2,413,894	3,402,971
Avg. indegree	13.52	17.44	9.83	10.03	5.33
Avg. outdegree	47.55	101.86	41.25	9.23	1.25
# classes	754	576,331	30,765	116,822	290
# relations	3,555	93,659	11,053	165	1,334

We can observe that DBpedia and YAGO have roughly the same number of instances, which is not surprising, due to their construction process, which creates an instance per Wikipedia page. Wikidata, which uses additional sources plus a community editing process, has about tree times more instances. It is remarkable that YAGO and Wikidata have roughly the same number of axioms, although Wikidata has three times more instances. This hints at a higher level of detail in YAGO, which is also reflected in the degree distributions.

OpenCyc and NELL are much smaller. NELL is particularly smaller w.r.t. axioms, not instances, i.e., the graph is less dense. This is also reflected in the degree of instances, which depicts that on average, each instance has less than seven connections. The other graphs are much denser, e.g., each instance in Wikidata has about 50 connections on average, each instance in DBpedia has about 60, and each instance in YAGO has even about 120 connections on average.

The schema sizes also differ widely. In particular the number of classes are very different. This can be explained by different modeling styles: YAGO automatically generates very fine-grained classes, based on Wikipedia categories. Those are often complex types encoding various facts, such as "American Rock Keyboardists". KGs like DBpedia or NELL, on the other hand, use well-defined, manually curated ontologies with much fewer classes.

---

[3] Freebase was discarded as it is discontinued, and non-public KGs were not considered, as it is impossible to run the analysis on non-public data.

[4] Scripts are available at https://github.com/dringler/KnowledgeGraphAnalysis.

Since Wikidata provides live updates, it is the most timely source (together with DBpedia Live, which is a variant of DBpedia fed from an update stream of Wikipedia). From the non-live sources, NELL has the fastest release cycle, providing a new release every few days. However, NELL uses a fixed corpus of Web pages, which is not updated as regularly. Thus, the short release cycles do not necessarily lead to more timely information. DBpedia has biyearly releases, and YAGO and OpenCyc have update cycles longer than a year.

3   Category-Specific Analysis

When building an intelligent, knowledge graph backed application for a specific use case, it is important to know how fit a given knowledge graph is for the domain and task at hand. To answer this question, we have picked 25 popular classes in the five knowledge graphs and performed an in-depth comparison. For those, we computed the total number of instances in the different graphs, as well as the average in and out degree. The results are depicted in Fig. 2.

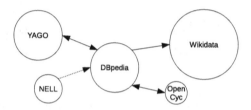

Fig. 1. Knowledge Graphs inspected in this paper, and their interlinks. Like for the Linked Open Data Cloud diagrams [8], the size of the circles reflects the number of instances in the graph (except for OpenCyc, which would have to be depicted an order of magnitude smaller).

While DBpedia and YAGO, both derived from Wikipedia, are rather comparable, there are notable differences in coverage, in particular for events, where the number of events in YAGO is more than five times larger than the number in DBpedia. On the other hand, DBpedia has information about four times as many settlements (i.e., cities, towns, and villages) as YAGO. Furthermore, the level of detail provided in YAGO is usually a bit larger than DBpedia.

The other three graphs differ a lot more. Wikidata contains twice as many persons as DBpedia and YAGO, and also outnumbers them in music albums and books. Furthermore, it provides a higher level of detail for chemical substances and particularly countries. On the other hand, there are also classes which are hardly represented in Wikidata, such as songs.[5] As far as Wikidata is concerned, the differences can be partially explained by the external datasets imported into the knowledge graph.

---

[5] The reason why so few politicians, actors, and athletes are listed for Wikidata is that they are usually not modeled using explicit classes.

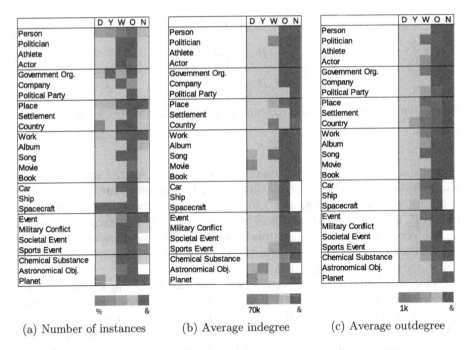

(a) Number of instances   (b) Average indegree   (c) Average outdegree

Fig. 2. Number of instances (a), avg. indegree (b) and avg. outdegree (c) of selected classes. D = DBpedia, Y = YAGO, W = Wikidata, O = OpenCyc, N = NELL.

OpenCyc and NELL are generally smaller and less detailed. However, NELL has some particularly large classes, e.g., actor, song, and chemical substance, and for government organizations, it even outnumbers the other graphs. On the other hand, there are classes which are not covered by NELL at all.

4   Overlap of Knowledge Graphs

Knowledge graphs on the Web are equipped with links connecting identical entities between those graphs. However, due to the *open world assumption*, those links are notoriously incomplete. For example, from the fact that 2,000 cities in knowledge graph A are linked to cities in knowledge graph B, we cannot conclude that this is the number of cities contained in the intersection of A and B.

Links between knowledge graphs can be determined using entity linkage approaches [5], e.g., interlinking all entities with the same name.

Given that there is already a certain number of (correct) interlinks between two knowledge graphs, we can also compute the quality of a linking approach in terms of recall and precision. Given that the actual number of links is C, the number of links found by a linkage rule is F, and that the number of correct links in F is F^+, recall and precision are defined as

$$R := \frac{|F^+|}{|C|} \tag{1}$$

$$P := \frac{|F^+|}{|F|} \tag{2}$$

By resolving both to $|F^+|$ and combining the equations, we can estimate $|C|$ as

$$|C| = |F| \cdot P \cdot \frac{1}{R} \tag{3}$$

For our analysis, we use 16 combinations of string metrics and thresholds on the instances' labels: string equality, scaled Levenshtein (thresholds 0.8, 0.9, and 1.0), Jaccard (0.6, 0.8, and 1.0), Jaro (0.9, 0.95, and 1.0), JaroWinkler (0.9, 0.95, and 1.0), and MongeElkan (0.9, 0.95, and 1.0). Furthermore, to speed up the computation, we exploit token-based blocking in a preprocessing step (where each instance is only assigned to the block of the least frequent token), and discarding blocks larger than 1M pairs.

As incomplete link sets for estimating recall and precision, we use the links between the knowledge graphs, if present. If there are no links, we exploit transitivity and symmetry, and follow the link path through DBpedia (see Fig. 1). NELL has no direct links to the other graphs, but links to Wikipedia pages corresponding to DBpedia instances, which we use to create links to DBpedia (indicated by the dashed line in the figure).

Figure 3 depicts the pairwise overlap of the knowledge graphs, using the 25 classes also inspected above, according to two measures: potential gain by joining the two knowledge graphs (i.e., the relation of the union to the larger of the two graphs), and the overlap relative to the existing KG interlinks.

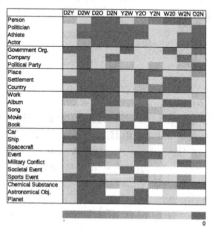

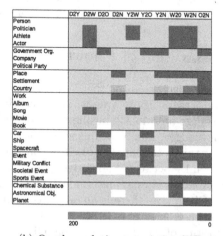

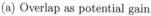

| (a) Overlap as potential gain | (b) Overlap relative to existing links |

Fig. 3. Number as potential gain (a) and relative to existing interlinks (b) of selected classes. D = DBpedia, Y = YAGO, W = Wikidata, O = OpenCyc, N = NELL.

Overall, we can observe that merging two graphs would usually lead to a 5% increase of coverage of instances, compared to using one KG alone. The largest potential gain most often comes from merging the larger knowledge graphs with NELL. We can therefore conclude that NELL is rather complementary to most of the other KGs under consideration. The most complementary classes, with an average gain of more than 10% across all pairs of knowledge graphs, are political parties and chemical substances. When looking at the overlap relative to the number of existing links, NELL has the weakest interlinking: e.g., for YAGO and NELL, the estimated overlap is more than eight times larger than the number of interlinks. The classes with the weakest degree of interlinking are countries (32 times larger overlap than explicit interlinks), movies (13 times larger), and companies (10 times larger).[6]

5 Conclusions and Recommendations

We have compared the coverage and level of detail for 25 popular classes. Some key findings from this comparison include:

- For person data, Wikidata is the most suitable source, containing twice as many instances as DBpedia or YAGO, at a similar level of detail.
- Organizations, such as companies, are best described in YAGO.
- DBpedia contains more places than the other KGs, including almost four times more cities, villages etc. than YAGO.
- While DBpedia and YAGO contain much more countries than Wikidata (due to the inclusion of historic countries, such as the Roman Empire), Wikidata holds the most detailed information about countries.
- Overall, DBpedia contains the largest number of artistic works, although details differ for subclasses: Wikidata contains more music albums and movies, while YAGO contains more songs. The most detailed information about artistic works is provided by YAGO.
- Cars and spacecraft are best covered in YAGO, while DBpedia is the better resource for ships.
- For events, YAGO is the most suitable source, both in terms of coverage and level of detail.
- NELL contains the largest number of chemical substances. The highest level of degree for chemicals, however, is provided in Wikidata.
- YAGO contains the largest number of astronomical objects.

Note that those numbers are not exhaustive, they merely demonstrate the need for a careful analysis of KGs before exploiting them for a project at hand.

---

[6] Note that it is not necessary that the linking approach is particularly good, as long as we can estimate its quality reasonably well. In our experiments, the agreement about the estimated overlap is rather high, showing an intra-class correlation coefficient (ICC) of 0.969. In contrast, the size of the actual alignments found by the different approaches differs a lot more, showing an ICC of only 0.646.

In addition to the question which knowledge graph serves a certain task best, another question is whether it makes sense to use *more than one* combined. Here, we have observed that there is often a considerable complementarity. Especially NELL is very complementary to the other KGs, although a lot less rich in details. Thus, the coverage can often be extended significantly by combining different KGs. This, however, requires refinement of the interlinking, since the interlinks are usually incomplete.

Summarizing: Although DBpedia, YAGO, Wikidata & co. are often perceived at somewhat similar to one another, our analysis has revealed that there are considerable differences. Hence, when deploying a public KG in a project, it makes sense to look at the details first before selecting one KG.

References

1. Carlson, A., Betteridge, J., Wang, R.C., Hruschka Jr., E.R., Mitchell, T.M.: Coupled semi-supervised learning for information extraction. In: Proceedings of the Third ACM International Conference on Web Search and Data Mining, pp. 101–110 (2010)
2. Färber, M., Ell, B., Menne, C., Rettinger, A., Bartscherer, F.: Linked data quality of DBpedia, Freebase, OpenCyc, Wikidata, and YAGO. Semant. Web (2016, to appear)
3. Lehmann, J., Isele, R., Jakob, M., Jentzsch, A., Kontokostas, D., Mendes, P.N., Hellmann, S., Morsey, M., van Kleef, P., Auer, S., Bizer, C.: DBpedia-A large-scale, multilingual knowledge base extracted from Wikipedia. Semant. Web J. **6**(2), 167–195 (2013)
4. Lenat, D.B.: CYC: a large-scale investment in knowledge infrastructure. Commun. ACM **38**(11), 33–38 (1995)
5. Nentwig, M., Hartung, M., Ngonga Ngomo, A.C., Rahm, E.: A survey of current link discovery frameworks. Semant. Web **8**(3), 419–436 (2017)
6. Paulheim, H.: Knowledge graph refinement: a survey of approaches and evaluation methods. Semant. Web **8**(3), 489–508 (2017)
7. Pellissier Tanon, T., Vrandečić, D., Schaffert, S., Steiner, T., Pintscher, L.: From Freebase to Wikidata: the great migration. In: Proceedings of the 25th International Conference on World Wide Web, pp. 1419–1428 (2016)
8. Schmachtenberg, M., Bizer, C., Paulheim, H.: Adoption of the linked data best practices in different topical domains. In: Mika, P., Tudorache, T., Bernstein, A., Welty, C., Knoblock, C., Vrandečić, D., Groth, P., Noy, N., Janowicz, K., Goble, C. (eds.) ISWC 2014. LNCS, vol. 8796, pp. 245–260. Springer, Cham (2014). doi:10.1007/978-3-319-11964-9_16
9. Suchanek, F.M., Kasneci, G., Weikum, G.: YAGO: a core of semantic knowledge unifying WordNet and Wikipedia. In: 16th International Conference on World Wide Web, pp. 697–706 (2007)
10. Vrandečić, D., Krötzsch, M.: Wikidata: a free collaborative knowledge base. Commun. ACM **57**(10), 78–85 (2014)

Classifyhub: An Algorithm to Classify GitHub Repositories

Marcus Soll[(✉)][(iD)] and Malte Vosgerau

University of Hamburg, Mittelweg 177, 20148 Hamburg, Germany
{2soll,2vosgera}@informatik.uni-hamburg.de

Abstract. The classification of repositories found on GitHub can be considered as a hard task. However, the solution of this task could be helpful for a lot of different applications (e.g. Recommender Systems). In this paper we present ClassifyHub, an algorithm based on Ensemble Learning developed for the InformatiCup 2017 competition, which is able to tackle this classification problem with high precision and recall. In addition we provide a data set of classified repositories for further research.

1 Introduction

GitHub is the largest [3] platform to organise and collaborate on different projects (so-called repositories). The diversity of *GitHub* repositories reaches from small LaTeX templates for homework up to huge software development projects. Because of this diversity *GitHub* is ideal for many research projects (e.g. influence of programming languages to code quality [10] or social studies [14]).

To gain additional value out of the large variety of repositories on *GitHub* it would be useful to classify these repositories into different disjunctive classes. Such *clustering* could be used for many tasks like, for example, recommendation (so-called *Recommender Systems*) [1,11]. Another application would be the improvement of search functions on *GitHub*.

In this paper we present *ClassifyHub*, an algorithm based on *Ensemble Learning* which tackles the *GitHub Classification Problem* and achieves high precision and high recall considering the hard task. This algorithm reached the final round in the InformatiCup 2017 competition, where the goal was to develop a complete software solution with a time frame of about 5 month. In addition we provide a data set with 681 classified repositories which can be used for further research.

2 Related Work

Ugurel et al. [15] classified source code archives into different application types (like *database* or *games*), however they did not focus their work on content types (like *educational* or *data set*) and furthermore only focused on application source code instead of arbitrary repositories (like repositories containing only images).

© Springer International Publishing AG 2017
G. Kern-Isberner et al. (Eds.): KI 2017, LNAI 10505, pp. 373–379, 2017.
DOI: 10.1007/978-3-319-67190-1_34

Kawaguchi et al. [6] proposed a system which classifies software in automatically generated categories. Again, the categories seem to focus on application types rather than content types. In addition, they used categories about the technology used (e.g. libraries), as well as the architecture of the software.

Maskeri et al. [8] proposed a system to automatically extract topics from the source code. These topics are more related to the implementation (like *SSL* or *Logging*) than to the content type.

3 GitHub Classification Problem

The *GitHub Classification Problem* (based on the InformatiCup 2017 task) is a problem from the area of classification. The task is the classification of repositories hosted on *GitHub* into exactly one of the following content categories:

- **DEV:** Software development projects and similar
- **HW:** Solutions for homework, exercises and similar
- **EDU:** Projects with educational purpose and similar
- **DOCS:** Documents with no educational intent and similar
- **WEB:** (Personal) websites
- **DATA:** Data sets
- **OTHER:** Repositories which do not fit in one of the above categories

Two aspects turn the *GitHub Classification Problem* into a hard tasks:

- There is a large variety of repositories on *GitHub*. One can find repositories with projects run by one person up to repositories with thousands of contributors (e.g. the Linux kernel).
- The classification of repositories is sometimes ambiguous - many projects can be classified into multiple categories.

4 Multi Classifier Solution

To tackle the *GitHub Classification Problem* we used an approach based on *Ensemble Learning* [13]: Through the combination of multiple *weak classifier* (which have to be better than random guessing) we get a single *strong classifier* which is correct on the majority of data. This works because each *weak classifier* added reduces the total error of the *strong classifier*. In our solution the probability of a class is equal to the average probability calculated by all *weak classifiers*, as shown in (1).

$$P(\text{class}) = \frac{\sum^{\text{classifier}} P_{\text{classifier}}(\text{class})}{N_{\text{classifier}}} \tag{1}$$

4.1 Weak Classifier Used

Each *weak classifier* presented in the following sections returns a value between zero and one which represents the probability with which the classifier classifies a repository into one of the classes. The total sum of all classes can be higher than one.

FileClassifier. Based on the class of the repository one will likely find different types of files in different repositories. A project of the class **DEV** is more likely to have files of the type *.cpp* (C++ source code), *.h* (C/C++ header) or *.java* (JAVA source code) while a repository of the **DOCS** class is more likely to have files of the type *.md* (Markdown) or *.pdf* (document format). Often, the file type is associated to the filename extension. The FileClassifer exploits this for classification. While learning, the FileClassifier monitors the distribution of extensions on the different classes (ignoring extensions which only occur once) as shown in (2). For classification, the probability of all known filename extensions in a repository will be averaged over all files as shown in (3).

$$P(\text{class}|\text{extension}) = \frac{N_{\text{extension in class}}}{N_{\text{extension in all classes}}} \tag{2}$$

$$P(\text{class}) = \frac{\sum^{\text{extensions}} P(\text{class}|\text{extension})}{N_{\text{files}}} \tag{3}$$

ReadmeClassifier. A lot of information about a project can be found in the self description which is usually found as a *README* file. Based on this description it is often possible to correctly classify the repository. To analyse README files we use a *Bag-of-words* representation followed by a classification using the *k-Nearest Neighbor* algorithm.

A *Bag-of-words* [12] is a special representation of a text where only the appearance of a word has a meaning but not the context in which the word appears. Although the context of the text is lost in this representation, it is still possible to get a lot of information out of it. In our case we collected words in all README files encountered during learning phase which only consist of letters and numbers (independent of capitalisation). All words that only occur once are removed. Based on the remaining words a list is created. During classification, every occurring word in the README is set to 1, all other to 0. For every README file one of these lists is created. These will then be used by the *k-Nearest Neighbor* algorithm [5] (using the Jaccard distance [2]). The probability of a class is equal to the distribution of classes with the smallest distance. To classify a new repository a Bag-of-words is created for the README file. After that the neighbourhood will be calculated. Based on the neighbourhood the probability of the classes is calculated.

MetadataClassifier. Another source for the classification of repositories is their meta data. *GitHub* provides an API to get a wide variety of meta data for repositories. For the creation of a *weak classifier* we chose the following meta data:

- Information whether the repository is a *fork*
- Information whether the repository has a website
- Size of repository
- Number of *stargazers* (equivalent to *likes*)

- Number of watchers
- Information whether the repository has a *wiki*
- Information whether the repository has *pages* (website hosted by *GitHub*)
- Number of *forks*
- Number of *bugs*
- Number of *subscribers*

These meta data is then used in a decision tree [5].

LanguageClassifier. An evidence of the class of a repository is the used programming language. *GitHub* provides a way to ask for the most used programming language in a repository. The LanguageClassifier uses the language returned by *GitHub* to calculate the probability of the different classes for a repository. This allows a broad classification of many repositories. While learning, the classifier observes the languages used for the classes and calculates the probability as shown in (4). The probability for a language not observed during training is $P(class|unknown\ language) = 0$.

$$P(\text{class}|\text{languange}) = \frac{N_{\text{class with language}}}{N_{\text{language}}} \qquad (4)$$

LanguageDetailsClassifier. The LanguageDetailsClassifier is based on the same idea as the LanguageClassifier. However, it uses the percentage distribution of programming languages in a repository instead of the main language (based on file size). The *GitHub* API is used to get the distribution of programming languages. Based on this, a decision tree [5] is build which is used for classification. Because of this, the LanguageDetailsClassifier has a more detailed basis but looses some generalisation in comparison to the LanguageClassifier.

NameClassifier. Although there is a huge variety in names for repositories, there seems to be some common patterns found in the names of repositories of the different classes. For example, one finds many repositories with words like 'dataset', 'list' or 'challenge' in their name in the **DATA** class. This can be exploited for classification. For this, we use the *k-Nearest Neighbor* algorithm [5] with the Levenshtein distance (cost 1 for replacement) [4] to calculate the distance between names.

CommitMessageClassifier. Whenever someone changes something in a repository (a so called *Commit*) there must be a description of that change. These descriptions often hold information which can be used for classification. As an example, a description 'Solution exercise 2' will hint at the **HW** class.

We use the same method here as for the *ReadmeClassifier*: All messages are put into a *Bag-of-word* [12]. The probability of a class is calculated using the *k-Nearest Neighbor* algorithm [5] using the Jaccard distance [2].

RepositoryStructureClassifier. Often, the structure of a repository gives evidence for the class of the repository. For example, if two repositories contain a folder named 'lab2' and one has the class **HW**, it is very likely that the second one also belongs to the same class.

RepositoryStructureClassifier exploits this for classification. It uses a similar algorithm compared to the *ReadmeClassifier*: The structure of a repository (consisting of paths of files, folders and similar) is converted to a *Bag-of-words* [12], which is then classified using the *k-Nearest Neighbor* algorithm [5] using the Jaccard distance [2].

4.2 Implementation

We implemented *ClassifyHub* in Python using scikit-learn [9] for many machine learning algorithms. The implementation has a high degree of parallelisation because all *weak classifiers* can run independently. To show the internals of our algorithm we implemented a user interface in Qt/PyQt5.

5 Data Set

For training and evaluation purpose we created a data set containing 681 repositories of all 7 classes. We focused on an almost equal distribution over all classes to prevent an overfitting to one single class. The data set contains repositories with a wide variety to match the variety of repositories found on *GitHub*, which were picked at random and classified by hand. This includes not using the main repository all the time but also *forks* which sometimes do not get updated. The distribution of classes in the data set can be found in Table 1.

Table 1. Distribution of classes in our data set

Class	Number repositories
DEV	127
HW	96
EDU	74
DOCS	77
WEB	95
DATA	86
OTHER	126
Sum	**681**

Table 2. Average results of a 10-fold cross-validation

Target class	Precision	Recall
DEV	0.5474	0.7189
HW	0.4933	0.5311
EDU	0.5299	0.3534
DOCS	0.6314	0.4192
WEB	0.6744	0.8051
DATA	0.7681	0.7178
OTHER	0.5484	0.5430
Average	**0.5990**	**0.5841**

6 Results and Discussion

We performed a *10-fold cross-validation* on our data set, which should give us a good overview (with slightly negative tendency) over the performance of our algorithm [7]. The results are shown in Table 2. With the combination of multiple *weak classifier* we were able to achieve both high precision (59.90%) as well as high recall (58.41%). This is a good result especially because the *GitHub Classification Problem* can be considered as a hard task due to the high variety of repositories (even within a class). In addition, the distinction between the different classes is often ambiguous, even for humans (e.g. the difference between source code for homework and normal software projects). This might lead to classifications which could be considered correctly by humans, but do not correspond to the labels in the data set.

Both, high precision and recall, is achieved over all classes (with minor differences). This is useful because based on the future application both high precision and recall might be needed:

- A high *precision* might be important if, for example, the classification will be used to improve search results because a human often does not want to look through many wrong results first.
- A high *recall* might be important e.g. for automatic recommendation (like in *Recommender Systems*) to show a high variety of results. A single wrong classification has less effect here, because there is no active search which would be interrupted.

7 Conclusion

In this paper we presented *ClassifyHub*[1], an algorithm which tackles the *GitHub Classification Problem* with high precision (59.90%) and high recall (58.41%). This is achieved through the usage of *Ensemble Learning*, which combines multiple *weak classifier* to a single *strong classifier*. In addition, we provide a data set[2] with 681 classified *GitHub* repositories which can be used for further research.

Acknowledgements. We would like to thank the organisers, the jury and all participants of the InformatiCup 2017, for which *ClassifyHub* was developed.

References

1. Adomavicius, G., Tuzhilin, A.: Toward the next generation of recommender systems: a survey of the state-of-the-art and possible extensions. IEEE Trans. Knowl. Data Eng. **17**(6), 734–749 (2005)
2. Cha, S.-H.: Comprehensive survey on distance/similarity measures between probability density functions. Int. J Math. Models Methods Appl. Sci. **1**(4), 300–307 (2007)

---

[1] https://github.com/Top-Ranger/ClassifyHub.
[2] https://github.com/Top-Ranger/ClassifyHub-data.

3. Gousios, G., Vasilescu, B., Serebrenik, A., Zaidman, A.: Lean GHTorrent: Github data on demand. In: Proceedings of the 11th Working Conference on Mining Software Repositories, MSR 2014, NY, USA, pp. 384–387 (2014). http://doi.acm.org/10.1145/2597073.2597126

4. Jurafsky, D., Martin, J.H.: Speech and Language Processing: An Introduction to Natural Language Processing, Computational Linguistics, and Speech Recognition, 2nd edn. Prentice Hall (2009)

5. Kantardzic, M.: Data Mining: Concepts, Models, Methods and Algorithms, 2nd edn. Wiley, Hoboken (2011)

6. Kawaguchi, S., Garg, P.K., Matsushita, M., Inoue, K.: Mudablue: an automatic categorization system for open source repositories. J. Syst. Softw. **79**(7), 939–953 (2006). http://www.sciencedirect.com/science/article/pii/S0164121205001822. Selected papers from the 11th Asia Pacific Software Engineering Conference (APSEC 2004)

7. Kohavi, R.: A study of cross-validation and bootstrap for accuracy estimation and model selection. In: Proceedings of the 14th International Joint Conference on Artificial Intelligence, IJCAI 1995, vol. 2, pp. 1137–1143. Morgan Kaufmann Publishers Inc., San Francisco (1995). http://dl.acm.org/citation.cfm?id=1643031.1643047

8. Maskeri, G., Sarkar, S., Heafield, K.: Mining business topics in source code using latent dirichlet allocation. In: Proceedings of the 1st India Software Engineering Conference, ISEC 2008, NY, USA, pp. 113–120 (2008). http://doi.acm.org/10.1145/1342211.1342234

9. Pedregosa, F., Varoquaux, G., Gramfort, A., Michel, V., Thirion, B., Grisel, O., Blondel, M., Prettenhofer, P., Weiss, R., Dubourg, V., Vanderplas, J., Passos, A., Cournapeau, D., Brucher, M., Perrot, M., Duchesnay, E.: Scikit-learn: machine learning in Python. J. Mach. Learn. Res. **12**, 2825–2830 (2011)

10. Ray, B., Posnett, D., Filkov, V., Devanbu, P.: A large scale study of programming languages and code quality in github. In: Proceedings of the 22nd ACM SIGSOFT International Symposium on Foundations of Software Engineering, FSE 2014, NY, USA, pp. 155–165 (2014). http://doi.acm.org/10.1145/2635868.2635922

11. Ricci, F., Rokach, L., Shapira, B.: Introduction to Recommender Systems Handbook, pp. 1–35. Springer US, Boston (2011). http://dx.doi.org/10.1007/978-0-387-85820-3_1

12. Salton, G., McGill, M.J.: Introduction to Modern Information Retrieval. McGraw-Hill Inc., New York (1986)

13. Seni, G., Elder, J.F.: Ensemble methods in data mining: improving accuracy through combining predictions. Synth. Lect. Data Mining Knowl. Discov. **2**(1), 1–126 (2010)

14. Tsay, J., Dabbish, L., Herbsleb, J.: Influence of social and technical factors for evaluating contribution in github. In: Proceedings of the 36th International Conference on Software Engineering, ICSE 2014, NY, USA, pp. 356–366 (2014). http://doi.acm.org/10.1145/2568225.2568315

15. Ugurel, S., Krovetz, R., Giles, C.L.: What's the code?: automatic classification of source code archives. In: Proceedings of the Eighth ACM SIGKDD International Conference on Knowledge Discovery and Data Mining, KDD 2002, NY, USA, pp. 632–638 (2002). http://doi.acm.org/10.1145/775047.775141

Bremen Big Data Challenge 2017: Predicting University Cafeteria Load

Jochen Weiner, Lorenz Diener[✉], Simon Stelter, Eike Externest,
Sebastian Kühl, Christian Herff, Felix Putze, Timo Schulze, Mazen Salous,
Hui Liu, Dennis Küster, and Tanja Schultz

Cognitive Systems Lab, University of Bremen, Bremen, Germany
{jochen.weiner,lorenz.diener,simon.stelter,eike.externest,Sebastian.Kuhl,
Christian.herff,felix.putze,timo.schulze,mazen.salous,hui.liu,
dennis.kuster,tanja.schultz}@uni-bremen.de

Abstract. Big data is a hot topic in research and industry. The availability of data has never been as high as it is now. Making good use of the data is a challenging research topic in all aspects of industry and society. The Bremen Big Data Challenge invites students to dig deep into big data. In this yearly event students are challenged to use the month of March to analyze a big dataset and use the knowledge they gained to answer a question. In this year's Bremen Big Data Challenge students were challenged to predict the load of the university cafeteria from the load of past years. The best of 24 teams predicted the load with a root mean squared error of 8.6 receipts issued in five minutes, with a fusion system based on the top 5 entries achieving an even better result of 8.28.

Keywords: Big data · Data analysis · Data challenge

1 Motivation

Technical advances in mobile devices and Internet technology, a growing range of devices connected to the Internet, and the general public's readiness to share data and personal information produce more and more data every day. This data accumulates to enormous datasets many of which are collections of unstructured data [3]. Datasets of this size can no longer be handled by trivial means. Instead they require specialist approaches to data generation, data acquisition, data storage and data analysis. These approaches for big datasets call for engineers and data scientists with expertise in data mining, machine learning and data analysis. Using these skills they can leverage big data, uncover latent knowledge hidden in the data and use the unstructured wealth of information to solve problems and extract answers to relevant questions.

We live in an "era of big data" [3]. Using large datasets and the appropriate computing power that is now available we can perform analyses which have not been possible in the past. The usage and analysis of this data will open new possibilities in research, both academic and industrial, and all aspects involved

© Springer International Publishing AG 2017
G. Kern-Isberner et al. (Eds.): KI 2017, LNAI 10505, pp. 380–386, 2017.
DOI: 10.1007/978-3-319-67190-1_35

in running a company. If encouraged and nurtured the availability of big data and knowledge in data analysis will drive future development of services, devices and the so-called "Internet of things".

To advance development of techniques applicable to the analysis of such datasets and to gain better understanding of specific sets of data, it has become common practice to hold competitions: Teams can make predictions about a dataset based on given training data and compete against each other to build the system with the best performance on held-out test data (usually not published until after the end of the competition), on platforms specifically built for such competitions [2].

A subcategory of these challenges is those organized specifically for students. Such competitions encourage the participants to familiarize themselves with techniques commonly used in data science and machine learning and allow them to compete specifically against their peers on a reasonably level playing field. One noteworthy competition is the Data Mining Cup, an international student competition with teams from over universities in over 20 countries [4].

2   The Bremen Big Data Challenge

The Bremen Big Data Challenge (BBDC) is a student challenge in the field of big data. This yearly event aims at sparking interest in data science among students. Each year the students are presented with a new big dataset and a task to solve on the dataset. As researchers with an interest in data analysis and lecturers tasked to prepare students for jobs in computer science we are very keen to spread our fascination of data and its analysis to students. Through the challenge as well as through our regular teaching we hope to show the students the diversity of tasks in big data and find talented students willing to take part in the variety of big data-related research at the University of Bremen.

The BBDC was created in 2016 and is open to all students in the federal state of Bremen. Interested students can sign up for a newsletter which keeps them updated with the latest BBDC news, and form teams of one to three participants. On the first of March we publish the big dataset and the corresponding task which is to be completed within 31 days. At the end of the challenge the best five teams are awarded monetary prizes. The data and the reference of the task are then published on the BBDC website [1].

In 2016 the task was to predict players' performance in an online game based on a history of past matches. In 2017 the task was to predict the load in Studentenwerk Bremen's cafeteria [8] on the campus of the University of Bremen.

Compared to other data analysis competitions, the BBDC is a competition that is limited to students local to the Bremen universities only. The task is chosen to allow even those with absolutely no prior experience in machine learning to participate, and the 2017 task directly relates to the lives of University of Bremen students.

Solution submissions for the BBDC 2017 are handled using an automated system that lets each team evaluate their solution on the test data three times a week (a total of 15 submissions which can be saved up). Each team that has submitted at least one solution can also see the leaderboard showing the currently best solution of each participating team.

3   The Bremen Big Data Challenge 2017

For the Bremen Big Data Challenge 2017 we cooperated with the Studentenwerk Bremen [8] which, among other services for students, operates the cafeterias on the campus of the University of Bremen. The question preceding this challenge was: Can we predict the load the main cafeteria on campus will have at a specific time? For this task we counted the number of receipts issued in every five-minute-slot from January 2009 to November 2016. The participants were given the data of these five-minute-slots for 2009 through 2015 and were asked to predict the numbers for the year 2016. The challenge is evaluated using the root mean squared error (RMSE) between the actual cafeteria load in the five-minute-slots and the load prediction.

With a very straight-forward analysis we can draw first conclusions about the data: There is no load around the beginning and end of each year. This is the time the cafeteria is closed between Christmas and the new year. The term in the winter semester usually runs from October to February and from April to July in the summer semester. From personal experience we know that the cafeteria is generally less crowded during the break (February to April and July to October) than during the term. And indeed, the data shows a much higher load during term than during break.

The data covers the whole time period from January 2009 through November 2016. This means that times at which the cafeteria did not issue any receipts (e.g. during the night) are also included. The whole period contains a total of 829,191 five-minute-slots. In 752,841 slots (90.8%) there was no load and there were receipts in 76,350 five-minute-slots (9.2%).

In the average working week all days have a similar distribution of the loads with a small load in the morning and a large peak around midday. The highest load occurs every day at the beginning of lunch time. The total load on an average day varies with considerably less receipt being issued on Fridays than on the other days. On an average day we observe the main load between 11:30 and 14:00 when lunch is served. During this period the load has several peaks, all of which occur five to ten minutes after a full or half hour. Our interpretation of this structure is that people meet for lunch at a full or half hour when their classes end and arrive at the cafeteria's checkout five to ten minutes later.

This first analysis shows that the cafeteria load depends on external information such as the semester times and (obviously) cafeteria closing times. Participants were therefore provided with additional data:

Semester times obviously influence the cafeteria load as described above. The dataset therefore includes the start and end of the term as well as any days without classes and the first-semester orientation week.

Possible cafeteria guests are the group who visit the cafeteria and cause the load there. For this reason the dataset contains the number of students enrolled each semester and the numbers of researchers, lecturers and university staff employed each year.

Weather may influence cafeteria load, since it is possible that fewer people will walk to the cafeteria during a storm or heavy rain. The dataset therefore includes hourly information on wind, rain and temperature, courtesy of Deutscher Wetterdienst [5].

Cafeteria menu varies every day and is available on the cafeteria's website. As some meals are more popular than others, the meals offered on a given day might also influence the load of the cafeteria on that day. The menu is provided as a textual description of each day's menu (the same information available to potential cafeteria visitors).

Participants were explicitly invited to include their own sources of additional information e.g. public holidays, days when the cafeteria was closed, or special events (such as conferences) held at the university.

4   The Course of the Bremen Big Data Challenge 2017

We developed a very straight-forward one-afternoon-baseline before we published the dataset and the task. In this baseline we take into account the whole data from 2009 through 2015 as training data. The system is based on semester times, the day of the week and the time of day. Term and break are handled separately. We calculate the mean of each five-minute-slot per weekday, e.g. the mean of all five-minute-slots starting at 12:00 on a Monday during lecture time. Then we assign this mean to the corresponding time-slots in the test data as the prediction for the year 2016. The prediction of the straight-forward baseline achieves an RMSE of 13.47. When preparing the data and for our baseline system we used the pandas [6] and scikit-lean [7] libraries.

A total of 121 students from all three big universities in Bremen showed interest in the challenge and signed up for the newsletter. 41 students from the University of Bremen and the Hochschule Bremen formed the 24 teams participating in the challenge. Figure 1 shows the progress of the leader's score during the challenge. The first submission with an RMSE of 17.81 was made on the sixth day of the challenge. By the 10th day of the challenge the best score had dropped below an RMSE of 10 and then slowly improved to the final score. The final winning submission with an RMSE of 8.60 was made 5 min before the end of the challenge. Table 1 shows the top 5 teams at the end of the challenge.

The number of participants show that students in Bremen are interested in big data and machine learning. Compared to 2016, there was a 10% increase in the number of participants. If the Bremen Big Data Challenge became more popular because of an increased awareness for big data among the students remains to be seen in the next installment of the BBDC in 2018. The results from the BBDC show that as hoped the majority of the teams performed better

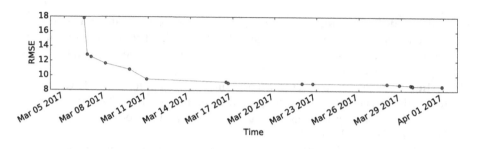

Fig. 1. The development of the leading team's score over time.

Table 1. Results of the challenge: The top 5 and a late-fusion combined system.

Place	RMSE	Submission time	
		First	**Final**
1	8.60	Mar 15 17:24:47	Mar 31 23:54:49
2	8.63	Mar 12 16:00:58	Mar 31 23:50:55
3	8.75	Mar 06 17:00:49	Mar 29 21:42:20
4	8.80	Mar 06 22:30:16	Mar 31 23:12:45
5	9.21	Mar 11 13:51:54	Mar 31 21:26:22
Fused	8.28		

than our explicitly very straight-forward baseline. The approaches of the first five teams are more complex and more powerful than our baseline, but not all of them used machine learning. This shows that teams could participate and achieve good results without deep knowledge of machine learning. Since this was possible, the teams used substantially different approaches:

The winning team considered the customer behaviour underlying the issued receipts: During the term many receipts are issued to students who timed their lunch to be in between lectures, resulting in multiple sale spikes. In contrast, during break students are not restricted by schedules and university staff make up a higher percentage of the customers, leading to a more shallow sales curve. To model this customer behavior they created template sales curves for the summer term, winter term and break: They averaged the receipts issued for each five-minute-slot and then normalized the standard deviation in this average day to one. For each day they predicted a scaling factor for the template sales curve. Multiplying the template sales curve with a predicted scaling factor results in their prediction for that day. The scaling factor was predicted by a regression tree with a maximum depth of 4. It was trained using year, month, day, weekday and semester time as features. The target was the standard deviation of sales (the scaling factor) on the day specified by the feature.

The second-place finisher predicted the receipt count directly using a 2 hidden layer (1000 and 300 ReLU units respectively) feed forward neural network trained using RMSprop (with a learning rate of 0.0005 and a batch size of 128).

In addition to the time, they also used weather information as additional features and excluded federal holidays during which the cafeteria was closed. The fourth place finisher used a similar technique (feedforward neural network with slightly different architecture), but did not use weather or holiday information.

While the first- and second place finishers used common machine learning techniques, the team that came in in third place used a rather simpler method for their system: They assigned each slot the average past value according to the mean of past slots with the same time-of-day, day of week, month and part of the academic year after smoothing out the data with a median filter.

The fifth-placing teams entry was special insofar as it was the only highly-placed entry that made use of the cafeteria menu: The system automatically grouped textually similar menus and used them (as well as time and weather features) as input for a gradient boosting regressor.

One similarity between all the winning entries is that they relied heavily on selecting which data to train their systems on: All of them chose to exclude data, sometimes using only the most recent year and often choosing to train their system only for times during which the cafeteria is known to be open and setting all other times to zero (or modeling them separately). While some systems are similar, they do appear to be learning different things: A late fusion of all the winning systems outputs (by taking their mean) results in a new system that outperforms each single system by a large margin.

On average the teams spent 10.5 days between their first and their last submission. None of the first five teams spent less time than average on the challenge and they used all their available submissions. This shows that time and dedication paid off. The best team's prediction missed the number of receipts issued in a five-minute-slot by just 8.6 receipts on average. The system based on the top 5 entries combined results achieved an even better result with an RMSE of 8.28.

5 Conclusion

Today, larger quantities of data and a wider range of data is available than ever before. Working with this data and using this data to answer relevant questions is not an easy task. The Bremen Big Data Challenge aims at sparking interest in data research among students in Bremen. The Bremen Big Data Challenge 2017 focused on the load of the Studentenwerk Bremen's university cafeteria. Participants were supplied with the cafeteria's load in five-minute-slots from 2009 to 2015 and supplementary data such as the cafeteria menu, semester times and weather. Their task was to predict the cafeteria load in the five-minute-slots of the year 2016. 24 teams participated in this year's challenge and achieved a range of good results with the best team's prediction missing the true number of receipts issued in a five-minute-slot by just 8.6 receipts. Combining the top 5 results the number of receipts issued is missed by only 8.28 receipts.

We will continue this tradition with the Bremen Big Data Challenge 2018.

Acknowledgements. We thank the Studentenwerk Bremen for providing us with the dataset for the Bremen Big Data Challenge 2017.

References

1. Bremen Big Data Challenge: https://bbdc.csl.uni-bremen.de/
2. Carpenter, J.: May the best analyst win (2011)
3. Chen, M., Mao, S., Liu, Y.: Big data: a survey. Mob. Netw. Appl. **19**(2), 171–209 (2014)
4. Data Mining Cup: http://www.data-mining-cup.de/en/dmc-wettbewerb/wettbewerb.html
5. Deutscher Wetterdienst - Archiv Monats- und Tageswerte: http://www.dwd.de/DE/leistungen/klimadatendeutschland/klarchivtagmonat.html
6. McKinney, W.: Data structures for statistical computing in python. In: van der Walt, S., Millman, J. (eds.) Proceedings of the 9th Python in Science Conference, pp. 51–56 (2010)
7. Pedregosa, F., Varoquaux, G., Gramfort, A., Michel, V., Thirion, B., Grisel, O., Blondel, M., Prettenhofer, P., Weiss, R., Dubourg, V., Vanderplas, J., Passos, A., Cournapeau, D., Brucher, M., Perrot, M., Duchesnay, E.: Scikit-learn: machine learning in Python. J. Mach. Learn. Res. **12**, 2825–2830 (2011)
8. Bremen, S.: http://www.stw-bremen.de/en

Towards Sentiment Analysis
on German Literature

Albin Zehe[(✉)], Martin Becker, Fotis Jannidis, and Andreas Hotho

University of Würzburg, 97074 Würzburg, Germany
{zehe,becker,hotho}@informatik.uni-wuerzburg.de,
fotis.jannidis@uni-wuerzburg.de

Abstract. Sentiment Analysis is a Natural Language Processing-task that is relevant in a number of contexts, including the analysis of literature. We report on ongoing research towards enabling, for the first time, sentence-level Sentiment Analysis in the domain of German novels. We create a labelled dataset from sentences extracted from German novels and, by adapting existing sentiment classifiers, reach promising F1-scores of 0.67 for binary polarity classification.

> *Und sie lebten glücklich bis ans Ende ihrer Tage.*   *(German fairy tales)*

1 Introduction and Related Work

The above quote is a common ending in German fairy tales. If you can not tell whether or not this ending is happy, you have already come across the problem this paper is concerned with: For Sentiment Analysis (SA), a task in Natural Language Processing, there exists a multitude of solutions tailored to specific datasets of English texts, but few for other languages - and none for our domain: German novels. We aim to change this, as SA can help to achieve a very interesting goal in the context of literature: a computer-readable representation of a story. One viable approach for story representation is the use of *sentiment trajectories* that describe the emotional state over the course of a novel. For example, a wedding could be recognised in such a trajectory by a spike in positive emotions, while the death of a protagonist would be accompanied by negative words. Such representations have previously been used in [2,4,12]. Similarly, [22] use sentiment trajectories to recognise one core element of a story's plot: the presence or absence of a Happy Ending.

Most of these previously used representations rely on relatively crude SA, using only word-level sentiment. In order to take into account negation, intensification etc., more complex systems have to be used. Such systems have been a field of active research for a while. For example, [13] proposes an SVM-based classifier relying on bag-of-words and syntactic features, as well as some manually crafted emotion features. Recently, Neural Network-based approaches have become increasingly popular, redefining the state-of-the-art in SA. One milestone was the introduction of RNTN [20] along with the Stanford Sentiment

© Springer International Publishing AG 2017
G. Kern-Isberner et al. (Eds.): KI 2017, LNAI 10505, pp. 387–394, 2017.
DOI: 10.1007/978-3-319-67190-1_36

Treebank (SST), which has since been used as a standard evaluation dataset. RNTN reached an accuracy of 85.4% on the SST. [5] and subsequently [6] proposed systems based on Convolutional Neural Networks, reaching accuracies of up to 88.1%. Paragraph Vectors [7] have also been reported to yield accuracies of up to 87.8% on the SST. Very recently, a system using a fundamentally different approach with unsupervised pre-training has achieved accuracies of 91.9% on the SST [17].

While working very well, these systems have only been used on English texts. In contrast to that, our goal is to introduce sophisticated methods for SA into the domain of German literature. To this end, we verify results from previously published approaches and evaluate their performance in our domain. To make this possible, we create the German Novel Dataset (GND), a set of sentences extracted from novels in German language, labelling these sentences with sentiment information using crowdsourcing. We adapt three state-of-the-art SA methods [6,7,13] forming a good basis for adaptation to German data, as they rely on a straightforward and understandable model. [17] is currently unsuitable for our evaluation, as its pre-training does not transfer well to other domains and is too time intensive to retrain. Overall, our work is an important step towards building a repository of advanced methods that can be used for the analysis of German literature.

The remainder of this paper is structured as follows: In Sect. 2, we define Sentiment Analysis and adapt existing approaches to German texts. Section 3 describes the English reference datasets and introduces our GND. Sections 4 and 5 report and discuss our findings. A summary and future work are given in Sect. 6.

2 Sentiment Classification

Generally, Sentiment Analysis refers to the task of assigning a label, called *polarity*, to a segment of text, describing whether it induces positive, negative or neutral feelings in a human reader. In this work, SA is defined as a sentence classification task, enabling classifiers to account for the effect of negation etc. Assume a corpus $C \subset S \times L$ of sentences $s \in S$ and polarity labels $l \in L$. For example, $c = (s, l) = (\text{"I love you."}, 1)$ represents a sentence s with a positive polarity l. We perform two classification tasks, distinguished by the set of possible polarities: (a) Binary classification: $L_{bin} = \{-1, 1\}$ and (b) Ternary classification: $L_{ter} = \{-1, 0, 1\}$.[1] A classifier of any kind is trained to predict the correct label given a sentence, that is, to learn a function $f \colon S \to L$ with $f(s) = l$.

We compare two different classifiers for our SA task: Support Vector Machines (SVMs) [3] and Convolutional Neural Networks (CNNs) [8]. To represent sentences for the SVM, we use two different feature generation methods, the *NRC Representation* [13] and *Paragraph Vector* [7]. For the CNN, we use the model from [6], which we refer to as *S-CNN*.

---

[1] Ternary labels are transformed into binary labels by omission of the neutral class (0).

SVM Classifier. In this paragraph, we give a short overview of the sentence representations used as input for the SVM.

NRC Representation. For the NRC Representation, a sentence is represented as the concatenation of different kinds of n-gram and syntactic features in combination with a set of sentiment features constructed manually from the EmoLex [14]. We use the TreeTagger [19] to get part-of-speech-tags required for the syntactic features. The representation employs a basic negation detection relying on a set of English negation words. In order to be applicable to German text, this list had to be translated. [2] Lemmatisation was not employed in n-gram generation, as it did not improve results, but was used for the lookup of words in the sentiment lexicon. For a full description of the features, we refer to [13]. Note that we do not use the full set of features described there, as we consider the following features to be irrelevant outside the context of tweets: all-caps words, hashtags, multiple punctuation marks, emoticons and elongated words. Also, using Brown Clusters has been shown to be ineffective in [13].

Paragraph Vector. The Paragraph Vector-Framework extends the word2vec-Framework [10,11] to create an embedding of a piece of text, for example a sentence, in a low-dimensional space. Following [7], we directly use this embedding as a feature vector for SA with Logistic Regression or other suitable classifiers/regressors. We use the implementation of Paragraph Vector provided by gensim [18] to train sentence embeddings on our GNC (see Sect. 3).

S-CNN. The S-CNN is a sentence classification method based on a Convolutional Neural Network. We use the variant referred to as "cnn-nonstatic" in [6]. While [6] uses word2vec embeddings pre-trained on a very large corpus of English news articles[3], to our knowledge, no embedding trained on such a large corpus is available for German. Again, we used gensim to train 300-dimensional word2vec embeddings on our corpus of German novels. An implementation of S-CNN is provided by the original author.[4] Only small changes had to be made to the code to make it compatible with German text, specifically the inclusion of the character "ß" and German umlauts to the regular expression used for preprocessing.

3   Datasets

In this section, we describe the datasets we use in our experiments. We use English reference corpora to verify results of the existing algorithms. Additionally, we extract a dataset of sentences from German novels and label it by crowdsourcing to evaluate the classifiers in our domain.

---

[2] We use the words "nicht" (not), "kein" (no), "ohne" (without), "nie" (never), "niemals" (never), "nirgends" (nowhere), "niemand" (nobody), and "keiner" (nobody) as negation markers.

[3] https://code.google.com/archive/p/word2vec/.

[4] https://github.com/yoonkim/CNN_sentence.

English SA Datasets. In order to validate the selected approaches as well as existing results, we use two standard English datasets. The first one is a dataset of tweets [15] used in [13]. It is downloadable via Twitter's API. Some differences may arise depending on the time of the download, but the distribution over the polarity labels was mostly unchanged from that in [13] (14% negative, 49% neutral and 37% negative for the training set of 6128 samples.). The second dataset is the Stanford Sentiment Treebank (SST) [20].

German Novel Dataset and Corpus. The *German Novel Dataset* (GND) was generated using a crowdsourcing approach. It contains 270 labelled sentences extracted from our German Novel Corpus (GNC) of over 600 novels in German language from the TextGrid Digital Library[5]. Of these sentences, 89 are labelled as "negative", 124 as "neutral" and 57 as "positive". The dataset is released along with this paper.[6]

Labelling Process. To create the GND, we extracted all sentences from the GNC containing at least three words and no more than 30 words or 1500 characters. These sentences were then ranked using the ratio $r = e^n w$, where e is the number of words in a sentence associated with emotions by the EmoLex [14] and w is the total number of words in the sentence. We evaluated $n \in \{1, 2, 3\}$ and selected $n = 3$ because it led to sentences that were emotional, but did not consist only of emotional words. [7] We selected the 210 highest ranked sentences and 90 additional sentences by random choice, resulting in 300 sentences for annotation. We developed a web interface for the annotation process.[8] The sentences were annotated for ternary polarity and the eight basic emotions defined in [16] using *Microworkers* and *CrowdFlower*.[9] An Inter Annotator Agreement was calculated and annotators were dropped, including all of their annotations, if they failed to meet a defined threshold. We kept only sentences with at least five annotations after filtering. The polarity of a training sample was selected by majority vote, while a sentence was marked as conveying an emotion if at least two annotators selected the emotion. For details on the annotation and selection process, see [21].

4   Results

Here, we briefly report the findings on the English datasets and give a more detailed description of our results on the German Novel Dataset (GND).

Validating Classifiers on English Datasets. To validate our implementations, we evaluated all classifiers on the Twitter Dataset and the SST, reproducing the results from [13] and [20]. On both datasets, the S-CNN gave better

---

[5] https://textgrid.de/digitale-bibliothek.

[6] https://www.dmir.org/datasets/german_novel_dataset.

[7] We also evaluated other selection schemes, but found that random selection yielded too many unemotional sentences, while $r = e$ preferred very long ones.

[8] Available on http://dmir.org/senticrowd/senticrowd. Login is possible with both "Microworkers-ID" and "Kampagnen-ID" set to "demo" in the upper form.

[9] http://www.microworkers.com and https://www.crowdflower.com.

results (F1-score of 0.86 for binary classification), but was much more sensitive to parameter selection. We were not able to reproduce the results from [7], using Paragraph Vectors as input for an SVM or Logistic Regression. Note that others were also unable to reproduce them and one author of [7] considers them to be invalid [9].

Evaluating Classifiers. All classifiers were evaluated on the GND and large parameter studies as well as some feature analysis were performed.

Results Using an SVM. We start by describing the findings from the SVM-based methods. For both the NRC features and the Paragraph Vectors, we used a linear kernel SVM. For the Paragraph Vectors, we additionally employed an RBF-kernel. To optimise parameters, we did a grid search over 20 values for C evenly spaced on the log-scale from 10^{-2} to 10^{2} and (where applicable) $\gamma \in \{0.01, 1, 10\}$. We report micro-averaged F1-scores[10] over all classes in the respective task. All scores are calculated as the average over 10 independent runs of 10-fold cross-validation. There were no major differences between runs (usually much less than 5%).

We reached an F1-score of 0.43 for ternary and 0.67 for binary classification respectively using a linear SVM trained on NRC features. Using Paragraph Vectors as input to an SVM led to similar results. While these scores are not on par with those on English datasets, they are far above those a majority baseline would achieve (F1-score ≈ 0.5 for binary classification). There was no dependency of the linear SVM on the value for C in the range we searched. Using an RBF kernel made the classifier much more dependent on hyper- parameter selection, but did not improve the results overall.

Results using S-CNN. We use random search [1] to jointly optimise Dropout rate d, number of filters n per filter size and filter size s. We draw about 80 parameter combinations uniformly from $d \in [0.0, 0.5]$, $n \in [100, 500] \subset \mathbb{N}$ and $s \in [2, 10] \subset \mathbb{N}$, as recommended in [23]. After sampling a filter size s, we use $s-1$, s and $s+1$ in parallel for the CNN. The only parameter with clear influence on the results is s. Using smaller values clearly outperformed larger ones, as shown in Fig. 1. Generally, the S-CNN performed comparably or slightly worse than an SVM trained on NRC features, with F1-score up to 0.67 for binary classification.

5 Discussion

On the German Novel Dataset (GND), all three methods yielded comparable results. However, the SVM trained on NRC features is much less dependent on hyper- parameter selection and requires less time to train than the S-CNN. While training an SVM on Paragraph Vectors is also fast, the training of these embeddings requires much time. We therefore consider the SVM trained on NRC features to be the most suitable classifier for our task at the current state.

---

[10] http://scikit-learn.org/0.17/modules/generated/sklearn.metrics.f1_score.

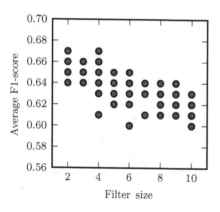
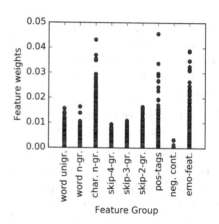

Fig. 1. Dependency of the S-CNN on the filter size for binary polarity classification on the GND. A datapoint corresponds to a specific combination of the three tuned hyper-parameters.

Fig. 2. Absolute weights assigned to feature groups by a linear SVM. Blue dots are individual feature weights, red dots group averages. Weights for all classes plotted together.

To gain some further insight into the relevance of individual features, we plotted the weights assigned to all NRC features by a linear SVM trained on the full GND. Figure 2 shows the resulting plot comparing the average weight of our feature types during classification. The manually constructed emotion features (*emo-feat.*) obviously are most important to the classification. Similarly, the *pos-tag* features play an important role, which may be due to their ability to capture specific sentence structures. Word n-grams ($n > 1$) and skip-n-grams (except, to some degree, $n = 2$) have only small influence, which is not surprising considering their sparsity in the small GND. Unigrams have some relevance, but are, interestingly, much less important than character-n-grams. We assume this is due to the fact that character n-grams can actually group together different words with the same stem, helping generalisation. Assuming that the filters in the S-CNN capture information similar to n-gram features[11], these findings are consistent with those for the CNN. There, smaller filter sizes (i.e., corresponding to lower order n-grams) performed best.

While the results achieved on the GND are certainly not on par with those on the English datasets, this can most likely be explained by the training set that is at least an order of magnitude smaller than the English sets. The performance being far above that of simple baselines and the interpretability of the feature weights show that the NRC features are able to capture information that is useful for polarity classification on German literary text.

---

[11] http://www.wildml.com/2015/11/understanding.

6   Conclusion and Outlook

In this paper, we have presented first steps towards introducing more complex SA methods to the domain of German literature. This is a prerequisite for plot representation and other interesting tasks in the Digital Humanities. To this end, we introduced a unique dataset of sentences extracted from German novels that have been manually labelled with polarity information and basic emotions. Our annotation interface can easily be used to extend this dataset in the future. While the results are not on par with English SA, we have shown that the features and classifiers are generally applicable in our domain and can recognise signals that are useful for SA on German novels.

In future work, we will expand our dataset to enable training of more expressive models, possibly also creating French and Spanish datasets, and introduce domain- specific features to improve classification accuracy.

References

1. Bergstra, J., Bengio, Y.: Random search for hyper-parameter optimization. JMLR **13**, 281–305 (2012)
2. Elsner, M.: Abstract representations of plot struture. LiLT **12** (2015)
3. Joachims, T.: Text categorization with support vector machines: learning with many relevant features. In: Nédellec, C., Rouveirol, C. (eds.) ECML 1998. LNCS, vol. 1398, pp. 137–142. Springer, Heidelberg (1998). doi:10.1007/BFb0026683
4. Jockers, M.L.: A novel method for detecting plot, June 2014
5. Kalchbrenner, N., Grefenstette, E., Blunsom, P.: A convolutional neural network for modelling sentences. In: Proceedings of the 52nd ACL, pp. 212–217
6. Kim, Y.: Convolutional neural networks for sentence classification. In: Proceedings of the 2014 Conference on EMNLP, pp. 1746–1751 (2014)
7. Le, Q.V., Mikolov, T.: Distributed representations of sentences and documents. In: ICML, vol. 14, pp. 188–1196 (2014)
8. LeCun, Y., Bottou, L., Bengio, Y., Haffner, P.: Gradient-based learning applied to document recognition. Proc. IEEE **86**, 2278–2324 (1998)
9. Mesnil, G., Mikolov, T., Ranzato, M., Bengio, Y.: Ensemble of generative and discriminative techniques for sentiment analysis of movie reviews (2014). arXiv:1412.5335
10. Mikolov, T., Chen, K., Corrado, G., Dean, J.: Efficient estimation of word representations in vector space (2013). arXiv:1301.3781
11. Mikolov, T., Sutskever, I., Chen, K., Corrado, G., Dean, J.: Distributed representations of words and phrases and their compositionality. In: NIPS (2013)
12. Mohammad, S.: From once upon a time to happily ever after: tracking emotions in novels and fairy tales. In: LaTeCH 2011, pp. 105–114. Association for Computational Linguistics, Stroudsburg, PA (2011)
13. Mohammad, S.M., Kiritchenko, S., Zhu, X.: Nrc-canada: building the state-of-the-art in sentiment analysis of tweets. In: SemEval-2013 (2013). arXiv:1308.6242
14. Mohammad, S.M., Turney, P.D.: Crowdsourcing a word-emotion association lexicon. Comput. Intell. **29**(3), 436–465 (2013)
15. Nakov, P., Kozareva, Z., Ritter, A., Rosenthal, S., Stoyanov, V., Wilson, T.: SemEval-2013 task 2: Sentiment analysis in twitter (2013)

16. Plutchik, R.: A general psychoevolutionary theory of emotion. Theor. Emotion **1**, 3–31 (1980)
17. Radford, A., Jozefowicz, R., Sutskever, I.: Learning to generate reviews and discovering sentiment (2017). arXiv:1704.01444
18. Řehůřek, R., Sojka, P.: Software framework for topic modelling with large corpora. In: Proceedings of the LREC 2010 Workshop on New Challenges for NLP Frameworks, pp. 45–50. ELRA, Valletta, Malta, May 2010
19. Schmid, H.: Probabilistic part-of-speech tagging using decision trees. In: New Methods in Language Processing, p. 154 (2013)
20. Socher, R., Perelygin, A., Wu, J.Y., Chuang, J., Manning, C.D., Ng, A.Y., Potts, C., et al.: Recursive deep models for semantic compositionality over a sentiment treebank. In: Proceedings of the EMNLP, vol. 1631, p. 1642 (2013)
21. Zehe, A.: Sentiment Analysis on German Novels. Master's thesis (2017)
22. Zehe, A., Becker, M., Hettinger, L., Hotho, A., Reger, I., Jannidis, F.: Prediction of happy endings in german novels. In: Cellier, P., Charnois, T., Hotho, A., Matwin, S., Moens, M.F., Toussaint, Y. (eds.) DMNLP@PKDD/ECML, pp. 9–16, July 2016
23. Zhang, Y., Wallace, B.: A sensitivity analysis of (and practitioners' guide to) convolutional neural networks for sentence classification (2015). arXiv:1510.03820

Author Index

Printed in the United States
By Bookmasters